D1121488

3 1210 00058 9962

Word for Word

By Edward C. Pinkerton

A VERBATIM BOOK

Distributed to libraries by
Gale Research Company, Detroit, Michigan

ISBN No.: 0–930454–06–5

VERBATIM

Box 668

Essex, Connecticut 06426, U.S.A.

VERBATIM

2 Market Square

Aylesbury, Buckinghamshire, England

Keyboarding, programming, processing, index extraction and typesetting by:
    Alexander Typesetting, Inc.
    Indianapolis, Indiana

Printing and binding by:
    Vail-Ballou Press, Inc.
    Binghamton, New York

Typographic and system design by:
    Laurence Urdang

to Denny,
for her help, her encouragement,
and her forbearance

For the most part our words come deviously, making their way by winding paths through the minds of generations of men, even burrowing like moles through the dark subconsciousness. Fancied likenesses, farfetched associations, ancient prejudices have acted upon them. Superstition, misapprehension, old fables, mythological taboos, the jests of simpletons and the vaulting imaginations of poets have all played a part in shaping them. During their labyrinthine journeys in time and space they have often changed their form, spelling, pronunciation and, especially, their sense.

John Moore, *You English Word*

Foreword

You start to look up a word in the dictionary. As you flip through the pages a more intriguing entry catches your eye. You pause to examine this other word, its definition, its etymology; a reference sends you leafing through more pages to check out yet another entry. The new word has further suggestions to "see THIS, THAT and OTHER." You turn to THIS . . . and are off on a word hunt that takes you further and further afield, expanding in several directions at the same time. Twenty minutes or two hours later you come back to earth with the realization that you have completely forgotten the word that prompted you to turn to the dictionary in the first place. If you have experienced this sort of capricious, involuntary dictionary-rambling, then you will find this book interesting, for it is based on a kind of controlled dictionary-rambling: all the words discussed in each chapter are descended from one root.

That there are Indo-European roots to the English language and word families derived from those roots is something that most of us know from our elementary school sessions with etymology but have never delved into very deeply. Our practical use of etymology is confined to using our knowledge of Latin and Greek roots and stems to help us decipher words in the Romance languages and English loanwords that have obviously been borrowed from such sources. I was not severely bitten by the word-origin bug until one day several years ago when, while leafing through an etymological dictionary, I was struck by the fact that cognate words are often of such disparate form and meaning that no one looking at them in alphabetical order would imagine that they were descended from the same root. It was the existence of these sometimes striking—not to say bizarre—disparities that prompted me to write a series of short articles, linking superficially different but linguistically related words, that were published by the Baltimore *Evening Sun* during 1972–1973. The longer forays here presented grew out of those brief essays and are the result of several years of sleuthing through linguistic materials.

Baltimore   Edward C. Pinkerton
August 1981

Acknowledgments

Lines and sentences from pieces published in the Baltimore *Evening Sun* are scattered throughout the pages of this book. Of great help to me in getting the book into shape have been:

Laurence Urdang, editor of VERBATIM, not only by his moral support and encouragement, but by his excellent advice and skillful editing;

Professor Robert A. Fowkes, of New York University, most of whose penetrating suggestions have been followed;

And especially Dr. H. Craig Melchert, of the Harvard University Department of Linguistics, who has vetted the entire manuscript and who has been so helpful in straightening out particularly thorny matters and pointing out pitfalls that I have come to regard him as a collaborator. Even so, some of his suggestions (very few) have not been followed, and the final onus is with me, as is not only proper, but inevitable.

E.C.P.

Table of Contents

Introduction

The existence of a Proto-Indo-European language is not a fairy tale, although it was one of the Grimm brothers, Jakob, who formulated what is popularly known as "Grimm's law," a statement in historical terms of the correspondences of consonants in Germanic tongues like English, German, Gothic ... and those in the classical languages like Latin, Greek, and Sanskrit. Grimm's success in showing that the correspondences among these languages were regular was a great step forward in establishing the historical study of language as a legitimate science. Grimm's law also confirmed that these languages, along with many others, were descended from the same ancestral tongue, called Proto-Indo-European by some, Indo-European by most. German scholars prefer *Indogermanisch*.

Jakob Grimm was not the first to make this discovery. Sir William Jones, a British colonial in India, had reached the same conclusion in 1786, and by 1816 Franz Bopp had already written a comparative grammar of Sanskrit, Greek, Persian, and Germanic. In fact, others before Jones had suggested a relationship between the languages of Persia and India and those of Europe; however, Jones's statement is remembered because it signaled the beginning of an era in which the study of the classical languages of Persia and India by European scholars led to the establishment of comparative Indo-European studies. In fairness it should be pointed out that the gist of Grimm's law (see below) had also been set forth by the Danish scholar, Rasmus Rask, in an essay written in 1814 and published in 1818, in time to influence Grimm's formulation, which appeared in 1822. This is not to diminish the contributions of Grimm himself, whose monumental *Deutsche Grammatik* is considered one of the foundation stones of Indo-European linguistics.

Prior to the late 18th century it had been generally assumed in the Western and near-Eastern world that all human language must be descended from Hebrew. Wasn't Hebrew the language of Genesis and the Garden of Eden, presumably spoken until the confusion of tongues inflicted on mankind at the time of the building of the Tower of Babel? Even as late as 1828 the great American lexicographer Noah Webster believed that "the primitive language of man," spoken by "the descendants of Noah ... on the plain of Shihar ... must have been the original Chaldee," the language of Chaldea, the native land of Abraham; and that "all the words of the several great races of men ... must have been derived from the common Chaldee stock."

Such views are now considered naive and scientifically impossible, though one can find in current linguistic literature speculations on such reconstructed entities as Proto-Indo-Hittite, Proto-Indo-Etruscan, and even a universal Proto-Speech of the Upper Paleolithic, postulated as ancestral to all contempory western and near-eastern languages; such a language would make cousins of the Indo-European and Semitic languages.

In this book we are content to follow the standard authorities as far back as they go (some go further than others), to indicate disagreements when they seem important enough, and to indicate what is speculative.

Assume for a moment that all traces of Latin had been destroyed, including the Vulgate Bible and all Medieval Latin records, and that the only witnesses to the existence of this ancient tongue were the various Romance languages: Italian, Provençal, French, Spanish, Catalan, Portuguese, Rumanian and Rhaeto-Romanic. Latin would then be known as "Proto-Romance," and scholars would undoubtedly attempt to reconstruct it in the same way that they have reconstructed Proto-Indo-European. Such an attempt to rebuild Latin from the evidence remaining in its daughter languages was in fact made in order to test the reliability of the methods used in reconstructing proto-languages; and the resultant Proto-Romance shows an 85% correspondence to Classical Latin as it was actually written.

In a similar way Proto-Indo-European has been reconstructed by generations of scholars laboriously comparing the grammars and lexicons of all the known Indo-European languages, especially the older Germanic ones like Gothic, Old Norse, Old High German, Old English; the older Italic languages like Latin, Faliscan, Oscan, Umbrian; the older Celtic languages including Gaulish, Old Irish, Old Cornish, Old Welsh; the older Baltic tongues: Old Prussian, Lithuanian; older Slavic languages: Slavonic, Old Russian; old Iranian tongues: Old Persian, Avestan; ancient Indic languages: Sanskrit, Pali, the ancient Prakrits; and ancient Greek, Armenian, Albanian. The researchers even discovered in the process a few languages that had not been known to be Indo-European, like Hittite and Tocharian A and B.

The resultant Proto-Indo-European language not unnaturally has features that seem odd or even alien to a speaker of any of the living descendant tongues, just as Latin is a strange-sounding but vaguely familiar language to Italians and Rumanians, rather more alien to Russians and Lithuanians. According to modern linguistic theory, the consonantal sounds of Proto-Indo-European are those indicated by the letters p, t, k, kw; b, d, g, gw; bh, dh, gh, gwh; s, m, n, r, l, y, w, and a "laryngeal glide" indicated by the character ∂, called a "schwa" and sounding something like "h" when used as a consonant. I say "as a consonant" because one feature of Proto-Indo-European was that the sounds indicated by m, n, r, and l, and by y, w, and ∂ could also serve as vowels. When so used they sound like the sounds of the final syllables in *bottom*, *button*, *butter*, and *bottle*, like *i*, *u*, and the indistinct vowel sound of the *e* in *quiet* or the *a* in *ago*, and they are written *m̦, n̦, r̦, l̦, i, u,* and *ə*.

In migrating to the various descendant languages, the consonants sometimes went through sound shifts or phonetic change. This is what *Grimm's law* is about, for what Jakob Grimm formulated was the observed fact that, as a general rule, when in initial position or immediately preceded by the accented syllable:
Indo-European (IE) *p, t, k* sounds (voiceless stops) become Germanic *f, th, h* (fricatives),
Indo-European (IE) *b, d, g,* sounds (voiced stops) become Germanic *p, t, k* (voiceless stops),
Indo-European (IE) *bh, dh, gh* sounds (voiced aspirated stops) become Germanic *b, d, g* (voiced stops).
Furthermore, the IE sounds *kw, gw,* and *gwh* show changes parallel to Germanic *hw, kw* (or *k*), and *gw* (or *g*).

While this was going on in the migration to Germanic, the first six consonantal sounds moving from Indo-European to Latin and Greek (the sources of the other great portions of the English vocabulary) were not changing at all, and remained *p, t, k; b, d, g.* However, the voiced aspirated stops *bh, dh, gh* were devoiced to the Greek aspirates *ph, th, kh* and to Latin *f* (or *b*), *f* (or *d*), and *h*; while *kw* became Latin *qu* (no change) or *c* (= *k*) and Greek *p, t,* or *k*. The sound *gw* remained in Latin after *n* (*gu*) and became *v* (= *w*) elsewhere; in Greek *gw* resulted in *b, d,* or *g;* and *gwh* became Latin *f* and Greek *ph, th,* or *kh*.

Of the other consonants, *m, n, r, l* remained the same in Germanic, Latin, and Greek; *s* remained the same in Germanic and Latin but changed to *h* in Greek; *y* remained in Germanic (spelled *j* > English *g* or *y*), and also in Latin (spelled *i,* later *j*); in Greek *y* became *h* or *z.* The sound *w* remained Germanic *w,* becoming Latin *u* (no change) and Late Latin *v;* it disappeared in Greek after appearing in Old Greek as digamma (ϝ).

The correspondences among Indo-European, Greek, Latin, Germanic, English, and (High) German consonantal sounds are tabulated on the next pages.

Indo-European	Greek	Latin	Germanic	English	German	
p	p	p	f	f	f/v	(v pronounced [f])
t	t	t	th	th	d	
k	k	c (k)	h	h	h	
kw	p/t/k	qu/c (k)	hw	wh	w	(pronounced [v])
b	b	b	p	p	p/pf	
d	d	d	t	t	z	(pronounced [ts])
g	g	g	k	k/c	k	
gw	b/d/g	u/v/gu	kw/k	qu/c	k/qu	
bh	ph	f/b	b	b	b	
dh	th	f/d	d	d	t	
gh	kh	h/g	g	g/y	g	
gwh	ph/th	f	gw/g	w/g	w	(pronounced [v])
s	h	s	s	s	s	
w	—	u/v	w	w	w	
y	h/z	i/j	j	y	j	

m, n, l, r: no change

Examples: [A form preceded by an asterisk is a hypothetical reconstruction, that is, it has not yet been found in any attested source.]

Indo-European	Greek	Latin	Germanic	English	German	
*pə ter	patēr	pater	*fadar	father	Vater	
*trei-	treis	tres	*thrijiz	three	drei	
*kerd-	kardia	cor, cordis	*herton-	heart	Herz	
*kwo- *kwi-	tis 'who?' poteros 'which one?' ouki 'not'	qui, quod cui, cuius	*hwa, *hwi-	who, what	wer, was	
*bak- 'staff'	bakterion 'staff'	baculum 'rod'		peg	pegel	(Low German)
*beu 'to swell'	boubōn 'groin' (>bubonic)	bulla 'bubble' (>boil)	*puk 'swelling'	pock	Pocke pfoche (dialectal)	
*dekm	deka	decem	*tehun	ten	zehn	
*gen- 'to beget'	genea 'race'	gens 'clan'	*kunjam 'family'	kin	Kind 'child'	
*gwei- 'to live'	bios 'life'	vivus 'alive'	*kwi(k)waz	quick quitch grass	keck, kweck 'lively' quecke 'quitch grass'	

Indo-European	Greek	Latin	Germanic	English	German
*gwem- 'to come' 'to go'	bainein 'to go'	venire 'to come'	*kuman	come	kommen
*gwelbh-	delphus 'womb' delphis 'dolphin' (because of its shape; >dolphin)				
*gwen- 'woman'	gunē 'woman' (>gynecology)		*kwēniz	queen	
*ongw- 'to salve'		unguentum 'salve'			
*bhel- 'to bloom'	phullon 'leaf'	flos 'flower'	*blomon	bloom	Blume
*bhardhā		barba 'beard'	*bardaz	beard	Bart
*dhwer- 'door'	thura 'door'	foris 'outdoors'	*duram	door	Tür 'door'
*medhyo		medium	*midjiz	middle	mittel
*gher- 'to enclose'	khortos 'enclosure'	hortus 'garden' (>horticulture)	*gardaz	garden, yard	Garten
*ghredh-		gradus 'step' (>grade)			
*gwher- 'warm'	thermos 'warm'	formus 'warm'	*warmaz	warm	warm
*gwhen- 'to strike'	epephnon 'I killed'	offendere 'to hit'	*gunthjo 'war, battle'	gun	
*seks	hex	sex	*seks	six	sechs
*weid- 'to see'	idein 'to see'	videre 'to see'	*witan 'to look after'	wit, wise	wissen
*wreg- 'to push'	eirgein 'to shut up'	urgere (>urge)	*wrekan	wreak, wreck	
*yeug- 'to join'	zugon 'yoke'	iugum, jugum 'yoke'	*yukam	yoke	Joch
*yē- 'to throw'	hienai 'to throw'	jacere 'to throw' (>jet, jetty)			

As already noted, the Indo-European sonants *m̥, n̥, l̥,* and *r̥,* and *u, i, ə* were used as vowels. The other Indo-European vowels were *e, o,* and *a,* which along with *i* and *u* could be either short or long.

A characteristic of Indo-European is the phenomenon known as *ablaut, apophony,* or *gradation.* This is a system of internal vowel changes, serving to signify different shades of meaning of the same general thought. English-speakers are familiar with this device, since it is what characterizes the "strong" verbs, those that use only internal vowel changes to indicate past tenses and that are sometimes accompanied by related nouns, for example,

sing, sang, sung; song
write, wrote, written; writ
do, did, done; deed, doom

(By contrast, "weak" verbs are those that form their past by the addition of a dental or alveolar, *d* or *t,* as in *walk, walked; sleep, slept; bring, brought.*)

In Indo-European, ablaut affects the vowels *e* and *o,* of which *e* is the basic form. The "*e*-grade" form can change to "*o*-grade"; for example, Indo-European **ped-* 'foot' is *e*-grade in Latin *pes, pedis* 'foot' and *o*-grade in Greek *pous, podos* 'foot.' Or the vowel can disappear entirely, giving the "zero-grade" form, as in Indo-European **wreg-* 'to push,' zero-grade form **wr̥g-* in Latin *urgere* 'to urge.' But the descendant languages usually managed to put one vowel or another back into the combination, as in:

Indo-European **men-* 'to think,' zero-grade **mn̥-* in Germanic **(ga-) mundi* > English *mind*; or
Indo-European **pelə-* 'to fill,' zero-grade **plə-* in Germanic **fulnaz* > English *full.*

The vowel shifts among the Indo-European languages are so complicated and in many cases still so uncertain that it is not feasible to draw up a chart of the changes comparable to that drawn up for the consonant changes.

English traces its direct descent from Proto-Indo-European back by way of Middle English (1100–1500), preceded by Old English, sometimes called Anglo-Saxon (mid-7th century to 1100). English is one of the West Germanic tongues, a designation it shares with German, Low German, Yiddish, Dutch, Flemish, Afrikaans, and Frisian; in other words, all these languages were originally the same one, spoken by the branch of the Germanic-speaking people who moved to the west sometime in prehistory during the breakup of the speakers of Common Germanic—which goes back still further into prehistory, to the period before the separation into West Germanic, East Germanic (> Gothic) and North Germanic (> Old Norse > Faeroese, Icelandic, Norwegian, Swedish, Danish). Thence we go back by unknown stages to Proto-Indo-European, which was actually being spoken at a time no one is sure of, but probably before 4000 B.C.

While English is structurally and historically a Germanic language and while in an average written or spoken English sentence a majority of the words will be Germanic in origin, it is a fact that fewer than half of the words in the English vocabulary are inherited Germanic words, and more than half are borrowed from other Indo-European languages—mostly Medieval and Old French—and various non-Indo-European languages. The first borrowings discernible in Old English come from the contacts of the Germanic speakers with the Greco-Roman civilization, with the Celtic Gauls who occupied much of southwestern Europe, and with their relatives across the Channel, the Britons. Some of these words are still in use:

street, Old English strǣt, from Late Latin strāta 'laid down, paved,' used elliptically for via strāta 'paved road'

cheese, Old English cēse, from Germanic *kasjus, from Latin caseus 'cheese'

wine, Old English wīn, from Common Germanic *winam, from Latin vīnum (for *winom) 'wine'

cook, Old English cōc, from Latin cocus, coquus 'cook'

dish, Old English disc, from West Germanic *diskaz, from Latin discus, from Greek diskos 'quoit'

church, Old English cirice, from West Germanic *kirika, from Late Greek kurikon, for (dōma) kuriakon '(house) of the Lord'; from Greek kurios 'lord'

bishop, Old English bisc(e)op, from Vulgar Latin *biscopus, from Late Latin episcopus, from Greek episkopos 'overseer' (epi 'on' + skopos 'watcher')

priest, Old English prēost, via Vulgar Latin *prester from Late Latin presbyter, from Greek presbuteros 'elder'

cross, Old English cros, from Old Irish cross, from Latin crux, crucem 'cross'

bin, Old English binn 'manger,' from Celtic *benna 'manger'

brock 'badger,' Old English broc, from Celtic *brokka- 'badger'

As can be seen from their meanings ('church, bishop, priest, cross') some of these words were adopted under the influence of missionaries seeking to convert the heathen Germans to Christianity. Those efforts continued after the invasion of Britain by the Angles, Jutes, and Saxons during the 5th and 6th centuries, invasions that pushed the Christian, British- and Latin-speaking Britons to the west and south, to Wales, Cornwall, and across the Channel to Brittany. The Christianization of the Anglo-Saxons and consequent Latin influence on the language reached full flood in 597 when Ethelbert, king of Kent, was baptized by St. Augustine, first archbishop of Canterbury and Apostle to the English (also known as St. Austin, and not the Numidian bishop).

The next events that had a noticeable influence on the English vocabulary were the Viking invasions of the 9th and 10th centuries and the Danish conquest of the early 11th century. The Scandinavian sea-rovers and Danish monarchs spoke North Germanic tongues that go under the name Old Norse, which has since separated into Icelandic, Faeroese, Norwegian, Swedish, and Danish. Long before the formal takeover of the kingdom by Canute the Dane, the Norsemen had been establishing permanent settlements on the coasts of Britain, especially in the northeast, and living in uneasy proximity with the Anglo-Saxons. The two languages were similar enough so that they could be mutually understood, and as a result many Norse words and idioms crept into the English speech, often displacing native words and becoming accepted English usage. Examples are

they, Middle English *thei*, from Old Norse *their* 'those,' influenced by Old English *thā* 'those,' and replacing Old English *hī, hīe* 'they' (similarly, *them* and *their*)

egg, from Old Norse *egg*, replacing Middle English *ey*, from Old English *aeg*

sky, from Old Norse *skȳ* 'cloud,' cognate with Old English *sceo* 'cloud'

get, from Old Norse *geta*, cognate with Old English **gietan*

ugly, from Old Norse *uggligr* 'to be feared,' from *uggr* 'fear'

skirt, from Old Norse *skyrta* 'shirt,' living alongside *shirt*, from Old English *scyrta* 'shirt'

loose, from Old Norse *lauss* 'loose, free, empty,' cognate with Old English *lēas* 'free from, without,' ancestor of the English suffix *-less* 'without'

anger, from Old Norse *angra* 'to grieve, to vex,' from *angr* 'grief'

By far the most important external event to have a bearing on the course taken by the English language was the Norman conquest of 1066. In the subsequent 200 or more years, English, "once the name of a national vehicle of culture, became little more than a generic term for a congeries of kindred dialects" (Kemp Malone in *RHD*)—spoken, moreover, by a conquered people in a conquered country where the ruling class spoke a language that was a kind of French. (It was Anglo-French or Anglo-Norman, derivatives of Norman French and Northern Old French. The conquering Normans were descendants of Norsemen who had invaded, conquered and settled north central France, but who had given up their Scandinavian tongue and adopted a French dialect and French culture.) For a period of more than two hundred years, many members of the English-speaking community, both high and low, were of necessity bilingual, a situation that was bound to have an effect on both vocabulary and idiom. Among the common English words that can be traced to this period are

very, Middle English *verray* < Old French *ver(r)ai* < (ultimately) Latin *vērus* 'true' (modern French *vrai* 'true') *jolly,* Middle English *jolif* 'lively, jovial' < Old French *jolif* < (?) Old Norse *jōl* 'midwinter festival,' cognate with *yule* (modern French *joli* 'pretty')

beef, Middle English *boef* < Old French *boef, buef* < Latin *bovem,* accusative of *bos* 'ox, bull, cow' (modern French *boeuf* 'ox, bull; beef')

mutton, Middle English *moto(u)n* < Old French *moton,* probably of Gaulish origin (modern French *mouton* 'sheep; mutton')

castle, Anglo-Norman, from Old Northern French *castel,* variant of Old French *chastel* < Latin *castellum* 'little fort' < Latin *castrum* 'emcampment' (modern French *château*)

engine, from Old French *engin* < Latin *ingenium* 'innate quality; mental powers,' hence 'clever (*ingenious*) contrivance'

curfew < Anglo-Norman *coeverfu* < Old French *cuevrefeu* "cover-fire" (modern French *couvre-feu*)

—and many more. Some of the English idioms traceable to French are, as listed by John Orr in *Old French and Modern English Idiom,*

by heart < *par coeur* < *par choeur* 'by chorus' = 'in chorus; by rote'

cut short from French *couper court*

used to from Old French *user de*

The progressive present (*I am going*) was current in Old French and may have helped in the development of this very idiomatic English usage. (The progressive in other tenses—*I was going, I shall be going,* and so on are also used in Spanish.) Perhaps even the use of the verb *to do* as an auxiliary, so characteristic of English—*We don't have any. How do you know? I don't think so*—was helped along by "the use of *faire* with the infinitive (by 13th century) pupils coping with French, as a means of sidestepping difficulties encountered in the conjugation of their French verbs. If so, any similar trend in their native speech would thereby be encouraged" (John Orr, *op. cit.* Mr. Orr goes on to say and demonstrate that "there are cases where the syntactical use of individual English words can only be satisfactorily explained by that of their French equivalents.")

  With the revival of English as a literary language in the 14th century, signaled by the writings of Chaucer, the new writers did not (successfully) revive many of the Old English literary words that had fallen into disuse, like *wanhope* 'despair,' *inwit* 'conscience,' and *again-bite, ayenbite* 'remorse'; instead, they adopted and adapted words from Medieval and Old French and from Medieval and classical Latin. Latin, it should not be forgotten, had continued to be used as a second (or third) language by persons of education: by the clergy, in the courts, and in the keeping of town and manorial records. It was the accepted vehicle for "serious" works and was used by writers into the 18th century. Since the educated Englishman, whether of Anglo-Saxon or Norman descent, wrote and spoke Latin as fluently as any of his peers on the continent, it is not possible to determine in many cases whether words were taken into English from French or from Latin.

With the full flowering of the Renaissance in Britain, the revival of interest in the learning of the ancient world, the new experimental science, and the new explorations opening up the Americas and the far East, exotic words flowed into English from all directions: Latin, Greek, and Arabic words from the revival of learning; new Latin words coined by the new scientists; outlandish words for outlandish products, like *tobacco, potato,* and *tomato* from the Americas, *tea* from China and *coffee* from Africa; contemporary words from foreign languages, Dutch (*boom* 'spar,' *free-booter*), German (*Kindergarten, meld*), Italian (*infantry, opera*), Spanish (*corral, fiesta*), Portuguese (*fetish, palanquin*), Scandinavian (*skoal, iceberg*), Russian (*samovar, knout*), and so on.

Because a preponderance of English loanwords come from Modern, Medieval, and Old French—and most of which, in turn, come from Latin—it will serve us to examine some of the changes that took place as Latin and Vulgar Latin were transformed into the various stages of French. Of all the Romance languages, French has eroded and distorted the ancestral Latin the most, perhaps because the language had first to be learned by the Celtic Gauls, who adapted it to fit their native modes of speech and then transmitted it to the conquering Germanic Franks and Burgundians who, like the Normans after them, gave up their Germanic speech for the more cosmopolitan Romanic. Perhaps the most noticeable feature in Old French is the frequent loss by syncope of the internal consonants of the ancestral Latin word, making the new word almost unrecognizable as a descendant of the older. For example:

Old French *sur* < Latin *sēcūrus* 'free from care, safe' (English *sure, secure*)

Old French *conter* < Latin *computāre* 'to sum up, to reckon' (English *count, compute*)

Old French *hostel* < Latin *hospitālis* 'of a guest; hospitable' (English *hostel, hotel; hospital*)

Old French *sire* < Latin *senior* 'older' (English *sire, sir, senior; señor, signor . . .*)

Old French *leial, loial* < Latin *lēgālis* 'of the law' (English *legal, loyal*)

Old French *deintie* < Latin *dignitas* 'worthiness, merit' (English *dainty, dignity*)

French has also dropped the terminal (originally inflectional) syllable, unlike Italian, Spanish, Portuguese, and Rumanian.

Another feature of English borrowing from French and Latin is that it took place at different times and from different stages of the source languages, so that the same basic word is frequently borrowed in different forms, as in

Latin *hospitālis* > *hostel* (from Old French), *hotel* (from modern French), *hospital* (from the Latin)

Latin *fragilis* 'easily broken' > *frail* (from Old French *fraile*), *fragile* (from the Latin)

Latin *gentilis* 'of the (same) clan' > *gentile* (from Late Latin *gentilis* 'pagan'); *genteel, gentle, jaunty* (from Old French *gentil* 'well-born.' Modern French *gentil* means 'amiable')

Greek *diskos* > Latin *discus* 'quoit, flat circular object to be thrown in competition; dish' > *discus, disc, disk; dish* (from Old English *disc*), *dais* (from Old French *deis* 'table')

Special note should be made of Latin *c-*, pronounced [k]. In French, its pronunciation before *-e-* and *-i-* was "palatalized" to [s] (*cent, cirque*); but before *-a-* in standard French it changes to *ch-*, pronounced [sh,] as in: *chanter* < *cantāre; chauffer* < *calefacere; chapitre* < *capitulum*. Other changes of note:

Latin *-āticum* > Old French *-age:*
Latin *viāticum* 'money for a journey' > Old French *veiage* > English *voyage*
Latin *silvāticum* 'of the woods' > Old French *sauvage* > English *savage*
Vulgar Latin **corāticum* 'of the heart' > Old French *corage* > English *courage*

Latin *s-* + consonant > Old French *es-* (modern French *é-*), English *es-* or *s-:*
Latin *status* > Old French *estat* (modern French *état*) > English *estate, state*
Latin *spatium* > Old/Modern French *espace* > English *space*
Latin *spina* 'thorn; spine' > Old French *espine* (modern French *épine*) > English *spine*

Old French *-iss-* > English *-ish:*
finiss(ent) > *finish*   *periss(ent)* > *perish*   *aboliss(ent)* > *abolish*

Germanic **w* > Old French *gu-*, modern French *gu-* or *g-* :
Germanic **wardōn* > Old French *guarder* (modern French *garder*) > English *guard*
(Germanic **wardaz* > Old English *weard* > English *ward*)
(Germanic **wardan* > Norman French *warder* > English *warden*)
Germanic **werr-* 'confusion' > French *guerre* 'war', Spanish *guerra* 'war' > Spanish *guerrilla* "little war" (Old High German *werra* 'strife' > English *war*)

As modern English is descended from Middle English (1500 < 1100), which is descended from Old English (1100 < 7th century A.D.), so are the other west European languages arranged historically into the somewhat arbitrary divisions of Modern, Middle, and Old. In the West Germanic languages of High German, Low German, and Dutch, the usual dividing lines are, as in English, 1100 and 1500: anything before 1100 is classified as "Old," anything after 1500 as "Modern," with "Middle" in between. However, "Middle French" is reckoned to be the French of the 14th, 15th, and 16th centuries; but the term is no longer in favor in some linguistic circles, where the era mentioned is considered to be the "final period of Old French." (*AHD*). Old French itself dates from the 9th century (801, the year after Charlemagne's coronation as emperor—obviously an arbitrary date). In this book I have used the term "Medieval French," which is to be understood as covering the French of the 13th–15th centuries (1201–1500).

Old Norse is reckoned to be the North Germanic language prior to 1350 (*MW3*).

Latin is split up into many eras: Old Latin, 6th century B.C. to 240 B.C.; Anteclassical, 240 B.C. to 80 B.C.; Classical Latin, 80 B.C. to 180 A.D.; Late Latin, 180 to 600; Medieval Latin, 600 to 1500; New Latin or Modern Latin, 1500 to the present—with the added complication of Vulgar Latin, the spoken language of the people that "is scantily recorded . . . but attested by inscriptions and established by comparative evidence as the chief source of the Romance languages." (*MW3*)

The situation with Greek is somewhat different in that classical Greek appears in four preeminent dialects: the Ionic (the language of Homer); Attic (taken as standard); Aeolic; and Doric. Classical Greek continued to the 2nd century A.D., at which point it is classified as "Late Greek" till the end of the 6th century. "Medieval Greek" lasts till the end of the 15th century; and "New Greek" is the name given to the modern tongue. (*MW2*)

Edward C. Pinkerton

Bibliography

Adams, J. Donald, *The Magic and Mystery of Words*. Holt, Rinehart & Winston, New York, 1963

The American Heritage Dictionary of the English Language, William Morris, Editor. American Heritage Publishing Co. and Houghton Mifflin Co., Boston, 1969

Barnett, Lincoln, *The Treasure of Our Tongue*. Alfred A. Knopf, New York, 1964

Bloomfield, Leonard, *Language*. Alfred A. Knopf, New York, 1963

Bense, J. F., *A Dictionary of the Low-Dutch Element in the English Vocabulary, Parts I-V*. H. Mitford, London, 1926–1939

Bloch, O. and W. von Wartburg, *Dictionnaire étymologique de la langue française*. Presses Universitaires de France, Paris, 1950.

Bodmer, Frederick, *The Loom of Language*, Lancelot Hogben, editor. W. W. Norton, New York, 1944

Boielle, James and de V. Payen-Payne, *A New French and English Dictionary (Cassell's New French Dictionary)*. Funk & Wagnalls, New York, 1903

Boisacq, Emile, *Dictionnaire étymologique de la langue grecque*. Winter, Heidelberg, 1950

Breul, Karl, *Heath's New German and English Dictionary*. Heath, New York, 1939

Carroll, John B., *The Study of Language*. Harvard University Press, Cambridge, 1953

Dauzat, Albert, *Dictionnaire étymologique de la langue française*. Larousse, Paris, 1957

Edgren, Hjalmar, *An Italian and English Dictionary*. Holt, New York, 1937

Ekwall, Eilert, *The Concise Oxford Dictionary of English Place Names*. Oxford University Press, Oxford, 1960

Ernout, A. and A. Meillet, *Dictionnaire étymologique de la langue latine*. Klincksieck, Paris, 1951

Ernst, Margaret, *The Executive's In a Word Book*. Belmont Books, New York, 1963

Feyerabend, Karl, *Langenscheidt Pocket Greek Dictionary*. McGraw-Hill, 1969

Gerdon, James D. *The English Language, an historical introduction.* Crowell, New York, 1972

Goldberg, Isaac, *The Wonder of Words.* D. Appleton-Century, New York, 1938

Handford, S. A. and Mary Herberg, *Langenscheidt Shorter Latin Dictionary.* McGraw-Hill, 1960

Dictionary of the Bible, edited by James Hastings. Revised edition by Frederick C. Grant and H. H. Rowley. Charles Schribner's Sons, New York, 1963

Holt, Alfred H., *Phrase and Word Origins.* Dover Publications, New York, 1961

Hook, J. V., *History of the English Language.* Ronald Press, New York, 1975

Hulbert, J. R., *Dictionaries: British and American.* James Root, André Deutsch, London, 1956

Jespersen, Otto, *Growth and Structure of the English Language,* 9th edition. Basil Blackwell, Oxford, 1962

Lewis, C. S., *Studies in Words.* Cambridge University Press, Cambridge, 1967

Liddell, H. G. and R. Scott, *Greek-English Lexicon.* Clarendon Press, Oxford, 1925-1940

Mencken, H. L., *The American Language.* Alfred A. Knopf, New York, 1936

Mencken, H. L., *The American Language, Supplement One.* 1945

Mencken, H. L., *The American Language, Supplement Two.* 1948

Menninger, Karl, *Number Words and Number Symbols.* The M.I.T. Press, Cambridge, Mass. 1970

Moore, John, *You English Word.* Lippincott, Philadelphia, 1962

Morris, William and Mary, *Dictionary of Word and Phrase Origins.* Harper and Row, New York, 1962

Myer, M., *The Roots of Modern English.* Little, Brown, Boston, 1966

Orr, John, *Old French and Modern English Idiom.* Basil Blackwell, Oxford, 1962

The Oxford Dictionary of English Etymology, edited by C. T. Onions, with the assistance of G.W.S. Friedrichsen and R.W. Burchfield. Clarendon Press, Oxford, 1966

The Oxford English Dictionary, the Compact Edition of (reproduced micrographically). Oxford University Press, Oxford, 1971

Partridge, Eric, *Origins: a Short Etymological Dictionary of Modern English.* Macmillan, New York, 1958

Pedersen, Holger, *The Discovery of Language,* translated by John Webster Spargo. University of Indiana Press, Bloomington, 1962. (Originally published as *Linguistic Science in the Nineteenth Century*, Cambridge, Mass., 1931)

Pei, Mario, *The Families of Words*. Harper and Brothers, New York, 1962

Pei, Mario, *The Story of the English Language*. Lippincott, Philadelphia, 1967

Pokorny, Julius, *Indogermanisches etymologisches Wörterbuch*. Francke, Bern, 1951-1959

Pope, M. K., *From Latin to French with Especial Consideration of Anglo-Norman*. Manchester University Press, Manchester, 1934, reprinted 1956

Price, H. T., *Foreign Influence on Middle English*. University of Michigan Contributions in Modern Philology, Ann Arbor, 1947

Pyles, Thomas, *The Origins and Development of the English Language, second edition*. Harcourt Brace Jovanovich, New York, 1971

Ramondino, Salvatore, editor, *The New World Spanish-English and English-Spanish Dictionary*. New American Library, New York, 1969

The Random House Dictionary of the English Language, Jess Stein, Editor in Chief, Laurence Urdang, Managing Editor. Random House, New York, 1966

Rosten, Leo, *The Joys of Yiddish*. McGraw-Hill, New York, 1968

Sapir, Edward, *Language: an Introduction to the Study of Speech*. Harcourt Brace, New York, 1955

Serjeantsen, Mary S., *A History of Foreign Words in English*. Routledge & Kegan Paul, London, 1935, second impression 1961

Skeat, W. W., *An Etymological Dictionary of the English Language*. Cambridge, 1910

Sledd, James H. and Gwin J. Kolb, *Dr. Johnson's Dictionary*. University of Chicago Press, 1955

Starnes, DeWitt T. and Gertrude E. Noyes, *The English Dictionary from Cawdrey to Johnson, 1604-1755*. University of North Carolina Press, Chapel Hill, 1946

Tacitus, *On Britain and Germany*, translated by H. Mattingly. Penguin Books, Harmondsworth, England, 1948; reprinted 1954

Walshe, M. O'C., *A Concise German Etymological Dictionary*. Routledge & Kegan Paul, London, 1952

Webster's New International Dictionary of the English Language, Second Edition, unabridged, William Allen Neilson, Editor in Chief; Thomas A. Knott, General Editor; Paul W. Carhart, Managing Editor. G. & C. Merriam, Springfield, Mass., 1941

Webster's Third New International Dictionary, unabridged, Philip Babcock Gove, Editor in Chief. G. & C. Merriam, Springfield, Mass., 1961

Weekley, Ernest, *Concise Etymological Dictionary*. Dutton, New York, 1952

How to Use This Book

The first thing to do is to read *Word for Word*. Because it contains such a great amount of information, highly condensed, you will probably wish to read one chapter at a time, which is why the chapters are relatively short. To identify the various kinds of information in the book, it will be useful—at first—to refer to the following explanations:

1. A word under discussion is printed in small capital letters: For example, the following passage appears at the opening of Chapter XIV:

> CRUMBS in the CRIB? CRUMBLING CRUMPETS in the CRADLE? CRANK up your CROQUET mallet and watch the ENCROACHERS CRINGE and CREEP away!

In the following paragraph, each of these words is explained and the ways in which they are related is discussed in detail. Not only are their sources given, but the author pinpoints the ways their meanings have changed, which languages they sprang from, and many other interesting facts about their history.

2. During the course of tracing these (and many other) words back to their sources, their original forms in other languages are given. In all cases, these words (or, in some cases, phrases) are shown in italic type, many with their original accents. In some instances, where the original language might not have been written in the Roman alphabet (for example, Sanskrit, Russian, or Greek), the word has been transliterated. All foreign languages are always clearly identified. Here is a passage illustrating this style:

> Old Norse *krōkr* has an equivalent in Frankish **krōk*, antecedent of French *croc.* . . .

It will be noted that the second italicized word is preceded by an asterisk. This is not to call attention to a footnote (there are no footnotes in this book) but to employ a symbol used by linguists to mark a form that they believe may (or should) have existed at one time during the development of the language identified but for which they have no written evidence.

It must be remembered that the further back certain languages are traced, the sparser the extant writing available for study; likewise, some languages, though of more recent vintage, might not have been used by a large population of speakers or by a civilization that attended much to the keeping of records. Thus, linguists have found gaps in the developments of certain forms. Typically, a later form of the same word may differ from an earlier one both by lacking a consonant sound and by exhibiting an apparent change in sound in a vowel; depending on the language, linguists may theorize about the "shape" of an intermediate form for which no written evidence exists (as far as is known at the time)—a form that *theoretically* should be spelled a certain way—and then write it with an asterisk as hypothetical. Often, later evidence confirms linguists' hypotheses about some of these forms, but not always, of course: certain changes that might have taken place in the undocumented past might well have been brought about by a conquering people, by some anomalous, unknown event, or simply by a change of speech habit. With literacy controlled by very few until quite recently in the history of man, influences tending to standardize dialects or to "freeze" a particular form of a language seldom existed.

3. In single quotation marks are found the meanings, or glosses, of the words printed in small capitals and in italics. Where these are closely related, they are separated within quotation marks by commas; where the senses are somewhat less closely related, they are separated by semicolons; and in those cases where a particular sense may have a special label (shown in parentheses preceding the given sense), the quotation marks are closed before a following semicolon and then opened again to make clear the somewhat more distant relationship of meaning. Here are some examples from the first page of Chapter XIV:

> Also, CROCHET 'needlework made by looping thread with a hooked needle' [French crochet 'small hook,' diminutive of croc] and CROTCH-ET 'a small hook'; (music) 'a quarter note'; 'an odd notion,' hence CROTCHETY 'full of eccentricities.'

4. In the square brackets are interpolated etymologies given at the spot so that the thought needn't be reintroduced later on. Here is another example of this bracketing technique:

> Another probable derivative of Frankish *krok 'hook' is CROQUET 'a lawn game in which players using long-handled mallets drive balls through a series of hoops' [from Northern French croquet 'a small hook'].

5. Some forms are given with a hyphen; these are either prefixes (pre-), suffixes (-ing), or root forms (Indo-European root *ger-). These should not be confusing, because they are always identified.

6. It will be seen that the lines of text are numbered from beginning to end. That has been done because it was felt that the book contained so much detailed information on every page that it would be difficult to return to some bit of data again, once it had been read. Also for that reason, a detailed Index will be found beginning on page 319. Because the same item may appear several times within a few lines in the text, only the first instance appears in the Index; if an item is repeated in the text within fewer than 25 lines, no further listing for it appears in the Index; if the item is repeated after the 25-line minimum, a new Index listing is shown.

In addition to including almost every citation for every word printed in small capitals and italics in the text, the Index contains listings for all of the meanings listed in the book. As it would be impossible to list these words with their alternatives—providing, in effect, a thesaurus—we have been content to list key words from the glosses, giving as full a description in each case as is feasible.

Abbreviations and Symbols

AHD	*American Heritage Dictionary*
EP	Eric Partridge, *Origins*
M.O'C. Walshe	M.O'C. Walshe, *A Concise German Etymological Dictionary*
MW2	Merriam-Webster's *New International Dictionary*, 2nd edition
MW 3	Merriam-Webster's *New International Dictionary*, 3rd edition
ODEE	*Oxford Dictionary of English Etymology*
OED	*Oxford English Dictionary*
Pei	Mario Pei, *The Families of Words*
RHD	*Random House Dictionary*

* (before a root or word) unattested, hypothetical; extrapolative
\> yields, leads to, whence
\< derived from, descended from, following after

Word for Word

I

Actors, Demagogues, Ambassadors, *and* Navigators

People go agog over DEMAGOGUES; children reluctantly follow PEDAGOGUES; and congregations gather in SYNAGOGUES. All this -AGOGUEry should lead somewhere, for the element *-agogue* stems from the Greek noun *agōgos* 'leader,' which comes from the Greek verb *agein* 'to lead, to drive'; and *agein* derives ultimately   5
from the Indo-European root **ag-* 'to drive' (so close is leading to driving).

The DEM- in DEMAGOGUE comes from the Greek *dēmos* 'the common people.' In ancient Athens, a *dēmagōgos* was a leader of the people or of a popular faction. Nowadays, a DEMAGOGUE is 'a   10
rabble rouser; a political agitator who appeals to the passions and prejudices of the mob in order to obtain power.' These are unfavorable senses that were already gaining ground in Athens during the Peloponnesian wars (fifth century B.C.).

An ancient Greek *paidagōgos* was originally 'a slave who led   15
a boy to and from school' (the girls didn't go to school), rather than what he later became, a PEDAGOGUE 'one entrusted with the education of children; a schoolteacher' [Greek *pais*, *paidos* 'child']. Greek *paidagōgos* was adopted into Latin as *paedagōgus* 'a slave in charge of children; guardian, leader.' As time went by,   20
the emphasis shifted from 'in charge of' to 'instructor of'; and by the time of Medieval Latin, a fellow-traveling verb had developed: *paedagōgāre* 'to instruct, to teach.' The accusative of the present participle of *paedagōgāre*, *paedagōgāntem*, which is quite a mouthful, may have telescoped into Italian *pedante* 'teacher,   25
schoolmaster.' *Pedante* is the source of English PEDANT (obsolete) 'a schoolteacher'; 'one who insists on strict adherence to formal rules in matters of learning' [via French *pedant*, *pédant*]. But evidence for the development of Medieval Latin *paedagōgāntem* into Italian *pedante* is lacking, and one analyst suggests that the   30

ped- in *pedante* is equivalent to *ped-*, *piede* 'foot'; hence, *pedante* = 'going on foot' = 'a servile follower.' As for the word SYNA-GOGUE 'the congregation of a Jewish community for religious worship,' it comes from the Greek *sunagōgē* 'assembly'; from
35   *sunagein* 'to lead together.' *Sunagōgē* has been used as the term for the Jewish congregation since the third century B.C., when the Hebrew scriptures were put into Greek by the seventy learned translators of the Septuagint, as their rendering of the Hebrew *keneṣeth* 'assembly' (compare *Knesset* 'the Israeli parliament').
40   There is yet another -AGOGUE 'leader': MYSTAGOGUE 'one who prepares candidates for initiation into the mysteries of a religion' [from Greek *mustagōgos*, *mustēs* (literally) 'close-mouthed; an initiate'], as well as the adjective HYPNAGOGIC 'inducing sleep' [Greek *hupnos* 'sleep'] as a barbiturate does or a
45   dull lecture.
There is also a shortened form of Greek *agōgos* 'leader, guide,' to wit, *agos* 'leader, captain.' A variant of *agos* shows up as part of the Greek word *stratēgos* 'leader of an army; general' which is formed on *stratos* 'army' + *-ēgos* equivalent to *agos*
50   'leader, captain.' *Stratēgos* gives rise to the English words STRAT-EGY 'the art of directing large military operations' [from Greek *stratēgia* 'office of a general'] and STRATAGEM 'an act of general-ship; a maneuver designed to outwit the enemy' [from Greek *stratēgēma*].
55   Also formed on *agein* 'to lead' and *agos* 'leader' is CHORAGUS 'the leader of the chorus in a Greek drama' [via Latin from Greek *khoragos*, *khorēgos* (*khoros* 'chorus')]. (Note: The English word *agog* 'full of intense interest' comes from Medieval French *en gogues* 'full of merriment' according to most authorities.)
60   Anyone who has watched a wrestling match has seen physical AGONY written on the face of a wrestler pinned to the mat in a toehold. To one who associates the word AGONY with the mental anguish of Christ in the garden of Gethsemane, this illustration taken from sports may seem flippant; but it is in fact peculiarly
65   apt, as the etymology will show. AGONY 'intense pain' is based on Greek *agōnia* 'struggle, contention; labor; fear, agony,' which in turn stems from Greek *agōn* 'place where athletic contests are held'; hence, 'contest' (originally *agōn* meant simply 'assembly place,' and intermediately 'place of festive celebrations'). *Agōn*,
70   *agōnia*, and AGONY, like the -AGOGUE words, stem from the Indo-European root *ag-* 'to drive' via the Greek verb *agein* 'to drive; to lead,' which has secondary or extended meanings of 'to celebrate; to keep a festival.' The conclusion to be drawn is that among the Greeks a festive assembly was spiced with sporting games, much
75   as a county fair in the United States is enlivened by horse races

and prize contests (*athletic* means, literally, 'for a prize' from *athlon* 'prize'). The prize example of festive sporting games is the Olympics, which traditionally were first held in 776 B.C., when they consisted of a simple foot race, and continued with a gradually expanding agenda until they were banned in the 4th century A.D. because they had become too professionalized. (They were revived in 1896 and are now becoming professionalized all over again.)

The succession of meanings of Greek *agōnia* ('struggle, contention > labor > fear > agony') sounds something like the pleasant torture a baseball fan goes through toward the end of a season when his team is in the thick of the fight for the pennant. The English word based on *agōnia* is AGONY 'a violent struggle; the suffering of intense pain.'

Where there is a contest there must be contestants. A Greek contestant in an *agōn* was called *agōnistēs* 'one contending for a prize; an advocate; an actor' (another suggestive sequence of meanings; cf. Milton's sacred drama, *Samson Agonistes*). Greek *agōnistēs* is preserved in the English words AGONIST 'one engaged in a struggle; one beset by conflicts'; ANTAGONIST 'adversary' [*anti-* 'against']; and PROTAGONIST 'the leading character in a drama' [*proto-* 'first'].

So much, for now, for Greek words derived from the Indo-European root **ag-* 'to drive.' In Latin this root shows up most clearly in the verb *agō, agere, ēgi, āctum* 'to drive, to lead; to set in motion; to do, to act, to perform; to manage.' It is a verb that has many Latin meanings and an enormous progeny of English words. Among the most important is ACT 'a deed; a thing done; to do something; to perform; to behave' [from the Latin past participle *āctum* 'done; deed, action'; and *āctus* 'done; performance; a driving']. ACT is a word of many derivatives and compounds, of such easily perceived meanings that most of them can be listed without comment: words like ACTION; ACTIVE; ACTIVITY; ACTIVATE; ACTOR (original Latin meaning was 'driver, shepherd'; hence, 'manager,' but the sense 'performer in a play' also developed in Latin); ACTUAL; ACTUALITY; ACTUATE; ACTUARY (obsolete) 'a clerk of a law court'; 'a statistician who computes insurance risks' [from Latin *āctuārius* 'shorthand writer; registrar of documents']; ENACT 'to pass a bill of legislation (= an ACT); to represent or reproduce, as on a stage' (using ACTORS); TRANSACT 'to carry through negotiations'; and REACT 'to perform another time; to respond to a stimulus.' Now the derivations become less obvious: EXACT (literally) 'to drive out, to force out'; 'to require, to demand; strictly in accordance with facts, accurate' [from Latin

80

85

90

95

100

105

110

115

120   *exigere* (for *exagere), *exāctum* 'to drive out; to demand; to examine; to weigh'].

An EXACTING master is a "demanding" one. One can imagine him standing by, whip in hand, EXAMINING the products of one's labors, "weighing" the profitable ingots. The tie-in of 'weighing'
125   and 'accuracy' with 'driving out' was gradually lost in the minds of the Latin speakers, for the related nouns *exāmen* [from **exag(s)men*] 'swarm (of bees); multitude' and *exāmen* 'tongue of a balance, examination, consideration' were felt by them to be two different words. *Exāmen* 'tongue of a balance' leads to *exāmināre*
130   'to weigh accurately; to examine' and to English EXAMINE 'to scrutinize in detail.'

A related noun, which appeared in Late Latin, is *exagium* 'a weighing, a balance,' perhaps borrowed from the almost synonymous Greek word, *exagion* 'a testing'; but more likely the borrowing went the other way. From *exagium* there developed the
135   Vulgar Latin verb *exagiare 'to weigh out,' which evolved into Old French *essaier, assaier* 'to test, to try out,' with related nouns *essai, assai*. These are sources of the English words ESSAY 'to try; an attempt; a short composition on a single subject' and ASSAY 'to
140   examine by trial and experiment; to subject to chemical analysis.'

Adopted directly from Latin *exigere* 'to drive out; to demand' is EXIGENT 'urgent; excessively demanding' [from the Latin present participle *exigens* 'exacting'] and intimately related is EXIGU-OUS (etymologically) 'weighed exactly'; 'scanty, meager' [from
145   Latin *exiguus* 'scanty, short (in weight)']. Note that Latin *exiguus* has already taken on the sense 'short weight,' rather than its literal meaning, 'exact weight.' One gets the impression that a vendor who didn't allow a little over the measure was considered niggardly. (A similar sense development is seen in French *étriqué*
150   'scanty' derived from Old French *estriquer* 'to remove excess grain from a measure with a strickle.' (See line 9704.)

Finally we have REDACT 'to edit; to put into proper literary form' [from Latin *redigere, redactum* 'to bring back; to collect']; REDACTOR 'editor' (the *red-* prefix is a variant of *re-* 'back, again'
155   used before a vowel in some words); and RETROACTIVE 'applying to a period prior to enactment' [*retro-* 'backwards'].

An AGILE AGENT will AGITATE constantly and COGENTLY, until his client's AGENDA is filled. These busy, nimble words also come (via Latin *agere* 'to drive, to lead; to set in motion') from the
160   Indo-European root **ag-* 'to drive': AGENT 'a means by which something is done; one who acts (for another)' [from Latin *agens* 'setting in motion,' present participle of *agere*]; AGENDA 'a list of things to be done' [from the Latin gerundive *agendum*, plural *agenda* '(things that) must be done']; and AGILE 'nimble, able to

move easily' [from Latin *agilis* 'easily moved; quick' (*-ilis* 'tending   165
to')].

From the Latin compound *cōgere* [for *co-* + *agere*] 'to drive
together' we get English COGENT 'forcibly convincing' [from the
present participle *cōgens* 'compelling'].

The Latin suffix *-itāre*, added to a verbal root, has what is   170
called a "frequentative" effect: it indicates that the action of the
verb takes place repeatedly—sometimes so often as to be constantly. Thus, *-itāre* added to *ag(ere)* 'to drive, to lead; to set in
motion' gives us Latin *agitāre* 'to set in motion frequently, to set
in constant motion; to shake, to toss up and down.' From this   175
comes English AGITATE 'to move briskly; to perturb; to excite the
mind; to stir up public interest.' Latin *agitāre* developed
extended meanings of 'to celebrate, to keep a festival' (compare
Greek *agein*, line 71); 'to consider, to deliberate' ('to set things
astir in one's mind'); hence, 'to discuss, to debate.' These last   180
meanings may seem to have been more than one verb could
handle, because simple *agitāre* was reinforced with the intensify-
ing prefix *cō-* (literally) 'together with' to make *cōgitāre* 'to stir up
one's mind together with; to reflect upon, to think.' This is the
source of English COGITATE 'to take careful thought.' ("*Cōgitō,*   185
ergo sum," quoth Descartes.)

There are numerous Latin compounds in which *agere* 'to
drive' takes the form *-igere*, providing the impulse for a large
range of activities, as reflected in the following English words:
FUMIGATE 'to subject to smoke' [from Latin *fūmigāre* (*fūmus*   190
'smoke')]; FUSTIGATE 'to beat with a club' [from Late Latin
fūstigāre (*fūstis* 'club')]; NAVIGATE 'to control the course of a
ship; to direct one's course' [from Latin *nāvigāre* 'to make a ship
go, to sail' (*nāvis* 'ship')]; LITIGATE 'to subject to a lawsuit' [from
Latin *lītigāre* 'to dispute' (*līs, lītis* 'contention; lawsuit')]; OBJUR-   195
GATE 'to rebuke sharply' [from Latin *obiūr(i)gāre* 'to scold';
(literally) 'to bring a lawsuit against' (*ob-* 'against' + *iūs, iūris*
'law' + *agere*)]; and CASTIGATE (literally) 'to make pure, to make
chaste'; 'to punish; to criticize severely' [from Latin *castīgāre* 'to
reprove, to punish' (from Latin *castus* (etymologically) 'cut off   200
from'; 'pure, chaste')]. Purity achieved by "cutting off" results in
some interesting comparisons, in terms of semantic development.
Note these cognates: CHASTE, CASTE, and CASTRATE. Latin
castīgāre 'to reprove, to punish' evolved into Old French *chas-*
tier, whence Middle English *chastien*, and English CHASTEN,   205
CHASTISE 'to punish.' The English loanword INTRANSIGENT (literally) 'not transacting; refusing to compromise' comes from a
French loanword borrowed from Spanish *los intransigentes* 'the
noncompromisers,' the name of a Spanish party of extreme repub-

210 licans, circa 1873 [from Latin *in-* 'not' + *trānsigere, trānsāctum* 'to drive through, to transact; to come to an understanding']. Note, also, AMBIGUOUS 'leading around; capable of being interpreted in more than one way' [from Latin *ambiguus* 'inclined to both sides; of uncertain nature'; from *ambigere* 'to wander about; to doubt'

215 (*ambi-* 'on both sides, around' + *-igere* for *agere* 'to lead')].

The element *ambi-* 'on both sides, around' is also seen in AMBIDEXTROUS, AMBIVALENT, AMBIENCE; and it is cousin to the Greek *amphi-*, seen in AMPHITHEATER, AMPHIBIOUS. Both Greek and Latin forms stem from the Indo-European root **ambhi-*

220 'around' (as does English BY). Celtic also had the form **ambi-* 'around' and, like the Latin speakers, the Celtic speakers combined it with the root **ag-* 'to drive' to make a compound, **ambagto-* 'one who is sent around.' **Ambagto-* showed up in Gaulish as **ambactos* 'vassal, servant (messenger)' and was

225 adopted into Latin by Quintus Ennius and later by Julius Caesar in the form *ambactus* 'vassal, envoy.' Latin *ambactus*, after passing through divers Germanic tongues, eventually gave rise to Medieval Latin *ambactia* 'mission,' which was extended to form the verb **ambactiāre* 'to send on a mission' and the noun

230 **ambactiator(em)* 'one sent on a mission, a messenger.' To give the word its current English spelling: AMBASSADOR 'a diplomatic official of the highest rank' [from Old French *ambassadeur*; from Old Italian *ambasciator*]. Medieval Latin *ambactia* 'mission' survives in English in EMBASSY, and at one time or another the

235 title of the official who presides over an embassy has been spelled variously *embassador, embassadour, embassiator, imbassator, inbassetour.* (There are thirty-four spellings listed in the *Oxford English Dictionary.*) There is yet another word, this one archaic, that descends from these same two Indo-European roots, **ambhi-*

240 'around' and **ag-* 'to drive': AMBAGE 'an indirect pathway; a roundabout way of speaking' [from Middle English *ambages* 'circumlocution,' an adoption of Latin *ambages* 'a roundabout way']. Thus it should surprise no one that the statements of AMBASSADORS are often AMBIGUOUS, since they are couched in

245 AMBAGES.

There follows a list of English words descended by way of Latin and French from the Indo-European root **ag-* 'to drive' in some of which that root is so disguised as to be imperceptible: PURGE 'to purify' [via Old French *purger* from Latin *pūrgāre* (for

250 *pūrigāre*) 'to cleanse' (*pūrus* 'pure, clean')]; COAGULATE 'to become a solid mass' (said of a liquid) [from Latin *coāgulāre* 'to curdle,' from *coāgulum* 'rennet,' from *cōgere* (for **coagere*) 'to drive together']. The *-ulum* suffix is here instrumental: 'that which drives the curds together.' Also from Latin *cōgere*, ultimately, is

CACHE 'a hiding place; a store of hidden goods' [from the French,   255
from *cacher* 'to hide'; from Vulgar Latin **coacticare* 'to compress,
to stow away'; from Latin *coāctum* 'gathered together,' past
participle of *cōgere* 'to drive together.'] CACHE was borrowed by
English-speaking Americans from the vocabulary of the French-
Canadian *coureurs de bois* and *voyageurs*, who roamed Louisiana   260
when that province extended all the way from the Gulf of Mexico
to the Rockies and the Canadian border; but it was also used as
early as 1595 by Sir Francis Drake, who wrote: "The inhabitants
. . . hid theyr treasure in casshes."

From an older meaning of French *cacher* 'to press, to crush'   265
(represented in modern French by *écacher* 'to crush') comes the
noun CACHET 'a seal on a letter or document; a mark of distinction' ("the seal of approval"), borrowed from the French.

Also traceable to Latin *cōgere*, according to some, is SQUAT
'to sit on one's heels; short and thick' [from Old French *esquatir*   270
'to flatten thoroughly'; *es-* (= *ex-*, used as an intensifier) + *quatir*,
catir 'to press flat'; from Vulgar Latin **coactire* 'to press together,'
formed on *coactus*, past participle of *cōgere* 'to drive together']. A
dialectal variant of SQUAT in the north of England was *swat*, and
an obsolete meaning of SQUAT is 'to lay flat with a blow'; put   275
these two together and you have SWAT 'to hit a crushing blow; to
hit at; a sharp blow; a long hit in baseball, especially a home run.'
Babe Ruth was known as "the Sultan of Swat"; the reaction to this
by the real ruler of Swat, which is a state in northwestern
Pakistan ruled not by a sultan, but by a *wali* ('governor'), is   280
unknown.

There is also PRODIGAL 'recklessly wasteful,' a back formation
from PRODIGALITY [from Medieval Latin *prōdigālitās* 'wasteful-
ness'; from Latin *prōdigus* 'wasteful,' from *prōdigere* 'to drive
forth, to squander' (from *prōd-* = *prō-* 'forth, away' + *-igere* for   285
agere)]. But, "prodigious" as was the welcome-home feast that his
father had prepared for the PRODIGAL son, the words *prodigy* and
prodigious are not related to PRODIGAL.

Switching back to Greek, we come across an example of Indo-
European **ag-* 'to drive' in the Greek adjective *axios* (for **agtios*)   290
'weighing as much as; worth, equivalent; worthy.' If one should
wonder how the notion of 'worth' evolved from the notion of
'driving,' he would have to imagine the semantic sequence to
have been something like: 'to drive > to force > to force out > to
examine > to weigh > to be worth.' (Remember Latin **exagmen*,   295
exāmen 'the pointer of a set of scales; examination'; furthermore,
Greek *agein* 'to drive, to lead' has an extended sense of 'to
estimate, to weigh.')

From Greek *axios* 'worthy' there developed the verb *axioun* 'to value as worthy; to take for true,' and the noun *axiōma* 'valuation, estimation; that which is thought worthy; that which is taken for true.' The noun *axiōma* was used by Aristotle and has been used by all western philosophers and mathematicians since to mean 'a self-evident principle,' an AXIOM 'a proposition that is taken for granted; a self-evident truth.' A related word is AXIOLOGY 'the study of the nature of values.'

Another Greek word that may possibly be descended from Indo-European **ag-* 'to drive' is *agra* 'chase, hunting; a catching, a seizure' (drive > pursue > catch > seize). This is seen in English in the medical terms PODAGRA 'a seizure of the foot; gout' [Greek *pous, podos* 'foot'] and PELLAGRA 'skin seizure; a diet-deficiency disease marked by skin eruptions' [Latin *pellis* 'skin'].

II

Angry Anxiety, Hangnails, *and* Quinsy

Discovering a new HANGNAIL on one's finger is annoying but hardly a cause for ANGER or ANXIETY, though an especially painful AGNAIL may cause some ANGUISH. These words of worry and woe have come into English by various routes from the Indo-European root *angh- 'tight, painful.' The word HANGNAIL 'a small piece of partly detached dead skin alongside a fingernail' is a folk-etymological adaptation of AGNAIL (obsolete) 'a corn on the foot; an inflammation about a fingernail or toenail; a hangnail' [from Old English *angnaegl* 'a corn on the foot']. The later meanings of AGNAIL result from a misconstruing of the sense of the element -*naegl* in Old English *angnaegl*, which comes from Germanic *ang-* 'compressed, painful' + Old English *naegl* 'nail.' This -*naegl* did not originally refer to fingernails or toenails but to the shape of a 'clavus,' a corn on the foot, a 'hard, round-headed excrescence fixed in the flesh,' a 'painful spike (in the flesh)'; hence a nail, the Latin meaning of *clāvus*. However, the fact that other painful spots occur in the neighborhood of fingernails and toenails was too much for the folk-etymological sense of the English speakers, so the meaning was transferred to maladies of those digital extremities, and the word *angnaegl* was eventually "corrupted" into HANGNAIL, quite a different thing from a corn. In Scotland, Old English *angnaegl* became ANGER-NAIL. Here the *ang-* element has been interpreted to mean ANGRY 'inflamed,' which is closer to the original meaning than 'hanging.' The English word ANGER meant (originally) 'that which pains or afflicts,' then (obsolete) 'the passive feeling of suffering that pain produces,' and finally 'wrath, ire, hot displeasure.' It was adopted directly from Old Norse *angr* 'trouble, affliction; grief, sorrow.' The shift in meaning from 'the cause of pain' to 'passive suffering' to 'active resentment' is somehow exhilarating, like the downfall

315

320

325

330

335

340

of a bully. Note that the 'painful' connotations of the word ANGER still linger in the use of the adjective ANGRY 'inflamed,' as in 'an ANGRY sore' and in dialectal English ANGER 'inflammation of a wound or sore.'

Indo-European *angh- 'tight, painful' shows up in modern German as *eng* 'narrow, tight' and *engen* 'to pinch.' It is also present in a German word that has been taken into English as a psychological term, ANGST 'a feeling of anxiety.' ANXIETY [Latin *anxietās*] springs from the Latin for ANXIOUS 'worried, upset about a matter whose outcome is uncertain' [from Latin *anxius* 'troubled, uneasy'; from *angere, anxi* 'to squeeze; to feel pain'].

Also derived from Indo-European *angh- 'tight, painful' is ANGUISH 'agonizing pain; mental torment' [from Old French *anguisse*; from Latin *angustia* 'narrowness, difficulty, distress,' from *angustus* 'narrow']. Latin *angustus* 'narrow' also survives in Spanish *angosto* 'narrow' and *angostura* 'narrowness.' The Venezuelan city now known as Ciudad Bolívar, built on the Orinoco river at the head of ocean-going navigation, where the river "narrows," was originally known as ANGOSTURA because of its location. Certain trees in the area had a peculiarly aromatic bark that was found to be beneficial as a tonic; it was called "ANGOSTURA bark" and is still used as a tonic and as an ingredient in ANGOSTURA Bitters. ANGINA 'any disease in which spasmodic suffocating attacks occur, such as croup or diphtheria' is from Latin *angina* 'quinsy'; from Greek *ankhonē* 'strangulation,' from *ankhein* 'to strangle'; or from Latin *angere* 'to strangle.' ANGINA pectoris is (literally) 'strangulation of the chest.'

The ancient Greek word for 'dog collar' is *kunankhē* (literally) 'dog throttle' [from *kuōn* 'dog' + *ankhein* 'to strangle']. *Kunankhē* was also used to mean 'sore throat,' and this meaning was taken into Medieval Latin in the form *quinancia*. *Quinancia* evolved into Old French *quinencie*, which was adapted into Middle English as *quinesye*, whence English QUINSY 'a severe inflammation of the throat.'

III

Artists, Arithmeticians, *and* Harmonious Armadillos

The ARMADILLO's ARMATURE is ingeniously ARTICULATED to allow him to move with HARMONIOUS COORDINATION; but even so, he looks slightly ARTHRITIC as he clanks about the countryside. The word ARTICULATED here means 'consisting of segments united by joints,' while ARTICULATE means 'speaking clearly and expressively,' a figurative extension of meaning that had already been made in Latin (*articulō* 'I speak distinctly'). All of these words trace back to the Indo-European root **ar-* 'to fit together.'

The place where things fit together is called a 'joint,' or in Latin *artus* and in Greek *arthron*—formed on the Indo-European root **ar-* by way of the suffixed forms **ar-tu-* and **ar-dhro-*, respectively. It is from the Greek *arthron* 'joint' that we get the element *arthr-*, *arthro-* found in a number of scientific terms, for example, ARTHRITIS 'inflammation of the joints.' (The suffix *-itis* has come to mean 'inflammation of,' but all it meant originally was 'of the,' the Greek word *nosos* 'disease' being understood. Thus, ARTHRITIS is short for *arthritis nosos* 'disease of the joints.') Other examples are ARTHROPOD (literally) 'jointed foot; one of a phylum of articulated invertebrates with jointed limbs' (insects, crustaceans, arachnids, myriapods); ARTHROSIS 'a connection between bones; a degenerative process in a joint' [*-osis* 'process, condition']; and ANARTHROUS 'lacking joints'; (grammar) 'used without an article' [Greek *a-*, *an-* 'not, without'].

Latin *artus* 'joint' has a diminutive, *articulus* 'a (small) joint; a part, a division'; hence, 'a division of time, a moment, a precise point; a crisis.' Latin *articulus* has been adopted into English as ARTICLE (obsolete) 'a joint connecting two parts of the body'; (archaic) ' "a nick of time that joins two successive periods" ' (*OED*); 'a juncture in time, a critical moment; especially "the ARTICLE of death" ' (Latin, *in articulo mortis* 'at the moment of

380

385

390

395

400

405

death'); 'a distinguishable item' (an ARTICLE of clothing; an ARTICLE of the Constitution); 'a part of speech (*the*; *a, an*) used with nouns to indicate definiteness or indefiniteness.' Also from *articulus > articulāre* are ARTICULATE(D), noted earlier.

The contrary notions of 'dividing things up' and 'fitting things together' are basic to the kind of manipulative intelligence that human culture rests upon; the concept conveyed by the Indo-European root **ar-* 'to fit together' is thus a fundamental one. It shows up most characteristically in the Latin words *ars, artis, artem* 'skill, profession; science, knowledge' adopted into English by way of Old French as ART 'skill in doing anything as the result of study and practice'; ' "human effort to imitate, supplement, alter or counteract the work of nature" ' (*AHD*); 'a formal branch of learning.' During the Middle Ages, seven such ARTS, or branches of learning, were taught in the colleges. They were thought of as "subjects requiring only to be acquired and practised" (*OED*), since their main principles had already been investigated and established. Known as the liberal arts, they were grammar (Latin grammar, that is), logic, and rhetoric (the trivium), and arithmetic, geometry, music, and astronomy (the quadrivium). (See line 10624.) Students who reached prescribed levels of proficiency in these disciplines were awarded degrees of Bachelor of Arts and Master of Arts.

Besides the seven liberal arts there are the more prestigious, less utilitarian fine arts (French *beaux arts*), which may be defined as 'those arts that are intended to be beautiful rather than useful': drawing, painting, sculpture, and architecture (the arts of design), literature, drama, music, and the dance. (Note that music is both a liberal art and a fine art.)

And let us not overlook ARTIST 'a practitioner of one of the fine arts; especially a painter or sculptor' but, basically, anyone who has mastery over his work technique, be it polishing shoes, performing surgery, or operating a bulldozer. Then there is the word ARTISTE, which is ARTIST with a French accent, originally applied to musical and theatrical performers but now extended to modistes, hairdressers, cooks, and other skilled craftsmen. Says the *OED* of ARTISTE: "a re-introduction of the French word in consequence of the modern tendency to restrict *artist* to those engaged in the fine arts, and especially painting." The earliest example of ARTISTE given in the 1972 *OED Supplement* is dated 1823.

Other derivatives of ART are ARTFUL 'skillful, ingenious; crafty, deceitful'; ARTLESS 'without guile, naive; lacking skill, crude'; ARTIFICE (obsolete) 'the making of something by skilled workmanship'; 'a clever device; a wily stratagem; trickery, deceit;

ingenuity, skill' [from Latin *artificium* 'skill, ingenuity'; from *artifex* 'craftsman' (*-fex* 'maker' from *facere* 'to make')]; ARTIFICIAL; ARTIFACT 'an object produced by human workmanship' [*factum* 'something made; deed, exploit']; ARTISAN 'a skilled workman' [via Old French from Italian *artigiano* 'a mechanic'; from Vulgar Latin *artitiānus*; from Latin *artītus* 'skilled in arts'; from *artīre* 'to instruct in the arts'].

The Latin word *ars*, *artis* and its brood of derivatives all imply a skill 'a way of putting things together; a way of doing, a way of acting.' On the other hand, something that does nothing at all except resist all efforts to make it move is said to be INERT 'unable to act or move' [from Latin *iners* 'without skills; inactive' (*in-* 'not' + *ars* 'skill')] and to exhibit INERTIA 'a resistance to motion or change' [from Latin *inertia* 'unskillfulness, laziness']. The Latin word was adapted to modern physics by the German astronomer, Johannes Kepler (1571–1630).

Somewhat closer to the original idea of 'joining' and 'fitting together' is Latin *armus* 'shoulder, shoulder blade; upper arm.' The resemblance of this Latin word to English ARM 'an upper limb of the human body' is not as obvious as it looks, for the relationship is collateral: ARM comes to English from Indo-European **ar-* 'to fit together' by way of Germanic **armaz* (a cognate of Latin *armus*) and Old English *earm*.

On the other hand, the English word ARMS 'weapons' is borrowed from the Latin *arma* 'tools, weapons; armor.' The inference seems unavoidable that tools, weapons, and armor were called *arma*, ARMS because they are wielded by men's upper limbs and carried on their shoulders.

Latin *arma* 'weapons' gives rise to a small glossary of related terms. For example, ARMY 'a large body of men organized for warfare' [from Medieval French *armee*; from Medieval Latin *armāta* 'the armed one' (feminine past participle of Latin *armāre* 'to furnish with implements; to arm')]. In Classical Latin, the masculine plural *armāti*, along with the more usual *miles*, *militis*, was used to mean 'soldiers,' while the word for 'army' was *exercitus* 'the disciplined.' Other examples are ARMAMENT 'the weapons and supplies of war' [from Latin *armāmenta* 'tackle, ship's gear; tools' (*-menta*, plural of *-mentum* 'product of, means of')] and ARMADA 'a fleet of warships, especially the ill-fated Spanish fleet that sailed to attack Britain in 1588' [from Spanish *armada* 'navy, fleet'; from Medieval Latin *armāta* 'army, fleet']. The Spanish use of *armada* to mean 'war fleet' may derive elliptically from the Latin phrase *classis armata* 'armed fleet.' More examples: ARMADILLO (literally) 'the little armored one'; 'a mammal of sub-tropical America, protected by armorlike jointed

bony plates' [from Spanish *armado* 'armored' + the diminutive suffix *-illo*]; ARMOR 'defensive covering' [from Medieval French *armure, arměure*; from Latin *armātūra* 'armor; armed soldiers'];
500 and ARMATURE 'a structure having a protective function; a piece of soft iron connecting the poles of a magnet, preserving and increasing its magnetic power.' Apparently it was the 'preserving and increasing' of power that prompted the name ARMATURE, which has been carried over into electrical engineering. Still
505 more examples: ARMORY 'armor collectively; a storehouse for weapons and military equipment; a place where arms are manufactured' [from Middle English *armurie*; from Old French *armoirie*, influenced by Old French *armure, arměure*]; ARMORIAL 'pertaining to heraldic arms; a book containing coats of arms';
510 heraldic ARMS 'insignia borne originally on the shields of fully armed knights to distinguish them in battle' (hence, properly called "ARMORIAL bearings"); coat of ARMS 'a vest of rich materials embroidered in colors and worn over a knight's armor to identify him; a surcoat embroidered with armorial bearings; any
515 emblem having a symbolic function similar to that of armorial bearings'; ARMIGER 'a squire or scutcheon bearer; an armorbearer for a knight' [an adoption of Latin *armiger* 'bearing arms; shield-bearer' (*-ger* 'bearing, carrier' from Latin *gerere* 'to carry')]; ARMOIRE 'a large cabinet or wardrobe' [from Old French *armoire*,
520 variant of *armaire*; from Latin *armārium* 'chest, cupboard, closet']. ARMOIRE goes back to the 'tools, utensils' meaning of Latin *arma*. A doublet of ARMOIRE is the now mostly ecclesiastical or dialectal AMBRY, AUMBRY 'a place for keeping things; a recess in a church for storing sacramental objects' [from Middle
525 English *aumbry, aumery, almerie*; from Old French *almarie*, *aumaire*; from Medieval Latin *almārium*, a dissimilated form of Latin *armārium* 'cupboard']. At the end of this productive list come ARMISTICE 'a stoppage of hostilities' [via French from New Latin *armistitium* (*-stice, -stitium* 'stoppage,' from Latin *sistere*,
530 *stiti* 'to cause to stand')] and ALARM (literally) 'to arms!'; 'a warning of approaching danger; a feeling of apprehension' [via Old French from Old Italian *all'arme* (literally) 'to the weapon; to arms!' (Latin *ad* 'to' + *illa* 'that' (> 'the') + *arma*)]. The archaic variant ALARUM came about through the prolonging of the word
535 when shouting it out as a warning. During the 17th century, ALARM was often spelled *all-arm* "everyone arm," due to the erroneous belief that the word arose from this combination.

Latin *armus* 'shoulder, upper arm' has a diminutive, *armilla*, with a specialized meaning of 'an armlet, an arm ring; a bracelet,'
540 and, in Medieval Latin, 'a metal ring.' On *armilla*, the New Latin adjective *armillaris* was formed, whence French *armillaire* and

English ARMILLARY 'consisting of iron rings,' which is seen in
ARMILLARY sphere 'an astronomical model with solid rings representing the principal celestial circles.'

There are related words in Greek having to do with 'joints'   545
and 'fitting together' that contain the element ãrm. Here, the ˙
represents 'an aspirate, spiritus asper, rough breathing' that is
transliterated into the Roman alphabet as h. Among such Greek
words are *harmos* [<*ar-smo-] 'joint; shoulder; groove,'
harmozein 'to fit together,' and *harmonia* 'union, concord, conso-   550
nance; proportion,' and English HARMONY 'a combination of
elements producing a consistent and pleasing whole; agreement
of sentiment; the simultaneous sounding of different musical
notes.' Hence, HARMONIOUS, HARMONICS, HARMONICA, HARMO-
NIZE, HARMONIUM, etc.   555

The rest of the words included in this chapter may or may not
derive from the Indo-European root *ar- 'to fit together'—linguists
are far from agreement on the matter. The semantic connections
seem strong enough to some linguists to warrant putting the forms
together, since the phonology (sound changes) and morphology   560
(structure of the root and stem) do not absolutely prevent it. But
the derivation of the following words from Indo-European *ar- 'to
fit together' has been denied by linguists of equal repute.

With this caveat in mind, we proceed to an excellent example
of the way abstract meanings grow out of the metaphorical use of   565
homely, concrete terms, provided us by the Latin word, ōrdō,
ōrdinem whose original meaning was 'a row of threads in a loom.'
There aren't many things more homely and concrete than a row of
threads in a loom, but from this humble source come, first, the
notion of 'a series, an array' and then such grand abstractions as   570
'rank, class; regularity, rule.' Finally is yielded ORDER 'systematic
arrangement of the parts of a whole; the condition in which
everything is in its proper place and performing its proper
function; to arrange things systematically; to direct that certain
things be done' [from Old French *ordre*, earlier *ord(e)ne*; from   575
Latin ōrdō, ōrdinem 'series; order']. The Latin stem ōrd- is
thought by some to be a variant form that the Indo-European root
*ar- 'to fit together' assumed by way of "the suffixed variant form
*ōr-dh-" (AHD); certainly the semantics "fit together." English
ORDER also means 'rank,' as in the ORDERS of the hierarchy   580
(deacon, priest, bishop, etc.) and 'a group of people living under
the same discipline,' as in the Franciscan ORDER and the ORDER
of the Round Table. Other offspring of Latin ōrdō, ōrdinem 'a row
of threads in a loom,' adopted into English are ORDAIN 'to decree;
to invest with priestly authority, to confer Holy Orders upon'   585
[from Norman French *ordeiner* or Old French *ordener*; from Latin

ōrdināre 'to arrange, to set in order']; ORDINANCE 'a decree; an authoritative command' [via Old French and Medieval Latin from Latin *ōrdināns* 'arranging,' present participle of *ōrdināre* 'to set in
590   order']; and ORDNANCE 'military weapons collectively, and the means of keeping them operative.' ORDNANCE is actually a syncopated variant of ORDINANCE and thus, etymologically, means 'an arranging.' The *i*-less spelling dates from the 17th century; the military meaning, originally synonymous with 'artillery,' dates
595   from the 14th. Semantically, the connection may be traceable to the manner in which weapons or weapon bearers are arranged in rows, or ranks. *Artillery*, despite its spelling, is not related to our root. The commonest of these cognates, fittingly, is ORDINARY 'occurring in the regular course of events; average, commonplace'
600   [from Latin *ōrdinārius*]. A "colloquial U.S." (*OED*) or dialectal alteration of ORDINARY that changed not only the pronunciation and spelling, but also the meaning—pejoratively, for the most part, though in some instances the word connotes a grudging admiration, as when commenting on the stubbornness of a mule—
605   is: ORNERY, ONERY 'common; of poor quality; lazy, shiftless; mean, cantankerous, bad-tempered; stubborn; eccentrically independent.' Stemming from the same source are EXTRAORDINARY; ORDINATE 'arranged in rows'; INORDINATE 'not regulated; excessive, immoderate'; COORDINATE 'one of a set of numbers that
610   determines the location of a point on a map or graph; to harmonize in a common effort'; SUBORDINATE 'subject to the authority of another'; and INSUBORDINATE 'rebelling against authority.'

Intimately related to Latin *ōrdō, ōrdinem* 'a row of threads on a loom' is the Latin verb *ōrdior, ōrdiri* 'to set the threads on a
615   loom; to begin to weave'; hence, 'to begin, to commence.' A compound with the same sense is *exōrdior, exōrdiri* 'to lay the warp (out); to begin to weave; to begin' and a related noun is Latin and English EXORDIUM 'a beginning.' A more frequently encountered relative is PRIMORDIAL 'existing at the very begin-
620   ning; first, original' [from Late Latin *prīmōrdiālis*, from Latin *prīmōrdium* 'first beginning' (*prīmus* 'first')].

An interior decorator may use some such term as "color COORDINATION" to describe some of the effects he strives for. COORDINATE comes ultimately from Latin *co-* + *ōrdinātus*
625   'arranged,' past participle of *ōrdināre* 'to set in order, to arrange.' *Ordināre* is (apparently—but perhaps only apparently) the ancestor of a contracted form *ōrnāre* 'to fit out, equip; to decorate, embellish.' Doesn't the embellishing and decorating of things often consist to a great extent in arranging them in a pleasing
630   order? In any event, that Latin *ōrnāre* 'to fit out' is related to *ōrdināre* 'to set in order' and hence to Indo-European *ar- 'to fit

together' in the opinion of some etymologists. English descendants of Latin *ōrnāre* are ORNAMENT 'anything used to beautify'
[from Latin *ōrnāmentum* 'equipment; decoration']; ORNATE 'elaborately decorated'; ADORN 'to embellish; to put ornaments on'   635
[from Latin *adōrnāre* 'to fit out; to embellish'] (a Roman lady's
maid was called an *ōrnātrīx*); and SUBORN 'to induce (someone)
by underhanded means to do something unlawful' [from Latin
subōrnāre 'to supply secretly; to suborn' (*sub-* 'under' + *ōrnāre*
'to equip, to supply')].   640
     We come now to the greatest 'fitter-together' of history, the
human REASON. According to some laborers in the field of
etymology, the word REASON is descended from yet another
variant of the Indo-European root **ar-* 'to fit together,' this one
taking the form **rē-* and leading to Latin *rērī, ratum* 'to think, to   645
judge; to count, to calculate.' The past participle *rat(um)* gives
rise to the noun *ratiō, ratiōnem* 'a reckoning; calculation; reasoning.' Adopted from these forms into English, usually by way of
Old French, are REASON 'the ability to think logically; the basis
for a belief; the motive for an act' [from Old French *reisun*; from   650
Latin *ratiō, ratiōnem*]; RATIO 'a numerical relation between two
similar things'; RATION 'a fixed portion'; RATIONAL 'based upon
logical thought'; RATIONALE 'a logical basis'; RATIONALIZE 'to
give a logical explanation (of); to provide plausible but untrue
reasons for (one's behavior); to convert (a business, a process) to   655
more efficient methods'; RATE 'a quantitative measurement
against a fixed quantity of something else' (e.g., miles per hour or
cents per pound) [from Medieval Latin *rata* 'fixed, calculated';
past participle of Latin *rērī, ratum* 'to calculate']; RATIFY 'to give
formal sanction to' [from Medieval Latin *ratificāre* 'to make fixed'   660
(*-ficāre* < *facere* 'to make')]; and ARRAIGN 'to call before a court to
answer charges' [from Old French *araisnier* 'to call to account';
from Vulgar Latin **adrationāre* (Latin *ad-* 'to' + *ratiō*
'reckoning')].
     'Counting' and 'reckoning' are similar to READING in these   665
respects: all three activities involve the powers of reason and all
require eventually the making and understanding of abstractions
with the help of symbols. The same Indo-European root variant
*rē- (of **ar-* 'to fit together') that is said to underlie Latin *ratiō* 'a
reckoning' manifests itself in the Germanic tongues with words   670
whose meanings have to do with interpreting, advising, and
reading. Thus, Indo-European **rē-* leads, by way of the suffixed
form **rē-dh-*, to Germanic **rēdan*, one of whose descendants is
Old English *rǣdan*, ancestor of English READ 'to interpret the
meaning of (a dream; a riddle); to foretell' (to READ someone's   675
fortune); 'to ascertain the nature of something by careful scrutiny'

(He READS the sky for signs of the weather; I can READ him like a book); 'to peruse and understand something written.' Spelled with the archaic spelling REDE 'to give advice; to interpret' the
680   word itself is archaic, but the meaning points to a relationship with the very much alive German words, *Rat* 'advice, counsel; council'; *Rathaus* 'council house; town hall'; and RAT(H)SKELLER 'town-hall cellar'; (U.S.) 'a below-street-level restaurant' patterned on the cellar of a German town hall, where beer and food are
685   sold. (The archaic -*h*- is preserved in the U.S. spelling.)

Old English *rǣdan* 'to read, to interpret; to counsel' is also related to English RIDDLE 'a statement requiring interpretation; a statement intentionally worded in a puzzling manner' and to the suffix -*red* indicating 'counsel.' It is found in the proper names
690   ALFRED 'elf counsel' [Old English *ælf* 'elf' + *rǣd* 'counsel'] and ETHELRED 'noble counsel' [Old English *æthele* 'noble' (compare German *edel* 'noble')]. Old Norse *radh* 'counsel' is said to be lurking in the name RALPH 'wolf counsel' [from Middle English *radulf;* from Old Norse *radhulfr* (*radh* 'counsel' + *ulfr* 'wolf')].
695   Old English *rǣdan* 'to advise, to read, to interpret' has an extended meaning 'to rule, to decide,' which gave rise to the noun *rǣden* 'rule; condition' and to another -*red* suffix seen in English HATRED 'violent dislike' [from Middle English *hatereden*; from Old English *hete* 'hate' + *rǣden* 'condition'] and KINDRED 'a
700   group of related people' [from Middle English *kinrede, kindreden;* from *kin* 'persons of common ancestry' + *rǣden* 'condition']. The first *d* in KINDRED may be what is called "epenthetic," which means merely that it is a sound inserted in the middle of a word. (Compare the *d* in *thunder*, which comes from Old English
705   *thunor*, and the *b* in *nimble*, from Middle English *nemel*, Old English *næmel*.) Then again, but not as likely, the first *d* in KINDRED may come from the *d* in *kind* 'descent, kin.'

We get back to the mathematical significations seen in Latin *ratiō* 'calculation, reckoning' in the case of yet another suffix -*red*,
710   this one meaning 'number,' derived from Germanic **rath* 'number,' and found in the English word HUNDRED 'ten tens' (literally) 'the *hund* number' [where *hund* is from Latin *cent(um)* ('100'); from Indo-European **dkm̥-tom* + -*red* 'number'].

There is, according to some, one more variant of the Indo-
715   European root **ar-* 'to fit together, to be dealt with.' It is **rī-* or **(a)rī-* 'to arrange,' manifested in Greek *arithmos* 'number, amount, quantity,' which is the progenitor of English ARITHMETIC 'the science of numbers' [via Old French and Latin from Greek *arithmētikē* (*tekhnē*), '(the art) of counting,' from *arithmētikos*,
720   from *arithmein* 'to number, to count up'] and LOGARITHM (literally) 'ratio-number'; 'one of a set of arithmetical functions used to

simplify calculations.' Logarithms were invented and named by the Scottish mathematician John Napier (1550–1617). He coined his word from Greek *logos* 'ratio, proportion' + *arithmos* 'number.'   725

The Indo-European root variant *(a)rī- 'to arrange' is also detected by some in Latin *rītus* 'religious usage, ceremony,' the source of English RITE 'a ceremonial act that has been sanctioned by custom' and RITUAL 'prescribed ceremonial acts' [from Latin *rītuālis*].   730

Finally, and most tenuously, from Indo-European *ar-* 'to fit together,' and the "suffixed (superlative) form *ar-isto-*" (AHD) comes Greek *aristos* 'the best, bravest, noblest (? best fitted)'; whence English ARISTOCRACY 'rule by the best; a hereditary ruling class' [Greek -*kratia*, from *kratos* 'strength, power;   735 dominion'].

IV

Ave atque Vale; Salutes
and Wassails

"What's good about it?" is the surly response sometimes heard to a cheery greeting of "Good morning!" This misanthropic reply is based on the (purposely) mistaken assumption that the
740   greeter is making a statement, when actually he's expressing a wish; since *Good morning!* is short for 'God give you a good morning,' as *Good-bye* is short for 'God be with ye.' And so with the other greetings. Most SALUTATIONS and VALEDICTIONS are made up of similar good wishes or of expressions of SOLICITUDE
745   for the other's health. The word SALUTE 'a sign expressing good will' comes from the Latin *salūs, salūtis* 'health' and the VALE- of VALEDICTION 'an act of saying good-bye' is the imperative *valē!* 'be healthy!' of the Latin verb *valēre* 'to be well; to be strong.'
        Latin *salūs* 'health, well-being' derived from the variant
750   suffixed form **sal-u-* of the Indo-European root **sol-* 'whole' ('unbroken, all in one piece,' hence 'healthy'). One adjectival form related to Latin *salūs* is *salvus* 'safe, unhurt, preserved' and the imperative of the concomitant verb *salvēre: salvē! salvēte!* 'be in good health!' was used by Roman citizens to mean both 'hail!'
755   and 'farewell!' Latin *salvus* became Old French *sauf, sauve(r)*; these were adopted into Middle English and led to modern English SAFE 'free from harm'; and SAVE 'to keep from harm; to rescue.' Other English borrowings that trace back through Old French to Latin *salvus* are SALVAGE 'the act of saving; what is
760   extracted in usable condition from wreckage'; SALVATION 'preservation from destruction'; SAVIOR 'one who saves another'; SALUTARY 'producing a wholesome effect'; and SAGE 'a plant of the genus *Salvia* whose aromatic leaves are used in cooking' [from Old French *sauge*; from Latin *salvia* 'the healing plant']. Bor-
765   rowed directly from Latin in the 16th century is SALUBRIOUS

'conducive to health and well-being' [from Latin *salūbris* 'healthful'].

A cognate from the Italian that has developed equivocal meanings (if one is thinking in terms of 'good health') is SALVO 'a military or naval salute consisting of the simultaneous discharge   770
of firearms; the timed discharge of artillery pieces; the simultaneous release of a rack of bombs from an aircraft' [from Italian *salva*; from Latin *salvē* 'greeting!'].

While we are speaking of things dangerous it is a good time to bring up the word SALVER 'a tray for serving food or beverages;   775
a tray on which anything is presented, such as letters or visiting cards.' These are innocuous enough meanings, but their semantic origin is not; for SALVER comes from the Spanish verb *salvar* 'to pretaste the food or drink of a nobleman to make sure it isn't poisoned' by way of the Spanish noun *salva* > French noun *salve*   780
'a tray for presenting objects to the king.' These meanings are no longer current in either French or Spanish; their source is the Late Latin verb *salvāre* 'to save' from Latin *salvus* 'safe, unharmed.' (The noun *salve* 'a medical ointment, something that soothes' comes from a different root.)   785

Another Latin adjective derived from our Indo-European root **sol-* 'whole' (this one by way of the extended form **sollo-*) is *sollus* 'whole, entire.' *Sollus* appears as an element in Latin *sollicitus* (literally) 'wholly moved; tossed, stirred up, agitated'; therefore, 'troubled' or, in today's vernacular, 'all shook up.' (The   790
-citus element means 'moved, set in motion' from *ciēre* 'to set in motion' and is the same as that found in English ex*cite*, in*cite*). The meaning of English SOLICITOUS 'full of concern, anxious' is not quite so stirred up. A related noun is English SOLICITUDE 'uneasiness, disquiet, anxiety; urgently attentive care' [from Latin   795
sollicitūdō].

The Latin verb *sollicitāre* (literally) 'to set wholly in motion' means 'to move violently, stir, agitate, shake; to disturb, annoy; to incite'; also, 'to plow.' The English verb, borrowed from the Latin by way of Medieval French/Old French *solliciter*, has softened   800
considerably into SOLICIT (obsolete) 'to disquiet; to fill with concern'; 'to entreat a person to do something; to importune' and SOLICITOR 'a person who seeks favors, purchases, or contributions.' In some U.S. city, state, and governmental departments a SOLICITOR is also 'a law officer.' (The Solicitor General is an   805
officer appointed by the President to assist the Attorney General.)

In French, Latin *sollicitāre* became *solliciter* 'to solicit, to petition,' but it is also the source of the reflexive verb *se soucier* (*de*) 'to care, to be concerned, to be anxious (about).' From this there developed the negative present participle/adjective INSOU-   810

CIANT 'careless, thoughtless, heedless,' which has been adopted into English with the more lighthearted meaning 'blithely indifferent, carefree.' The attendant French noun *souci* 'anxious care, worry' is part of the cheerful phrase *sans souci* 'without care' 815   which Frederick the Great chose as the name for his splendid palace at Potsdam.

Another Latin word based on *sollus* 'whole, entire' is *sol(l)emnis*, sometimes spelled *sol(l)ennis* 'annual, periodic; ceremonial, solemn.' *Sollennis* was once thought to derive from *sollus* 820   'entire' + *annus* 'year' ('that takes place every year'). This derivation still appears in some modern dictionaries, but most etymologists now account the element *-emnis, -ennis* as of obscure origin. The English borrowing is SOLEMN 'marked by a sober realization and acceptance' [via Old French/Medieval French *solem(p)ne*].

825   From Indo-European **sol-* 'whole' and the suffixed form **sol-ido-* comes Latin *solidus* 'dense; massive, solid, hard,' obviously the ancestor of English SOLID 'of the same substance throughout.' However, the Latin word has three rather more unexpected descendants in English SOLDIER, SOLDER, and SOU 'a coin of 830   small value.' These can be explained as follows: At one point in the evolution of Latin, the phrase *solidus nummus* meant something like the English expression 'hard cash' (*nummus* means 'coin'; the plural *nummi* 'money'). Eventually the *nummus* part of the Latin phrase was dropped, and the word *solidus* took on the 835   meaning 'coin.' During the reign of Constantine I, the *solidus* was officially established as a gold coin worth 25 denarii. During Late Latin times *solidus* was shortened to *soldus*. In Old French it was further shortened to *soulde*, and in this form it meant 'pay' or 'wages'—especially 'army pay.' The fighting man who accepted 840   these *souldes* as his army pay was called a *souldeour* or SOLDIER 'one who serves in an army.' (The *OED* lists sixty-seven different ways this word has been spelled in English: *sawgeour, sawdyour, sojor, sodger*, etc.)

As the name of a coin, Late Latin *solidus* became Old French 845   *sol, soul* plural *soux, sous*, whence Modern French SOU 'a 5-centime piece, 1/20th of a franc,' a far cry in value from the Roman gold coin. As for SOLDER 'a metal alloy used, when melted, to join metallic surfaces,' it comes from Latin *solidāre* 'to make solid, to strengthen' by way of Medieval French *solder*, 850   *souder* 'to solder.'

Our Indo-European root **sol-* 'whole' shows up in Greek as *hol-*, with initial aspiration having replaced the sibilant *s-*. (The change from Indo-European initial **s-* to Greek initial *h-* is a regular sound development.) Hence, Greek *holos* 'whole, complete, 855   entire, all.' *Holos* is represented in English by many scientific terms (like the recent coinages *hologram* and *holography*), as well as by HOLOCAUST 'a sacrificial offering that is wholly consumed by fire; a conflagration' [from Greek *holokauston*, from *holokaustos* 'burnt whole' (*kaustos* 'burnt'; cf. *caustic*)]; HOLOGRAPH 'a document written entirely in the handwriting of the person whose signature it bears' [from Greek *holographos* 'written in full']; HOLISM 'a philosophy that can be summed up: the whole is greater than the sum of its parts'; and CATHOLIC (literally) 'concerning the whole; universal, general, all-inclusive' [via Old French and Late Latin from Greek *katholikos*, from *katholou* 'in general, universally' (from *kata* 'concerning, according to' + *holou* '(of) the whole')].

It might seem plausible that English WHOLE, which has exactly the same meaning as Greek *holos*, would be that word's cognate. But it isn't. Coincidentally, English WHOLE, as well as the English word HEALTH and the English greeting HAIL! are descendants of a different Indo-European root **kailo-* 'whole, uninjured.' Indo-European **kailo-* underlies Germanic **hail-* (or **khail-*) and **hailaz* (**khailaz*). In Old Norse, Germanic **hailaz* became *heill* 'sound, healthy.' English adopted Old Norse *heill* as the salutation HAIL! 'be healthy!' A sidelight is cast on the drinking habits of the denizens of Britain during the late Middle Ages by the word WASSAIL 'a festivity characterized by much drinking; a drink made of ale or wine spiced with roasted apples and sugar' [from the phrase *waes haeil!* 'be in good health!'; from Old Norse *ves heill*]. *Waes* is a form of the verb *to be*, represented in modern English by *was*. The expression *waes haeil* was used from the 12th century on as "a salutation when presenting a cup of wine to a guest, or drinking the health of a person, the reply being 'Drink-hail!'" (*OED*). Other descendants of Indo-European **kailo-* 'whole, uninjured' and Germanic **hail-* are HALE 'sound, in good health'; HEAL 'to make whole, to restore to health'; HEALTH 'the state of being of an organism with regard to its functioning'; and WHOLE 'sound, healthy; not divided' [from Middle English (*w*)*holle, hole, hool*; from Old English *hāl*]. The *w-* did not appear until the 15th century, at a time when many words formerly spelled with initial *ho-* were being spelled *who-*; the *w-* corresponds to a widespread dialectal pronunciation with *w-*. Note, also, HOLY 'kept inviolate, kept intact; set apart for religious purposes; associated with a divine power' [from Old English *hālig*]. *Hālig* was used in Old English as a translation of the Latin *sacer* 'sacred, holy'; the connection with 'wholeness' is probably in the sense of 'that which is inviolable.' HALLOW 'to set aside as holy' is another member of the family. A cognate is the

900   personal name OLGA 'holy' [from Russian; from Old Norse *helga*
       'holy'].

       The greeting *Hello* does not seem to fit in here, although
       Mario Pei in *The Story of Language* traces it to the Anglo-Saxon
       (Old English) expression *hal beo thu* 'whole be thou,' which
905   would make *Hello* a cognate of HAIL. However, other etymolo-
       gists do not go along with this derivation; instead, they link *Hello*
       with earlier *Hullo, Holla, Hollo, Hallo, Halloo*, etc., exclamations
       used to incite dogs to the chase or to call attention at a distance.
       These are either of echoic origin or from the French *holà* 'stop';
910   from *ho* 'halt' + *là* 'there.'

       We come now to the Latin *vale!* 'be well!; farewell, good-
       bye'; the imperative of the verb *valēre* 'to be strong, to be well.' A
       derived Latin word is *valētūdō* 'state of health,' which could also
       mean either 'good health' or 'poor health.' However, the adjective
915   *valētūdinārius* wound up with the meaning 'invalid,' and that is
       the sense that has survived in English VALETUDINARIAN 'a chron-
       ic invalid.' Note that the word INVALID '(a person) disabled by
       injury or illness; falsely reasoned; null, ineffective' is itself
       derived from the same root, and means (literally) 'not strong' (*in-*
920   'not' + *validus* 'strong').

       The Indo-European source here is **wal-* 'to be strong.' One
       might think that English *well* 'in good health' would spring from
       this same source, but *well* comes from the root **wel-* 'to wish, to
       will.' Not all the Latin descendants of **wal-* 'to be strong' have to
925   do with health; Latin *valēre* 'to be strong, to be well' developed
       the extended senses of 'to be powerful; to have influence; to be
       worth.' It evolved into the Old French verb *valoir* 'to be worth'
       from whose feminine past participle *value*, we have borrowed
       English VALUE 'worth.' Other cognates are VALID (archaic) 'of
930   sound health'; 'correctly reasoned; efficacious; having legal
       strength'; VALOR 'bravery' (linked here to strength); VALIANT
       'brave'; AVAIL 'to be of value; to be of use to'; PREVAIL 'to be the
       strongest; to be currently predominant'; EQUIVALENT 'of equal
       value'; AMBIVALENT coined by Freud to mean 'characterized by
935   conflicting feelings of love and hate, attraction and revulsion; "on
       the fence"' [from AMBIVALENCE 'coexistence of conflicting atti-
       tudes in one person'; from German *Ambivalenz* (*ambi-* 'on both
       sides')]; and CONVALESCE 'to regain strength' [*-esce* indicates
       'beginning to'; the *con-* is an intensive].

940   From the Latin present participle/adjective *valens* 'being
       strong; in good health' came Late Latin *valentia* 'strength, capac-
       ity'; whence English VALENCE 'the capacity to interact; a number
       representing a capacity to interact.' *Valentia* is also used as a
       place name meaning 'place of strength.' Note French *Valence*, a

textile town in southeastern France where drapery materials are   945
made, such as are used in VALANCES 'short ornamental draperies
hung across the tops of windows, four-poster beds, and similar
structures.' Also VALENCIENNES 'a town in north central France; a
type of lace' and VALENCIA 'a city and province of eastern Spain,'
for which are named a variety of orange, varieties of almonds,   950
onions, and peanuts, and a kind of woven fabric once used for
waistcoats. *Valens* 'strong' was also used as a personal name.
There was an emperor Valens of the Eastern Roman Empire, from
A.D. 364 to 378, with the derivative *Valentinus*, whence VALEN-
TINE '3rd-century martyr, patron saint of lovers; a card or gift sent   955
as a token of love'—not to forget Rudolph Valentino, preeminent
lover of the silent films. There is also the proper name VALERIE
from the Latin *Valerius*, name of a Roman gens, or clan, after
whom the eastern European province of *Valeria* was named,
place of origin of the plant and drug known as VALERIAN.   960

In Germanic, the Indo-European root **wal-* 'to be strong'
manifests itself as **waldon*, **walthan* 'to rule, to govern' (he who
is strongest, rules), antecedents of German *walten* 'to rule' and
English WIELD (obsolete) 'to have sovereign power over'; 'to exert
(power or influence); to handle (an ax, sword, etc.)' [from Middle   965
English *welden*; from Old English *wieldan, wealdan*].

A Germanic personal name that may incorporate the root
*wal- 'to be strong' is WALTER 'army commander' [from Norman
French *Waltier*; probably from Old High German *Walthari*; from
waltan 'to govern' + *hari* 'army.']. If this derivation is correct,   970
then WALTER is equivalent to another given name HAROLD 'army
commander' [from Old Norse *Haraldr*; from Germanic **harja-
waldaz* (**harjaz* 'army' + *waldaz* 'commander')]. **Harja-waldan*
is thought by many to be the ancestor of English HERALD 'an
officer whose duties were to make pronouncements and carry   975
messages between sovereigns; one who specializes in armorial
insignia, or HERALDRY; a messenger; one that foreshadows,' even
though the semantics don't fit. Other personal names incorporating **wal-* 'to be strong' include GERALD 'spear wielder' [from Old
French *Giraut*; from Old High German *Gēr(w)ald* (*gēr* 'spear' +   980
waldan 'to rule')]; REGINALD 'wielder of power' [from Old English *Regenweald* (*regen* 'power' + *weald* 'force')]; RONALD 'ruler
of the gods' [from Old Norse *Rögnvaldr* (*rögn* 'decreeing powers,
gods' + *valdr* 'ruler')]; and ARNOLD 'eagle power' [from Old High
German *Arenwald* (*arn* 'eagle' + *wald* 'power')].   985

Finally, there is *avē!* 'Hail!' as in *avē! Maria* 'Hail! Mary.'
This is from the defective verb *avēre*, found chiefly in the
imperatives *avē, avēte* (present) and *avētō* (future) 'Hail! Farewell!' The word is not of Indo-European descent and has no

990   English cognates. Some speculate that the Romans adopted *avē*
       from the Carthaginian, or Punic, *ḥwy* 'Live!' (The *atque* in the
       phrase *ave atque vale* 'hail and farewell' means 'and, and also,
       and moreover').

V

Biscuits *ain't* Zwieback;
Two, Twelve, *and* Twenty

Those irascible TWINS, the DUELING TWOSOME of TWEEDLE-
DUM & TWEEDLEDEE were not invented by Lewis Carroll but   995
were in the first instance TWO rival composers, Giovanni Battista
Bononcini and George Frederick Handel, who vied for the favor
of opera and oratorio fans in 18th-century London. The rivalry
began in 1716, and the contestants were given the sobriquets of
Tweedledum and Tweedledee by the satirical poet John Byrom   1000
in 1725.

The verb to *tweedle* 'to whistle, to produce a succession of
shrill sounds' is thought to be echoic; but there is another,
dialectal *tweedle* that is associated with *twiddle* 'to play with; to
rotate without purpose,' described as a blend of *twirl* and *fiddle*.   1005
Twirl may be a combining of TWIST and *whirl*, and thus we arrive
at TWIST 'to entwine two or more strands of thread; to turn.' It is
based on the notion of "twoness" and therefore a cognate of TWO
and TWIN. Of the words in the dictionary that begin with *tw*-
more than half have meanings that involve the notion of   1010
TWONESS, or DUALITY, beginning of course with the word TWO
itself, which comes from Old English *twēgen* (masculine), *twā*
(feminine and neuter), *tū* (neuter), and is related to

German *zwei, zwo*[1]	Latin *duo*	Greek *duo (dyo)*	1015
Dutch *twee*	Italian *due*	Russian *dva, dve*	
Old Frisian *twā, twēne*	French *deux*	Lithuanian *du*	
Old Norse *tveir, tvaer, tvau*	Spanish *dos*	Old Irish *dau, dō*	
Gothic *twai, twos, twa*	Romanian *doui, doua*	Sanskrit *dva, dvi*	
Indo-European *°dwō, °duwō*			

[1] *zwo* is an obsolete feminine noun only used for clarity to distinguish *zwei* from *drei*, three.   1020

A direct descendant of Old English *twēgen* is TWAIN 'a set of two'; as in "never the TWAIN shall meet." The pseudonym, *Mark Twain*, adopted by Samuel Clemens, came from the Mississippi riverboat cry meaning 'by the mark two fathoms,' called out while sounding the ever-changing depths and shallows of that temperamental river. TWAIN also means 'asunder, into two parts,' as in "the nation was split in TWAIN by the slavery issue." Then there are TWIN 'one of two offspring born at the same birth'; TWINE (originally) 'string composed of two strands twisted together'; and TWIST 'to combine two strands into a thread.' The verb to TWIST had an earlier and opposite meaning of 'to divide in two'; this sense can still be detected in the German cognate *Zwist* 'disunion, discord; quarrel.' The meaning 'to combine two into one' came later, with the more usual modern sense of 'to turn, to wrench, to wring' somewhere in between, chronologically. Related is TWILL 'a fabric with diagonal parallel ribs' [from Old English *twili(c)* 'two-threaded'; a partial translation of Latin *bilix* 'with a double thread' (*bi-* + *līcium* 'thread')]. In a similar way, the fabric *drill* means 'three-threaded' [from German *drillich*; from Latin *trilix* 'triple-threaded']. In Scotland, TWILL was spelled and pronounced TWEEL, which leads us to TWEED 'a rugged woolen fabric usually in a twill weave,' originally a trade name that combined the associations of a TWEELED (TWILLED) fabric with the Scottish river Tweed.

Getting away from fabrics, we come to the word TWIG (originally) 'something forked, or divided in two'; 'a small branch' [from Germanic **twigga* 'a fork.' Compare German *Zweig* 'branch, scion']. Duality also lurks in the prepositions BETWIXT, BETWEEN 'in the space separating, or connecting, two objects' [from *be-* 'by' and relatives of *twēgen, twā, tū*]. Inseparably related to TWO are these other number forms TWICE 'two times' [the *-ce* was once an *-es* genitive ending meaning 'of one'; cf. *once, thrice*] and TWELVE (literally) 'two left, two remaining (over ten)'; 'ten plus two.' In Old English, TWELVE was spelled *twelf(e)*, and in Germanic, **twa-lif-*. *Eleven* was spelled **ainlif*. This is evidence that the number sequence at one time stopped at ten. In other words, man got as far as ten and then counted "one left over, two left over, lots more." Eventually he counted out a second set of ten, and so reached TWENTY (literally) 'two tens' [from Germanic **twēgentig* (**-tig* 'ten')].

The English prefix TWI- can mean either 'two' or 'half,' as exemplified by TWILIGHT 'half-light; light between night and day' and TWIBILL 'a battle-ax with two cutting edges; a mattock; a digging tool with one vertical blade like an ax, and one horizonal blade like an adze.' Then there is the hybrid baseball term

TWINIGHT 'designating a doubleheader that starts in the late afternoon.'

The verb to TWEAK to 'pinch or twist sharply' is not in this group, though it is a fact that tweaks are administered with two fingers, the thumb and forefinger. The German word for 'tweak' is *zwicken*, but etymologists carry the word back only as far as Germanic **twik-* 'to pinch.' A relative of TWEAK is TWITCH 'to move suddenly; to nip as if with pincers.' A word that is dismissed as echoic is TWANG 'the sound of a plucked bowstring; a nasal vocal sound.' The word TWEEZERS 'a small pincerlike tool' has nothing whatever to do with *two*, even though the tool in question is made up of two moving parts. TWEEZERS comes from *etuis*, the plural of French *étui*, 'a case for holding small articles.' (See line 10084.)

To get back to a word that may have some connection with TWO, we have TUB 'a round, open, flat-bottomed vessel.' TUB can be traced to Middle Low German *tubbe*, where its lineage stops. But the German mathematician Karl Menninger, in his book *Number Words and Number Symbols*, sees a possible relationship with German *Zuber*, *Zober* 'a two-handled tub; a butter firkin,' which in Old High German was spelled *zubar* or *zwibar*. This last spelling seems to betray the presence of an element for *two*: *zwi-* 'two' + *-bar* 'handled' [from the Germanic **beran* 'to carry, to bear']. Menninger also sees an analogy with German *Eimer* 'pail, bucket' from *ein-* 'one' + *-bar* 'handled.' In other words, a pail was a container with one handle, Old High German *einbar*, while a tub was a container with two handles, *zwibar*.

The derivation of TUB may be DUBIOUS, but there is no DOUBT, DUBIETY, DUBITATION, DUBITANCY, DUBIOSITY, or DUBIOUSNESS about the derivation of the next few words. In Latin, the Indo-European root **d(u)wō* 'two' shows up as *duo* 'two; both,' and *duo* has come into English by way of Italian, with a musical meaning DUO 'two performers singing or playing together' in a DUET 'a musical composition for two performers' [from Italian *duetto*, diminutive of *duo* 'duet']. (The Italian for 'two' is *due*.) Latin *duo* 'two' is also evidenced in English DUODECIMO 'a page size of one printer's page folded twelve times; a book made up of pages this size'; DUODECIMAL 'pertaining to the number twelve' [from Latin *duodecim* 'twelve' (*duo* 'two' + *decem* 'ten')]; and DUODENUM (literally) 'of twelve'; 'the first portion of the small intestine.' DUODENUM is short for the Latin phrase *intestinum duodenum digitorum*, intestine of twelve digits (fingers' breadths), indicating the length of the duodenum [from Latin *duodeni* 'twelve each']. *Duodenum digitorum* is a translation of the Greek *dōdekadaktulon* 'twelve fingers' breadths' (*dō-* < **dwō*

1070

1075

1080

1085

1090

1095

1100

1105

1110

'two' + *deka* 'ten' + *daktulon* 'finger, finger's breadth'). In addition, we have DUAL 'composed of two parts, double' [from Latin *duālis*]; DUPLE 'consisting of two' [from Latin *duplus*
1115 'double,' the antecedent of Old French (whence English) DOUBLE 'twice as much,' whence DOUBLET (originally) 'stuff made of two materials'; 'a close-fitting jacket worn by men in the 16th and 17th centuries; a pair of similar things; one of a pair' [Old French *doublet*] and DOUBLOON 'an old Spanish gold coin' [from Spanish
1120 *doblón*, augmentative (enlarging) form of *doble* 'double']. The coin was so called, originally, because it had the value of two gold escudos, according to some authorities, which would make the doubloon or *doblón* the equivalent of a Spanish pistole. However, others say the doubloon was worth two pistoles, while still others
1125 say a doubloon was worth four pistoles, or eight escudos, or sixteen pesos (= pieces of eight reales). The two escudos (or one pistole) value seems the most likely, since *pistole* was not the Spanish name for any coin, but a facetious name invented by Frenchmen (originally *pistolet*). DOBLÓN is defined as a coin
1130 worth two escudos in the very dictionaries that say that a DOUBLOON is a coin worth eight escudos (at the same time deriving the second word from the first).

8 REALES = 1 PESO = 1 SPANISH DOLLAR = 1 PIECE OF EIGHT
2 PESOS = 1 ESCUDO
1135
2 ESCUDOS = 1 DOBLON = 1 DOUBLOON = 1 PISTOLE

Note, also, DUPLEX 'twofold; a two-floor apartment' [from Latin *duplex, duplicis* 'twofold' (*duo* 'two' + *plexus* 'folded')]; DUPLI-CATE 'to double; to make a copy of'; and DUPLICITY 'double-
1140 dealing; deliberate deceptiveness; speaking with forked tongue.'
The masculine accusative of Latin *duo*, to wit, *duos*, evolved into Old French *deus*, later *deux*. These forms were taken over into Middle English as *deux, dewse*, eventually yielding DEUCE 'the two-spot at dice or playing cards; a roll of dice totaling two';
1145 (tennis) '40-all.'
DEUCE! is also used as a mild oath, as a word meaning bad luck, and as a euphemism for the devil. These uses seem also to derive from Latin *duos* 'two' but by way of Low German *duus* 'deuce' a roll of two at dice, from the annoyed exclamation of a
1150 player making this roll, since it is crap, the lowest possible score. Another numerical word is DOZEN 'a set of twelve' [from Old French *dozeine*, from Old French *doze* 'twelve'; from Latin *duodecim*].
Leaving the strictly numerical for a while, we come upon the
1155 Latin word *dubius* meaning 'uncertain, undecided, irresolute' and its English derivative DUBIOUS 'uncertain, questionable.' The *du-*

of these words is related to Latin *duo,* 'two' while the *-bius,*
-bious comes from Indo-European **bheu-* 'to be,' so that the
complete words etymologically mean 'to be (at) two; to be
hesitating between two alternatives.' Latin *dubius* is kin to the   1160
rare Latin verb *dubāre* 'to be of two minds' and to its more
frequently encountered extended form *dubitāre* 'to doubt; to
hesitate.' *Dubitāre* became Old French *douter* and was borrowed
into Old English as *douten*; whence English DOUBT 'to be
undecided about; to distrust; to tend to disbelieve.' The *-b-* was   1165
put back into the English spelling by Latinists, but it has never
been pronounced in English.

Also springing from Latin *dubius* are DUBITABLE 'subject to
doubt'; INDUBITABLE 'unquestionable'; and DUBIETY 'uncer-
tainty.' Because one tends to fear what one is uncertain about, the   1170
Medieval French verb *redouter* 'to fear' (literally) 'to doubt back
at' led to the adjective *redoutable* 'formidable, frightening,'
whence English REDOUBTABLE 'awesome; to be feared.' The verb
to REDOUBT 'to dread' is archaic, and the noun REDOUBT 'a small
defensive fortification' comes from a different source altogether   1175
[via Medieval Latin *reductus* 'a concealed place']. (See line 3527.)

One might think that the English word DUEL 'a prearranged
combat between two persons' should be in this group, and there
are some etymologists who would agree, as did the ancient
Romans themselves. Others say that to make a connection   1180
between DUEL and Latin *duo* 'two' is folk etymology. The attested
facts are that in archaic Latin the word *duellum* meant 'war,' and,
following a trend in early Latin to change *du-* followed by a
vowel to *b-,* that *duellum* became Classical Latin *bellum* 'war.'
The archaic *duellum* continued to be used poetically and was   1185
revived in Medieval Latin with the signification of 'judicial single
combat; trial by wager of battle,' on the theory that God would
see to it that the right prevailed. Medieval Latin *duellum* became
Italian *duello,* French and English *duel.*

The phonetic change in early Latin from *du-* + vowel to *b-* is   1190
also evidenced by the Latin adverb *bis* 'twice,' derived from an
earlier *duis* (*dvis*). The cry of "Bis! Bis!" is still heard in Italian
and French concert halls, exploding from enthusiastic audiences
with a meaning of 'Again! Again! Encore!' As a prefix, *bis-* and its
variants *bi-* and *bin-* are found in many English compounds,   1195
including BICYCLE 'a two-wheeled velocipede' [Greek *kuklos*
'wheel circle']; BIPED 'an animal with two feet' [Latin *pes, pedis*
'foot']; BIPOD 'a stand having two legs (and feet)' [Greek *pous,
podos* 'foot']; BINOCULAR 'using two eyes' [Late Latin *oculāris* 'of
the eye; from *oculus* 'eye']; BIFOCAL 'having lenses that correct   1200
for both nearsightedness and farsightedness' [Latin *focus* 'fire-

place'] (see line 5406); BINAURAL 'hearing with two ears; relating to sound transmission from two sources' [Latin *auris* 'ear']; BILA-BIAL 'having two lips; pronounced with both lips' [Latin *labium* 'lip']; BILINGUAL 'speaking two languages' [Latin *lingua* 'tongue, language']; BICEPS (literally) 'two-headed'; 'any muscle having two points of origin' [Latin -*ceps*, from *caput* 'head']; BICUSPID 'having two points, like the crescent moon, or a premolar tooth' [Latin *cuspis* 'point, head of a spear']; BISECT 'to cut into two parts' [Latin *sectus* 'cut'; from *secāre* 'to cut']; BIPARTITE 'having two parts' [Latin *pars, partis* 'part']; BIPARTISAN 'supported by two parties' [Italian *partigiano* 'one who takes the part of (another), a supporter']; BINARY 'composed of two parts; of a number system based on two' [Late Latin *bīnārius;* from *bīnī* 'two by two']; BINOMIAL 'consisting of two terms' [Greek *nómos* 'portion, division; usage']; and BISSEXTILE (literally) 'twice sixth, second sixth'; 'pertaining to a leap year.' If you're wondering what "twice sixth"or "second sixth" can possibly have to do with leap year, it's like this:

Prior to 154 B.C., the Roman year began on March 1st, called by the Romans the calends of March, making February the last month of the year. This explains why September, October, November, and December were the Romans' seventh, eighth, ninth, and tenth months. It also explains why leap-year day comes in February, the "last" month. The extra day of leap year was not inserted by the Romans after the *last* day of February but after the *sixth* day before the calends of March, giving them two "sixth days" before the calends. The intercalary day was therefore known as *dies bissextus ante Calends Martias.* The Romans did not count up from the first, as we do, but down to the Nones (the 5th or 7th), the Ides (the 13th or 15th), and the calends (the first).

Possibly the commonest English word beginning with *bi*- 'two, twice' (along with BICYCLE, BIKE) is BISCUIT (literally) 'twice-cooked' [Old/Medieval French *bescuit*; from Latin *bis* 'twice' + *coctus*, past participle of *coquere* 'to cook']. Of the spelling of this word the *OED* remarks: "the regular form in English from the 16th to the 18th century was *bisket* as still pronounced; the current *biscuit* is a senseless adoption of the modern French spelling without the French pronunciation." Not only is the spelling senseless, but in the United States the etymological sense has become senseless. The original "twice-cooked" BISCUIT was a kind of unraised bread formed into flat cakes and baked hard. Americans now call these edible objects *crackers,* and our modern *biscuits* are not twice baked at all, but a variety of "quick bread made in a small shape and raised in the baking by some leavening agent other than yeast." (In Britain, however, American *crackers* are still called *biscuits*.) Old-time biscuits were more like hardtack, or sea biscuit. Another substance that is subjected to two cookings is ZWIEBACK (literally) 'twice-baked'; 'a type of bread baked first as a loaf and later cut into slices and toasted' [adopted from German *zwieback* 'twice-baked' (bread); 'rusk']. Note that the German *zwi(e)-* is a cognate of English *twi-* and Latin *dui-* > *bi-*.

BISQUE is a thick, rich soup made by boiling down fish, flesh, or fowl. To most etymologists this word is of obscure origin, but Karl Menninger fearlessly asserts that the name arose because a BISQUE is twice (hence thoroughly) cooked.

Note, also, BIFURCATE 'to divide into two branches, to fork' [from Latin *bifurcus* 'two-pronged' (*furca* 'fork')] and BIGAMY 'the act of marrying a second spouse while still legally married to the first' [from Late Latin *bigamus* (Greek *gamos* 'marriage')].

A word that belongs in this group, although the spelling has been changed, is BALANCE (etymologically) 'having two plates'; 'a beam supported exactly in the middle having pans of equal weight suspended from its extremities' [from Vulgar Latin **bilancia*; from Late Latin *bilanx* 'having two plates' (*lanx, lancis* 'plate; scale')].

In the temporal sphere we have BIWEEKLY 'happening every two weeks'; (sometimes) 'happening twice a week; semi-weekly'; BIMONTHLY 'every two months'; (sometimes) 'twice a month'; BIYEARLY 'every two years'; (sometimes) 'twice a year'; BIENNIAL 'every two years; lasting two years' [from Latin *biennium* 'space of two years']; and BIANNUAL 'happening twice each year; semi-annual.'

In the United States and France, a BILLION = a thousand million = 1,000,000,000, while in Great Britain and Germany, a BILLION = a million million = 1,000,000,000,000, or what Americans call a *trillion*. The British/German meaning is the original. The word itself, BILLION, was coined in the 16th century by French arithmeticians who prefixed Latin *bi-* to the *-illion* of *million*. *Million* derives from the Italian *millione* (now *milione*) and etymologically means 'a great thousand' [Latin *mille* 'a thousand' + the augmentative (enlarging) suffix *-one*]. In Classical Latin, a 'million' was expressed as *decies centena milia* 'ten hundred thousand,' while in Medieval Latin it became *mille milia*, 'a thousand thousand.'

In addition, we have Latin *bīnī* 'two by two' used with the prefix *com-* 'together with' in the Late Latin verb *combīnāre* 'to join two by two,' antecedent of French *combiner*, adopted into English as COMBINE 'to join in physical union.' This by no means exhausts the listing of *bi-* 'two' words. Others include BIAXIAL,

BICARBONATE, BICAMERAL, BICENTENNIAL, BICORN, and many more.

1295 The Greek word for 'two' is *duo* or *dyo*, depending on how one transliterates the Greek upsilon. As a prefix, *duo*, *dyo* is usually shortened to *di-*, as in English DIPLOMA (literally) 'twice folded, twofold'; 'a state paper; an official document; a certificate indicating that a course of study has been completed.' In Greek *diplōma* means 'a paper folded double; a letter of recommenda-
1300 tion; a document conveying a license or privilege.' The Latin speakers enlarged on this last sense and gave the word a special meaning that Karl Menninger explains as follows:

> The Roman emperors often granted certain rights and
> privileges to veteran soldiers upon their discharge from
1305 > service. These were originally inscribed in the inner
> surfaces of *two* bronze tablets which were . . . closed
> against each other; a wire was [then] drawn through
> two holes drilled in the center, twisted together several
> times, and the two ends held with a wax seal. This
1310 > was a "diploma," an imperial writ specifying certain
> rights and privileges. Today a "diplomat" still presents
> his "diploma," his written credentials, to the foreign
> government to which he is accredited. [*op. cit.*, p. 173]

Actually, the word DIPLOMAT 'one appointed to represent his
1315 government vis-à-vis the governments of other nations; one who possesses skill in dealing with others' was not so easily arrived at. It has a distinct international flavor (the secondary sense of 'a tactful person' arose metaphorically after the 'foreign relations' meaning had been established), but the Greco-Latin *diplōma* did
1320 not have to do with international relations, simply with 'documents.' The New Latin adjective *diplōmaticus* was not even coined until 1681, when the French Benedictine monk Jean Mabillon, who was interested in documents of all kinds, dreamed it up. He wrote a book entitled *De re diplōmatica*, in which he
1325 attempted to develop a critical method for determining the authenticity of historical documents. The new word, *diplōmaticus*, was picked up by historiographers, who used it in works about historical documents, especially those involving international affairs. By the time of the French Revolution, the phrase
1330 *corps diplomatique* had come to mean 'the body of representatives of foreign governments in residence in a capital city.' The words DIPLOMAT and DIPLOMACY are back-formations from this specialized sense of DIPLOMATIC, from which all notions of 'twice folded'—the original meaning of Greek *diplōma*—have disap-
1335 peared. (In this regard, we note that modern institutions of learning make a point of *not* folding their diplomas, so there will be no creases in case their recipients should want to have them framed.)

Other English words with the Greek *di-* 'two' prefix are
DIPLOID 'double'; DIPTYCH 'an ancient writing tablet of two   1340
leaves hinged together; a picture painted on two tablets connected by hinges' [Greek *ptukhē* 'fold']; DIMITY 'a sheer cotton
fabric made by weaving two or more threads as one' [Greek *mitos*
'thread']; DIPHTHONG (literally) 'two sounds'; 'a speech sound
consisting of two vowel sounds' [Greek *phthongē, phthoggē*   1345
'voice, sound']; DICHOTOMY 'division into two parts' [Greek
dikhotimia, from *dikhotomein* 'to split asunder' (*dikha* 'in two,
asunder' + *tome* 'cut, stroke')]; and DILEMMA 'a situation requiring a choice between two equally repugnant or equally attractive
alternatives' [Greek *lēmma* 'proposition, assumption'].   1350

VI

Bloody Blessings

It was not customary for newly converted Anglo-Saxon Christians to be BLESSED by their priests with the BLOOD of sacrificial animals, yet those same Anglo-Saxons chose to translate the Latin word *benedīcere* 'to speak well of, to commend; to bless, to
1355 sanctify by making the sign of the cross over' with the Anglo-Saxon word *blētsian, bloedsian* 'to consecrate with blood' [based on the Germanic *blōthisōjan* 'to mark with blood' from *blōtham* 'blood']. Our present-day English verb, to BLESS 'to sanctify, to invoke divine favor upon,' is directly descended from these
1360 sanguinary progenitors.

The *Oxford English Dictionary* remarks that the idea expressed by Old English (Anglo-Saxon) *blētsian* was similar to that which prompted the Israelites to streak their doorposts with lambs' blood on the day of the first Passover "to mark them as
1365 holy to the Lord and inviolable to the destroying angel." One of the strongest notions lurking behind the word to BLESS is that of being made safe from harm, by divine or magical means. It was some such idea that the missionaries were trying to get across to the heathen Anglo-Saxons, that is, that a Christian benediction, or
1370 BLESSING, was similar in effect to the pagan sprinkling of sacrificial blood.

Latin *benedīcere* is a translation of Greek *eulogein* and has nothing to do with blood sprinkling. Both words have etymological meanings of 'to speak well of, to eulogize, to praise,' but both
1375 developed in Christian usage the extended meanings of 'to make holy, to sanctify, to bless.' *Eulogein* and *benedīcere*, as used by the Church Fathers, were in turn translations of the Hebrew *bārak* (literally) 'to bend, to bend the knee; to worship, to praise God; to invoke blessings upon.' Thus, English to BLESS has
1380 swirling about it connotations of bending the knee, worshiping,

eulogizing, and sprinkling with blood. It should be very efficacious indeed if there is anything to logomancy, or word magic.

Another association that sprang up in the popular mind was with the noun *bliss* 'serene happiness,' the assumption being that *bliss* is a condition that a BLESSED person eventually arrives at. 1385 However, there is no etymological connection. *Bliss* traces back to Germanic *blīthiz* 'gentle, mild, merciful,' which is also the ancestor of English *blithe* 'gay, cheerful; carefree.'

English is the only one of the Germanic languages that developed words with the meanings of BLESS, BLESSED [from 1390 Germanic *blōtham* 'blood']. Other English derivatives from this source that are similar to German derivatives are BLOOD 'the red liquid circulating in the arteries and veins of man and the higher animals' [Old English *blōd* (German *Blut*)]; and BLOODY 'stained with blood' [German *blutig*]. BLOODY is also used by the British 1395 as an intensive, meaning (to quote the *Oxford English Dictionary* in a definition that was written some time before March 1887): "*Very . . . and no mistake. . . .* In general use from the Restoration (1660) to *c*1750; now constantly in the mouths of the lowest classes, but by respectable people considered 'a horrid word,' on 1400 a par with obscene or profane language." The *OED* goes on to say of this usage that "there is good reason to think that it was at first a reference to the habits of the 'bloods' or aristocratic rowdies of the 17th and beginning of the 18th *c*. The phrase 'bloody drunk' was apparently = 'as drunk as a blood' (cf. 'as drunk as a lord'). 1405 There is no ground for the notion that 'bloody' has connection with the oath ' 'sblood!' " However, the *Oxford Dictionary of English Etymology* contradicts all this by stating that the expletive BLOODY is "probably from the interjection *blood*, *'sblood* (for *God's blood*)." John Orr, in *Old French and Modern English* 1410 *Idiom*, sees BLOODY as a translation of Medieval French *sanglant* 'bleeding,' saying: "Despite the *OED*'s assertion . . . and . . . conjecture . . . there can be little doubt that . . . it is an adjectival device which, like *sanglant* from *par le sang Dieu*, enabled the oath to be introduced syntactically as a means of robust, if 1415 somewhat indeterminate, vituperation." (He gives this fine example of a Medieval French oath: *sanglant bougre d'ung vieil thoreau*.) Cognate with BLESS and BLOOD is BLEED 'to emit blood' [German *bluten*].

A strange fact about Germanic *blōtham* is that it has no 1420 cognates in the other Indo-European languages. The Latin word *sanguis* from which English has acquired 'sanguine, sanguinary' is also of obscure origin.

VII

Boorish Husbands, Beings in Bondage

A BOWERY bum must sometimes think all his NEIGHBORS
1425 BOORS, the whole CABOODLE of them. He might be surprised to
learn that a BOOR is (etymologically) 'a farmer' and the BOWERY 'a
farm.' The word BOOR 'peasant; a rude, unrefined person' comes
from the Dutch *boer* 'a farmer.' This is the same word encountered in the phrase, "the BOER war," which refers to a conflict
1430 (1899–1902) between the Dutch colonists of the Orange Free
State and the Transvaal Republic on one side, and the British
fighting with and on behalf of their South African colonists on the
other. (The British won, but today's Union of South Africa is more
Dutch, or Afrikaner, than it is British.)
1435 The Germanic root underlying BOOR and *boer* is *bū- 'to
dwell,' a root with many other inherited and borrowed English
descendants that come to us, some by way of Dutch, some
through Old English, Old Norse, Old Danish, and German. One
of the most familiar is NEIGHBOR (etymologically) 'near fellow-
1440 dweller'; 'one who lives nigh, or nearby' [from Old English
nēahgebūr, from *nēah* 'near' + *gebūr* 'dweller, farmer'; from the
collective prefix *ge-* 'fellow, together' + *būr* 'dwelling, cottage'].
Old English *būr* 'a dwelling, a cottage' evolved into English
BOWER 'a cottage; a leafy retreat; a boudoir.' There is another
1445 BOWER 'the jack of trumps' in certain card games—euchre, for
instance—but this BOWER comes from the German cognate *Bauer*
'farmer; jack (in playing cards).' (The Dutch also use *boer* with
the playing-card meaning.) Also in this group is BOWERY 'a farm
owned by a Dutch colonist in early New York' [from Dutch
1450 *bouwerij*, from *bouwen* 'to cultivate, to till'].
Straight from Old English—and almost as strange to modern
ears—is the word for that dwelling place for kine, the BYRE
'cowshed, barn' [from Old English *bȳre* 'stall, hut'; from Ger-

manic *būrjam 'dwelling']. In Old Norse, bȳr had the meaning,
enlarged from 'dwelling,' of 'village.' This Scandinavian bȳr   1455
survives in the suffix -by, found in many English place names
(RUGBY, DERBY, GRANBY, WHITBY). The local rules and customs
of the Middle-English-speaking people who lived in these and
other towns were known as BYLAW, BYRLAW 'village law; the
local customs of a rural district whereby disputes as to bounda-   1460
ries, trespasses of cattle, etc., were settled without going into law
courts; a regulation dealing with internal, organizational matters,
made by the members of the organization.' Thus, the BY- in
BYLAW has to do with villages and organizations, and is not
related to the preposition/adverb by 'close to; through the use of.'   1465
A medieval serf was—and a modern farmer in a sense still
is—bound to the soil. It is a condition known as BONDAGE
(etymologically) 'the condition of being a dweller on the land, a
householder and tiller of the soil'; 'villeinage; the state of being a
freeman in all respects except duties toward a feudal lord;   1470
serfdom; slavery, captivity' [from Anglo-Latin bondāgium; from
Old English bōnda 'householder'; from Old Norse bōndi, būandi
'tiller of the soil'; from the present participle of Old Norse būa 'to
dwell']. The above definitions, which are arranged in historical
order, show a distinct downward trend in social standing from   1475
freeman to slave. The reason for this semantic deterioration is,
simply, the Norman Conquest. Before 1066, an Anglo-Saxon/
Norse bōnda or būandi was 'a free man tilling his own soil,' but
after the Conquest the land was owned by the new king, who
parceled it out among his nobles. The farmer/peasant was suffered   1480
to remain on it only after paying homage to his feudal lord,
becoming in effect a villein. Because of these restrictions and
because of the similarity of the word bōnda 'husbandman' to the
unrelated words band, bond, bind, and bound that have connotations of fetters and of being tied, the word BONDAGE became   1485
associated in usage with 'the condition of being fettered.' Etymologically, nevertheless, the fettering "bonds" of matrimony, Wall
Street, liquor warehouses, and insurance companies are not
related to the BOND- of BONDSERVANT, BONDMAN, BONDMAID,
BONDSLAVE, and the kind of BONDSMAN that means 'a person   1490
required to work without pay.' However, the other kind of
bondsman 'one who puts up surety for another' obviously derives
from the bond that means 'written obligation' [from the Indo-
European root *bhendh- 'to bind'].
Another English word related to BONDAGE, BOWER, NEIGH-   1495
BOR, and BOOR is HUSBAND (etymologically) 'house-dweller'; 'the
male partner in a marriage' [from Old English hūsbonda; from
Old Norse hūsbōndi; hūs 'house' (from Germanic *husam) +

bōndi, bōandi, būandi, present participle of *bōa, būa* 'to dwell'].
1500 That the origins of the word HUSBAND have to do with house and
land is further evidenced by meanings that survive in the words
HUSBANDRY 'the cultivation of plants; the raising of livestock;
farming'; HUSBANDMAN 'a farmer'; and HUSBAND (verb) 'to administer as a good housekeeper; to manage with thrift and prudence.'
1505 Judging by the work of some laborers in the field, we are
dealing here with three variants of a Germanic root: **bū-, *bō-*,
and **bu-. *Bū-* is at the bottom, so to speak, of BOWER, BOOR,
NEIGHBOR, BYRE, and BYLAW, while **bō-* generates BOWERY,
BONDAGE, and HUSBAND [the last two via Old Norse *bōa, būa* 'to
1510 dwell']. This Old Norse verb *būa* 'to dwell, to live' developed an
extended sense of 'to prepare,' so that the past participle *būinn*
had a meaning of 'prepared, ready.' Old Norse *būinn* came into
Middle English as *boun* 'prepared, ready to go,' and Middle
English *boun* has had a *-d* tacked on to become modern English
1515 BOUND 'headed for, going toward' (homeward BOUND, outBOUND,
inBOUND). (This is one of four different English words spelled *b*,
o, u, n, d. The *-d* was added perhaps under the impression that
Middle English *boun* was related to *bound* 'destined, fated,'
which is a past participle of *bind* 'to tie, to make certain' and no
1520 etymological kin.)
Also from the root **bō-* is BOOTH (originally) 'a temporary
dwelling'; 'an enclosed compartment' [from Old Danish *bōth*].
A house, or dwelling place, or booth, is something that
someone has to BUILD 'to erect, to construct' [from Old English
1525 *byldan* 'to construct a dwelling,' from *bold*, variant of *botl* 'a
dwelling'; from Germanic **buthla(m)*]. Here we have the Germanic **bu-*, in **buthla(m)*, but right away we get a variation to
Germanic **bōthla*, antecedent of Middle Dutch *bōdel* 'property,
riches' and Dutch *boedel* 'effects, estate.' This was borrowed into
1530 English as BOODLE 'a collection, a lot; counterfeit money; bribe
money; swag, loot, plunder.' BOODLE arose as a colloquial expression in the United States, apparently an adaptation of Dutch
boedel 'the whole of one's possessions,' as early as 1699, "but it
did not acquire the meaning of money until the 1850s, and was
1535 apparently not used to signify political bribes and loot until after
1880." (*HLM*) The semantic connection of 'the whole of one's
possessions' with 'to dwell' is, possibly, that a man's dwelling is
usually his most valuable possession and that people tend to
gather their valuables together in their dwellings. BOODLE has an
1540 intensive form in CABOODLE 'the lot' (kit and CABOODLE, the
whole CABOODLE) [possibly a shortening of *kit and boodle*, or the
ca- may be a variation of the intensive prefix *ker-*, as in *kerflop*]. A
friend with State Department connections supplies the informa-

tion that in the foreign service, *kit and boodle* has been
metathesized into BOODLE kit 'a package of local currency given   1545
to junketing congressmen by functionaries at U.S. embassies,'
currency that the congressmen spend as they see fit.

Can one tell an IMP by his PHYSIOGNOMY? or a BUMPKIN by
his PHYSIQUE? These are DUBIOUS propositions, hardly subject to
PROOF. The words discussed up to now have been derivatives of   1550
the Germanic roots *bū-, *bō-, *bu- 'to dwell.' But these roots are
themselves descended from an Indo-European root, *bheu-, with
the more fundamental meaning of 'to grow, to cause to grow' and
extended meanings of 'to be, to exist.'

The most obvious English descendant of *bheu- 'to grow; to   1555
be' is the verb to BE (originally) 'to become'; 'to exist; to occupy a
certain place' [from Old English *bēon* 'to come to be, to become'].
There are only three forms of this word in use: BE—used in the
imperative, the subjunctive, and the infinitive; BEING—the present participle/gerund; and BEEN—the past participle. Other parts   1560
of the verb 'to BE—*am, is, are, was, were*—come from different
roots. (See line 8478.) Also, the prefix *be-*, as in *become, befriend*,
and *between*, is not from the verb BE but is related to English *by*,
Latin *ambi*, and Greek *amphi*.

One remaining Germanic manifestation of Indo-European   1565
*bheu- 'to be; to grow' with derivatives surviving in English
is (possibly) *baumaz 'a growing thing, a tree,' whence modern
German *Baum* 'tree' and English BEAM (obsolete) 'a tree'; 'a large
piece of squared timber; the breadth of a ship; an oscillating lever
attached to a pivot; a shaft, column, or ray of light; electromag-   1570
netic rays; a directional radio signal' (on the BEAM) [from Old
English *bēam* 'tree; post; ray of light'] and BOOM 'a long spar
extending from the mast of a ship; the mast of a mobile crane; any
device resembling a ship's boom used to maneuver a piece of
equipment into a desired position' [from Dutch *boom* 'a tree, a   1575
pole']. In Dutch and Flemish, a little tree is called a *boomken*, a
word possibly used by Dutch seafarers to mean 'a little boom.' In
any case, *boomken* was (probably) taken over into English as
BUMKIN, BUMPKIN 'a short spar projecting from the deck of a ship';
(? originally) 'a Dutchman'; 'a simple-minded rustic' [-*ken* and   1580
-*kin* are diminutive suffixes], but BUMPKIN may come from Middle
Dutch *bommekijn* 'a little barrel.'

Germanic *baumaz 'tree' also lives on in English BAUM
marten (literally) 'tree marten'; 'the fur of the European pine
marten' [a partial translation of German *Baummarder* 'tree mar-   1585
ten, pine marten'].

The Indo-European root *bheu- 'to be' lurks, unsuspected by
most, in the -*bus*, -*bius* endings seen in the Latin word *superbus*

'being above; haughty; excellent,' whence English SUPERB. It
1590 occurs also in *probus* 'being straightforward; upright, honest,'
whence English PROBE, PROBITY, PROOF, PROVE, PROBABLE,
PROBATION, etc. And, finally, we can see it in *dubius* 'being two;
of two minds; doubtful,' whence English DUBIOUS, DOUBT,
REDOUBTABLE, etc. (See line 1173.) The -*bus*, -*bius* endings are
1595 presumed to have evolved from Indo-European *bheu- by way of
intermediate forms like *-bhw-o- and *-bhw-io-, only to wind up,
in English SUPERB, as the one-letter suffix -*b*. This is transmogrified, in PROOF, into -*f* [from Middle English *prof, pref, preve*;
from Old French *proeve, preve, prueve*; from Late Latin *proba*;
1600 from Latin *probus* 'upright, honest; being straightforward'].

Indo-European *bh-, which changes to -*b*- in the body of the
Latin words *superbus, probus*, and *dubius*, should, according to
the rules of sound correspondences, change at the beginning of a
Latin word to *f*-. Therefore, we find Indo-European *bheu- 'to be'
1605 manifesting itself in Latin in the forms *fuī, fuistī, fuit*, etc. 'I have
been, thou hast been, he has been,' etc.; *fueram, fuerās*, etc. 'I
had been, thou hadst been,' etc.; *fuerō*, etc. 'I shall have been,'
etc.; in the subjunctive perfect *fuisse* 'to have been'; and in
futūrus 'about to be.' Of all these, only the future participle
1610 *futūrus* has an English descendant, which was borrowed from
Old French *futur*, FUTURE 'time that is yet to be.'

The transformation of Indo-European *bh- into Latin *f*- at the
beginning of a word is also seen in the verb *fieri* 'to become, to
grow; to spring up,' the equivalent of Old English *bēon* 'to
1615 become.' The imperative/subjunctive of *fierī* is *fiat* 'let it be
(done).' *Fiat* is used in English as a substantive: FIAT 'an arbitrary
order.'

In Greek, Indo-European *bh- changed, not to *f*-, but to *ph*-,
now pronounced like *f*- but originally pronounced like the -*ph*- in
1620 *uphill*. Likewise, *bh- was presumably pronounced like the -*b H*-
in *Bob Hope*. Indo-European *bheu- 'to be, to exist; to grow, to
cause to grow' shows up in Greek in four different words
beginning with *ph*-, each word a source of modern scientific
terms. The Greek words are *phusis* 'birth, growth; nature'; *phuton*
1625 'a plant, a tree'; *phulon* 'family, tribe, race'; and *phuein* 'to make
grow, to engender.' From *phusis* 'birth, growth; nature' and its
adjective *phusikos* 'of nature; natural,' English has taken these
words: PHYSICS 'the science of matter and energy' [from Latin
physica 'natural science'; a plural form taken from Greek *ta*
1630 *phusika* 'natural things,' the title of Aristotle's treatises on natural
phenomena]; PHYSIC (obsolete) 'physics'; (archaic) 'knowledge of
the human body and its diseases'; 'a medicine or drug; a cathartic'; PHYSICIAN 'one who deals with the human body; a medical

doctor'; PHYSICAL 'of the body' (as distinguished from *mental* 'of
the mind'); 'of material things'; and PHYSIQUE 'the proportions   1635
and development of the human body' [from French *physique*
'physical']. All the *physio-* words form a part of this set, as well,
notably, PHYSIOLOGY 'the study of bodily processes' and PHYSIO-
THERAPY 'treatment of the body by physical means' [*therapeia*
'service'], as well as the somewhat different PHYSIOGNOMY (liter-   1640
ally) 'understanding the nature of'; 'the art of judging character
from facial features; facial features' [*gnōmōn* 'judge, one that
knows']; in the last sense, this is sometimes shortened to PHIZ
[from Greek *phusiognōmonia* 'judging of nature; the judging of a
man's nature by his features']. The notion that a person's nature   1645
and temper are most clearly revealed by his face has been used
by conmen and other swindlers to their great advantage.

Also from *phusis* 'birth, growth; nature' and its adjective
phusikos 'of nature; natural' comes METAPHYSICS (literally) 'after
physics'; 'that branch of philosophy that concerns itself with the   1650
investigation of the nature of ultimate reality.' The Greek preposition *meta* means 'with, among, after,' but in order to give the
compound word METAPHYSICS an intelligible referent, the *meta-*
has been interpreted as meaning 'beyond,' with the result that
METAPHYSICS means '(studies) beyond physics.' This is some-   1655
times further interpreted to signify 'study of the supernatural or
transcendental.' Historically, however, the word METAPHYSICS
comes from the phrase *ta meta ta phusika* (literally) 'the after-the-
physics'! This designation was given by Andronicus of Rhodes, a
first-century B.C. editor of Aristotle's works, to those works of   1660
Aristotle's that came after (*meta*) his treatises on natural science
(*ta phusika*). Thus, *ta meta ta phusika* = 'the (things) after the
natural (things)' = the works of Aristotle that came after the works
on physics (in the traditional order in which they were handed
down). Another compound using *phusis* is MONOPHYSITE 'one   1665
who believes in the single nature of Christ.'

Based on Greek *phuton* 'a plant, a tree' is PHYTON 'a unit of
plant structure; the smallest part of a plant that will grow after
being cut off.' The prefix *phyto-* 'plant, vegetable' is found in
PHYTOLOGY 'the study of plants; botany'; PHYTOGNOMY (obsolete)   1670
'the art of deducing the properties of plants from their appearance' (compare PHYSIOGNOMY); PHYTOPSYCHE 'a soul or spiritual
essence conceived as innate in plant life'; and PHYTOPHAGOUS
'feeding on plants' [*phagein* 'to eat']. The suffix *-phyte* 'a plant
with a certain character or habitat' is found in AEROPHYTE =   1675
EPIPHYTE 'air plant; a nonparasitic plant that grows on other
plants' [*epi* 'on, upon']; MICROPHYTE 'a minutely small plant';
HYDROPHYTE 'a plant that grows in water'; THERMOPHYTE 'a

plant that likes high temperatures'; and, at least metaphorically,
1680   NEOPHYTE (literally) 'newly planted'; 'a new convert to a religion;
a beginner.'

Based on Greek *phulon* 'family, tribe, race' are PHYLON 'a
genetically related group; a tribe or race'; PHYLUM 'a division of
the plant or animal kingdom whose members are assumed to have
1685   a common ancestor; a large grouping of related languages'; and
PHYLE 'a political subdivision of ancient Greece based on kin-
ship,' corresponding to the Roman *tribus* 'tribe.'

Based on the Greek *phuein* 'to engender, to make grow,'
besides some technical terms, is the Greek compound *euphuēs*
1690   'well-grown; shapely' (*eu-* 'well, pleasant'). *Euphuēs* was adopted
by the Elizabethan writer John Lyly as the name of the protagonist in two of his books, books that were characterized by an
overly elegant style of writing. This conjuncture led to the
coinage of the English word EUPHUISM 'affected elegance of
1695   language' (not to be confused with *euphemism*). (See line 4972.)
One of the earliest technical terms incorporating *phuein* 'to cause
to grow' was the Greek *emphuein* 'to implant' with past participle
emphutos 'implanted, engrafted.' By Late Latin/Medieval Latin
days, Greek *emphutos* had been altered to Latin *impotus* 'a graft,'
1700   implying a Vulgar Latin verb **impotare* 'to engraft.' **Impotare* or
impotus led to Old English *impian* 'to engraft,' whence the Old
English noun *impa* and English IMP (obsolete) 'a young shoot of a
plant or tree; a scion; a young child; a scion of a noble family'; 'a
child of the devil, a child of hell; an evil spirit; a mischievous
1705   child; to graft feathers onto the wing of a bird (in falconry).' There
is also a folk etymology of IMP that makes it out to be a shortened
form of *impious*.

Lastly, from Indo-European **bheu-* 'to be; to grow' is the
Welsh *bod* 'to be,' which was softened, or "lenited," to *-fod* in the
1710   Welsh word EISTEDDFOD (literally) 'a being seated; a sitting, a
session'; 'a festive assembly of poets and musicians.'

VIII

Bucolic Bovines, Beefy Presbyters

A BUCOLIC scene should include a COW or two (KINE), a hillock covered with BUTTERCUPS, and Little Boy Blue practicing on his BUGLE. In the nursery rhyme it's a horn, but the word BUGLE is much more BUCOLIC. BUGLE comes from the Latin *būculus* 'little ox,' and what could be more BUCOLIC than an ox?

Both BUGLE and COW descend from the Indo-European root **gwou-* 'ox, bull, cow.' Indo-European **gw-* at the beginning of a word regularly evolved into Greek *b-* along one line of descent and into Germanic **k-* along another. Therefore, **gwou-* became Greek *bous* 'cow, ox, bull' and Germanic **kōuz*, whence Old English *cū*, plural *cȳ(e)*. *Cū* changes into COW 'a mature female of the bovine family, a she-elk, -moose, -elephant, -whale, etc.'; and *cȳ(e)* (genitive *cȳna*, *cūna*) into archaic KINE 'cows.'

Normally, **gwou-* would have developed into Latin **vos*, **vovis*, but the actual Latin word is *bōs*, *bovis* 'ox, bull; cow,' probably from the Oscan or Umbrian. In modern zoology, *bōs* is used as a genus term: BOS 'ruminant quadrupeds that include wild and domestic cattle.' It is from the Latin form, as altered by Old French, that we get the English word BEEF 'a full-grown ox, bull, cow or steer; or its meat' [from Old French *boef*; from Latin *bovem*, the accusative of *bōs*]. The modern French word is *boeuf*, but the French word for BEEFSTEAK 'a slice of beef suitable for frying or broiling' is *bifteck*, an adaptation of the English word. This early example of Franglais was apparently introduced by the Vicomte de Chateaubriand, writer and diplomat, who was an émigré in England from 1792 to 1800, fleeing the French Revolution, and French ambassador to Great Britain in 1822, representing Louis XVIII. The French have taken the *bifteck* thing a step further by calling bear steak *bifteck d'ours*.

1715

1720

1725

1730

1735

1740

Also based on Latin *bos, bovis* are BOVINE 'pertaining to an animal of the genus Bos' [from Late Latin *bovīnus*] and BUGLE (originally) 'a wild ox; a buffalo'; 'a bugle-horn; a musical instrument made from the horn of a wild ox; a brass musical instrument 1745 without keys' [from Old French *bugle*; from Latin *būculus* 'little ox,' diminutive of *bōs*].

Coming to English through Latin but ultimately based (probably) on the Greek cognate *bous* 'cow, bull, ox' is BUFFALO 'any of several species of oxen' [from Italian *bufalo*; Spanish *búfalo*; or 1750 Portuguese *bufalo* (now *bufaro*); from (Late) Latin *būfalus*, from Latin *būbalus*, an adaptation of Greek *boubalos*, properly a kind of African antelope, but applied to a wild ox; probably based on Greek *bous* 'cow, bull, ox']. There are domesticated buffalo and there are untamable buffalo and there is the American bison, also 1755 commonly called a "buffalo," but in reality only distantly related to those species. The bison's first cousin, both biologically and etymologically, is the European *wisent*, an animal that is almost extinct, except for protected herds on reservations.

Buffalo hide is made into a superior leather with a fuzzy, 1760 velvety finish, once very popular as a material for military uniforms. This leather was called by the French, *buffle*, which is also their word for BUFFALO. *Buffle* was adopted into English and shortened to BUFF (obsolete) 'a buffalo'; 'a military coat made of buffalo (or ox, or bison, or elk) leather; a polishing tool whose 1765 rubbing surface is covered with buff leather; to polish with leather; the bare human skin' (in the BUFF); 'an enthusiast about going to fires' [originally, a New York City volunteer fireman; from the color of their uniforms]; 'an enthusiast about a special field of knowledge.' Also based on Greek *bous* 'cow, ox' are 1770 BUCOLIC 'pastoral, pertaining to herdsmen' [via Latin *būcolicus* from Greek *boukolikos*, from *boukolos* 'cowherd'] (the Greek element *-kolos* being accounted for as related to Latin *colere* 'to cultivate'; see line 10967); BUCEPHALUS (literally) 'ox-headed'; 'the war-horse of Alexander the Great' [*kephale* 'head']; BOUSTROPHE- 1775 DON (literally) 'turning like oxen (in plowing)'; 'an ancient way of writing in alternate directions: one line from left to right, the next line from right to left, and so on' [*strephein* 'to turn']; BOSP(H)ORUS (literally) 'ox river, passage, ford'; 'a strait connecting the Black Sea and the Sea of Marmora, separating European 1780 from Asiatic Turkey; a strait connecting two seas or a lake and a sea' [from Greek *Bosporos* (*poros* 'passage, ford, river')]; and, possibly, BUTTER 'the solidified fat of milk' [via Latin *būtȳrum* from Greek *bouturon* (literally, perhaps) 'cow-cheese' (*turos* 'cheese')]. If BUTTER belongs here, then so does BUTTERCUP 'a 1785 common wildflower with glossy yellow petals,' formerly called

BUTTERFLOWER. It wasn't until the 18th century that English speakers combined BUTTERFLOWER with *gold-cup* or *king-cup* to form BUTTERCUP. Also, BUTTERFLY 'an insect with four broad, colorful, nonfolding wings.' A common species of butterfly is yellow in color, and this may account for the name; but another explanation is that the insects were once believed to "steal" milk and butter. (An old German name for the creatures is *Milchdieb* 'milk-thief.') 1790

A relative of Greek *bous* 'ox, cow' may be craftily concealed in the word PRESBYTER 'an elder in the early Christian church; a priest; an elder' [via Late Latin from the Greek comparative form, *presbuteros* 'elder, chief'; from *presbus* 'old man']. PRESBYTER carries with it connotations of 'taking precedence, leading the way' because etymologically, according to some, Greek *presbus* breaks down into *pres-* 'in front' + *-bus* 'ox; the lead ox, the leader of the herd.' Others, however, connect the *-bus* of *presbus* with the Indo-European root *gwā-* 'to go,' so that the word etymologically means simply 'going in front.' 1795 1800

A PRESBYTERIAN church is one in which "no higher order than that of presbyter or elder is recognized, the *bishop* and *elder* of the New Testament being held to be identical" *(OED)*. The Greek word *presbuteros* was taken over into ecclesiastical Late Latin as *presbyter* and evolved variously into Vulgar Latin *prester*, Old High German *prēster*, German *Priester*, Old French *prestre*, French *prêtre*, and, in an unexplained way, into Old English *prēost* and English PRIEST 'one whose office is to perform public religious functions.' 1805 1810

Greek *presbus* 'old man' gives us the combining form *presby-* 'old age' found in the ophthalmological term PRESBYOPIA 'a defect of vision associated with advancing age' [*ōps* 'eye']. This defect is marked by the inability to distinguish small objects, such as newspaper print, at close range. (When this condition occurs for reasons other than advancing age, it is called *hyperopia* or, in the vernacular, *farsightedness*, which in this case doesn't mean to see far-off things better, but not to see close-up things so well.) 1815 1820

Even better camouflaged than the 'lead ox' in *presbuteros* are the Greek oxen in HECATOMB 'a large-scale sacrifice; a public sacrifice, to the gods, of 100 oxen' [via Latin from the Greek *hekatombē* (*hekaton* '100' + *-bē*, from *bous* 'ox')]. Another medical term that incorporates our Greek element is BULIMIA, BULIMY (literally) 'ox hunger'; 'a perpetual, insatiable appetite for food' [New Latin, from Greek *boulimia* (*limos* 'hunger')]. 1825

The scientific name for the musk-ox is OVIBOS (literally) 'sheep-ox' [Latin *ovis* 'sheep' + *bōs* 'ox'].

1830   Possibly meriting inclusion in this group is that vexatious
word BOTHER 'trouble, annoyance; to pester, to annoy; to take
pains.' This word is usually accounted of obscure origin, although
all authorities agree in assigning it to the Anglo-Irish arena.
Attempts have been made to link BOTHER with Old Irish *bodhar*
1835   'deaf,' Irish *bodhraim* 'I deafen,' Old Irish *buadrim*, and Irish
buadhrim 'I vex, I annoy.' Some trace Old Irish *buadrim* 'I vex'
further back to the Indo-European root **gwōu-* (with a long *ō*)
'dung; disgust, annoyance,' "doubtless a derivative of **gwou-*
'cow, bull.'" This would make the exclamation BOTHER! first
1840   cousin to another, vulgar, expression of disapproval (and disbe-
lief). BOTHER may also have influenced (and been influenced by)
another word of obscure origin, POTHER 'a commotion; a state of
nervous agitation.'
        Before we leave the BOVINES, we should point out that the
1845   English word *bull*, though it starts with *bu-* and stands for the
male of the species, does not come from Indo-European **gwou-*
'cow, bull,' but from Indo-European **bhel-* 'to swell,' and also
that the word COWSLIP 'an Old-World primrose' literally means
'cow droppings.'
1850   Ferdinand is the name of a prominent BOVINE who was also a
student of BOTANY, and loved to thrust his PROBOSCIS into
fragrant bouquets of flowers. (Strictly speaking, a bull does not
have a proboscis, but since Ferdinand is a highly anthropomor-
phic creation, the term seems applicable.) Being ruminant herbi-
1855   vores, bovines are grazers. The Greek word meaning to graze is
boskein, and the Greek word for 'pasture; herb; fodder' is *botanē*.
Botanē is accounted by some to be of obscure origin, but others
link it with *boskein* 'to graze,' with Latin *bōs* 'cow,' and thus with
our Indo-European root **gwou-* 'cow, ox.' *Botanē* is the ultimate
1860   source of English BOTANY 'the science of plant life' [by way of
Latin *botanicus* and Greek *botanikos*], and *boskein* 'to graze' has
an English descendant in PROBOSCIS 'the long, flexible snout of
an animal (as an elephant, tapir, shrew); an unusually long human
nose'; [from Greek *proboskis* 'an elephant's trunk; a means of
1865   providing food' (*pro-* 'in front' + *boskein* 'to feed')].
        There are some etymologists who would include in the
*gwou- 'ox, bull, cow' group the English word BOY 'a male child;
any male; a waiter, messenger, porter, field hand or other male
servant.' The suggested derivation from Indo-European **gwou-*
1870   'ox' begins with Greek *boeiai (dorai)* 'ox(hides); thongs made of
oxhide.' Such thongs were used as fetters for slaves, a practice
that gave rise to the Vulgar Latin word *boiae* 'fetters, a slave
collar' and the associated verb **imboiāre* 'to fetter, to enslave.'
*Imboiāre leads to Old French *embuier* and Norman French

*embuié, *abuié 'fettered; a male servant.' *Embuié, *abuié were   1875
then decapitated and borrowed into Middle English as *bwey, bye,*
boye (originally) 'a male servant; a youth.' If all this is true, the
automatic aversion among U.S. black male adults to the appellation *boy* has etymological as well as socio-psychological grounds.
Other derivations of BOY trace the word back to the Indo-   1880
European root of BROTHER (*bhrāter-*) and make it kin to modern
German *Bube* 'youth, knave.'

IX

Charging Chariots, Careening Carriages

When motor CARS were first being developed, they were called "horseless CARRIAGES." In the palmy 1920s, a smooth-faced sheik in plus fours might refer to his roadster as his CHARIOT. The airport limousine of the 1970s somewhat resembles the old-time, horse-drawn or motorized CHARABANC (literally) 'carriage with benches'; 'a long, light vehicle with several rows of forward-facing seats across its width; a sight-seeing bus' [from the French *char à bancs*]. The French word, however, was not used for buses or limousines but for wagonettes and jaunting cars.

We are dealing here with offspring of the Indo-European root **kers-* 'to run.' These words come to us from the Celtic **karros* by way of the Gaulish noun *carros*, which is said to have been adopted into Latin as *carrus* 'wagon, cart.' *Carrus* evolved into Late Latin *carra* and Old Northern French *carre*, and was adopted into Middle English as *carre*, whence modern English CAR 'a wheeled conveyance; a boxlike conveyance' (cable CAR, elevator CAR); 'an automobile.' Latin *carrus* 'wagon, cart' is the base of many other English words, such as CARRY 'to transport; to convey while supporting' [from Old Northern French *carier*, from *carre* 'cart']. Today we CARRY things in our arms or in our pockets and handbags, and baseballs CARRY over the fence to produce home runs; but the word originally meant 'to transport in a vehicle,' as does a motor CARRIER 'one that conveys (goods, passengers, diseases).' Note, also, CARRIAGE 'the act of carrying; the manner in which one holds one's body while walking; a transportation charge; a machine part that holds and moves another part; a four-wheeled passenger vehicle' (including peram-bulators) [from Old Northern French *cariage*, from *carier* 'to transport in a vehicle']; CAREER (originally) 'a racecourse'; 'a charge at full tilt; a path or course, as of the sun through the skies;

1885

1890

1895

1900

1905

1910

progress through a profession' [from Medieval French/French
carrière 'racecourse, career'; from Provençal *carriera* 'road, highway'; from the Medieval Latin phrase *via carrāria* 'carriage road'   1915
from Latin *carrus*]; CARIOLE 'a small one-horse carriage' [via
French from Old Provençal *carriola*, diminutive of *carri* 'chariot';
from Vulgar Latin **carrium*, from Latin *carrus*]; and CAROCHE 'a
stately coach of the 17th century' [from Old French/Medieval
French *carroche*, from Old Italian *carroccio* 'war chariot' (of   1920
Italian republics: a car of state that accompanied the army); based
on *carro* 'wagon,' from Latin *carrus*].

Oddly enough, the English word *cart*, so similar in meaning
and spelling to CAR, comes from entirely different sources, to wit,
Old Norse *kartr* 'cart' and Old English *craet* 'carriage.' (See line   1925
3160.) *Cart* was perhaps also influenced by Old Northern French
carete, diminutive of *carre* 'wagon.'

The observant reader will have noticed that most of these
words beginning with *ca-* have been acquired from Latin by way
of Northern French. This is to be expected, since in standard   1930
French, Latin *c-* followed by *-a* regularly becomes *ch-*, as in *char
à bancs*. *Char* 'carriage, car, chariot' is the regular French descendant of Latin *carrus*, which in Old Northern French (and Middle
English) becomes *carre*. Another *ch-* word that was borrowed by
English is CHARIOT 'an ancient two-wheeled, horse-drawn vehi-   1935
cle used in war, in races, and in processions; a light four-wheeled
carriage' [from Old French *chariot*, based on *char* 'wagon'].
French has two derivative forms of the basic *char* 'carriage, car':
charette 'a cart, usually two-wheeled' and *chariot* 'a wagon, a
wain, usually four-wheeled.' Both these forms were used in   1940
English through the 16th century, but in English pronunciation
the stress shifted to the first syllable of each word, and the two
became confused and, in effect, fused. *Charrette* (*charette*,
charet) fell into disuse before the middle of the 17th century. It
has been reintroduced, however, in architects' jargon, with the   1945
French *ch-* (*sh-*) and the stress on the second syllable, in CHAR-
RETTE, CHARETTE 'a final intensive effort to finish a project in
architectural design before a deadline.' The usage arose, perhaps,
because architectural drawings were transported by cart; others
say because of "the idea of speed on wheels" (*RHD*). The French   1950
names for the Big and Little Dipper are *le grand chariot* and *le
petit chariot*. The Latin word for chariot is *currus*. (See line 2082.)
A relative to these is CHARGE 'a load that can be carried at one
time; an order; a responsibility; to load a gun; to attack violently'
[from Old French *charg(i)er* 'to load, to place a burden upon';   1955
from Late Latin *carricāre* 'to load a wagon,' from Latin *carrus*
'wagon']. A gimmick that has become popular in baseball parks as

a way of sparking a home-team rally is the sounding of a bugle call, sol$_1$ do$_2$ mi$_2$/ sol$_2$ ... mi$_2$/ sol$_2$ ...... /, over the stadium loudspeakers. This is followed by a roar from the crowd of "Charge!" But it is said that the bugle call used is a signal not for "Charge!" but for "Water your horses!" A cavalryman's horse was called a CHARGER because he was trained to dash heedlessly into the fray. This is not the earliest meaning of CHARGER, which is, simply, 'one that loads,' just as the original sense of to CHARGE is 'to load,' as in "to charge a furnace (with ore)" and "to charge a rifle" = to load it. (To CHARGE a purchase at the store is to put a "load" on your credit.) The sense of to CHARGE 'to rush against in a hostile way' is linked semantically with the idea of placing a loaded weapon in position for action.

The 'loading' connotations of CHARGE become more apparent when we consider its doublet CARGO 'the freight carried in a vehicle' [from Spanish cargo 'burden, charge'; from Late Latin carricāre, from Latin carrus 'wagon'].

In Italian, caricare first meant 'to load,' then 'to overload,' hence 'to exaggerate.' ('To overload' is also an obsolete meaning of English CHARGE.) From the sense 'exaggeration' came the Italian caricatura and English CARICATURE 'exaggeration by means of deliberate distortion.'

The Latin speakers had another wheeled vehicle, besides the carrus, whose name they also borrowed from the Gauls: the carpentum 'a two-wheeled carriage,' apparently an adoption of Celtic *carpentom. An artisan who manufactured these carriages was an artifex carpentārius, or 'carriage-maker'—carpentārius for short—whence Old Northern French carpentier, borrowed into English as CARPENTER 'an artificer in wood' (Samuel Johnson's definition); 'one who builds and repairs wooden objects.'

The Indo-European root *kers- 'to run' is also manifested in Latin cursus 'a running; a place for running,' a substantive use of the past participle of currere 'to run.' Cursus became Old French cours, course (influenced by Italian corsa 'a running'), and was borrowed into English as COURSE 'the action of moving onward' (the COURSE of the sun, the COURSE of events, as a matter of COURSE); 'the path or direction of running' (a river's COURSE); 'a systematic succession' (a COURSE of studies, a COURSE of dishes in a meal); 'to move swiftly; to pursue.' A COURSER is either 'a swift horse' or 'a dog trained to chase game by sight rather than scent,' and a CORSAIR is 'a privately owned vessel authorized to attack enemy vessels; a privateer; a pirate; a swift pirate ship,' especially those of the so-called "Barbary pirates." CORSAIR traces back through Old French corsaire, Provençal corsari, and Old Italian corsaro to Medieval Latin cursārius 'plundering one,' from

Medieval Latin *cursus* 'hostile excursion, inroad; plunder,' from Latin *cursus* 'a running.'

Of the possibility that the island of Corsica was named after these pirates, the *Oxford English Dictionary* says: "a piece of Italian popular etymology and animosity." However, the Old Italian word *corsaro* 'one who makes hostile excursions' did, apparently, migrate into (Old) Serbian, where it was transformed into *kursar, hursar, husar* 'pirate' and was thence adopted into Hungarian/Magyar as *huszar*, originally, 'highway robber,' later, 'cavalryman.' It was in the latter part of the 15th century that the word was attached to light horsemen of the Hungarian army, and this military designation as well as a typically Hungarian dress uniform were later adopted by other European armies, giving us the German *Husar*, the French *houssard, hussard*, and the British/English HUSSAR 'a member of a light cavalry regiment.' A suggested alternative derivation of HUSSAR is through Byzantine Greek *koursōrios*, from *koursōr*, but influenced by Medieval Latin *cursārius*, from Latin *cursor* 'runner.'

Other English borrowings from the family of Latin *currere*, *cursus* are PRECURSOR 'one who runs ahead' [Latin *praecursor* 'forerunner, scout']; CURSORY 'while running; hasty and superficial' [Latin *cursōrius*, from *cursor* 'runner']; CURSIVE 'running, flowing' [from the Medieval Latin phrase *scripta cursiva* 'flowing script'] (said of writing in which the letters are joined together); DISCURSIVE 'rambling' [from Medieval Latin *discursīvus* 'a running to and fro' or 'in all directions' (*dis-* 'asunder')]; DISCOURSE 'conversation' [from Late Latin *discursus* 'conversation,' from Latin *discursus* 'a running to and fro']; CONCOURSE 'a running together; a crowd; a broad thoroughfare'; INTERCOURSE 'a running between; an interchange; communication'; RECOURSE 'a running back again; something that is turned to for aid'; EXCURSION 'a running out; an outing, a short trip'; INCURSION 'a running in; an invasion'; and possibly COARSE 'common, ordinary; of inferior quality; consisting of large particles; lacking in fineness or delicacy.' The word COARSE would seem to have been originally used of cloth. Many scholars are of the opinion that COARSE is a special sense of COURSE 'the usual; ordinary, common,' but others put it in the category "of obscure origin." "That it should be based on the phrase *of course* 'customary, usual' seems to be chronologically impossible," says the *Oxford Dictionary of English Etymology*, inasmuch as the phrase *of course* dates from the 16th century and COARSE 'ordinary, common' from the 14th. Yet another writer, noting an earlier spelling *cowarce*, breaks this down into *cow* + *arse*, and opines that COARSE is "apparently [an] adjectival use of [an] abusive vulgarism."

2005

2010

2015

2020

2025

2030

2035

2040

2045

From compounds of Latin *currere* 'to run' English has borrowed INCUR 'to run into; to bring upon oneself'; OCCUR (obsolete) 'to run to meet; to run against'; 'to happen' [*oc-* < *ob-* 'toward, against']; RECUR 'to happen again'; CONCUR 'to happen at the same time; to agree'; and SUCCOR (literally) 'to run under'; 'to run to the aid of' [from. Latin *succurrere* 'to run under, to run to help' (*suc-* < *sub-* 'under')].

Via Old French *corant, curant*, based on the Latin present participle *currēns* 'running,' comes English CURRENT 'now in progress; circulating; a steady flow' (of water, electricity, etc.). The modern French form, *courant*, is used in English in the phrase *au courant* (literally) 'in the current'; 'up-to-date, in the know,' and in the name of a venerable Connecticut newspaper, the Hartford COURANT. (However, the word *currant* 'the small, sour fruit of plants of the genus *Ribes*,' comes from an entirely different source, to wit, via Anglo-French *raisins de corauntz* 'raisins of Corinth,' from the name of the Greek seaport that exported the fruit.) Other reflexes of this productive root are COURANTE 'a French dance of the 17th century characterized by running steps to an accompaniment in triple time; the second movement of a classical suite'; COURIER 'runner; diplomatic messenger' [from Medieval/Old French *courrier*, from Old Italian *corriere*, from *correre* 'to run'; from Latin *currere* 'to run']; COUREUR (DE BOIS) '(woods) runner; a French-Canadian woodsman who trapped and traded pelts with the Indians' [French *coureur* 'runner,' from *courir* 'to run,' from Latin *currere* 'to run']; and CURRICULUM (literally) 'a running course'; 'the courses of study offered by an educational institution' [from Latin *curriculum* 'a running; a race-course; a race-chariot']. A former carriage, light, open, two-wheeled, and drawn by two horses, was known as a CURRICLE during the 18th and 19th centuries [from Latin *curriculum* 'race-chariot']. An interesting cognate is CURULE 'of superior rank; privileged to sit in the curule chair' [from Latin *curulis* 'belonging to a chariot']. The *sella curulis* 'curule chair' was originally a throne mounted on a chariot, or *currus*. It was shaped like a camp stool, inlaid with ivory, with curved legs but without a back, and was reserved for the use of the highest magistrates in ancient Rome. And in the same family may be CORRIDOR 'a hallway; a passageway' [via French, from Old Italian *corridore* 'a runner,' but with the meaning of Old Italian *corridoio* 'a running place,' from Vulgar Latin *curritorium*, based on Latin *currere*]; CORRIDA (de toros) 'a running (of bulls); a bullfight'; and CORRAL 'an enclosure for livestock; to round up (livestock).' Here we have some more differing of opinion. Some trace CORRAL back through the Spanish *corral* and Portuguese *curral* to Latin *currere*

'to run,' citing either Spanish *correr* 'to run' and *corro* 'a ring, a circle' or Vulgar Latin *currale 'an enclosure for vehicles' and deriving KRAAL 'a village of South African natives, such as   2095
Hottentots or Kaffirs; an enclosed stockade for livestock' from Portuguese *curral*, and hence from the Latin. Others, however, think that the sequence went the other way, that *kraal* was originally a Hottentot word and is the sire of Portuguese *curral* and Spanish *corral*.   2100

X

Chief Cadet; Capriccioso da Capo

"You, sir, are a CAD!" is an old-fashioned expression, but many of us still know what it means. According to the *Oxford English Dictionary*, a CAD is "a fellow of low, vulgar manners and behaviour," and the editors add that this is "an offensive and insulting appellation." Such were not, however, the original meaning and intent of the word. CAD is a shortened form of CADDIE, which in 18th-century Scotland and England meant '"a lad who waits about on the lookout for chance employment as a messenger, odd-job-man, etc."' (*OED*). CADDIE later came to mean '"a golf-player's attendant who carries his clubs"' (*OED*). Such lads were of course looked down upon by public-school boys and collegians, and it was among these would-be nobs that the term CAD developed its pejorative connotations. Going further back, we find that the word CADDIE is itself a popular mispronunciation of the French word *cadet*, whose primary meaning in French is 'younger son,' hence 'younger brother,' hence 'young fellow.' The signification of English CADET 'a student in a military or naval school' stems from the fact that before the French Revolution the younger sons of the French nobility regularly entered upon military service to make careers for themselves. The French term *cadet* was "originally applied to Gascon officers (younger sons of noble families) at the French court" (*ODEE*). (It will be remembered that d'Artagnan was a Gascon.) Going even further back, we discover that a *cadet* is, etymologically, 'a little head (of the family).' (Compare the formal title of *master* for 'a young boy.') French *cadet* evolved, by way of Gascon *capdet* 'little chief, captain' and Late Latin *capitellum* 'little head,' from Latin *caput* 'head' and ultimately from the Indo-European root **kaput* 'head.'

A host of English words have been borrowed from Latin   2130
caput 'head' and its derivatives. Some of them are obvious ones,
like CAPTAIN 'head man, leader' [from Medieval French/Old
French *capitain(e)*, from Late Latin *capitāneus* 'chief'] and CAPI-
TAL 'head city; an uppercase letter' (standing at the head of the
word or sentence); 'first, chief; first-class; calling for the death   2135
penalty' (CAPITAL crime, CAPITAL punishment) [via French from
Latin *capitālis* 'of the head; chief']. The last meaning traces back
to execution by DECAPITATION 'beheading.'

Then there is another CAPITAL 'accumulated wealth, especially when used to create more wealth.' This meaning stems   2140
from senses acquired by the Medieval Latin word *capitale*, the
neuter of *capitalis* used as a noun with the senses of 'goods,
property, principal.' Etymologically, the word *principal* means 'of
the prince, of the "first" man.' Similarly, *capital(is)* means 'of the
chief, of the head man.' One may assume that the accumulated   2145
wealth that CAPITAL stands for was originally property that be-
longed to the chief or prince as representative of the tribe.

There is yet another CAPITAL 'the head of a pillar, usually
ornamented in a distinctive style' [from Late Latin *capitellum*],
and, differently spelled CAPITOL 'a citadel on the head of a hill;   2150
the national temple of Rome; the edifice of Congress in Washington; the statehouse of one of the United States' [from Latin
Capitōlium 'the chief (temple)']. The Roman temple was dedicated to Jupiter Optimus Maximus and was erected on the
Tarpein, or Saturnian Hill, later called the CAPITOLINE.   2155

Also derived from Latin *caput* 'head' are CAPITULATE (literally) 'to list under headings, or chapters'; (obsolete) 'to list terms
(of surrender)'; 'to come to terms; to surrender' [from Medieval
Latin *capitulāre*; from Late Latin *capitulum* 'chapter'; from Latin
capitulum 'small head']; RECAPITULATE 'to list again under head-   2160
ings; to summarize'; and per CAPITA 'per person'; (literally) 'by
heads.'

In the words listed so far, Latin *caput* 'head' has changed to
capit-. A further change to *cipit-* and less obvious semantic
relationships are found in the words PRECIPICE 'a sheer cliff'   2165
[from Latin *praecipitium* 'precipice'; from *praeceps, praecipitis*
'headfirst; headlong; steep'] and PRECIPITATE (literally) 'to throw
head first'; 'to cast down headlong; to hurl down'; (meteorology)
'to condense and fall'; 'to hurry'; (adjective) 'moving rapidly;
moving hastily' [from Latin *praecipitāre* 'to cast down headlong;   2170
to hasten; to ruin'; from *praeceps, praecipitis* 'headfirst, steep'
(*prae-* 'in front, first' + *caput* 'head')]. The *-ceps* element seen in
praeceps 'head' is also evidenced in the anatomical words BICEPS
(literally) 'two-headed'; 'any muscle that has two points of origin,

2175   or heads; especially the large muscle in the upper arm' [New
Latin, from Latin *biceps* 'two-headed; having two peaks'] and
TRICEPS 'a large three-headed muscle along the back of the upper
arm.' Two other anatomical words, in which our element *caput*
'head' takes the form of *-ciput*, are OCCIPUT 'the back of the skull'
2180   [from Latin *occiput* (*oc-* < *ob-* 'in back of')] and SINCIPUT 'the
upper half of the cranium' [from Latin *sinciput* 'brains,' earlier
*senciput; from *sēmi* 'half' + *caput*].
The reader is here reminded that Latin *c-* followed by *-a-*
changes in French to *ch-*, as in the sequences Latin *capra* >
2185   French *chèvre* 'she-goat'; Latin *caballus* > French *cheval* 'horse';
Latin *castellum* > French *château* 'castle'; and Latin *capitulum*
'small head' > Old French *chapitre* > English CHAPTER 'a
subheading of a book; a branch of an organization.' There is also
the architectural term CHAPITER 'the capital of a column.'
2190   In another Old French derivation, subsequently adopted by
English, the *-u-* of *caput* disappears, and the resultant *-pt* is
simplified to *-t(t)*, so that we get the following sequence: Latin
capitale 'property' > Old French *chatel* > English CHATTEL
(obsolete) 'property, goods, money'; (obsolete) 'livestock, CAT-
2195   TLE'; 'any movable possession; a slave.' However, in Old Northern French, the "Latin-*c*-followed-by-*a*" rule does not apply, and
we have the sequence Latin *capitale* > Old Northern French
catel > English CATTLE (obsolete) 'property, goods'; 'livestock,
especially bovines.'
2200   Latin *caput* 'head' may or may not be the ultimate source of
English CAP 'a covering for the head; anything that serves as a
covering' (bottle CAP, ice CAP) [from Late Latin *cappa* 'hood,
cloak'; probably from Latin *caput* 'head']. Note the "probably."
Other words that etymologists use to hedge on this relationship
2205   are "possibly," "perhaps," "irregularly," "akin to," and "uncertain." Note also that the meaning 'cloak' is already attached to the
Late Latin *cappa*, indicating a combined sense of 'cloak with
hood attached.' The *Oxford English Dictionary* comments: "The
presumption is that the name [*cappa*] was transferred from a
2210   woman's . . . head-covering . . . to the 'hood' of a cloak, and then to
the cloak or 'cape' having such a hood, and thus to a priest's
'cope.'" As this quotation suggests, a cognate word denotes the
'cloak' only: CAPE 'a sleeveless garment fastened at the throat and
hanging over the shoulders' [via French *cape*, from Provençal
2215   *cape* and Spanish *capa*; from Late Latin *cappa*]. ESCAPE (literally)
'out of the cloak'; 'to break out of confinement; to elude capture;
to avoid disaster' [from Old Northern French *escaper* '"to take off
one's cloak"' (*AHD*), 'to get out of'; from Vulgar Latin **excappāre*
(*ex-* 'out of' + Late Latin *cappa* 'cloak')]; ESCAPEE, ESCAPEMENT

'an arrangement of pawls and toothed wheels or racks for regulat-   2220
ing mechanical movements, as in a clock or typewriter' (the
reference is to the pawls "escaping" from the teeth). ESCAPADE 'a
breaking loose from confinement and restraint; a prank, a lark, an
adventure.' A doublet of CAPE, arriving in English through an Old
English borrowing from Latin, is COPE 'a long, sleeveless ecclesi-   2225
astical garment worn on ceremonial occasions' [from Old English
-cāp, in cantelcāp 'a kind of cope'; from Medieval Latin cāpa,
variant of cappa; from Late Latin cappa]. Based on CAPE is
CAPOTE 'a long cloak, usually with a hood; the movable top of a
buggy' [from French capote, a diminutive of cape]. Based on   2230
COPE is COPING 'the top part of a stone or brick wall, usually
slanted to shed water,' and consisting of COPESTONES = CAP-
STONES.

Late Latin cappa 'hood, cloak' became Old French chape
'hood, cope, covering,' and in this form was borrowed into   2235
English as CHAPE 'the metal tip of a scabbard.' However, it was
from the Vulgar Latin diminutive *cappellus > Late Latin/Medi-
eval Latin cappellus that the French word CHAPEAU 'hat' evolved,
by way of Old French chapel 'head covering, hat, wreath.' Old
French made a diminutive of a diminutive with chapelet 'little   2240
wreath,' seen in English CHAPLET 'wreath or garland for the
head; prayer beads' (with one third the number of beads as a
rosary). The name CHAPLET was applied to the prayer beads not
because they were worn on top of the head when not being used
in prayer, but because a chapelet was originally 'a wreath of   2245
roses,' and each prayer-bead was carved in the shape of a rose.
This also explains why prayer-beads are called rosaries 'rose
gardens' [from Latin rosārium 'rose garden'].

From the feminine of Medieval Latin cappellus, cappella
'little cape' came Old French chapele, source of English CHAPEL   2250
'a Christian place of worship, smaller than a church.' The explanation of this seeming non sequitur is that the cappella 'cloak' of the
Frankish saint Martin, bishop of Tours (died 399), after being
preserved for centuries as a sort of talisman, was deposited by the
Frankish kings in a specially constructed shrine called, because of   2255
the relic it sheltered, a cappella. From this circumstance, any
sanctuary housing a holy relic was called a cappella > chapele >
CHAPEL, and then any building of worship smaller than a
church—places that had formerly been called oratories (literally)
'places of prayer.' The persons in charge of a cappella were called   2260
cappellāni, whence Old French chapelain and English CHAPLAIN
'a clergyman attached to a chapel; a clergyman attached to a
military unit.' A CAPPELLA is 'singing in the manner of a chapel;

in the manner of a band of choristers; without instrumental
2265   accompaniment' [from Italian *cappella* 'chapel'].

For some reason, French fishermen who seined the waters of
the north Atlantic saw a resemblance between the codfish they
caught there and a chaplain, for they gave the fish the name
capelan, derived from the Provençal *capelan, cappellan* 'chaplain'
2270   from Medieval Latin *cappellānus.* French-Canadians adopted the
name *capelan,* but they transferred it to a much smaller ocean fish
that they used as bait for cod. The change in meaning filtered
back to the old country, and the name was also adopted into
English, in the forms CAPELAN, CAPELIN, CAPLIN, and CAPLING 'a
2275   small, edible marine fish related to the smelts.' (The modern
French word for 'cod' is *morue. Capelan* is now used in French to
denote the smaller fish, also with the meaning of 'a beggarly
(needy) priest.')

An English word that is similar in appearance and origin but
2280   not in meaning is CAPELINE 'a small steel skullcap worn by
medieval foot soldiers; a cap-shaped bandage for the head or for
the stump of an amputated limb; a kind of woman's hat with a
small crown and wide brim' [from Medieval French *capeline*;
from Old Provençal, Italian, or Medieval Latin *capelina* 'little
2285   hat'; from Late Latin *cappa* 'head covering, cloak'].

Other words traceable to Latin *caput* 'head' are CHAPERON 'a
hood formerly worn by nobles and, after the 16th century, by
ladies; a person who accompanies a young unmarried woman in
public; one who oversees a meeting or gathering of unmarried
2290   persons' [from French *chaperon* 'hood; chaperon'; from Old
French *chape* 'head covering,' from Late Latin *cappa*] and CAPAR-
ISON 'ornamental trappings for a horse; fine clothing' [from Medieval French *caparasson,* from Old Spanish *caparazón* (related to
Provençal *caparasso* 'a hooded cloak'), from *capa* 'hood, cloak'].
2295   Ladies who find themselves mentioned in the society pages as
having been seen "elegantly CAPARISONED" (at the opera, cotil-
lion, benefit, dog show) might ponder the modern Spanish meanings of ancestral *caparazón,* which are 'CAPARISON'; 'horse
blanket'; 'feedbag'; and 'insect's or crustacean's shell.' Note, also,
2300   CAPUCHE 'a hood on a cloak,' especially the long pointed cowl
worn by a CAPUCHIN monk [from Italian *cappuccino* 'hooded
one'; from *cappuccio* 'cowl'; from Late Latin *cappa* 'hood']. The
CAPUCHIN monkeys of South America are so called because of the
hoodlike tufts of hair on their heads. Also from Latin *caput* 'head'
2305   are KÉPI 'a French military cap' [from Swiss German *käppi,*
diminutive of German *Kappe* 'cap'; from Late Latin *cappa* 'head
covering'] and CAP-À-PIE 'from head to foot' [via Old French, from

Old Provençal *de cap a pe* (Latin *caput* 'head' + *pēs* 'foot')].
Modern French has it turned around to *de pied en cap.*

As Latin *capra* became French *chèvre* 'nanny goat' and as 2310
Latin *capillus* became French *cheveu* 'hair of the head,' so did
Latin *caput* [via Vulgar Latin **capum*] become French CHEF
'CHIEF, head man; head cook.' *Chef/chief* has these English
compounds: KERCHIEF 'cover-head' [from Old French *couvrechef*
(*couvrir* 'to cover')]; ACHIEVE (literally) 'to bring to a head'; 'to 2315
accomplish' [from Old French *achever*, from *a-* 'to' + *chef* 'head'];
and MISCHIEF 'damage, destruction; malicious behavior; pranks.'
MISCHIEF etymologically has the sense of 'mis-achievement,' of
'something that has been brought to an unfortunate conclusion,
end, head.' It comes from Old French *meschef*, from *meschever* 2320
'to meet with misfortune' [*mes-* 'amiss, ill'; from Latin *minus*
'less'].

A French architectural term sometimes used in English is
CHEVET (literally) 'head-covering, opening for the head'; 'the apse
of a church; the rounded east (head) end of a church, behind the 2325
chancel' [from French *chevet* 'apse; pillow, bolster, head (of a
bed)'; from Latin *capitium* 'head-covering,' from *caput* 'head'].
There is another obsolete, French word that contains the element
chevet 'head (of a bed),' and that is *bechevet* 'double bedhead'
[*be-* < Latin *bis* 'twice, in two ways']. *Bechevet* did not mean an 2330
ordinary double bed, with two pillows and two bolsters, but a bed
with a headboard at each end. That is, the sort of bed that could
be used comfortably by one of the two-headed face cards in a
deck of playing cards, something like the sleigh beds popular in
the 1820s and 1860s. Obsolete *bechevet*, shortened to *bêche*, is 2335
part of the stamp collector's word TÊTE-BÊCHE (literally) 'head-
double-head'; (French) 'top against bottom; head against foot; a
pair of inverted stamps'; 'concerning a pair of stamps inverted in
relation to one another.' Note that TÊTE-BÊCHE contains two
French words for *head*: *tête* [from Vulgar Latin **testa* 'head'; from 2340
Late Latin *testa* 'skull'; from Latin *testa* 'pot; shell, covering'] and
chevet 'head (of a bed)' [from Latin *caput*]. (The *bêche* in *tête-
bêche* is not the same as that in *bêche de mer* 'a sea-cucumber of
the South Pacific and Indian oceans; a lingua franca of the
southwest Pacific that combines English and Malay.' The latter 2345
bêche is an alteration of Portuguese *bicho* 'worm.')

We mentioned earlier the French word *cheveux* 'hair of the
head' derived from Latin *capillus* 'hair of the head, hair of the
beard.' *Capillus* is considered by most authorities to be of obscure
origin, but some believe that it may come from Latin *caput* 'head' 2350
+ *pilus* 'hair.' If this suggestion should be true, we would have to
add the following to our *caput* derivatives: CAPILLARY 'concern-

ing or resembling a hair; fine, slender, of a very small diameter; one of the minute blood vessels that connect the arteries to the
2355 veins'; CHEVELURE 'a head of hair' [from Old French *chevel(e)ure*, from Latin *capillātūra* 'the hair of the head']; and DISHEVELED 'with one's hair in disarray, unkempt; disarranged, with one's clothing in disorder' [from Old French *descheveller* 'to loosen one's hair' (*des-* (< *dis-* 'apart') + *capillus* 'hair of the head')].
2360 We are left with a residue of semantically wide-ranging words that are descended from Latin *caput* 'head.' For example, CAPO-RAL 'a strong, dark tobacco' [from French *tabac de caporal* 'corporal's tobacco'; from Italian *caporale* 'corporal, head of a squad']. Remember "Sweet Caporal" cigarettes? *Tabac de caporal*
2365 was more expensive than and superior to *tabac de soldat*. It would seem from this derivation that our English word denoting the Army rank of CORPORAL 'the lowest rank of noncommissioned officer' is an example of folk etymology, whereby an alteration of spelling makes this noncom the leader of a *corpus* 'body (of
2370 men),' rather than the 'head man,' he started out to be. At least that is what many of the authorities indicate; but some think it happened the other way around. They trace the military CORPO-RAL back to a 5th-century Venetian-Latin form, *corporalis*, and opine that this later became assimilated to Italian *capo* 'head' to
2375 make Italian *caporale*, whence French *caporal*, perhaps as a contraction of the phrase *capo corporalis*. In this event, English CORPORAL, which comes from an early modern French *corporal*, would represent a reversion to or a survival of the original spelling of the word. More words descended from Latin *caput*
2380 'head' include CAPE 'a point or head of land thrust out into the sea' [from Old French *cap* 'cape,' from Old Provençal, from Latin *caput* 'head']; da CAPO 'from the head' ('from the beginning,' a musical direction to repeat a passage); CAUDILLO 'in Spanish-speaking countries, a military leader with political aims' [Spanish
2385 *caudillo* 'leader, chieftain'; from Late Latin *capitellum* 'small head']; CABEZON (literally) 'big head'; 'a large edible Pacific ocean fish' [augmentative (enlarging) form of Spanish *cabeza* 'head'; from Vulgar Latin *capitia* 'head']; CAPRICCIOSO (a musical direction) 'in a lively, improvisatory manner'; and CAPRICE 'a
2390 whim; a musical work in an improvisatory style; a CAPRICCIO'; (literally) 'a head with hair standing on end, like a hedgehog's spines' [from Italian *capriccio*, from *capo* 'head' + *riccio* 'hedge-hog']. The original meaning of Italian *capriccio* was 'horror.' The modern sense is due to an association with *capra* 'goat; frisky,
2395 sportive.' But some writers derive *capriccio* directly from *capr(o)* 'goat.'

A common English word that is related collaterally to Latin *caput* 'head,' by common descent from the Indo-European root **kaput*, is HEAD 'the division of the body that contains the brains, eyes, ears, nose and mouth' [from Old English *hēafod*, from Germanic **haubitham*, **haubidam*; **haubutham*, **haubudam*]. The difference in the vowel sounds between Latin *caput* and Germanic **haubid-* gives the linguist some trouble. They agree, nevertheless, that the relationship is there. In English HEAD, the inner *-b-* of **haubitham* has disappeared, but note the cognate German *Haupt* 'head, leader,' seen in *Hauptmann* > Polish *hetman* > Russian ATAMAN 'a Cossack leader.' Some linguists link **kaput* with Indo-European **kap-* 'to grasp,' the base of Latin *capere* 'to seize; to take, to contain' > *capture, catch, capable, receive*, etc., the basic idea being 'vessel' (*MW2*).

2400

2405

2410

XI

Chilly Glaciers, Gelid Glances

A GLACIER is a CHILLING place. If you lost your way on one for any length of time, your blood and bone marrow would turn to JELLY and eventually CONGEAL, and you would have become GLACIATED, that is, frozen. These words having to do with cold
2415   are descended from the Indo-European root *gel- 'cold; to freeze.' Typical Latin derivatives of *gel- are the verb gelāre 'to freeze' and the noun gelū (also gelum, gelus) 'frost; cold; ice' (all pronounced in Latin with a hard g). Typical English borrowings from these Latin words are GELID 'cold, frozen, icy' [from Latin
2420   gelidus, 'icy cold'; from gelū 'ice'] and CONGEAL 'to solidify, as by freezing; to coagulate' [via Old French congeler from Latin congelāre 'to freeze solid; to harden' (con- = cum 'together, with')].

Not frozen, but in a semisolid state when cool, is GELATIN(E)
2425   'animal jelly; a glutinous protein substance obtained from animal tissues by prolonged boiling' [via French from Italian gelatina 'jelly,' diminutive of gelata 'frost'; from the feminine past participle of Latin gelāre 'to freeze']. Gelatin is the consolidating element in some kinds of JELLY 'a semisolid food with a resilient
2430   consistency' [from Middle English gely, geli; from Old French gelee; from Latin gelāre, gelāta]. A GEL is 'a jellylike material formed by the coagulation of a colloidal liquid' [short for GELATIN], and the verb to JELL 'to become firm and gelatinous; to fall into place; to become clear and definite' is an American back-
2435   formation from JELLY.

The Latin word for 'frost,' gelū, can also mean 'ice,' but the more usual Latin word for 'ice' is glaciēs. (The -e- between the g- and the -l- of Indo-European *gel- has been "frozen out," leaving only *gl-. This is known as a "zero-grade" form, because the
2440   vowel sound has been reduced to zero.) Latin glaciēs is the

source of French *glace* 'ice' and of French and English GLACIER 'a field or river of ice, formed of snow compressed into ice by the pressure of its own weight' [via dialectal French *glacier* from French *glace* 'ice'; from Late Latin *glacia*, from Latin *glaciēs* 'ice']. The corresponding adjective is GLACIAL 'pertaining to 2445 glaciers; icy cold; hard as ice; slow-moving' [from Latin *glaciālis* 'icy']; and there is a verb GLACIATE 'cover with ice or snow; alter by the action of ice; freeze' [from Latin *glaciāre* 'to turn to ice'].

In English we use the French *glacé* 'iced, glazed,' past participle of *glacer* 'to freeze; to ice; to glaze,' as a verb GLACÉ 'to 2450 ice, to glaze; to incrust with a thin layer resembling glass.' However, those similar-sounding words, *glass, gloss, glaze,* and *glazier,* do not come from Latin *glaciēs* 'ice,' nor from Indo-European **gel-* 'to freeze,' but, along with *glint, gleam, glitter* and *glad,* from the similar-sounding root **ghel-* 'to shine.' 2455

However, some noncold, nonfreezing words have come to English from Latin *glaciēs* 'ice' by way of borrowing from French, to wit, GLACIS 'a gentle slope, an incline; a slope extended in front of a fortification so that it can be swept by the defenders' fire' [from French *glacis* 'slope,' from Old French *glacier* 'to slide, 2460 as on ice'] and GLANCE 'to strike obliquely and veer off; to look briefly.' The two meanings of GLANCE may originally have been two different words. A synonymous English verb, **glace,* was in use up to the 14th century and even later in some dialects. Both GLANCE and **glace* are thought to be derived from Old French 2465 *glacier* 'to slide, as on ice,' but how the -*n*- got into GLANCE is a moot question. It was already present in the earlier English forms *glench, glens, glaunche, glence, glaunse, glawnse, glanss,* and *glaunce.* Some suggest that this -*n*- comes from an association with Middle English *glenten* 'to glint,' while others explain it as 2470 owing to the influence of *lanch* 'to set in motion, to launch.' The question is as unsettled as ever.

Germanic descendants of Indo-European **gel-* 'cold; to freeze,' following the rules of sound correspondences, show up in English with the initial **g-* changed to a *k-* sound, as in COLD 'of a 2475 low temperature; lacking heat' [from Old English *ceald,* from Germanic **kaldaz* 'chilled, frozen' (the equivalent of Latin *gelatus*)]. (The final -*d* in COLD is structurally a past participle suffix, equivalent to the -*ed* in COOLED or CHILLED or to the -*atus* in *gelatus*.) Clearly related are COOL 'moderately cold; to make 2480 less warm' [from Old English *cōl,* from Germanic **koluz*] and CHILL 'to lower the temperature (of); a sensation of coldness' [from Old English *c(i)ele,* from Germanic **kaliz*].

Finally, we have the archaic verb, to KEEL, which has nothing to do with ships' bottoms, but means 'to cool; to prevent a pot 2485 from boiling over by stirring and skimming' [from Old English *cēlan*; from Germanic **kōljan* 'to cool'; from **kōluz* 'cool']. English KEEL 'to cool' is the equivalent of German *kühl* 'cool' and *kühlen* 'to cool,' both being examples of umlaut, a sound change

2490   caused by the tendency of a vowel to be pronounced the same as a vowel or semivowel in a following syllable (now usually lost). It refers especially to the moving of a back vowel toward the front of the mouth, caused by a following *-i-* or *-j-*. It would follow that the *-ee-* in English KEEL 'to cool' and the *-üh-* in German *kühl, kühlen*

2495   were caused by partial assimilation to the *-j-* of Germanic **kōljan*.

German is dotted with umlauts, especially in plurals and diminutives: *Mann* 'man,' *Männer* 'men'; *Haus* 'house,' *Häuser* 'houses'; *Brot* 'bread,' *Brötchen* 'roll'; *Magd* 'maid,' *Mädchen* 'girl.' Other examples of the result of umlaut in English are MEN

2500   (< **manniz*); BED (< **badjan*); GEESE, MICE, TEETH, and KITTEN (plurals of GOOSE, MOUSE, and TOOTH, and diminutive of CAT).

XII

Clefs, Claviers, *and* Claustrophobia

An ENCLAVE is a territorial dollop completely surrounded by a foreign land. The CONCLAVE of cardinals, gathered to elect a new pope, must remain in chambers until its deliberations have reached a CONCLUSION. And what these words have in common   2505
with CLEFS, CLAVIERS, and CLAUSTROPHOBIA is that they're all related to Latin *clāvis* 'key; lock,' *clāvus* 'nail,' *clāva* 'club,' and *claudere* 'to close, to shut.' The common ancestor is the Indo-European root **kleu-* 'hook, peg.'

One pauses here to ponder the semantic relationships. The   2510
idea of a door or gate is surely lurking in the background, since the common denominator of the meanings has to do with closing something up and keeping it closed. A door or gate can be locked with a hook and a peg. The peg could have the shape of a nail, or if it is big enough, a club, and the tapered shape is just right for   2515
wedging securely into a hook. A modern key is in effect a refined version of the pegs that serve to lock and unlock gates.

Of our four Latin words, *clāvis* 'key; lock' has been most borrowed from by English. Among the borrowings is CLEF (literally) 'key'; 'a symbol on a musical staff indicating the pitch of   2520
the notes.' CLEF is the French descendant of Latin *clāvis*. There are three musical clefs, G, F, and C. These notational devices are only figuratively "keys," unlike the solidly material keys of a CLAVIER 'the keyboard of an organ, piano, or harmonium; a piano or other keyboard stringed instrument; a dummy keyboard.' The   2525
second meaning was taken into English from the German *Klavier* 'piano'; but ultimately all the meanings come from the French *clavier* 'key bearer; key ring, key frame, keyboard.'

A CLAVICHORD is an early keyboard instrument, predecessor of the piano. Literally, the word means 'key-string' [*chorda*   2530
'string']. The clavichord could not be played with variations of

volume. However, a later invention, the piano, could; which is why it was called *pianoforte* 'soft-strong, soft-loud' and why it superseded the clavichord. This ends the musical portion of our disquisition, except to mention that an early name for the harpsichord was CLAVICEMBALO or CLAVICYMBAL and that there is (or was) such an instrument as a CLAVIHARP 'a harp played by means of a keyboard.'

Nonmusical words containing the element *clāvis* 'key' include CLAVIS 'a key; a glossary'; CLAVICLE 'the collarbone' [from Latin *clāvicula* 'small key'] (so called because of its shape); and CLAVIGER 'keeper of the keys' [*gerere* 'to carry']. (There is another CLAVIGER 'one that carries a club' [from *clāva* 'club' + *gerere*]. Neither word enjoys a wide circulation.) More words descended from Latin *clāvis* 'key' are CONCLAVE (literally) 'with a key'; (obsolete) 'a private chamber'; 'a private meeting; "the set of apartments within which, since 1274, the cardinals of the Roman Catholic Church are continuously secluded while choosing a pope"' (*MW2*) [from Latin *conclāve* 'room; (room that can be locked) with a key'] and ENCLAVE (literally) 'locked in'; 'any distinctly bounded area enclosed within a larger area' [from (Old) French *enclaver* 'to enclose, to hem in'; from Vulgar Latin **inclāvāre* 'to lock in'].

The *-l-* of Latin *clāvicula* 'small key' seems to have disappeared from a French word thought by some to be its descendant: *cheville* 'peg, pin, bolt; plug.' *Cheville* has been adopted into English with both a figurative and a literal meaning: CHEVILLE 'a meaningless or redundant word or phrase used to fill out the meter of a verse; a peg of a stringed musical instrument.' An Old Northern French cousin of *cheville* is ancestor to English KEVEL 'a sturdy belaying pin or cleat for holding the heavier cables of a ship' [from Old Northern French *keville*, from a Late Latin meaning of *clāvicula* 'bolt, bar']. The Late Latin meaning of *clāvicula* 'bolt, bar' supposedly from Latin *clāvicula* 'small key,' sounds as if these speakers thought the word to derive from *clāva* 'club' or *clāvus* 'nail,' more than from *clāvis* 'key.' No doubt the Romanic (Vulgar Latin) speakers were as confused as any barbarian by these three similar-sounding words. Etymologists, who often lack the evidence required to arrive at definite conclusions, figure two English borrowings from Latin *clāvus* 'nail' to be CLAVUS 'a corn on the foot' (compare *agnail*, line 319) and CLOVE 'an East Indian spice' [from Middle English *clow(e) of gilofer*, from (Old) French *clou de girofle; clou* 'nail' from Latin *clāvus* 'nail'], so called because the shape of a clove bud resembles that of a nail. There is a problem as to how Middle English *clow(e)-* came to be pronounced as in modern English CLOVE. One suggestion is that the *clow of gilofer* was influenced by the Middle English *clove* 'one of the small segments of a separable bulb,' as in "a clove of garlic." This *clove* comes from a different source, to wit, the archaic past participle *clove* of the verb *cleave* 2580 'divide by force.' (While we're on the subject of words that do not derive from our Indo-European root, let us mention three that seem very similar in appearance and meaning but that are nevertheless not related: *claw* 'sharp nail on the toe of an animal'; *clue* 'an indication that aids one in solving a puzzle; a key'; and 2585 *club* 'a heavy stick.') Another English borrowing from Latin *clāvus* 'nail' is CLOY (obsolete) 'nail'; 'glut, satiate, especially with something sweet' [from obsolete *ac(c)loy* 'to drive in a nail,' hence 'to stop up, to choke up; to clog, to satiate'; from Old French *encloer*, from Medieval Latin *inclāvāre* 'to nail in']. 2590

Latin *clāva* 'club' is ancestor to English CLAVATE 'club-shaped; thickened at one end,' CLAVIFORM 'club-shaped,' and CLAVICORN 'a family of beetles having club-shaped antennae.'

Remembering that in classical Latin, -*v*- (pronounced *w*) and -*u*- were indicated by the same letter, one can see at a glance that 2595 the Latin verb *claudere/clavdere* 'to close, to shut' is related to Latin *clāvis* 'lock; key,' *clāvus* 'nail,' and *clāva* 'club.' The past participle of *claudere* is *clausus, clausa, clausum*. These lead us eventually to English CLAUSE 'a distinct stipulation in a formal document; a word group containing a subject and a predicate' 2600 [from Medieval Latin *clausa*, a back formation from or equivalent to Latin *clausula* 'close, conclusion']—in other words, a 'closed' word group, a group that has a beginning and an end; properly, 'the close of a rhetorical period.' The Latin masculine past participle *clausus* led to the English verb CLOSE 'to shut; to bring 2605 to an end,' as well as the adjective CLOSE 'shut fast; secretive; near; precise' (CLOSE reasoning), and the noun CLOSE 'an enclosed place; the precinct of a cathedral or abbey.' However, according to some, this substantive meaning comes from Latin *clausum* 'enclosure,' a substantive use of the neuter past partici- 2610 ple. A diminutive of CLOSE 'enclosure' is CLOSET 'a small enclosure' [-*et* = -*ette*]; 'a storage space equipped with a door or other barrier.' Compound forms of -CLOSE are ENCLOSE 'to shut in; to surround on all sides' [from Old French *enclore, enclos(e)*; from Vulgar Latin **inclaudere*, a variant of Latin *inclūdere* 'to shut in'] 2615 and DISCLOSE 'to uncover, to reveal' [from Old French *desclore, desclos(e)*, from Medieval Latin *disclaudere* 'to open that which has been closed'].

The Latin speakers put together many compound verbs based on *claudere* 'to close' in the form -*cludere*. English has borrowed 2620 INCLUDE 'to contain; to have as a part' [from Latin *inclūdere* 'to

shut in']; EXCLUDE 'to shut out' [from Latin *excludere* 'to shut
out'; also, 'to hatch']; CONCLUDE 'to bring to a close' [from Latin
concludere 'to shut up closely; to bring to an end']; SECLUDE 'to
2625   set apart from others' [from Latin *secludere* 'to shut apart' (*se-*
'apart')]; PRECLUDE 'to put a barrier in front of; to make impossible by previous action' [from Latin *praecludere* 'to shut off' (*prae-*
'in front of')]; OCCLUDE 'to cause to become closed; to prevent the
passage of; to bring the upper and lower teeth together in proper
2630   alignment' [from Latin *occludere* 'to shut up' (*oc-* < *ob-* 'toward')];
and MALOCCLUSION 'faulty alignment of the teeth.' These verbs
all have their corresponding nouns and adjectives: INCLUSION,
INCLUSIVE; EXCLUSION, EXCLUSIVE, etc. There is also the biological ECLOSION 'the emergence of an adult insect from a pupal case'
2635   [from French *éclosion* 'hatching'; from Vulgar Latin **exclaudere*
'to hatch out'; from Latin *excludere* 'to hatch']. The list of English
borrowings from Latin *claudere* 'to close' is not yet exhausted.
Among those remaining to be mentioned is RECLUSE 'one who
withdraws from the world to live in seclusion' [from Old French
2640   *reclure*, *reclus(e)*, from Late Latin *recludere* 'to shut up'; from
Latin *recludere*, *reclūsus*, which means both 'to open' and (rarely)
'to close']. The earlier Latin meaning of 'to open' exemplifies a
use of the prefix *re-* to mean ' "in a contrary direction so that what
has been done is annulled" ' (*ODEE*) and ' "an undoing of some
2645   previous action" ' (*OED*). Thus, *recludere* could mean 'to unclose,
to open.' As time passed, the originally less frequent meaning 'to
close' outstripped and eventually obliterated the earlier, opposite
meaning 'to open.' Also borrowed from Latin *claudere* 'to close' is
CLOISTER 'a place devoted to religious seclusion' [from Old
2650   French *clostre*, from Medieval Latin *claustrum* 'an enclosure, a
room in a monastery'; from Latin *claustrum*, plural *claustra*
'locks, barriers, gates; cage']. Latin *claustra* 'locks, barriers, gates;
cage' is the source of the New Latin compound CLAUSTROPHOBIA
'a fear of confined spaces.' "Confined spaces" on a decorative
2655   surface are called CLOISONNÉ (literally) 'partitioned'; 'a kind of
enamel work in which the surface to be decorated is divided into
designs by thin strips of metal set on edge' [from French *cloison-
ner* 'to partition'; from Old French *cloison* 'partition'; from Vulgar
Latin **clausiō(nem)* 'enclosure'].
2660   There is a possibility that the Indo-European root **kleu-*
'hook, peg' is also the source of the Germanic form **hluta-* 'lot,
portion.' The semantic development is obscure, but one can
speculate that LOTS were chosen by having people draw different
lengths of sticks (pegs), as is sometimes still done when choosing
2665   sides in a game. Germanic **hluta-* evolved into Old English *hlot*,
whence English LOT 'an object used in making a choice by

chance; a prize in a drawing; a portion; fate; a large amount'
(often plural LOTS). Germanic *hluta- also became Frankish *lot
and migrated to Italy, where it was adopted as *lotto* 'lottery.' It
went back to France as *loto*, and on to England as LOTTO 'a game   2670
of chance involving cards with rows of numbers, and numbered
discs drawn by lot: the predecessor of bingo.' *Lotto* 'lottery' was
not enough for the Italians; they also had to coin the word
lotteria, whence French *loterie*, Dutch *loterij(e)*, and English
LOTTERY 'a scheme for the distribution of prizes by chance   2675
drawings.'

Old French/Medieval French made a verb out of Frankish
lot, to wit, *aloter* 'to distribute by lot.' This is the source of
English ALLOT 'to apportion' and ALLOTMENT 'that which is
apportioned.'   2680

XIII

Crabbed Epigrams, Graphic Graffiti

A DIAGRAM is a GRAPHIC way of getting information across, as is a GRAPH. GRAFFITI, on the other hand, are usually meant to be EPIGRAMMATIC. These words all spring from the Greek verb *graphein* 'to scratch, to engrave; to draw, to write' and the related
2685   Greek words *graphē* 'picture, drawing; writing' and *gramma* 'a letter of the alphabet.' (These associated meanings indicate a tribal remembrance that the letters of the alphabet were originally drawings, or PICTOGRAPHS: *alpha* was once a drawing of an ox's head and derives its name from a Phoenician word related to
2690   Hebrew *āleph* 'ox.' Similarly with *beta* < *bēth* 'house'; *gamma* < *gimel* 'camel'; *delta* < *dāleth*, and so on.)

    Another Greek word related to *graphein* 'to scratch, to write' is *graph(e)ion* 'a stylus; an ancient writing instrument for use on papyrus or parchment'; also 'an instrument for writing on waxed
2695   tablets, having one of its ends sharp.' Greek *graphion* 'stylus' was transliterated into Latin as *graphium*, which evolved into Old French/Medieval French *grafe*, *greffe*. Sometime before the 14th century, because of the resemblance of a *grafe* 'stylus' to the sliced shoot of a plant prepared for grafting, the meaning was
2700   enlarged to include the horticultural operation known as GRAFT-ING 'the uniting of a shoot with a growing plant by splicing.' Old French *grafe* was adopted into English in the form *graff*, but that spelling is now archaic, and the altered spelling, GRAFT, is preferred. This was probably derived from the past participle and
2705   past tense, *graffed*. The figurative meaning of GRAFT 'the unscrupulous use of one's position to derive profit; bribery' thus has connotations of tapping someone else's stock with one's own illicit sap-suckers. (However, this derivation of GRAFT 'bribery' is questioned by some.)

Most English words borrowed from Greek *graphein* 'to   2710
scratch, to write' and its relatives have something to do with
writing or drawing. For example, DIAGRAM 'a drawing designed to
clarify the relationship among the parts of a whole' [from Greek
diagramma 'a drawing, a figure' (*dia* 'through, by means of' +
gramma 'a drawing')] and GRAPH 'a diagram that represents the   2715
vacillations of a variable' [Greek *graphē* 'a picture'], such as the
fluctuations of stock prices from day to day. Also from the same
source are GRAPHIC 'pertaining to written or pictorial representa-
tions; pictorial as opposed to written; vividly described' and
GRAFFITI 'anything written or drawn on rocks or walls so as to be   2720
seen by the public.' This is the plural of the Italian GRAFFITO 'an
inscription scratched on rocks or walls or on artifacts made of
plaster, stone, or clay.' There is also the term in decorative arts,
SGRAFFITO 'designs produced by scratching a top coat of plaster
to reveal an undercoat of contrasting color.' (Most writers agree in   2725
tracing *graffito* to Greek *graphein* 'to scratch,' but some derive it
from Italian *graffio* 'a hook,' which is related to Old High German
krapfo 'hook, clasp,' and English *grape*. See line 2895.) More
words borrowed from Greek *graphein* 'to scratch, to write' are
EPIGRAPH 'an inscription engraved in a durable material, as on an   2730
ancient temple or monument; a quotation at the beginning of a
book or chapter' [from Greek *epigraphē* 'inscription,' from
epigraphos 'written upon' (*epi* 'on, at; upon')]; EPIGRAM 'epigraph; a short poem expressing a single thought; a terse, witty,
often paradoxical saying' [from Greek *epigramma* 'inscription'];   2735
and GRAM or GRAMME 'a metric unit of mass and weight.' A
KILOGRAM or KILOGRAMME is 'one thousand grams' [French *kilo*,
adapted from Greek *khilioi* 'one thousand']. English GRAM,
GRAMME comes to us via Old French from Late Latin *gramma* 'a
small weight,' from Greek *gramma* 'a letter of the alphabet;   2740
something drawn; a small weight.' How the meaning, 'a small
weight' came about is unexplained. Yet another English borrowing is GRAMMAR 'the study of the systems underlying the formal
features of a language; a theory specifying the manner in which
all sentences of a language are constructed' [from Old French   2745
gramaire, an irregular formation from Latin *grammatica*; from
Greek *grammatikē* (*tekhnē*) '(art) of alphabetical characters; the
art of reading and writing']. In classical times, *grammatikē* and
grammatica meant the study of the Greek and Latin languages in
all their aspects, including literature and rhetoric. (The Greeks   2750
and Romans scorned all other languages as barbarian babble.)
However, with the arrival of the Middle Ages in western Europe,
gramaire, or GRAMMAR, meant chiefly the study of Latin, the
language of the learned. English grammar was largely ignored

2755   until the 16th century, and even then it was studied with the intent of forcing it into the Latin mold, a disservice whose results are still being felt.

Reading and writing were rare skills in medieval times. Those who possessed them were looked upon with awe and were
2760   supposed by the populace to be equally familiar with magic, alchemy, astrology, and other occult matters. Consequently the word GRAMMAR was superstitiously used to denote such mysteries as witchcraft, sorcery, and necromancy. In Scotland the word appeared, with the first -r- changed to an -l-, in the forms
2765   glammar, glamer, and GLAMOR 'magic, enchantment, spell.' "When devils, wizards or jugglers deceive the sight they are said to cast glamour over the eyes of the spectator"— Allen Ramsay, 1721 (OED). The modern meaning is closer to 'an elusive, mysteriously exciting and often illusory attractiveness.' Sir Walter
2770   Scott introduced this word with its new meaning into literary English, and all theatrical press agents are forever in his debt.

That the elements gram and graph are closely related is illustrated by two old-fashioned words for record-player: PHONO-GRAPH (literally) 'sound-writing' and GRAMOPHONE (literally)
2775   'written sound' [Greek phōnē 'voice, sound']. "Talking phonograph" was the phrase first used to describe Thomas Edison's invention of 1877, for the word PHONOGRAPH had been used earlier as a synonym for PHONOGRAM 'a written symbol representing a spoken sound.' The word GRAMOPHONE, criticized by some
2780   as an incorrect formation, was coined by the inventor Emile Berliner in 1887. His "talking machine" recorded the sonic vibrations on discs instead of Edisonian cylinders.

There are many words ending in -gram with meanings having to do with writing, drawing, or recording something or other. For
2785   example, CARDIOGRAM 'the tracing made by a cardiograph'; CARDIOGRAPH 'an instrument that records the movements of the heart' [kardia 'heart']; CRYPTOGRAM 'something written in a secret code' [kruptos 'secret']; IDEOGRAM 'a symbol that represents an idea without expressing a word for it' (for example, highway signs and
2790   Arabic numerals); MONOGRAM 'a design formed of two or more letters fused into one'; PROGRAM or PROGRAMME (literally) 'written before'; 'a listing of the order of scheduled events; a procedure for solving a problem' [via French and Late Latin from Greek programma 'a written public notice'; from Greek
2795   prographein 'to write in public']; TELEGRAM (literally) 'written at a distance' [tēle 'far off']; ANAGRAM 'a word formed by reordering the letters of another word' [from New Latin anagramma, based on Greek anagrammatizein 'to transpose letters' (ana- 'back,

again' + *gramma* 'letter')]; CHRONOGRAM; SPECTROGRAM; THER-
MOGRAM, etc.   2800

The Greek word *tetragrammaton* means 'consisting of four
letters,' but the TETRAGRAMMATON is 'a combination of four
Hebrew letters, transliterated as YHWH or JHVH, that stands for
Yahweh, the God of the Old Testament.' Since the 3rd century
B.C., devout Jews have considered this name to be ineffable and   2805
"not to be spoken." Therefore, they have substituted for the
sacrosanct name the less awesome *adōnāi* 'my Lord(s)' or *Elōhim*
'God(s).' The popular but incorrect Christian version of the
Tetragrammaton, *Jehovah*, is the result of a scholarly error: the
insertion between the consonants *J-H-V-H* of the vowel sounds   2810
from *adōnāi* (the vowels not being written in Hebrew).

English words that incorporate the element *graph* are even
more numerous than those based on *gram*. One example is
GRAPHITE 'a soft black, lustrous carbon, the "lead" of "lead
pencils"' [from German *Graphit*], given this name in 1789 by a   2815
German geologist, because it is used for writing. More examples
include GRAPHOLOGY 'the study of handwriting'; MONOGRAPH 'a
treatise on one particular subject'; and PARAGRAPH 'a division of a
written work; a sign marking such a division' [from Medieval
Latin *paragraphus* 'a sign marking a new section in writing'; from   2820
Greek *paragraphos* (literally) 'written alongside; a horizontal line
used to mark a change in speakers in a dialogue']. The modern
form of the sign, used chiefly in scholarly works and proofreading,
is ¶. The horizontal line is still used in French typography to
mark dialogue. Continuing the list, we have SEISMOGRAPH 'an   2825
instrument for recording vibrations of the earth' [Greek *seismos*
'earthquake,' from *seiein* 'to shake']; CALLIGRAPHY 'beautiful
handwriting' [*kallos* 'beauty']; CACOGRAPHY 'bad handwriting;
incorrect spelling' [*kakos* 'bad']; ORTHOGRAPHY 'correct spelling'
[*orthos* 'straight, correct']; STENOGRAPHY 'writing in shorthand'   2830
[*stenos* 'narrow, scanty']; GEOGRAPHY; OCEANOGRAPHY; TOPOG-
RAPHY; LITHOGRAPHY, etc.

So much for the English words acquired from Greek *graphein*
'to write, to scratch,' a list that is added to constantly. The Indo-
European root underlying all these words is **gerebh-* 'to scratch.'   2835
*Gerebh- shows up in Germanic, following the rules of sound
correspondences, with the initial **g-* changed to **k-*. An example
is Germanic **kerban*, which evolved into West Germanic **kerfan*
> Old English *ceorfan* 'to cut' > English CARVE 'to divide into
pieces by cutting; to cut into desired shapes.' At one time, CARVE   2840
was the ordinary word used in English to express any notion of
cutting. (The verb *cut* doesn't appear until the 13th century, and
is of obscure origin. See line 9136.)

Related to CARVE is the carpentering and mining term KERF
2845 'a notch made by cutting.' Another possible relative, derived from
Germanic *krabb-, is Old English *crabba* > English CRAB 'a
marine crustacean,' certainly a "scratchy" animal. Some assign
CRAB to the same family as CARVE and Greek *graphein* 'to
scratch,' but others suggest a relationship with Old High German
2850 *krapfo* 'a hook,' commenting that "the creature may have been
named from its claws." Crabs are noted for traveling sideward, or
at what the dictionaries call "a perverse gait"; consequently, a
person who is labeled a CRAB, CRABBED, CRABBY 'is one who is
cross-grained, cross-tempered, perverse, contrary.' There may be
2855 a cross-pollination of meaning here with another CRAB, this one
the CRAB apple 'the wild apple' [from Scandinavian *skrabba* 'fruit
of the wild apple,' of unknown origin].

It seems that the game known as CRAPS 'a gambling game
played with dice' was originally called CRABS. *Crabs* was an 18th-
2860 century English slang expression for a roll of dice, in the game of
hazard, that turned up two aces (known today as "snake eyes") or
CRAP 'a throw of 2, 3, or 12 on the first roll in the game of craps
that causes the shooter to lose his bet.' As the name of the game,
crabs did not catch on among the British, but it was taken up by
2865 French speakers and altered to *craps* in Louisiana French. From
the gaming rooms of New Orleans it was borrowed into American
English to flower anew in the subculture of gamblers.

Related to Old English *crabba* 'crab' is Germanic *krabiz*,
which was adopted into Medieval French, via Frankish *krabītja*,
2870 as *crevice* (modern French *écrevisse*) > Middle English *crevis(e)*
> English CRAYFISH, CRAWFISH 'a freshwater crustacean resem-
bling the lobster, but much smaller.' The Middle English *-vis* has
been changed to -FISH by folk etymology. (The modern German
word is *Krebs*.)

2875 Yet another possible English member of the *gerebh- 'to
scratch' family is the verb to CRAWL 'to drag the body along the
ground' [from Old Norse *krafla* 'to crawl, to creep'; from Germanic *krab-]. CRAWL is used to describe the way many animals
get around, but not particularly crabs, since crabs tend to scuttle.
2880 The semantic connection between a root meaning 'to scratch' and
the act of crawling might be found in the marks that are scratched
on the ground by animals like snakes and turtles.

XIV

Crooked Crullers, Crumbling Crumpets

CRUMBS in the CRIB? CRUMBLING CRUMPETS in the CRADLE? CRANK up your CROQUET mallet and watch the ENCROACHERS CRINGE and CREEP away! This parody of advertising verbiage makes very little sense, but it does serve to showcase some of the CROTCHETY words that have been lumped together by etymologists as descendants of a hypothetical Indo-European root *ger-. These are all Germanic words beginning with a kr- sound, sometimes changed to gr- in words that have passed through Romance languages. The words fall into two semantic groups: those with meanings of 'curved, crooked, bent' and those meaning 'a rounded object; a collection; a container.'

We start with the most obvious "crooked" English word: CROOK 'a hook; something bent or crooked; a curved tool; a shepherd's staff; a bishop's crosier; one who is not honest in his business dealings' [from Middle English crōk; from Old Norse krōkr 'hook']. Old Norse krōkr has an equivalent in Frankish *krōk, antecedent of French croc 'hook, crook; fang' and croche 'crooked, bent,' from which English has borrowed CROCHE 'a small knob at the top of a deer's antler,' also called a CROCKET (see below), CROCHET 'needlework made by looping thread with a hooked needle' [French crochet 'small hook,' diminutive of croc], and CROTCHET 'a small hook'; (music) 'a quarter note'; 'an odd notion,' hence CROTCHETY 'full of eccentricities.'

Another probable derivative of Frankish *krōk 'hook' is CROQUET 'a lawn game in which players using long-handled mallets drive balls through a series of hoops' [from Northern French croquet 'a small hook']. Apparently the game was named after the mallets, which were originally hooked sticks. The word croquet in Old Northern French also meant 'a shepherd's crook,' and in some modern French dialects it means 'a hockey stick.' The game

2885

2890

2895

2900

2905

2910

of croquet was brought to Ireland from France sometime in the first half of the 19th century and was introduced from Ireland into
2915 England in 1852. In an *Encyclopaedia Britannica* entry dated 1877, an ivory turner of London recalls "having made a set of croquet implements for Ireland over 40 years ago"—that is to say, before 1837. (Imagine playing croquet with ivory mallets!)

The English word CROCKET = CROCHE (obsolete) 'a style of
2920 hair curl worn by both sexes in the Middle Ages'; 'a small ornament resembling curled leaves placed on inclined surfaces in Gothic architecture' (notably Cologne cathedral), is also descended from Old Northern French *croquet* 'a small hook.' (But the word *croquette* 'a small cake of minced food coated with
2925 bread crumbs and fried' comes from the French verb *croquer* 'to crunch,' of imitative origin.) From Old French *croc* 'hook' there evolved the verb *crochir* 'to become bent like a hook,' which possibly came over into Middle English as *crochen, crouchen,* later English CROUCH 'to stoop with the limbs pulled close to the
2930 body.' A Medieval French compound from the same source was *encrochier* 'to seize with a hook,' borrowed into English as ENCROACH (obsolete) 'to seize wrongfully'; 'to intrude upon the rights of others.' Medieval French *croche* 'crook, crosier' may also have led to English CROTCH 'a stake with a fork-shaped top, used
2935 as a prop; the fork of a tree; the angle formed by the joining of two legs,' but some think it more likely that CROTCH is a variant of CRUTCH 'a staff with a crosspiece to fit under the armpit'; (nautical) 'a fork-shaped timber' [from Middle English *crucche,* from Old English *crycc,* from Germanic **krukjō*].

2940 Possibly related to all these Germanic words, and themselves from the Germanic root **kruk-,* are Medieval Latin *crucca* 'a crutch' and *croccia* 'a pastoral crook.' *Croccia* evolved into Old French *croce, crosse* 'a bishop's staff,' whence *crocier, crossier* 'the bearer of the bishop's staff.' (Note that the Old French word
2945 *crosse* means 'a bishop's staff' and not 'a cross.' Keep this in mind, and what follows may not be too confusing.) Old French *crocier, crossier* came over into English as CROSIER, CROZIER (obsolete) 'the bearer of a bishop's staff'; 'a bishop's staff resembling a shepherd's crook, and symbolizing the bishop's pastoral function
2950 as keeper of the flock; a cross-staff, or processional cross; a cross or crucifix mounted on a long pole.' This confusion between the cross and the crook is not hard to understand, since the Latin word *crux, crucem* 'cross' is so similar in form and meaning to the Medieval Latin *crucca* 'crook, bishop's staff.' However, Latin *crux*
2955 and its English descendant (by way of Old Norse and Old Irish) *cross* 'an upright post with a transverse piece near the top' are not related to the Germanic words associated with the notion of

'hook, crook.' Latin *crux* became Old French *croiz,* while the Germanic root **kruk-* became Old French *croce,* modern French *crosse.* In Old French, a 'cross-bearer' was a *croisier,* while a 'crook-bearer' was a *crocier* or *crossier.* The two sources were never confused in French, but it's easy to see why they became so in English.

2960

The French word *crosse* 'bishop's crook; hockey stick' has been taken into North American English with another meaning, in the game of LACROSSE 'a game of American Indian origin, resembling field hockey except that the ball is carried, thrown through the air, and caught in a long-handled racket with a hooked ending across which netting has been strung' [from the Canadian French *(jeu de) la crosse* '(game of) the hooked stick']. (The American Indian name for the game was *baggatiway.*)

2965

2970

Another game that used to be played with "hooked sticks" is CRICKET 'an outdoor game played with bats, a ball, and wickets.' Up to the 17th century, cricket bats were hockey sticks, and the ball was bowled along the ground at the wicket, rather than hurled through the air as it is now. The game itself dates back to before 1598. The etymology of the word is uncertain, but it may derive from French *criquet* 'a game of skill; a stick serving as a mark or goal in a bowling game.' (The "stick" would be the wicket rather than the bat.) In any case, this French word *criquet* may stem from Medieval Flemish *krick(e)* 'a stick for leaning upon,' which would make it a relative of CRUTCH, CROOK, and the rest. However, some writers derive Old French *criquet* 'wicket or bat in a ball game' from *criquer* 'to click,' from the clicking of the ball against the wickets.

2975

2980

2985

Another kind of hook is a CRANK 'a part of an axis bent at right angles, and sometimes fitted with a handle for turning, thus imparting a rotary motion to a shaft; something crooked; a grouch; a person with a fixation or obsession.' Associated with the figurative meanings is the adjective CRANKY 'ill-tempered, peevish; eccentric, crotchety.' However, these senses may have been influenced by Dutch *krank* 'weak, sick, ill.' All of these words come from a Germanic source that conveys the notions of 'bending, curling up,' as in English CRANK, or of 'shrinking, becoming ill,' as in German *krank* 'sick.' The English CRANK is an ablaut derivative of the Old English verb *crincan, cranc, cruncen,* a variant of *cringan, crang, crungen* 'to yield, to fall dead'; (earlier) 'to draw oneself together, to curl up,' or, using a modern English derivative, to CRINGE 'to cower, to shrink back.'

2990

2995

A related word that has to do with 'drawing together' and 'curling up' is CRINKLE 'to wrinkle; to form numerous short turns and twists (in).' Etymologically, CRINKLE means 'to bend fre-

3000

quently.' It stems from the base that gives us Old English *crincan* 'to draw together, to contract.' More related words include CRIN-
3005 GLE (nautical) 'a small ring of rope or metal fastened to the edge of a sail' [from Low German *kringel*, diminutive of *kring* 'ring, circle'] (the rope CRINGLES are made by bending and curling); CRAMP 'a violent, involuntary contraction of a muscle' [from Old French *crampe*; related to Old High German *krampfo*, and
3010 modern German *Krampf* 'cramp, convulsion']; and CRAMP 'a metal bar with a right angle bend for holding together blocks of stone, timbers, etc.' [from Medieval Dutch *crampe* 'a hook']. Both CRAMPS derive ultimately from the same Germanic source; thus we have 'squeezing-hooks,' which are 'bent,' associated with 'a
3015 contraction of a muscle.' Note, also, CRAMPED 'compressed, squeezed together'; CRAMPON 'a hinged pair of hooks for lifting stones, timbers, etc.; one of the spikes set into a steel framework to fit onto boots, for walking on ice' [from Old French *crampon*]; CRIMP 'to pleat, to press into small regular folds; to obstruct, to
3020 inhibit; something that inhibits' [from (Medieval) Dutch *krimpen* 'to shrink'; related to Old English *gecrympan* 'to curl']; CRUMP (obsolete) ' "crooked; said chiefly of the body or limbs; from deformity, old age, or disease" ' (*OED*) (CRUMP-back, CRUMP-footed); (obsolete) 'to curl up.' The adjective and verb CRUMP are
3025 no longer with us, but the following derivative is: CRUMPLE (etymologically) 'to curl up often'; 'to crush together; to become wrinkled.' The participle CRUMPLED 'curved, crooked' is found much earlier than other parts of this verb. A late example (probably before 1750) is seen in the nursery rhyme, *The House*
3030 *that Jack Built*: "This is the Cow with the Crumpled Horn, that tossed the Dog, that worried the Cat . . . ." In Scottish, a CRUMMIE is ' "a cow with *crumpled* or crooked horns" ' (*OED*). However, neither of these adjectives means that there is anything damaged or wrong about the horns, simply that they are curved.
3035   Then there is the famous English CRUMPET 'a light bread, similar to a muffin, but cooked on a griddle.' *The Oxford English Dictionary* gives us this 1769 recipe for tea crumpets: "Beat two eggs very well, put to them a quart of warm milk and water and a large spoonful of barm; beat in as much flour as will make them
3040 rather thicker than a common batter," and cook on a griddle. *Barm* is 'the froth that foams on the top of fermenting malt liquors' used to leaven bread and therefore, 'a leaven.' The authorities vary from "perhaps" to "probably" in deriving CRUM-PET from a word that appears in Wycliffe's translation of the Bible
3045 (1382): *crompid* (*cake*) '(cake that is) curled up.' These were apparently thinner griddle cakes than the ones described in 1769.

Speaking of curly cakes and other good things to eat reminds us of that gastronomical delight, the CRULLER 'a small twisted cake made of rich batter fried in deep fat' [from Dutch *krulle*, from *krullen* 'to curl']. CRULLER got into our language and diet by way of the Knickerbockers of Nieuw Amsterdam > New York. However, Middle English already had the forms *crollid*, *crulled*, and *crouled*, all meaning 'curled,' based on the adjective *croll(e)*, *crul(le)* 'curly,' source of the verb *croul*, *kurl*, *courl*, whence modern English CURL 'to twist or form into ringlets.'

3050

3055

Other words in *cr-* having to do with 'contracting, bending over' are CREEP 'to move with the body close to the ground' [from Old English *crēopan*, from Germanic **kreupan*]; CRIPPLE 'one who creeps or limps; one who is partly disabled' [from Old English *crypel*]; and, possibly, CREEK (Great Britain) 'a small inlet or bay'; (U.S. and former British colonies) 'a small stream' [from Old Norse *kriki* 'a bend, a nook'], influenced by Old French *crique* 'cove, creek,' a word that probably also comes from the Norse. With regard to the different meanings of CREEK in Great Britain and the United States and other former colonies, *The Oxford English Dictionary* suggests that this came about because early explorers of the New World, Australia, and New Zealand gave the name CREEK to various indentations in the coast line that they observed from their ships. However, when these inlets were later explored more extensively, they often led to small tributary streams, sometimes "of great length; but they retained the designation originally given, and *creek* thus received an application entirely unknown in Great Britain."

3060

3065

3070

Our Indo-European **ger-* root changed to Germanic **kr-* to yield Germanic **krappon* 'a hook; a hook for harvesting grapes.' Under Romanic influence *kr-* changed to *gr-* in Old French (*craper>*) *graper* 'to harvest grapes (with a hook),' whence Old French (*crape>*) *grape* 'what has been harvested with a hook; a bunch of grapes' and English GRAPE 'a smooth-skinned, juicy berry that grows in clusters on vines.' (The French word for the fruit is *raisin*. The French word *grappe* still means 'a bunch of grapes; a cluster of fruit.') In addition, we have GRAPESHOT 'a cluster of small iron balls formerly used as a cannon charge.' Also descended from Germanic **krappon* 'a hook' are GRAPPLE 'an iron shaft with claws at one end for grasping and holding; to seize with one's hands and arms, as in wrestling' [perhaps via Old French *grapil*, from Provençal *grapil*, diminutive of *grapa* 'hook'] and GRAPNEL 'a small anchor with three or more flukes or claws' [from Norman French **grapenel*, diminutive of Old French *grapon* 'hook']. (The modern French is *grap(p)in*.)

3075

3080

3085

3090

The second group of words lumped together as descended from the Indo-European root *ger- has meanings of ' "a rounded mass, a collection, a round object, a vessel, a container" ' *(AHD)*. The evolution of French *grappe* 'a bunch of grapes' from a word
3095 meaning 'a hook for harvesting' exemplifies how some of these semantic linkages developed.

Among the "collection" words are GROUP 'an assemblage of persons or objects' [from French *groupe*, from Italian *gruppo* 'a cluster, a knot'; from Germanic *kruppaz* 'a round mass'] and
3100 CROP 'a harvest; the seasonal yield of a product' [from Old English *crop(p)* 'cluster, bunch; ear of corn']. CROP has a more primitive sense of 'a swollen protuberance or excrescence,' yielding modern English CROP 'the craw of a bird, a pouchlike enlargement of the gullet; the handle of a whip'; (obsolete) 'the
3105 top part of a plant; an ear of corn, a young sprout'; 'to cut off the stems or tops of plants; to cut short.' Etymologically related is another 'rounded mass,' CROUP 'the posterior part of the back of a quadruped; the place behind the saddle of a riding horse' [from Old French *croupe* 'hindquarters,' from Germanic *krūppo*]. It is
3110 from this rather undistinguished position that we acquire the word CROUPIER (literally) 'one who rides behind another on a horse's back'; (obsolete) 'a gamester's assistant'; 'one who presides at a gaming table, collecting and paying off the bets; one who sits at the foot of the table as assistant chairman of a public
3115 dinner party.' The semantic sequence went something like this: 'riding pillion on a horse' > 'going halves with a gambler and standing behind him as he plays' > 'standing behind and assisting the banker at a game of basset' (an obsolete game resembling faro) > 'raking in the losing bets and paying off the winners at a
3120 gaming table.' The sense of 'assistant chairman at a dinner party' seems to be a side development, perhaps from 'assistant banker'; it dates back to 1785 or before.

A small 'round object' that has broken away from a larger one is called a CRUMB 'a small fragment or piece; a small particle of
3125 bread; to break into small pieces' [from Old English *cruma*, from Germanic *krumjan*]. The noun CRUMB is related to Latin *grūmus* 'a small heap; a hillock.' The final -*b* of CRUMB, which is not pronounced, is a late arrival. It was first tacked on in the 16th century, and the spelling *crum* was permissible up to the 19th.
3130 This intrusive -*b* originally developed in the related verb CRUMBLE 'to keep breaking into small pieces.' In CRUMBLE the -*b*- is now pronounced, though it still isn't in CRUMBY, CRUMMY 'full of crumbs'; (slang) 'contemptible, no good.' The slang meaning is a turnabout, for in 18th/19th century British slang, CRUMMY meant
3135 '(of a woman) plump, full-figured; pretty.'

'Round objects' often serve as 'containers.' In this category we have CROCK 'an earthenware vessel' [from Old English *crocc(a)*] and CRUET 'a small glass bottle' [from Norman French *cruet*, diminutive of Old French *crue* 'flask']. Both of these are related to German *Krug* 'pitcher.' Note, also, CRUSE 'a jar or pot   3140
for holding water, oil, honey, etc.' [from Middle English *crouse*; related to Old English *crūse* and Middle Dutch *cruyse*].

Another 'rounded object' and 'container' is a CRIB (originally) 'a manger; a feeder, a barred trough for fodder'; 'a small building with slotted sides for storing corn; a child's bed with high sides; a   3145
wooden framework; a wicker basket'; (slang) 'to steal; to plagiarize'; 'a word-for-word translation of a text' [from Old English *crib(b)* 'manger']. The name of the card game CRIBBAGE apparently comes from CRIB 'the discarded cards used by the dealer in scoring in cribbage,' although no one is sure how this   3150
usage arose. More 'rounded objects' and 'containers' are CRÈCHE (French) 'manger, crib'; 'a representation of the Nativity scene; a foundling hospital' [from Old High German *kripja* 'crib'] and CRADLE 'a bed for a baby, especially one mounted on rockers; a supporting framework' [from Old English *cradol*]. CRADLE is   3155
related to Old High German *kratto* and dialectal German *kratte* 'basket.' "Old English *cradol* ... might be a diminutive form, literally 'little basket'" *(OED)*. Also related to German *kratte* 'basket' is English CART 'a light, wheeled vehicle' [either from Old Norse *kartr*, or by metathesis from Old English *craet* 'car-   3160
riage,' or both]. Some surmise that CART has been influenced by Old Northern French *carete*, a diminutive of *car*. (See line 1925.) This conjecture is vociferously denied by others.

Finally, the British and Scottish word CROFT 'a small enclosed field, usually adjacent to a cottage' is thought by some to   3165
belong to this group, because of the underlying sense of something 'rounded, curved.'

XV

Dignified Doctors, Doctrinaire Disciplinarians

Teaching and learning are two sides of the same coin, so it seems fitting that the Latin words for these activities, *docēre* 'to
3170   teach' and *discēre* 'to learn,' are closely related and stem from the same Indo-European root, **dek-* 'to conform (to), to accept.' Learning comes before teaching; in effect, teaching is 'causing to learn,' so that the now ungrammatical expression, "That'll learn you," is not so far off the mark. (*To learn* meaning 'to teach' was
3175   correct English as late as the 1800s. Benjamin Disraeli wrote in 1844, "Learn to know the House; learn the House to know you.")
Descended from Latin *docēre, doctum* 'to teach' is DOCTOR (obsolete) 'a teacher'; (obsolete) 'a learned man'; 'one who holds the highest academic degree in a specified discipline; a person
3180   trained and licensed in the healing arts' [from Latin *doctor* 'teacher, instructor']. The Latin word for 'a learned man' was *doctus* (and for 'physician' was *medicus*). Thus, the word *doctor* has made a complete volte-face in meaning from 'one who teaches' to 'one who has been taught (has learned) a great deal.'
3185   Latin *docēre* also yielded English DOCENT (literally) 'teaching'; 'a teacher or lecturer who is not a regular faculty member; one who conducts tours of a museum or other institution' [from Latin *docent-*, present participle of *docēre* 'to teach']. DOCENT was adopted into English from the German *Docent* (now *Dozent*) 'a
3190   university teacher,' especially a *Privatdozent* 'an unsalaried university lecturer who is remunerated by students' fees.' In some U.S. colleges, DOCENT specifies ' "an academic rank between the doctorate and instructor" ' (*MW2*). More English descendants of Latin *docēre* include DOCILE 'teachable; submissive' [from Latin
3195   *docilis* 'easily taught']; DOCTRINE 'something that is taught; dogma' [via Medieval/Old French from Latin *doctrīna* 'instruction']; DOCTRINAIRE 'inflexibly attached to certain teachings'

[from the French]; INDOCTRINATE 'to imbue with opinions, beliefs, points of view'; and DOCUMENT (obsolete) 'teaching'; (obsolete) 'that which serves to prove something'; 'something written that furnishes information or evidence' [via Medieval/Old French from Latin *documentum* 'lesson'].

Latin *discēre* 'to learn' has these English descendants: DISCI-PLE 'one who attends upon another for the purpose of learning from him' [from Old English *discipul*, influenced by Old French *deciple*, both from Latin *discipilus* 'pupil, scholar']; DISCIPLINE (obsolete) 'instruction imparted to scholars'; 'a branch of instruction, a department of learning; instruction having as its goal a prescribed kind of conduct; observance of prescribed rules of conduct' [via Medieval/Old French from Latin *disciplīna* 'instruction']; and DISCIPLINARIAN 'one who believes in strict enforcement of prescribed rules of conduct.'

As noted, one definition of the English word DOCTRINE is DOGMA 'a belief formally considered to be absolute truth.' *Dogma*, a Greek word, was adopted by Latin speakers to mean 'philosophic principle, tenet.' In Greek, however, it meant primarily 'an opinion,' with secondary meanings of 'a decree,' that is, 'a principle that is declared to be valid, a doctrine.' These meanings are much more flexible than the English meaning of DOGMA. Even more revealing, Greek *dogma* is derived from the verb *dokein* 'to think, to suppose'; or (looking at the other side of the coin) 'to seem, to appear to be.' This is a manifestation of the famed Greek attitude of skepticism, that is, the notion that things are not what they seem to be. This attitude culminated paradoxically in the Platonic "ideals," which were thought truly to exist in the highest realms of being, while sense impressions were held to be illusory.

The Greek verb *dokein* 'to think, to suppose; to seem, to appear to be' is cousin to Latin *docēre* 'to teach' and *discēre* 'to learn,' since all are descended from the Indo-European root *dek- 'to conform (to), to accept.' The semantic evolution in the case of *dokein* must have been along the lines of 'to accept what seems to be.' The human mind, however, has a long history of disliking uncertainty and longing for certainty, so that the word *dogma*, from meaning merely 'opinion based on what seems to be,' has wound up as one of the most inflexible terms in the English language, meaning 'a belief held to be absolute truth and not subject to doubt.'

Greek *dokein* 'to think, to suppose' has another derivative similar to *dogma* 'opinion; decree': *doxa* 'opinion, notion; expectation.' *Doxa* is an element in the English words DOXY 'opinion, especially religious opinion'; ORTHODOX (literally) 'having the

right opinion'; 'adhering to traditional beliefs' [*orthos* 'right, true']; HETERODOX (literally) 'differing in opinion'; 'not in agree-
3245 ment with accepted beliefs' [*heteros* 'other']; and PARADOX (origi-nally) 'a statement that is contrary to accepted opinion'; 'a seemingly contradictory statement that is nevertheless true; an assertion that is self-contradictory' [from Greek *paradoxos* 'unex-pected, incredible' (*para* 'beyond')].

3250 While we're with the Greek, let us mention another English word derived from that language that incorporates the Indo-European root **dek-* 'to conform (to), to accept': the technical rhetorical term SYNECDOCHE 'a figure of speech in which a less inclusive term is used for a more inclusive one, or vice versa'
3255 [from Greek *sunekdokhē* 'joint expectation; joint interpretation' (from *sun-* 'together with' + *ekdokhē* 'expectation, interpretation, acquisition from'; from the verb *ekdekhesthai* 'to acquire from, to learn from'; from *ek-* 'out of' + *dekesthai* 'to take, to receive')]. "A part for the whole, or the whole for a part" is the formula for
3260 synecdoche. An example is "the herd consisted of twenty *head*," meaning twenty animals. Another example is "*the law* was pursuing us on his motorcycle," meaning 'a policeman.'

Adherence to beliefs or opinions is one kind of 'acceptance' found in words that stem from Indo-European **dek-* 'to conform
3265 (to), to accept.' Cognate words having to do with social, personal, or decorative 'acceptability' are exemplified by the Latin verb *decēre* 'to be fitting, to be suitable,' whose present participle, *decent-* 'becoming, seemly,' leads to English DECENT 'acceptable; conforming to recognized standards of propriety.' The primary
3270 meanings of DECENT in present-day English have to do with modesty, but there are secondary senses of 'kind, generous,' as in "He's a decent sort" and of 'adequate, moderately satisfying,' as in "He makes a decent salary." In Elizabethan days, the English word still retained some of an extended Latin meaning of 'hand-
3275 some, beautiful.' Francis Bacon wrote of "Decent & Beautifull Arches, as High as the first story" (1625).

Similarly, English DECOROUS 'characterized by seemly behavior' [from Latin *decōrus* 'fitting, seemly'] and DECORUM 'conformity to social conventions' had their origins in Latin *decor*,
3280 *decōris* 'comeliness, elegance' and *decus, decoris* 'ornament; deed of honor, exploit.' These also give us the English DECOR 'the arrangement and embellishment of rooms, stage settings, etc.' [from French *décor*] and DECORATE 'to adorn; to confer a medal upon' [from Latin *decorāre* 'to embellish; to honor'].
3285 Some etymologists also include the Latin adjective *dexter* 'right, on the right hand; propitious, suitable; skillful' among the cognate Latin words having to do with 'what is fitting' and 'what

is favorable.' This is the ancestor of English DEXTER 'of the right
side' and DEXTEROUS 'adroit, skillful.' But others postulate
a separate Indo-European root, *deks- 'right.' One of these, Eric   3290
Partridge (*Origins*, p. 150), goes on to say of *deks- 'right' that it is
"probably a reduction of Indo-European *dekos (cf. Latin *decus*)
'that which is fitting,' hence 'favourable, good,'" and therefore a
tie-in with *dek- 'to conform (to), to accept.'

Also from Latin *dexter* 'on the right hand; propitious; skillful'   3295
are DEXTERITY 'adroitness' [from Latin *dexteritās* 'skillfulness'];
AMBIDEXTROUS 'capable of using either hand with equal facility;
deceitful, hypocritical' [*ambi*- 'on both sides']; and DEXTROSE 'a
sugar found in living tissues and derived synthetically from
starch.' The sugar is called DEXTROSE because it is DEXTROROTA-   3300
TORY 'rotating the plane of polarized light toward the right, or
clockwise,' much as certain vines are described as being DEX-
TRORSE 'spiraling in a clockwise direction' [from New Latin
dextrorsus (from *dexter* + *versus* 'turned toward')]. A DESTRIER
(archaic) 'a war-horse, a charger' [from Old French, from Late   3305
Latin *dextrārius* (*equus*) 'right-hand (horse)'] was so called
because the knight's squire led the charger with his right hand
while managing his own horse with his left.

There are a number of cognate words that have to do with
DIGNITY 'personal worth; self-respect that inspires the respect of   3310
others' [from Old French *dignete*, from Latin *dīgnitās*, from
dīgnus 'fitting, worthy']. *Dīgnus* traces back to Indo-European
*dek- through primitive Latin *decnos* and the suffixed root form,
*dek-no. The -k- changed to -g- owing to assimilation by the
following nasal -n-, as in Greek *dogma*, derived from *dokein*. A   3315
person who is deemed "worthy" is sometimes DIGNIFIED or
'honored with an elevated rank,' and thus made into a DIGNITARY
'one who possesses exalted rank.' Having achieved this eminent
position he will not, one hopes, look down upon his fellows with
DISDAIN 'a feeling of contempt for what is regarded as beneath   3320
one; to look down upon with contempt' [from Latin *dēdignāri* 'to
consider unworthy,' by way of Vulgar Latin *disdignāre*, Old
French *desdeignier*, and Middle English *desdeyn(en)*]. Similarly,
Latin *dīgnāri* 'to deem worthy' became Old French *deignier*.
Present-day English preserves some of that spelling in the word   3325
DEIGN 'to think it suitable to one's dignity (to do something); to
condescend.' Of course, if something occurs that one regards as
unworthy, one is filled with INDIGNATION 'the feeling excited by
what is base, unjust or mean.' If one is lucky, the villain who has
aroused one's ire will suffer a punishment that is CONDIGN   3330
'deserved, merited.' CONDIGN is now used in English only with
reference to the notion of 'let the punishment fit the crime.'

However, the ancestral Latin word, *condīgnus*, meant merely
'very worthy' [*con-* = *cum* 'with,' used to intensify the meaning].
3335   Timidly bringing up the rear in this parade of worthiness is
the delicate word DAINTY 'exquisite; of refined taste; delicious,
choice.' DAINTY is now a rather precious word, but it traces back
through Old French *deintie* to Latin *dignitātem* 'worth, beauty;
dignity.'

XVI

From Dromedaries to Trampolines

One tends to think of camels as rather slow-moving, cud-   3340
chewing beasts of burden with bad tempers and complexly
folding legs. These are all true attributes except the first. Camels
are not necessarily slow; in fact the word DROMEDARY 'the one-
humped or Arabian camel' comes from the Greek *dromas,
dromados* 'running, fleet,' by way of Late Latin *dromedārius,*   3345
short for *camēlus dromedārius* 'running camel,' and originally
meant 'a camel of unusual speed, bred and trained especially for
riding,' usually, but not necessarily, of the one-humped variety.
Thus, it should be possible to have a "Bactrian dromedary,"
though this sounds like a contradiction in terms.   3350
The Arabs have indeed bred camels for swiftness as Europe-
ans have bred thoroughbreds for racing; and Arabs do indulge in
camel races. However, I have never heard of a **kamelodrome,*
which would be the dromedary's equivalent to the thoroughbred's
HIPPODROME 'an oval track for horse and chariot races, with tiers   3355
of seats for the spectators' [from Greek *hippodromos* 'horse
racetrack' (*hippos* 'horse' + *dromos* 'racetrack')]. In most American cities that have a *Hippodrome* it turns out to be a moving-
picture theater. The Hippodrome in New York, however, was
converted into a jai alai fronton. In a previous existence, it was   3360
once used for six-day bicycle races and other such events, and it
was originally built for racing motorcycles, if not horses.
Greek *dromos* 'a running' came to mean 'a racecourse' as well
as the race itself, and from that, 'any large open space where
contests are held,' as in VELODROME 'an arena where bicycle   3365
races are held' [*velo-* from *velocipede* 'swift-footed,' an early name
for bicycles] and AERODROME (originally) 'a course for practice or
contests with flying machines'; 'an airport.' Then there are the
following nonracing terms that incorporate the element *-drom-:*

3370 SYNDROME (literally) 'a running together'; 'a group of symptoms that occur together'; PRODROME (literally) 'running before, forerunner'; 'a symptom of the onset of a disease'; and PALINDROME (literally) 'running backward'; 'a word, phrase or sentence that reads the same backward as forward' [palin 'back, backwards'].

3375 (Examples of palindromes are madam, reviver, and a man, a plan, a canal, Panama!) Other words with the element -drom- include ANADROMOUS (literally) 'running upward'; (of salmon, shad, etc.) 'ascending rivers at certain seasons for breeding' and CATADROMOUS (literally) 'running downward'; (of eels, etc.) 'descending

3380 rivers to the sea to spawn.'

Underlying Greek dromos 'a running' is Indo-European *der-, the base of roots meaning 'to run; to walk, to step.' *Der- shows up in Germanic languages with the initial d- changed, regularly, to t-, as in English TREAD 'to walk on; the horizontal part of a step

3385 in a staircase; the part of a wheel that makes contact with the ground.' From TREAD it is an easy step to TREADLE 'a pedal or lever operated by foot' and TREADMILL 'a mechanism operated by walking on the moving steps of a wheel, or on an endless belt.'

Walking was the way most of the Indo-European speakers got

3390 about, though their own feet were sometimes spared, and it was the hooves of oxen and horses that did the treading. The pathways that became worn between communities are known as "TRADE routes" because they were made by the constant treading of feet. The English word TRADE comes from the Middle Low German

3395 trade 'a course, a track, a path.' This early meaning is lost in the English word, which has acquired the senses of 'commerce,' relating to the goods that are carried along the trade routes, and of 'occupation, especially one involving skilled labor,' which ties in with the whole business of traveling along pathways by providing

3400 the goods of commerce that are TRADED. So we wind up with phrases like TRADE mark, TRADE union, and TRADE winds, which used to blow the commerce along the trackless paths of the ocean.

English TREAD, which comes from Old English tredan, has an Old High German cousin, tretan 'to step, to walk,' with an

3405 intensive form, trottōn 'to tread, to step.' This is a remote cousin of English TROT 'to move at a brisk jogging gait.' 'Really stepping' is not an unusual way to think of the pace of a TROTTER since harness-racing horses pick their feet up and put them down again in a hurry. [TROT is Germanic in derivation but came into English

3410 by way of Old French troter and Vulgar Latin *trottare (modern French has it trotter, modern German, trotten).]

Another, unpleasant way of putting one's foot down is to step on a TRAP 'a device for catching and holding animals' [from Old English traeppe 'a snare'; from Germanic *trep- 'something into

which one steps.' There is another kind of TRAP 'a steplike   3415
configuration in igneous rocks,' also called TRAPROCK. Quarried
and broken up, traprock is used extensively in road building. The
words TRAP and TRAPROCK were adapted into English from the
Swedish word *trapp*, from *trappa* 'stair.' They were coined
because such rock occurs in masses rising up above one another   3420
like so many "steps." The verb to TRIP 'to stumble; to cause to
stumble' [from Middle Dutch *trippen* 'to hop, to skip'] may be
looked upon as an ablaut variant of the verb to TRAP, both
phonetically and semantically, since TRIPPING is a sort of narrow
escape from being TRAPPED. English TRIP also has the sense of 'to   3425
move lightly and nimbly,' as in the catch phrase, to "trip it lightly
as we go, on the light fantastic toe." It also has the substantive
sense of TRIP 'a going from place to place; a journey.' In one of its
updated usages, a TRIP is 'a protracted hallucination induced by
drugs.' That the word TRAP originated with notions of 'stepping'   3430
is demonstrated by the nasalized forms TRAMP 'to step heavily; a
vagrant or hobo' (who foots it around the country); 'a cargo vessel
that has no regular schedule; a promiscuous woman' and TRAM-
PLE 'to step on repeatedly.'

Finally we have the word TRAMPOLINE ' "a sheet of strong,   3435
taut canvas attached with springs to a steel frame and used for
acrobatic tumbling" ' (*AHD*). TRAMPOLINE comes to us via Spanish *trampolin* 'springboard,' from the Italian *trampolino* 'a performance on stilts,' from *trampoli* 'stilts.' We have seen acrobats
turn somersaults on stilts, but the connection between stilts and a   3440
trampoline is not obvious; I suppose it's "a heavy step." In any
event, Italian *trampoli* 'stilts' is traceable to the Germanic root
*tramp- 'to step heavily,' and thence to Indo-European **der-*, the
base of roots meaning 'to run; to walk, to step.'

XVII

The Duke Ties One On

3445   *Il Duce* 'the leader' was the epithet Mussolini chose for himself while he was CONDUCTING his campaign toward dictatorial power. He could have chosen *duca*, another Italian word for 'leader,' but *duca* also means 'DUKE,' and Mussolini's appeal was not along the lines of traditional aristocracy, but those of dema-
3450   goguery. Therefore, he chose the word *duce*, whose everyday meaning in Italian is 'captain, military leader; guide.'
      The source of all three words, *duce*, *duca*, and DUKE, is Latin *dux* 'leader, guide; commander, ruler.' *Dux* (for **ducs*) is kin to the Latin verb *dūcere*, *ductum* 'to draw, drag, pull; to lead, guide,
3455   conduct.' The latter is ancestor to a multitude of English words, including all those ending in *-duce* and *-duct*, like ABDUCT 'to carry off by force' [from Latin *abdūcere*, *abductum* 'to carry off, to lead away']; SEDUCE 'to lead astray; to entice into a state advantageous to the enticer' [from Latin *sēdūcere* 'to lead aside' (*se-*
3460   'apart, aside')]; TRADUCE (obsolete) 'to translate' (French *traduire*); 'to slander' [from Latin *trādūcere* 'to lead over; to expose to ridicule' (*trā-* < *trāns* 'across, over')]; EDUCE 'to draw out, elicit' [from Latin *ēdūcere* 'to draw out' (*ē-* < *ex-* 'out; from')]; and EDUCATE 'to provide with knowledge and training' [from
3465   Latin *ēducāre*, *ēducātus* 'to bring up (out of ignorance)']. The older Latin form, *ēdūcere*, was also used to mean 'to bring up, to rear, to educate,' but it was largely replaced by the "durative" (continuing) *ēducāre* 'to keep on drawing out.' More descendants from Latin *dūcere*, *ductum* 'to draw, drag, pull; to lead, guide,
3470   conduct' are REDUCE (obsolete) 'to bring back'; 'to diminish, to lower' [from Latin *redūcere* 'to lead back']; DEDUCE (archaic) 'to lead forth'; 'to derive; to draw a conclusion from a general principle' [from Latin *dēdūcere*, *dēductus* 'to lead away, to lead forth']; DEDUCT 'to take away, to subtract' [*dē* 'away from'];

INDUCE (literally) 'to lead into'; 'to persuade; to reach a general 3475
conclusion from the study of particulars' [from Latin *indūcere*,
inductus 'to lead in']; INDUCT 'to place ceremoniously into office;
to enroll for military service'; PRODUCE 'to bring forth' [from Latin
prōducere, *prōductum* 'to lead forth']; PRODUCT 'what has been
brought forth' [*prō* 'before, in front of']; INTRODUCE (literally) 'to 3480
lead inside'; 'to identify and present' [from Latin *intrōdūcere* 'to
lead into']; ADDUCE 'to bring forward (as proof)' [from Latin
addūcere 'to lead to']; CONDUCE (literally) 'to lead together'; 'to
lead to a desirable result' [from Latin *condūcere*, *conductus* 'to
lead together; to hire']; and CONDUCT 'to lead or guide; to 3485
transmit'; (reflexive) 'to behave'; 'the act of leading or guiding;
behavior.' CONDUCT first appeared in 13th-century English as
conduyt, adopted from Medieval/Old French *conduit*, but the
spelling was refashioned in the 16th century to conform with the
Latin. The earlier spelling remains in CONDUIT 'a channel or pipe 3490
for carrying fluids; a duct for enclosing electric wires.' CONDUCT
'to lead' has an agential noun CONDUCTOR 'one who leads' (e.g., a
symphony orchestra); 'one in charge' (of a railroad train, streetcar;
tour); 'a substance that transmits' (heat CONDUCTOR, electric
CONDUCTOR). 3495

In Italian, the railway and orchestra CONDUCTOR is a *condut-*
tore, but Italian has another, very similar, noun, CONDOTTIERE
'military leader, captain.' The latter was used throughout western
Europe in the 14th to 16th centuries to denote ' "a leader of a
band of mercenary professional soldiers; ... any one of the 3500
soldiers; ... an adventurer" ' (*MW2*). Some etymologists trace this
word to Italian *condotto* 'leadership' + the agent-suffix *-iere*.
Others, noting that a secondary meaning of Latin *condūcere* is 'to
hire, to contract for,' and that of Latin *conductor* is 'hirer,
contractor,' derive it from Latin *conductus* 'a hired soldier'; plural 3505
conducti, *conductorum* 'mercenaries.'

Conduire, the French verb derived from Latin *condūcere* 'to
lead together,' means, among other things, 'to drive,' in the sense
that one drives a team of horses, a car, or a boat. In the nautical
sense, the French word has come over into English to give us two 3510
of the few nautical terms taken from the French: CON(N) 'to direct
the steering of a vessel; the station of the pilot of a vessel' [from
earlier *cond*, from Middle English *condue*, *condie*, from Old
French *conduire* 'to conduct'] and CONNING tower 'an armored
pilothouse on a warship.' Since the CONNING tower of a subma- 3515
rine is 'a raised, enclosed observation post,' this CONNING might
be confused with the etymologically unrelated verb *to con* 'to
examine carefully' (related to *can* 'be able,' *ken* 'perception,' and

know). Etymologically, the CONNING in CONNING tower has to do
3520 with steering rather than observing.

Another compound not so obviously borrowed, via French,
from Latin *dūcere* 'to lead' is SUBDUE 'to bring under control'
[from Medieval/Old French *so(u)duire*, from Latin *subdūcere* 'to
lead away, to withdraw']. The Latin meaning is quite different
3525 from the English, because, as the word developed in Anglo-
French, the sense became confused with that of Latin *subdere* 'to
put under.' Note, also, REDOUBT 'a small defensive fortification'
[from Old French *redoute*, adapted from Italian *ridotto*, from
Medieval Latin *reductus*, 'a refuge, a retreat'; from the past
3530 participle of Latin *redūcere* 'to lead back, to withdraw']. The *-b-*
was inserted in REDOUBT by errant pedants who associated the
word with *redoubtable* 'to be feared,' from Latin *dubitāre*. (See
line 1173.)

More obviously derived from Latin *dux* 'leader' and *dūcere*
3535 'to lead, to draw' are DUCHY 'a dukedom; the territory controlled
by a duke' and DUCAT 'a coin bearing the effigy of a duke, or
coined by a duchy' [via Medieval/Old French from Old Italian
ducato, from Medieval Latin *ducātus* 'duchy']. A silver DUCAT
was coined by the Norman, Roger II of Sicily, Duke of Apulia, in
3540 1140. The first gold ducats were minted by the Doge of Venice
and bore the legend: "Sit tibi, Christe, datus quem tu regis iste
ducatus" 'May this DUCHY which Thou rulest be dedicated to
Thee, O Christ.' More derivatives of Latin *dux* 'leader' and *dūcere*
'to lead' are DOGE 'the elected chief magistrate of the old
3545 Republics of Venice and Genoa' [via French from the Italian
doge, Venetian variant of *duce* 'leader']; DUCT 'a tubular passage'
[from Latin *ductus* 'a leading; a conduit']; AQUEDUCT 'a conduit
for transporting water; an elevated structure for carrying water
over a valley' [from Latin *aquae-ductus* (*aqua* 'water')]; VIADUCT
3550 'a bridge for carrying a road over a valley, gorge, or other roads'
[*via* 'road']; DOUCHE 'a jet of water or air applied to the body'
[from French *douche* 'shower-bath'; from Italian *doccia* 'shower-
bath; water pipe'; from *doccione* 'conduit pipe'; from Latin
ductiō 'a leading, a conveying']; and, possibly, DOCK 'the water-
3555 way alongside a pier where ships are received; a pier or wharf; a
platform for loading and unloading cargo' [from Middle Low
German and Middle Dutch *docke*]. "Probably" according to some,
"perhaps" according to others, DOCK may stem from Vulgar Latin
**ductia*, or Latin *ductiō* 'a conveying.' But most scholars put this
3560 word in the "of obscure origin" category.

The Indo-European root from which all these words stem is
**deuk-* 'to lead, to draw.' According to the rules of sound corre-
spondences, Indo-European initial **d-* becomes Germanic **t-*.

Indo-European *k regularly becomes Germanic *h, but under
certain accentual conditions it becomes Germanic *g instead. So   3565
we should not be too surprised to see the Indo-European root
*deuk- 'to lead, to draw' transformed into English as TUG 'to pull
at vigorously,' as a TUGboat pulls at a barge, CONDUCTING, or
'leading, drawing, pulling' it across the water. (Remember that the
Latin verb dūcere also has the sense of 'to drag.') [TUG comes   3570
from Middle English tuggen, toggen, from Germanic *tiuhan, the
base of Old English tēo(ha)n, tugon 'to pull']. These forms have
close correspondents in modern German ziehen 'to pull,' past
tense zog, Zug 'a pulling, drawing; railway train,' and -zog
'leader,' seen in Herzog (etymologically) 'army commander; duke'   3575
(Heer 'army').
        English relatives of TUG are TOW 'to pull along by a line'
[from Middle English towen, from Old English togian; from
Germanic *tugon]; TAUT 'pulled tight' [from Middle English
tought, perhaps a variant past participle of towen (see TOW,   3580
above)]; TUCK 'to pull up into a fold; to put into a snug place'
[from Middle English tu(c)ken 'to tug at; to punish'; from Old
English tūcian 'to punish, to torment']. The semantic development is not very clear here, but it is the 'pulling at' sense that has
survived. A TUCKER was (originally) 'a fuller of cloth; one that   3585
pulls out burls and loose threads and teases the nap'; (later) 'one
that makes tucks.' "All TUCKERED out" is an Americanism for "all
tired out," exhausted from overexertion (from fulling too much
cloth?). The TUCKER in bib and tucker was a piece of lace or the
like worn by women around the top of the bodice, in the 17th and   3590
18th centuries. Note, also, TIE 'to pull together and secure with a
knot' [from Old English tīgan, from tēag 'a rope'; from Germanic
*taugo]. One might expect to find tight here, but most authorities
trace this word to a different source.
        Harking back, Latin ēdūcere and ēducāre 'to bring up, to   3595
rear,' the last word fits in semantically with them: WANTON
(etymologically) 'without bringing up'; 'undisciplined; mali-
ciously cruel; unchaste' [from Middle English wantowen; from
Old English wan- 'lacking, without' + togen, past participle of
tēon 'to bring up, to draw']. (See line 10491.)   3600

XVIII

Dynamic Belladonna, Debonair Beldames

BELLADONNA (literally) 'beautiful lady' is, in fact, 'deadly nightshade,' a poison. A BELDAME (literally) 'a beautiful lady' is, in reality, 'a hag, a virago; a fury; an ugly, loathsome old woman.' CLARABELLA 'bright-beautiful' is sometimes 'a Disneyesque cow'

3605   (Claribel) or (musical) 'an eight-foot organ stop, producing "soft, sweet tones"' (*AHD*).

The one element common to these three words is *bel(la)*, from Latin *bellus*, *bella*, *bellum* 'handsome, pretty, fair, charming, fine' (and later, in Romance languages, 'beautiful').

3610   Before going any further, we must mention a sound change that took place, from Old Latin *du-* to classical Latin *b-*. We have already seen an example of this in the shift from archaic *duellum* 'war,' to classical *bellum* 'war.' (See line 1181.) There is another Latin *bellum*, this one the neuter of the adjective *bellus*, *bella*,

3615   *bellum* that means 'handsome, pretty, fair,' etc. These *b-* words also come from an archaic *du-* form, to wit: *duenelos*, *-a*, *-um*. Furthermore, *duenelos* is a diminutive of archaic Latin *duenos* (>*duonos*), *-a*, *-um* 'good,' another word that made the sound shift, to become classical Latin *bonus*, *bona*, *bonum* 'good.' Before

3620   we get off this merry-go-round, we might as well mention the adverbial form of *duenos*, that is, *duene*, which became classical Latin *bene* 'well.' So we have the related Latin words *bellus* 'pretty,' *bonus* 'good,' and *bene* 'well,' all represented by many English borrowings. For example, BONUS (literally) 'good' (mascu-

3625   line); 'a gift given in addition to the usual remuneration; an extra dividend.' *The Oxford English Dictionary* offers the opinion that this usage, which dates back to the late 18th century, was originally Stock Exchange slang and represents an uneducated use of the Latin word *bonus* 'good,' to mean *bonum* 'a good

3630   thing.' More examples are BONNY (Scottish) 'handsome, pretty, pleasing to the eye'; (Scottish) 'fine; healthy, robust' [of uncertain origin, but perhaps from Old French *bon* 'good,' from Latin *bonus*] and DEBONAIR (literally) 'of good stock'; 'urbane and carefree; of a gentle, gracious disposition' [from Old French *debonair*, from the phrase *de bon(ne) aire*, where the *aire* is derived from Latin *ager* 'field; place,' in the sense of 'place of origin']. The modern French *débonnaire* means 'good-natured, compliant.' Derived from the same root are BONNE (literally) 'good woman'; 'a French nursemaid' [from French *bonne* 'nursery-maid, lady's maid']; BONBON (literally) 'good-good'; 'a kind of candy' [a baby-talk reduplication from the French]; and BONHOMIE 'good nature; a pleasant disposition' [from French *bonhomie* 'good nature,' from *bonhomme* 'a good-natured man']. BONNE, BONBON and BONHOMIE all have a strong French flavor and might be considered foreign words by some. Also on the borderline of naturalization are the French phrases beginning with *bon* that are sprinkled throughout English writing and conversation. For example, BON mot 'a quip, a clever saying' [*mot* 'word']; BON vivant 'one who lives well and enjoys good food and drink' [*vivant* '(one who is) living']; and BON voyage 'Have a good trip.' Just as surely descended from the French but so thoroughly naturalized as to have lost its Frenchness is BOON 'jolly, convivial' (in the phrase, BOON companion); 'kind, generous' [from Middle English *bone* 'good,' from Medieval/Old French *bon* 'good']. (This is not the same word as *boon* 'request, favor,' as in "Grant me this boon," which comes from Old Norse.) (See line 4953.) Note, also, BOUNTY (obsolete) 'human goodness; kindness'; 'generosity, liberality; a premium paid out for specified acts, like joining the army or killing a wolf' [from Old French *bonte(t)*, from Latin *bonitātem* 'goodness,' from Latin *bonus* 'good'].

Latin *bonus, bona* evolved into Spanish *bueno, buena*, with the diminutive forms *bonito, bonita* (the Latin *-o-* changes to Spanish *-ue-* only when stressed). *Bonito, bonita* have their own meanings of 'pretty; neat,' and it is possible that *bonito* 'pretty' is the source of the name of the fish BONITO 'a game and food fish resembling tuna.' It is so called, according to some, because of its beautiful appearance; but others list the origin of this fish's name as unknown or uncertain, and the Spanish Academy maintains that it comes from the Arabic *bainīth.* On the other hand, Arabic *bainīth* looks, to *The Oxford English Dictionary*, like an adaptation of Spanish *bonito.*

Another Spanish word derived from Latin *bonus* 'good' is BONANZA (Spanish) 'fair weather; prosperity'; 'a rich vein of gold or silver ore; a stroke of good fortune' [from Vulgar Latin **bonacia*]. **Bonacia*, which is attested in Medieval Latin, was

3635

3640

3645

3650

3655

3660

3665

3670

3675

formed on the analogy of Latin *malacia* 'calmness at sea,' as though that word were based on Latin *malus* 'bad.' If a dead calm at sea is 'bad' (and it was in the days of sailing ships), then fair, breezy weather should be 'good' or *bon*(*us* + *mal*)*acia* or *bonacia*.

3680 Actually, *malacia* 'calmness at sea' comes from Greek *malakia* 'softness' and is (probably) related to Latin *mollis* 'soft' rather than *malus* 'bad.'

A Latin phrase that has been taken over into English where it serves as an adjective is BONA *fide* (literally) 'in good faith';

3685 'genuine.'

From the Latin adverb *bene* 'well' we have acquired English compounds whose meanings are explained elsewhere in this book (see Index), such as BENEDICTION, BENEFIT, BENEFACTOR, and BENEVOLENT, as well as BENIGN 'of a gentle disposition; promot-

3690 ing well-being; not malignant' [via Old French from Latin *benignus* 'kind, good-natured'; from **benigenus* 'well-born' (*genus* 'birth, origin')]. BENNET(T), a family name as well as a boy's given name, comes from Latin *benedictus* 'blessed,' as does BENNET 'a kind of herb' [via Middle English (*herb*) *beneit* and Old French

3695 (*herbe*) *beneite, benoite,* from Medieval Latin (*herba*) *benedicta* 'blessed herb'].

A variety of words come to us from Latin *bellus, bella, bellum.* For example, BELLADONNA 'a poisonous Eurasian plant; deadly nightshade; a drug derived from the roots and leaves of

3700 this plant' [from the Italian *bella donna* 'fair lady']. BELLADONNA is "said to be so named because in Italy a face cosmetic was made from it" (*ODEE*). But E. Hamilton in *Flore Homoecop* (1851) states that the drug is called BELLADONNA "because it was employed by Leucote, a famous poisoner of Italy, to destroy the

3705 beautiful women" (*OED*). Drops of belladonna, which enlarge the pupil, are used in eye examinations, and another theory holds that Italian ladies used to place a drop of belladonna in each eye to make them resemble deep, limpid pools (as a result of the enlarged pupils). Also, BELDAM(E) (obsolete) 'grandmother'; 'an

3710 old woman, especially an ugly one' [from Middle English *beldam* 'grandmother' (*bel-* 'grand-' + *dam* 'mother'); from Old French *bel*(*le*) 'beautiful,' used as a respectful prefix + *dame* 'lady']. In modern French, *belle-dame* is the name given to the plant goosefoot. However, the prefixes *beau-* and *belle-* are regularly

3715 used to indicate the relationships of '-in-law' and 'step-.' Thus a *belle-mère* (literally) 'beautiful mother' is either a mother-in-law or a stepmother.

Other English borrowings of French *beau, bel, belle* 'beauti-ful, handsome, fine' are BEAU 'a dandy' (BEAU Brummel); 'a girl's

3720 sweetheart'; BEAU geste 'a gracious gesture'; BEAU monde 'fash-

ionable society' [*monde* 'world']; BEAU ideal 'perfect beauty' [BEAU is here a noun]; BEAUX arts 'fine arts,' and possibly HOBO 'a migratory worker; a vagrant' [? from the salutation, "Ho, beau"]. "Ho! beau" is "known to have been a tramps' formula of address in the 1880s and 1890s," according to Eric Partridge; surely a   3725
sarcastic formula! Other writers mention this suggestion without endorsing it, while many authorities list HOBO as of unknown origin. Additional English borrowings include BELLE 'a beautiful girl; the most attractive woman at a given occasion or place' (the BELLE of the ball); BELLES lettres 'fine letters; literature of   3730
esthetic value'; BEAUTY 'physical loveliness' [from Old French *beaute, bealte,* from Vulgar Latin **bellitātem,* from *bellus* 'pretty']; EMBELLISH 'to make beautiful, to adorn' [from Old French *embel(l)ir, embelliss(ant)*]; and BELLEVUE, BELVEDERE, and BELLA VISTA, all meaning 'beautiful view.'   3735

Not so obvious is BIBELOT 'a trinket, a small decorative object' [from Old French *beubelot,* diminutive of *belbel* 'pretty-pretty']. Also derived from Old French *belbel* 'pretty-pretty,' according to some, is BAUBLE 'a trinket; a jester's baton, topped by a grotesquely carved head with ass's ears, carried as a mock   3740
scepter,' but others list BAUBLE as from Old French *baubel* [of unknown origin]. *The Oxford English Dictionary* states that BAUBLE is a blend of Old French *baubel* [of uncertain etymology but possibly from the same root as *babble* and *baby*] and a Middle English word, *babyll* 'to waver, to oscillate.'   3745

There is a possibility that the Latin verb, *beāre, beātus* 'to bless, to make happy' is another cousin to be added to the trio of *bonus, bene,* and *bellus.* This would make relatives of the English words BEATITUDE 'blessedness, supreme happiness'; (capitalized) 'one of the declarations made by Jesus at the Sermon on the   3750
Mount' ("Blessed are they who . . .") [from Latin *beātitūdo* 'happiness']; BEATIFY 'to make supremely happy'; (Roman Catholicism) 'to declare officially that the soul of a dead person is enjoying heavenly bliss' [from Late Latin *beātificāre* 'to make happy'] and the names BEATRICE, BEATRIX 'she who makes   3755
happy' (feminine of **beator*).

If one remembers that Latin *bonus, bene, bellus* evolved from archaic Latin words beginning with *du-*, it will not come as a surprise that the Indo-European root they derive from is **deu-*. However, the meanings ascribed to this root may come as a   3760
surprise: 'to honor, to revere'; (earlier) 'to do honor, to do reverence'; (and most primitively) 'to do, to perform.' Thus, semantically: Indo-European **dwenos* > Archaic Latin *duenos* > Latin *bonus* 'working, useful' > 'good'; **dwene > duene > bene*

3765   'performing efficiently' > 'well'; *dwenelos > duenelos > bellus
'performing well' > 'neat, trim, pretty.'
   The Greek derivatives of Indo-European *deu- 'to do honor;
to perform' have meanings of 'performing' rather than of 'honoring.' The Greek stem is dun-, evidenced by the verb dunasthai 'to
3770   be able, to have the strength to.' Greek dun- is transliterated into
the Latin alphabet as dyn- and is seen in English DYNE 'the force
necessary to impart an acceleration of one centimeter per second
per second to a mass of one gram' [via French from Greek
dunamis 'power,' from dunasthai 'to be able']; DYNAMIC 'pertain-
3775   ing to energy; vigorous, powerful' [from French dynamique, from
Greek dunamikos, from dunamis 'power']; DYNAMO 'a generator; a
forceful person' [from German Dynamoelektrischemaschine]; and
DYNAMITE 'a powerful explosive made from nitroglycerin.' The
last name was coined by Alfred Nobel, the inventor of dynamite.
3780   And, rounding off the list, is DYNASTY 'a succession of rulers of
the same family' [via French dynastie or Late Latin dynastia from
Greek dunasteia 'power, sovereignty'; from dunastēs 'sovereign,
ruler,' from dunasthai 'to be able'].

XIX

East of Austria

Daylight dawns in the EAST. Another kind of dawn, that of a new growing season, begins around EASTER. The name of the Germanic goddess of spring, originally a dawn goddess, is *Austrōn*, a name that evolved in Old English into *Eastre* or *Eostre*. In Homeric Greek, the word for 'dawn' is *ēōs*; in Attic Greek, *heōs*; in Aeolic Greek, *auōs*; in primitive Latin, it is *ausōsa*; and in Latin, *aurōra*. (Primitive Latin -*s*-, when it occurs between two vowels, becomes Latin -*r*-. Compare *flos, floris, flora*; *genus, generis, genera*.)   3785   3790

The similarities between these words for 'dawn' and 'spring' are not coincidental. They bear witness that the words all spring from the same source, which is the Indo-European root *awes-*, variant *aus-* 'to shine.' Furthermore, the words all have to do with the sun, its rising in the east, its approach to full vigor in the springtime, and, for the Indo-European speakers, its location in the southern skies.   3795

In modern German, the word for EAST is *Ost*. EASTER is *Ostern*, and the country we know as AUSTRIA is *Österreich* 'eastern realm.' The word AUSTRIA is a 10th-century Latinization of medieval German *ostaricchi*, and it introduces directional confusion, for *auster* in Latin means 'south,' while the Germanic *austro-* indicates 'east' (the Latin word for 'east' is *oriens* 'rising'). Some authorities list Latin *auster* 'the south wind, south' as of obscure origin, but others link *auster* to *aurōra* (< *ausōsa*) 'dawn' and, therefore, to the shining EAST and to *awes-* 'to shine.' It does seem a plausible derivation, since, for people living in the tropic of Cancer, the south side is the sunny side. (The more usual Latin word for south is *merīdiēs* 'midday,' which also evinces a solar orientation.)   3800   3805   3810

The Latin adjective *austrālis* 'of the south' gave rise to a phrase used by 16th-century explorers and cartographers to
3815   denote the islands of the south Pacific, to wit, *terra austrālis* 'southern land.' The phrase gave way to the geographical term AUSTRALIA, which, by the 19th century, was restricted to the island-continent of that name, formerly New Holland and New South Wales, rather than to all of AUSTRALASIA 'Oceania; Micro-
3820   nesia, Melanesia, Polynesia, Australia, New Zealand, and the Malay Archipelago.'

Other derivatives of Indo-European *awes-, *aus- 'to shine' are OSTROGOTH 'east Goth' [? 'shining, splendid Goth,' as opposed to *Visigoth* 'west Goth,' ? 'good, brave, noble Goth'];
3825   OSTMARK 'east mark, the monetary unit of East Germany'; AURORA 'flashing luminosity in the sky' [from Latin *aurōra* 'dawn']; AURORA borealis 'flashing luminosity in northern skies' [Latin *boreās*; Greek *boreas* 'the north wind, north']; AURORA AUSTRALIS 'night luminosity in southern hemisphere skies' [Latin
3830   *auster* 'the south wind, south']; EOCENE 'new dawn; the geologic era marked by the rise of the mammals' [Greek *ēōs* 'dawn' + *kainos* 'new, strange']; EOHIPPUS (literally) 'dawn horse'; 'a small extinct American mammal with four toes on the front feet and three on the hind feet; ancestor of the horse' [Greek *hippos*
3835   'horse']; and EOLITHIC (literally) 'of the dawn stones'; 'pertaining to the earliest Stone Age' [Greek *lithos* 'stone'].

XX

Elusive Illusions, Ludicrous Interludes

These are things to be wary of: "a mockery and an ILLUSION," and "a snare and a DELUSION." One is warned by the first cliché to avoid being misled and by the second to look out for traps, but there is no inkling that the words ILLUSION and DELUSION   3840
originally had to do with games and sports. Connotations of playfulness do still linger around the related words ELUDE and ALLUDE, though not so obvious as those that surround PRELUDE and INTERLUDE. The sportive aspect shows up grotesquely in the word LUDICROUS (obsolete) 'playful; witty, humorous'; 'ridicu-   3845
lous; giving rise to derisive laughter.'

The source of all these words is Latin *lūdus* 'play, game; pastime' and the allied verb *lūdere* 'to play, to sport; to play with; to baffle; to ridicule.' However, the source of Latin *lūdus* and *lūdere* is a matter of conjecture. One writer suggests a Celtic   3850
origin, citing Old Irish *lōid* 'a song, a poem' and an Old Celtic root *leut- or *lut- 'to be joyous,' as well as Greek *loidoros* 'abusive, insulting' (play, playful abuse, and abuse being not far apart). Others postulate an Indo-European root, *leid- 'to play, to jest,' with the caveat that the Latin words *lūdus, lūdere* may be of   3855
Etruscan, ergo non-Indo-European origin.

Whatever its source, Latin *lūdus* proved very serviceable to the Latin speakers. From 'game, play' it came to mean 'elementary school'; a transition that might puzzle some young school-goers. In another direction it came to mean 'public games,   3860
spectacles,' as in the Roman *lūdi publici*, which included athletic competitions, horse and chariot races, and theatrical presentations. Eventually, *lūdus* even meant 'gladiatorial school.' A *lūdia* was either 'a female stage dancer' or 'a gladiator's wife,' while a *ludicrum* was either 'a toy, or public games,' and as an adjective,   3865
ludicrus meant either 'playful' or 'of public games.' Early mean-

ings of English LUDICROUS, though now obsolete, included 'playful, witty, humorous.' In a similar way, the 'playful' connotations
of the following English compounds have largely disappeared:
3870   ALLUDE (obsolete) 'to make game of, to mock'; (obsolete) 'to make
a play on words'; 'to make an indirect reference to' [from Latin
allūdere 'to play with, to touch playfully; to approach by stealth'
(*al-* < *ad-* 'toward')]; ELUDE 'to avoid by adroitness; to baffle'
[from Latin *ēlūdere* 'to win at play; to parry; to avoid']; DELUDE
3875   'to mislead; to deceive the judgment of' [from Latin *dēlūdere* 'to
mock, to deceive']; COLLUDE 'to connive; to act together secretly';
and COLLUSION 'a secret agreement for a deceitful purpose' [from
Latin *collūdere* 'to sport with' (*col-* < *com-* 'with')]. Latin *collūdere* had also developed the meaning of 'to have a secret
3880   understanding with' and *collūsiō*, the sense of 'secret understanding.'
    A PRELUDE is 'something that is played beforehand; an
introductory performance' [from Latin *praelūdere* 'to play beforehand; to say as preface'], while an INTERLUDE was (originally) 'a
3885   dramatic representation of a light or farcical nature introduced
between the acts of medieval mystery plays'; (archaic) 'any
popular drama'; 'a short musical piece played between other
compositions; an intervening episode' [from Medieval Latin
interlūdium 'performance between acts'] or ' "a game between
3890   two periods of business, hence something light introduced to
relieve heaviness" ' (*EP*).
    We are left with the seldom encountered PROLUSION 'a
preliminary exercise; a trial performance; an introductory essay'
and the ubiquitous ILLUSION (obsolete) 'derision, mockery'; 'an
3895   erroneous perception of reality; something that deceives by creating a false impression' [via Old French from Latin *illusiō(nem)*
'mockery'; from *illūdere* 'to sport with; to jeer at' (*il-* < *in-* 'into,
against')].

XXI

Elves, Alps, *and* Albinos

Sir Laurence OLIVIER and ALFRED Lunt have more than one thing in common: besides being widely acclaimed actors they are both descended from ELVES—or, rather, the names ALFRED and OLIVIER are both thought, by some linguists, to contain the equivalent of the Old English word *ælf* 'elf.' This possibility is fairly easy to see in ALFRED [from Old English *Ælfræd* 'elf council']. (The *-ræd* is a cognate of German *Rat* 'counsel; council,' as in *Bundesrat* 'Federal Council.') The possible ELFISH ancestry of OLIVIER is not so evident, since the common French noun, *olivier*, means simply 'an olive tree.' However, the personal name OLIVIER is an Old French alteration, no doubt influenced by the tree's name, of a Germanic personal name corresponding to Old English *Ælfhere* 'elf army' (compare German *Heer* 'army'). The name OLIVIER was adapted into Middle English as OLIVER, which means, therefore, 'elf army.'

In early Germanic myth, ELVES were 'supernatural beings supposed to possess formidable magical powers.' The superstitious people of the Dark Ages believed in them implicitly and were properly terrified of them, since these tiny creatures could cause great harm if angered and do great good if pleased. Mothers hoped, by giving a child a name such as *Ælfræd* or *Ælfhere* to enlist the elfin band on the infant's side.

The word *ælf* comes from Germanic **albaz*, meaning, possibly, 'a white, ghostlike apparition.' A cognate is German *Alp* 'elf, bad spirit; nightmare,' a Middle High German form of which was *alb*. The German speakers devised another personal name based on this form of the word, to wit, *Alberich* 'ruler of elves.' (Old High German *rich* 'ruler' is a cognate of Latin *rex* 'king.') German *Alberich* was adapted by Medieval French as *Auberi*, and has come into English as AUBREY. The name *Alberich* 'ruler of elves'

3900

3905

3910

3915

3920

3925

also had an influence, through the Frankish tongue, on Old
3930 French *Auberon*, source of English OBERON 'king of the fairies.'
Oberon appears as a character in Shakespeare's *A Midsummer
Night's Dream.*

The kingdom over which Alberich > Oberon ruled could
have been called in Old English **ælfrīce* 'elf-kingdom, fairyland'
3935 [*rīce* 'realm'], if the Old English speakers had thought up that
word. Perhaps they did. It is not attested, but some etymologists
think that the Scottish word ELDRITCH 'weird, unearthly, eerie'
may be an alteration of Old English **ælfrīce* by way of Scottish
elphrish, although this theory does not satisfy all investigators.
3940 Another, less appealing, elfin king is the ERLKING 'an evil
spirit of Germanic mythology and folklore,' typically represented
as a perpetrator of cruel tricks on children [from German
Erlkönig]. *Erlkönig*, if taken at face value, means 'king of alder
(trees)'; but it is a mistranslation of Danish *ellerkonge, elverkonge*
3945 'king of the elves.'

Besides causing nightmares, the elves were held responsible
for inflicting various diseases on mankind and his chattels. They
were also believed to steal children, substituting changelings.
Therefore, a changeling was called an OAF 'an elf's child, a goblin
3950 child; a misbegotten, deformed, or idiot child; a half-wit, dolt,
fool; a stupid or clumsy person' [from Old Norse *aelfr* 'elf']. In
early English, OAF was spelled variously *ouph, aufe, aulfe*, and
some believe that it is simply a variant of Old English *ælf*
without any Old Norse intervention.
3955 As already mentioned, Germanic **albaz* may mean 'a white,
ghostlike apparition.' In Old High German, *albiz* means 'swan,' a
white bird. Through this glimmering notion of 'whiteness' may be
detected a possible relationship with the Latin word *albus*
'white.' *Albus* is the ultimate source of several English borrow-
3960 ings, the simplest of which is ALB 'a long white garment worn by
a priest when he celebrates Mass' [from Middle English *albe,
aube*; from Old English *albe*, adapted from the Medieval Latin
phrase *vestis alba* 'garment of white']. The alb is worn underneath the chasuble and over the cassock. This white garment is a
3965 vestige of the early days of the Church, when all good Christians,
according to Edward Gibbon, wore nothing but white, since "gay
apparel ... (was) supposed to unite the double guilt of pride and
sensuality." Gibbon continues: "In their censure of luxury the
fathers (condemned) false hair, garments of any colour except
3970 white, instruments of music, vases of gold or silver, downy
pillows (as Jacob reposed his head on a stone), white bread,
foreign wines, public salutations, the use of warm baths, and the
practice of shaving the beard, (which constituted) a lie against our

own faces, and an impious attempt to improve the works of the creator."   3975

In Latin, an *album* is a 'blank, white tablet,' from the neuter of *albus* 'white.' Today, a newly purchased photograph ALBUM 'a bound volume of blank pages; a miscellaneous collection of musical compositions in one binding; a set of phonograph records' often has black pages, but they are blank (and the word blank   3980 comes from Old French *blanc* 'white').

Other borrowings from Latin *albus* 'white' include ALBUMEN 'the white of an egg' [from Latin *albūmen* 'the white of an egg'] and ALBINO 'an organism lacking normal pigmentation, such as an animal with white fur and pink eyes' [from the Portuguese *albino*   3985 'whitish,' from *albo* 'white']. On the other hand, a person with AUBURN hair has hair of reddish-brown, even though the word itself comes, via Old French, from Medieval Latin *alburnus* 'whitish.' Note also that in Middle English, *alborne, aborne* meant 'blond, fair-haired.' The explanation of this anomaly is that   3990 in the 16th and 17th centuries, the English word·was sometimes spelled *abron, abrune, abroun,* and these spellings "probably originated, or at least encouraged, the idea that *auburn* was a kind of brown, and so helped to modify the signification of the word" (*OED*).   3995

Having mentioned Medieval Latin *alburnus* as the source of AUBURN, we should note the botanical term ALBURNUM 'sapwood; newly formed outer wood of a tree, usually lighter in color than the heartwood.' While we're on the subject of trees, consider the ABELE 'white poplar' [from Dutch *abeel,* from Old French *abel,*   4000 *aubel*; from Medieval/Late Latin *albellus* (literally) 'little white,' diminutive of Latin *albus* 'white'].

A French word for 'dawn' is *aube* (which also means ALB) [from the Vulgar Latin **alba* 'dawn,' from the feminine of *albus* 'white']. The use of *alba* to mean 'dawn' is "probably elliptical for   4005 (the phrase) *alba lux* 'the pale white light of dawn'" (*EP*). The Spanish word for 'dawn' is also *alba,* as is an Old Provençal word. From either Spanish *albada* or Provençal **aubada* 'an occurrence at dawn,' French speakers derived (or constructed) the word AUBADE 'a morning serenade; a musical composition intended to   4010 be played or sung at dawn.' AUBADE is considered to be a naturalized English word: "The crowing cock .../Sang his aubade with lusty voice and clear" (Longfellow).

We come to two words about whose origins there is some disagreement. One is DAUB 'to smear with an adhesive substance,   4015 such as plaster; to apply paint with crude, hasty strokes.' Most etymologists derive DAUB from Latin *dēalbāre* 'to whitewash, to plaster' [*dē-* 'completely'+ *albāre* 'to whiten'], by way of Old

French *dauber* 'to plaster.' However, a few suggest that DAUB
4020   comes from Old French *adouber* 'to mend, to repair,' influenced
by Spanish *adobar* 'to plaster.' They refer to Spanish ADOBE 'a
sun-dried, unburned brick of clay and straw,' supposedly a derivative of *adobar*, from Medieval Latin *adobāre* 'to adorn.' This
raises further complications, because many etymologists derive
4025   Spanish *adobe* and *adobar* from the Arabic *aṭṭōb(a)* < *al-ṭōba* 'the
brick,' of Egyptian or Coptic origin. (Note that the French verb
adouber 'to mend, to repair' is the same one used in chess circles
to mean 'to adjust a piece.')

One turns with a sigh to ALBION 'the ancient name for Great
4030   Britain.' It is more or less agreed that this name is Celtic in origin,
based on the Celtic element **alb-*, to which some give the
meaning 'high,' and others the meaning 'white.' If the latter be
true, then there may be something to the theory that Great Britain
was called ALBION because the first landfall one sees when
4035   crossing the Channel from France is the celebrated white cliff
formation near Dover. A small spanner is thrown into this theory
by the discovery that the Irish-Gaelic name for Scotland is *Alba*,
that the name *Albion* has often been limited to Scotland, and that
the Medieval Latin word *Albanus* meant 'Scottish.' The puzzle
4040   may be resolved when we consider the word ALP 'a high mountain,' which in English is a back-formation from *Alps*, the name of
the mountain chain in south central Europe. The name of the
Alps (Latin *Alpēs*, Greek *Alpeis*) is also most likely Celtic in
origin. Compare Gaelic *alp* 'a high mountain' and Irish *ailp*, *alpa*
4045   'a protuberance, a high mountain.' There may be a possible
connection with Celtic **alb-* 'white,' in that high mountains tend
to be snow-covered and therefore white. (The cliffs of Dover are
white because they are made of chalk.)

The Indo-European for all the above words is **albho-* 'white.'
4050   Two final words that may well be cognates are Greek *alphos* 'dull
white leprosy' and Hittite *alpas* 'cloud.'

XXII

Ethereal Edifices

What, if anything, is so EDIFYING about an EDIFICE? One definition of EDIFICE is 'a building; especially a large or massive structure.' The verb to EDIFY means ' "to instruct and improve; especially in moral and religious matters" ' (*MW2*). This is an instance of the figurative sense of a word almost blotting out the literal sense, for the original sense of to EDIFY was 'to build, to construct of the usual building materials'; but its later, quasi-religious sense of 'to build up character and spirituality' is now by far the more usual meaning.

Etymologically, the suffixes *-fy* and *-fice* indicate the 'making' of something. They derive from the French *-fier*, from the Latin *-ficāre*, *-ficere*, the combining form of *facere* 'to make.' In the word EDIFY, that "something" is obviously an *edi-*. *Edi-* comes from the Latin *aedēs*, *aedis* 'a temple, a sanctuary; a room'; (earlier) 'a dwelling, a house'; (originally) 'a hearth.' The original edifice was a fireplace, perhaps even something like a barbecue pit, since the Latin words *aedēs* and *aedificāre* 'to build houses' stem from the Indo-European root **aidh-* 'to burn.' It gives one a homey feeling to learn that an early word for 'a dwelling place' presumed the warmth of a hearth.

However, by Classical Latin times the meanings of these words had progressed far beyond the primitive sense of fire and heat, for a Roman *aedīlis* or AEDILE was 'a government official in charge of public buildings, public works, and the grain supply.' An AEDILE also furnished the populace with public games, such as chariot races and gladiatorial contests—at his own expense! Thus the office was an influential but costly political post. It was once occupied by Julius Caesar on his way to political supremacy. He borrowed most of the money for his public games from

4055

4060

4065

4070

4075

4080

Crassus, and went into debt, by his own account, for almost one hundred million sesterces, about $5,000,000.

The Indo-European root *aidh- 'to burn' is also evidenced by the Greek verb aithein 'to kindle; to burn brightly' and by the
4085 related noun aithēr 'the upper air, the clear sky, where the sun shines so brightly.' The ancients had a notion that the atmosphere becomes hotter the higher one rises, despite the evidence of the snow-capped mountains. (Witness the myth of Icarus, whose wax-coated wings melted when he flew too close to the sun.) Greek
4090 aithēr leads to Latin aether and English ETHER (originally) 'the heavens, the clear sky beyond the clouds.' The word ETHER has acquired additional philosophical and scientific meanings. A 1798 definition in the Dictionary of the Arts and Sciences reads: "Æther, an imaginary fluid supposed by several authors, both
4095 ancient and modern, to be the cause of gravity, heat, light, muscular motion, and, in a word, every phenomenon of nature. Perrault represents it as 7200 times more rare than air; and Hook makes it more dense than gold itself."

The word ETHER has a more specific and down-to-earth
4100 chemical meaning of '$C_4H_{10}O$, a volatile liquid used as a solvent and anesthetic.' ETHER is also the source of the first syllable of ETHYL 'a univalent organic radical, C_2H_5' [-yl, indicating a radical, from Greek hulē 'matter, stuff']. These seem crassly materialistic meanings when contrasted with the sense of the derivative
4105 adjective ETHEREAL 'delicate, dainty, exquisite; highly refined.' However, ethyl gasoline is highly refined but also highly danger-ous if allowed to come into contact with the skin; so parlous are the refinements of modern technology.

Another Latin word descended from our Indo-European root
4110 *aidh- 'to burn' [by way of the "suffixed form *aidh-sto-" (AHD)] is aestās, aestātem [<*aestotātem] 'summer, summer heat, sum-mer weather.' Latin aestātem evolved into modern French été 'summer,' but the English borrowings, which are few and rarely used, come directly from the Latin. They include ESTIVATE (or
4115 AESTIVATE) 'to spend the summer' [from Latin aestivāre 'to pass the summer']. Some people escape the cities' summer heat by estivating in a mountain retreat or at the seashore; and certain mollusks aestivate, or fall into a summer sleep, when the heat is great (compare hibernate). Also, ESTIVAL (or AESTIVAL) 'belong-
4120 ing to summer' (the ESTIVAL solstice) [from Latin aestīvus].

Not really having to do with heat, but rather with certain boiling, bubbling phenomena that resemble the results of heat applied to water, is ESTUARY 'the lower end of a river where the current meets and mingles with the ocean tides' [from Latin *aestuārium* 'inlet of the sea'; from *aestus* 'tide, surge, seething; 4125 summer heat, fire'].

A Germanic descendant of Indo-European **aidh-* 'to burn,' by way of the same **aidh-sto-* that begat Latin *aestas* 'summer,' is English OAST 'a kiln for drying hops, malt, or tobacco' [from Old English *āst*, from Germanic **aistaz*]. 4130

Finally, from the suffixed form **aidh-lo-*, perhaps, comes Germanic **ail-* and Old English *āl* 'fire,' evidenced in English ANNEAL (originally) 'to set on fire'; 'to temper by heating and gradually cooling' [from Old English *onǣlan*; from *on* + *ǣlan* 'to set fire to'; from Old English *āl* 'fire'; related to Old English *ǣld* 4135 'fire' and *ād* 'funeral pyre'].

XXIII

Facts, Fetishes;
Anathema, Doom

Primitive people have a FACULTY for FASHIONING FETISHES, while the less primitive make a FETISH of FASHION—and that's a FACT. We have here a string of words derived ultimately from the
4140   Latin verb *facere* 'to make, to do.' *Facere* is one of the most prolific of Latin words in terms of its English progeny, which includes all words ending in *-fect*, *-ficient*, *-feit* and *-fy*. What's more, Latin *facere* is cousin to the ubiquitous English verb, to DO, as well as to English DOOM, DEEM, and DEED. These are all
4145   descended from the Indo-European root **dhē-* 'to set, to put.' (Indo-European **dh-*, when used as the initial sound, regularly changes to Latin *f-*, to English *d-*, and to Greek *th-*.)
The past participle of Latin *facere*, *factus*, *factum* 'made, done; what has been done' is the source of a long list of English
4150   words. We start with FACT 'something that has been done; something that is demonstrably true'; FACTOR 'an agent; something that contributes to a result'; (literally) 'a maker, a doer' [from Old French *facteur*; from Latin *factor* 'an oil-presser; a maker, a doer']; FACTORY 'a trading station where agents (factors) transact
4155   business; a MANUFACTORY; a place where goods are manufactured'; and MANUFACTURE 'to fabricate; to make goods by processing raw materials'; (literally) 'to make by hand' [from Medieval/Old French *manufacture*, from Late Latin *manufactus* 'made by hand' (*manus* 'hand')]. FACTORY comes ultimately from
4160   Late Latin *factōrium* 'oil-press,' which is based on the principal meaning of Latin *factor* 'oil-presser.' The prevalence of this meaning of *factor* is an indication of the importance of vegetable oils (especially olive oil) in ancient times.
Two compounds of *factor* 'doer' used in modern English are
4165   BENEFACTOR 'one who gives financial aid'; (literally) 'one who does good' and MALEFACTOR 'an evil-doer; a criminal.' MALEFAC-

TOR comes to English straight from the Latin, but BENEFACTOR is a Late Latin development, based on Latin *benefactiō*, from *benefactus*, past participle of *beneficere* (*bene facere*) 'to do good (to).' Note, also, FACTION 'a contentious clique'; (literally) 'a making; a manner of doing.' The Latin word *factiō, factiōnem* 'a making, a doing' acquired early in Roman history the more generally used meaning of 'party, sect.' The word was applied in a specialized sense to the teams of charioteers who competed in the public games (*lūdi publici*, see line 3861), and who were distinguished from one another by the color of their costumes. These sports *factiōnes* vied for the favor of the populace, and some of the plebs opted for one *factiōnem*, some for another. Subsequently the word was transferred from the teams to their supporters. The fighting among the Blues and Greens led to such widespread rioting during the reign of Justinian that it became a major civic problem. This contentiousness underlies the meaning of English FACTION and is mirrored in the adjective FACTIOUS 'divisive; giving rise to dissension' [from Latin *factiōsus* 'partisan'].

In addition to *faction*, Old French had another version of Latin *factiōnem*, which was *facon, fazon* (Old Northern French *fachon*). *Facon* became Medieval and Modern French *façon*, and was adapted into Middle English as *facioun, fasoun*, whence modern English FASHION 'a way of making something; style, mode, custom; to form in a certain way.' FASHIONING 'forming in a certain way' is implied in the adjective FACTITIOUS 'artificially produced; lacking genuineness' [from Latin *factīcius, factītius* 'made by art']. Latin *factīcius, factītius* 'made by art' became Portuguese *feitiço*, a word used by the Portuguese explorers of Africa as a noun meaning 'a charm; sorcery; something that works by magical art.' Portuguese *feitiço* was adapted into French as *fétiche*, whence English FETISH 'an inanimate object supposed to possess some magical power.' A FETISH may be something natural, such as an animal's foot, or something artificial, such as a carved figure. By extension, anything that is the object of irrational devotion, from a child's teddy bear to a theological tenet, may be called a FETISH.

Speaking of things ARTIFICIAL brings us to ARTIFACT, ARTEFACT 'an object made by human workmanship' [from Latin *arte* 'by art' + *factum* 'made']. The English word doesn't appear until 1821. It was perhaps coined with Italian *artefatto* 'artificial' in mind. Much older is ARTIFICE 'an artful contrivance; skill, ingenuity; trickery' [from Latin *artificium* 'skill; a work of art; a trick'; from *artifex* 'one who makes by art; artist']. The taint of deceptiveness and spuriousness lingers in the English word ARTIFICIAL

4170

4175

4180

4185

4190

4195

4200

4205

4210

'man-made; not natural; pretended; stilted,' even though man is now surrounded by, if not drowned in, the products of his artifice. The vowel change in compounds of Latin *facere* to *-ficere* has already been seen in *beneficere* and *artificium*. Other *-fic-* derivatives adapted into English are BENEFICIAL 'having a good effect'; BENEFICENT 'doing good'; MALEFICENT 'doing evil'; BENEFIC 'beneficent'; and BENEFICE 'a fief; a landed estate granted in feudal tenure' (the lord is "doing good" to the vassal); 'an ecclesiastical living; a church office endowed with fixed assets, and the revenues therefrom.' A similar sound change that took place later is seen in BENEFIT 'anything that promotes well-being' [from Norman French *benfet*, from Latin *benefactum* 'a good deed'].

Compounded from *dē-* 'of, off, away from' + *facere* are DEFICIENT (etymologically) 'making off; doing away'; 'lacking' [from Latin *dēficiens*, present participle of *dēficere*, *dēfectus* 'to fall off, to be wanting; to abandon'] and DEFICIT 'a shortage'; (literally) 'it is lacking' [via French *déficit* from Latin *deficit*, third person singular of *dēficere*]. Note that in *dēficere*, the past participle becomes *dēfectus* (not **dēfactus*). The vowel change from *-a-* to *-e-* holds true for most compounds in *-ficere*. In the case of *dēfectus*, it leads to English DEFECT 'the lack of something; an imperfection; to desert; to go over to the enemy'; (literally) 'abandoned, deserted.'

The *-c-* of the Latin past participle *factus* 'done, made' and that of the noun *factum* 'deed, event' disappear in Old French, and we get *fait, fet*. These are adapted into English as FEAT 'an outstanding deed; an achievement.' Of similar derivation are FEATURE 'the make-up or appearance of something' [from Medieval/Old French *faiture*, from Latin *factūra* 'a making, a formation']; FEASANCE (legal) 'the performance of an obligation'; MALFEASANCE 'the doing by a public officer of something that is legally unjustified' [from *mal-* 'bad' + Medieval/Old French *faisance* 'doing,' from *faire* 'to do,' from Latin *facere*]; and FEASIBLE 'doable' [from Medieval/Old French *faisible*].

Old French *fait* 'done' is seen in the Old French compound *desfait* 'undone,' past participle of *desfaire*, from Medieval Latin *disfacere* 'to undo, to destroy.' *Desfait* appears in English as DEFEAT 'to undo, to vanquish; to thwart; loss of a contest.' The Latin past participle *factus, -fectus* > Old French *fait, fet* sometimes turns up as *-feit*, seen in English COUNTERFEIT 'to make a fraudulent imitation of; to feign' (*contra* 'opposite, over against'); (literally) 'made in contrast to'; and SURFEIT 'to overdo, to make in excess; to satiate' [from Old French *surfeit*, from Vulgar Latin **superfactum*, from **superficere* 'to overdo' (*sur-* < *super*)]. (How-

ever, SUPERFICIAL has a different origin. See line 4423.) In this set
is FORFEIT 'to lose the right to by error or neglect'; (literally) 'to
do outside (the limits of respectability)'; (obsolete) 'to be guilty of
a misdeed' [from Old French *forfet*, from *for(s)faire*, from Medi-   4260
eval Latin *forisfacere* 'to commit a crime' (*forīs* 'outside,
beyond')]. Latin *afficere*, *affectus* 'to do something to' is a compound of *ad* 'to, toward' and *facere* 'to do,' yielding English
AFFECT 'to have an influence on; to produce an EFFECT upon; to
touch the emotions of'; AFFECTION 'the act of influencing; the   4265
state of being influenced; a feeling of fondness'; and AFFETTUOSO
(music) 'with warmth and feeling' (Italian). Also from *afficere*,
affectus, but by way of Latin *affectāre* 'to aim at, to strive after,' is
another English verb, to AFFECT 'to feign, to put on a pretense of,'
as well as the related noun AFFECTATION 'artificial behavior   4270
adopted to impress others.' Centuries later a compound similar to
Latin *afficere*, *affectus* was formed in Old French, to wit, *afaire*,
which means simply 'to do,' rather than 'to do to.' Old French
afaire was borrowed into Middle English as *afere*, whence
English AFFAIR 'what has to be done; anything that is done'   4275
(world AFFAIRS, a love AFFAIR); 'any object or contrivance' (a
ramshackle AFFAIR).

Another Latin compound *conficere*, *confectus* 'to put
together, to make ready' gives us English CONFECT 'to prepare by
combining ingredients'; CONFECTION 'the act of compounding;   4280
putting together; a sweet preparation, such as candy or preserves';
CONFETTI (Italian) 'candies, bonbons'; ' "small sweets used as
missiles at a carnival" ' (*ODEE*); 'small discs of paper thrown at
celebrations'; CONFITURE 'jam, preserves'; COMFIT 'candies, preserves'; and DISCOMFIT 'to defeat utterly; to make uneasy'; (liter-   4285
ally) 'to take apart': "to un-put-together" [via Old French
desconfire, *desconfit*, from Vulgar Latin **disconfecere*, **disconfectus*]. (The stronger meaning, 'to defeat utterly,' is the older.)

From the Latin compound *efficere*, *effectus* 'to make out; to
produce, to bring about, effect' come English EFFECT,   4290
EFFECTIVE, EFFECTUAL, EFFICIENT, EFFICACIOUS, and (originally
Scottish and North of England dialectal) FECKLESS 'effectless;
ineffective; dispirited; irresponsible.' More Latin compounds
include *inficere*, *infectus* 'to put in; to steep, to stain, to poison'
yielding English INFECT, INFECTIOUS, and DISINFECTANT; *per-*   4295
ficere, *perfectus* 'to make thoroughly, to complete' giving English
PERFECT 'complete; flawless' and PARFAIT 'a frozen dessert made
of cream, eggs, sugar and flavoring'; (literally) 'perfect' [from
French *parfait* 'perfect' from Latin *perfectus*]; and *praeficere*,
praefectus 'to put in front; to appoint to a command' from which   4300
English PREFECT 'an overseer; a high administrative official' is

derived. Still more compounds of Latin *facere*, *-ficere* are *prōficere*, *prōfectus* 'to make forward; to advance, to make progress' which give us English PROFICIENT 'skilled, facile'; (obso-
4305   lete) 'advancing toward perfection' and PROFIT 'to be of benefit; to make a gain; a gain'; (obsolete) 'to make progress'; *reficere*, *refectum* 'to remake, to restore, to refresh, to revive' which yield English REFECTION 'refreshment with food and drink'; REFECTORY 'a room where meals are served' [from Late Latin
4310   *refectōrium* 'dining room']; and *sufficere* 'to put under; to substitute; to be adequate' from which English SUFFICE and SUFFICIENT are derived.

Less obvious compounds are OFFICE 'a place where work is done; a public position'; (literally) 'a doing of work' [via French
4315   from Latin *officium* 'performance of duty'; from *opus* 'work' + *facere* 'to do' (see line 7735)] and PROLIFIC 'producing in abundance'; (literally) 'making offspring' [Latin *prōlēs* 'offspring' + *-fic*]. From the Latin imperative *fac!* 'Do!, Make!' come FACSIMILE 'Make it similar!; an exact copy, a reproduction' and FACTO-
4320   TUM 'Do everything!; a servant who takes care of everything for his employer.' FACTOTUM traces back to Medieval Latin phrases like *dominus factotum* 'Lord Do-it-all, an absolute ruler,' and *Johannes factotum* 'John Do-everything, a Jack-of-all-trades.'

Two other words based on Latin *facere* that have reached
4325   English by way of Spanish and Portuguese are HACIENDA 'a farming, ranching, mining or manufacturing establishment in the country; a plantation with a dwelling on it'; (literally) 'things to be done' [from Spanish *hacienda* 'domestic employment > employment > place of employment > estate'; from Latin *facienda*
4330   'things to be done'] and FAZENDA 'a Brazilian hacienda; especially, a coffee plantation.'

From the verb *fac(ere)* 'to do' Latin formed an adjective *facilis* 'doable; easy.' In Old Latin the corresponding adverb was *facul*, later replaced by *facile*. Latin *facilis*, *facile* give rise, via
4335   Old French, to English FACILE 'easy; done with little effort' and FACILITY 'ease; aptitude; something that is provided as a convenience.' But Old Latin *facul* 'easily' also begat Latin *facultās* 'ability, power' and Medieval Latin *facultās* 'a branch of learning,' whence English FACULTY 'ability, capacity; an inherent
4340   power; the teaching staff and administration of a school'; (obsolete) 'art, trade, occupation, profession.' On the other side of the coin is the word DIFFICULTY 'something not easily done' [from Latin *difficultās*, from *difficilis*, earlier *difficul* (*dif-* < *dis-* 'not')].

We encountered the element *-fex* 'maker' in the Latin word
4345   *artifex* 'maker by art; artificer, artist, craftsman.' This same *-fex* appears in Latin *pontifex* 'a member of the highest college of

priests.' Etymologically, *pontifex* means 'bridgemaker, bridge-builder' (Latin *pons, pontis* 'bridge'), and there has been much speculation as to why the Roman priests were so named. One hypothesis is that because Rome was a city of bridges (across the Tiber), control of those bridges gave them their start to power. Another is that the bridges in question are figurative, "sky-bridges to the gods"; a third that 'bridgemaker' is a poetic way of saying 'waymaker' = 'pathfinder'; and a fourth hypothesis is that the *ponti-* element is an assimilation of an Oscan-Umbrian word, *puntis,* meaning 'propitiatory offerings.' This last explanation would yield *pontifex* 'maker of propitiatory offerings,' a fairly accurate definition of a priest. Still another theory is that *pontifex* is "probably from Etruscan, reshaped by folk etymology to mean 'bridge-maker' " (*AHD*). *Pontifex* is the source of English PONTIFF 'a bishop; the Pope' and PONTIFICATE 'to administer the office of bishop; to behave with pompous authority.'

Of the English words based on Latin *facere* 'to make, to do,' there remain to be mentioned those ending in *-fy,* a suffix that has reached English by way of French *-fier,* from Latin *-ficāre,* from *-ficere.* The suffix *-fy* has been useful to English—some think overly useful—in that it has been borrowed to coin many hybrid words by combining it with non-Latin elements, as in PRETTIFY 'to make pretty' and UGLIFY 'to make ugly.' Most of the *-fy* words are self-explanatory: AMPLIFY 'to make wider, to enlarge' [*amplus* 'large, ample']; BEATIFY 'to make blessed(ly happy)' [*beatus* 'prosperous, blessed']; BEAUTIFY; CLARIFY; DANDIFY; EDIFY 'to uplift'; (literally) 'to make a building; to build' [*aedēs* 'room; temple']; FALSIFY; GLORIFY; HORRIFY [*horrere* 'to bristle']; IDENTIFY [*idem* 'the same']; JOLLIFY; LIQUEFY; MODIFY 'to moderate; to make changes in'; (originally) 'to keep within bounds' [from Latin *modificāre* 'to measure; to delimit' (*modus* 'measure; manner')]; NOTIFY 'to make known; to give notice'; OSSIFY; PETRIFY; QUALIFY [*qualis* 'of what kind']; RECTIFY [*rectus* 'straight']; SATISFY [*satis* 'enough']; TERRIFY [*terrere* 'to frighten']; UNIFY; and VERIFY [*verus* 'true'].

There remain two English words based on Latin *facere* 'to make, to do' that betray their origin scarcely at all in their current spellings. One is CHAFE 'to heat by rubbing; to irritate by rubbing; to become annoyed'; (obsolete) 'to heat, to warm' [from Medieval/Old French *chaufer* 'to warm,' from Vulgar Latin **cal(e)fāre,* from Latin *calefacere* 'to make warm' (*calere* 'to be hot')]. While the sense of CHAFE 'to heat' is obsolete in most instances, it remains alive in the compound CHAFING dish 'a pan suspended over a heating device for keeping food warm.' The Old French *chaufer* leads to modern French *chauffer* 'to heat' and the agent-noun CHAUFFEUR 'fireman, stoker; professional driver of limousines or trucks'; (literally) 'one that makes heat.'

Another Latin word that is perhaps related to Latin *facere* 'to make, to do' is *faciēs* 'shape, outward appearance, aspect, look; face.' Many writers agree in accepting this relationship, one explaining the semantic link between *facere* and *faciēs* with the phrase for *faciēs* '"form imposed on something"' (*AHD*). This may be the equivalent of 'to make something take on a certain appearance.' However, other writers believe Latin *faciēs* to be related to Latin *fax* (earlier *facēs*) 'torch,' from the Latin root **fac-* 'to appear, to shine.'

English words based on Latin *faciēs* 'face' include, most obviously of all, the Latin word itself used as an English word: FACIES 'outward appearance' and the Latin phrase *prima* FACIE 'on first appearance; at first view; on the face of it, before closer inspection' a legal term used of evidence that is sufficient to establish a fact unless rebutted. Also based on Latin *faciēs* 'face' are FACE 'outward appearance; the most significant surface of any object; countenance, visage' [via Old French from Vulgar Latin **facia*]; FACADE 'the face of a building; the front of anything; a false front' [via French from Italian *facciata*, from *faccia* 'face, appearance']; and FACET 'little face; one side of a many-sided object' [from French *facette* 'little face'].

Some include the Latin adjective *facētus* 'finely made, elegant; witty' as a relative of Latin *faciēs* 'face, aspect,' and, consequently, the Latin noun *facetia* 'a witty or humorous saying.' The latter is the source of English FACETIOUS 'playfully humorous, flippant' [French *facétieux*]. Others, however, label Latin *facētus* "of obscure origin" or are noncommittal.

Definitely related to *faciēs* > FACE are SURFACE 'the outermost layer of anything' [from the 16th-century French word SURFACE, based on Latin *superficiēs* 'surface']; SUPERFICIAL 'of the surface; lacking in depth' [from Late Latin *superficiālis*]; DEFACE 'to damage the surface of' [from Old French *desfac(i)er* (Latin *dē-* 'an undoing,' or *dis-* 'apart, asunder')]; and EFFACE 'to remove from the surface; to cause to disappear, to erase' [from Old French *effacer* 'to remove the face' (*ef-* < *ex-* 'out of, away from')].

There is a possibility that the (Late) Latin suffix *-fārius* (< *-fāriam*) '-doing, -sided, -fold' derives from Indo-European **dhe-* 'to set, to put.' If so, it would make *facere* and *faciēs* cousins to the series of multiplicative adjectives that starts with BIFARIOUS 'two-fold; ambiguous'; TRIFARIOUS 'facing three ways'; MULTIFARIOUS 'having great diversity'; OMNIFARIOUS 'of all varieties.'

Already mentioned is the development of Indo-European *dh- into Latin f- when used as an initial letter. However, when the *-dh- migrates into the middle of a Latin word, it changes more simply into *-d-. Thus, the Indo-European root *dhē- 'to put' combined with the prefix *kom- 'with' to form *kom-dhe, becomes Latin condere 'to put together, to compose.' (*Kom-dhe uses the zero-grade form of *dhē-; the e is a schwa, phonetically the vowel in English speech exemplified in about, crier, visible, violin, and circus.) A variant of condere, which 'puts things together' in a culinary way, is condire, conditum 'to make savory; to pickle, to preserve.' The past participle, conditum, gave rise to the obsolete English verb condite 'preserve with salt, sugar, spices and the like.' From the related Latin noun condimentum 'spice, seasoning' comes English CONDIMENT 'a seasoning for food.'

Latin condere, conditum 'to put together' developed secondary meanings of 'to store up,' hence 'to hide, to bury.' This secretive significance was reinforced in the compound verb, recondere, reconditus 'to hoard, to conceal' (literally, 'to put back together with'), whence the adjective reconditus 'put out of the way, hidden.' This was borrowed into English as RECONDITE 'concealed, hidden; abstruse; removed from ordinary understanding.' Another furtive compound of Latin condere 'to put together; to hide' is abscondere 'to hide away,' ancestor of English ABSCOND 'to hide oneself away; to leave secretly.' Latin abscondere 'to hide away' has an unexpected offspring in English SCONCE 'a wall bracket for candles'; (obsolete) ' "a lantern or candlestick with a screen to protect the light from the wind and a handle to carry it by" ' (OED) [by way of the Latin past participle absconsus and the Medieval Latin phrase lanterna absconsa 'hidden lantern']. What happened is that the lanterna was dropped out of the phrase, and absconsa shortened into Medieval Latin (a)sconsa, whence Old French esconse 'lantern, hiding place,' which was borrowed into English as SCONCE. (The verb to ensconce 'to put in a secure place' comes from a different sconce meaning 'a small fort,' from an entirely different root.)

From an "extended o-grade form" (AHD) of *dhē- 'to put, to set,' that is, *-dhōt-, comes the Latin suffix -dōs, -dōtis evidenced in SACERDOTAL 'pertaining to priests' [from Latin sacerdōs, sacerdōtis 'priest; one who performs sacred rites' (sacer 'holy, sacred')]. (However, some authorities attribute Latin -dōs, -dōtis to Indo-European *dō- 'to give.')

*Dhō-, an o-grade form of Indo-European *dhē- 'to put, to set,' which gave us Latin -dōs, -dōtis 'performer,' also provides us with a bridge to the Germanic/English forms mentioned earlier as deriving from this root, such as DO 'to perform, to execute; to

4440

4445

4450

4455

4460

4465

4470

4475

4480

make' [from Old English *dōn* 'to do,' from Germanic **dōn*]. The *-n* in Old English *dōn* 'to do' and Germanic **dōn* is an infinitive ending, thus different from that in the modern English word to DON 'to put on (a garment).' In the English word, the *-n* stands for
4485 'on,' since DON is simply a contraction of DO ON, that is, 'put on.' The case is similar with DOFF 'to take off (a garment)' [from DO OFF 'put off'], the dialectal DOUT from DO OUT 'put out' a light, fire], and DUP [from DO UP 'open' a latch].

Other compounds of DO are TO-DO and ADO 'fuss, commo-
4490 tion.' ADO is a contraction of AT DO, which means 'to do' in the northern English dialects, where 'at' is used to form the infinitive. Note, also, UNDO 'to reverse, to annul; to untie.' The past tense of DO is DID, and from there it is a simple ablautish step to DEED 'an act; something that has been done; an instrument in writing that
4495 effects some legal disposition' [from Old English *dǣd* 'a doing, a deed'; from Germanic **dēdiz*, from Indo-European **dhē-ti-* 'something set down, something done'].

A similar kind of 'setting down, laying down, decreeing' is involved when judgments are made as to what is to be done, as
4500 reflected in the Indo-European **dhō-mo-* > Germanic **dōmaz* > Old English *dōm* 'judgment, law, decree' > English DOOM 'a sentence of punishment; irrevocable destiny, usually to an adverse fate; death, ruin, destruction'; (obsolete) 'a decree.' DOOMSDAY is the day of the Last Judgment, but the DOMESDAY
4505 Book (pronounced and sometimes spelled DOOMSDAY) is merely the record of the "Grand Inquest," a survey and census made of the lands of England, their ownership, value, and taxability, at the behest of the Norman conqueror, William, in 1085–86. There had been other earlier DOOMBOOKS 'codes of Old Teutonic laws,'
4510 especially one attributed to Alfred the Great, king from 871 to 899 of the West Saxons. The kind of thinking that went into compiling DOOMBOOKS and pronouncing DOOMS was denoted by the related verb to DEEM 'to judge, to consider, to have an opinion'; (obsolete) 'to pronounce judgment, to sentence, to doom' [from Old
4515 English *dēman*, from Germanic **dōmjan*; from *dōmaz* 'doom']. The shift from the long *-ō-* of **dōmjan*, back in the throat, to the *-ee-* of DEEM, forward in the mouth, is an example of umlaut, caused here by partial assimilation to the (now lost) *i*-glide sound (spelled *-j-*) in the following syllable. The DOOM of judgments,
4520 laws, and decrees has a cognate in Russian DUMA 'a council; the Russian parliament, established in 1905 and abolished in 1917' [from Russian *duma* 'thought, meditation'; from Gothic *dōms* 'judgment']. Another cognate is the English suffix -DOM 'condition or state; office or jurisdiction,' as in FREEDOM 'state of being free';
4525 KINGDOM; BOREDOM 'condition of being bored'; and CHRISTEN-

DOM—a suffixal use of Old English *dōm* 'judgment, statute, jurisdiction.'

It was mentioned earlier that Indo-European **dh*- in initial position changes to *th*- when migrating to Greek. So it is that, as a cognate of English DOOM 'decree, sentence, what has been laid down,' we find Greek *thema* 'what has been laid down or posed; a proposition.' Greek *thema*, by way of Latin and French, gives us English THEME 'a topic of discussion; an underlying subject expressed in works of art; a basic melody that recurs in a musical composition.' Then there is ANATHEMA 'the great curse of the Church, formally handing a person over to Satan; anything consigned to damnation' [from Greek *anathema* 'execration']. Greek *anathema* did not start out with such a dread, execratory sense, for it was originally a variant of *anathēma* 'a consecrated gift, votive offering, a thing set up to the gods,' from Greek *anatithenai* 'to set up, to dedicate' (*ana* 'up' + *tithenai* 'to put, to place'). But, as Emile Benveniste has shown, that which is sacred to (reserved for) the gods is at the same time accursed (off limits) to men. In fact, Latin *sacer* (> *sacred*) has this double sense, and the same duality is found in other Indo-European languages. Thus, the difference between a long *ē* and a short *e* is all that separates *anathēma* 'consecrated gift' from *anathema* 'execration.'

Closely related to Greek *thema* 'proposition' is Greek *thesis* 'a setting, a placing; a proposition; the setting down of the foot or lowering of the hand in marking time; a statement.' *Thesis* leads to English THESIS 'a proposition maintained by an argument; a dissertation'; (music) 'the downbeat(s) of a measure'; (prosody) 'the unstressed part of a foot.' Note that the musical and prosodic meanings are exact opposites (ANTITHESES). The discrepancy arose as the result of a misunderstanding by Late Latin writers of the meaning of the Greek term. *Thesis* means 'a lowering (of the foot or hand in marking time),' but these writers took it to mean 'a lowering (of the voice in reading poetry),' and consequently applied the term to the unstressed syllables in poetry.

Thesis has many compounds, among them ANTITHESIS 'the exact opposite; the juxtaposition of contrasting ideas' [from Greek *antithesis* 'opposition,' from *antitithenai* 'to put against']; SYNTHESIS 'the combining of substances to form a whole; the uniting of elements or simple compounds into more complex compounds'; SYNTHETIC 'artificially created' [from Greek *sunthesis* 'a putting together' (*sun-*, *syn-* 'with')]; and HYPOTHESIS 'an unproved proposition used as a basis for argument or experimentation; an assumption; a conjecture' [from Greek *hupothesis* (literally) 'a putting under; a supposition'; from Greek *hupotithenai* 'to put under' (*hupo* 'under')]. (Note that *supposition* also means,

literally, 'a putting under.') Three more examples: PARENTHESIS
'a comment inserted into a sentence that would be grammatically
complete without it; the curved lines used in writing to mark off
such comments' [from Greek *parenthesis* 'a putting in beside'
4575   (*para* 'beside' + *en* 'in' + *tithenai* 'to put')]; EPITHET 'a word or
phrase added to a person's name and used to identify or characterize him' (William the Conqueror, Philip the Fair, Jack the Ripper,
Mac the Knife); 'a term used to characterize a person or thing'
(Silent Cal, the cold war); 'a term of abuse or contempt'
4580   (meathead, dingbat) [from Greek *epitheton* (literally) 'put on; an
added word']; and METATHESIS 'transposition of sounds within a
word' [from Greek *metathesis* 'transposition, putting after' (*meta*
'after, denoting change')]. "Eastren" for "eastern," and "Fallstaff"
for "Fastolph" are examples of metathesis. Some of these transpo-
4585   sitions take hold and change the form of the word permanently.
For instance, English *bird* was, in Old English, *brid(d)*, and
English *carnival* comes from Italian *carnevale*, which was originally, however, *carnelevare* 'the removal or putting away of meat.'
(The Mardi Gras carnival takes place on the eve of Lent, when
4590   the eating of meat is restricted.) Another *thesis* compound is
PROTHESIS 'a placing before; the addition of a phoneme at the
beginning of a word' (to make the word easier to pronounce or for
other phonetic or linguistic reasons). For example, a Spanish-
speaking person speaking English might say 'United Estates.' A
4595   historical example of prothesis is the evolution of Latin *status*
into Spanish *estado* and Old French *estat*, modern French *état*,
English ESTATE and STATE. PROTHESIS also has a meaning in the
Eastern Orthodox Church of 'placing before' in the sense of 'the
preparation of the eucharistic bread and wine for consecration,'
4600   and in Greek antiquity it meant 'an exhibition, a show,' specifi-
cally, 'the laying out of a corpse.' Similar enough to cause
confusion is PROSTHESIS 'the artificial replacement of a part of the
body' [from Greek *prosthesis* 'an adding' (*pros* 'in addition to')].
       Also related to Greek *thesis* 'something put or placed' is
4605   Greek *thēkē* 'a container, case, cover; where things are placed.'
Greek *thēkē* was adopted into Latin as *thēca* 'a case, a covering,
an envelope, a sheath,' whence, via New Latin, English THECA
'the spore case of a moss capsule; the outer covering of the pupa
of certain insects.' Latin *thēca* is the ancestor of West Germanic
4610   *tēca*, which is the antecedent of Middle Dutch *tīke*, Middle
English *tikke*, and English TICK 'the cloth cover of a pillow or
mattress' and TICKING 'the tightly woven fabric used to cover
pillows and mattresses.' The element -*theca*- shows up in APOTH-
ECARY 'a druggist, a pharmacist;', (etymologically) 'one who puts
4615   (things) away'; (obsolete) 'one who keeps a store of nonperishable

commodities, such as drugs, spices and preserves' [from Late Latin *apothēcārius* 'warehouseman,' from Latin *apothēca* 'storehouse,' from Greek *apothēkē* 'receptacle,' from *apotithenai* 'to put away']. Greek *apothēkē* lost its initial *a-* and went through a few other changes to emerge as Old Provençal *botica*, and *botica* led 4620 to French, whence English BOUTIQUE 'a small retail shop; a specialty shop.' In Spanish, by similar metamorphoses, Latin *apothēca* changed to BODEGA 'a warehouse; a wine cellar'; (American Spanish) 'a grocery store.' Thus, a Spanish-American *bodeguero*, a Rue de Rivoli *boutiquier*, and a Main Street APOTH- 4625 ECARY are etymological cousins. Two more words related to Greek *thesis* are BIBLIOTHECA 'a storehouse of books; a library' [*biblion* 'book'] and HYPOTHECATE 'to pledge (property) as security without transfer of title'; (literally) 'to place under' [from Medieval Latin *hypothēcāre*, from Late Latin *hypothēca* 'pledge, 4630 mortgage'; from Greek *hupothēkē*, from *hupotithenai* 'to place under; to mortgage'].

According to at least one writer, another member of this word family is Greek *thēsauros* 'a storeroom, a treasure room,' ancestor of Latin and English THESAURUS 'a book of synonyms and 4635 antonyms; a treasury or storehouse of knowledge,' but most authorities give no origin for Greek *thēsauros*. What is known is that from Latin *thēsaurus* there evolved the Vulgar Latin *tresaurus*, forerunner of Old French *tresor*, Middle English *tresor, tresour*, and English TREASURE 'stored wealth.' 4640

There remains one cognate that comes to us as a loanword from modern Irish, and reminds us semantically of English DOOM 'decree' and Russian *duma* 'parliament'. That is Irish DAIL 'assembly,' seen only in or with reference to, the DÁIL ÉIREANN 'the assembly of Eire; the lower legislative house of the Republic of 4645 Ireland' [Irish *dáil*, from Old Irish *dāl* 'assembly'].

XXIV

Famed Prophet Abandons Euphemisms

Foot-slogging INFANTRYMEN of any war are not looking for FAME or INFAMY, but they might consider it DEFAMATORY if told that they were a bunch of INFANTS. Nevertheless, etymologically,
4650 that is what they are, since Latin *infāns* 'a young child' is the source of the English word INFANTRY 'foot soldiers' [via French from Italian *infanteria*, from Italian *infante* (obsolete) 'foot soldier, young man; infant'].

Somewhere between Latin *infāns* and Old Italian *infante*, the
4655 meaning was expanded to include 'young man.' Since it was the lot of unpropertied young men lacking influence or influential families to be drafted first and given the most rigorous assignments, so it is that the body of foot soldiers came to be known in Italian as *infanteria* "young-men-ery." A similar meaning of the
4660 cognate English word INFANT still prevails, for in the eyes of the law, an INFANT is 'a minor; any person under the age of 21' [from Middle English *enfaunt*, from Old French *enfant*, from Latin *infāntem*].

Infāns, *infāntem* has some more obvious derivatives than
4665 INFANTRY, such as INFANTILE 'childish' and INFANTICIDE 'the killing of a newborn or recently born child,' as well as two specialized instances in Spanish and Portuguese INFANTE 'a younger legitimate son of the king of Spain or Portugal'—the eldest son and heir is the *principe* 'prince'—and INFANTA 'any
4670 legitimate daughter of a king of Spain or Portugal.' There are also obsolete aphetic (beheaded) forms in English, such as *faunt* 'infant,' *fauntekin* 'little infant,' and *fauntelet* 'a little child,' which indicate that little Lord FAUNTLEROY was, etymologically, Lord 'Child-the-king; the king-child.'
4675 Actually, 'young child' is a secondary meaning of Latin *infāns*, the primary meaning being 'speechless,' which seems an

appropriate epithet for a baby, but hardly for an infantryman. Etymologically speaking, then, a baby remains an INFANT until he learns how to talk.

Infāns, infāntem is a compound of the prefix in- 'not' + fāns   4680
'speaking,' the present participle of the Latin verb for, fārī, fātus 'to speak, to say; to tell.' To tell what? A tale, of course, or Latin fābula 'narration, account, story,' from which derives English FABLE 'a story of highly marvelous happenings; a fiction'; "a didactic story of which a moral forms an integral part" (Brewer)   4685
[from Old French fable, from Latin fābula]. The third, restricted sense of FABLE applies to a form of literature in which anthropomorphized animals talk and display other kinds of human behavior. FABULISTS like Aesop, LaFontaine, Dryden, Harris, Thurber, et alii poke fun in their FABULOUS tales at the foibles of mankind.   4690

Latin fābula also means 'conversation,' and this sense is reflected in English CONFABULATE 'to converse together' and its shortened form CONFAB 'a get-together for the purpose of talking something over' [from Latin confābulārī 'to talk together']. Two similar words are AFFABLE 'easy to talk to; amiable' [from Latin   4695
affābilis, from affārī 'to speak to' (af- < ad- 'to')] and INEFFABLE 'unspeakable; not to be uttered' [from Latin ineffābilis; from in- 'not' + effārī 'to speak out' (ef- < ex- 'out')].

Based on the past participle of fārī, fātus 'to speak' is Latin fātum (literally) 'spoken; what has been spoken, an utterance; a   4700
prophetic declaration; divine will' and English FATE 'the power that predetermines destiny; doom.' The ultimate fate of all is death, and if death comes in an accident, that accident is termed FATAL 'causing death; FATEFUL,' and the victim becomes a FATALITY.   4705

The Romans deified Fate, dividing it into three goddesses, Nona, Decuma, and Morta, collectively the Parcae, or Fāta 'FATES.' In Vulgar Latin, however, the neuter plural Fāta was taken for a feminine singular, and by the time this fateful word got into Old French, the fearsome goddess had been syncopated   4710
and demoted to a mere faie or fae, whence English FAY 'a diminutive supernatural being possessed of magical powers.' The works of enchantment performed by faies, faes were known in Old French as faerie, and this word was used in English to mean 'the land of the fays; fays, collectively; enchantment.' However,   4715
by the late 14th century, the word was being used for the creatures themselves, in the form FAIRY 'a minor supernatural being capable of helping or hindering human endeavors.' In Italian, as in Vulgar Latin, the neuter plural Fāta became the feminine singular fata 'fay, fairy.' One of the most renowned of   4720
these creatures was Fata Morgana 'Morgan le Fay,' the sister of

the legendary King Arthur of Britain. This particular fairy was a
great one at creating mirages, so that today, a FATA MORGANA is a
'mirage,' "especially one seen at the Strait of Messina, between
4725 Calabria and Sicily; so called because regarded as the work of the
fairy of this name" (*MW2*).

The Roman *Fāta* were goddesses. The name, coming from
fārī, *fātus* 'to speak,' ·literally means 'things spoken; prophetic
utterances; divine will.' From the same root as *fārī*, *fātus*, *fātum*,
4730 *fāta* come Latin *fās* 'divine law; what has been uttered by the
gods' and its opposite *nefās* 'sin, wrong, crime.' *Nefās* has an
adjective, *nefārius* 'sinful, criminal,' which yields English NEFA-
RIOUS 'evil, impiously wicked.' (Some writers, however, list *fās*,
nefās, *nefārius*, and NEFARIOUS as derived from Indo-European
4735 **dhē-* 'to set, to put.')

Finally from Latin *fārī*, *fātus* 'to speak' comes the compound
form PREFACE 'an introductory statement' [from Latin *praefātiō* 'a
saying beforehand,' from *praefārī* 'to say in advance'].

Kissin' cousin to Latin *fārī*, *fātus* 'to speak' is Latin *fatērī*,
4740 *fassus* 'to confess, to acknowledge.' An intensified compound of
fatērī is *confitērī* 'to confess with; to avow, to make known,' past
participle *confessus*, whence Late Latin *confessāre*, Old French
confesser, and English CONFESS 'to admit; to disclose one's sins
to a priest; to avow,' as in "the new convert CONFESSED the true
4745 faith" (a throwback to the days of Roman persecution?). A CON-
FESSOR is both 'one who makes a confession' (in this sense also
spelled CONFESSER) and 'one who hears confessions,' as well as
'one who proclaims his faith in the face of danger, especially a
male saint who did not suffer martyrdom.' The third and fourth
4750 senses are the earliest meanings of the word in English (cf. Saint
Edward the Confessor, king of the English 1042–1066, called "the
CONFESSOR" because of his piety). CONFESSOR used to be pronounced with the accent on the first syllable; later, that pronunciation was reserved for 'one who proclaims his faith but does not
4755 suffer martyrdom'; now the word is usually pronounced with the
accent on the second syllable for all of its meanings. The first
person singular present indicative of *confitērī* is CONFITEOR 'I
confess; a prayer confessing sinfulness.'

Similarly formed from the Latin *profitērī*, *professus* and with
4760 an interesting variety of meanings, is English PROFESS 'to proclaim openly' "I profess myself to be a baseball fan."; 'to pretend'
"He professes to be a ballplayer." 'to practice a faith' "He
professes Buddhism." 'to claim a skill in' "He professes law."
[from Latin *prōfitērī*, *prōfessus* 'to declare publicly' (*prō-* 'in front
4765 of' + *fatērī* 'to confess')]. A PROFESSOR is 'a teacher of the highest
rank'; (obsolete) 'a member of a religious organization; one who

makes a public declaration; one who adheres to a faith; one who
teaches publicly.' A PROFESSION is 'an avowal' "a profession of
love; of faith"; 'an occupation requiring specialized study' "the
profession of veterinarian"; 'the body of practitioners of a given   4770
field' "a disgrace to the profession" and a PROFESSIONAL is 'one
who is qualified in a particular occupation' as well as 'one who is
paid for his services.'

The last of the Latin words from this root that have surviving
English derivatives is *fāma* 'report, rumor, public opinion,   4775
renown,' which yields English FAME 'the condition of being much
talked about; reputational renown'; (archaic) 'what people are
saying.' FAME does not necessarily denote good things that
'people are saying,' but the derogatory sense is not much in use
except in the phrase *house of ill* FAME 'brothel.' Other words of   4780
"bad" fame are found in the compound forms INFAMY 'a crime of
moral turpitude; an infamous act'; INFAMOUS 'having a reputation
of the worst kind'; and DEFAME 'to slander, to cast aspersions on a
person's reputation.'

All of the preceding Latin words stem from the Indo-Euro-   4785
pean root *bhā- 'to speak' and illustrate the sound correspondence
of Indo-European *bh- > Latin *f-*. Initial *bh- also evolves into
Greek *ph-* and Germanic *b-*, as further illustrated by the following cognates: Greek *phēmē* 'report, rumor' (the equivalent of
Latin *fāma*); Greek *phōnē* 'voice, sound'; Greek *phanai* 'to speak';   4790
and Germanic *bannan* 'to speak publicly.' English borrowings
from the Greek include EUPHEMISM 'an inoffensive word substituted for an offensive or disagreeable one'; (literally) 'good-saying'
[from Greek *euphēmein* 'to speak words of good omen' (*eus*
'good,' *eu* 'well')] and its opposite DYSPHEMISM 'an offensive or   4795
derogatory term substituted for an inoffensive or laudatory one'
[from Greek *dusphēmein* 'to speak evil words' (*dus-* 'badly, ill')].
(Isaac Goldberg, in *The Wonder of Words*, uses CACOPHEMISM
with this meaning [*kakos* 'bad'].) Also taken from Greek is
English BLASPHEMY 'reviling God; irreverence' [via Old French   4800
and Latin from Greek *blasphēmia*, from *blasphēmos* 'evil-speaking']. The *blas-* element is of obscure origin, perhaps related to
Greek *meleos* 'futile, unhappy,' according to some. However,
another writer ties *blas-* to Greek *blapsis* 'a harming, a hurting'
and *blaptein* 'to harm.' The Greek *blasphēmein* 'to speak evil, to   4805
speak profanely' was adopted into Latin as *blasphēmāre* 'to
blaspheme,' and in Late Latin the sense was mitigated to 'to
reproach' and picked up by Vulgar Latin as *blastēmāre*. *Blastēmāre* evolved into Old French *blasmer* (Modern French
blâmer), whence Middle English *blamen* and English BLAME 'to   4810
censure; to hold responsible for.'

Much more prevalent in English than derivates from Greek *phēmē* 'report, saying' are those from Greek *phōnē* 'voice, sound,' most notably the ubiquitous TELEPHONE (literally) 'far-off voice'
4815 [*tēle* 'at a distance']. Also, PHONOLOGY 'the science of speech sounds' [*logos* 'discourse, reason']; PHONETIC 'having to do with the sounds used in speaking' [*phōnētikos*]; PHONEME 'one of a small set of units considered to be the basic speech sounds of a language' [*phōnēma* 'an uttered sound']; HOMOPHONE 'a word that
4820 has the same sound as another but a different meaning' [*homos* 'the same']; PHONOGRAPH 'a machine made for reproducing sounds from a cylinder or disc' [*graphein* 'to write'—see line 2684]; POLYPHONY 'music in which two or more melodic lines are played or sung simultaneously; counterpoint'; (literally) 'many
4825 voices' [*polus* 'many']; DIAPHONY 'part singing in parallel motion at a fourth, fifth, or octave above or below the melody; organum' [*dia* 'through; in two']; and ANTIPHONY 'singing in responses' [*anti* 'opposite, over, against']. Also from Greek *phōnē* 'voice, sound' is ANTIPHON 'a composition sung responsively as part of a
4830 liturgy' [from Greek *antiphōna* 'sung responses,' from *antiphōnos* 'returning a sound']. Besides keeping its own form, Greek *antiphōna* evolved into Late Latin *antef(a)na*, whence Old English *antefn(e)*, Middle English *antempne*, *antem(ne)* and English ANTHEM (archaic) 'a composition sung in responses, by two voices
4835 or choirs; a hymn of praise.' The -*h*- in ANTHEM is intrusive. One 17th-century spelling is *anthymne*, indicating a tendency to explain the word as 'anti-hymn' or 'hymn sung responsively.' However, the word *hymn* has a different origin. The United States national anthem is not sung antiphonally, nor is it often
4840 sung EUPHONIOUSLY: there are critics who consider the melody of *The Star-Spangled Banner*, originally the music to which the poem, *To Anacreon in Heaven*, was set, as not EUPHONIOUS 'pleasing in sound.' More English derivatives of Greek *phōnē* 'voice, sound' include EUPHONY 'agreeable sound; the linguistic
4845 tendency to change speech sounds to make them easier to pronounce' [from Greek *euphōnia* 'good voice' from *euphōnos* 'well-voiced']; EUPHONIUM 'a tenor tuba; an organ stop with a soft, expressive tone'; and CACOPHONY 'harsh, jarring, discordant sounds; disagreeable sounds' [Greek *kakos* 'bad']. There
4850 shouldn't be too much disagreement about the euphoniousness of the referents of the next word, although some people may find disagreeable, hence cacophonous, the sounds sometimes made by a SYMPHONY 'a passage for instruments occurring in a vocal composition; a composition in sonata form, usually in four move-
4855 ments, written for a full orchestra; a large orchestra with well-proportioned instrumentation, but with the string sections pre-

dominating numerically'; (literally) 'together-sound; concord of sounds; harmony.'

Also descended from Greek *phōnē* 'sound, voice' are APHO-
NIA 'loss of speech as a result of damage to the organs of speech'   4860
[*a*- 'not'; cf. APHASIA, line 4875] and APHONIC 'affected with aphonia; unvoiced, mute.'

Introduced into English as recently as 1900, in the translation of J. Deniker's *The Races of Man*, are the terms FRANCOPHONE 'French-speaking' and ANGLOPHONE 'English-speaking.' These   4865
two words are most frequently used in discussing the population of Canada or other formerly colonial nations.

The adjective *phony, phoney,* meaning 'spurious, imitation,' has nothing to do with telephones or Greek voices. It is most likely an imported Irish/English thieves' cant word based on Irish   4870
fáinne 'finger ring,' phony, plated examples of which were fobbed off on the gullible as solid gold.

The last of the English borrowings from Greek *phanai* 'to speak,' *phatos* 'spoken,' and *phasis* 'utterance, statement' are APHASIA 'loss of the ability to speak or understand speech   4875
because of brain damage' [*a*- 'not']; DYSPHASIA 'impairment of the power to use or understand language' [*dys*- 'difficult']; TACHYPHA-
SIA 'very rapid speech' [*takhus* 'swift']; and PROPHECY 'a predic-
tion; a revelation of divine will'; (literally) 'a speaking beforehand; a speaking forth' [via Old French and Latin from   4880
Greek *prophēteia,* from *prophētēs* 'one who speaks forth, fore-
teller']. Hence, PROPHESY, PROPHET, etc.

The BANISHED BANDITS, ever BANAL, stashed their CONTRA-
BAND in an ABANDONED mine in the BANLIEUS of the BANNED village. Indo-European initial **bh-* becomes Germanic *b-*. There-   4885
fore, Indo-European **bha-* 'to speak,' the source of Latin *fāri,*
fātus 'to speak' and Greek *phanai, phatos* 'to speak' shows up in Germanic as **bannan* 'to speak publicly, to proclaim,' a word that was "used of particular kinds of proclamations in feudal and pre-
feudal custom; 'to proclaim under penalty, to summon to the levy,   4890
to declare outlaw' " (*AHD*).

All of the capitalized words in the foregoing alliterative sentence have arrived in English, by various routes, from Germanic **bannan* 'to proclaim,' for example BAN 'the gathering of the French king's nobles for war'; BANNS 'an ecclesiastical curse;   4895
excommunication; a prohibition; to prohibit by decree'; (origi-
nally) 'a summons to arms.' The verb to BAN is found in English earlier (Old English *bannan* 'to summon, to proclaim,' from Germanic **bannan*) than the noun BAN, which arrived in English via Old French *ban* 'proclamation, publication; summons; pro-   4900
scription, outlawry, banishment; assemblage of vassals' from Late

Latin *bannum* 'a proclamation commanding or forbidding under threat of penalty' (itself also from Germanic **bannan* 'to proclaim'). Two more of the aforementioned derivatives of Germanic

4905 **bannan* 'to proclaim' are BANNS 'public notice given in church of intended marriage' [from Old French *ban* 'proclamation,' from Medieval Latin *banna*, influenced by Old English *gebann* 'proclamation'] and BANAL 'commonplace, trite'; (originally) 'pertaining to (a summons to) compulsory feudal service required of all

4910 members of the community' [from Old French *ban*, from Frankish **ban* 'feudal jurisdiction']. The intermediate sense is "open to the use of all the community" (*OED*).

This Frankish **ban* 'feudal jurisdiction,' which is the equivalent and collateral of Late Latin *bannum, bandum* 'proclamation,

4915 proscription' (also of Germanic origin), shows up in two other words, one of them considered French when used in English, the other used freely in both languages. They are BANLIEU 'the territory outside the walls but inside the legal limits of a town; suburb'; (literally) 'place of jurisdiction' [French *lieu* 'place,' from

4920 Latin *locus* 'place'] and ABANDON 'to forsake; freedom from constraint'; (literally) 'to turn over to the jurisdiction of another' [from the Old French phrase (*metre*) *a bandon* '(to put) in one's power'; from *a* 'at, into' + *bandon* 'jurisdiction'].

Late Latin *bannum* 'proclamation commanding or forbidding

4925 under threat of penalty' led to Vulgar Latin **bannīre* and Old French *banir, baniss(ant)*, whence Middle English *banishen* and English BANISH 'to compel to leave the country.'

Meanwhile, in Italian, a -*d*- intruded itself into Vulgar Latin **bannīre* > Medieval Latin *bannīre* 'to proclaim; to proscribe,'

4930 resulting in Italian *bandire* 'to announce in church; to banish, to outlaw.' The past participle, *bandito* 'proclaimed; proscribed, outlawed,' was also used as a noun, meaning 'outlaw,' borrowed into English as BANDIT 'an outlaw.' The word was first popularized in English as *bandetto* with the plural *banditti* (for Italian

4935 *banditi*) 'outlaws,' a plural term used to refer to organized gangs of brigands, and sometimes understood as a singular. (One authority, harking back to the 'summons to arms' meaning of Germanic **bannan*, interprets Italian *bandire* as 'to have been summoned' > 'to band together,' making the *banditi* 'those who have banded

4940 together' rather than 'those outlawed.')

Related to Italian *bandire* 'to proclaim; to proscribe' is Italian *bando* 'proclamation; proscription,' from Late Latin *bannum, bandum*, of Germanic origin. What has been proscribed—but is being dealt in nevertheless—is called *contrabando* 'against the

4945 ban,' which yields English CONTRABAND 'goods prohibited by law' [via Spanish *contrabando*]. In earlier English it was *counter-*

bande, from French *contrebande*, but this term of cross-Channel smuggling was ousted by the Spanish/Italian word around 1600 because of the extensive illicit traffic with Spanish colonial possessions in the Americas.   4950

Finally from Indo-European **bhā-* 'to speak,' via the suffixed form **bhā-ni-*, come Germanic **bōniz* and Old Norse *bōn* 'prayer, request,' whence English BOON 'a favor; something gratuitously bestowed; a gratuitous benefit'; (obsolete) 'a prayer, a request' (although the ultimate relationship with **bhā-* 'to speak' is   4955 doubted by some). This BOON has been influenced by but is not the same as the *boon* in *boon* companion, which comes from Old French *bon*, Latin *bonus* 'good.' (See line 3654.)

XXV

Feathers Give Impetus

A baseball team that wins a major league PENNANT has to
4960 have a certain amount of PANACHE, but the team cannot claim to
have reached the PINNACLE of success until it wins the World
Series. PANACHE is not a common word; its literal meaning is 'a
plume of feathers, especially when used as an ornament for a
helmet,' but figuratively it is used to mean 'swagger, dash, verve,
4965 flamboyance,' all ingredients of a winning team.

As the pronunciation indicates, PANACHE comes from the
French, *panache*. The French borrowed it from the Italian *pennachio* 'crest, tuft of feathers,' derived from Late Latin *pinnāculum* 'little feather, small wing,' a diminutive of Latin *pinna*
4970 'feather, wing.'

Latin *pinna*, a variant of *penna* 'feather, wing,' had already by
classical Roman times acquired a secondary meaning of 'battlement: a parapet built on top of a wall with indentations for
defense' (although this *pinna*, which also means 'fin,' is consid-
4975 ered by some to be a different word from *pinna* = *penna*
'feather'). The semantic development is similar to the one that
prompts us to speak of the "wings" of buildings and of "flying"
buttresses. Thus, Late Latin *pinnāculum* or little *pinna* 'small
feather, small wing' is also 'a small battlement,' and its English
4980 descendant PINNACLE is 'a small spire on a roof or buttress.'
Pinnacles were used in Gothic architecture not for battle stations
or even primarily for ornament but to give additional weight to a
buttress or pier. In these Gothic structures the pinnacles were tall
and tapering, and this feature gave rise to the metaphorical sense
4985 of PINNACLE 'any tall, pointed formation, such as a mountain
peak; the highest point.'

Latin *penna* 'feather' is also the ancestor of English PENNON
'a narrow triangular flag that flies out like a long waving plume'

[from Old French *pen(n)on*, from *pen(n)e* 'feather, wing']. Pen- 4990
nons were originally borne on lances as the ensigns of knights
bachelors. The *-on* ending indicates 'largeness,' so that PENNON
etymologically means 'a huge feather.' PENNON was combined
with *pendant* 'hanging, something that hangs' to produce the
more widely used term PENNANT 'a long, narrow, often triangular
flag; the championship flag won in certain sports, chiefly profes- 4995
sional baseball.'

An early implement for writing with ink was a quill, the
horny barrel of a feather. Because of its origin, the implement was
called a PEN 'an instrument for writing with ink' [from Old French
penne 'feather, pen']. The modern French word for '(writing) pen' 5000
is *plume*, which also means 'feather'; modern French *penne*
means 'wing-feather, tail-feather.' A PENKNIFE was (originally) 'a
small knife used for sharpening quill pens.' Other members of
this sub-family of words are PENNATE 'feathered or winged';
PINNATE 'resembling a feather'; and PINION 'a bird's wing; one of 5005
the main flight feathers of a bird's wing; to remove or bind a
bird's flight feathers; to restrain by binding the arms; to confine'
[from Old French *pignon*, from Vulgar Latin **pinniō(nem)*, from
Latin *pinna* 'feather, wing']. The PINION that means 'cogwheel'
may or may not come from this same source, depending on which 5010
etymologist you believe. Many think so ("the teeth of a cog wheel
being compared to the crenellations of a battlement" (*OED*)), but
others trace this PINION to Old French *peigne* 'a comb' (which
also has teeth), and still others trace it to Latin *pīnea* 'pine-cone'
> French *pignon* 'pine nut.' 5015

There are two simple English words whose relationship (or
lack of it) with Latin *pinna* divides the etymologists. They are FIN
'an appendage of an aquatic animal used for propulsion, steering
and balance' and PIN. The Latin word for 'fin' is also *pinna*. There
is an obvious analogy between a bird's wings and a fish's fins, but 5020
the two words, *pinna* = *penna* 'feather, wing' and *pinna* 'fin' are
listed separately in Latin dictionaries, as though they were
distinct and unrelated words. English FIN comes from Old English *finn*, and is a cognate of Middle Low German *finne*, Middle
High German *pfinn*, and Medieval Dutch *vinne*. In the opinion of 5025
some writers, these Germanic words are ultimately related to both
Latin *pinna* 'fin' and *penna* 'wing,' but others declare FIN to be of
obscure origin, while a third party sees a possible connection
between FIN and *spine*, which takes us on a different tack
altogether. 5030

English PIN derives from Old English *pin(n)*, whose original
meaning was 'a peg' or ' "a small piece of wood, metal or other
solid substance, of cylindrical or similar shape, often tapering or

pointed, used for ... various purposes. .." ' (OED). The Oxford
5035   English Dictionary sees a connection in the 'pointedness' of pens,
pins, and quills, and states that PIN is "generally held to be an
adaptation of Latin pinna," an opinion shared by many. Others,
however, see a connection with Middle Irish benn 'point, peak,'
which is from a different Indo-European root.
5040   There is a similar lack of agreement on the derivation of the
English word PEN 'an enclosure' (pigPEN, playPEN); 'to confine'
(all PENT up). This PEN may well come from a root entirely
different from that of Latin penna, pinna, but it is nevertheless
true that pigs and babies are kept in their PENS by virtue of the
5045   PINS used to fasten the gates.
The Indo-European root underlying Latin penna 'feather' is
*pet- 'to rush, to fly.' The absence of the -t- of this root from
penna is explained by postulating an earlier Latin form, *pet(s)na.
The -t- was retained in other Latin words, notably in the verb
5050   petere, which starts out meaning 'to fall upon, to attack (to fly at),'
then shades off into progressively milder meanings of 'to make
for, to aim at, to pursue, to seek out,' and finally winds up with
the subdued sense of 'to request' and the meek 'to beg,' as in
PETITION 'an earnest request; to make a plea for a specified
5055   action' [via Old French from Latin peitiō(nem) 'attack, solicitation'; from petere 'to try to obtain']. Some of the fierceness comes
back in Latin appetere 'to try to seize; to desire violently,' from
whose past participle, appetītus 'strived for,' comes Latin appetītiō 'a longing for,' as well as English APPETITE 'an instinctive
5060   craving' [via Old French apetit].
Latin competere has the bland meanings of 'to be suitable, to
agree (to desire together),' and these senses can be discerned in
English COMPETENT 'sufficiently apt.' But competere also means
'to seek after along with others, to strive together, to vie,' as in
5065   English COMPETITIVE 'characterized by rivalry.' Some rivalries
can be very intense indeed, as any hockey player will tell you. An
observer of ice hockey and American football might justifiably
translate the word COMPETE as 'to assail (to fly at) one another; to
vie; to try to do (something) better than (someone else).'
5070   Latin impetere 'to attack' has the derivative noun impetus
'attack, violent impulse.' In English the word has been toned
down to the less violent meaning of IMPETUS 'a driving force, a
push.' The related Late Latin impetuōsus becomes English
IMPETUOUS 'impulsively vehement,' and from the same source
5075   comes the medical term IMPETIGO 'a skin disease characterized by
bursting pustules' [from Latin impetīgō, from impetere 'to attack']
The English word PETULANCE 'temporary or capricious ill
humor,' originally had the more contumacious meaning of 'inso-

lent behavior or speech; wantonness' [from Latin *petulāns* 'forward, wanton'; from **petulāre* 'to assail' (in jest), diminutive of 5080 *petere* 'to assail']. The semantic amelioration in the English word was probably helped along by the influence of the unrelated word *pet* 'a fit of peevishness.'

Other borrowings from Latin *petere* and its derivatives are REPEAT 'to say again, to do again'; (literally) 'to attack again' [via 5085 Medieval/Old French *repeter*, from Latin *repetere* 'to attack again, to repeat'] and PERPETUATE 'to cause to continue' [from Latin *perpetuāre*]. This is not an easy one to follow. The *per-* here means 'thoroughly, throughout,' and *-petuare* is an alteration of *petere*, meaning 'to rush forward, to go forward.' An intervening 5090 word was the Latin *perpes*, *perpetis* (literally) 'going forward thoroughly; uninterrupted.' From this arose the adjectives *perpetuus* 'uninterrupted; forever' > *perpetuālis* > English PERPETUAL 'eternal' and CENTRIPETAL 'moving (rushing) toward the center.' A related word is PROPITIOUS 'favorable, auspicious' [via 5095 Old French *propicius*, from Latin *propitius* 'favorable']. Latin *propitius* is kin to Greek *propetēs* 'falling forward,' hence 'inclined (to), well-disposed,' originally a religious term that supposedly meant that one can induce the gods to 'rush forward' on one's behalf. It is also true that when one PROPITIATES or 5100 'appeases' the gods in an effort to get them in a PROPITIOUS mood, one 'falls forward' on one's face. (Greek *propetēs* also means 'prostrate.')

The Indo-European root **pet-* 'to rush, to fly' loses its vowel in the "zero-grade suffixed form **pt-ero-*" (*AHD*), which manifests 5105 itself in Greek in the words *pteron*, *pterux* 'feather, wing; anything like a wing.' *Ptero(n)* and *pterux* have been adopted into English by way of New Latin (arbitrarily concocted scientific) words like APTERYX (literally) 'without wings; the New Zealand kiwi'; ARCHAEOPTERYX (literally) 'primitive wing; an extinct bird 5110 with lizardlike characteristics' (now thought to be dinosaurlike rather than lizardlike); and PTERODACTYL (literally) 'wing finger; an extinct flying lizard,' whose wings consisted of a flap of skin supported by a very long fourth digit (Greek *daktulos* 'finger'). Also, PTEROSAUR 'winged lizard; pterodactyls and other winged 5115 reptiles, now extinct.'

Ferns are similar in structure to feathers. The Greek word for 'fern' is *pteris*, *pteridos* 'winglike,' and PTERIDOLOGY is the New Latin word for 'the science of ferns.' PTERIDOPHYTE is the (New Latin) scientific word for plants that are ferns. 5120

Another Greek derivative of Indo-European **pet-* 'to rush, to fly' is *ptōma* 'fall, ruin, disaster; fallen body, corpse,' invented, presumably, on the principle that what flies up must fall down. In

1876, the Italian biologist Selmi, when announcing his discovery
5125 of poisonous nitrogenous materials produced by the putrefaction
of protein in corpses and other dead organic matter, coined the
word PTOMAINE [from Greek *ptōma* 'dead body, corpse']. This
coinage draws a reproof from the *OED*, which points out that the
combining form of *ptōma* is *ptōmat-*, so that the newly coined
5130 word should have been *ptomatine*. *Ptōma* 'corpse' itself comes
from the "reduplicated" verb *piptein* 'to fall.' (Reduplication is
the repetition of an element of a word, especially at the beginning, for grammatical purposes, just like a prefix or, if at the end, a
suffix.) In the derivatives of *piptein* that have been carried over
5135 into English, the reduplication has disappeared.

A compound of *piptein* 'to fall' is *sumpiptein* 'to fall in with,
to coincide, to happen,' yielding the derivative noun *sumptōma*
(literally) 'a happening together; chance, accident; occurrence,
phenomenon.' Taken into Late Latin as *symptōma*, this leads to
5140 English SYMPTOM 'something that indicates that something else
has happened; a departure from normal, indicating a disorder.'
(Compare *syndrome* 'a running together.') Other medical terms
derived from *piptein* 'to fall' are PTOSIS 'abnormal lowering of an
organ; drooping of an eyelid caused by muscle failure' and
5145 PROPTOSIS 'forward displacement of an organ.'

A nonmorbid derivative of **pet-* 'to rush,' by way of the *o*-
grade form **pot-*, is Greek *potamos* 'river.' Rivers may be thought
of as 'water rushing down hill,' especially in mountainous Greece.
This element is seen in English HIPPOPOTAMUS 'river-horse' and
5150 MESOPOTAMIA 'the land between rivers.'

We come finally to Germanic **fethrō*, Old English *fether*, and
English FEATHER, which is first cousin to German *Feder*, second
cousin to Greek *pteron* and Latin *penna* (for **pet(s)na*), all with
the same meaning.

XXVI

Flowery Flourished, Blossoming Bloomers

With a FLOURISH of his sword and a FLIRT of his horse's tail,   5155
the FLORID conquistador cantered off into the FLOWERY FLORIDA
countryside. An association between FLIRT 'to throw about jerkily; to play at courtship' and FLOWER is not made by the standard
dictionaries, which categorize FLIRT as imitative or of obscure or
unknown origin. However, Eric Partridge in *Origins* connects   5160
FLIRT with the archaic French verb *fleureter* 'to talk flowery
nothings, to make gallant speeches; to make love' which derived
from the noun *fleurette* (literally) 'a small flower; amorous discourse.' (It is unquestionably true that Modern French has taken
over the English FLIRT and concocted the Franglais *flirter*,   5165
flirteur, and *flirteuse*, discarding the older *fleureter*.)

In any case, English FLOURISH, FLORID, FLOWERY, and
FLORIDA are all borrowed from Latin *flōs*, *flōris*, by one avenue
or another; furthermore, they are etymologically related to English BLOOM and BLOSSOM by common descent from the Indo-   5170
European root **bhel-* 'to bloom, to thrive.'

The meaning of FLOURISH as used in the opening sentence
was arrived at by a semantic sequence that went something like
this: FLOURISH 'to blossom; to throw out leaves and shoots; to
make expressive gestures with the hands; to brandish, to wave   5175
about' [from Old French *florir*, *floriss(ant)*, from Vulgar Latin
*flōrīre, from Latin *flōrēre* 'to bloom']. Another meaning is 'to
thrive, to be prosperous,' as in the FLOURISHING Italian Renaissance city of FLORENCE, home of the FLORIN. Other derivatives of
Latin *flos*, *floris* 'flower' are FLORA 'plants collectively; the   5180
Roman goddess of flowers.' FLORA and FLORENCE ('blossoming')
are used as given names, with diminutives FLO, FLORRIE and
FLOSSIE. Also derived from Latin *flōs*, *flōris* 'flower' are FLORID
'flowery; overembellished; of a ruddy complexion' [from Latin

5185 *flōridus* 'flowery'] (some say by way of French *floride*) and
FLORIDA (Spanish) 'flowery; the southeasternmost part of the
United States.' The state is so named, not because Ponce de Leon
found it blooming with flowers in early 1513, but because he
arrived there at Eastertide, which in Spanish is sometimes called
5190 *Pascua Florida* 'the Feast of Flowers.' Yet another derivative of
Latin *flōs, flōris* is FLORESCENT 'beginning to bloom' (-*escent*
'beginning to'), not to be confused with fluorescent spelled with a
-*u*-, which means, literally, 'beginning to flow.' (See line 5323.)
Still more derivatives of Latin *flōs, flōris* include FLORENCE
5195 (literally) 'blooming' [from Latin *flōrentia,* from *flōrens* 'flowering,' from *flōrēre* 'to bloom, to thrive'] and FLORIN 'a gold coin
first issued at Florence in 1252' [from Italian *fiorino* 'little flower,'
from *fiore* 'flower']. (Latin *fl-* > Italian *fi-.*) The FLORIN was so
called because it was stamped with the figure of a lily. The Italian
5200 name of the city is *Firenze,* for *Fiorenza* 'flowering, flourishing.'
(Cf. *Fiorello* La Guardia, former mayor of New York, affection-
ately known as 'the little flower.')

Among the French derivatives of Latin *flōs, flōris* are *fleur de
lis* 'iris'; (literally) 'lily flower.' A stylized representation of the
5205 *fleur de lis* was used as an armorial bearing by the kings of
France. Note, also, FLEURET 'a light fencing foil'; (literally) 'little
flower.' The foil was so called because the protective button
on the tip of the blade resembles a flower bud. More French
derivatives of Latin *flōs, flōris* include FLOWER [from Old French
5210 *flo(u)r,* from Latin *flōs, flōrem*] and FLOUR (a variant spelling of
FLOWER) 'finely ground meal' [from Medieval French *flour de
farine,* from Latin *flōs farinae*]. Flour is made from the best meal,
or flower of the meal. A hybrid word is CAULIFLOWER (literally)
'flower cabbage' [from Italian *cavolfiore,* plural *caoli fiori* (Latin
5215 *caulis* 'cabbage, stalk')].

It's not much of a leap from FLOWERS to FOLIAGE 'the leaves
of growing plants,' which is another descendant of our Indo-
European root **bhel-* 'to bloom, to thrive,' by way of the *o*-grade
suffixed form **bhol-yo-,* which yields Latin *folium* 'leaf.' *Folium*
5220 evolved into Old French *foille,* whence *foillage* 'leafage,' borrowed into English and altered in the 17th century to FOLIAGE
due to the influence of Latin *folium. Folium* 'leaf' is used
unchanged in English as the scientific (New Latin) term FOLIUM
'a thin layer of rock; a kind of geometric curve resembling one
5225 blade of a cloverleaf.' From the ablative of *folium* we get FOLIO 'a
large sheet of paper folded once in the middle,' and from Old
French *foille* 'leaf' and its compounds we get FOIL 'a leaflike
design worked into stone or glass; a thin flexible sheet of metal; a
thin layer of bright metal placed under a gem to increase its

brilliance; anything that serves to set off something else by 5230
contrast.' A man's black-and-white evening dress serves as a FOIL
to his consort's gown. (But the *foil* of "Curses! foiled again!" is a
different word, as is, most authorities believe, a fencing *foil*.) Also
from Old French *foille* 'leaf' and its compounds are TREFOIL 'any
of various plants having compound leaves with three leaflets; any 5235
ornament having the appearance of a trifoliate leaf' (*trifolium*
'three-leafed plant; clover'); CINQUEFOIL 'a plant with five-lobed
leaves; an architectural design composed of five converging arcs'
[from Old French *cincfoille*, from Latin *quīnquefolium* 'five-leaf,'
a translation of Greek *pentaphullon*]; and MILFOIL 'the yarrow, a 5240
plant with many fine divisions of the leaf' [via Old French from
Latin *millefolium* 'thousand-leaf'].

'To strip a plant of its leaves' is to DEFOLIATE it, but to
EXFOLIATE means 'to remove in flakes, scales or leaves; to peel'
(skin, cuticle, the bark of a tree). A PORTFOLIO is 'a portable case 5245
for holding loose sheets of paper, drawings, etc., or the securities
held by an investor,' while a FEUILLETON is 'the feature section
of a European newspaper devoted to light literature, reviews, and
criticism'; (literally) 'a little leaf.'

In Greek, the **bh-* of the o-grade suffixed form **bhol-yo* 'leaf' 5250
changes *ph-*, yielding *phullon* 'leaf.' *Phullon* shows up in English
in the New Latin combining forms *phyllo-* and *-phyll*, as in
PHYLLOTAXY 'the arrangement of leaves on a stem' [*taxis* 'order']
and CHLOROPHYLL 'green pigment found in leaves and other
photosynthetic organisms'; (literally) 'green-leaf' [*khlōros* 'light 5255
green, yellow']. The proper name PHYLLIS means 'foliage of a
tree,' or 'a green bough.'

To resort to some learned phraseology, the Indo-European
root **bhel-* 'to thrive, to bloom' in the extended o-grade form
*bhlō- led to Latin *flōs* 'flower' (Indo-European **bh-* > Latin *f-*). 5260
The same **bhlo-* appears in Germanic **blō-mōn* (Indo-European
*bh- > Germanic **b-*), seen in English BLOOM 'flower; to flower;
a delicate powdery coating on fruit' [from Old Norse *blōm*
'flower']. There is another BLOOM 'a mass of iron or steel ready for
working' [from Old English *blōma*], that may or may not be 5265
related to BLOOM 'flower.' However, most definitely related to
BLOOM 'flower' is BLOOMER 'a plant that flowers.' There is also
another BLOOMER 'loose trousers gathered at the ankle and worn
under a short skirt; (plural) wide loose trousers gathered at the
knee and worn by girls as athletic costumes.' The garments were 5270
not named for the way they made their wearers look, but because
they were promoted by Amelia Jenks Bloomer, an American
suffragette (1816–1894) who advocated them as a mark of
women's liberation.

5275   An archaic English word meaning 'to bloom' is BLOW, as in
Shakespeare's: "I know a bank where the wild thyme blows,
Where oxlips and the nodding violet grows" (A *Midsummer
Night's Dream*). This BLOW is more frequently encountered in the
compound adjective FULL-BLOWN 'in full bloom.'

5280   The Old English equivalent and cognate of Old Norse *blōm*
'bloom, flower' was *blōstm*, *blōs(t)ma*, whence English BLOSSOM
'a flower, especially of a fruit tree or plant.' Each little leaf of
grass is called a BLADE 'the leaf of a grass; any thin structural
member; the cutting part of a tool' [from Old English *blæd*].

5285   The Indo-European root we have been exploring, **bhel-* 'to
bloom, to thrive,' is one of a family of roots having to do more
basically with 'swelling, flowing, overflowing.' For other, related
words see FLUID, next.

XXVII

Fluid Fluorescence; Mellifluous Affluence

A grammar school joke current in the 1870s was: "He opened the window, and INFLUENZA." Even way back then it was probably not a new joke, for the word INFLUENZA 'an acute, highly infectious disease, marked by fever, prostration, and severe aches and pains, that occurs in epidemic form,' was not new. In fact, the Italian word *influenza* has been in English since 1743, when a fierce epidemic of the disease spread from Italy throughout Europe. Before that, since 1504 or earlier, the word had been used in Italy with the sense of 'an epidemic' (*influenza di catarro, influenza di febbre scarlattina*). Literally, the word means 'an inflowing,' and comes from Medieval Latin *influentia*, from Latin *influere*, 'to flow in; to steal into.' The reason INFLU-ENZA was used to denote an epidemic disease was that the people of the era believed these pestilential visitations to be caused by an "astral INFLUENCE," or what astrologers would define as "an occult ethereal fluid flowing from the stars to affect the destiny of man."

The basic Latin verb is *fluere* 'to flow,' which has many English descendants such as INFLUENCE 'the power to produce effects by insensible means'; AFFLUENCE 'a plentiful supply of material goods'; (literally) 'a flowing toward' [*af-* > *ad-* 'toward']; EFFLUENT 'flowing out' [*ef-* > *ex-* 'out']; 'something that flows forth' (EFFLUVIUM, EFFLUX); CONFLUENCE 'a flowing together of two or more streams'; FLUENT 'flowing'; FLUID 'flowing'; SUPER-FLUOUS 'overflowing'; and MELLIFLUOUS 'flowing like honey; smooth and sweet' [*mel, mellis* 'honey'].

The related Latin word for 'a stream' is *flūmen*, whence the American English word FLUME 'a deep, narrow ravine; an artificial water chute' [via Middle English and Old French *flum*]. The related Latin word for 'a river' is *fluvius*, whence English FLU-

5290

5295

5300

5305

5310

5315

VIAL 'produced by the action of running water' [via Latin
5320   *fluviālis*].

Another (New) Latin word for 'flowing' is *fluor*, adopted into
the language of science to produce words like FLUOR, FLUORINE,
FLUORIDE, FLUORITE, FLUOROSCOPE, FLUOROMETER and FLUO-
RESCENCE, all having to do in one way or another with things in a
5325   state of FLUX 'a flowing' [from Latin *fluxus* 'flowing,' from *fluxus*,
past participle of *fluere* 'to flow']. An earlier form of the Latin past
participle *fluxus* is *fluctus*, also used as a noun to mean 'a current,
a wave,' and source of the verb *fluctuāre* 'to wave, to undulate,'
which yields English FLUCTUATE 'to rise and fall like the waves
5330   of the ocean; to vary irregularly.' Latin *fluxus* 'flowing' also led to
Old French *flux, flus* 'flux, flow; a flush (in playing cards),' which
was adapted into English with the last sense as FLUSH 'a hand in
cards consisting of cards all of one suit.'

There are other meanings of *flush* that are more closely
5335   related to 'a rush of flowing water' than a poker hand is. They
include 'to clean by a quick gush of water; to blush; to redden (by
a rush of blood to the skin); to be filled to overflowing; to be lined
up evenly.' However, the etymologists do not associate these
meanings with Latin *fluxus* 'flowing,' except as a passing influ-
5340   ence. They assign them instead to an imitative origin, influenced
by *flash, rush, gush,* and *blush,* that started with the sense of
'flying up suddenly' (like a startled covey of quail, *flushed* from
cover).

One might think that the English verb *to flow* must be
5345   descended from Latin *fluere* 'to flow,' but such is not the case:
indeed the two words are not even descended from the same
Indo-European root. Latin *fluere* traces back to Indo-European
bhleu- 'to well up, to overflow' and eventually to Indo-European
bhel- 'to swell,' while *flow* derives from Indo-European *pleu-*
5350   'to flow,' and is related to *fleet, fly,* and *pluvial.* (But one cannot
help wondering if Indo-European *bhleu-* and *bhel-* are not
ultimately related to *pleu-*.)

Another English word that is possibly derived from Indo-
European *bhleu-* 'to well up, to overflow' by way of Germanic is
5355   BLOAT 'to swell up with liquid, gas, or vanity' [from Old Norse
blautr 'soft, wet, soaked'; from Germanic *blaut-*]. When one is
'soft, wet, and soaked' is no time to be exposed, but that is just the
sense that seems to have developed in Middle Dutch *bloot*
'naked, exposed,' the source of an English word perhaps known
5360   only to backgammon players—BLOT 'an exposed piece in backgammon.' Also possibly derived from Indo-European *bhleu-* 'to
well up, to overflow' by way of Germanic is BLOT 'a spot, a stain.'
Some find that this BLOT has "no corresponding form . . . outside

English" (*OED*), while others refer to Icelandic *blettr* 'blot, stain' and Danish *blat* 'spot, blot,' and still others look for a source in 5365
Old French *blotte*, *blost(r)e* 'clod of earth.' BLOT is, however, ultimately of Germanic origin and perhaps traceable to another Indo-European root related to Indo-European **bhel-* 'to swell' (and therefore to Indo-European **bhleu-* 'to well up, to overflow'), to wit, **bhlei-* 'to blow, to swell.' Also from **bhlei-* are BLISTER 'a 5370
rounded swelling of the skin filled with watery matter' [from Old French *blestre* or Middle Dutch *bluyster*] and BLAIN 'a skin sore; a blister; a blotch' [from Old English *blegen* 'boil, blister,' from Germanic **blajinōn* 'a swelling' (*AHD*)]. BLAIN survives chiefly in the compound CHILBLAIN 'an inflammatory swelling of the hands 5375
and feet caused by exposure to cold.' A BLOTCH 'a discoloration of the skin' is thought to be a hybrid formed from *blot* and *botch* 'a swelling,' or an alteration of obsolete, synonymous *plotch*, or a combination of both processes (cf. *splotch*).

Two scientific terms based on Indo-European **bhleu-* 'to well 5380
up' reach us by way of Greek. They are PHLYCTENA 'a small blister' [from Greek *phluktaina* 'blister,' from *phlu(z)ein* 'to boil over'] and PHLOEM 'the food-conducting tissue of vascular plants' [from Greek *phloos* 'tree bark' ("swelling with growth" (*AHD*))].

For other words descended from **bhel-* 'to swell,' see Chap- 5385
ter XXVI, lines 5155 ff.

XXVIII

Focus on the Foyer

Any fool who FUELS flames in the FOYER of a theater will soon find the attentions of the security police FOCUSED on his person, and himself removed posthaste to the nearest place of
5390   detention. Such a pyromaniac could be laboring under the delusion that the word FOYER still meant what its ancestor meant, i.e., 'a fireplace.' The word FOYER 'the lobby of a theater or public building; an entrance hall' derives from Latin *focus* 'fireplace, hearth' by way of Vulgar Latin *focārium* 'fireplace,' Old French
5395   *fuier*, and Medieval/Modern French *foyer* 'a heated room.' In early theaters the auditoriums were poorly heated and playgoers were more than happy to get into 'a heated room' between acts. However, according to the *Oxford English Dictionary*, theatrical foyers were first provided for the performers rather than the
5400   spectators and were what are now called *greenrooms* 'waiting rooms in theaters or concert halls for the use of performers when off stage.'

In modern French, *foyer* still has the various meanings of 'fire-grate, hearth; firebox of a steam engine; bowl of a pipe;
5405   lobby, greenroom; focus.' In the Latin of classical Rome the ancestral term *focus* meant 'fireplace, hearth; fire-pan; altar; funeral pile; home and family,' and the *focus* 'hearth' was the dwelling place of the Lares, who were ancestral spirits and household deities.

5410   It was the German astronomer and mathematician Johannes Kepler who in 1604 first used the Latin word FOCUS to mean 'a point toward which lines converge,' and he is thought to have chosen this term because the rays of the sun, when refracted by a lens and brought to a FOCAL point on combustible material, are
5415   hot enough to start a fire.

In Late Latin, *focus* meant 'fire' and *focalia* meant 'fire things.' The latter word evolved into Old French *fouaille* 'a faggot, kindling,' whence Middle English *fewaile, feuel,* and English FUEL 'materials burned to produce heat.'

Any person prominently involved in a publicized controversy will be subjected to a FUSILLADE of questions from reporters whenever the opportunity presents itself. Luckily for the questionees, this is only a figure of speech, since a literal FUSILLADE is 'a discharge of many firearms, simultaneously or in rapid succession.' This definition doesn't specify what kind of firearms are being discharged, but a FUSIL is 'a light flintlock musket,' so called because it uses the spark of steel striking against flint to set off the gunpowder. 'Steel for striking fire' was called in Old French *fu(i)sil, foisil,* from Vulgar Latin **focile* 'of fire,' from Late Latin *focus* 'fire,' from Latin *focus* 'fireplace.' (But *fuse* 'length of combustible material,' *fuse* 'melt,' and *fusee* come from different sources.)

Late Latin *focus* 'fire' is also the ancestor of French *feu* 'fire,' a word that appears in the English compound CURFEW 'an ordinance requiring that certain activities cease at a stated time of night'; (literally) 'cover-fire' [from Medieval/Old French *covrefeu, cuevref(e)u*]. Modern curfews require, for instance, that juveniles be off the streets by ten or that no inning of a baseball game start after midnight; but during the early Middle Ages the curfew was a regulation that at a set hour of the evening, indicated by the tolling of a bell, all household fires must be covered over or extinguished, the purpose being to diminish the chance of conflagrations. By the 13th century the extinguishing of fires was no longer required, but the tolling of the bell continued to be heard in many localities at the appointed time, usually eight or nine o'clock, and it was still called the CURFEW bell: "The curfew tolls the knell of parting day" (Gray's *Elegy*); *Curfew Must Not Ring Tonight* (Rose Hartwick Thorpe).

In other Romance languages, Late Latin *focus* 'fire' became Italian *f(u)oco* 'fire,' as in the musical direction *con fuoco* 'with fire,' and Spanish *fuego* 'fire,' as in *Tierra del Fuego* 'land of the fire.'

The antecedents of Latin *focus* 'fireplace' are not known, although it is probably of non-Indo-European origin. (The Classical Latin words for *fire* were *ignis*, as in English *ignite*, *incendium* as in English *incendiary*, and *ardor*.) Therefore the similarities between English *fire* and the German cognate *Feuer* 'fire' on the one hand, and French *foyer* 'fire-grate' and *feu* 'fire' on the other are coincidental, since there is no established etymological connection between the two groups.

5420
5425
5430
5435
5440
5445
5450
5455
5460

FIRE and German *Feuer* are related, however, since they both come from the Indo-European root **pur-* 'fire,' which also leads to Greek *pur* 'fire' and the English loanwords PYRE 'a combustible pile, usually of wood, for burning a dead body as a funeral rite'
5465 [from Greek *pura* 'place where fire is kindled; funeral pile; burial place']; PYRITE 'fool's gold; iron disulfide'; and PYRITES 'any of various metallic sulfides' [from the Greek phrase *puritēs lithos* 'fire-stone; a mineral that strikes fire']. "Fire was obtained in the Bronze Age by striking a flint against a piece of pyrites" (W. B.
5470 Dawkins in the *OED*). Because of the spark-producing capability of pyrites, many fabulous properties were credited to it, such as being able to burn under water or warming the hands if pressed hard. Additional English loanwords include PYROMANIAC 'a fire-bug, an arsonist'; PYROTECHNICS 'fireworks'; and PYRACANTHA
5475 'fire thorn' (*akantha* 'thorn'), 'a shrub with bright red and orange berries.' Note, also, PYREX 'a trade name for heat-resistant glass'; PYROSIS 'heartburn'; (literally) 'fire condition'; and EMPYREAN 'the highest reaches of the heavens, believed by the ancients to be a realm of pure fire and light; the abode of God and the angels.'
5480   The expression "a PYRRHIC victory" means 'a victory won with staggering losses,' and dates back to the battle of Asculum, fought in 279 B.C. and won by King *Pyrrhus* of Epirus over the Romans with so many casualties on the winning side that the king exclaimed: "One more such victory over the Romans and we are
5485 utterly undone!" In Greek the word *purr(h)os** means 'fire-colored, red,' and it is possible that the king was so named because he was a redhead.
   The prosodic term PYRRHIC 'a metrical foot consisting of two short syllables' [from the Greek *purr(h)ikhē* 'a war dance'] is said
5490 to be named after its inventor, the poet-composer **Purr(h)ikhos*. It is tempting to speculate that the earliest Greeks performed their war dances (**purr(h)ikhē*) around bonfires (*pura*) as other primitive peoples did, especially since it is known that they cremated their slain heroes on PYRES. However, no hint of this possibility is
5495 given by the etymologists.

XXIX

Foreign Doors: Hors d'Oeuvres in the Faubourgs

In medieval London the residents of the city were called (in Anglo-French) *de(i)nzein* '(those) from within,' while the word for outsiders was *forein* '(those) outside the doors.' *De(i)nzen* was derived from Old French *deinz* and Latin *dē intus* 'from within,' and it eventually evolved into English *denizen* (and *deinz* became French *dans* 'within'). Anglo-French *forein, forain* is derived by way of Old French from Late Latin *forānus*, from Latin *forīs, forās* 'out of doors,' and it led to the modern English FOREIGN (obsolete) 'out of doors'; (obsolete) 'not belonging to one's family'; 'alien in character; introduced from outside; situated outside one's country.' (Latin *forīs* 'out of doors' became French *hors* 'out, beyond.' The -g- is not found in FOREIGN until the 17th century, and how it got there is not explained. Perhaps it was due to the influence of *reign* 'rule.' Cf. *sovereign* < Vulgar Latin **superanus*.)

Latin *forīs, forās* 'out of doors; from without; in public' are related to Latin *foris* 'door, gate,' and all are descended from the Indo-European root **dhwer-* 'door, doorway' (Indo-European **dh-* > Latin *f-*), which is also the ancestor of English DOOR 'a movable barrier serving to close or open a passage; an entranceway' [from Old English *dor* 'gate,' *duru* 'door']. (Modern German cognates are *Tür* 'door' and *Tor* 'gate.')

From the sequence of the historical meanings of FOREIGN, one gets the impression of man huddled indoors with the members of his immediate family, gradually extending his horizon to include his neighbors, his village, his town, his city, and finally his country. Thus, the word FOREIGNER has had its limits pushed further and further back.

A Latin word descended from Indo-European **dhwer-* 'door' that has been carried over bodily into English is FORUM (originally) ' "the enclosed space around a house" ' (*AHD*); 'the market-place of an ancient Roman city; a public meeting place; a place where public discussions and debate are carried on; a court, a tribunal.' The forum in Rome, established sometime before the

5530   6th century B.C., was an open-air, 'out-of-doors' place of assembly for the conducting of civic, judicial, and other public business. Because of these associations, the adjective of FORUM, FORENSIC, means 'pertaining to oratory and debate; pertaining to legal argumentation' (FORENSIC medicine) [from Latin *forēnsis* 'belong-

5535   ing to the forum'].

Another outdoorsy place is the FOREST (originally) 'a wood-land district belonging to the king and set aside for hunting'; 'an extensive tract of land covered with trees' [from the Medieval Latin phrase *forestem silvam* 'outside woods']. *Forestem silvam*

5540   or *forestis silva* was originally used with reference to the royal game preserve of Charlemagne. 'Outside' here obviously does not mean 'out-of-doors,' but either 'outside the public domain; reserved for royal use,' or 'outside the royal park (not fenced in), but reserved for royal use.' Thus the Medieval Latin word *forestis*

5545   had meanings similar to the Medieval Latin meaning of *forum*, which was 'court of the King's justice,' according to O. Bloch and M. von Wartburg. That the forest was the king's preserve is clearly evidenced by this 1598 definition: "A Forrest is certen Territorie of wooddy grounds and fruitfull pastures, priuileged for

5550   wild beasts and foules of Forrest, Chase and Warren, to rest and abide in, in the safe protection of the King, for his princely delight and pleasure." (John Manwood, *A Treatise and discourse of the lawes of the forrest*, quoted in the *OED*). Because of the status of the forest as a princely preserve, the FORESTER was ' "an

5555   officier of a forest of the King ... that is sworn to preserve the Vert and Venison of the same forest, and to attend vpon the wild beasts within his Bailiwick, and to attach offenders there" ' (*ibid.*) and is today 'one trained in the science of woodlands management.' (The discrepancies in the spelling and capitalization of

5560   *forest* in the John Manwood quotations may be explained by the fact that the second excerpt was taken from a 1615 edition.)

In only two of the many English verbs that begin with *for(e)* does that prefix derive from Latin *forīs* 'outside, out of doors.' Those two are FORFEIT 'to be required to give up something as

5565   punishment for a breach of the rules'; (literally) 'to do outside; to do something outside the permitted limits, to overstep the bounds'; (obsolete) 'to sin' [from Old French *forfet*, past participle of *for(s)faire* 'to commit a crime,' from Medieval Latin *forisfacere* 'to transgress'] and FORECLOSE 'to shut out; to deprive a mortga-

5570   gor of the right to redeem his property' [from Old French *forclos*, past participle of *forclore*, from Latin *forīs* 'outside' + *claudere* 'to close'].

More French than English is HORS *d'oeuvre* 'an appetizer'; (literally) 'outside of the work; not part of the regular meal.' (See line 7757.) Latin *forīs* > Old French *fors* changed to Modern French *hors* during the 13th–15th centuries. Also more French than English are HORS *de combat* 'out of the fight; disabled' and FAUBOURG 'a suburb'; (literally) 'outside the city' [from Medieval/ Old French *faubourg*, a variant influenced by *faux* 'false' of Old French *forsborc*; from Latin *forīs* 'outside' + Late Latin *burgus* 'fortified place, town']. The spelling with *fau-* indicates that the French speakers took seriously the idea that obsolete *fauxbourg* derived from Medieval Latin *falsus burgus* 'false town; not the town proper.' However, the earlier Old French spellings of *forsborc*, *forsbourg* point to the true derivation from Latin *forīs* 'outside' + Late Latin *burgus* 'fortified place, town' (this "Latin" word comes from Germanic **burgs* 'hill-fort'). A possible explanation for the change in spelling from *for-* to *fau-* may be found in the Middle High German word *falborgere* 'burgher of the pale,' where *fal-* means 'the pale; the space within the outer palisades of the town but beyond the town walls.' German scholars Latinized *falborgere* as *phalburgensis*, and from there it is only a step to the erroneous or punning translations *falsus burgensis* > *falsus burgus* > *fauxbourg*. The old faubourgs of Paris are 'suburbs' only in the same sense that Greenwich Village is a suburb of New York, for it is many years since they were outside the city limits.

Other descendants of Indo-European **dhwer-* 'door' are one English loanword from the Greek and one from Hindi and Persian. From the Greek we have THYROID 'an endocrine gland found in all vertebrates'; (literally) 'door-shaped' [New Latin, from Medieval Greek *thuroidēs* 'door-shaped,' from Late Greek *thureoeidēs* 'shield-shaped,' from Greek *thureos* 'a long shield,' from *thura* 'door']. From the Persian via Hindi we get DURBAR 'the court of an Indian prince' [from Hindi *darbār*, borrowed in turn from Persian *darbār* 'court' (*dar* 'door' + *bār* 'admission; audience')].

5575

5580

5585

5590

5595

5600

5605

XXX

The Fugitive's Refuge

The preludes and FUGUES of J. S. Bach have more than a FUGITIVE charm; their flowing polyphonic progressions afford a welcome if FUGACIOUS REFUGE from modernity. The linguistic
5610   source of these fleeting words is the Indo-European root *bheug- 'to flee.' *Bheug- doesn't have a large progeny in English, where its only descendants come to us as loanwords from Latin fugere 'to flee,' fugare 'to put to flight,' and fuga 'a running away.' There is one exception, however, the architectural term APOPHYGE 'the
5615   curvature at the top and bottom of the shaft of a column' [from Greek apophugē 'escape, flight' (apo 'away' + phugē 'flight')], surely a poetic way of describing an architectural feature.

Latin fuga 'running away' has come down to Italian as fuga 'escape, flight,' but Renaissance musicians also used the word to
5620   denote a FUGUE 'a polyphonic composition constructed on one or more short themes which are harmonized according to the laws of counterpoint.' This usage seems another flight of poetic fancy, however, one that aptly expresses the way the musical themes chase one another down the echoing corridors of memory. The
5625   Italian word fuga was adapted into French in the form fugue, but it first appears in English in 1597 with the spelling fuge.

Modern medicine has also adopted the word FUGUE to mean 'a prolonged pathological condition during which the patient is apparently aware of his actions, though on return to normal he has
5630   no recollection of them.'

Another loanword from Latin is FUGITIVE 'a person who is on the run, fleeing from something; passing quickly, fleeting' [from Latin fugitīvus, by way of Medieval/Old French fugitive; from fugitum, past participle of fugere 'to flee']. A secondary meaning
5635   of Latin fugitīvus is 'a runaway slave,' a meaning that reminds us

of the Fugitive Slave Laws passed by the U.S. Congress at various times (the first was in 1793).

What a fugitive is looking for is a REFUGE 'a place providing protection or shelter' [via Medieval/Old French from Latin *refugium* 'a place to flee back to,' from *refugere* 'to flee back'], and a REFUGEE is 'a person looking for a safe place.' What about a SUBTERFUGE 'a device one resorts to for escape or concealment'? This comes from Late Latin *subterfugium*, from Latin *subterfugere* (literally) 'to flee under' = 'to flee secretly' [Latin *subter* 'below, underhand, in secret'].

Another English word expressing this idea of 'fleeing, fleeting' is FUGACIOUS 'evanescent, lasting but a short time' [from Latin *fugāx*, *fugacis* 'swift, fleeing'], used of short-lived flowers or their parts. Note, also, LUCIFUGOUS 'avoiding or turning away from light' [*lux*, *lucis* 'light'].

Related to Latin *fugere* 'to flee' and *fuga* 'flight' is Latin *fugāre* 'to cause to flee; to drive away.' It is this transitive sense that is behind CENTRIFUGE 'a rotating device for separating materials of different density.' "CENTRIFUGAL force" is an expression first used by astronomers to explain why the planets don't fall into the sun. It also explains why artificial satellites don't fall to earth, why you can swing a bucket of water over your head without losing any of the water, and why your body sways to one side when you are going around a curve in a car. All these objects, planets, satellites, water, bodies, are being driven away from the center by the rotation. One may take note, also, of FEBRIFUGE 'any agent that reduces a fever' [from Latin *febris* 'fever' + *fugāre* 'to drive away']. A perennial Eurasian plant, *Chrysanthemum parthenium*, has the popular name FEVERFEW 'fever-chaser' [an alteration of Latin *febrifugia*].

Finally from Indo-European **bheug-* 'to flee' is the name given to the first coinage authorized by the U.S. Congress, in 1787, which was a copper coin designed by B. Franklin and popularly known as a FUGIO (literally) 'I flee,' so called because it had that Latin word inscribed on it, as well as a sundial and the admonition, "Mind your business."

Not the same root but similar enough to warrant inclusion here is Indo-European **bhegw-* 'to run away,' ancestor of Greek *phebesthai* 'to flee in terror' and its associated noun *phobos* 'panic, fear, flight.' *Phobos* has given rise to New Latin > English PHOBIA 'an irrational dread; an intense animosity.' PHOBIA has a few relatives, like PHOBIC 'relative to,' PHOBIAC 'one that,' PHOBISM 'condition of,' and innumerable compounds that refer to specific dreads, aversions, sensitivities and compulsions. For example, ACROPHOBIA 'dread of high places' [*akros* 'upper, top-

5640

5645

5650

5655

5660

5665

5670

5675

5680

most']; BATHOPHOBIA 'dread of depths' [*bathos* 'depth']; and
AGORAPHOBIA 'dread of open spaces' [*agora* 'marketplace, plaza'].
AGORAPHOBIA was apparently coined in 1873 by one Dr. C.
Westphal because a Greek AGORA 'marketplace, square, plaza' is
5685   open in contrast to the narrow streets of old cities. AGORA- has
always seemed to me a poor choice for the meaning intended,
because the 'marketplace' sense causes one to envision an area
cluttered with food stalls and stands of merchandise and throng-
ing with buyers and sellers, rather than the 'open space' of a
5690   deserted marketplace. Furthermore, Greek AGORA has a primary
meaning of 'meeting, congregation,' a sense that is not indicative
of open spaces, but rather one which would tend to make
AGORAPHOBIA mean 'dread of assemblies,' rather than 'dread of
open spaces.' In any case, 'dread of assemblies' is what is now
5695   called OCHLOPHOBIA 'a dread of crowds' [*okhlos* 'crowd, mob'] or
CLAUSTROPHOBIA 'a dread of enclosed places' [Latin *claustrum*
'bar, bolt']. ANGLO-, FRANCO-, GALLO-, GERMANO-, ITALO-, HIS-
PANO-, POLONO-, SINO-, etc. -PHOBIA is 'aversion toward anything
English, French, Gallic, German, Italian, Spanish, Polish, Chi-
5700   nese,' etc. Another PHOBIA compound is HYDROPHOBIA 'rabies in
human beings; dread of or aversion to water; resistance to
wetting' (as exhibited by ducks' wings, nylon, etc.) [*hudōr*
'water']. The reason that 'rabies in humans' is called HYDROPHO-
BIA is that the disease, after an incubation period of from three
5705   weeks to several months, manifests itself in a sense of dryness
and constriction in the throat that makes swallowing difficult and
results in convulsions following an attempt to drink water or even
at the sight or sound of water. More PHOBIA compounds include
DORAPHOBIA 'dread of furs' [*dora* 'hide, skin']; HERESYPHOBIA;
5710   PYROPHOBIA 'dread of fire' [*pur* 'fire']; and SYPHILOPHOBIA 'dread
of syphilis' [from *Syphilus*, protagonist of a 1530 Latin poem
Syphilis sive Morbus Gallicus 'Syphilis or the French Disease'],
written by a Veronese physician, Girolamo Fracastoro]. *Syphilus*,
a shepherd, is portrayed as the first sufferer from syphilis. Still
5715   more PHOBIA compounds are TOXICOPHOBIA 'dread of poi-
son(ing)' [(*pharmakon*) *toxikon* '(poison, drug) of an arrow'
(*toxon* 'arrow')]; ZOOPHOBIA 'dread of animals' [*zōon* 'animal'];
HELIOPHOBIA 'abnormal sensitivity to sunlight' [*helios* 'the sun'];
PHOTOPHOBIA 'painful sensitivity to light' [*phōs, phōtos* 'light'];
5720   CHROMOPHOBIC 'not readily absorbing stain' [*khrōma* 'color']; and
the ultimate PHOBOPHOBIA 'dread of fear.' This last PHOBIA is not
exactly the same but is similar to what F. D. Roosevelt had in
mind when he said: "The only thing we have to fear is fear
itself."

Indo-European *bhegw- 'to run away' has one English conse-   5725
quent that comes to us by way of the Germanic, namely, BECK 'a
small brook' [from Old Norse bekkr 'a stream,' from Germanic
*bakjaz 'a stream']. *Bakjaz is also the source of German Bach
'brook,' as in J. S. Bach, who (some listeners think) keeps running
on and on and on and on.   5730

XXXI

Habitual Duties;
Exhibitions *and*
Inhibitions

The GIVING of a GIFT creates a DEBT in the psyche of the recipient, who feels DUTY-bound to reciprocate. If he is not ABLE to do so, further friendship may be INHIBITED. GIFTS, DEBTS, DUTIES, ABILITIES and INHIBITIONS are all derived etymologically
5735   from the Indo-European root *ghabh- 'to give, to receive; to take.' All of them except GIFT have reached English by way of the Latin verb *habēre* 'to hold, to possess, to have.' Since one of the meanings of Latin *habēre* is 'to have,' it may be just as well to point out immediately that, despite the resemblance, English *to*
5740   *have* is not derived from Latin *habēre* 'to have.' The English word comes from Germanic *habēn*, from the Indo-European root *kap-* 'to grasp.'

On the other hand, French *avoir* 'to have' is a derivative of Latin *habere* and consequently so is the English weights-and-
5745   measures term AVOIRDUPOIS 'a system of weights based on a pound weighing 16 ounces or 7000 grains, and equal to 453.59 grams.' The word AVOIRDUPOIS looks as if it means 'to have some weight,' but etymologically and historically the word should be spelled *avoir-de-pois* or *averdepois* meaning 'possessions of
5750   weight; property whose value depends upon its weight.' The English word comes from the Old French phrase *aveir de peis*: *aveir* 'goods' + *de* 'of' + *peis* > *poids* 'weight' [Latin *habēre* + *dē* + *pēnsum*]. The substitution in the English word of *-du-* 'of the; some' for *-de-* 'of' was made "by some ignorant 'improver' *c.*
5755   1640–1650" (*OED*).

Another technical term, this one straight from the Latin, is HABEAS corpus 'a writ requiring that a person held in custody be brought before the court so that the lawfulness of his detention may be investigated'; (literally) 'thou shalt have the body (in
5760   court)' [the subjunctive/imperative *habeas* '(that) thou hast, thou

shalt have' + *corpus* 'body']. Another word straight from the Latin is HABITAT 'natural abode; the kind of environment that an organism normally lives in'; (literally) 'it inhabits' [the third person singular present tense of *habitāre* 'to inhabit, to dwell']. HABITAT was used in early natural histories, written in Latin, to   5765
indicate the geographical and topographical regions where a species HABITUALLY lives. The Latin verb *habitāre* comes from *habēre* 'to have, to possess,' and means 'to possess frequently,' hence 'to dwell in.' If one takes possession of a place frequently enough, one ends up residing there or is said to INHABIT 'to   5770
occupy as a place of settled residence.' People or animals that occupy a certain place are called its INHABITANTS, unless that place happens to be Canada or Louisiana where the people are French-speaking, in which case they are called HABITANTS 'mem-
bers of the race of original French colonists of Canada and   5775
Louisiana' [from French *habitant* 'inhabitant, resident'].

Living in the same place can get to be a HABIT 'a compulsive inclination to perform some act, acquired through constant repetition; a distinctive dress or costume' (a nun's HABIT, a riding HABIT) [from Latin *habitus* 'condition, state; dress, attire,' past   5780
participle of *habēre* 'to possess; to be characterized by'].

If a man and woman live together as husband and wife they are said to COHABIT (literally) 'to inhabit with,' whether married or not. The word is often used of couples not legally married, but this distinction is not implicit in the word.   5785

A fellow who is always to be found at a certain place is said to be a HABITUÉ 'a frequenter of a particular place or kind of place' [from French *habituer* 'to frequent,' from Late Latin *habituāre* 'to condition,' based on Latin *habitus* 'condition, state']. Late Latin *habituāre* 'to condition' also leads to English HABITUATE 'to   5790
accustom to by long practice; to fix in a habit.'

Similar in meaning to HABIT 'dress, attire' is French *habiller* 'to dress, to clothe; to make clothes for' and its negative *deshabiller* 'to undress.' *Deshabiller* has been adapted into English in the word DISHABILLE 'undress; the state of being only partially or   5795
very casually dressed' [from Latin *dis-* > Old French *des-*, indicating 'reversal' + *habiller* 'to dress']. *Habiller* 'to dress, to clothe' is an outgrowth from Latin *habilis*, whose basic meaning is 'holdable, easy to hold,' hence 'ready > suitable, fit.' *Habiller*, then, would be the end product of a sequence that went some-   5800
thing like 'to make ready > to render fit and suitable > to clothe.'

Also descended from Old French *habiller* 'to clothe' is English HABILIMENT(S) 'vestments, clothes,' and from its Latin antecedent *habilis* 'easy to hold; ready; suitable; manageable, handy' comes one of the handiest words in the English language,   5805

ABLE 'having sufficient power (to); skilled, talented' [from Medieval/Old French *able*, from Latin *habilis*]. In Modern French, the *h-* of Latin *habilis* has been restored to the spelling (but not to the pronunciation) to make *habile* 'skillful, clever, able,' sometimes used in English HABILE 'adroit, skillful; able.'

Although not etymologically related to the Indo-European root *ghabh-* 'to give, to receive; to take,' the ubiquitous suffixes *-ble, -able,* and *-ible* are associated in usage with ABLE because such words as *eatable* or *perishable* can be analyzed as 'ABLE to be eaten' or 'capable of perishing.' (They would be more correctly interpreted as 'fit to be eaten' and 'tending to perish.') The English suffixes come from Latin *-bilis*, denoting a passive tendency, as in *legibilis* 'readable, easily read,' or an active tendency, as in *terribilis* 'tending to cause terror.'

The *-able, -ible* suffixes have been adopted by English speakers almost on a do-it-yourself basis, so that the number of such words is limited only by the number of English verbs there are to attach the suffixes to, at least in nonce usage. In one case, the noun *knowledge* is so extended to make the adjective KNOWLEDGEABLE 'well-informed; capable of retaining knowledge'; (obsolete) 'perceptible.' KNOWLEDGEABLE is listed in some older dictionaries as colloquial, but it seems to have gained favor recently among the literati. Other noteworthy compounds are CAPABLE 'competent, efficient; (literally) 'able to hold; capacious' [from Late Latin *capabilis* 'able to hold, roomy,' based on *capere* 'to take, to hold'] and RELIABLE 'trustworthy, capable of being relied upon.' RELIABLE has been in frequent use since about 1850. Although sometimes decried by Britishers as an Americanism, it really isn't, since it was used as long ago as 1569 in Scotland and 1624 in England. Note, also, FRANGIBLE 'fragile, breakable.' Though much more frequent, Latin *-bilis* 'tending to' is in fact merely an extended form of Latin *-ilis* > English *-ile* 'tending to.' Note the similarity in meaning of *frangible, fragile* 'breakable,' *tangible, tactile* 'touchable,' *feasible, facile* 'doable,' *volatile* 'tending to fly away,' and, finally, HABILE 'skillful'; (literally) 'easy to hold, easy to handle.'

The English adjective ABLE 'having sufficient power, capable' underlies the verbs ENABLE 'to make possible; to supply with a means' and DISABLE 'to render incapable, to cripple,' both dating from the 15th century and having no Latin or French antecedents as compound words.

The evolution of Latin *habilis* > Old French *able* to English ABLE is paralleled by that of Latin *habilitās* to English ABILITY 'competence, skill' [by way of Medieval/Old French (*h*)*abilite, ablete*]. Latin *habilitās* 'ability, aptitude; fitness' also leads to the

Late Latin verb *habilitāre* 'to render fit, to qualify,' whence English HABILITATE 'to supply with the means'; especially 'to back a mining operation' [after Spanish *habilitar*]; or 'to qualify for an office' [after German *habilitieren*]. Note, also, the much more frequently used (especially in sociological jargon) REHABILI-   5855
TATE 'to restore to usefulness; to reinstate; to restore the good name of.'

So much for the English words acquired from simple Latin *habēre* 'to hold, to possess, to have.' In compound forms, Latin *habēre* often changes to *-hibere*, as manifested in English INHIBIT   5860
'to hold in, to hold back, to restrain' [from Latin *inhibēre* 'to hold in, to hold back, to restrain,' also 'to row backwards']. INHIBIT is a word much used in psychology, along with its noun INHIBITION 'the stopping or checking of an action; a psychic block.' More compounds from Latin *habēre* > *-hibere* are English EXHIBIT 'to   5865
show, to display'; (literally) 'to hold out' [from Latin *exhibēre* 'to hold forth, to display'] and PROHIBIT 'to prevent; to forbid'; (literally) 'to hold in front; forward' [from Latin *prōhibēre* 'to keep in check, to prevent, to forbid']. Semantically, some interpret Latin *prōhibēre* as meaning 'to hold forward,' hence 'out of the   5870
way,' hence 'to prevent,' hence 'to order the prevention of.' However, it seems just as logical for *prōhibēre* to mean 'to hold in front of,' hence 'to bar the way,' hence 'to prevent,' etc.

Less obviously borrowed from Latin *habēre* 'to hold' is this English word, much distorted by time and slurring tongues: 5875
BINNACLE 'the housing of a ship's compass'; (literally) 'little habitation' [from Early Modern English *bittacle*, *bitakle*, *biticle*; from Portuguese *bitácola* or Spanish *bitácula*, *bitácora*; from Latin *habitāculum* 'small dwelling,' from *habitāre* 'to inhabit,' from *habēre* 'to hold']. "The change from *tt* to *nn* may have been   5880
bridged by such a form as *biddikil*" (*ODEE*) or was perhaps brought about by the influence of *bin* 'receptacle.' Note, also, PROVENDER 'dry food for livestock; food' [from Old French *provend(r)e*, from Medieval Latin *prōbenda* 'fodder']. *Prōbenda* is an alteration, confusing *prae-* for *prō-*, of Latin *praebenda*, itself a   5885
contraction of *praehibenda* 'things to be held forth; things to be supplied' [from *prae* 'before, in front' + *habenda* 'things to be held,' gerund of *habēre* 'to hold']. Another descendant of Latin *praebenda* 'things to be supplied' is the ecclesiastical PREBEND 'a clergyman's stipend granted out of the estate of his church' and   5890
MALADY 'a sickness; any unwholesome condition' [from Old French *maladie*, from *malade* 'sick'; from the (Late) Latin phrase *male habitus* 'badly kept, in poor condition' (*male* 'badly,' *habitus* 'condition')].

5895   Similar to the telescoping of Latin *praehibenda* into *praebenda* is the contraction of *dehibēre* into *dēbēre* (literally) 'to hold from; to have by withholding payment,' hence 'to owe.' Latin *dēbēre* has weighty English descendants, like DEBIT 'owed; an item on the left hand side of an account in bookkeeping' [from

5900   Latin *dēbitum* 'due, debt,' past participle of *dēbēre* 'to owe']. Latin *dēbitum* 'debt' became Vulgar Latin **dēbita* but suffered the loss of its internal -*b*- while evolving into Old French *dette*. *Dette* came into Middle English in that form and was shortened to *det*, but Latinists worried about the missing -*b*- and many of

5905   them inserted it into their spelling of the English word, so that by the 16th century the spelling DEBT 'that which is owed' had become standard, although the -*b*- had never been pronounced in English. (Compare *doubt*, line 1164.) Another derivative of Latin *dēbēre* is DEBENTURE 'an unsecured bond; a certificate acknowl-

5910   edging debt' [from Latin *debentur* 'they are owed,' 3rd person plural passive of *dēbēre* 'to owe']. Latin *dēbēre* evolved into Old French *devoir* 'to owe.' *Devoir* was also used as a substantive meaning 'that which is owed; duty,' and was taken into English as (modern spelling) DEVOIR 'courteous attention, social duty' (to pay

5915   one's DEVOIRS to the hostess) [via Middle English *dever*]. The Middle English pronunciation of Old French *devoir* as *dever* has survived in modern English in the word ENDEAVOR 'to strive, to make an earnest attempt' [from the phrase *to put oneself in dever*, translating the French *se mettre en devoir* 'to make it one's duty'].

5920   The past participle of Latin *dēbēre* 'to owe' was drastically shortened from Latin *dēbitum* > Vulgar Latin **dēbūtum* to (the past participle of Old French *devoir*) Old French *deü* 'owed.' *Deü* has become modern French *dû*, *due* and English DUE 'owed as a debt; payable immediately; owing' (DUE to circumstances . . .);

5925   'scheduled' (the train is DUE at . . .). The negative of DUE, UNDUE, while retaining its literal sense of 'not due, not yet payable,' has acquired additional meanings of 'unseasonable' (one should not visit at UNDUE hours); 'excessive; illegal' (UNDUE influence).

        Apparently a coinage of the Anglo-French-speaking Normans

5930   in England is the word DUTY 'a moral obligation; what is owed; a course of action demanded by social tradition; a tax on certain transactions' [from Anglo-Norman *deweté*, *dueté*, based on Old French *deu* 'owed'], "as if ultimately from Latin **debitas, debitatem*" (*EP*).

5935   The Indo-European root **ghabh-* 'to give, to receive; to take' that gave us Latin *habēre* 'to hold' and its derivatives has also given us, by way of the variant form **ghebh-*, the English words GIVE, GAVE 'to make a present; to bestow' [from Old English *giefan, geaf*, from Germanic **giban*] and the associated noun GIFT

'a present; that which is given' [from Old Norse *gipt, gift,* from   5940
Germanic **giftiz*]. A grisly cognate is the German *Gift* (obsolete)
'a present, a gift'; (Middle High German, translating Late Latin
dosis 'a giving') 'a dose'; (modern German) 'poison.'

The compound verb FORGIVE 'to pardon; to give up claim of
requital' [from Old English *forgiefan,* from Germanic **fer-giban*]   5945
is said to be a translation of Medieval Latin *perdōnāre* 'to pardon,'
from *per* 'for, through' + *dōnāre* 'to give.' The Classical Latin for
pardon is *ignoscere* 'to overlook' or *venia dare* 'to give indulgence.' It seems just as plausible that the Medieval Latin was a
translation of the Germanic, as the *OED* conjectures when it says   5950
that *pardon* is "perhaps after Old High German *forgeben*
'FORGIVE.'"

XXXII

Haughty Old Alumni *and* Proliferating Adolescents

ADOLESCENTS usually imagine themselves to be ADULTS long before they have achieved that EXALTED state; on the other hand,

5955 they can't imagine themselves as ever growing OLD, even though they know that man has not yet succeeded in ABOLISHING old age. The secret syllable here is *-al-*, sometimes disguised as *-ol-* or *-ul-*. It is based on the Indo-European root *al-* 'to nourish,' a root that can be discerned with its original significance intact in the words

5960 ALIMENT 'food, nourishment' [from Latin *alimentum*, from *alere* 'to nourish'] and ALIMENTARY 'having to do with nutrition,' and lurking in the background of the word ALIMONY 'sustenance; maintenance, support; a court-ordered allowance for support' [from Latin *alimōnia* 'sustenance, nutriment'].

5965 Besides the verb *alere* 'to nourish' and the nouns *alimentum*, *alimōnia* 'nourishment,' Latin has an adjective *almus*, *alma*, *almum* 'nourishing, giving food, bountiful.' The Romans bestowed the epithet *alma mater* 'bounteous mother; foster mother' on certain goddesses, notably Ceres, the goddess of

5970 growing vegetation and agriculture, and Cybele, the Anatolian goddess of nature, ' "nourishing mother of men, giver of the arts of life, and founder and upholder of cities and nations' " (*MW2*). In English, the title of ALMA MATER 'foster mother' has been transferred to schools and colleges, as nourishers of the minds and

5975 characters of their students, who consequently are looked upon as their foster children. The Latin words for foster child are *alumnus*, *alumna*, words that also mean 'nurseling' and 'pupil.' Nowadays, in American English, ALUMNUS, ALUMNA mean 'a former student at a school, college or university,' though it was not so long ago

5980 that they also meant 'pupil.' In fact, the only definition given in the *Oxford English Dictionary* for ALUMNUS is: "The nurseling or pupil of any school, university, or other seat of learning." The word is marked as not naturalized, and the feminine ALUMNA is not even given. (This treatment has been updated in the *Supplement*, where ALUMNA is labeled "Chiefly U.S." The added definition of ALUMNUS is "Also, a graduate or former student." Examples are given of U.S. use, "esp. in *pl.*") Incidentally, there is another *alma* from the Italian meaning 'soul' that is sometimes mistaken for the *alma* of *alma mater*, which would make that phrase mean 'soul mother.' The Italian *alma* (and French *âme*) come from Latin *anima* 'soul; breath; breeze,' and have nothing to do with food or with *alma mater*.

Whatever is nourished tends to grow, to grow up, to grow older, and for a while to grow taller, that is, higher. To express the idea of 'growing though nourishment' there developed in Latin the verb *alēscere* (literally) 'to begin to nourish; to grow,' from *al-* + the inchoative ('beginning to') suffix *-ēscere*. From *alēscere* 'to grow' the Latin speakers developed the further compounded verb *adolēscere* [*ad* + *alēscere*] (literally) 'to grow toward' = 'to grow up.' *Adolēscere* has the present participle *adolēscēns* and the past participle *adultus*, ancestors of English ADOLESCENT 'growing up' and ADULT 'grown up.'

The 'growing' significance of Latin *alēscere* is apparent in English COALESCE 'to grow together; to unite' [from Latin *coalēscere*], but less obvious in the related noun COALITION 'a combination, a union; an alliance' [from Medieval Latin *coalitiō*], and scarcely noticeable in ABOLISH 'to do away with, to destroy; to annul' [via Old French *abolir, aboliss(ant)* from Latin *abolēscere* 'to wither, to disappear' inchoative form of *abolēre* 'to destroy; to take away'] or its related noun ABOLITION 'annulment; destruction' [from Latin *abolitiō* 'abolition, amnesty']. Classical Latin *abolēre* means 'to destroy,' but the etymological sense is 'to take nourishment away from,' which would seem equivalent to 'to starve to death.' Related, but less frequently encountered words are ALIBLE 'nourishing' [from Latin *alibilis*] and ALTRICIAL 'requiring nourishment and protection when newborn' [from Latin *altrīx, altrīcis* 'nurse, foster mother']. It should be pointed out that ADULT has nothing to do with either *adultery* or *adulterate*, both of which stem from Latin *ad* + *alter* 'other' and have a basic sense of corrupting or debasing with foreign ('other') ingredients.

To say that the PROLETARIAT is PROLIFIC is not only platitudinous, it is also tautological. The Romans called their PROLIFERATING poor, who had no land and no capital or other means of economic production, *proletarii*, because all they could produce was *prōlēs* 'offspring.' *Prōlēs* (for **prōoles, *prōales*) is another compound based on *alere* 'to nourish, to rear,' this time with the

prefix *prō-* 'forth, forward,' so that *prōlēs* means 'that which is grown forth' = 'offspring.' English offspring of *prōlēs* are PRO-
6030   LIFIC 'fertile; producing abundant fruit' [from Medieval Latin *prolificus* 'making offspring' (*-ficus* < *facere* 'to make')]; PROLIF-ERATE 'to reproduce rapidly' [from Medieval Latin *prōlifer* 'one who bears offspring' (*ferre* 'to bear')]; and PROLETARIAT 'men and women without property who have nothing to sell but their labor'
6035   and "nothing to lose but their chains." PROLETARIAT is a French word much bandied about since the days of Karl Marx. Another English derivative of *prōlēs* 'offspring' is PROLAN 'a hormone found in high concentration in the urine of pregnant women' which is harmful to rabbits.
6040   The classical past participle of Latin *alere* 'to nourish, to bring up' is *alitus*, but in earlier Latin it was *altus*. It is not a coincidence that the Latin word for 'high' is also *altus*, and that the Latin word for 'height' is *altum* (which also means 'depth'), for these words were originally those same archaic past participles
6045   *altus, altum* 'reared, nourished.' English has a few words whose relationship to Latin *altus* 'high' is immediately apparent. For example, ALTITUDE 'height above sea level' [from Latin *altitūdō* 'height, depth']; ALTIMETER 'an instrument for measuring height'; ALTO (originally) 'a high male singing voice, above tenor; the
6050   lowest female singing voice; CONTRALTO; and EXALT 'to place in a high position' [from Latin *exaltāre* 'to raise high'].
    The *Oxford English Dictionary* says that the word ALTAR 'a raised structure on which sacrifices to a deity are made' is from Latin *altare*, plural *altaria*, and that it probably originally meant
6055   'a high place,' from Latin *altus* 'high.' That derivation is disputed by some other authorities, including the *OED's* companion, the *Oxford Dictionary of English Etymology*, which defines *altaria* as 'burnt offerings, altar,' and offers that *altare, altaria* are related to Latin *adolere* 'to burn in sacrifice' and *olere* 'to smell.' The *ODEE*
6060   opinion is the more recent (1966), but some of the newer dictionaries, e.g. the *Random House* (also 1966) go along with the *altus* 'high' derivation.
    Latin *altus* 'high,' after a brush with Germanic **hauh(az)* 'high' (the source of German *hoch* and English *high*), evolved into
6065   Old French *haut* 'high' (the *h-* is no longer pronounced in French). From Old French *haut* English has borrowed HAUTEUR 'haughtiness, arrogance' [from French *hauteur* 'height; haughti-ness'] and HAUGHTY 'vain, arrogant' [from archaic *haught* 'high, exalted,' from Middle English *haute*, from Old French *haut*
6070   'high']. The spelling with *-gh-* was introduced late in the 16th century, probably through association with the *-gh-* in *caught* and *taught*, or *high* and *height*. However, these *gh's* represent gut-

tural sounds that were once pronounced, while the -gh- in
HAUGHTY has never been pronounced. Another English word
borrowed from Old French *haut* is HAUTBOY (literally) 'high-   6075
wood'; OBOE; 'a high-pitched double-reed woodwind' [from
French *hautbois*]. The OBOE spelling comes from the Italian, no
respecter of orthography. Note, also, HAWSER 'a rope used for
towing or mooring a ship'; (literally) 'lifter' [from Old French
haucier 'to lift,' from Vulgar Latin *altiāre*, from *altus* 'high'].   6080
(However, the *hawse* of the *hawsehole* through which the HAW-
SER passes is from a different root. See line 10925.) Yet another
English borrowing from Old French *haut* is ENHANCE 'to make
more valuable; to increase' [from Norman French *enhauncer*,
from Old French *enhaucer, enhalcier*, from Vulgar Latin *inal-*   6085
tiare 'to raise' (*in-* used intensively + *altus* 'high')].

In Germanic, the past participle formation parallel with Latin
altus 'high' was *aldaz* 'grown up, adult,' based on a verb similar
to Gothic *alan* 'to grow up' and Old Norse *ala* 'to nourish.' The
Old English word that evolved out of Germanic *aldaz* 'grown up'   6090
is *ald, eald*, ancestor of English OLD 'having a specified age;
having lived a long time'; ELDER 'senior, older; a governing
officer in a church'; and ALDERMAN 'the headman of a group; a
member of a municipal legislative body; a councilman.' For the
semantics of ALDERMAN compare Latin *senex* 'old man,' *senior*   6095
'older; elder,' and *senator* 'member of a legislative body.'

The -LD of OLD is also lurking in the word WORLD 'human
existence; the sum of human affairs; the earth; the universe' [from
Old English *weorold*, from Germanic *wer-ald-* 'man-era, the age
of man' (*weraz* 'man')], or "the age of the earth inhabited by   6100
mankind" (*EP*). The original meaning was closer to 'the sum of
human affairs' sense. The expansion of this once puny area to
encompass the universe coincides with man's increasing ability to
alter his environment.

Germanic *werald-* became Old High German *werald*, which   6105
lost first the -a-, then the -r-, to yield modern German *Welt*
'world.' English has borrowed a few word-phrases incorporating
this word, such as WELTSCHMERZ 'sorrow caused by the state of
human affairs'; (literally) 'world-pain,' and WELTANSCHAUUNG
'world outlook'; (literally) 'world-onlooking.'   6110

Finally, from the Greek, comes ALTHEA 'the genus of plants
that includes hollyhocks and marsh mallows; the rose of Sharon';
(literally) 'healer' [via Latin from Greek *althaia* 'marsh mallow;
healer'; from *althein* 'to nourish'; from Indo-European *al-* 'to
nourish'].   6115

XXXIII

Judgments *and* Verdicts: Contradictions *and* Predicaments

According to the DICTIONARY, a VERDICT is (literally) 'a true-saying,' though it doesn't always work out that way, as any JUDGE will tell you. The word JUDGE 'an arbiter' sounds like an Anglo-Saxon word, short and to the point, but in actuality it comes from the Latin *iūdex, iūdicem* 'he who speaks the law,' from *iūs* 'law' and the root of *dīcere* 'to speak.' Latin *iūdex* became Medieval Latin *jūdex*, and this or more likely the adjective *jūdicus* 'judicious' or the verb *jūdicāre* 'to judge' was syncopated and slurred into Old French *juge*, which was adopted with that spelling into Middle English. (The *-d-* was not inserted into the English word until the 16th century.)

Latin *dīcere* 'to speak' has the past participle *dictus, dictum* 'spoken.' The word DICTUM 'a maxim, an authoritative pronouncement' [from Latin *dictum* 'saying, maxim'] has been current in English since the 18th century; before that the word was more often *dict* or *ditton*. This same *dict* shows up in the word VERDICT 'the decision reached by a jury after a trial; a judgment' [from Middle English *verdit*; from Old French *veirdit*; from Latin *vērum* 'true' + *dictum* 'saying']. Before we leave the august company of the JUDICIARY we should note that another member of that etymological fraternity is the lowly word HOOSEGOW 'jail' [from Spanish *juzgado* (pronounced in Mexican Spanish "khoos-gado") 'tribunal, courtroom,' from *juzgar* 'to judge,' from Latin *jūdicāre* 'to judge'], part of our Southwestern U.S./Mexican-Spanish heritage.

In Italian, Latin *dictum* became *ditto, detto* 'saying, maxim; said.' *Ditto* is now obsolete in standard Italian, but survives in the Tuscan dialectal *ditto* 'said,' and English DITTO 'what has been said; the aforementioned thing (again).' Another Latin noun formed on the past participle *dictus* was *dictiō, dictiōn(em)* 'uttering, speaking, saying; word.' This has become English DICTION 'choice and use of words in speech and writing; enunciation.' From Latin *dictiō* there developed the adjective *dictiōnārius* 'of speaking, of words,' whence the phrase *liber dictiōnārius* 'book of words.' This was shortened in Medieval Latin to *dictiōnārium* > English DICTIONARY. 6150

There are numerous compounds of Latin *dīcere* 'to speak, to say' from which English has borrowed. From Latin *addīcere* (literally) 'to speak toward'; 'to assent; to award, to adjudge' comes English ADDICT 'one who has a compulsory craving, especially for drugs.' In Roman days the past participle *addictus* was used to mean 'a debtor; a bondsman; a slave,' and the reflexive verb *se addīcere* meant 'to give oneself up to.' From Latin *benedīcere* 'to speak well of, to commend' comes English BENEDICTION 'a blessing; a wishing of good fortune,' usually given with an invocation of God or the gods. A recently married male character in Shakespeare's *Much Ado about Nothing* is named *Benedick*. This is assumed to be a variant of BENEDICT 'he over whom a blessing has been spoken,' and the latter word has long been erroneously used to mean 'a newly married man,' especially one who has been a bachelor for a long time. But, as William Rose Benét points out in *The Reader's Encyclopedia*, *benedick* is the word for 'a newly married man,' while BENEDICT means, or should mean, 'a bachelor . . . a man of marriageable age, not married.' The reason for the appellation is that "St. Benedict was a most uncompromising stickler for celibacy" among his monkish followers. Shakespeare was making a wry comment on this usage of BENEDICT when he named his character, "caught in the snares of matrimony," *Benedick*. From Latin *condīcere* 'to talk together, to agree' and *condiciō* 'agreement, stipulation; state' comes English CONDITION 'a point of agreement; a stipulation; state of being.' The sense of 'stipulation,' as in "I'll take the job on CONDITION that I be given a free hand," is an obvious outgrowth from the sense of 'agreement.' The sense of 'state of being,' as in "this lawn is in very poor CONDITION" is not so easily arrived at, semantically. However, the Latin speakers already used the word *condiciō* with this sense. From Latin *contrādīcere* comes English CONTRADICT 'to speak against; to say the opposite to,' while Latin *ēdīcere* 'to speak out; to proclaim' gives us English EDICT 'a decree issued by an authority.' INDICT 'to accuse, to make charges against' is pronounced the same as INDITE 'to set down in writing; to compose.' These two were originally the same word, acquired from Old French *enditer* 'to make known, to indicate,' from Late Latin **indictāre*, based on *indictus*, past participle of Latin *indīcere* 'to proclaim' (war, for

6155

6160

6165

6170

6175

6180

6185

6190

instance); 'to impose' (taxes, for instance). INDICT and INDITE are
close kin to INDEX 'the forefinger; an alphabetical listing' [from
Latin *index, indicis* 'informer, betrayer; the forefinger']. The
American slang expression *to finger,* meaning 'to inform on; to
6195   point out as the intended victim,' fits in nicely with the Latin
meanings 'informer, betrayer.' It has a literal Latin parallel in the
verb *indicāre* 'to point out, to show; to disclose,' borrowed into
English as INDICATE 'to point out.' The association between 'the
forefinger' and 'an alphabetical listing' was exploited by the
6200   copywriter who coined the slogan: "Let your fingers do the
walking through the yellow pages."
        Now is as good a time as any to introduce a derivative of
Latin *dīcere* 'to speak,' to wit, *dicāre* 'to say solemnly, to proclaim.' It is manifest in the English compounds ABDICATE 'to
6205   disclaim, to disown; to renounce; to give up high office' [from
Latin *abdicāre* 'to disclaim, to reject' and *se abdicāre* 'to abdicate;
to proclaim oneself away from' (*ab-* 'away from')] and DEDICATE
'to consecrate; to devote; to set apart for a special purpose' [from
Latin *dēdicāre* 'to dedicate; to proclaim away from oneself' (*dē-*
6210   'away from')].
        We come now to a pair of first cousins, PREDICT 'to foretell'
[from Latin *praedīcere* 'to say in advance'] and PREDICATE 'to
affirm as an attribute; the part of a sentence that says something
about the subject' "the house is *white*" [from Latin *praedicāre* 'to
6215   declare in front of (others)']. Latin *praedicāre* 'to proclaim' has a
couple of unexpected English descendants. One is PREDICAMENT
'a troublesome situation'; (etymologically) 'what has been predi-
cated, or stated as an attribute'; (in logic) 'a category'; (archaic) 'a
specific condition,' or what any soap opera fan could have pre-
6220   dicted the heroine was going to get herself into. The other
unexpected English descendant of *praedicāre* 'to proclaim' is
PREACH (etymologically) 'to assert before (a congregation)' [from
Old French *prechier*]. (Preachers also predict what will happen to
you if you don't believe what they tell you and act accordingly.)
6225   From Latin *interdīcere* 'to forbid' ('to say between' = 'to intervene by speech') comes English INTERDICT 'to forbid; to interpose legally; to cut off by firepower, to lay down a barrage against'
[by way of Old French *entredit*, respelled after the Latin *interdic-
tum*], pronounced "interdite" by some artillerymen. Other com-
6230   pounds from *dīcere, dicāre* are MALEDICTION 'a curse; slander'
[Latin *maledictiō* from *maledīcere* 'to speak evil of']; VALEDIC-
TION 'something said when bidding farewell' [from Latin
valedīcere 'to say farewell']; and VINDICATION 'justification' [from
Latin *vindicāre* 'to champion, to defend; to avenge,' from *vindex*
6235   'protector; one who speaks for another in court']. The *vin-* ele-

ment is of unknown origin, but some speculate that it might come from Latin *vis, vim* 'power, strength, violence.' This would make *vindex* mean 'he who points to violence (done to the victim).' Latin *vindicāre* was syncopated into Old French *vengier, venger,* whence English VENGE, along with the compounds AVENGE, REVENGE, and VENGEANCE, all having to do with paying back dirty tricks. The past participle of Latin *vindicāre, vindicta,* was used as a noun to mean 'the freeing of a slave; rescue; vengeance.' *Vindicta* became Italian *vendetta* 'revenge,' adopted into English as VENDETTA 'a hereditary blood feud,' like that between the Hatfields and the McCoys. Someone who is VINDICTIVE is disposed to seek revenge. Related to Latin *praeiūdicāre* 'to judge beforehand' is English PREJUDICE 'a preconceived judgment' [via Old French from Latin *praeiūdicium* 'premature decision' (*iūdex, iūdicis* 'judge')].

Yet another derivative of Latin *dīcere* 'to speak' is Latin *dictāre, dictatum* 'to say often, to say loudly; to compose; to dictate,' source of English DICTATE and DICTATOR. Originally, Latin *dictator* was "the appellation of a chief magistrate invested with absolute authority, elected in seasons of emergency by the Romans" (*OED*). In a slip downhill from that eminence, Latin *dictātum* 'thing composed' evolved into Old French *ditie,* adapted into English as DITTY (originally) 'a composition, a treatise; a composition meant to be set to music; a simple song.' Finally, from Latin *dictāre* 'to compose,' borrowed into English was a word back in the Old English days, very popular in Middle English but now archaic except in poetic use (*bedight,* for example): DIGHT 'to dress, to adorn' [from Old English *dihtan* 'to arrange, to compose']. (Compare German *dichten* 'to compose, to write poetry,' and *Dichter* 'poet.')

The Indo-European root underlying all these talky, demonstrative words is *deik-* 'to point at, to show.' It is certainly easier to point at something than it is to tell about it verbally; however, when the object isn't in sight you can't point at it, and so you must say what you mean in words.

Indo-European *deik-* 'to point at, to show' has a variant *deig-*. A Latin derivative of *deig-* is *digitus* (originally) 'a pointer; a finger' and (because of the structural similarity) 'a toe.' Latin *digitus* leads to English DIGIT 'a finger or toe; any one of the Arabic numerals from zero to nine' (so called from the immemorial practice of counting on one's fingers). The drug DIGITALIS 'the dried leaf of the purple foxglove' is so named because it is made from plants of the genus DIGITALIS 'Eurasian herbs of the figwort family.' The plants are so named because of the fingerlike shape of the flowers (Latin *digitālis* 'of the finger').

6240

6245

6250

6255

6260

6265

6270

6275

6280

The Greek word for 'finger, toe' is *daktulos*, which, despite the *d-k-* pattern, is held to be of obscure origin. It is possibly Semitic, according to Eric Partridge, who in the same breath writes: "Nevertheless, I suspect that ... *daktulos* ... has root

6285   **dak-* akin to the *deik-* ... of *deiknumi* 'I show, point out,' the finger being the original pointer." Greek *daktulos* in its Latin spelling *dactyl(us)* is widely used in scientific words having to do with fingers and joints, and is also the source of English DACTYL 'a metrical foot of three syllables, long, short, short' ("All the

6290   king's/horses and/all the king's/men ..."), so called because it has three parts like the joints of a finger.

The Greek word *daktulos* was also used as the name of the fruit of the date palm; in fact the English word for that fruit, DATE 'the sweet oblong fruit of a tropical palm tree, *Phoenix*

6295   *dactylifera*,' is borrowed from Old French, from Old Provençal *datil*, from Latin *dactylus*, from Greek *daktulos*.

One more word involving Latin *digitus* 'finger' is PRESTIDIGI-TATOR 'a sleight-of-hand artist' [coined from French *preste* 'nimble' (< Italian *presto* 'ready, speedy' < Latin *praesto* 'ready, at

6300   one's service') + *digitus* 'finger']. This is not an old coinage, but a word invented circa 1830 by the French illusionist Jules de Rovère as a means of self-glorification. "One day the pompous title of *prestidigitateur* was visible on an enormous poster, which also condescended to supply the derivation of this breath-stop-

6305   ping word, *presto digiti* (activity of the fingers)" (Robert Houdin, quoted in the *OED*). PRESTIDIGITATOR is an alteration of an earlier word that has nothing to do with fingers, to wit, *prestigiator* 'juggler, conjurer,' based on Latin *praestigiae* 'illusions, deceptions,' for **praestrigiae*, from *praestringere* 'to bind

6310   (the eyes),' hence 'to dazzle.'

In Germanic, the Indo-European root **deik-* 'to point at, to show' manifests itself in the form **taikjan* 'to show,' ancestor of Old English *tǣcan* 'to show the way; to direct; to instruct' > modern English TEACH 'to communicate knowledge; to give

6315   instruction.' Related words are TOKEN 'a sign, a symbol; something that serves to indicate the existence of something else' [from Old English *tāc(e)n*, from Germanic **taiknam*] and TOE 'one of the digits of the foot' [from Old English *tā, tahe*, from Germanic **taihwō*]. Thus we find that our pedal extremities get into the

6320   DIGITAL act from two directions, Germanic and Latin. Another related word is TETCHY, TECHY 'easily irritated, peevish' [from Old French *tec(c)he, tache* 'blemish, fault,' from Late Latin **tacca*, from Gothic *taikns* 'sign']. TETCHED, TECHED 'slightly mad' is possibly from the same source. TETCHY is not, as I had

6325   thought, a dialectal variant of *touchy*, even though the meaning is

the same. However, according to some etymologists, *tetched*, *teched* is an alteration of *touched*.

The Indo-European root **deik-* 'to point at, to show' is evidenced in Greek by the verb *deiknunai* 'to show,' from whose compounds English has borrowed PARADIGM 'an example, a model; "a list of all the inflectional forms of a word taken as an illustrative example of the conjugation or declension to which it belongs"' (*AHD*) [from Greek *paradeigma* 'model, example,' formed on *paradeiknunai* 'to show alongside; to exhibit'] and POLICY 'a certificate of insurance.' This word has no connection with *policy* 'guiding principles,' or *politics* 'the art of government' (both from *polis* 'city'), but traces back by a tortuous chain of altered spellings through Old French *police*, Italian *polizza*, Medieval Latin *apodissa*, *apodixa*, and Latin *apodixis* to Greek *apodeixis* 'a showing, a demonstration; proof' [from *apodeiknunai* 'to show off, to display, to make known' (*apo* 'off, from')]. 6330 6335 6340

Dikein 'to throw' is another Greek verb that is traced by some to the Indo-European root **deik-* 'to point at, to show.' The semantic gap between 'showing' and 'throwing' is bridged by postulating an intermediate sense of '"to direct an object at"' (*AHD*). However, some etymologists propose an Indo-European root **dik-* 'to throw.' Whatever its ultimate derivation, the Greek verb *dikein* 'to throw' is the source of the several English words, some of which have nothing to do with 'showing' or 'throwing' (or 'saying'). One derivative of Greek *dikein* 'to throw' is DISCUS 'a flat circular plate thrown for distance in athletic competitions' [from Latin *discus*, from Greek *diskos* (for **dikskos*) 'discus; quoit,' from *dikein* 'to throw']. The flat circular shape of the discus gave rise to extended meanings in Greek and Latin, and consequently in English DISC, DISK 'any thin, flat, circular plate' and DISH 'a shallow, concave container' [from Old English *disc*]. 6345 6350 6355

The idea of circularity was lost in Late Latin days when the word *discus* acquired the sense of 'table,' that is, unless all the people ate from a round table in those days, which they didn't. (Late Latin *discus* leads directly to German *Tisch* 'table'). The Italian speakers changed *discus* to *desco* 'table, board; desk,' which traced back into Medieval Latin *desca* 'desk,' thence into Middle English as *deske* > English DESK. 6360

Finally, the much-traveled 'athletic-saucer-turned-table/desk' *discus* became Old French *deis* 'table,' a word adopted into Middle English to mean 'a high table in a hall,' then 'the raised platform' on which such a high table rested. The modern English form is DAIS 'a raised platform, as in a lecture or dining hall.' 6365

XXXIV

Kneeling in the Pentagon

Some people think of KNEES as knobby, angular protuber-
6370   ances that are better covered up with skirts or trousers, and some
people think that the PENTAGON, with five angles and an indeterminate number of knobs, should be not so much covered up as
diverted from the public treasury. The word PENTAGON 'a closed
plane geometrical figure with five sides' [via Latin *pentagōnum*
6375   and Greek *pentagōnon* from Greek *pente* 'five' + *-gōnon* 'angled,'
from *gōnia* 'angle'] is one of a long line describing various
POLYGONS 'closed plane geometrical figures bounded by three or
more sides' (*polus* 'many'). There are words to describe polygons
with any number of sides and angles, for example, triangle,
6380   square, PENTAGON, HEXAGON, HEPTAGON, OCTAGON, NONAGON,
DECAGON, etc. You won't find them all in the dictionary, though;
what you have to do is find the Greek word for the number of
sides, Latinize it, interpose *-a-* if necessary, and add *-gon*.
There are also the angular words DIAGONAL 'passing through
6385   from angle to angle' (*dia* 'through') and GONIOMETRY 'the science
of measuring angles' (*metron* 'measure'). (Greek *gōnia* 'angle' also
means 'corner, cornerstone, carpenter's square.')
The Indo-European root for Greek *gōnia* and English *knee* is
*genu-, with variants **gneu-*, **gōn-* 'knee, angle.' In the Germanic
6390   languages, the **g(e)n-* became *kn-*, as in German *Knie* 'knee,'
knien 'kneel,' and English KNEE 'the joint in the middle part of
the leg' and KNEEL 'to rest on bended knees.' (The initial *k-* is
still pronounced in modern German.)
In Latin, the basic form of the Indo-European root turns up
6395   unchanged in appearance except for a long *-ū*, to make *genū*
'knee' (a 'knee' in Greek is *gonu*, with a short *-o-*). In Late Latin,
genū was combined with the verb *flectere* 'to bend' to produce
genuflectere 'to bend the knee; to kneel in worship' > English

GENUFLECT 'to kneel briefly by bending one knee.' A related but
seldom encountered adjective is GENICULATE (literally) 'like a   6400
little knee; bent at an abrupt angle' [from Latin *geniculātus*
'knotty,' from *geniculum*, diminutive of *genū* 'knee'].

Another adjective, this one of disputed origin, is GENUINE
'authentic, real, true, pure' [from Latin *genuīnus* 'innate, natural'].
Many etymologists trace Latin *genuīnus* to Latin *genus* 'birth,   6405
race,' which is related to *genere* 'to beget' and the Indo-European
root **gen-* 'to give birth.' Others, however, interpret *genuinus* as
originally meaning 'placed on the knees,' the reference being to
an ancient custom in which a father acknowledges his paternity
by placing the baby on his knees. According to this theory,   6410
genuīnus originally derived from *genū* 'knee,' and was later
associated with *genus* 'race.'

There is another Indo-European root **genu-*, this one meaning 'jawbone, chin.' Jawbones and chins are certainly angular, and
the possibility that there was an ultimate relationship with **genu-*   6415
'angle; knee' further back in prehistory is not unthinkable. From
*genu- 'jawbone, chin' come Greek *genus* 'jaw, chin' and the
related *gnathos* 'jaw, mouth.' *Gnathos* is perceptible in English
PROGNATHOUS 'having jaws that project forward.' The stem *gnath-*
was used to coin scientific words referring to jaws, mandibles, and   6420
jawlike appendages, for example, GNATHIDIUM, GNATHOPODITE,
and GNATHOSTEGITE, as well as GNATHOMETER 'an instrument for
measuring angles of the jaw.'

Along the Teutonic line, Indo-European **genu-* 'jawbone,
chin' evolved into Germanic **kinnuz*, whence German *Kinn*   6425
'chin' and English CHIN [from Old English *cin(n)*].

Both of these Indo-European roots signifying angular objects
regularly gave rise to Germanic words beginning with *k-* or *kn-*. It
is intriguing to come across another list of *kn-* words derived from
the similar root **gen-* 'to compress into a ball,' a root that is   6430
described as "the hypothetical base of a range of Germanic words
referring to compact, knobby bodies and projections, sharp blows,
etc." (*AHD*), especially since jaws, chins, and knees fall into the
category of "knobby projections." The connection between
knobby bodies and sharp blows apparently is that the blows are   6435
often delivered by the bodies, as when one KNOCKS on a door
with one's KNUCKLES. One of these *kn-* words is KNOB 'a rounded
protuberance' [from Middle Low German *knobbe*, from Germanic
*knub-]. In slang, KNOB is sometimes used to mean 'head,' with
the spelling shortened to NOB. There is another NOB 'a person of   6440
wealth or high social position' that some authorities suggest may
derive from NOB 'head,' though others list this word as of obscure,
uncertain origin. A variant of Middle Low German *knobbe* 'knob'

was *knubbe* 'a knot in a tree.' *Knubbe* came into English as KNUB,
6445   now usually spelled (in the U.S.) NUB 'a knob or protuberance;
the gist of a story; the heart of a problem.' NUB has the diminutives NUBBLE 'a small protuberance' and NUBBIN 'a stunted ear of
corn; a small protuberance.' More *kn-* words are KNOT 'a hard
place or node, especially of a tree; what one makes when one
6450   KNITS; any tie or bond; the marriage bond' [from Old English
cnotta, from Germanic **knut-*]; KNIT 'to form by interlacing a
single thread into interconnecting loops; to draw together'; (archaic) 'to form by tying knots' [from Old English *cnyttan* 'to tie in a
knot,' from Germanic **knut-*]; and KNOUT 'a leather scourge for
6455   flogging criminals' [via French from Russian *knut* 'a knotted
whip,' from Old Norse *knūtr* 'a knot']. "The Knout is a thick hard
Thong of Leather of about three Foot and a half long, fasten'd to
the end of a handsome Stick, about two Foot and a half long, with
a Ring or kind of Swivle like a Flail at the end of it, to which the
6460   Thong is fasten'd." (Captain John Perry, *The State of Russia
under the Present Czar*, 1716, quoted in the *OED*). Still more *kn-*
words include KNUR 'a bump or knot, as on a tree trunk'; KNAR 'a
knot or burl on a tree'; KNURL 'a knob, knot or similar protuberance'; GNARLED 'knotty or misshapen' [variant of *knurled*]; and
6465   possibly KNACK 'the ability to do something adroitly and intui-
tively.' KNACK has had the meaning of 'trick, dodge; an adroit or
ingenious method of doing something' since the days of Chaucer
and Wyclif (14th century), but it also meant 'a sharp blow' and
was thus similar in meaning to the related KNOCK 'to strike with a
6470   hard blow' [from Old English *cnocian*, from Germanic **knuk-*]. In
German, a *Knack* is 'a cracking noise,' and a KNACKWURST is 'a
sausage whose skin cracks open when bitten into' [German *Wurst*
'sausage']. While we're on the subject of food we should mention
Italian GNOCCHI 'dumplings made of flour or semolina, boiled and
6475   then baked' [from Italian *nocchio* 'knot in wood,' from Germanic
*knuk-], and French QUENELLE 'a dumpling of forcemeat' (finely
ground meat or poultry) [probably from Middle High German
knödel, diminutive of *knode* 'knot']. At least one etymologist
suggests the possibility that English NOODLE 'a ribbonlike strip of
6480   dehydrated dough' [from German *Nudel*] is from the same source
as German *Knödel* 'dumpling.'

Still in the comestible line, a KNAPSACK (literally) 'a bite-bag;
an eating-bag; a bag for carrying supplies on one's back' [from
Low German *knappsack* or Dutch *knapzak* (*knappen* 'to crack, to
6485   bite, to eat' + *sack, zak* 'bag')] is obviously related to KNAP 'to
bite, to snap, to nibble; to strike, to rap.' Other related *kn-* words
are KNUCKLE 'one of the protuberances formed by the joints of the
fingers' [from Middle Low German *knokel*, from Germanic **knuk-*];

KNOLL 'a small rounded hill' [from Old English *cnoll*, from Germanic **knul-*]; KNELL 'to toll a bell' [from Old English *cnyllan*   6490 'to strike,' from Germanic **knul-*]; KNIFE 'a sharp blade with a handle' [from Old English *cnīf*, from Germanic **knib-*]; and KNEAD 'to press and squeeze methodically with the hands' [from Old English *cnedan*, from Germanic **kneth-*].

XXXV

Legends Defy Logic, Lexicons, *and* Catalogues

6495   The military prowess of the Roman LEGION is LEGENDARY, and many a LECTURE has been given on the subject. The problem here is to understand how words with such varied meanings as LEGION, LEGEND, and LECTURE all sprang from the same source.

6500   That source is the Latin verb *legere, lectum*, which originally meant 'to gather, to collect,' then expanded its semantic area to include the senses of 'to choose, to receive,' and eventually developed meanings of 'to read, to read aloud; to recite.' One explanation put forward to explain this semantic evolution is that the difficult task of reading the scratchings and carvings that made

6505   up early writing was described by the phrase *legere oculis* 'to gather with the eyes,' that is, 'to assemble the written characters optically so as to make sense out of them.' When one considers that in the earliest days of writing, words were not separated by spaces as they are now but all run together, thisexplanationmakesso

6510   mesensesinceoneseyesreallyhavetoworktomakeoutwritinglikethis. Furthermore, the letters on one line would run from left to right, on the next line from right to left with the letters reversed. For example, Ж for K and Ǝ for E, et cetera, then again from left to right and so on. This practice was given the name *boustrophedon*,

6515   meaning 'as the ox plows' consecutive furrows in a field.

When we consider that the English verb *to gather* has a figurative sense of 'to understand, to deduce, to draw as an inference,' the Latin sequence 'to gather > to choose > to read' is easier to accept. The 'to gather' meaning of *legere* can still be

6520   detected in related nouns, like *legiō, legiōnem* 'a Roman legion; the major unit of the Roman army consisting of 3000 to 6000 infantry troops and 100 to 200 cavalrymen.' The inference one draws is that the men 'chosen' for their strength, courage, and military skills were 'gathered' together into a combat force by the

state. Latin *legiō*, *legiōnem*, by way of Old French *legion*, gives us   6525
English LEGION 'a military force, an army; a large number, a
multitude.' Similarly, from Latin *legūmen* (etymologically) 'what
one gathers or picks; peas, beans, vegetables,' via French *légume*
comes English LEGUME 'any of certain related plants that bear
seeds in pods, including peas, beans, clover, and alfalfa; any   6530
edible vegetable.' The idea of 'gathering' firewood is at the
bottom of Latin *lignum* (for **legnom*) 'firewood, wood; tree.'
Lignum has been used in the coining of scientific words like
LIGNUM 'woody tissue'; LIGNIFY 'to turn into wood'; LIGNITE 'a
variety of coal intermediate between peat and bituminous coal.'   6535
(The derivation of *legūmen* from the root of Latin *legere* is not
universally accepted.)

'Gathering' implies picking and choosing, and this idea of
'selectivity' is evident in several compound words formed on
legere, *lectus* (whose combining form is sometimes *-ligere*). For   6540
instance, SELECT 'to choose from among several' [from Latin
sēligere, *sēlectus* (literally) 'to gather apart; to pick out, to select'
(*sē-* 'apart')] and ELECT 'to select by vote; to choose' [from Latin
ēligere, *ēlectus* 'to pick out, to choose' (*e-* = *ex-* 'out')]. *Eligere*,
ēlectus has some satellite words whose relationship is not imme-   6545
diately apparent, for example, ELITE (literally) 'picked out,
choice; the choice part or segment; a group regarded as superior'
[from French *élite*, from Old French *eslite*; either as past participle of *eslire*, from Vulgar Latin **exlegere*, variant of Latin *eligere*
'to pick out, to choose,' or from Medieval Latin *ēlecta*, alteration   6550
of Latin *ēlectus* 'choice, select,' from *eligere*]; ELIGIBLE 'qualified
to be chosen' [(possibly via French) from Late Latin *ēligibilis*];
and ELEGANT 'fastidiously tasteful' [(possibly via French) from
Latin *ēlegāns*, *ēlegāntis* 'choice, fine, tasteful']. The Latin word is
in the form of a present participle of an otherwise nonexistent   6555
verb, **ēlegāre*, related to *ēligere* 'to choose, to pick out.' The
etymological sense of *ēlegāns* is 'choosing carefully,' so it must
have been applied to the chooser before it came to be applied to
the thing chosen. Another word related to *ēligere*, *ēlectus* is
COLLECT 'to gather together, to assemble; to demand and obtain   6560
payment; a short prayer said "at the congregation" (*ad collectam*)'
[from Latin *colligere*, *collectus* 'to bring together, to collect' (*col-*
< *com-* < *cum* 'with, together')]. COLLECT has two not easily
recognizable relatives. The first is CULL 'to pick out from others'
[from Old French *cuillir*, *coillir*, from Latin *colligere*]. The mod-   6565
ern French is *cueillir* 'to pick; to gather; to take up,' with related
noun *cuiller*, *cuillère* 'spoon.' To CULL is often used with the
implication of 'rejecting,' that is, of picking out inferior specimens
to be discarded; but this is not always the case, as in "he CULLED

6570   the best passages from the poet's work." As a noun, a CULL is
always something inferior. The second, rather hidden relative of
COLLECT is COIL (literally) 'a gathering together; to wind together
in concentric rings' [from Old French *coillir*, etc.], said of rope, of
metal lengths (coil springs), or the length of a snake.

6575   Not quite as bad as being a CULL is being an object of
NEGLECT 'the omission of proper attention; disregard of duty';
(literally) 'not chosen' [from Latin *neglēctus*, past participle of
neglegere, negligere 'to disregard, to overlook' (*neg- < nec- < ne*
'not')]. Other borrowings from Latin *negligere* 'to disregard, to

6580   overlook' are NEGLIGIBLE 'unworthy of attention; safely overlooked'; NEGLIGENT 'culpable, careless' (via French); and NEGLI-
GEE 'careless, slovenly; unstudied, casual; in undress, in informal
or unceremonious attire; a loose gown worn by women of the 18th
century; a woman's loose dressing gown, usually of soft, delicate

6585   fabric'; (literally) 'neglected' [via French].

As the derivation of the word indicates, 'being choosy' or
knowing what choice to make is at the bottom of the mystery of
INTELLIGENCE 'the capacity for knowledge and understanding;
mental acuteness; the obtaining and distribution of information'

6590   [from Latin *intelligentia, intellegentia,* from *intelligere, intellegere* 'to perceive, to understand'; (literally) 'to choose from
among' (*intel- < inter* 'between, among')]. The past participle of
Latin *intellegere* 'to understand' is *intellectus,* a word the Latin
speakers made into the following noun meaning 'perception,

6595   discernment': INTELLECT 'the ability to learn and reason as
distinguished from the ability to feel and will.' Thus, that much-
abused word INTELLECTUAL 'given to study, reflection and speculation, especially on large or abstract issues,' etymologically
applies to anyone who is using his brains to figure something out,

6600   from automobile mechanic to cosmologist. The 'understanding,
comprehending' sense of Latin *intellegere* shows up most plainly
in English INTELLIGIBLE.

The meanings of the English word DILIGENCE 'perseverance,
assiduity; devoted and painstaking application to accomplish an

6605   undertaking' are very similar to those of the ancestral Latin word
diligentia, which is translated 'carefulness, attentiveness, accuracy; frugality.' The associated Latin verb *dīligere, dīlectus* means
'to esteem highly, to prize,' senses elaborated from an etymological meaning of 'to gather apart' (Latin *dis-* 'apart' + *legere* 'to

6610   gather'). Thus the semantic sequence seems to be the following:
'choosing and setting apart' > 'cherishing' > 'devoting oneself to
constantly.'

Fans of western movies will recall another meaning of the
word DILIGENCE 'a stagecoach; a large closed public horse-drawn

carriage formerly used for long journeys.' This meaning arose 6615
from another sense of the word that was current in the 15th
century, i.e., 'haste, speed.' (Perhaps, if one 'devotes oneself
constantly' to a project, that project will be accomplished 'speed-
ily.') The 'stagecoach' sense of DILIGENCE is elliptical for the
French phrase *carrosse de diligence* 'speed coach.' *Diligence* had 6620
this same sense of 'public stagecoach' in Dutch and German, also
in Italian in the form *diligenza*, and in Spanish as *diligencia*.

If Latin *dīligere, dīlectus* means 'to esteem highly,' then
Medieval Latin *praedīligere, praedīlectus* should mean 'to esteem
highly in advance.' However, the pundits translate it as 'to prefer, 6625
to love more; to choose before others.' An English borrowing by
way of French is PREDILECTION 'a favorable prepossession, a
predisposition toward, a preference formed as a result of personal
leanings.'

There is yet another English word containing an element 6630
from Latin *legere* 'to gather,' but in this case the 'gathering' is
illicit, and in effect 'stealing, purloining.' The word is SACRILEGE
'the desecration of anything regarded as sacred'; (literally) 'the
stealing of sacred things' [from Latin *sacrilegium* 'temple robbery,' from the phrase *sacra legere* 'to purloin sacred things,' from 6635
sacer 'sacred' + *legere* 'to gather, to pick up; to steal'].

Up to now we've been dealing with the 'to gather' sense of
Latin *legere, lectus*, but remember that an extended meaning of
this verb is 'to read, to read aloud; to recite.' English borrowings
along these lines include LEGIBLE 'capable of being read' [from 6640
Late Latin *legibilis* 'readable'] and LECTURE (originally) 'a reading'; (later) 'a reading aloud'; (eventually) 'an exposition of a
subject before an audience; a solemn scolding' [via Old French
from Medieval Latin *lectūra* 'a reading, a reading of Scripture,'
based on Latin *lectus*, past participle of *legere* 'to read']. Nowa- 6645
days, a good lecturer speaks extemporaneously from notes, or at
least tries to give that impression. More English borrowings are
LECTOR 'a cleric of the second lowest order in the early Christian
church whose chief duty was to read the lessons in the church
service'; (literally) 'reader' [Latin *lēctor* 'reader']; and LECTERN 'a 6650
reading desk; a stand that serves as a support for the notes of a
speaker' [via Old French *let(t)run* from Medieval Latin
lect(ō)rīnum, from *lectrum* 'reader's thing']. (*Lectrum* is traced
further back to early Medieval Latin **lectorium* 'a place for
reading' by Eric Partridge.) Belonging to the same group is 6655
LESSON 'a portion of Scripture read aloud for instruction as part of
a church service; one of the segments into which a course of
instruction is divided'; (literally) 'act of reading' [from Old French
lecon, from Latin *lectiō, lectiōnem* 'a reading, a reading aloud'].

6660   (Compare Spanish *leccion.*) A reversion to the original Latin
spelling is seen in LECTION 'a reading from Scriptures as part of a
church service; a reading from a text found in a particular copy or
edition' and LEGEND 'an explanatory caption accompanying a
map, chart, or illustration; an inscription on an object such as a
6665   coin or coat of arms; a story coming down from the past, especially one that is popularly regarded as historical but is not
verifiable'; (literally) 'thing(s) to be read.' LEGEND comes to
English by way of Old French *legende* from Medieval Latin
legenda which, according to most interpreters, was a neuter plural
6670   gerund meaning 'things to be read.' Because of the *-a* ending, the
theory says, *legenda* came to be thought of as a feminine singular
noun and was used to denote 'the biography of a saint.' However,
the *Random House Dictionary* etymologist (Kemp Malone) states
that Medieval Latin *legenda*, "so called because appointed to be
6675   read on respective saints' days, literally 'lesson to be read,' " is a
substantive use of the feminine singular gerund. In either case,
the original meaning of English LEGEND was 'the story of the life
of a saint,' while a later meaning was 'a collection of saints'
biographies; stories of a similar character.' The best-known such
6680   collection was written in the 13th century by Jacobus de
Voragine, archbishop of Genos and was popularly known as
Legenda Aurea 'the Golden Legend.' The current meaning of
LEGEND 'a story coming down from the past' dates from the 17th
century.
6685   When we turn to the Greek language we find that the verb
legein, lektos, like its Latin cognate *legere, lectus,* means 'to
gather, to pick out,' with extended meanings of 'to read, to recite.'
However, in its later semantic evolution *legein, lektos* broke into
other semantic areas, developing meanings of 'to count; to
6690   recount, to tell; to speak, to say, to declare; to express any
communication by word of mouth.'
       Similarly, the associated Greek noun *logos* originally meant 'a
counting, a reckoning' but later developed a host of meanings that
can be categorized under the following headings: (I) 'word; the
6695   word by which the inward thought is expressed: speech, saying,
speaking, discourse, tale, story' and (II) 'the inward thought or
reason itself: reason, reflection, deliberation, account, relation,
proportion, ratio.'
       In Greek philosophy *logos* signified 'reason; the manifesta-
6700   tion of reason conceived as constituting the controlling principle
of the universe.' In early Christian theology the term *logos* was
used to mean 'the creative thought and will of God,' identified
with the second person of the Trinity, that is to say God the Son,
incarnated as Jesus Christ. This explains the opening lines of the

Gospel according to St. John: "In the beginning was the Word   6705
(*Logos* = Jesus Christ), and the Word was with God, and the
Word was God," which is a statement of the orthodox view that
God the Son (Jesus Christ) is of the same substance as and
coexistent with God the Father. This view was later denied by
Arius, but was reaffirmed by Athanasius and upheld by the first   6710
council of Nicaea in A.D. 325.

English words acquired from Greek *legein* 'to gather' include
ECLECTIC 'choosing what seems to be best from diverse sources;
rejecting a single, unitary and exclusive interpretation' [from
Greek *eklektikos*, from *eklektos* 'selected,' past participle of   6715
eklegein 'to pick out' (*ek-* 'out of')] and ANALECTS 'leftovers from a
feast; literary gleanings; collections of miscellaneous writings';
(obsolete) 'crumbs from the table' [from Greek *analekta* 'things
gathered up,' from *analegein* 'to pick up' (*ana-* 'up')]. The Latin
speakers adapted *analecta* from the Greek and used it as a   6720
masculine singular noun meaning 'a slave who removes food left
over at the table.'

The 'to speak' signification of Greek *legein*, *lektos* is reflected
in the related Greek noun *lexis* (for **legsis*) 'phrase, word;
speaking, diction' and the adjective *lexikos*, *lexikon* 'of words; of   6725
speaking, of diction.' *Lexikon*, used elliptically for the phrase
lexikon biblion 'book of words, book of diction' has been adapted
into English as LEXICON 'dictionary; the vocabulary peculiar to a
particular profession, subject, or other group' "the LEXICON of
youth, the LEXICON of art criticism." Also stemming from the 'to   6730
speak' sense of Greek *legein*, *lektos* are DIALECT 'a regional
variety of a language' [from Greek *dialektos* 'discourse; the
language of a country,' past participle of *dialegesthai* 'to converse'
(*dia-* 'one with another' + *legesthai*, middle voice of *legein* 'to
speak')] and DIALECTIC 'the art of arriving at the truth by disclos-   6735
ing the contradictions in arguments and overcoming them through
discussion or debate' [from Greek *dialektike* (*tekhnē*) '(the art) of
discourse,' by way of Latin and French]. One of the earliest and
perhaps the best known of all DIALECTICIANS was Socrates;
however, credit for the invention of the question-and-answer   6740
dialectic method is given by Aristotle to Zeno of Elea (5th century
B.C.). In medieval times, DIALECTIC was the word used for what
we now call *logic*, although later philosophizing by Kant, Hegel,
and Marx has given the word DIALECTIC special meanings, all of
them having to do with contradictions and their resolution.   6745

In two other English words coined from Greek elements we
find that the 'speech' meaning of *lexis* has become associated with
the 'reading' meaning of Latin *legere*, mainly because these are
scientific terms invented in comparatively recent years and using

6750   what is called *New Latin* 'Latin and Greek as used in scientific description and classification.' Those words are DYSLEXIA 'a disturbance of the ability to read' [from Latin *dys-* < Greek *dus-* 'faulty, bad, diseased' + *-lexia* 'reading'; from Greek *lexis* 'word, speech'] and ALEXIA 'a disorder in which cerebral lesions cause

6755   loss of the ability to read; word blindness' [from Greek *a-* 'not, without' + *lexis* 'speech,' construed to mean 'reading']. The 1933 *Oxford English Dictionary Supplement* says that this coinage is "badly formed," after the example of *agraphia* 'inability to write,' on Greek *a-* 'not, without' + *lexis* 'speech,' *legein* 'to speak' being

6760   confused with Latin *legere* 'to read.' ALEXIA was coined circa 1878; DYSLEXIA appeared much later. (While the latter is not in the 1933 *OED Supplement*, it is in the Addenda (new words) section of *Merriam-Webster's New International*, 1950 edition.)

        When it comes to Greek *logos* 'counting, reckoning, propor-

6765   tion, ratio, word, talk, proverb, discourse, reason, etc.' there is a superabundance of English borrowings. We start, logically enough, with LOGIC 'the study of the principles of reasoning' [from the Greek phrase *hē logikē tekhnē* 'the art of reasoning,' from *logikos* 'rational; of reasoning,' from *logos* 'reason,' via (Late)

6770   Latin *logica* and (Old) French *logique*]. Another English borrowing is LOGARITHM 'the exponent indicating the power to which a fixed number called the base must be raised to produce a given number'; (literally) 'number ratio, number reckoning' [from Greek *logos* 'ratio, reckoning' + *arithmos* 'number']. This word was

6775   coined in 1614 by John Napier, the Scottish mathematician who invented logarithms. More English borrowings from Greek *logos* include LOGISTIC 'skilled in calculation; the art of calculation, especially in arithmetic' [from Greek *logistikos* 'skilled in calculation,' from *logistēs* 'calculator,' from *logizein* 'to calculate'] and

6780   LOGISTICS 'the procurement and distribution of military matériel and personnel.' LOGISTICS is a military science that most assuredly takes a lot of reckoning and calculating by the brass, and especially by the quartermaster corps. However, many authoritative works maintain that the word *logistics* used in this sense is

6785   derived not from Greek *logos* 'reckoning,' but from French *logis* 'dwelling, quarters' (as in *quartermaster*), and *loger* 'to dwell,' related to English *lodge, lodging*. Other authorities remain silent on this derivation, thus allowing one to assume that both *logistic(s)* are traceable to Greek *logistikos*. Some of the less common

6790   English words that begin with *logo-* are LOGOGRAM = LOGOGRAPH 'a symbol used to represent an entire word' (e.g., $, ', #, %, &) [from Greek *logos* 'word' + *gramma* 'letter' or *graphein* 'to write']; LOGO = LOGOTYPE 'a single piece of typeface with a composite, like a slogan, a trademark, an emblem' [Greek *tupos*

'impression']; LOGOMACHY 'contention in words that have little or   6795
no relation to reality'; (literally) 'word-battle' [Greek *makhē* 'battle, fight']; LOGOMANIA 'abnormal talkativeness; a form of insanity
in which there is great loquacity' [Greek *mania* 'madness,
frenzy']; and LOGORRHEA 'pathologically excessive talkativeness'
[Greek *-rrhoia* 'a flowing,' from *rhein* 'to flow'].   6800

Many English words ending in *-logue* are associated with the
theater, such as PROLOGUE 'a speech addressed to the audience at
the beginning of a play; opening remarks' [*pro* 'before' + *logos*
'speech']; EPILOGUE 'a speech directed to the audience at the end
of a play; closing remarks' [*epi* 'after, in addition']; DIALOGUE   6805
'conversation carried on between two or more persons; conversation written for and spoken by actors on the stage' [*dia-* 'through;
between, one with another']; and MONOLOGUE 'a soliloquy; a
scene in which a person of the drama speaks by himself' [*monos*
'alone, only']. MONOLOGUE is also used to mean 'a continuous   6810
series of jokes or stories delivered by a lone performer.' (The
original meaning of English MONOLOGUE was 'one who does all
the talking.') Note, also, DUOLOGUE 'a conversation confined to
two people; a dramatic piece for two actors' [*duo* 'two']; coined
circa 1864 on the pattern of MONOLOGUE. Then there is the   6815
DECALOGUE 'the Ten Commandments' [*deka* 'ten' + *logos* 'order,
command']. In the words CATALOGUE 'a systematic listing with
descriptions of the listed items' [via Old French from Late Latin
catalogus, from Greek *katalogos* 'a counting up; an enrollment
list,' from *katalegein* 'to pick out, to count up' (*kata* 'down,   6820
entirely' + *legein* 'to collect, to enumerate')] and ANTHOLOGY ' "a
collection of the flowers of verse, i.e., small, choice poems,
especially epigrams, by various authors; originally applied to the
Greek collections so called," and later "extended to other literary
collections," including hymnals' (*OED*); (literally) 'flower-gather-   6825
ing' [via Latin *anthologia* from Greek *anthologia* 'a collection of
flowers; a collection of poems "made up into a nosegay" ' (*L&S*)],
the *-logue* and *-logy* revert to the meaning of 'collecting,
enumerating.'

Most English words ending in *-logy* are the names of sci-   6830
ences, such as ARCHAEOLOGY 'the study of extinct or prehistoric
peoples' [*arkhaios* 'ancient, primitive,' from *arkhē* 'beginning' +
logos 'account']; BIOLOGY 'the science of life' [*bios* 'life']; and
COSMOLOGY 'the study of the structure and dynamics of the
universe' [*kosmos* 'order; the world; the universe']. However,   6835
there are many *-logy* words that are not the names of sciences.
Two of these have to do with literature: TRILOGY 'a series of three
closely related dramas or other literary compositions' and
TETRALOGY 'a series of four dramas or literary compositions'

6840   [*tetra-* < *tetora* 'four']. In the ancient Greek theater, a *tetralogia* was a series of three tragedies and one satyric play, the last being a kind of burlesqued tragedy in which the chorus is dressed as satyrs. (This *satyric* is not the same word as *satiric*, even though a *satire* is also a kind of poking fun.) A Greek *trilogia* consisted of

6845   the three tragedies without the satyric play.

Another set of *-logies* is used to name different kinds of comparisons, for example, ANALOGY 'similarity in certain respects between things otherwise dissimilar' [from Greek *analogia* 'proportion, correspondence' (*ana* 'up to, according to' + *logos* 'ratio,

6850   proportion')]; HOMOLOGY 'similarity in position, structure or function' [from Greek *homologia* 'agreement' (*homos* 'same')]; and HETEROLOGY 'dissimilarity of apparently similar bodily parts due to difference in origin' [New Latin, from Greek *heteros* 'other' + *logos* 'ratio, relation']. An analogy is a comparison that can take

6855   the form "A is to B as C is to D," "London is to England what Paris is to France," or "She takes to skiing the way a duck takes to water." However, if you were to say that "arms are to a human as flippers are to a seal, or wings to a bird, or pectoral fins to a fish," a grammarian would agree that these are ANALOGIES, but a

6860   biologist would tell you that the organs indicated are not ANALOGUES but HOMOLOGUES 'likenesses in structure owing to evolutionary development from the same part of a remote mutual ancestor.' To a biologist, an ANALOGUE is 'an organ similar in function to an organ of another animal or plant but different in

6865   structure and evolutionary origin,' like a fish's gills and a mammal's lungs. According to the definitions given, a biological ANALOGUE is ipso facto HETEROLOGOUS.

Another English word ending in *-logy* is APOLOGY 'admission of a wrong or discourtesy done, accompanied by an expression of

6870   regret'; (originally) 'something said or written in justification of what may appear to others to be wrong' [from Greek *apologia* 'a speech in defense' (*apo* 'away from')]. The second usage is not often encountered today, but it explains such book titles as *An Apologie or Defence of our Dayes, Apologie of Syr Thomas More,*

6875   *Knyght, An Apology for the Bible,* and Cardinal Newman's *Apologia pro Vita Sua,* where the apologetic words are translatable as 'justification, defense.' Nowadays, following Newman's lead, the Greek/Latin word *apologia* is more often used when the sense of 'defense' is intended. The use of APOLOGY to mean 'the

6880   admission of a wrong done' dates from the late 16th century.

An interesting cognate in this group is EULOGY 'a speech in praise of someone; praise; an oration honoring someone recently dead' [via Medieval Latin *eulogium* from Greek *eulogia* 'praise' (*eu* 'well' + *logos* 'speaking')]. During the Middle Ages, the

Medieval Latin word *eulogia*, borrowed from the Greek, was   6885
confused with Latin *ēlogium* 'an inscription, especially one on a
tombstone; an epitaph,' and the Medieval Latin *eulogium* was
formed. As a consequence French *éloge* and archaic English *elogy*
came to have meanings of 'words spoken in praise.' Latin *ēlogium*
'inscription, epitaph' is thought to be a folk-etymological altera-   6890
tion of Greek *elegeion* > English ELEGY 'a song or poem expressive of sorrow' [from Greek *elegos* 'lament']. Despite their
appearance, Greek *elegos*, *elegeion* are not thought to be related
to the *legein*, *logos* words, but to be of non-Greek origin. Yet
another English word ending in *-logy* is IDEOLOGY 'a theory of   6895
the origin of ideas; a systematic scheme of ideas about life and
society' [from French *ideologia*, from Greek *idea* 'form, idea' +
logos].

In the study of LOGIC we come across the word SYLLOGISM 'a
form of deductive reasoning consisting of two premises and a   6900
conclusion: *Dogs have four legs. Jackson is a dog. Therefore,
Jackson has four legs* [from Greek *sullogismos* 'a reckoning
together'; (*sul-* < *sun* 'with, together' + *logismos* 'reckoning')].
Ancient Greek also had the words *antilogos* 'contradictory' and
antilogia 'controversy, contention,' from *antilogein, antilegein* 'to   6905
speak against, to gainsay.' English borrowings are the seldom
used ANTILOGY 'a contradiction in terms,' and a later coinage
(1902) ANTILOGISM 'an inconsistent triad of propositions in logic,'
such that if any two of them are true, the opposite of the third
must also be true. Other kinds of logical misreasonings go by the   6910
name of PARALOGISM 'fallacious or illogical reasoning; a logical
fallacy of which the reasoner is unconscious' [*para* 'amiss' +
logismos 'reckoning']. One kind of paralogism is known as "affir-
mation of the consequent," exemplified by the following reasoning: *If it rains, they cancel the game. The game has been   6915
canceled. Therefore, it rained.* Another formal fallacy is called
"denial of the antecedent," as if, in the example already given,
another reasoner were to retort: "Well, it didn't rain, so the game
hasn't been canceled." In both examples (adapted from *MW3*), the
game could have been canceled for reasons other than rain.   6920

A final loanword from Greek *legein, logos* is HOROLOGE 'time-
piece, clock' [via Old French *orloge* and Latin *hōralogium* from
Greek *hōrologion* 'hour-teller' (*hōra* 'time of day, hour' + *legein*
'to tell')].

All of the words discussed in this chapter so far stem from   6925
either Latin *legere* 'to gather, to read,' Greek *legein* 'to gather, to
speak,' or Greek *logos* 'saying, reasoning.' They can all be traced
further back to the Indo-European root **leg-* 'to collect.' It is
thought that Latin *lēx, lēgis* 'law, covenant,' with all its concomi-

6930   tant English words (LEGISLATE, LOYAL, PRIVILEGE, etc.), is also
        most probably derived from this same root, as an offshoot of *legere*
        (*lēx* 'law; a collection of rules'). These words have been gathered
        together in a different chapter entitled LOYAL LEGISLATORS.

            Only one English word of Germanic derivation can be traced
6935   back to Indo-European **leg-* 'to collect' (with derivative meanings
        of 'to speak'). That word is LEECH 'a bloodsucking worm'; (archa-
        ic) 'a physician, a surgeon' [from Old English *lǣce*, from Ger-
        manic **lekjaz* ' "one who speaks magic words" ' (*AHD*)]. One can
        almost hear the shaman/witch doctor intoning his incantations.
6940   The sense 'bloodsucking worm' was originally attached to a
        different word, but became assimilated to LEECH 'physician'
        because of the formerly widespread practice among doctors of
        bleeding patients as a cure for almost any kind of ailment.

XXXVI

Liquidating Delinquents
and Derelicts

When a bank borrower becomes DELINQUENT in payments on a LOAN, the LENDING bank would be DERELICT in its duty if it didn't send a few nudging reminders, that is, unless the bankers intended to RELINQUISH their claim, something bankers are not prone to do. 6945

The English words LEND 'to give temporarily' [from Old English *lǣnan*, from Germanic **laihwnjan*] and LOAN 'a temporary gift' [from Old Norse *lān*, from Germanic **laihwniz*], parts of our Germanic inheritance, are related etymologically to Latin *linquere* and Greek *leipein*, both of which have meanings of 'to leave, to abandon, to quit, to forsake.' The common ancestor of all these words is the Indo-European root **leikw-* 'to leave,' which also carries no suggestion of the 'promise to pay back' that is implicit in LEND and LOAN. (In modern German, *leihen* means both 'to lend' and 'to borrow.') 6950 6955

*Leikw-, *leipein*, *linquere*, *lend*, *loan*, and *leihen* seem to have little in common but the initial *l-*. The etymologists explain the relationships in the following way: The basic form of the root is **leikw-*. In migrating to Greek, the *-kw-* changed to *-p-*, a regular evolution, to yield *leipein*. A "nasalized zero-grade form" of the root is **linkw-*, that is, the *-e-* has disappeared ("zero-grade") and an *-n-* has appeared ("nasalized"). Thus, **linkw-* leads to Latin *linquere*. An "o-grade form" of the root **loikw-* (the *-e-* has been replaced by an *-o-*) leads to Germanic **laihw-*, where the *-o-* has changed further to *-a-* and the *-kw-* to *-hw-*, another regular evolution. Germanic **laihw-* then leads by various suffixes, elisions and additions to *lend*, *loan*, and *leihen*. The *-d* of LEND, for instance, is an old past tense and past participle ending that became incorporated into the word on the analogy of words like *bend*, *send*, and *wend*. 6960 6965 6970

Latin *linquere* 'to leave, to abandon' has the compound
6975   *dēlinquere* 'to leave undone; to fail in one's duty; to commit a
crime,' whose present participle *dēlinquēns* has been borrowed
into English as DELINQUENT 'failing to do what is required by
law.' Another Latin compound, *relinquere*, *relictus* 'to leave
behind,' became Medieval French *relinquir*, *relinquiss(ant)*,
6980   whence English RELINQUISH 'to give up something desirable.' An
associated Latin adjective, *reliquus* 'left behind,' with substantive
plural *reliquiae* 'remains, fragments' yielded Old French *relique*
> English RELIC 'something that has survived the passage of
time.' The Latin past participle *relictus* has been Anglicized as
6985   RELICT 'a surviving remnant of an otherwise extinct form of life; a
living fossil; a widow.' Latin also has an intensified form of
relinquere 'to leave behind,' to wit, *dērelinquere* 'to abandon
utterly, to forsake completely,' whose past participle *dērelictus*
has given English the hyperemphatic DERELICT 'grossly neglect-
6990   ful of duty; abandoned; a vessel abandoned on the high seas; a
social outcast,' where the intensive Latin prefix *dē-* has the
meaning of 'down to the bottom, down to the dregs; completely.'
    "Related by some to this root but more likely a separate Indo-
European form" (*AHD*) is **wleik-* 'to flow, to run,' represented in
6995   Latin by the verbs *liqui* 'to flow,' *liquēre* 'to be clear, to be
liquid,' and *liquāre* 'to melt, to dissolve.' When 'flowing, melting,
dissolving' take place, something is obviously 'leaving' from
where it just was to go someplace else. This may be a semantic
bridge to **leikw-* 'to leave' strong enough to support the aye-
7000   sayers, who receive guarded support from *The Oxford Dictionary
of English Etymology*, Eric Partridge, and from Mario Pei. Cognates or not, the following are some of the English words
borrowed from these Latin wellsprings: LIQUID 'flowing; clear,
transparent' [possibly via Old French *liquide*, from Latin *liquidus*,
7005   from *liquēre* 'to be fluid'] and LIQUOR 'any flowing substance, like
water, milk, blood, sap, juice; any alcoholic beverage; a distilled
alcoholic beverage' [via Old French *licour* from Latin *liquor*
'fluidity; a fluid; the sea']. The Latin spelling has been reestab-
lished in English, but not the pronunciation of the *-qu-*. People
7010   refer to distilled beverages as *hard liquor*; this means by implication that beer and wine are *soft liquor*, and that soft drinks aren't
liquor at all, although by the first definition they are. Another
English borrowing is LIQUIDATE 'to make clear, to render unambiguous; to settle a debt; to wind up a business; to convert into
7015   cash; to abolish; to wipe out by killing' [from Late Latin *liquidāre*
'to melt']. The meaning of LIQUIDATE 'to wipe out by killing' is a
comparatively recent usage, introduced by totalitarian regimes (cf.
Russian *likvidirovat* 'wipe out') as a euphemism for the methods

they used to get rid of their opposition. Note, also, LIQUEFY 'to
make liquid, to melt' [from Old French *liquefier*, from Latin   7020
liquefacere 'to melt'].

An otherwise nonexistent past participle of *liquēre* 'to be
liquid, to flow' is *lixus*, attested in the adjective *prōlixus* 'poured
forth; extended, abundant,' whence English PROLIX 'verbose.'
Etymologically, *prōlixus* means 'poured forth; flowing forward.'   7025
English PROLIX is used of a speaker who goes on and on, and on,
and on, and on ... until his hearers' eyelids are drooping (the
word is also used of writers).

The Greek representative of Indo-European *leikw-* 'to leave'
is *leipein* 'to leave, to abandon.' Two English words that can be   7030
traced back to Greek *leipein* are ECLIPSE 'the partial or complete
obscuring of one celestial body by another; to reduce in importance by comparison' (Hank Aaron ECLIPSED Babe Ruth's home
run record) [from Greek *ekleipsis* 'a forsaking, a disappearing' by
way of Latin *eclīpsis* and Old French *eclipse*; from *ekleipein* 'to   7035
leave out'] and ECLIPTIC 'the apparent path of the sun through the
stars of the zodiac,' so called because it is on this great circle of
the celestial sphere that eclipses occur. The noun ECLIPTIC is also
used for a great circle drawn on the terrestial globe at an
approximate angle of 23°27′ to the equator, which is the amount of   7040
the angle between the planes of the earth's equator and its orbit
around the sun (the obliquity of the ecliptic) that accounts for the
latitude of the tropic of Cancer and the tropic of Capricorn at
approximately 23°27′, above and below the equator. Another
English word that traces back to Greek *leipein* is ELLIPSIS 'the   7045
omission of words necessary to a grammatically correct construction' [from Latin *ellīpsis*, from Greek *elleipsis* 'deficiency, defect';
from *elleipein* 'to leave in, to leave behind; to leave out' (*el-* < *en*
'in')]. For example, "How come?" for "How did this come to
happen?" Or telegraphic communications such as "Departure   7050
delayed arrive eight." Note, also, ELLIPSE 'a regular oval figure.'
A circle seen obliquely shows the form of an ellipse. The word
ELLIPSE is a back formation from ELLIPSIS, coined by mathematicians for abstruse reasons involving the idea of 'falling short of,
deficient.' The conic section called an ELLIPSE is so called   7055
"according to Appolonius of Perga, because the square on the
ordinate is equal to a rectangle whose height is equal to the
abscissa and whose base lies along the latus rectum but falls short
of it." (*ODEE*) Now you know.

Two unexpected words pop up as descendants of the Indo-   7060
European root *leikw-* 'to leave.' They are ELEVEN and TWELVE.
Etymologically, most of the experts agree that these words mean
'one leave' and 'two leave,' or 'one left over' and 'two left over,'

that is, left over after subtracting ten. *Ten* is one of the great
landmarks in the evolution of counting. As Ovid puts it:
This number was held in great honor by men in those days:
Because that is the number of fingers on which we reckon . . . . the numerals increase to ten, and from there We begin
again a new round. (Ovid's *Fasti III*, quoted in Karl Menninger's *Number Words and Number Symbols*.)
The Germanic forms of ELEVEN and TWELVE were **ainlif-* and
*twalif-. These numbers must have first been named 'ten-and-
one-left' and 'ten-and-two-left.' Modern German has reduced
them to the minimal forms of *elf* and *zwölf*. Some of the
aforementioned experts think that Germanic **-lif* may derive from
Indo-European **leip-* (see below, next) instead of Indo-European
*leikw-. Compare Tocharian *lip-* 'be left over.' In Lithuanian, the
suffix *-lika* 'left over,' from Indo-European **leikw-* 'to leave,' is
used all the way from eleven to nineteen.
    That winds up our discussion of the English derivatives of
the Indo-European root **leikw-* 'to leave.' However, there seems
to be a curious omission here: the English word LEAVE is not
included. LEAVE certainly looks and sounds like a member of this
family, not to mention being semantically the same. But the
experts tell us that English LEAVE derives from the Indo-European root **leip-* 'to adhere, to be sticky.' This meaning is exactly
opposite to that of LEAVE 'to go away from.' (Compare also Greek
leipein 'to leave, to abandon,' which begins with the same letters
as our reconstructed root **leip-* 'to adhere.') The fact is that there
is a duality in the notion of 'leaving,' since the verb can be both
transitive and intransitive. When something LEAVES the premises—say, a rabbit, startled by a dog—it also LEAVES something
behind, i.e., its spoor, its scent, and (it hopes) the dog. We have
already seen that some derivatives of **leikw-* 'to leave' refer to
what is left behind, as in RELIC, ELEVEN, and have noted the
opposition of meaning in the related German *leihen* 'to lend; to
borrow.' If such an anomaly can exist in a modern language it
could have existed earlier. Semantically, psychologically, and
phonologically, the two roots, **leikw-* 'to leave' and **leip-*
'to adhere' are similar enough to warrant the suspicion that in
"Pre-Proto-Indo-European they were the same.
    The most important English derivative of the Indo-European
root **leip-* 'to be sticky, to adhere' is not LEAVE 'to go away from;
to allow to remain behind' "I LEFT my keys in the car" [from Old
English *lǣfan*, from Germanic **laibjan*], but LIFE 'the interval
between the birth of an organism and its death; the quality that
distinguishes functioning organic matter from inorganic or dead
organic matter' [from Old English *līf*, from Germanic **lībam*] and

the accompanying verb to LIVE 'to continue in existence as a functioning organism; to dwell' [from Old English *lifian, libban*; from Germanic *līben*]. The semantic connection between **leip-* 'being sticky' and LIVING is explained by the sequence: 'to be sticky' > 'to adhere' > 'to remain, to stay' > 'to stay alive' > 'to live' (*EP*). LIFE and LIVE have many associated words, such as LIVELY 'animated,' LIFELESS, LIFELIKE, LIVING 'the means of maintaining life' (to earn a LIVING), LIVELIHOOD, LIVER¹ 'one who lives,' and LIVER² 'a large glandular organ in vertebrate animals.' LIVER² was spelled *lifer* in Old English. It was formerly thought to be the blood-producing organ. Directly from German is the word LEBENSRAUM 'room to live; territory deemed necessary to a nation's economic well-being.' Several nations have decided that their LEBENSRAUM includes the offshore waters up to 200 miles.   7110

7115

7120

Also descended from Indo-European **leip-* 'to be sticky' are Greek *lipos* 'fat' and *liparos* 'fatty, oily,' both used as combining forms in scientific words like LIPOMA 'a tumor consisting of fatty tissue' [*-oma* indicates 'a tumor'], LIPEMIA 'excess fat in the blood' [*haima* 'blood'], and LIPAROID 'fatty.'   7125

There is another word spelled *leave*, this one meaning 'permission,' as in "by your *leave*," and "absent without *leave*." One might think that *leave* 'permission' must be related to LEAVE 'to go away from,' since a soldier on *leave* LEAVES his station. However, such is not the case, since *leave* is the offspring of yet another Indo-European root, **leubh-* 'to care, to desire; to love.'   7130

XXXVII

Loyal Legislators
Legitimize Delegated
Privileges

When ALLEGATIONS of ILLEGITIMACY are launched, one
7135 hopes for LOYALTY from COLLEAGUES, whether in LEGISLATIVE
or COLLEGIATE halls. These words all stem from Latin *lēx, lēgis*
'law,' originally 'religious law,' but the field of reference was later
enlarged to include the generalized concepts of legal formulas
and contracts.
7140   There is a possibility that Latin *lēx* 'law' is derived from the
Indo-European root **leg-* 'to collect,' with the basic meaning of 'a
collection of rules.' This would make *lēx* 'law' cousin to Greek
logos 'discourse' and consequently to English LOGIC, a comforting
thought to LEGISLATORS and LEGALISTS.
7145   The Latin word *lēx* is itself used in Anglo/American jurispru-
dence, but with a consciousness that one is using Latin (and
largely Medieval Latin at that), in phrases like *lex loci* 'the law of
the place: the law of the *loc*ale where the contract is drawn up';
lex situs 'the law of the site: the law of the place where the thing
7150 (*res*) is *situ*ated'; *lex actus* 'the law of the act: the law of the place
where the act was done'; *lex fori* 'the law of the forum: the law of
the court where the proceedings are conducted'; *lex mercatorum*
'the law of the merchants: commercial law'; *lex scripta* 'written
law: the statute law'; *lex non scripta* 'unwritten law: the common
7155 law'; and *lex Salica* 'the Salic law: Germanic law of the Salian
(Merovingian) Franks, codified near the end of the fifth century
A.D.' The Salic law is of historical interest because the portion
dealing with the noninheritance of land by women was interpreted in France as governing dynastic succession, with the
7160 meaning that no woman should rule and that the succession to the
throne could not pass through a woman. This factitious interpretation was made to further the claims of the house of Valois in the
contest between Philip VI of France and Edward III of England

that marked the beginning of the Hundred Years' War. It is also
the reason that France has never had a ruling queen.

English words borrowed from Latin *lēx, lēgis* 'law' are LEGAL
'having to do with law' [via Medieval/Old French from Latin
lēgālis]; LEGISLATE 'to pass laws,' a back formation from LEGISLA-
TOR 'lawmaker' [from Latin *lēgis lātor* 'proposer of law']; and
LEGITIMATE 'lawful; genuine' [from Medieval Latin *lēgitimātus*,
past participle of *lēgitimāre* 'to make lawful,' from Latin *lēgitimus*
'lawful'].

The Latin verb springing from *lēx, lēgis* is *lēgāre* 'to entrust
(to someone) by law; to depute, to commission; to bequeath.'
Flowing from Latin *lēgāre, lēgātus* are the English words LEGATE
'emissary'; LEGATEE 'one who has inherited a legacy'; LEGACY
'something handed down by a predecessor' [via Medieval/Old
French *legacie* from Medieval Latin *lēgātia]*; DELEGATE 'an
agent, a deputy; to appoint a deputy; to entrust to another' [from
Medieval Latin *dēlēgātus* 'deputy,' from Latin *dēlēgāre, dēlēgātus*
'to send away; to entrust']; and RELEGATE 'to consign; to send
into exile' [from Latin *relēgāre, relēgātus* 'to dispatch, to banish'].

Your COLLEAGUE is not someone you went to COLLEGE with.
Etymologically the words COLLEAGUE and COLLEGE are related
as parent to offspring, with a basic significance of 'commissioned
together.' They are as follows: COLLEAGUE 'a fellow member, an
associate' [via French *collegue* from Latin *collēga* 'partner in
office'] and COLLEGE 'a body of persons engaged in common
pursuits; a body of clergy living in common; a society of scholars;
a school of higher learning' [via Medieval/Old French from Latin
collēgium 'colleagueship; association, guild, fraternity,' from *collēga* 'partner in office']. There is a divergence of opinion among
the experts as to whether the *-lēg-* of Latin *collēga* and *collēgium*
is traceable to *lēgāre* 'to depute, to choose as one's lieutenant' or
to *legere* 'to collect, to gather; to choose.' The second derivation
would relegate the words COLLEGE and COLLEAGUE to the
LEGION, LEGEND group (Chapter XXXV, lines 6525, 6663.). There is
another, seldom encountered *colleague* in English, a verb meaning 'to enter into an alliance with.' This *colleague* comes from the
Indo-European root **leig-* 'to bind,' which is also ancestor to
legato 'tied together' and *league*.

A peculiar situation exists with regard to the two words
ALLEGE 'to state positively but without proof' and ALLEGATION
'an unsupported assertion.' They certainly look and sound as if
they should be etymologically related and are in fact used as verb
and noun for the same circumstances. The *OED*, however, noting
the soft *-g-* in ALLEGE and the hard *-g-* in ALLEGATION, unequivo-

7165

7170

7175

7180

7185

7190

7195

7200

7205

cally states that they are not etymologically related, and this view
is shared by many others.

7210   The derivation of ALLEGATION is straightforward enough: it
comes via Old French from Latin *allēgātiō* 'a sending of negotia-
tors; a bringing forward, a citing,' from *allēgāre, allēgātus* 'to send
on a mission; to adduce; to allege' [*ad* + *lēgāre*]. On the other
hand, ALLEGE derives from Norman French *alegier*, from Old

7215   French *esligier* 'to free from legal difficulties,' from Vulgar Latin
exlītigāre 'to clear at law; to acquit' [Latin *ex-* + *lītigāre* 'to carry
on a lawsuit'].

       'To get out of legal entanglements' or 'to acquit,' which seems
to be the gist of the meaning of Vulgar Latin *exlītigāre*, is hardly

7220   the same as 'to allege'; indeed, the use of ALLEGE often indicates
that someone is getting into legal difficulties. But in medieval
England, Norman French *alegier* 'to acquit' was Latinized erroneously into *adlēgiāre* (as if from *ad legem*), and the meaning of
adlēgiāre and English ALLEGE shifted eventually to agree with

7225   that of Latin *allēgāre* 'to cite, to adduce; to allege.'
       Since a secondary meaning of Latin *allēgāre* is 'to allege,' it is
by the seemingly obvious path, Latin *allēgāre* > English ALLEGE,
that some trace the ancestry of the English word. However, this
derivation is rejected by the *OED* and others because *allege* is

7230   pronounced with a soft *-g-*. According to the workings of sound
correspondences, if the derivation of ALLEGE had been from Latin
allēgāre via Old French *alleguer*, the English word would be
alleague, with a hard *-g-*.

       Also from Latin *lēx, lēgis* 'law' is the second element of the

7235   compound word PRIVILEGE 'private law; an ordinance referring to
an individual; a right granted to a class of persons; a special right
granted to an office' [via Old French from Latin *prīvilēgium* 'a law
relating to one person' (*prīvus* 'private, individual')]. (But for
sacrilege see line 6632.)

7240   Finally, Latin *lēgālis* 'having to do with law' evolved into Old
French with the usual syncopating of the internal consonant, so
that *lēgālis* became Old French *leial, loial* 'legal; faithful to one's
obligations,' whence English LOYAL 'faithful, steadfast.' (The
English word LAW comes from Old English *lagu* 'a code of rules,'

7245   from Old Norse *lagu*, plural of *lag* 'what has been laid down,'
from Germanic *lagam*, from the Indo-European root *legh-* 'to
lie, to lay.')

XXXVIII

Luminous Lucy, the Illustrious Lunatic

LUCY (Lucille Ball) is one of those Hollywood LUMINARIES whose LUMINOSITY is as real as it is apparent; the LUSTER of her comic talents LIGHTENS and ILLUMINATES the scene, even though   7250 she is seldom LUCID and her behavior is often LUNATIC. The words we are dealing with here all have to do with LIGHT, and their Indo-European root is *leuk- 'light, brightness.' The inherited Germanic words are comparatively few, including LIGHT 'the essential condition of vision; the opposite of darkness; luminous   7255 radiant energy' and LIGHTEN 'to grow less dark; to make less dark; to flash or shine brightly.' It is from the 'flashing' sense of LIGHTEN that we get the noun LIGHTNING (=LIGHTENING) 'the flash of light that accompanies a discharge of atmospheric electricity.' (These words are not related to light 'not heavy' and lighten   7260 'to make less heavy.') Used nowadays in a figurative sense is the compound verb ENLIGHTEN 'to give knowledge of truth to,' which originally had the literal meanings of 'to illuminate; to cause to shine.' All of these words trace back to Indo-European *leuk- 'light' by way of Old English lēoht, līht (pronounce the -h-) and   7265 Germanic *liuhtam or *leuhtam.

The o-grade Indo-European form of the root, *louk- 'light,' leads to another Germanic form, *lauhaz 'clearing,' cognate of Sanskrit loká(s) 'open space,' Lithuanian laūkas 'field,' Old High German lōh 'thicket,' and Latin lūcus 'grove.' *Lauhaz gave rise   7270 to Old English lēah 'place where the sun shines; meadow,' whose modern English descendant is LEA 'grassland, meadow.' (Old English lēah 'meadow' is not related to the proper name Leah, which comes from the Hebrew and means 'wild cow.')

In Latin, Indo-European *leuk- 'light' evolved into lūx (for   7275 *lūcs) 'light, daylight,' a word also used in English as LUX 'the international unit of illumination, equal to one lumen per square

meter' (as well as the trade name for a brand of soap). Latin *lūx*,
lūcis 'light' is the probable source of the proper names LUCIUS,
7280   LUCIA, and LUCY, and the undoubted source of the name LUCIFER
(literally) 'bearer of light; light-bringer'; 'the morning star; a kind
of friction match; Satan' [from Latin *lūcifer* 'light-bringing; the
morning star' (*ferre* 'to bring')]. (Latin *lūcifer* is a loan translation
of Greek *phōsphoros*.) In the Vulgate translation of *Isaiah* xiv, 12,
7285   there is a reference to *Lucifer* (the translator's rendition of
Hebrew *hêlēl* 'daystar,' here an epithet for the king of Babylon) as
having fallen from the heavens, which led some Christian interpreters of the Bible to believe that *Lucifer* was the name of Satan
before his fall, when he was the proudest of heaven's archangels.
7290   As the name for a friction match, *Lucifer* was preceded and
rivaled for a while by *Promethean* (1831).
    The Latin verb associated with *lūx* 'light' is *lūcēre* 'to shine,
to be bright,' with present participle *lūcēns* 'shining.' Latin
lūcēns, *lūcentis* has been borrowed into English as LUCENT
7295   'giving off light, shining,' more often encountered in the compound form TRANSLUCENT 'transmitting light diffusely so that
objects cannot be distinctly perceived'; (literally) 'shining
through.' Also deriving from Latin *lūcēre* 'to shine' is the Latin
adjective *lūcidus* 'bright, shining; clear,' whence (perhaps via
7300   French *lucide* or Italian *lucido*) English LUCID 'shining, bright;
clear; easily understood' and the intensive compound PELLUCID
'admitting the maximum passage of light; transparently clear' [*pel-*
< *per-* 'through, throughout']. From Latin *lūcidus* 'clear' there
developed the Late Latin verb *ēlūcidāre* 'to make completely
7305   clear,' antecedent of English ELUCIDATE 'to clarify, to explain' [*ē-*
< *ex* 'out,' used here with the sense of 'completely'].
    Other Latin derivatives of *lūx*, *lūcis* 'light' are *lucerna* 'lamp,
oil-lamp' and *lucubrare* 'to work by lamplight' > English LUCU-
BRATE 'to work by night, "to burn the midnight oil."' That the
7310   results of such work are not necessarily of high quality is attested
by the later meanings of LUCUBRATION 'nocturnal study; the
product of such study; any elaborate literary composition; an
overlabored or artificial work; pedantry in speech and writing.'
    Then there are the NOCTILUCA 'a genus of bioluminescent
7315   marine organisms that, when grouped in large numbers, make the
seas phosphorescent' [from Latin *noctilūca* 'night light; the moon'
(*nox*, *noctis* 'night')].
    Latin speakers had another word for 'light,' to wit, *lūmen* (for
*lucmen or **lucsmen*) 'light, lamp; daylight; splendor; eye, win-
7320   dow, opening.' In some senses *lūmen* is a synonym for *lūx*, and
both are descended from the same Indo-European root, **leuk-*
'light, brightness.' The modern scientific meaning of LUMEN is

'the unit of luminous flux; the amount of light emitted in a solid angle of one steradian by a uniform point source of one candle.' LUMEN also has biological meanings having to do with tubular organs such as blood vessels and intestines, the reference being to the 'opening' significance of Latin *lūmen*. But most English borrowings from Latin *lūmen* have to do with 'light' or 'brightening,' as in LUMINOUS 'shining, brilliant, bright'; LUMINARY 'an object that gives light; a notable person; a star'; ILLUME (poetic) 'illumine'; ILLUMINE 'illuminate'; and ILLUMINATE 'to throw light on; to make understandable; to adorn a text with flourishes and designs or miniature pictures in brilliant colors or precious metals, as in medieval manuscripts' [from Latin *illūmināre* 'to light up' (*il-* < *in-* 'into')]. The 'adorn a text' meaning comes from Medieval Latin *illūmināre* 'to illuminate books.' *Illūmināre* became Medieval French *enluminer*, which was borrowed into Middle English as *enluminen*, suffered the loss of the initial *en-* to become Middle English *lumine(n)*, dwindled still further to *limnen*, and finally evolved into modern English LIMN 'to draw or paint; to describe'; (obsolete) 'to decorate in color' [but some etymologists trace LIMN back through Middle English *lumine(n)* to Old French *luminer* < Medieval Latin *lūmināre* 'to light up'].

Yet another Latin cognate of *lūc-* is *Lūcīna* 'the Roman goddess of childbirth,' an epithet of Diana in her capacity as the moon goddess and helper of women in childbirth, from *lūcīnus* 'bringing to light.' An archaic English meaning of LUCINA is 'midwife.' From a related Indo-European form, **leuksna*, comes the shortened Latin word *lūna* 'the luminous one; the moon.' Based on *luna* 'the moon' are English LUNATIC 'insane'; (literally) 'affected by the phases of the moon; moonstruck.' The popular slang version is LOONY. More English words based on *luna* 'the moon' are LUNAR 'pertaining to the moon'; SUBLUNAR, SUBLUNARY 'earthly, mundane'; (literally) 'beneath the moon'; CISLUNAR, CISLUNARY 'relating to space between the earth and the moon'; TRANSLUNAR, TRANSLUNARY 'relating to space beyond the moon; unworldly or ethereal'; LUNATE 'shaped like a crescent moon'; LUNETTE 'a crescent-shaped ornament'; (*plural*, obsolete) 'eyeglasses' (from the shape of the lenses); (literally) 'small moon.' *Lunettes* is still the common French word for 'eyeglasses.'

Related to all these luminous words is Latin *lūstrāre* (for **lūcstrāre*) 'to light up, to illuminate, to brighten.' *Lūstrāre* gave rise to the Italian verb *lustrare* 'to polish; to sparkle,' whence the adjective *lustro* 'polished; shining' > French *lustre* 'brightness' > English LUSTER 'the quality of shining with reflected light.' Other English borrowings are ILLUSTRIOUS 'famous, renowned' [from Latin *illūstris* 'full of light; famous'] and ILLUSTRATE 'to set in a

7325
7330
7335
7340
7345
7350
7355
7360
7365

clear light; to make clear; to provide with explanatory or decorative pictures.'

7370 There is another Latin verb *lūstrāre* that means 'to purify by expiation,' with the related noun LUSTRUM 'a ceremonial purification undergone by the entire Roman population after the census, every five years.' According to some etymologists these two *lūstrāres* are really one and the same verb, with a literal meaning

7375 'to brighten' and a figurative meaning 'to purify.' However, others account them as two separate words from different sources, associating *lūstrāre* 'to purify' and *lūstrum* 'expiatory sacrifice' with Latin *lavāre* 'to wash.' While we are talking about disagreement among experts, we may as well point out that the English

7380 word LUXURY 'a mode of life characterized by material abundance; indulgence in costly food, dress or furnishings' [via Old French *luxurie*; from Latin *luxuria* 'rankness; extravagance; riotous living'] is thought by a few to be akin to Latin *lūx* 'light' by way of the Latin noun *luxus* 'excess, extravagance; splendor,' but

7385 that most associate *luxus* 'excess' with the Latin adjective *luxus* 'disjointed, sprained' and the verb *luxāre* 'to dislocate,' from the Indo-European root **leug-* 'to bend, to turn.'

We must now go back to Indo-European **leuk-* 'light' and consider some Greek descendants of that luminous root that have

7390 affected the English vocabulary, notably the combining forms *leuco-*, *leuko-*, and *leuk-*, which have the sense of 'whiteness, colorlessness,' and are taken from Greek *leukos* 'bright; white, clear.' These meanings are evidenced in the English words LEUCOCYTE 'a white blood corpuscle' [-*cyte* 'cell' from Greek

7395 *kutos* 'hollow vessel']; LEUKEMIA 'a disease involving uncontrolled proliferation of the white blood corpuscles' [-*emia* from Greek -*aimiā*, from *haima* 'blood']; LEUCITE 'a white or gray mineral; potassium aluminum silicate'; LUCITE 'the trade name of a transparent acrylic resin'; and LEUCOMA 'a dense white opacity

7400 in the cornea' [Greek -*ōma*, an abstract nominal ending]. (-*Oma* in medical parlance indicates a tumor.) Also from the Greek is ALYSSUM 'a genus of plants also known as madwort' [from Greek *alusson* 'madwort,' from *a-* 'not' + *lussa* 'rage; rabies']. This plant was thought to be a cure for rabies. Greek *lussa* 'rage, fury,

7405 madness; rabies' is descended from Indo-European **leuk-* 'light, brightness.' The semantic explication given is that the derivation came about "from the gleaming eyes characteristic of " madness or rabies (*AHD*).

Presumably also having to do with gleaming eyes is the name

7410 of the LYNX 'a genus of wild cats' [from Latin *lynx, lyncis*, from Greek *lunx* (*lugx*)] (possibly a nasalized form of **lux*), "as if from its shining eyes, but more likely of obscure origin" (*AHD*).

The Medieval French form of Latin *lynx, lyncis* > Vulgar
Latin *luncia* was *lonce*. *Lonce* was misinterpreted as standing for
l'once, so that the animal thus became *once* in French. This   7415
mistake has been corrected, and a French *lynx* is once again a
lynx, but the name *once* has been preserved and transferred to
another wild cat, spelled in English OUNCE 'the snow leopard; a
large feline of the highlands of central Asia.'

XXXIX

The Mannerly
Amanuensis Maneuvers
Manure

7420   Women's liberationists are seeking EMANCIPATION; they want to cast off their MANACLES and be free to MANAGE, MANEUVER, MANIPULATE, and MAINTAIN their own affairs in their own MAN-NER with their own well-MANICURED hands, and COMMAND their own not-so-MANIFEST destinies. All of these words have to do
7425   ultimately with 'hands' and 'handling,' and they stem from Latin *manus* 'hand,' from the Indo-European root *man- 'hand.'
         In some words the sense of 'hand' is still literal rather than figurative, for example, MANUAL 'by hand; the keyboard of an organ played by hand (rather than by the pedals); a handbook'
7430   [from Latin *manuālis* 'of the hand'] and MANUSCRIPT 'a composition written by hand' [from Medieval Latin *manūscrīptus* 'hand-written']. Note, also, MANUFACTURE 'to make a finished product out of raw materials'; (literally) 'to make by hand' [from Old French *manufacture* 'handiwork,' from Late Latin *manūfactus*
7435   'handmade']. Today, MANUFACTURED usually implies 'made by machine' and is thus antonymous rather than synonymous with *handmade*.
         In zoology, the Latin word MANUS means 'the end of the foreleg in vertebrates,' whether it be a hand, a paw, a claw or a
7440   hoof. Another word in which the 'hand' sense is manifest is MANACLE 'handcuff' [from Medieval/Old French *manicle*, from Latin *manicula* 'little hand']. Latin and French -i- became English -a- by assimilation to such words as *tentacle*, *oracle*, *miracle*, and *spectacle*.
7445   A word in which the 'handling' sense is clear enough but whose etymology is not quite so straightforward is MANIPULATE 'to operate by skillful use of the hands; to manage shrewdly; to tamper with' [ultimately from Latin *manipulus* 'a handful']. The *-pulus* element is of unknown origin, but some think that it stems

from the root of Latin *plere* 'to fill.' Latin *manipulus* 'a handful, a 7450
bundle' came to mean (in Roman army lingo) 'a bundle of hay on
a pole used as a standard by a company of soldiers' and eventually the 'company of soldiers' itself, or a MANIPLE 'a subdivision of
the Roman legion consisting of 60 or 120 men.' In Medieval Latin
the word *manipulus* 'a handful' was occasionally used to mean 7455
'something carried in the hand; a workman's tool, a bowl, a staff;
(and sometimes) a servant,' although its principal use was an
ecclesiastical one. In the western church, the name *manipulus*/
MANIPLE was given to 'one of the Eucharistic vestments, consisting of a strip of stuff from two to four feet in length and worn 7460
suspended from the left arm near the wrist of the celebrant . . . ;
said to have originally been a napkin held in the left hand for the
purpose of wiping the tears shed for the sins of the people'
(*OED*). Another interpretation of the symbolism of the ecclesiastical MANIPLE is that it represents the cord in which Jesus's hands 7465
were bound, while a 19th-century church dictionary states that
the maniple was originally used to wipe away the perspiration
from the face.

Meanwhile erudite members of the scientific world in the
18th century devised the French noun *manipulation*, based on a 7470
nonexistent Latin verb **manipulāre*, from *manipulus* 'a handful.'
Thus the new word was promptly naturalized into English,
Italian, Spanish, and Portuguese to denote 'the methods of handling apparatus and materials in chemical experiments.' The verb
to MANIPULATE soon followed and proved so useful that it was 7475
adopted into medical and everyday use, so that by 1855 Herbert
Spencer could write that "the hand has been moulded into fitness
for manipulating things," in a kind of reverse definition of the
word.

Other compound words in which the element acquired from 7480
Latin *manus* still has something to do literally with 'hands' are
MANICURE 'care of the hands and fingernails' [*cura* 'care']; LEGER-
DEMAIN 'sleight of hand'; (literally) 'light of hand' [from Medieval/
Old French; from *leger* 'light' + *de* 'of' + *main* 'hand'; from Latin
manus 'hand']; and QUADRUMANOUS 'having four hands, or four 7485
feet with opposable first digits,' said of the QUADRUMANA, a
zoological group that includes all the primates except man.

For untold generations working with his hands has been the
lot of man. The Latin phrase for this fact of life is *manū operārī*
'to work by hand.' Compressed into one word this became the 7490
Medieval Latin noun *man(u)opera* 'handwork,' and *man(u)opera*
was transmogrified into Old French *manuevre, maneuvre*, a word
that has two English descendants of vastly different meanings.
They are MANOEUVRE, MANEUVER 'an adroit move; an artfully

7495   contrived plan; a military move; a military exercise involving two opposing sides' and MANURE (obsolete) 'to work the soil by hand'; 'to enrich the earth with dung or compost; animal dung or compost used to enrich the soil.' (See line 7775.)

7500   The human hand is still faintly visible in the last two words, but it disappears from view in MANIFEST 'obvious, clearly apparent; to show plainly; a cargo or passenger list' [from Latin *manifestus* 'seized by the hand; palpable; obvious']. The *-festus* element is obscure and is variously interpreted as meaning 'struck, gripped, given, taken.' Note, also, MANIFESTO 'a public

7505   declaration' [from the Italian *manifesto* 'manifestation']; MANUMIT 'to free from slavery'; (literally) 'to send from the hand' [from Latin *manumittere* 'to set free,' from *manū ēmittere* 'to send away from one's hand' (*ēmittere* 'to send out, to let go')]; and MANCI-PATE (literally) 'to take into hand'; (obsolete) 'to enslave' [from

7510   Latin *mancipāre* 'to sell,' from *manus* 'hand' + *capere* 'to take']. What interests us about this obsolete word is its opposite, EMANCI-PATE 'to set free; to release from parental control.' Another English word where the hand element is no longer visible is MANAGE 'to exert control over'; (literally) 'to handle' (originally)

7515   'to train (a horse)' [from Italian *maneggiare* 'to handle (a horse),' from Vulgar Latin *manidiāre* 'to handle']. No one seems to have an explanation for the element *-diare* that became Italian *-ggiare* and English *-ge*. The spelling with the second vowel *-e-* is still retained in the English word MANÈGE 'the art of horsemanship;

7520   the training of horses' [from French *manège*, from Italian *maneggio*, from *maneggiare* 'to train a horse'].

        The notion of gentling animals 'by hand' is also present in the infrequent English word MANSUETUDE 'gentleness, mildness' [from Latin *mānsuētūdō* 'tameness,' from *mānsuēscere* 'to accus-

7525   tom to the hand, to tame,' from *manus* 'hand' + *suēscere* 'to accustom to; to become accustomed']. Latin *suēscere* comes from *sui* 'one's own' + *-ēscere*, a verbal ending indicating 'beginning, becoming,' and thus means 'becoming one's own.' Latin *mān-suētus* 'tamed, accustomed to the hand' is the source, by way of

7530   Vulgar Latin *mānsuētīnus* 'tamed; watchdog,' > Old French *mastin* 'watchdog' > Middle English *mastif*, of English MASTIFF (etymologically) 'tamed'; 'a large, powerful dog of an ancient breed, used as a watchdog and hunter.' The endings in *-f(f)* are explained in a variety of ways, depending on which dictionaries

7535   one consults. One source says that they are due to the influence of Middle English *-if* '-ive,' another that they are the result of a confusion and blending of Old French *mastin* 'watchdog' with Old French *mestif* 'a mongrel dog' (a different word), a third postulates a Vulgar Latin form *mansuetīvus*, which would yield

the *-if* ending, while yet another assumes that the English   7540
speakers first picked up the parallel Provençal word *mastis*
'watchdog' and later assumed on grammatical grounds that this
must be the nominative singular of the (nonexistent) Old French
*mastif. Related semantically are MAINTAIN 'to keep up, to carry
on'; (literally) 'to hold in the hand' [from Old French *maintenir*,   7545
from Medieval Latin *manūtenēre*, from Latin *manū tenēre* 'to
hold in the hand'] and MANNER 'a way of acting'; (*plural*) 'a code
of social conduct; mores'; (literally) 'a way of handling' [from
Norman French *manere*, from Old French *maniere*; from Vulgar
Latin *manuāria, from Latin *manuārius* 'of the hand'].   7550
    Somewhat more exotic words based on Latin *manus* and
French *main* 'hand' are AMANUENSIS 'one who takes dictation;
secretary; one who copies manuscripts' [from Latin *āmanuēnsis*
'secretary,' from the Latin phrase *ā manū*, short for *servus ā manū*
'slave at hand' + *-ēnsis* 'belonging to'] (sometimes used as a   7555
euphemism for 'ghostwriter') and MORTMAIN 'institutional possession of property; the condition of land held by ecclesiastical
corporations'; (literally) 'dead hand' [from French *mortemain*
'dead hand,' from Medieval Latin *mortua manus*], so called
because ecclesiastics were deemed in medieval law to be civilly   7560
dead. A similar term is the feudal *manus mortua*, which denotes
the custom whereby serfs had no testamentary rights to the
disposition of their possessions, which reverted to the lord if the
serf had no legitimate offspring. In the same set is MANQUÉ
'lacking, defective; unfulfilled, frustrated' [from French *manquer*   7565
'to fail; to lack,' from Italian *mancare*, from *manco* 'lacking,' from
Latin *mancus* 'maimed,' from Indo-European **man-ko-* "'maimed
in the hand'" (*AHD*)].
    An extension of Latin *manus* 'hand' is found in Latin *manica*
'a long sleeve (that reaches to the hand),' as well as its attendant   7570
adjective *manicātus* 'with long sleeves.' These forms lead to the
botanical MANICATE 'interwoven into a mass that can be easily
stripped off, like a sleeve' and the gastronomical MANICOTTI 'a
kind of pasta shaped like sleeves, usually served with a filling of
chopped ham and cheese' [plural of Italian *manicotto* 'muff,'   7575
augmentative of Italian *manica* 'sleeve']. In French, Latin *manica*
became *manche* 'sleeve.' Because of its shape, that is the name
given by the French to *la Manche* 'the English Channel.'
    We have seen Latin *manus* 'hand' compounded with *operārī*
'to work' (MANEUVER, MANURE), *ēmittere* 'to send out, to let go'   7580
(MANUMIT), *capere* 'to take' (EMANCIPATE), and *tenere* 'to hold'
(MAINTAIN), but the most far-reaching compound of *manus* was
that made with *dāre* 'to give,' which resulted in Latin *mandāre* 'to
give into one's hand; to charge someone with; to order, to

7585   COMMAND.' (However, some etymologists ascribe this Latin element, -dāre, to the root that gives us English do, that is, Indo-
European *dhē- 'to put,' as in Latin condere 'to put together.' This
would yield mandāre 'to put into one's hand.') Mandāre is the
base of the following English words: MANDAMUS (literally) 'we
7590   order'; 'a writ issued by a high court ordering something done';
MANDATE 'an authoritative command; election results interpreted
as a go-ahead sign on party policy' [from Latin mandātum 'charge,
order,' from the past participle of mandāre]; and MANDATORY
'obligatory.' Compoundings give us COMMAND 'to direct with
7595   authority; to give orders to; an order' [via Old French comander
from Late Latin commandāre]. The com- 'with, together' is used
here as an intensifier, to make the word more forceful. Cognate
with these are COMMANDEER 'to force into service' [from Afrikaans
kommande(e)ren, from French commander 'to command']; COM-
7600   MANDO 'a small fighting force especially trained for quick raids';
(originally) 'a force of Portuguese or Boer troops called up for an
expedition against the natives' [from Dutch commando (whence
Afrikaans kommando), from Portuguese commando 'command'];
and DEMAND 'to ask for peremptorily' [from Old French demander
7605   'to ask,' from Latin dēmandāre 'to hand over, to entrust']. This
word has gone through a semantic reversal since the Classical
Latin days when it meant 'to hand over, to entrust.' It now means
as good as the opposite, 'to ask for.' This change had already
taken place in Vulgar Latin, probably because of the 'to order'
7610   sense of Latin mandāre. The French demander means simply 'to
ask, to request,' rather than 'to demand, to insist upon.' More
compoundings include COUNTERMAND 'to reverse an order' [con-
tra 'opposite to'] and REMAND 'to order back; to send back for
further procedure' [via Old French remander from Medieval
7615   Latin remandāre; from Late Latin remandāre 'to send back word;
to repeat a command'].
        In addition to Late Latin commandāre 'to order,' Latin
mandāre 'to entrust, to charge with' has an altered intensive form
in Latin commendāre 'to commit to the care of; to recommend,'
7620   the base of two English words with virtually synonymous meanings: COMMEND 'to praise; to represent as worthy' and RECOM-
MEND 'to praise as worthy or advisable; to cite as deserving of
patronage' [from Medieval Latin recommendāre].
        Finally we have MAUNDY Thursday (literally) 'Mandate
7625   Thursday,' the anniversary of the day of the Last Supper when
Jesus, according to John xiii, 34, said to the assembled apostles:
"A new commandment (mandātum novum) give I unto you, that
ye love one another." The words mandātum novum were used as
the first words of the antiphon sung at the commemorative

observances of Holy Thursday, so that it became known as 7630
"*Mandatum* Thursday." *Mandatum* evolved into Old French
Mande and English MAUNDY.

Except for proper names, we have in English only one word
that may stem from Indo-European **man-* 'hand' by way of the
Germanic. In Germanic, the notion 'hand' developed a secondary 7635
sense of 'a guiding hand,' hence 'protector, protection.' The
Germanic word **mund* is possible ancestor of English MOUND
(originally) 'to build a hedge or fence around a field'; 'a pile of
earth or rocks heaped up for protection or concealment; an
artificial elevation of earth' [from Old Norse *mund* or Middle 7640
Dutch *mond* 'protection']. Not all etymologists accept this derivation of MOUND. Germanic **mund* also yields Old English *mund*
'hand; protector.' Two proper names from these sources are
EDMUND 'protector of property' [Old English *ēad* 'riches, possessions; property'] and RAYMOND 'counsel protection' [from Old 7645
French *Raimund*, from Frankish *Raginmund* (**ragin* 'counsel,
decree' + **mund* 'protection')].

XL

Opera *and* Hors d'Oeuvres

In order to OPERATE a mechanism with OPTIMUM effect, whether it's a COPYING machine in an OPULENT OFFICE or a 7650 MANURE spreader down on the farm, one OFTEN has to MANEUVER various switches, levers, buttons or other gadgets. What all these words have in common with hors d'OEUVRES is descent from the Indo-European root *op- 'to work; to produce in abundance.'

Those interested in classical music know that the works of 7655 certain composers are listed by their OPUS number and that the Latin word *opus* means 'work, composition.' The plural of *opus* is *opera* 'works,' which was transformed, already in Latin, into a feminine singular noun meaning 'work; effort, exertion, pains.' It has come down to Italian where it still means 'work' but also 7660 OPERA 'a drama in which music forms an essential part, especially singing.' An OPERETTA is (literally) 'a little opera.' The term is used of lightweight works in which much of the dialogue is spoken, in contrast to grand opera, where all the dialogue is sung.

Since Latin *opera* means 'work' it is easy to understand 7665 English OPERATE 'to make work, to cause to function; to bring about a desired effect' [from Latin *operārī*, *operātus* 'to work, to labor']. Latin *operārī* also gives us the phrase *modus operandi* 'way of working, the manner (mode) in which something operates; the way a person works.' Other obvious relatives are COOPERATE 7670 'to work together'; INOPERATIVE 'not working'; and INOPERABLE 'not capable of being used; not suitable for surgery.' The second meaning pertains to the special medical use of the verb OPERATE to mean 'to perform surgery.'

Getting back to the Indo-European root *op-, we note that the 7675 second meaning hypothesized is 'to produce in abundance.' In some parts of the world, nature does the producing while man has only to gather and enjoy the results; but this was apparently not so in the hypothetical world of the Indo-European-speakers, since 'to produce in abundance' is equated with 'to work.'

The earliest form of *op- found in Latin is *ops, opis 'abundance; strength.' The nominative singular *ops is not found in Latin literature, but the word does exist as the proper noun OPS 'an ancient Italian goddess of the harvest.' The plural of *ops is opēs 'wealth, riches, resources,' and from the same source comes the Latin adjective opulentus 'wealthy' > English OPULENT 'immensely wealthy; luxurious, lavish.' *Ops, opis 'abundance,' in the form -ōpia, is compounded with com- 'together with' in Latin cōpia 'plenty, abundance,' seen in English CORNUCOPIA 'horn of plenty.' The adjectival form of cōpia is cōpiōsus 'plentiful, abundant' > English COPIOUS 'yielding plenty, affording ample supply.' 7680

7685

7690

In Medieval Latin, cōpia acquired the meaning of 'a transcript.' Before the printing press was invented, the only way of copying and thus making more plentiful the ancient writings, those storehouses of wisdom, was by transcribing them manually over and over again. Such a handmade transcript was called a cōpia. The related Medieval Latin verb was cōpiāre, which was adapted into Old French as copier > English COPY 'to duplicate; to imitate; material to be set in type.' 7695

Having plenty of everything is an enviable situation to be in. Apparently the Latin speakers thought this was just about the best situation there could possibly be, since (according to some etymologists) their word for 'best,' optimum, is a derivative of *ops, opis 'abundance, plenty' (in other words, being 'best' is a result of being wealthiest). In English OPTIMUM means 'the most favorable condition for a particular situation.' (However, other etymologists ascribe Latin optimum to a different Indo-European root, *op- 'to choose,' thus optimum 'most desired.' Still others trace optimum to the preposition ob 'before, in front of' + superlative ending, thus optimum 'most in front.') 7700

7705

7710

The philosophical notion that the world we live in is the best of all possible worlds, enunciated by Leibniz in 1710 and ridiculed by Voltaire in Candide (1759), was called OPTIMISM (by Jesuit scholars in 1737). Leibniz's reasoning was that since God is omniscient he knows all possible worlds, and since he is omnipotent he could create whatever world he chose, and since he is omnibenevolent he would and did choose to create the best world. The word is now used more loosely to mean a kind of cheerful hopefulness: OPTIMISM 'a belief that everything will turn out all right in the end.' 7715

7720

The Latin element omni- seen in OMNISCIENT, OMNIPOTENT, and OMNIBENEVOLENT is considered by most etymologists to be of obscure origin, but some associate it with our Indo-European root *op- 'to produce in abundance,' and derive Latin omnis 'all' from *op- through the suffixed form *op-ni- (AHD), reasoning that the idea of 'abundance' led to the idea of 'all.' Omni- as a prefix is omnipresent in English, and most of its compounds are self-explanatory. One word that is not so obviously a derivative of Latin omnis is BUS 'a large motor vehicle for carrying passengers' [a shortened form of Latin omnibus 'for all,' dative plural of omnis 'all']. The first omnibuses were horse-drawn. They were given their name in France: voiture omnibus 'carriage for all' ca. 1828 (OED).

Getting back to the 'work' signification of *op-, we come upon Latin officium 'service, kindness; duty, obligation.' Officium (for *opificium) is analyzed as a compound based on the roots of Latin opus 'work' and facere 'to make, to do.' The etymological meaning of officium is thus 'performance of work.' English borrowings, via Old French, include OFFICE 'a place where work is done; a position of authority given to a person' and OFFICER 'a person to whom a position of authority has been given.' Most of the related English words are semantically obvious (OFFICIAL, OFFICIATE), except perhaps OFFICIOUS 'excessively forward in offering one's services.' This comes from Latin officiōsus, which has favorable meanings of 'obliging, courteous,' which were also early meanings of the word in English. The derogatory sense is first noted by the OED in a 1602 quotation. Then there is the pharmaceutical term OFFICINAL 'a drug kept in stock that may be had without special preparation,' as opposed to a magistral drug that is specially formulated for a particular case. An officīna in Latin was 'a workshop or manufactory,' while in Medieval Latin the word was used to stand for 'the storeroom in a monastery where provisions, medicines and other necessities were kept.' Thus an OFFICINAL medicine is one 'taken from the storeroom.'

Latin opera 'work' evolved into Old French oevre, uevre > Modern French oeuvre, a word best known to English-speaking partygoers from the French tongue twister hors d'OEUVRES (literally) 'outside of work'; 'a side dish; an appetizer served before a meal.' Early uses of the phrase in English, now obsolete, carried meanings of 'outside of the ordinary course of things; something rare.' In French, the phrase (sans the final -s) also means 'outbuilding; digression, episode.' (It does not mean 'outside of work' in the sense of 'leftover.')

Consistent with this strange new way of spelling Latin opera, the Latin phrase manū operārī 'to work by hand,' became, by way of Medieval Latin manūopera 'manual work,' Old French manuevre, maneuvre. The Modern French spelling is manoeuvre

'working; (military) drill; contrivance, laborer.' The British spelling is also MANOEUVRE, while the American spelling is MANEUVER 'an adroit or dexterous move; a military or naval exercise; to 7770
manipulate into a desired position.' These meanings no longer have to do with handwork and are more a question of brainwork and planning. The Old French *maneuvrer* 'to work by hand' had a variant, *manouvrer*, meaning 'to till the soil by hand.' *Manouvrer* came into Middle English as *maynoyren*, *ma(y)nouren*, and eventually 7775
evolved into MANURE (originally) 'to till the soil'; 'to cultivate; to enrich the land with fertilizer; organic fertilizer; the dung of barnyard animals.'

Old French *uevre*, *oevre* 'work' also acquired a meaning of 'custom,' perhaps because work was what most people were most 7780
accustomed to. This usage led to the obsolete English word *ure* 'custom, use, practice' and the current compound INURE 'to make used to something by prolonged subjection' [via Middle English *enewren*].

Finally, the English word OFTEN 'frequently, repeatedly, 7785
many times,' which carries with it the connotation of an 'abundance' of whatever is taking place, is possibly descended from our Indo-European root *op- 'to produce in abundance; to work,' by way of Germanic *oft- 'frequently.' In that case, it is also related to Latin *ops, opis; opus.* 7790

XLI

Peculiar Fellows'
Pecuniary Peculations

If an IMPECUNIOUS FELLOW, acquitted of charges of cattle rustling, were somehow to embezzle back the FEE he'd paid his lawyer, it would be a pretty PECULIAR PECUNIARY PECULATION. The reason for the barnyard references is that all the capitalized words, from IMPECUNIOUS FELLOW to PECULATION, can be traced to words meaning 'cattle.'

The Indo-European root of all these words is *peku- 'wealth, movable property.' One of the earliest forms of wealth in a nomadic culture was livestock or *cattle*, a word that nowadays means 'animals of the bovine tribe,' but that formerly included all domesticated animals. Thus, it was no accident that the Latin word *pecū*, which originally meant 'flocks, herds,' later came to mean 'money.'

English loanwords that retain the monetary sense of Latin *pecū* include PECUNIARY 'pertaining to money' [from Latin *pecūnārius*, from *pecūnia* 'property in cattle; riches; money']; PECUNIOUS 'well provided with money' [from Latin *pecūniōsus* 'rich, wealthy']; and the much more frequently encountered negative IMPECUNIOUS 'without funds, penniless.'

More abstract, so that even the sense of 'wealth, riches' is lost, is PECULIAR 'standing apart from others; unusual, eccentric'; (originally) 'belonging to an individual as his own personal property' [from Latin *pecūliāris* 'one's own; as private property'; from *pecūlium* (literally) 'a little herd' > 'wealth in cattle; personal property, a small > sum of money'] . . . ' "that small part of a herd given as his own private property to the slave acting as herd[sman]; hence private property." ' (*EP*). If one of these herdsmen or a slave in charge of other kinds of property appropriated some of the lord's goods to his own peculiar uses, the commission of this misdeed was known by the word *pecūlārī* 'to embezzle.' The past participle *pecūlātus* 'embezzlement (of public money)' is the base of English PECULATION 'embezzlement; the stealing of goods entrusted to one; the appropriation of another's property unlawfully to one's own use,' said especially of the misuse of public funds.   7825

A word that gets us back to the animal members of this word-family, by way of Italian *pecora* 'ewe, sheep,' is PECORINO 'a Romano cheese made from ewe's milk.'

Indo-European **peku-* 'wealth, movable property' turns up in Germanic as **fehu-* (Indo-European **p* > Germanic **f*; Indo-   7830
European **k* > Germanic **h*). In Frankish, Old Saxon, and Old High German, *fehu* meant 'cattle,' while in Old English **fehu* took the forms *feoh, fioh* 'cattle.' (Note, however, that Gothic *faihu* seems to have meant 'money' and not 'cattle.') In modern German Indo-European **peku* is *Vieh* (pronounced "fee") 'cattle,'   7835
and there is an obsolete English *"fee"* meaning 'livestock; movable property in general; money.' This Old English *fee* is perhaps cousin to another FEE (originally) 'an inherited estate in land, held on condition of homage and service to a superior lord'; 'an inherited estate in land; a fixed charge made by an institution; a   7840
charge for professional services' [from Old French *fe, fiu*; related to Medieval Latin *feodum, feudum* 'feudal estate']. Other possible relatives are FIEF 'a fee; a feudal estate' and FEUDALISM 'a social system that results from land being held on condition of homage and service by a vassal to a lord.' (The latter has nothing to do   7845
with *feud* 'a quarrel between two families'.) Presumably, FEE, FIEF, FEUDAL(ISM) and Medieval Latin *feudum* trace back to a Frankish compound **fehu-ōd* 'cattle-property,' but there is no explanation of how the meaning was transferred from 'cattle, movable property' to 'an estate in land,' which of all property is   7850
the least movable. (The *OED* states that this etymology "must be rejected. . . . The ultimate etymology is uncertain.")

In Old Norse, Germanic **fehu* evolved into *fē* 'cattle; property; money,' and was combined with another Germanic word **lagam* > Old Norse *lag* 'a laying down,' to produce Old Norse   7855
fēlagi 'one who lays down money (in a joint undertaking); a partner.' Old Norse *fēlagi* became Old English *fēolaga* > Middle English *felawe* > Modern English FELLOW (obsolete) 'a partner'; 'an associate; one of the same kind as another; a man, a boy.'

Some etymologists identify our Indo-European root **peku*   7860
'wealth, movable property' with another root, **pek-* 'to pluck wool; to comb.' This allows one to speculate that the abstract notion of 'wealth' may have arisen because of the wool and yarn that were obtained from the sheep rather than because of the animals themselves. If the two roots are indeed the same, we   7865

have several more English words, from Latin *pecten* 'comb,' to add to our list. They are: PECTEN (zoology) 'any structure resembling a comb'; PECTINATE 'having teeth like a comb'; and PEIGNOIR (literally) 'a garment to be worn while combing the hair'; 'a 7870 dressing gown' [from the French; from French *peigner* 'to comb the hair,' from Latin *pectināre*].

In Greek, **pkt-*, a zero-grade extended form of the root, developed. Not surprisingly, this unwieldy consonant cluster lost its initial *p-*, leaving us with words like *kteis*, *ktenos* (for **pkte-* 7875 *nos*) 'comb,' and these English borrowings: CTENOID 'comblike' [*ktenoeidēs*]; CTENOPHORA 'a phylum of marine animals bearing eight rows of comblike cilia for locomotion' [*-phore* 'bearing']; and CTENIDIUM (zoology) 'a comblike structure' [New Latin *-idium* from Greek *-idion*, a diminutive suffix].

7880 On the Germanic side, the Indo-European root **pek-* 'to pluck wool; to comb' may have taken an angry twist, for it seems to have developed into Germanic **feht-* 'to fight,' Old English *feohtan* and English FIGHT 'to contend with physically,' possibly in a manner similar to the way one contends with snarls in wool 7885 when trying to comb it. A suggested semantic progression is: 'to pluck, to pull out > to scuffle > to fight.' (However, some etymologists associate English *fight* with Latin *pugnus* 'a fist,' and therefore a different Indo-European root.)

According to Mario Pei, the *Faeroe* Islands of the North 7890 Atlantic, between the Shetlands and Iceland, are so named because they are the *Sheep* Islands.

XLII

Peerless Umpires, Imperious Nonpartisans

A NONPAREIL is 'an individual of unequaled excellence; a nonesuch, a paragon; a small disc of chocolate covered with sugar pellets; a size of type between agate and minion; a painted bunting.' We may be sure that the exalted status of NONPAREIL 'nonesuch, paragon' is an apotheosis toward which all baseball UMPIRES strive. We may be equally sure that no baseball player, living or dead—certainly not Leo Durocher, that "practically PEERLESS leader"—would agree that any umpire ever achieved such status. Nevertheless, etymologically speaking, UMPIRE and NONPAREIL are almost the same word, since they both have the basic meaning of 'not equal,' and they both stem from Latin *par* 'equal.'

From Latin *par* 'equal' there developed Old French *per* 'equal; peer; one of a pair (of contestants)' and its opposite *nonper* 'non-equal; not one of a pair (of contestants); a third party.' *Nonper* had a variant *nomper* that went into Middle English as *noumpere*; "*a + noumpere*" was misapprehended as "*an + oumpere*," and the word became in Modern English UMPIRE 'a third (not equal) party who arbitrates between contestants' (where the notion of 'not equal' has the sense of 'impartial'). On the other hand, Latin *par* 'equal' had a Vulgar Latin diminutive **pariculus* that evolved with syncopation into Old French *pareil* 'equal; like.' *Pareil* had the negative counterpart *nonpareil* 'not to be equaled; matchless.' Q.E.D.

In addition to UMPIRE and NONPAREIL a number of English words have been borrowed from Latin *par* and Old French *per* 'equal,' among them PEER 'an equal in rank' [from Old French *per, peer* (Modern French *pair*)]. The phrase *peer group* is a current sociological catchword for 'those who share a common background.' The original peer group was the *douzepers* 'twelve

7895

7900

7905

7910

7915

7920

equals, twelve peers,' who in medieval French romances were the twelve bravest of Charlemagne's knights, the legendary paladins who constituted his personal entourage, Roland, Oliver, etc. In England, the word PEER was used to designate male members of the nobility, such as dukes, marquises, earls, viscounts, and barons. The House of Lords is made up of such, so that the word has a general meaning of 'a man of high rank, a nobleman.' Also from Latin *par* and Old French *per* 'equal' are PEERLESS 'without equal'; PAR 'equal footing' (on a PAR with); 'normal' (up to PAR); 'the number of strokes necessary for an expert player to complete a hole in golf'; PARITY 'equality, equivalence' [from Latin *paritās* 'equality']; IMPARITY 'inequality'; DISPARITY 'inequality; state of being disparate' (DISPARATE is a related word, but it comes from Latin *disparāre* 'to separate'); the word PAIR means 'two equals, two of a kind; two things of similar form intended to be used together' (gloves, shoes); 'one object composed of two similar and associated parts' (scissors, eyeglasses); 'a mated couple' [from Old French *paire*, from Latin *paria* 'equals, equal things,' neuter plural of *par*]. In Modern French, *un pair* (masculine) means 'a peer, a fellow; par, equality,' while *une paire* (feminine) means 'a pair, a couple,' and the adjective *pair* means 'even (opposed to *odd*); similar.'

Pair 'even' and *impair* 'odd' are calls made by croupiers at the roulette tables of Monte Carlo and at French casinos. Speaking of roulette, we have another gambling cognate in the French word *pari* 'bet, wager; gambling stake,' from Old French *parier* 'to bet; to make equal'; from Vulgar Latin **pariāre*, from Latin *pār* 'equal.' *Pari* 'bet' is used in English in the word, originally a phrase, PARImutuel (literally) 'mutual stakes'; 'a system of racetrack betting that automatically adjusts the odds according to the amount wagered on each entrant.' Also associated with betting but borrowed ultimately from the Italian is PARLAY 'to compound a bet and its winnings on two or more events; to adapt an asset successfully to a sequence of circumstances' [via French *paroli* from Neapolitan Italian *paroli* 'a pair of dice,' from *paro* 'a pair'].

A more recherché word for 'fellow, equal, peer' is COMPEER 'a person of equal rank; a comrade' [from Medieval/Old French *comper*, from Latin *compār* 'like, similar; comrade' (*com-* < *cum* 'together with')]. (There may be an admixture here from French *compère* < Medieval Latin *compater* 'godfather, crony.') Latin *compār* 'like, similar' leads to the Latin verb *comparāre* 'to bring together as equals, to pair, to match,' to COMPARE 'to liken; to represent as being equal; to examine for similarities and differences' [from Medieval/Old French *comparer*].

A twist is given to the notions of 'equal status, rank, position on the social scale' by the last of our words based on Latin *pār* 'equal,' DISPARAGE (literally) 'to deprive of rank'; (obsolete) 'to degrade (someone) by marrying (her) to a man of inferior rank'; 'to belittle' [from Old French *desparagier* 'to cause to marry unequally'; from Latin *dis-* 'depriving of' + Old French *parage* 'equality of rank,' from *per* 'peer']. One gathers that the reduction in rank caused by being married to a person inferior to oneself applied only to females (all the examples cited in the *OED* refer to women). Presumably a man did not so lower himself, but raised the woman to his higher level. In other words, the woman took the rank of her husband, whether higher or lower.   7970

7975

Latin *pār* 'equal' is of uncertain origin, perhaps or probably related to Latin *parāre* 'to get, to obtain; to equip.' A semantic bridge between *pār* 'equal' and *parāre* 'to get, to obtain' is furnished by the supposition that Latin *paria* 'equal things' (the plural of *pār*) was "originally a term of barter, akin to Latin *parāre* to value equally [and] *comparāre* to compare" (*MW2*), since bartering is a way of 'obtaining.'   7980

'To value equally' is not the classical sense of *parāre*, which means rather 'to get, to obtain, to buy, to acquire,' hence 'to furnish, to provide,' hence, to PREPARE 'to get in readiness; to furnish ahead of time' [from Latin *praeparāre* 'to make ready' (*prae-* 'before, in front' + *parāre* 'to furnish')].   7985

The Indo-European root of all of the preceding words is *per(ə)* 'to get in return; to grant, to allot,' an extension of that most prolific of all Indo-European roots, *per-*, the "base of prepositions and preverbs with the basic meaning of 'forward, through,' and a wide range of extended senses such as 'in front of, before, early, first, chief, toward, against, near, around, at'" (*AHD*). Among the progeny of *per-* is the prefix *prae-* > *pre-* 'before, ahead of.' Thus Latin *praeparāre* and English *prepare* are ultimately reduplications of the Indo-European root *per-*.   7990

7995

The 'bartering' sense of Vulgar Latin *paria* 'a pair,' Latin *paria* 'equal things,' and *parāre* 'to value equally; to buy, to acquire' would seem to imply putting two things near each other so they could be *compared*.   8000

There are many English loanwords based on Latin *parāre* 'to get, to buy; to equip, to prepare.' One of the most obvious, surprising because of its simplicity, is the verb PARE 'to trim by cutting off the outside part' [from Old French *parer* 'to make ready; to trim; to prepare,' from Latin *parāre*]. Thus "to 'prepare' an apple is to *pare* it" (*EP*). Old French *parer* 'to trim' also acquired the meaning of 'to adorn, to embellish,' leading to Modern French *parure* 'ornament, adornment; finery' and *parure*   8005

8010

de diamants 'set of diamonds,' whence English PARURE 'a set of matched jewelry.'

Some see a possibility that English SPAR (cockfighting) 'to strike out with the feet and spurs'; 'to practice boxing; to bandy
8015   words in an argument' is a descendant of Latin *parāre* by way of Italian *sparare* (from *ex* + *parāre*) 'to kick out (as a horse does),' and Early Modern French *s'esparer* 'to kick, to fling out the feet' (Modern French *s'éparer*, a term used in manège). Most writers, however, trace English *spar* 'to practice boxing' to Old English
8020   *sperran* 'to strike,' to a form of unknown origin, or to the root of English *spur, spurn.*

The 'defending, warding off, shielding' sense seen in PARRY is also evidenced in the prefix *para-* 'defense against' (from Italian *para!* 'defend!'), as found in the words PARASOL 'a shield against
8025   the sun' [via French from Old Italian *parasole*] (The French for 'umbrella' is *parapluie* 'defense against rain,' from Latin *pluvia* 'rain.'); PARACHUTE 'a protective device against falling rapidly through the atmosphere' [French *chute* 'fall']; and PARAPET (literally) 'a chest-protector'; 'a wall protecting soldiers from enemy
8030   missiles' [from Italian *parapetto* 'a chest-high wall' (*petto* 'chest,' from Latin *pectus*)]. From the New World, but not frequently heard any more, is PARFLECHE 'a shield against arrows; rawhide soaked in lye and dried on a stretcher' [from Canadian French *parer* 'to ward off' + *flèche* 'arrow']. "In an Indian village . . . the
8035   hand that scrapes the parfleche rules the camp" (G. B. Grinnel, 1899, quoted in *OED*). While we're on the subject of defensive devices, we should include the word RAMPART 'a broad defensive embankment on which a parapet is raised; a protective barrier' [via Old French from *ramparer* 'to fortify' from *re-* 'again' +
8040   *emparer* 'to defend,' from Old Provençal *amparar, antparar,* from Vulgar Latin **anteparāre* 'to prepare before'].

In Spanish, an extended meaning acquired by the Romanic *parāre* was 'to stop.' In fact, 'to stop' has now become the primary sense of Spanish *parar,* though it also means 'to parry,' and, in
8045   American-Spanish, 'to stand up.' In the days when horses were the principal means of swift locomotion, Spanish *parar* came to mean 'to stop a horse, to make a horse stand.' It was *parada* 'a stopping, a standing,' especially of men on horseback, hence of cavalrymen, hence of soldiers of any kind, the past participle of
8050   *parar* that led to the meaning of PARADE 'an assembling of troops to hear orders read or as preparation for a march.' The PARADE ground was the place where these assemblies took place. Compare the military command, "Parade rest!," upon hearing which the soldier assumes a formal attitude next to "Attention!" in
8055   strictness, without moving or talking. These are not the meanings

that spring to the mind of a Norteamericano when he hears the word, for in the United States, the principal meaning of PARADE is 'a march or procession.' What has happened is that Latin *parāre*, in its migrations to the Romance languages, developed three groups of senses: 'defend, shield' (PARRY, PARASOL), 'adorn, bedeck, display' (PARURE, Easter PARADE), and 'stop, stand' (PARADE ground, PARADE rest). Thus, English PARADE has connotations from all three groups, but mostly the second and third.

From Latin compounds of *parāre* 'to obtain, to prepare, to furnish' we have acquired English REPAIR 'to restore to good condition' [from Old French *reparer*, from Latin *reparāre* 'to get back, to acquire again; to repair']. (*Repair* 'to betake oneself,' as in "He repaired to his country estate," is a different word, from Late Latin *repatriāre* 'to return to one's country.' *Impair* 'to diminish, to worsen' does not belong here either since its *-pair* comes from Latin *peior* 'worse.')

The compounding of *in-* with *parāre* is found in Latin *imperāre* (originally) 'to prepare against' (*in-* 'against'), therefore 'to give orders against,' therefore 'to command.' *Imperāre* was destined to become one of the grandest words in Roman history, for the commander of a Roman army was called *imperātor*, and this word became "a title of honor bestowed on a victorious general by the acclamation of the army on the field of battle. This title was afterward conferred by the senate on Julius Caesar and on Augustus ... and ... was adopted by all the subsequent rulers of the empire except Tiberius and Claudius" (*OED*). It is the antecedent of English EMPEROR 'a sovereign ruler over conquered or otherwise consolidated peoples' [by way of Old French *empereor*]. The territory over which an emperor holds sway is called an EMPIRE [via Old French from Latin *imperium* 'command, sway, dominion']. The simple 'to order, to command' meaning of Latin *imperāre* is still seen in English IMPERATIVE 'expressing a command; not admitting denial,' while the more sweeping connotations are evident in IMPERIOUS 'domineering, overbearing' and IMPERIALIST 'extending control over other nations.' More English derivatives of Latin compounds with *parāre* include APPARATUS (literally) 'what has been made ready toward an end'; 'gear, equipment, rigging; a machine or group of machines' [from Latin *apparātus* 'tool, engine,' from the past participle of *apparāre* 'to equip' (*ad* 'toward' + *parāre* 'to prepare')]; APPAREL 'clothing, garments' [from Old French *apareil* 'preparation; furnishings'; from Vulgar Latin **appariculāre* 'to make fit, to fit out,' from Latin *apparāre* 'to make ready']; and SEPARATE (literally) 'to prepare apart from'; 'to set apart; to divide' [from Latin *sēparāre* 'to separate, to divide' (*sē-* 'apart')].

8060
8065
8070
8075
8080
8085
8090
8095
8100

Latin *sēparāre* led to Vulgar Latin **sēperāre*, which became Old French *sevrer* 'to separate' (later 'to wean, to deprive of'), which led to English SEVER 'to divide into parts; to cut off.' By a slightly different route we get SEVERAL 'existing apart; individual' (They

8105   went their SEVERAL ways); 'more than one, but not many' [from Norman French *several*; from Medieval Latin *sēparālis*; from Latin *sēpār* 'separate'].

Living organisms are constantly getting or begetting off-spring, and the Latin verb for this activity is also descended from

8110   the Indo-European root **per(ə)-* 'to get in return; to grant, to allot,' and thus closely allied to Latin *parāre* 'to get, to prepare, to furnish.' It is *parere* 'to produce young, to give birth; to beget.'

From the present participle of *parere*, *parēns* 'producing young,' comes the Latin noun *parēns* (plural *parentēs*) 'father,

8115   mother, progenitor' > English PARENT 'a father or mother.' From the Latin past participle *partum* 'given birth' comes English POSTPARTUM 'occurring shortly after childbirth,' and from the future participle *parturus* 'about to give birth,' and the conse-quent Latin verb *parturīre* 'to be in labor,' we have English

8120   PARTURIENT 'about to give birth' and PARTURITION 'childbirth.'

The suffixes *-parous* and *-para*, from Latin *-parus*, *-para*, indicate 'bearing,' hence 'producing,' as seen in the English words OVIPAROUS 'producing eggs that hatch outside the mother's body' and VIVIPAROUS 'giving birth to living offspring that have

8125   developed within the mother's body,' and the combined OVOVI-VIPAROUS 'producing eggs that hatch within the female's body.' Speaking of viviparous animals, the Latin word for VIPER 'a venomous snake,' is *vīpera*, and the ancient Romans themselves believed that this word derived from an earlier **vivipara* 'that

8130   which bears living young,' since some of these snakes are indeed viviparous or ovoviviparous. This is an etymology that many etymologists accept, but other etymologists associate VIPER with *vibrate*. Latin *vīpera* 'viper' evolved into Old French *guivre* and Old Northern French *wivre* 'serpent, viper,' which lead to Eng-

8135   lish WIVERN, WYVERN 'a chimerical animal depicted as a winged dragon with eagles' claws and a serpentlike tail' and WEEVER 'a fish with venomous spines,' common off the coast of Europe.

The suffix *-parus* 'producing' also lurks, truncated, in the Latin word *pauper* (literally) 'producing little; poor; a poor man,'

8140   from *pau(cus)* 'little' + *-par(us)* 'producing,' originally used to describe infertile soil. Latin *pauper* appears unchanged in Eng-lish as the noun PAUPER 'a person without money, property or other wealth; one living on charity.' Adjectivally, Latin *pauper* evolved into Old French *povre* > Middle English *poure* and

8145   English POOR 'having little wealth; inferior,' while Latin *paupertās* yielded Old French *poverte* > English POVERTY 'the condition of being poor.'

From Latin *parere* 'to beget, to produce; to procure' there developed a compound verb, *reperīre* 'to procure for oneself, to acquire,' and a related noun *repertōrium* 'a place for acquisitions; a storehouse; a catalogue, a listing.' *Repertōrium* is the antecedent of Old French *repertoire* > English REPERTOIRE, REPERTORY 'the stock of pieces that a performer or a company is prepared to present.'

The Indo-European root **per-*, **per* 'to grant, to allot; to get in return' presupposes that what is 'allotted' is divided up into PART(S) 'a portion, segment, fraction, division or piece of a whole; a geographic region' (foreign PARTS) [via Old French and Old English from Latin *pars*, *partem* 'portion, part; region']. The English loanwords based on *pars*, *partem* are multifarious, including PART 'to divide' (He PARTED his hair. The Red Sea PARTED); 'to leave, to depart' (PARTING is such sweet sorrow); PARTIAL 'incomplete; favoring one person or PARTY' [via Old French from Latin *partiālis*]; IMPARTIAL 'disinterested; not favoring one side over another'; PARTY 'a division' (a PARTY of troops); 'a side in a contract or dispute' (the PARTY of the first part); 'one of opposing sides' (the Republican and Democratic PARTIES); 'a group gathered for pleasure' (a birthday PARTY) [from Old French *partie*, feminine past participle of *partir* 'to divide,' from Latin *partīre* 'to divide, to part']; PARTICLE 'a small part' [from Latin *particula*, diminutive of *pars* 'part']; and PARTICULAR 'attentive to small details; belonging to a small unit; not universal' [via Old French from (Late) Latin *particulāris*]. A Vulgar Latin diminutive of the Latin diminutive *particula* 'a small part' was **particella*. In Old French, **particella* was syncopated into *parcelle*, which was taken over into Middle English and has become Modern English PARCEL 'a part; a small part' (part and PARCEL); 'a division or portion of land; to divide into allotments; a package; a group.' In the last sense PARCEL is sometimes pronounced and spelled PASSEL 'a bunch.' More English loanwords based on *pars*, *partem* include PARSE 'to break a sentence down into its parts of speech' [from the Latin phrase *pars ōrātiōnis* 'part of speech'] and PARTITION 'something that divides an area into smaller sections; the act of dividing into parts' [via Old French from Latin *partītiō(nem)* 'a sharing; a division,' from *partitus*, past participle of *partīre* 'to divide, to part']. Latin *partītiō*, *partītiōnem* led to Old French *parçon* 'a share, a sharing; booty' and the agential noun *parçonier* 'one who shares.' *Parçonier* was adapted into Middle English and English as PARCENER = COPARCENER 'a joint heir in an undivided estate,' and, in a variant form influenced by

PART, as PARTNER 'one who shares in an activity with another, or others.' Note, also, PARTICIPATE 'to take part in; to PARTAKE.'

PARTAKE is a back-formation from *partaking* < Middle English *part taking*, a translation of Latin *participātiō* 'participation,' 8195 which is based on *particeps* 'partaker,' from *pars, partis* 'part' + *-ceps* 'he who takes,' from *capere* 'to take.' Related words are PARTICIPANT = PARTAKER = PART TAKER. Still more English borrowings based on Latin *pars, partem* are PARTICIPLE 'an auxiliary verb form that takes part in certain tense constructions, 8200 and may also stand alone as an adjective' [from Old French *participle, participe,* from Latin *participium* 'that which takes part'] and PARTISAN 'one who takes the side of another militantly' [via French from Italian *partigiano* (dialectal *partisano, partezan*)]. The *-igiano, -isano, -ezan* suffixes derive from Vulgar 8205 Latin **-ēse* + **-iano,* from Latin *-ēnsis* + *-iānus* (*ODEE*).

Prefixed compounds of Latin *pars, partis* 'share, part' lead to many English words. Among them is APART 'separated, one from another; off to one side; in pieces; to pieces' [from the Old French phrase *a part* 'to the side']. Old French *a part* is presumably from 8210 a Vulgar Latin phrase **ad partem,* but some etymologists trace it instead to Latin *ā parte* < *ab parte* 'on the side.' Another English word based on prefixed compounds of Latin *pars, partis* 'share, part' is APARTMENT 'a dwelling place that is one of two or more in the same building' [from French *appartement,* from Italian 8215 *appartemento* 'separate suite of rooms,' from *appartare* 'to separate'], although some etymologists trace APARTMENT to Medieval Latin *appartīmentum,* from *appartīre* 'to divide, to apportion.' Related words are APARTHEID (literally) 'apart-hood'; 'separateness; racial segregation with the purpose of maintaining white 8220 supremacy' [from Afrikaans *apartheid*]; COMPARTMENT 'a subdivision separated by partitions' [via (Medieval) French *compartiment* from Italian *compartimento,* from *compartire* 'to share,' from Late Latin *compartīri* 'to divide, to share with']; DEPARTMENT 'a division of a larger unit' [from French *département,* from 8225 Old French *departir* 'to divide']; DEPARTURE 'the act of leaving; parting from (someone, somewhere)' (compare the slang expression *to split* 'to leave'); COUNTERPART 'one that occupies the same position as another in a different system; opposite number' [*counter-* < *contra* 'opposite']; IMPART 'to give a share of; to 8230 communicate (to)' [from Latin *impartīre* 'to cause to share in']; and REPARTEE 'a witty reply' [from French *repartie,* from *repartir* 'to retort,' from Old French *repartir* 'to depart again; to reply promptly'].

A cognate of Latin *pars, partis* 'share, part' is Latin *portiō,* 8235 *portiōnis* 'a share, a portion,' whence English PORTION 'a section of a whole.' Latin *portiō* was first attested in the phrase *prō portiōne* 'for (its) share; proportionally' ("perhaps assimilated from *prō partiōne" (*AHD*)). The phrase *prō portiōne* was used as a translation of Greek *ana logon* 'according to the reckoning, proportionate' > *analogia* 'proportion' (> *analogy*). Following this lead, Cicero coined the Latin word *prōportiō* as a translation of Greek *analogia*. *Prōportiō* has been adopted into English as PROPORTION 'the relationship between the parts and the whole; comparative dimensions.' Note, also, APPORTION 'to allot a share to' [from Medieval/Old French *apportionner*, from Latin *ad* 'to' + Old French *portionner* 'to portion out'].

8240

8245

Finally, a special sense of Old French *parti* 'divided' was 'striped, variegated,' whence Middle English *party* 'divided into different colors,' amplified in Modern English into PARTICOL-ORED 'pied; of different colors.'

8250

XLIII

Porch Sports

A PORT is 'a harbor, especially one that has facilities for loading and unloading cargo.' A PORT is also figuratively a 'gate' or 'doorway' between the hinterland it serves and the other countries of the earth. This blend of meanings is a reflection of
8255 the ancestral Latin words *porta* 'gate, entrance, passageway' and *portus* "originally a 'mountain pass and a gate, a door'; basically, therefore, a 'passage,' hence a 'harbour'" (*EP*), 'harbor, haven, refuge' as well as the related Latin verb *portāre* 'to transport, to carry.' One of the many English borrowings from these Latin
8260 words is PORT 'the left side of a ship, seen facing forward,' so called because in earlier days the steering-board or rudder was carried on the right side of a vessel (*starboard* 'steer-board'), making it necessary to come alongside a wharf on the left or PORT side (formerly called *larboard* 'loading side'). Note, also, PORT 'a
8265 fortified wine of Portugal.' This PORT is short for Portuguese *o porto* 'the port.' The wine was named after the city of Oporto (Portuguese *Porto*), a seaport on the Douro river. In the Middle Ages Oporto was called *Portus Cale* 'the port of Cale,' consequently, its hinterland was called *Portucale* > PORTUGAL (the
8270 Roman name was *Lusitania*). More English borrowings from Latin *porta*, *portus*, and *portāre* are PORTHOLE 'a small circular window in a ship; an opening in machinery for the passage of steam or fluids'; PORTAL 'a gateway, doorway, entrance' [via Old French from Medieval Latin *portāle*, neuter of Latin *portālis* 'of a
8275 gate']; PORTICO 'a pillared, roofed walkway leading to the entrance of a building' [from Italian *portico*, from Latin *porticus* 'porch, colonnade, arcade']; PORCH 'a covered entrance to a building; a veranda' [from Old French *porche*, from Latin *porticus*]; PORTIÈRE 'a curtain hung over a doorway' [from the
8280 French, feminine of *portier* 'doorkeeper,' from Medieval Latin

portārius, *portāria* 'belonging to a door']; PORTE-COCHÈRE 'a
carriage entrance into a courtyard; a porch roof over a driveway
entrance to a building' [from the French *porte* 'door' + *cochère*
'for carriages']; and PORTCULLIS 'a sliding grille that can be
lowered to block the entrance to a castle' [from Medieval French   8285
porte coleïce 'sliding door'; *coleïce* from Vulgar Latin *cōlātīcius*
(cf. Old French *couler* 'to slide'); from Latin *colāre* 'to strain,'
from *cōlum* 'sieve']. Compare *coulisse, coulee, colander*. The
name of the medieval barriers was coined because they were
built to slide up and down in grooves embedded in the gateway.   8290
Coincidentally, a portcullis also has the appearance of a giant
sieve. These Latin forms also yielded PORT (military) 'to carry a
weapon diagonally across the body so that the barrel or blade is
opposite the left shoulder'; PORTLY 'characterized by a stateliness
of bearing; corpulent'; PORTFOLIO 'a folder for carrying sheets of   8295
paper, drawings, etc.'; 'an inventory of investments' [from Italian
portafogli (*fogli* 'leaves,' *foglio* 'leaf,' from Latin *folium* 'leaf')];
PORTMANTEAU 'suitcase'; (literally) 'carry-cloak; coat-carrier'
[from French *portemanteau*: *manteau* 'mantle, cloak, coat']; PORT-
AGE 'the labor of carrying goods'; PORTERAGE 'a charge for   8300
carrying goods; carrying boats overland between waterways' [from
Medieval French *portage*; from Medieval Latin *portāgium*,
portāticum; from Latin *portāre* 'to carry']. The third meaning,
'carrying boats overland,' was originally American, a borrowing
from the language of the French-Canadian *coureurs de bois* and   8305
voyageurs. Note, also, PORTER 'a carrier of baggage; a doorman, a
gatekeeper; a dark beer made from charred malt.' The first and
second meanings descended through two different words. The
first, 'a carrier,' comes to English from Old French *porteour*, from
Late Latin *portātor*, from the verb *portāre*; while the second, 'a   8310
doorman,' has been borrowed from Old French *portier*, from
Latin *portārius* 'gatekeeper,' from *porta* 'gate.'
     As for the beer, this PORTER is short for *porter's beer* or
porter's ale, and the beverage was so called because it was
consumed by porters and other low-income laborers. It was   8315
probably intended to be a poor man's stout. Porter must have
been a popular drink in the early 19th-century United States,
because the word PORTERHOUSE 'a tavern, an alehouse, a chop-
house' became a generic American-English term for an establishment where malt liquors, chops, and steaks were served. A   8320
favorite cut of beef at one of these establishments in New York
was given the name PORTERHOUSE steak 'a cut taken from the
thick end of the short loin, between the sirloin and the tender-
loin,' which was washed down, of course, with a couple of pints
of porter. Yet another English descendant from Latin *porta*,   8325

portus, and *portāre* is PORTAMENTO (music) 'a smooth glide from tone to tone' [from Italian *portamento* 'a carrying']. PORTAMENTO is usually done with the voice, a bowed string instrument, or a slide trombone, but is also possible on a keyed wind instrument. More derivatives from the same Latin words are EXPORT 'to ship goods out of a country' and IMPORT 'to cause goods to be shipped into a country.' But IMPORT also has an abstract meaning of 'to imply, to carry a meaning; to be significant, to be of consequence, to be IMPORTANT.' Note, IMPORTANT 'of great value or significance' [from Medieval Latin *importāns*, present participle of *importāre* 'to mean, to be significant,' from Latin *importāre* 'to carry into']. Similar to the abstract meaning of IMPORT 'to imply' is the meaning of PURPORT 'to profess outwardly, to imply; to convey to the mind' [from Old French *purporter, porporter* 'to embody, to contain,' from Medieval Latin *prōportāre* 'to carry forward'].

A word that has strikingly different literal and figurative meanings is DEPORT 'to expel from a country' and 'to behave (oneself).' From the second meaning comes the noun DEPORT-MENT 'behavior, conduct; bearing, demeanor' [from Early Modern French *déporter* 'to behave,' from Latin *dēportāre* 'to carry away']. English words synonymous with DEPORT, DEPORTMENT are COMPORT, COMPORTMENT [from Medieval French *(se) comporter* 'to behave (oneself),' from Latin *comportāre* 'to carry together, to support']. In Modern French only *se comporter* retains the meaning of 'to behave.' *Se déporter* now means 'to desist; to remove oneself from,' and the nonreflexive *déporter* has the sense 'to deport, to exile.' Note, also, TRANSPORT 'to carry from one place to another; to enrapture, to carry away with strong emotion' [via Old French from Latin *trānsportāre* 'to carry over'] and REPORT 'to carry back; to tell about; an explosive noise' [via Old French *report, reporter* from Latin *reportāre* 'to carry back']. In French, the related words *rapport, rapporter* are semantic workhorses, with such varied meanings as 'report, evidence, relation, communication, affinity, harmony, ratio, bearing, revenue, produce' and 'to account for, bring back, report, ascribe, trace, yield, revoke, reimburse, quote, direct.' From these meanings English has borrowed RAPPORT 'emotional affinity; a relationship of mutual trust' [from French *rapport* 'harmony, relation, affinity,' from *rapporter* 'to bring back; to carry back to, to respond' (*re-* 'back, again' + Latin *apportāre* 'to bring to, to carry')]. Also going back to Latin *porta, portus*, and *portāre* are SUPPORT 'to carry from underneath; to hold in position; to maintain by providing food, shelter and clothing; to withstand, to tolerate' [from Medieval/Old French *supporter*, from Latin *sup-*

portāre 'to carry up toward, to carry, to bring up' (*sup- < sub* 'under, up toward')] and DISPORT 'to play, to frolic, to divert (oneself)' [from Medieval/Old French (*se*) *desporter* 'to divert, to amuse (oneself),' from Latin *dis-* 'apart from' + Old French *porter* 'to carry']. The idea is one of being 'carried away' from serious   8375
matters by indulgence in amusements and diversions. DISPORT is mostly a literary word nowadays, but it is of special interest as the direct ancestor of that pervasive modern word SPORT (archaic) 'amorous dalliance'; 'a pastime or game; mockery, jesting' (to make SPORT of); 'one who leads a fast life; an individual exhibit-   8380
ing a sudden deviation from type.' Although the insatiable appetite for organized sports is of comparatively recent origin, the word SPORT, a shortened form of DISPORT, has been in English since the 15th century. The Italian word for 'sport' is *diporto*, while in Spanish it's *deporte*. (The Latin word is *lūdus* 'play,   8385
game,' yielding *ludicrous*. The Roman 'public games,' including theater, horse and chariot races, athletic contests, gladiatorial contests, and contests with or among wild animals, were called *lūdi publici*. See lines 3861ff.)

We can't leave our discussion of English borrowings from   8390
Latin *portus* 'port,' *porta* 'gate,' and *portāre* 'to carry' without mentioning a small subfamily of words that originally had to do with seafaring and a mariner's constant interest in the way the wind blows, though their present-day meanings have no necessary connection with things maritime. The words are based on   8395
Latin *opportūnus* (literally) 'toward port' [*op- < ob* 'toward' + *portus* 'port'; cf. *Portūnus* 'god of harbors']. *Opportūnus* was coined by the Latin speakers to describe a favorable wind that would blow one's ship toward its destination. It later acquired figurative meanings of 'favorable, suitable, appropriate' > English   8400
OPPORTUNE 'suited to a particular purpose; occurring at an advantageous moment'; OPPORTUNITY 'an advantageous combination of circumstances; the right moment to make a move'; and OPPORTU-NIST 'one who is looking for and ready to take advantage of any opportunity for self-advancement.' Such a felicitous coinage   8405
called for an opposite, so the Latin speakers invented *importūnus* 'not toward port' or 'without a port; unsuitable, unfavorable; troublesome' (instead of *inopportūnus* 'inopportune,' which didn't come along until Late Latin times). *Importūnus* leads to English IMPORTUNE (obsolete) 'to anger'; 'to annoy with frequent   8410
requests,' IMPORTUNATE 'irksomely persistent,' INOPPORTUNE 'untimely.'

Latin *portus, porta, portāre* stem from the Indo-European root **per-* 'to lead; to pass through,' a form of an even more fundamental root **per-*, which has a basic meaning of 'through,'   8415 forward.' Following the rules of sound correspondences, Indo-European *per- 'to lead; to pass through' shows up in Germanic languages in the forms fer-, far-, fir-, fjor-, führ, as witnessed by the English words FARE 'passage money; a paying passenger; to 8420 travel' (WAYFARER, THOROUGHFARE); 'to get along' (How FARES the republic? FAREWELL, WELFARE); 'food and drink' (bill of FARE) [from Old English faran 'to get along; to go on a journey,' from Germanic *faran]; FERRY 'a boat that transports people and goods across a body of water' [from Old English ferian or from 8425 Old Norse ferja 'ferryboat,' from Germanic *farjōn or *farjan 'ferry']; and FIRTH 'a long narrow inlet of the sea; a FJORD. Both the English and the Norwegian word come from Old Norse fjördhr or fjörthr, from Germanic *ferthuz, and both are cousins to English FORD 'a shallow place in a river where a crossing can 8430 be made on foot' [from Old English ford, from Germanic *furduz], although FIRTHS and FJORDS are waterways that lead into a land mass, while FORDS are passageways across water.

Turning to the 'to lead' significance of Indo-European *per- 'to lead, to pass through,' we come upon the originally-German-8435 but-eventually-internationally-infamous word FÜHRER 'leader; Hitler' [from German führen 'to lead; to carry, to convey']. German has many other related words, such as Fuhre 'transport; cart-load,' Fahrt 'journey,' fahren 'to travel,' and Fähre 'ferry.'

Another related word, coming from the Greek and therefore 8440 retaining the Indo-European initial *p-, is English PORE 'a minute opening or passageway' [from Latin porus, from Greek poros 'passageway, thoroughfare']. A compound of Greek poros 'thoroughfare, path' is Greek emporos 'on the path; traveler; trader, merchant,' whence emporion 'a trading place, a market,' adapted 8445 into Latin and English as EMPORIUM 'a market place; a large retail store; a commercial establishment aspiring to grandeur.'

There remains a scattering of related words stemming from Indo-European *per- 'to lead; to pass through.' For example, EUPHRATES (literally) " 'good to cross over' " (AHD); 'a Mesopota-8450 mian river' [via Latin and Greek from Avestan huperethwa (hu-'good' = eu- 'good']; GABERDINE, GABARDINE (literally) '(cloak) of a pilgrimage; a pilgrim's cloak'; 'a long coarse garment worn during the Middle Ages; a kind of twill' [influenced by Spanish gabardina from Medieval French galvardine > Old French gal-8455 levardine; from Middle High German wallevart 'pilgrimage' + French -ine, attributive suffix]. The *per- element is found in the syllables -berd- and -bard-, which represent a Gallicization of Middle High German vart 'journey,' from Old High German faran (Modern German Fahrt). The original word was Middle 8460 High German wallevart, where walle- stands for 'wandering,'

from *wallen* 'to wander' (Modern German *Wallfahrt* 'pilgrimage').
Wallevart was adapted into Old French as *gallevard(ine)*,
gauvard(ine), and Medieval French *galvard(ine)*, the attributive
-ine being added to indicate 'of the,' that is '(cloak) of the
pilgrimage.' Hence *galvardine* Spanish *gabardina* > English   8465
GABARDINE, GABERDINE. Thus Middle High German *walle - vart -
(ine)* yielded, ultimately, Medieval French *ga - bard/berd - ine*
'wandering journey, of the.' Also related to Indo-European **per-*
'to lead; to pass through' is FERDINAND (literally) 'one who goes
on risky journeys'; 'adventurer' [from Germanic **fardi-nanth-*,   8470
from **fardi-* 'journey' + **nanthi-* 'risk' (*AHD*)].

Finally, some writers assign FERN 'a flowerless, seedless
plant having fronds with divided leaflets and reproducing by
spores' [from Old English *fearn*] to this group, the semantic
association being 'having feathery fronds,' from Germanic **farno*   8475
'feather, leaf,' from Indo-European **porno-* 'feather, wing, "that
which carries a bird in flight"' (*AHD*).

XLIV

Presence *and* Absence

Two words that an English speaker learns early in life are AM and IS. A check with the dictionary will verify that these words, dissimilar as they are phonetically, are both derived from the same Indo-European root: *es-* 'to be,' by way of the first person singular form *es-mi* and the third person singular form *es-ti*.

It is easy enough to see how IS is derived from *es-*, especially when we have such corroborative testimony as that provided by the following cognates: Dutch *is*, German *ist*, French *est*, Latin *est*, Greek *esti*, Sanskrit *asti*, Hittite *eszi*, and, as mentioned, Indo-European *es-ti*. A majority of these forms have a *-t-* involved in their endings. It seems possible that this *-t-* is the remnant of an ancient personal pronoun, because the reconstructed form from which English AM descends is *es-mi*, and the chances are that this *-mi* ending is the remnant of a personal pronoun (compare *mich, mir, migo, mihi, me, moi*).

Indo-European *es-mi*, losing the *-s-* sound, evolved into Old English *eam*, English AM, Old Norse *em*, Gothic *im*, Old Irish *am*, Greek *eimi*, Armenian *em*, Albanian *jam*. In primitive Latin, Indo-European *es-mi* probably became *esem*, whence Latin *sum* 'I am,' the latter influenced by the first person plural *sumus* 'we are.' French and Spanish have shed the *-m* of Latin *sum* to become *(je) suis* and *(yo) soy*, while in Italian the *-m* has been replaced by *-n-*, in *(io) sono* 'I am.'

(The English verb *to be* in its various forms has elements of the following four Indo-European roots sprinkled through it: *es-* 'to be,' whence AM, IS; *er-* 'to set in motion,' whence ARE, ART; *wes-* 'to dwell, to delay,' whence WAS, WERE; and *bheu-* 'to exist, to become,' whence BE, BEING, BEEN. See Chapter VII, lines 1556ff.)

The Latin infinitive 'to be' is *esse*. *Esse* has no present participle, but if it did the form would be **essens* 'being.' What Latin does have is a noun based on that nonexistent present participle, to wit, *essentia* > English ESSENCE 'being; the basic underlying substance of a thing; the quality of a thing that gives it its identity.' This is a probing word, an attempt to get to the core of things by giving it a name. Latin *essentia*, a translation of the cognate Greek *ousia* 'the being, substance, essence of a thing,' was used by ancient and medieval philosophers to denote the four elements, that is, the four ESSENTIAL elements, earth, water, air, and fire, of which in varying combinations the physical world was supposedly comprised. Many became dissatisfied with this analysis of the make-up of the universe, so the medieval natural philosophers postulated and kept searching for what they called *pemptē ousia* = *quinta essentia* 'the fifth ESSENCE,' or QUINTES-SENCE 'the substance of which the heavenly bodies were once thought to be composed, and which was also thought to be latent in all things.' The extraction of the fifth essence by distillation or other methods was one of the great goals of alchemy; modern science has since determined that there are at least 103 elements, plus an undetermined number of isotopes. Meanwhile the word ESSENCE has acquired such rarefied meanings as 'the inherent unchanging nature of a thing as distinguished from its attributes or its existence, a spiritual or incorporeal entity,' as well as the more mundane 'an extract of a substance that retains its funda-mental properties in concentrated form; an extract in a solution of alcohol.' Perfumes are called ESSENCES, and in French, *essence* is used to mean 'gasoline.' As for the word QUINTESSENCE, it has come to be mainly a superlative for ESSENCE, that is 'the most nearly perfect and rarest extract or distillation.'

Now is as good a time as any to introduce the seldom encountered philosophical term ENS (plural ENTIA) 'existence or being as an abstract concept.' This word was a creation of Latin-speaking philosophizers, who coined it as a present participle (in lieu of **essens*) to fill the vacant niche in the paradigm of *esse* 'to be.' The coinage was made in order to translate Greek *ón* 'being.' It was formed on the analogy of Latin *absēns, absentis* 'being away, absent,' present participle of *abesse*, and *praesens, praesentis* 'at hand, present,' from *praeësse* 'to be before, to be on hand,' except that in those analogous words the present participle is formed by adding *-sēns, -sentis*. (It is worth noting that the Latin morpheme indicating the present participle is *-ēns, -entis*, or *-āns, -antis*.)

Latin *absēns, absentem* and *praesēns, praesentem* are the bases of the English loanwords ABSENT 'away, not at hand';

8510

8515

8520

8525

8530

8535

8540

8545

8550

(reflexive) 'to take leave'; and PRESENT 'at hand; now; a gift; to give a gift; to introduce.' ENS, ENTIA is not encountered in daily use, but it spawned the two more frequent words ENTITY 'a particular and discrete unit' and NONENTITY 'something that does not exist; a totally insignificant person or thing.'

Nonentities are *per se* UNINTERESTING. This brings us to another compound Latin verb based on *esse* 'to be,' that is, *interesse* 'to be between, to intervene; to matter, to be of concern' (*nobis interest* 'it is of concern to us'). The infinitive *interesse* was used as a noun in Medieval Latin to mean 'compensation for damages, compensatory payment,' and *interesse* was adopted into Middle English with meanings of 'a legal share of ownership; concern; benefit, compensation.' However, influenced by Old French *interest* 'damage, loss,' the English spelling changed to INTEREST 'concern; curiosity, inquisitiveness; involvement with or participation in something; a legal claim or share in a business or other property; the price paid for borrowing money.' This is the place to note that the currently accepted opposite of the English adjective INTERESTED 'concerned' is UNINTERESTED 'not concerned, not interested,' while the adjective DISINTERESTED means 'not influenced by interest; impartial, unbiased.' Thus judges, baseball umpires, and other arbiters are *disinterested* third parties who make decisions in disputes between other *interested* parties. The use of *disinterested* as a synonym for *uninterested* is considered nonstandard by most authorities, but such use is widespread nevertheless. In the 17th century the accepted usage was exactly the opposite, that is, *disinterested* meant 'unconcerned, not interested,' and *uninterested* meant 'impartial, unbiased.' The *OED* records the 'not interested' meaning for *disinterested* as "obsolete" (1896), but in the *OED Supplement* we are advised to delete the "obsolete" since the usage is making a comeback.

The Latin verb *prōdesse* 'to be useful, to be beneficial' has a survivor in the drinking toast PROSIT! (literally) 'may it be beneficial!'; 'may it do (you) good! your health!' (*prō* 'in behalf of'). This toast originated in Germany and Austria, probably among the beer-drinking university students. Note that the -*d*- in *prōdesse* is what used to be called "euphonic," that is, put between vowels to avoid a hiatus. It persists only when the syllable following *prō*-begins with a vowel (the -*d*- is not present in *prōsit*). The Latin word *prōdest* 'it is advantageous' evolved into the Late Latin phrase *prōde est*, and *prōde*, euphonic -*d*- and all, was thus transformed into an adjective meaning 'advantageous, useful, beneficial.' By the time this Late Latin adjective *prōde* got into Old French in the forms *prod, prud, proz, pruz*, its meaning had changed to 'good, gallant, brave.' However, when the word came

into English in the 11th century, its meaning took a pejorative
turn, and late Old English *prūd*, *prūt* meant 'having a high
opinion of oneself; arrogant, haughty,' which are some of the
meanings retained by the modern English form of the word,   8600
which is PROUD 'pleasurably satisfied with an accomplishment;
self-respectful.' We haven't come to the end of the story of Latin
prōdesse with the euphonic -*d*-. There were other developments;
for example, Old English *prūt*, *prūd* had the substantival derivatives *prȳte*, *prȳde*, which became English PRIDE 'self-respect;   8605
excessive self-esteem; a company of lions' (a "quasi-umlaut derivative," according to the *OED*, because it was not formed until c.
1000). From Old French *prud* there developed the compound
nouns *prud'homme* 'an upright, honest man,' and *prudefemme* 'a
strong woman; a modest woman.' *Prudefemme* was later short-   8610
ened to *prude*, still with the laudatory sense of 'good, respectable,
modest, virtuous.' However, the French word eventually developed the same derogatory sense found in English PRUDE 'a
person who is excessively concerned with being or seeming to be
proper, modest and virtuous.' In French, *prude* is still a femine   8615
noun, while in English it may be applied to PRUDISH persons of
either sex. (Note that being a *prude* has nothing to do with
prudence. See line 11341.) Old French *prud*, with nominative forms
pruz and *proz*, is also the ancestor of Modern French *preux*
'gallant, doughty, valiant,' a sometime English word, especially in   8620
the phrase PREUX chevalier 'gallant knight.' In its evolution the
Old French word *prud* went through the Medieval French forms
preu and *prou*, and developed the related noun *proesse* 'valor.'
Prou and *proesse* have come into English as PROW 'valiant,
gallant' and PROWESS 'distinguished bravery; extraordinary   8625
ability.'
    As noted, Old French *prou* evolved from Late Latin *prōde*
'advantageous.' This explains why *prou*, besides the adjectival
meanings of 'good, gallant, brave,' also had the substantival
meaning of 'advantage,' hence 'profit.' A Norman French verb   8630
incorporating this meaning was *emprouer* 'to turn to profit, to
make a profit in.' *Emprouer* became Anglo-French *emprower*,
whence, influenced by *prove* and *approve* (no relatives), sprang
English IMPROVE 'to increase the value of; to make better; to get
better.'   8635
    One more compound verb is REPRESENT 'to present again; to
be present in the place of; to act as a deputy for; to bring clearly
before the mind.'
    A remaining English loanword based on Latin *esse* 'to be' is
the seldom encountered ADSUM 'I am present,' from Latin *adesse*   8640

'to be at; to be present,' sometimes used when answering a roll call.

It was mentioned in passing that *eimi* is the Greek form of (*I*) *am*, that Greek *ōn* means 'being,' and that Greek *ousia* means 'essence, substance.' *Ousia* gave rise in the 4th century A.D. to a group of Christian theological terms having to do with the nature of the 'substance' of God and the Trinity, the ensuing dispute resulting in the long-lasting heresy of Arianism. The controversy centered on the sameness, similarity, or differentness of the substance of God the Father and the substance of God the Son. The Athanasians claimed that they were the same, the Arians thought that they were different, and a third group maintained that they were similar but not identical. The Greek terms in which these arguments were couched were HOMOOUSIA, HOMO-OUSIAN 'identity in substance' (*homos* 'same'); 'holding to the doctrine of the Nicene Creed that Jesus Christ the Son of God is of the same substance as God the Father; an Athanasian'; HOMOI-OUSIA, HOMOIOUSIAN 'similarity but not identity in substance'; 'holding to the doctrine that God the Son is similar to but not of the same substance as God the Father' [*homoios* 'like, similar']; and HETEROOUSIA, HETEROOUSIAN 'difference in substance' [*heteros* 'other']; 'holding that the substance of God the Son is different from that of God the Father; an Arian.' To anyone but a theological student these once life-or-death controversies seem remote and almost unreal. They do serve, however, as an example of the expression *jot and tittle*, since it was the *jot* 'iota, the letter *i*' that caused all the commotion. (A *tittle* is a small mark used in writing, such as the dot over the letter *i*, or the etymologically related Spanish *tilde*.)

The Greek present participle *onto(s)* 'being' is used as a combining form in words of scientific and philosophic import, notably ONTOGENY 'the biological development of an individual from single cell to adulthood' [*genea* 'birth, generation'] and ONTOLOGY 'the branch of philosophy that deals with being.'

In Sanskrit, Indo-European **es-* 'to be' appears as *as-; su-* is a Sanskrit prefix meaning 'well, good'; while *-ti* is a suffix that forms nouns from verb stems. Put all of this together and you get *svasti* 'well-being, fortune, welfare; good luck!' Add the adjectival suffix *-ka*, and *svasti* becomes SWASTIKA 'an ancient cosmic or religious symbol in the shapes 卐 , 卍 .' One may assume from its derivation that the swastika was originally a good-luck charm or talisman. Unfortunately, its adoption as the official symbol of the Nazis, who called it *das Hakenkreuz* 'the hook-cross,' has given the symbol an entirely new connotation.

A related word from the Hindi is SUTTEE 'the obsolete Hindu   8685
practice of a widow's cremating herself on her husband's funeral
pyre' [from Sanskrit *satī* 'good woman; faithful wife.']. To a
Westerner there seems to be nothing good or lucky about this
custom, now forbidden by law. *Satī* 'good woman; faithful wife' is
also the feminine of *sat, sant* 'good, wise, genuine.' *Sat, sant* is   8690
etymologically the present participle of the Sanskrit verb *as* 'to
be,' and therefore means 'being, existing.' Semantically the connection would seem to be that what 'is' or 'exists' is 'real' and
therefore 'genuine,' and what is real or genuine can be construed
as being, necessarily, 'good, faithful, wise, etc.'   8695
  The optimistic notion that what is is real, and therefore true,
and therefore good, is contradicted by the dour Germanic cognate
SIN 'a transgression of religious law; a serious offense' [from Old
English *syn(n)*, from Germanic **sun(d)jō* 'sin']. Here what is is
real, all right, and therefore true, but in this case 'bad.' The   8700
semantic tie-in with the Indo-European root **es-* 'to be' can be
summed up as follows: "the fact of guilt exists, the true verdict is
guilty, it is true, the sin is real" (*AHD*). The modern German
word is *Sünde* 'sin,' and a Latin relative is *sōns, sontis* 'guilty;
criminal, sinner.' ["*Sōns, sontis* is the real (present) participle of   8705
esse, long since specialized in meaning and disassociated from the
verb."—H. Craig Melchert.] Note the similarity of these words
with the forms of the verb *to be*: German *sind* '(we, you, they)
are,' and Latin *sunt* 'they are.'
  Another Germanic cognate is **santhaz* 'existing; true.'   8710
*Santhaz evolved into Old English *sōth* 'truth, verity' and archaic
English *sooth* 'truth; telling the truth; agreeing with.' The word is
still current in the compounds SOOTHSAYER 'a speaker of truth
and wisdom; a prognosticator' and FORSOOTH 'in truth; certainly,
indeed,' nowadays an archaism used in jest. The adjectival use of   8715
sooth < *sōth* led to the verb SOOTHE (originally) 'to prove to be
true; to declare to be true'; 'to blandish, cajole or please a person
by agreeing with him; to placate, to mollify; to ease or relieve
pain.'
  According to many pundits the final *-s* of English YES 'it is so;   8720
as you say' also stems from Indo-European **es-* 'to be,' hence the
word may be thought of as meaning 'yea, is.' YES derives from
Old English *gēse*, a contraction of *gēa sī* 'yea it be.' A suggested
alternative derivation from Old English *gēa swā* 'yea, so' is
dismissed by the *OED* as "phonologically inadequate."   8725
  The word ETYMOLOGY 'the study of the origin and historical
development of words' is based on the Greek word *etumon* '"the
essential meaning of a word seen in its origin"' (*RHD*), the neuter
of *etumos* 'real, true, actual.' *Etumos* is related to Greek *eteos*.

8730   'true' (from *setos 'being, existing; true') and by some scholars to Latin esse 'to be' and English sooth 'truth,' and consequently to our Indo-European root *es- 'to be.' The OED cites the 19th-century philologist Karl Brugmann who wrote that "etumos is for a prehistoric *s-etu-m-os, from 's, weak grade of Old Aryan *es 'to

8735   be' + suffixes," but other, more modern etymologists account eteos 'true' and consequently etumos, etumon as of obscure origin.

        Finally, from an extended form of the Indo-European root *es- 'to be,' to wit, *esu- 'good,' we get the Greek adjective eus

8740   'good, brave, valiant, noble,' and adverb eu 'well, properly.' Eu-serves as a prefix in many Greek words that have been adopted into English, such as EUGENICS 'the study of hereditary improvement by genetic control' [from Greek eugenēs 'well-born']; EUPHONY 'agreeable sound' [euphōnos 'sweet-voiced']; EULOGY

8745   'great praise' [eulogia 'praise, fair-speaking']; EUPHORIA 'a feeling of well-being' [euphoros 'easily borne']; and EUTHANASIA 'an easy or painless death' [thanatos 'death'].

        One might think that the Sanskrit su- 'well,' mentioned earlier with reference to swastika, would also be derived from the

8750   root *esu- 'good,' and indeed many scholars do now relate su- to *esu- 'good' and to *es- 'to be.' However, this development in linguistic theory has not yet found its way into the reference books, which agree in postulating another Indo-European root, *su- 'well, good.' If *es- 'to be,' *esu- 'good,' and *su- 'good' are

8755   all variants of the same root, that would make cognates of the words EUPHRATES (see line 8459) and HYGIENE (see line 8910).

XLV

Quick Vivacious Amphibians

If a *bon vivant* were to wander off into a nearby swamp and become entrapped in a QUICKSAND, he wouldn't be QUICK or *vivant* for long unless someone rescued him P.D.Q. A *bon vivant* is '(someone who is) living well; one who enjoys good food and drink' [from the French; from *bon* 'good' + *vivant* 'living,' present participle of *vivre* 'to live']. Similarly, the original meaning of the English adjective QUICK is 'living; endowed with life' (the QUICK and the dead); 'lively, brisk; fast, speedy; mentally acute; raw exposed flesh' [from Old English *cwic(u)*, from Germanic **kwi(k)waz*]. All derive from the Indo-European root **gwei-* 'to live.'

The Old English spelling was *cwic, cwicu.* The *qu-* spelling didn't appear until the 13th century, introduced by the Norman French, who took it from Latin. But the Latin word corresponding to *cwicu* was *vīvus* (pronounced "weewus") 'living, alive,' from the verb *vīvere* 'to live, to be alive,' ancestor of French *vivre* and of such English loanwords as VIVID 'lifelike; making a strong impression' and REVIVE 'to bring back to life.'

Semantically, the English word QUICK still retains its meaning of 'living, alive' in the sense 'a raw painfully sensitive spot or area of exposed flesh,' and also in the sense of QUICKENING 'the first movement of the fetus in the uterus felt by the mother' and QUICKEN 'to come to life; to become more rapid.' QUICK also has 'almost alive, as if alive' meanings in the compounds QUICKSAND 'a bed of sand that yields easily to pressure, causing objects resting on its surface to sink deeper and deeper if they move' and QUICKSILVER 'mercury; a silver-white metallic element, the only metal that is liquid at ordinary temperatures.'

Some English words are quite obviously borrowed from Latin *vīvus* and *vīvere* 'to live,' like VIVACIOUS 'animated, lively' [from

8760

8765

8770

8775

8780

8785

Latin *vīvāx* 'lively, vigorous'], the English equivalent of Italian *vivace* 'lively, briskly,' used as a musical direction. Note, also, VIVARIUM 'a place where living animals are kept, for food or for observation,' such as a fishpond. More obvious English borrowings from Latin *vīvus* and *vīvare* 'to live' include VIVIPAROUS 'giving birth to living offspring' [*parere* 'to give birth']; OVOVIVIP- AROUS 'producing eggs that hatch within the female's body' (See also line 8123); VIVISECTION 'cutting into the body of a living animal' [*secāre* 'to cut']; VIVA! '(long) live! hurrah for!' [Italian, from Latin *vivat* 'may he live']; VIVE! '(long) live! hurrah for!' [the French version]; and SURVIVE 'to remain alive; to outlive' [via Anglo-French *survivre* and Old French *sourvivre*, from Latin *supervīvere* 'to survive'].

Other borrowings are not so obvious, for example CONVIVIAL 'fond of feasting and drinking in good company' [from Late Latin *convīviālis*; Latin *convīvālis*, from *convīvium* 'a banquet']. The Latin verb *convīvere* literally means 'to live together,' but it came to have the extended meaning of 'to eat together,' and then 'to feast together.' A *convīva* was 'a table companion' and a *convīvātor* 'a host.' Another not-so-obvious borrowing is VIANDS 'articles of food' [ultimately from Latin *vīvenda* 'things to be lived on'; by way of Vulgar Latin **vi(v)anda* and Medieval/Old French *viande* 'food']. In Modern French, *viande* means 'meat,' dating from the 15th-century meaning of 'flesh as food.' Note, also, VIPER 'a common European venomous snake' [from Medieval French *vipere*, from Latin *vipera*; possibly from earlier **vivipera* 'that which produces living young' (See line 8127)].

The past participle of Latin *vīvere* 'to live' is *vīctus*, and derived from this is the Latin noun *vīctus* 'means of living, food, nourishment.' In Late Latin, *vīctus* developed an adjectival form *vīctuālis*, plural *vīctuālia*, which evolved into Old French *vitaille*, borrowed into Middle English as *vitaile* > English VITTLE, VICTUAL 'a food for human consumption.' Since the 16th century the English word has been spelled VICTUAL after the Latin model, but the pronunciation remains "vittle."

Another Latin noun based on the life-giving root *vī-*, from Indo-European **gwei-* 'to live' is *vīta* 'life.' *Vīta* is the base of the English loanwords VITAL 'necessary to the continuation of life'; VITALITY 'the capacity to live; energy, exuberance'; and VITAMIN 'any of a group of essential food elements.' This last word was coined in 1912 by the Polish-born biochemist Casimir Funk, who is credited with the discovery of vitamins. The original spelling was *vitamine*, "because it was first believed an amino-acid was present, the spelling being later modified in order to avoid the suggestion" (*ODEE*).

Latin *vīta* evolved into French *vie* 'life.' The related French adjective VIABLE 'capable of living; able to maintain a separate existence,' was first recorded in 1539. Adopted into English in the 19th century, VIABLE is currently a popular word in socioeconomic jargon. For a while, however, it had a competing sense and derivation, since some writers took the element *via-* to be from Latin *via* 'road, way,' and used *viable* to mean 'capable of being traversed.'   8835

French and Latin phrases based on *vīvere* 'to live' that have currency in English include (modus) VIVENDI 'mode of living; way of life; a compromise between contending parties'; VIVA (voce) 'with the living voice; oral, orally'; and (qui) VIVE (literally) '(long) live who?'; 'alert.' The last phrase was originally a sentinel's challenge to a would-be passer, the equivalent of English "Who goes there?" However, in French, the sentry is not asking the passer to identify himself, but to say whom he favors (the king of France or the king of England, for instance). The words are used in English in the phrase *on the qui vive* 'on the alert.'   8840   8845

The initial **gw-* of Indo-European **gwei-* 'to live' was replaced by Old English *cw-* in *cwicu* 'living,' and by Latin *v-* in *vīvus* 'living.' In Greek this **gw-* was supplanted by the *b-* of *bios* 'life' (and also by the *z-* of *zōē* 'life,' as we shall see later). To account for the form *bios* one writer postulates intermediate forms **guiuos* and **biwos* (*EP*), while another proposes the "suffixed variant form" of the root, **gwiy-o-* (*AHD*). However it was arrived at, the Greek word *bios* 'life' is still with us, and has given rise to a spate of English words through borrowing and compounding, to wit, BIOGRAPHY 'a written account of a person's life' [*graphein* 'to write']; BIOLOGY 'the science of life' [*logos* 'account, discourse']; BIOPSY 'the examination of tissue taken from a living body' [*opsis* 'a seeing, a viewing']; AMPHIBIOUS 'living both on land and in the water' [*amphi* 'on both sides; on all sides']; ANTIBIOTIC 'against life; a substance that destroys microorganisms'; ANTIBIOSIS 'an association between two or more organisms that is injurious to one of them'; SYMBIOSIS 'the intimate living together of two dissimilar organisms in a mutually beneficial relationship' [from Greek *sumbioun* 'to live with' (*sul-* < *sun* 'with')]; CENOBITE 'a member of a religious group living together' [from Greek *koinobion* 'communal life' (*koinos* 'common, general')]; MICROBE 'a minute form of life' [*mikros* 'small']; and many scientific terms like BIOCHEMISTRY, BIODEGRADABLE, BIOPHYSICS, BIONICS, etc.   8850   8855   8860   8865   8870

As mentioned earlier the Indo-European root **gwei-* 'to live' also produced Greek *zōē* 'life,' as well as *zōos* 'alive,' *zōon* 'living being, animal,' and *zēn* 'to live.' The metamorphosis of Indo-European initial **gw-* into Greek initial *z-* is unusual, since the   8875 regular evolution is to Greek *b-*, *d-*, or *g-*. (Initial *ž-* occurs regularly in Old Slavic, where Indo-European **gwei-* 'to live' is represented by *žive* 'alive, living,' *živetŭ* 'he lives,' and *žiti* 'to live.')

Almost all English borrowings from the Greek words based on *zō-* are scientific in nature, even the popular ZOO, which is a shortened form of ZOOLOGICAL garden, from ZOOLOGY 'the science of animal life' [from New Latin *zŏologia*]. Then there is the combining form *azo-* 'lifeless,' a chemical term indicating the presence of a nitrogen group, coined in the form AZOTE 'nitrogen' [from Greek *a-* 'not' + *zōē* 'life'] in 1787 by the French chemists Lavoisier and de Morveau from their observation that nitrogen cannot take the place of oxygen in supporting life. The geological term AZOIC 'without life' refers to periods in the earth's history before the appearance of life.

The suffix forms *-zoon*, plural *-zoa* indicate 'animal organisms,' as in PROTOZOA 'single-celled organisms' [*protos* 'first']; SPERMATOZOON 'the fertilizing gamete of a male animal' [*sperma* 'seed']; and ENTOZOA 'animals that live within other animals' (e.g., tapeworms) [*entos* 'within'].

A related word that goes back to the days when astronomy and astrology were the same subject is ZODIAC 'a band of the celestial sphere extending about eight degrees to each side of the ecliptic and representing the path of the planets, the sun, and the moon.' ZODIAC traces back to the Greek phrase *kuklos zōidiakos* 'circle of signs, circle of figures,' from *zōidion* 'sculptured figure,' a diminutive of *zōion* 'animal; figure, picture.' Coincidentally or not, seven of the twelve signs in the thirty-degree divisions of the celestial sphere were named for animals: *Aries* 'the Ram,' *Taurus* 'the Bull,' *Cancer* 'the Crab,' *Leo* 'the Lion,' *Scorpio* 'the Scorpion,' *Capricorn* 'the Goat (horned),' and *Pisces* 'the Fishes.'

A Greek cognate in which the initial **gw-* of Indo-European **gwei-* 'to live' has been replaced by *-g-* is found in the compound word *hugieia* (literally) 'well-living; good health,' personified as *Hygeia* 'the goddess of health.' *Hugieia* is based on Indo-European **su-gwiyes-ya* (*AHD*), from **su-* 'well, good' (see line 8754.) + **gwei-* 'to live.' Related adjectives are *hugiēs* 'healthy' and *hugieinē* 'of good health,' whence French and English HYGIENE 'the cultivation of conditions conducive to good health.'

Finally, "a term of the alchemists applied to ardent spirits or unrectified alcohol, sometimes applied to ardent spirits of the first distillation" (*OED*) is AQUA VITAE 'water of life; alcohol; strong liquor; brandy, whiskey.' We find this Latin phrase translated into French *eau de vie* 'water of life; cognac,' and adapted into Scandinavian *akvavit*, whence English AQUAVIT 'a clear alcoholic liquor distilled from potato or grain mash and flavored with caraway seed.' AQUA VITAE is also translated into Irish Gaelic *uisce beathadh*, Scottish Gaelic *uisge beatha*, whence *usquebaugh*, *usquebae*, *whiskybae*, whence (for short) WHISKEY, WHISKY 'a strong alcoholic liquor distilled from grain mash' [Old Irish *uisce* 'water' + *bethad*, genitive of *bethu* 'life']. Actually, the shortened form WHISKEY stands simply for Old Irish *uisce* 'water,' as *vodka* means 'little water' in Russian.

XLVI

Sculptured Scallops, Scalped Skulls

8930   SCALLOPS are SHIELDED from the outside world by their
SHELLS, and fish are safeguarded to a lesser extent by their
SCALES, but a bald man's SCALP provides scant protection from
the elements. Most of these words have something to do with
protection or covering, and one might expect a similar sheltering
8935   meaning in their root. They are in fact, however, based on the
Indo-European root *skel- 'to cut, to split, to separate,' seemingly
because the objects they stand for are in one way or another the
products of 'separation.'
One Germanic derivative is *skaljō 'a piece cut off; a shell.'
8940   *Skaljō gave rise to Old English scell, sciell, whence English
SHELL 'the hard covering of an animal, egg, nut, etc.; a hollow
structure,' as well as such Germanic cousins as Dutch schel 'pod,
rind, scale, shell,' German Schale 'shell, skin, rind, pod, acorn
cup,' and Old Norse skel 'seashell.' MW2 lists thirty-four defini-
8945   tions of the noun SHELL, ranging from "a hard rigid covering of an
animal" to "a light racing boat" and "the part of a loom in which
the reed is fitted."
A closely related word is the Germanic *skālō, ancestor of
English SCALE 'a thin horny plate on the skin of animals,
8950   especially fish' [from Old French escale 'husk, cup,' from West
Germanic *skāla]. The Modern French word for 'fish scale' is
écaille, which stems from Germanic *skaljō and is therefore a
close cousin to English SHELL, while the Modern French descendant of Old French escale is écale 'husk (of nuts); shell (of peas).'
8955   Another Old French word for 'shell,' from some Germanic source
possibly related to our *skel- 'to separate' words, is escalope,
surviving in the English loanwords ESCALLOP, SCALLOP 'a kind of
mollusk having a fan-shaped shell with a radiating fluted pattern.'
When something similar to this 'radiating fluted pattern' is used

as an ornamental border on garments, the garments are said to be   8960
SCALLOPED. The Italians also borrowed Old French *escalope*
'shell' as a cookery term, that is, *scaloppa* 'a thinly sliced fillet (of
meat, especially veal).' These fillets curl up like "shells" when
cooked in a wine or tomato sauce, and the dish is known as
SCALOPPINE or SCALLOPINI.   8965

The English word SCALP (originally) 'the cranium'; 'the skin
covering the top of the head; the hairy integument cut from the
top of a person's head as a battle trophy' has no Germanic
relatives with the same meaning, the closest being Old Norse
skálpr 'sheath' (others are dialectal Danish *skalp* 'shell, husk' and   8970
Dutch *schelp* 'shell'). The third sense of SCALP, 'battle trophy,'
has passed from English into French, German, and Swedish since
the discovery of the North American continent. It is this sense
that underlies the word SCALPER 'one who sells tickets to a sold-
out performance at prices higher than the established rate.' The   8975
money-hungry operators are compared to American Indians on
the warpath.

Despite the lack of Germanic relatives to SCALP with the
same meaning, there is a similar-sounding English word with a
closely related meaning. How much closer can a relationship be   8980
than that between scalp and SKULL 'the bony case that encloses
and protects the brain'? But this word is also in an etymological
limbo. The *OED* explains that the locality of the early examples of
SKULL (13th and 14th centuries in the forms *scolle, schulle,
skulle*) is against any connection with Old Norse *skoltr*, Norwe-   8985
gian *skolt, skult*, and Swedish *skult, skulle*, all of which mean
'skull,' or with Norwegian *skul, skol* 'shell (of nuts and eggs).' The
AHD goes along with this disclaimer by listing SKULL as "of
obscure origin," *EP* is content to include SKULL ("essentially a
hard, bony case") in the same listing as SHELL, Old High German   8990
scala, and Old Norse *skel* 'seashell.' *MW2* comes right out and
states that SKULL is akin to English SHELL, while *MW3* says that it
is akin to Swedish *skulle* "—more at SHELL," and the *RHD*
maintains that Middle English *scolle* stems from the Scandinavian: "cf. Swedish dialectal *skulle* 'skull' and Norwegian dialectal   8995
skol, skul 'shell (of an egg or nut).' " The source-seeker is left to
draw his own conclusions, but he'll probably agree with the
ODEE's comment (after stating that SKULL is of unknown origin)
that the word is "remarkably similar to synonymous Old Norse
skoltr."   9000

People have been known to use skulls and shells as drinking
cups, so it's not surprising to find this idea hidden away in a
related English word, though it may be surprising to learn that
that word is SCALE(s) (originally) 'drinking bowl(s)'; 'an instru-

9005   ment or machine for weighing' [from Old Norse *skål* 'a drinking
vessel made from a shell; a bowl; a scale of a balance,' from
Germanic **skēlō*]. The clue here is that this word is usually
plural like *trousers* or *scissors*, a reminder that SCALES were
balances with a pan or bowl hanging from each end of a beam that
9010   is horizontally suspended at its center. It is each one of these
bowls that is a SCALE. Old Norse *skål* 'a drinking vessel' is also
the source of the toast SKOAL! [Danish and Norwegian *skaal!*
Swedish *skal!*]. Semantically this toast is similar to English
"Bottoms up!" Among English speakers, the Scandinavian *skoal!*
9015   was first current in Scotland, following a visit to Denmark in 1589
by James VI of Scotland and later by James I of England. James
married a Danish princess in 1589, so there was probably much
skoaling going on during his visit. (That the SCALE for measuring
weight is exactly the same spelling as the *scale* for measuring
9020   distances on a map is purely coincidental, since the second *scale*
comes from Latin *scala* 'ladder, staircase.')

Before we get away from the derivatives of Indo-European
*skel- 'to cut, to split, to separate' that have to do with shells,
scales, and outer layers, mention must be made of the word
9025   SHALE 'a kind of easily split rock' [from Middle English *shale* 'a
shell, a husk,' from Old English *sc(e)alu*, from Germanic **skālō*]
(See line 8948). The Middle English sense of *shale* 'a shell, a husk'
is now obsolete or dialectal. *Shale* was also used as a verb
meaning 'to remove the shell from a nut,' a transitive sense later
9030   used intransitively to mean 'to cleave, to split or separate into
smaller fragments,' said especially of rocks. A 1712 quotation in
the *OED* reads: "a Stone unfit for Building because in the raising
it cleaves or shales into many small uneven Pieces." It is from
this usage that we probably have the modern sense of the word
9035   which denotes the SHALE rock that is mined to recover residual
oil. Note that SHALE combines the 'protective coating' connotations of SHELL with the 'splitting, separating' meanings ascribed
to Indo-European **skel*. Note, also, SHELLAC = SHELL LAC 'lac
melted and run into thin plates.' SHELLAC is a translation of the
9040   French phrase *laque en écailles* 'lac in thin plates' (*écaille* 'scale,
shell'). LAC is 'the resinous secretion of an insect of southern
Asia, the lac insect, variously identified as *Coccus lacca,
Tachardia lacca*, or *Laccifer lacca*.' Yet another derivative of
Indo-European **skel-* 'to cut, to split, to separate' having to do
9045   with shells, scales, and outer layers is SHIELD 'a broad piece of
defensive armor' [from Old English *sceld, scild, scield*; from
Germanic **skelduz* 'a split piece of wood, a board.']. It is not to be
assumed that early warriors merely picked up a board to serve as
a shield (the regular fighting gear was no doubt wrought by

competent craftsmen), but the idea certainly seems to be there as   9050
a tribal memory. In Modern German the word for 'shield' is
Schild, a form that makes up the second half of the family names
ROTHSCHILD 'red-shield' and HOCHSCHILD 'high-shield.'

Many etymologists think that the word SHELTER 'protective
cover from the elements, similar to that provided by a roof and   9055
walls' derives from Middle English *sheltron*, from Old English
scieldtruma (literally) 'shield-troop'; 'a group of men with shields;
a close compact body of troops,' who in the event of attack
provided SHELTER for themselves by locking SHIELDS together to
form a roof and wall (Latin *testudo*). However, the *OED* states   9060
that this theory "seems untenable" because of chronological
difficulties: *sheltron* had been obsolete for a hundred years before
the first example of SHELTER appears.

The 'split piece of wood' meaning turns up again in Ger-
manic **skelf-*, Middle Low German *schelf*, Middle English *shelfe*,   9065
and English SHELF 'a thin, flat, usually long and narrow piece of
wood used to support objects.' Although Modern English *sh* is a
symbol for a single sound, in other, older forms of Germanic *sh*
was *sk*, where the *s* and *k* were more obviously separate. If the
initial *s-* of **skelf-* weakened just as the *-k-* acquired a more   9070
aspirated form, one would be left with **helfe*, a formation sugges-
tively similar to Old English *healf* 'one side of something with
two sides,' whence English HALF 'one of two equal parts' [from
Germanic **halbaz* 'divided, cut in two, split'; from Indo-European **kelp-*, variant of **skel-* 'to cut'].   9075

The initial *s-* is back in Germanic **skulō* 'a division.' This
word developed senses of 'a multitude, a crowd' (in the way that
an Army *division* is 'a large gathering of troops') in Old English
scolu and Middle Low German and Middle Dutch *schōle*, all
meaning 'multitude.' The English SHOAL 'a great multitude (of   9080
fish)' comes from one of these words, no one is sure which. The
English SCHOOL 'a large group of fish of the same species
swimming together' comes from Middle Dutch *schōle*, whence
Middle English *scole*, and is the equivalent of Modern Dutch
school 'group, troop.' (Totally unrelated is the *school* where   9085
lessons are taught, which is from Latin *sc(h)ola* 'leisure devoted
to learning; school,' from Greek *skholē* 'work of leisure; disputation; school.' Also unrelated is English *shoal* 'a sandy elevation at the bottom of a body of water,' which is related to *shallow*.)

We come upon a word not really expected in this company,   9090
that is, SKILL 'proficiency, ability, dexterity' [from Old Norse *skil*
'discernment'; from Germanic **skeli-*], related to the Old Norse
verb *skilja* 'to separate, to distinguish.' One who is SKILLFUL is
adept at 'discerning' just what moves he has to make. This

9095   semantic sequence is similar to the development of Latin *scīre* 'to know,' whence *science* 'knowing,' from the sense 'to separate one thing from another' implicit in the Indo-European root **sek-* **skei-*, 'to cut.'

The corpus of descendants from Indo-European **skel-* 'to cut,
9100   to split, to separate' that we are dissecting also includes some Latin derivatives from which English has borrowed. Among these English loanwords is the dissector's tool a SCALPEL 'a surgeon's knife; a small straight knife with a keen blade used for dissecting' [from Latin *scalpellum* 'little knife, scalpel'; from *scalper, scal-*
9105   *prum* 'chisel, knife']. The associated Latin verb is *scalpere* 'to scratch, to cut, to carve.' A modification of *scalpere* is *sculpere, sculptum* 'to carve, to cut, to chisel,' and a person who makes a practice of carving, cutting, and chiseling is known as a SCULPTOR 'a maker of statues and graven images' [from Latin *sculptor*
9110   'stonecutter, sculptor']. The objects a sculptor produces are known as SCULPTURE 'carved, chiseled, modeled, cast, or welded figures in three dimensions' [from Latin *sculptūra*].

Dropping the *s*- from *sculptor* would give us **culptor*, which is not far from the Latin noun *culter* 'knife, razor; plowshare,' the
9115   source of English COLTER (or, british, COULTER) 'a knife or cutter attached to the beam of a plow to cut the sward in advance of the plowshare' [via Old English 'culter' (possibly influenced by Old French *coltre*)]. (Semantically, Latin *culter* 'plowshare' comes very close to Latin *cultor* 'farmer' and *cultus* 'tilling, cultivation,'
9120   but there no etymological connection has been established. See lines 10968ff.)

Latin *culter* 'knife' has a diminutive, *cultellus* 'little knife,' which became Romanic **cultellāceum* 'a big little knife,' which in turn evolved into Provençal and Old French *coutelas*, whence
9125   obsolete English *coutelace, cuttleax, cutlash*, whence Modern English CUTLASS 'a short heavy sword with a curved, single-edged blade.' (*Short* and *long* are relative terms, but a *cutlass* is undoubtedly a 'big little knife.') Latin *cultellus* also gave rise to French *couteau* 'knife' and Italian *coltella* 'big knife,' and through
9130   Late Latin *cultellārius* 'knife-maker' to French *coutelier*, whence English CUTLER 'one who makes, repairs, or sells knives or other cutting instruments.' Note, also, CUTLERY 'cutting instruments and tools; implements used as tableware' [from French *coutel(l)erie*].

9135   What with CUTLASSES, CUTLERS, and CUTLERY, one might expect a tie-in at this point with the English verb and noun *cut* 'to penetrate with a sharp edge; a gash, an opening made by a sharp object,' but this is not to be. English *cut*, from Middle English *cute, cutte, cutten, ketten, kitten,* is one of those elusive words

that seem to appear out of nowhere, without antecedents. Middle   9140
English *cute* put in an appearance at the end of the 13th century,
and, along with its variant spellings, was in common use by the
14th. However, there is no attested Old English form of the word,
and none in West Germanic. There is also no corresponding verb
in French or other Romance language. The only cognates are   9145
found in Swedish dialectal *kåta* 'to cut,' Norwegian *kutte*, and
Icelandic *kuta* 'to cut with a little knife,' and Icelandic *kuti* 'a
little blunt knife.' These suggest a Germanic root of **kut-*, **kot-*,
and some connection between *cut* and the Danish invasions of
the 9th century. However, if this is so, where the English word   9150
was living in the four hundred years between the 9th and 13th
centuries is a mystery.

XLVII

Simple Sincerity

9155

9160

9165

9170

9175

9180

SOME people SEEM to think it UNSEEMLY to give a SIMPLE answer; usually these SAME people tend to make every utterance a HOMILY. The Indo-European root underlying these SEEMINGLY DISSIMILAR words is *sel- 'one, the same.' This is not the root that gives us the word *one*: that is *oino- 'one, unique.' Nor is it the root that gives us the words *monad, monotone,* etc.: that is *men- 'small, isolated.'

Two different roots meaning 'one' may seem like one too many, but they point out different aspects of the concept of 'oneness.' *Oino- 'one, unique' relates to the aloneness, the solitariness of being one, while *sel- 'one, the same' refers to collective unity, the oneness of being of the same kind or of representing a union. It becomes apparent that 'sameness' rather than 'uniqueness' is the pervasive connotation of *sel- 'one' when we examine its English descendants. For example, SIMILAR 'alike' [via French *similaire* from Latin *similis* 'like'] and SIMILE 'a figure of speech that likens certain aspects of two different things' (He's as stubborn as a mule. She looks like a scarecrow) [from Latin *simile* 'comparison,' from the neuter of *similis* 'like'].

In addition to *simile* as the neuter for *similis* 'like,' the Latin speakers had an Old Latin neuter, *simul,* that they used as an adverb to mean 'at one time, at the same time; at once.' Between *simile* and *simul* and the prefixes *ad-* 'at, toward' and *dis-* 'asunder, in two,' we come up with the following English loan-words: SIMULATE 'to make like; to imitate; to feign' [from Latin *simulāre* 'to make like']; SIMULACRUM 'an image; something formed in the likeness of something else' [from Latin *simulācrum* 'likeness, image']; and SIMULTANEOUS 'happening at the same time.' SIMULTANEOUS is a 17th-century English coinage created on the analogy of *instantaneous* or *momentaneous.* French does

not record the equivalent *simultané* until the 18th century, while
Medieval Latin *simultāneus* has the different meaning of 'simulated; pretended, assumed.' More English loanwords include   9185
SIMILITUDE (= SIMILARITY) and ASSIMILATE 'to make like; to cause
to resemble; to absorb' [from Latin *assimilāre, assimulāre* 'to
make like, to copy']. ASSIMILATION is used as a technical term in
phonetics to denote a phenomenon that the word itself exemplifies, that is, 'the alteration of one sound in a word so that it   9190
becomes similar to or the same as an adjacent sound.' In ASSIMI-
LATE the *-d-* of Latin *ad-* was assimilated to the *s-* of *similāre* to
change *adsimilāre* to *assimilāre*. Note, also, DISSIMILATE 'to make
unlike' [New Latin, from Latin *dis-* + *similāre*]. Again, DISSIMILA-
TION is used in phonetics as a technical term meaning 'the   9195
changing of like sounds to unlike sounds.' Examples are Latin
marmor > French *marbre* > English *marble*, where the second
-m- dissimilates to *-b-*, and the second *-r-* to *-l-*, and Latin
peregrīnus > Late Latin *pelegrīnus* (>English *pilgrim*), where
the first *-r-* dissimilates to *-l-* (compare *peregrine*). New Latin   9200
dissimilāre does not appear until the 19th century, but a related
word that has a genuine Latin antecedent is DISSIMULATE 'to
conceal one's true intentions' [from Latin *dissimulāre* 'to hide, to
disguise']. This has a semantic content remarkably like that of
DISSEMBLE 'to disguise the true nature of; to feign; to mask,' and   9205
with good reason, for the two words are doublets, both descending from Latin *dissimulāre*. (In French, *dissembler* did not mean
'to feign, to mask,' but merely 'to be unlike.') The intrusion of *-b-*,
which took place as the word evolved from Late Latin into Old
French, is not an unusual occurrence with words containing an   9210
-m-. Compare Latin *humilis* > French, English *humble* and Latin
numerus > French *nombre* > English *number*.

Other English loanwords based on Latin *simulāre/similāre*,
with an intrusive Old French *-b-*, are SEMBLANCE 'outward
appearance; similarity' [via Medieval/Old French from Old   9215
French *semblant* 'seeming,' present participle of *sembler* 'to
seem, to resemble'; from Latin *simulāre* 'to make like']; RESEM-
BLE 'to look like' [from Old French *resembler*]; ENSEMBLE (literally) 'together; at the same time'; 'two or more units that make up
a complementary whole' [from the French; from Latin *insimul* 'at   9220
the same time']; and ASSEMBLE 'to come together; to bring
together' [from Old French *as(s)embler*, from Vulgar Latin
*assimulāre (*ad-* + *simul* 'together; at the same time')].

Simul, similis, and *simile* are not the only forms in which the
Indo-European root **sem-* 'one, the same' made its way into   9225
Latin. There is also Latin *singulus* 'one each; single,' whence
English SINGLE 'alone, unaccompanied, sole; not divided; unmar-

ried' [by way of Medieval/Old French]; SINGULAR 'being the only one; extraordinary' [from Latin *singulāris*]; and SINGLET 'an unlined woolen garment; an unlined waistcoat; an undershirt' [formed by analogy with *doublet* 'a lined jacket worn by men in the 14th–18th centuries']. Note, also, Latin *simplus* 'simple; one-fold, multiplied by one,' whence English SIMPLE 'not compli-cated; easy; unadorned' [via Old French]. Or SIMPLE may come from Latin *simplex, simplicis* 'simple; unmixed; folded once,' whence SIMPLICITY [< Latin *simplicitās*]. Another form of the Indo-European root **sem-* 'one, the same' is Latin *semper* 'ever, always.' The 'oneness' of Latin *semper* lurks in the notion of 'once for always.' The *-per* element is thought to stem from Indo-European **per-* 'through; during,' so that etymologically *semper* means 'one-during' = 'all of time' (all of anything can be con-ceived of as 'one').

Latin *semper* 'ever, always' is familiar to Americans by its presence in such mottoes as the Marine Corps' *semper fidelis* 'ever faithful,' the Coast Guard's *semper paratus* 'always ready,' and Virginia's *sic semper tyrannis* 'thus always to tyrants.' Other-wise it is found in SEMPRE (a musical direction) 'in the same manner throughout' [from Italian *sempre* 'always'] and SEMPITER-NAL 'perpetual' [(possibly via Old French) from Latin *sempiternus* (*semper* 'ever' + *aeternus* 'eternal')]. Still another form of Indo-European **sem* 'one, the same' is Latin *sincērus* (literally) 'of one growth; unadulterated, pure; honest' (Indo-European **ker-* is the root of the *-cērus* element. Compare *crescent, create*) whence English SINCERE 'honest, straight-forward.'

Except for obvious extended forms like SINCERITY and SIM-PLETON, the preceding covers most of the English words from Indo-European **sel-* 'one, the same' acquired as loanwords from Latin. When it comes to the Germanic, the list is not as long, but it includes three words that are well-nigh indispensable to Eng-lish. The first is (the) SAME 'identical, none other; similar, like' [from Old Norse *same, sama, samr,* from Germanic **samaz*]. (*Same* appears in Old English only in the adverbial phrase *swā same* 'likewise.') The two other Germanic loanwords are SOME 'one of a number; an indefinite number, but not a large number; an unspecified person or thing' [from Old English *sum* 'one, a certain number'] and SEEM 'to have the semblance of; to give the impression of'; (obsolete) 'to be suitable to, to BESEEM' [from or akin to Old Norse *soema* 'to conform to,' from *soemr* 'fitting, agreeable,' by umlaut from Germanic **sōl-*]. The semantic bridge between **sel-* 'one, the same' and the obsolete meaning of SEEM 'to be suitable' seems to be something like this: 'sameness >

semblance > congruity > agreeability > suitability.' This obsolete meaning also throws light on the current meaning of SEEMLY
'suitable; in good taste; handsome.'   9275
How the transition from *sel- 'one, the same' to SOME 'an
indefinite number' took place can be detected in such phraseologies as "You'll find out one day" = "You'll find out SOME day."
As for the suffix -SOME, it retains the notion of 'likeness, similarity'
inherent in *sel-, intimating 'a tendency toward the quality   9280
indicated by the first element' of the compound word, as in
AWESOME 'inspiring awe,' BURDENSOME 'tending to be a burden,'
and TROUBLESOME 'causing trouble.' In some instances the meaning of the first element is now obscure, or different from the
present-day meaning, as in NOISOME (obsolete) 'annoying'; 'harm   9285
ful; offensive' [from noy, for annoy; from Old French enui, from
Latin in odiō 'in hatred'] and HANDSOME (originally) 'easy to
handle'; 'generous; pleasing in appearance; good-looking.' From
'easy to handle' to 'good-looking' may seem a long semantic jump,
but the English speakers made it somehow, via: 'handy > conve   9290
nient > suitable > moderately large > generous > pleasing >
pleasing in appearance > good-looking' (all intermediate meanings attested in the OED). Note, also, WINSOME (etymologically)
'joyous'; 'winning, attractive' [from Old English wynsum, from
wyn(n) 'joy'] (related to win, since to win is a joy, and a joyous   9295
person is attractive) and TOOTHSOME 'pleasing to the taste.'
Compare "to have a sweet tooth." At one time the teeth were
thought to have something to do with the sense of taste. Other
phrases that bear this out are "It makes my teeth water" = "It
makes my mouth water" and "He loves his tooth" = "He likes to   9300
eat."
Not many English words are borrowed from the Russian, and
most of those that are are concerned with things typically Russian.
For example, these two words descended from Indo-European
*sel- 'one, the same,' SAMOVAR (literally) 'self-boiler'; 'a metal urn 9305
with a tap, in which water is boiled for making tea' [from Russian
samo 'self' + varit' 'to boil'] and SOVIET (etymologically) 'a
speaking together'; 'a council; a popularly elected assembly of the
USSR, on a national, regional, or local level' [from Russian sovet,
from Old Russian sŭvĕtŭ, from su 'together' + vĕtŭ 'council'].   9310
Vĕtŭ is from a Russian root meaning 'to speak,' from Indo-
European *weit- 'to speak.'
In Sanskrit, in the word SANSKRIT 'the literary language of
India' [from saṁskṛta 'put together; refined, polished' (saṁ
'together' + kṛ 'to make, to do')], the SAN- element is a derivative   9315
of our Indo-European root *sel- 'one, the same,' here meaning
'together.' The word for the vernacular languages of India, Pra-

krit, means 'made before; original, natural,' from *prakrta* 'natural, vulgar.' Sanskrit was the first Indo-European language to have a written grammar, since it was codified prior to the 4th century B.C. The Prakrits that existed 'before' (according to their name) and simultaneously with Sanskrit have flowed on after and divided into numerous streams. Today the Prakrits' descendants have developed into about 25 different languages ranging from Assamese and Bengali to Romany, Sinhalese, and Urdu.

The *sam* 'together' element also appears in the Indic words SAMSARA, SAMHITA, SANGH, and SANDHI (literally) 'a linking, a placing together'; 'a phonetic change caused by the mutual influence of words placed together,' as, for example, in the pronunciation of *did you* as "didja" or *don't you* as "doncha."

We get around finally to the Greek, where we find that the initial **s-* of our Indo-European root **sem-* 'one, the same' has gone through the characteristic sound shift to become *h-*, as evidenced by the derivative adjective *homos* 'one and the same' (from the suffixed *o*-grade root form **sol-o-*). *Homos* and its relative *homoios* 'similar' are the source of some prefixes much used in learned and semi-learned   English words, such as HOMOGENIZED 'made the same consistency throughout' [-*genēs* 'born, produced']; HOMOSEXUAL 'participating in sexual acts with someone of the same sex'; and HOMONYM 'the same name; a word that is pronounced the same as another, but that has a different spelling and meaning' [*onoma* 'name']. Examples include *hear, here; their, there; right, wright, rite, write..* Note, also, HOMO-GRAPH 'the same spelling; a word that has the same spelling as another but a different origin and meaning,' for example, the *bow* of ship's *bow*, that of *bow* and scrape, and that of *bow* and arrow); HOMOPHONE 'the same sound; a word pronounced exactly like another but not necessarily spelled like it,' for example, *bare* 'undressed,' *bear* 'to carry,' and *bear* 'the animal'; HOMEOPATHY 'medical treatment based on the use of drugs that produce effects similar to those produced by the disease itself' [*pathos* 'suffering']; HOMOLOGOUS 'having the same relative function, structure'; HOMOCENTRIC[1], HOMOZYGOUS, HOMEOCHROMATIC, HOMEOZOIC, HOMOOUSIAN, and HOMOIOUSIAN. The related elements *homou* 'together' and *homalos* 'level, even; average' are not so obvious in the following English words: HOMILY 'a sermon; a tediously moralizing lecture or reproof' [from Old French *omelie*, from Late Latin *homīlia*, from Greek *homilia* 'a living together; conversation, instruction; assembly,' from *homilos* 'crowd' (*homou* 'together' + *ilē* 'troop, band')] and ANOMALOUS (literally) 'not level, not average'; 'irregular, deviating from the norm' [*an-* 'not' + *homalos* 'even'].

Indo-European *sem- 'one, the same' has a compound zero-grade form *smma that yields Greek hama 'together with, at the same time,' seen in HAMADRYAD 'a wood nymph who is the spirit of a tree; the king cobra' [from Greek hamadruas ' "one together with a tree" ' (AHD); drus 'tree']. As if naming the large venomous snake after a wood nymph were not enough of an imaginative stretch, the biologists have also given the name HAMADRYAS to the sacred baboon, a baboon of North Africa and Arabia venerated by the ancient Egyptians.

The m with a small circle under it, -m̥-, is a syllabic -m- as in hm. In Greek hama (< *sm̥ma) it is replaced by -a-, and likewise in Greek hateros (*sm̥-tero-) 'one of two; other,' which has a doublet heteros that is the source of modern borrowings. The element *tero- is the same one that shows up in Latin alter (< *al-tero 'other of two') and English other (<*an-tero- 'other of two'). Thus the same Indo-European root *sem- 'one, the same' yields the Greek words for 'same' homos (< *som-o-s) and 'other' heteros (< *sm̥-tero-s).

As an English prefix, HETERO- is not as widely used as HOMO-, but it often supplies the opposite term to a HOMO- word, as in HETEROGENEOUS (opposed to HOMOGENEOUS) 'consisting of dissimilar elements'; HETEROSEXUAL (opposed to HOMOSEXUAL) 'participating in sexual acts with one of the opposite sex'; HETEROOUSIAN (See line 8661.); HETERONYM (opposed to HOMONYM but similar to HOMOGRAPH) 'a word that is spelled the same as another but has a different pronunciation and meaning' (sow 'a female pig,' sow 'to scatter seed'); HETERODOX (opposed to orthodox) 'holding other than the usual beliefs; unorthodox' [doxa 'opinion']; and HETEROSIS 'superior qualities arising from cross-breeding' [-osis indicates 'condition'].

Greek is the only Indo-European language having an immediate influence on English that adapted the root *sem- 'one, the same' to form the cardinal number 'one,' which it did in the forms heis (masculine) and hen (neuter), after going through the unattested stages *hems > *hens (AHD). The feminine is mia. Greek heis and hen have had little effect on English except in the formation of such ultra-learned words as HENOTHEISM 'belief in one supreme god, but not excluding belief in other gods' [theos 'god'] and HENDECAGON 'a polygon with eleven sides' [deka 'ten,' gonia 'angle'].

Another Greek derivative of Indo-European *sem- 'one, the same,' via the zero-grade root form *sm̥-, is the prefix ha- 'together; one,' evidenced in Greek haplous 'onefold; simple, single,' whence English HAPLOID 'having the basic number of chromosomes, that is, the normal number present in a germ cell' [from Greek *haploidēs* 'onefold' (*ha-* 'one' + *-ploos* '-fold' + *eidos* 'shape')] and HAPLOSIS 'reduction of the number of chromosomes

9410   by meiotic division.' In some cases the Greek prefix *ha-* 'together, one' is unaspirated, leaving simply *a-*, as in ACOLYTE 'one path; one who treads a pathway with another; follower; attendant' [via Old French from Medieval Latin *acolytus*, from Greek *akolouthos* 'follower'; *a-* 'together, one' + *keleuthos* 'path'].

9415   Greek *adelphos* 'brother' comes from *a-* 'one' + *delphus* 'womb,' and means (etymologically) 'from one (the same) womb.' *Adelphos* gives us English ADELPHOGAMY 'a marital relationship in which brothers have a wife in common' [*gamos* 'marriage'], as well as the botanical suffix -ADELPHOUS (etymologically) ' "in a

9420   brotherhood" ' (*AHD*); 'having bundles of stamens united by their filaments,' and the place name PHILADELPHIA (etymologically) 'brotherly love' [*philos* 'lover']. This *a-*, indicating 'togetherness, oneness,' is not to be confused with the prefix *a-* (< *an-*) 'without; not; opposite to.'

XLVIII

Skinny Saxons; Sickles
and Scythes

SAWS, SICKLES, and SCYTHES are all tools that cut. SECTIONS   9425
and SEGMENTS are what things are cut into. INSECT literally
means 'cut into,' and to SKIN an animal is to cut its hide off. The
common ancestor of these words is the Indo-European root *sek-
'to cut.' The words come to English, some inherited through the
Germanic, some borrowed from Latin, and one in both ways.   9430
    In a few Germanic derivatives, the *-k- of Indo-European
*sek- is replaced by -g-, as in Germanic *sagō 'a cutting tool, a
saw,' whence English SAW 'a thin metal blade with sharpened
teeth, used for cutting' [from Old English *sagu, sage*]. (The
Modern German word is *Säge.*) English SAW also gives us   9435
SAWYER 'one who saws wood for a living' and SEESAW 'a teeter-
totter; an up-and-down or back-and-forth motion,' perhaps
because the up-and-down or back-and-forth motions resemble the
movements of sawing wood. SEE- is a playful reduplication of
-SAW, and SEESAW may have been a nursery-rhyme word before it   9440
became attached to the playground device, for the *OED* says it
was "used as part of a rhythmical jingle, apparently sung by
sawyers, or by children imitating sawyers at their work."
    Another Germanic derivative of Indo-European *sek- 'to cut'
is *segithō, which evolved into Old English *si(g)the* and Modern   9445
English SCYTHE 'a long curved blade attached to a long two-
handed handle, used for mowing tall grasses.' The -c- in SCYTHE
is intrusive, inserted by erroneous association with Latin *scindere*
'to cut.' The etymologically correct spelling, favored by Samuel
Johnson, is *sithe.* A small one-handed scythe is a SICKLE 'a curved   9450
blade with a short handle, used for cutting tall grass' [from Old
English *sicol, sicel*]. SICKLE is the word that came to English by
way of both Latin and Germanic. It was adopted prehistorically,
that is to say in the early centuries of the Christian era, by West-

9455   Germanic speakers from Vulgar Latin *sicila, a variant of Latin
         sēcula 'sickle.' Compare Latin secāre 'to cut.' There is another
         Latin word sēculum, saeculum that means 'generation, age; cen-
         tury' and, in Church Latin, 'the world, temporality,' as opposed to
         the Church and spirituality (>English secular). Latin saeculum is
9460   of obscure origin, but by coincidence, Father Time, that symbol
         of temporality (saeculum) is usually depicted carrying a scythe
         (sēcula 'sickle').
             Turning from implements that cut to what has been cut, we
         come upon English SKIN (etymologically) 'that which one peels
9465   off'; 'the integument of an animal stripped from its body; pelt,
         hide; the epidermis; to flay' [from late Old English scinn; from
         Old Norse skinn; from Germanic *skinth-]. Note that the Indo-
         European *sek- has been shortened to sk- (zero-grade form). The
         guttural -k- > -g- is palatalized in English SEDGE 'a grasslike plant
9470   with solid, sharp-edged stems' [from Old English secg, from
         Germanic *sagjaz 'plant with a cutting edge']. Old English secg
         and Germanic *sagjaz are masculine, while the feminine Old
         English secg and Germanic *sagjō mean 'sword.' This sharp-
         edged name was used by the Anglo-Saxons to translate Latin
9475   gladiolus 'little sword,' another plant with a cutting name. A 1398
         translation of a 13th-century dissertation, On the Properties of
         Things, states that "sedge is an herb most hard and sharp; the
         stalk thereof is three cornered, and cutteth and carveth the hand
         that it holdeth."
9480   A sharp Anglo-Saxon cutting implement was the seax 'knife,
         dagger, sword; battle-ax,' from Germanic *sa(k)hsam 'knife,
         sword.' *Sa(k)hsam may also be the source of SAXONS 'a Ger-
         manic people who dwelt in what is now Holstein in northern
         Germany as early as the 2nd century A.D.,' the second half of the
9485   name of those hyphenated people, the Anglo-Saxons. Some of
         these tribesmen, along with the Angles and Jutes, conquered the
         Britons on their own island of Britannia and had by the 7th
         century colonized most of what is now England, while the Old
         Saxons remained in Germany. The AHD labels the derivation of
9490   SAXON from Germanic *sa(k)hsam as "traditional, but quite
         doubtful." In any case, Latin was an intermediary in the forma-
         tion of the modern word SAXON. The progression goes as follows:
         Germanic *sa(k)hsam > Latin Saxō, Saxōnes > English Saxon.
             Knife-wielders or not by name, the invading Saxons eventu-
9495   ally gave their name to many areas of England, and thence to
         innumerable U.S. towns and counties, such as ESSEX, WESSEX,
         SUSSEX, and MIDDLESEX 'East, West, South, and Middle Saxony.'
         Old English seax 'knife, sword' became Modern English SAX 'a
         short curved one-edged sword or dagger, used by the ancient

Celts and Germans; a chopping tool for trimming the edges of roofing slates.' The name of this tool has a variant, that is dear to the hearts of all Scrabble players: ZAX. 9500

In Latin, the word *saxum* means 'a large stone; a fragment of rock, a rock; a stone wall.' This word is also traced to the Indo-European root **sek-* 'to cut.' Some etymologists illuminate the 9505 connection between 'stone' and 'to cut' by describing a stone as 'a broken-off piece' (*AHD*), while others point out that knives were originally made of stone (*MW2*), thus linking our Germanic forebears with the Stone Age (compare Germanic **sakhsam* 'knife' and Latin *saxum* 'stone'). Latin *saxum* has few English descen- 9510 dants, and those are not very common words. Among them is SAXIFRAGE (literally) 'stone-breaker'; 'a genus of plants of the temperate regions' [from Latin *saxifraga (herba)* 'stonebreaking (herb)': (*frangere, frēgī, frāctum* 'to break')]. These plants com- monly grow in the crevices of rocks, and no doubt their roots help 9515 make the crevices larger, thus contributing to the breakup of the rock. However, the Roman naturalist Pliny believed the herbs to have lithontriptic virtues (dissolving kidney and bladder stones), thus accounting for their name. A Spanish name for the plants is *saxifrax*. It is possible that the Spanish word was blended or 9520 confused with an Amerindian word to give us SASSAFRAS 'a genus of aromatic trees of the laurel family.' Note, also, SAXICOLOUS 'growing on rocks; living among rocks' [*colere* 'to dwell'].

There is little explaining required about the ancestry of Latin *secāre, sectum* 'to cut,' which obviously springs from the Indo- 9525 European root **sek-* 'to cut.' The English loanwords borrowed from Latin *secāre, sectum* and its derivatives are almost as obvious, for instance, those words with the suffix *-sect*, like BISECT 'to cut in two'; DISSECT 'to cut apart'; INTERSECT 'to cut through or across' [*inter* 'amid']; TRANSECT 'to cut across'; RESECT 9530 (obsolete) 'to cut back, to pare down'; 'to cut off part of' (but not "to cut again") [from Latin *resecāre, resectum* 'to cut back, to cut a part of; to curtail']; INSECT (literally) 'cut into'; 'a class of animals characterized by having bodies segmented into three major divisions' [from Latin *insectum* 'cut into']. As a name for the 9535 animals, Latin *insecta* is a literal translation of Aristotle's *entoma* (singular *entomon*) 'cut into.' One look at an ant explains why these words were felt to be descriptive. Other loanwords are SECTION 'a piece or portion of anything; the act of cutting; the surgical separation of tissue' [from Latin *sectiōn(em)* 'a cutting']; 9540 SECTOR 'the geometrical figure formed by two radii and the intercepted arc' [from Latin *sector* 'cutter']; SECANT 'a geometrical line that cuts another' [from Latin *secāns, secānt(em)* 'cutting,' present participle of *secāre* 'to cut']; and SECTILE 'capable of

9545 being cut' [from Latin *sectilis* 'cuttable']. Before -*l*-, the voiceless -*k*- sound is replaced by the voiced -*g*- sound in Latin *segmen* 'a piece cut off' and *segmentum* 'a strip of brocade used in trimming,' whence English SEGMENT 'one of the pieces into which something is divided.'

9550 Not so obvious—and not so certain, either—is the development of RISK 'danger, hazard; to take a chance' [from French *risque*, from Italian *risico*, *risicare* 'to run into danger'; from Vulgar Latin **resecum* 'that which cuts off; danger, risk at sea,' from Latin *resecāre* 'to cut off' (*AHD*)]. Not all etymologists carry the derivation this far. Most stop at Italian *risico*, *risicare*, which 9555 they declare to be of uncertain, unknown, and much debated origin. One etymologist, in the *Random House Dictionary*, presumably Prof. Kemp Malone, traces *risico* to Greek *rhiza* 'root; cliff,' through the meaning 'to sail around a cliff.' Note, also, 9560 NOTCH 'a V-shaped cut or indentation' [from *an otch*, from Old French *o(s)che*, from *o(s)chier* 'to make a notch,' from Latin *absecāre* 'to cut off' (*AHD*)]. Most etymologists stop at Old French *oschier*. The *ODEE*, however, suggests a derivation from Latin *inoccāre* 'to harrow in.' The apparently very obvious *sect* 'a small 9565 faction within a larger group' is not from Latin *secāre* 'to cut' at all, but stems rather from Latin *secta* 'sect, faction; path, way,' from *sectus*, archaic past participle of *sequi*, *secutus* 'to follow.' Finally, the English word SAIL 'a sheet of canvas attached to the mast of a vessel or the arm of a windmill to catch the wind' [from 9570 Old English *seg(e)l*; from Germanic **seglam*] is also of unknown origin, according to some, although others believe that **seglam* originally meant 'a cut piece of material,' and is kin to SAW, SICKLE, SCYTHE, and all the other progeny of Indo-European **sek*- 'to cut.'

XLIX

The Staggering Detachment

With victory at STAKE, midst the STACCATO of machine-gun   9575
fire, the STAGGERING DETACHMENT ATTACKED the STOCKADE.
The common ancestor of these unlikely linguistic cousins is the
Indo-European root *steg- 'pole, stick.' The semantic connection
between root and offshoot is most apparent in the English word
STAKE 'a piece of wood sharpened at one end; a vertical post to   9580
which an offender is bound for execution by burning' [from Old
English staca, from Germanic *stak-]. This is not quite the same
STAKE as that indicated in the phrase "with victory at stake,"
where STAKE means 'the reward given to the winner of a contest;
a share in an enterprise; a bet.' It is possible, however, that these   9585
usages trace back to the practice of marking land boundaries with
STAKES to indicate what belongs to whom.

The 'poles' or 'sticks' postulated by the Indo-European root
*steg- are also apparent in the word STOCKADE 'a defensive
barrier made of strong poles' [from obsolete French estocade,   9590
estacade, from Spanish estacada 'staked,' from estaca 'stake,' from
Germanic *stak-]. One might expect to find in this group the
words stick 'a long slender piece of wood,' and stock 'a tree trunk
deprived of its branches,' but they have been assigned to the
different roots *steig- 'to stick; pointed' (Chapter LI, lines 9890ff.),   9595
and *steu- 'to push, stick, beat' (Chapter LII, lines 10056ff.). There
is, however, some disagreement among the etymologists about
these relationships. A word that does belong to the *steg- 'pole,
stick' family is STACK 'a pile of things arranged in an orderly
manner; to arrange in a pile' [from Old Norse staccr 'haystack,'   9600
from Germanic *stakkaz]. When the objects being arranged in
such special order are playing cards, cheating is implied, and the
person who has the cards STACKED against him has little chance
of winning. A cluster of chimneys (a very 'neatly arranged' pile) is

9605   also called a STACK, and from this usage comes the compound
SMOKESTACK 'a large vertical exhaust pipe; the funnel of a
steamboat; the chimney of a steam locomotive.'

Besides being used to mark boundaries and execute heretics,
stakes are used to secure tents and to fasten one thing to another,
9610   that is, to ATTACH 'to fasten onto; to connect as an adjunct part; to
seize, to arrest' [from Old French *atachier, estachier*, from Old
French *estache* 'stake,' from Frankish **stakka* 'stake' (< Germanic
*stak(ōn))]. The Italian version of ATTACH is *attaccare*, from Old
Italian **estacare*, from Gothic **stakka* 'stake' (*AHD*), from Ger-
9615   manic **stak-*. This same Italian *attaccare* is also used as a
shortened form of the phrase *attaccare battaglia* 'to attach battle'
= 'to join battle,' and when so used, *attaccare* 'to join (battle)' has
the meaning of ATTACK 'to assault, to set upon with vigor.' The
French speakers took up this meaning, with the spelling *attaquer*,
9620   and from French the word came into English, in the late 16th
century, spelled ATTACK. (The word is not found in Shakespeare.)

From the notion of ATTACH 'to fasten' it is a simple step to
that of 'to unfasten,' to DETACH 'to disconnect by separating; to
send (troops) on a special mission'; (etymologically) 'to unstake'
9625   [from French *détacher*, from Old French *destachier* (*des-* 'apart' +
atachier)]. This verb leads to the noun DETACHMENT 'separation;
a military unit separated from its group and sent on a special
mission; aloofness.' As the Italian for ATTACH is *attaccare*, so the
Italian for DETACH is *distaccare*. The regular past participle of
9630   *distaccare* is *distaccato* 'detached.' There is also an aphetic form
where, initial *di-* is dropped, leaving us with STACCATO
'detached; composed of distinct, abrupt sounds.'

Not all the dictionaries one searches through will agree with
these derivations (of ATTACH, ATTACK, DETACH, and STACCATO)
9635   from Germanic **stak-* 'stake.' Some of the older ones, like the
OED and *MW2*, as well as the *Random House* (1966), trace these
words to the root of English *tack* 'small nail,' Old Northern
French *taque*, and Old French *tache* 'fibula, clasp; a large nail,' of
obscure origin. Eric Partridge in *Origins* seems to point a way out
9640   of this impasse by suggesting that Old French *tache* 'clasp,
fastening' is "apparently aphetic for Old French-Medieval French
estache 'a stake,' from Frankish **stakka*." The *AHD*, however,
derives *tache, tack* ("perhaps") from an entirely different Indo-
European root, **dek-* ' "referring to a fringe, lock of hair, horsetail,
9645   etc.," ' from which they also derive *tail* and "perhaps" *tag* 'a loose
hanging piece,' *taco*, and *shako*.

We have one more English derivative of Indo-European
*steg- 'pole, stick' to note: STAGGER 'to move unsteadily on one's
feet; to cause to sway; to arrange in zigzag rows' [from earlier

English *stacker*, from Old Norse *stakra* 'to keep pushing,' from   9650
staka 'to push, to cause to stumble' (< Germanic **stak-*)], presumably by pushing with a stick.

L

The Streakers Have Struck

The early seventies' fad of STREAKING was no doubt another way of STRIKING out at what were felt to be overly STRINGENT
9655 RESTRICTIONS of society, though some members of the older generation STRESS that too many RESTRAINTS have already been abandoned. What we have STRUCK here is a rich etymological vein of derivatives from the Indo-European root *streig- 'to stroke, to rub, to press,' with differences of meaning associated
9660 with ablaut variations (STRIKE, STRUCK, STROKE, STREAK, STRICKLE) and nasalization (STRAIN, STRINGENT). One is struck, for instance, by the disparity in meaning between the related verbs STRIKE 'to hit sharply' and STROKE 'to rub lightly, to caress,' especially since STROKE is also a noun with the primary sense of
9665 'a blow given or received,' and numerous other rather violent applications, such as a lightning STROKE, a sunSTROKE, an apoplectic STROKE, the STROKE of a sword. Only rarely does STROKE denote anything so gentle as 'a caressing touch,' like the STROKE of a feather. Yet it is a fact that the gentler meaning was the
9670 earlier, and that the 11th-century meaning of to STRIKE was 'to rub lightly, to smooth, to level.' This meaning persisted through the 19th century and still survives in some trades, for instance masonry, where to STRIKE means 'to dress and smooth with a trowel.' On the other hand, the more violent meaning of 'to deal a
9675 blow' dates back only to the 13th century, although it is now by far the more common. (The OED lists 88 meanings under the heading STRIKE, verb, and fills 9½ pages in explaining and illustrating them.)

Another early meaning of to STRIKE is 'to lower,' as in to
9680 STRIKE sails, to STRIKE one's colors, to STRIKE a tent, to STRIKE a stage set. This meaning is probably the source of another sense dating from the 18th century, that of 'to refuse to work in order to

obtain concessions from an employer' which was originally used with the sense 'to strike tools,' that is 'to lay down tools.' Other meanings of STRIKE are 'to go, to proceed' (He STRUCK out across the field); (baseball) 'to swing at a pitched ball and miss; a pitch of the ball across home plate at a height between that of the batter's shoulders and that of his knees'; 'to reach an agreement' (to STRIKE a bargain). *MW2* notes of this last sense: "Perhaps in imitation of the Latin *foedus ferire*, to STRIKE a compact, so called because an animal was *struck* and killed as a sacrifice on such occasions." Still more meanings of STRIKE include 'to make an impression; to coin, to mint; to draw a line through.' If that line is made broad enough, we have a STREAK 'a long narrow mark differentiated by color or texture from its surroundings; a short interval, a brief run; to mark with stripes; to move at high speed.'

STRUCK, the past tense and past participle of STRIKE, has already been mentioned. -STRUCK is also used as a combining form with the sense of 'smitten, wounded, transfixed,' as in *horror-struck, moon-struck, awe-struck.* Another past participle, STRICKEN, is more common in the combinations *grief-stricken, panic-stricken, conscience-stricken.* One more meaning of the verb STRIKE is 'to make a measure (of grain, flour, or the like) level with the rim by scraping off the excess' with a STRICKLE 'a straight piece of wood with which surplus grain is scraped off level with the rim of a measure; an instrument for whetting scythes; various tools used for smoothing and leveling in carpentry, masonry, metal casting' [from Old English *stricel*].

The Old French version of STRICKLE was *estrique*, from the verb *estriquer* 'to pass a stick over a measure to remove excess grain,' probably (*AHD*) from the Middle Dutch *striken* 'to pass one thing over another; to strike.' Old French *estrique* became, by aphesis (beheading) and the addition of a diminutive ending, *tricot* 'a short stick, a cudgel,' also 'knitting,' an activity in which two sticks are passed one over the other. The French verb is *tricoter* 'to knit,' and in English, a TRICOT is 'a knitted fabric.' (In Modern French we have the cognates *trique* 'a cudgel,' *triquet* 'a tennis bat,' and *étriqué* 'scanty, narrow' < 'level measure' as opposed to a 'heaping measure.')

The English word STRICKLE also bears a resemblance to the Latin word *strigilis*, which is not surprising, since they both trace back to the Indo-European root **streig-* 'to stroke, to rub, to press.' *Strigilis* is Anglicized as STRIGIL 'an instrument used by the ancient Greeks and Romans for scraping perspiration from the skin after exercising or in the steam bath.' *Strigilis* is related to the Latin verb *stringo, stringere, strictum*, which has contrasting meanings of 'to touch lightly, to graze' and 'to draw tight together, to contract.' The *OED* affirms that these meanings indicate "two etymologically distinct verbs of coincident form," and then goes on to illustrate this by pointing out different meanings of the English word STRICTURE (from the sense of 'to touch lightly') 'an incidental remark; an adverse remark'; (from the sense of 'to draw tight, to contract') 'a binding, a tightening'; (medical) 'a morbid narrowing of a canal or duct' (*-ure* < Latin *-ura* 'act of, process of'). If the two Latin verbs are etymologically distinct, then Latin *stringere* probably comes from Indo-European **strenk-/*streng-* 'tight, narrow,' a group into which many etymologists place the words (through *prestigiator*) STRINGENT 'tight, constrictive; strict, rigorously binding' [from the present participle *stringēns, strin-gentem* 'drawing tight'] and STRICT 'enforcing discipline, not permissive; rigidly conforming, devout; precise, exact, rigorous' [from Latin *strictus* 'tight, narrow']. Despite its own 'narrow' significance, Latin *strictus* 'tight, narrow' has a wide assortment of words among its progeny. *Strictus* evolved into Old French *estreit, estroit* (Modern French *étroit* 'narrow, strait'). Going into Middle English *estreit* dropped the initial *e-* to become *streit,* whence Modern English STRAIT 'tight, narrow; a narrow passage of water connecting two large bodies of water'; (often plural) 'a position of difficulty' (sore STRAITS); STRAITEN 'to make narrow; to afflict with difficulties' (STRAITENED circumstances); STRAIT-laced 'wearing a garment that is tightly laced; excessively strict'; and STRAIT jacket 'a long-sleeved garment used to bind the arms against the body,' as a method of restraining violent patients or prisoners. (*Straight* and *straighten* are from a different source, related to *stretch.*) Another Old French version of Latin *strictus* that evolved by way of Vulgar Latin **strictia* is *estrece, estresse* 'narrowness, oppression.' *Estrece, estresse* became, or at least influenced, Middle English *stresse* 'hardship, distress,' and English STRESS 'a force that tends to strain a body; emphasis.' (STRESS is also an aphetic form of DISTRESS. See below.) In Italian, Latin *strictus* became *stretto* 'narrow, strait, tight.' In music we have STRETTO 'a close succession or overlapping of voices in a fugue; the crowding of answer upon subject to produce a climactic effect.' A related musical term that also provides us with a bridge back to Latin *stringere, strictum* 'to draw tight, to contract' is STRINGENDO 'played with an increasing tempo; accelerando' [from Italian *stringendo* 'tightening,' from *stringere* 'to tighten'].

The Latin infinitive *stringere* 'to draw tight, to contract' yielded Old French *estreindre,* whence Middle English *streyne, strayne,* whence English STRAIN 'to pull, stretch tight; to exert to the utmost; to pass through a filter' (or STRAINER); 'an excessive demand on one's resources.' When it comes to English compound words borrowed from this Latin source, we find a series of double and triple forms, such as RESTRAIN 'to hold back; to deprive of freedom' [via Old French *restraindre*]; RESTRICT 'to keep within limits' [both from Latin *restringere*, *restrictum* 'to bind back, to restrict']; CONSTRAIN 'to compel; to keep within bounds'; CONSTRICT 'to make smaller; to squeeze'; and CONSTRINGE 'to cause to contract' [all three ultimately from Latin *constringere*, *constrictum* 'to bind together']. And from Latin *distringere*, *districtum* 'to draw asunder, to torture; to keep from uniting' are DISTRAIN 'to seize property in order to compel payment of debts' [via Old French *destraindre*] and DISTRESS (legal) 'to hold property against the payment of debts'; 'to bring into difficult circumstances, to subject to severe strain; the condition of being in need of immediate assistance' [from Old French *destresse*, *destrece* 'narrow passage, strait,' from Vulgar Latin *districtia* 'narrowness,' from Latin *districtus* 'tortured']. The meaning 'to subject to severe strain,' with the initial *di-* dropped off, yielded the English word STRESS. The Latin past participle *districtus* had by Medieval Latin times become a noun meaning 'area of jurisdiction,' whence English DISTRICT 'a geographical unit marked off for some special purpose'; ASTRICT 'to bind within narrow limits'; and ASTRINGENT 'having the power to draw soft organic tissues together' [from Latin *astringere*, *astrictum* 'to draw together' (*a-* < *ad* 'to, at, toward')].

9775

9780

9785

9790

9795

Unexpected in this company and of a curious derivation is the English loanword PRESTIGE 'the power to command admiration; a commanding position in men's minds derived from general esteem.' What makes the derivation curious is that PRESTIGE comes from a Latin phrase meaning 'to blindfold,' *praestringere oculos* 'to bind up the eyes,' hence 'to blind, to dazzle' (with one's skill or brilliance). This meaning was developed by the speakers of Classical Latin, but not in an approving sense, for their word *praestigiae* (for *praestrigiae*) meant 'conjuring tricks; illusions, deceptions.' Up to the 17th century, the derived French noun *prestige* meant 'deceits, impostures, delusions, juggling or cozening tricks,' as translated by Randle Cotgrave in his *Dictionarie of the French and English Tongues* (1611). The modern French meanings are 'fascination, magic spell; prestige.' (Latin *prestigiātor* 'conjuror; cheat' had some influence on the coining of the word *prestidigitator* 'sleight-of-hand artist.' See line 6297.)

9800

9805

9810

Undoubtedly derived from Indo-European *strenk-* 'tight, narrow' is the Anglo/Germanic word STRING 'a cord, thicker than thread; a set or series of related things' [from Old English *streng*, from Germanic *strangi-*]. String is used to tie things together by drawing the cord tight. A STRINGED instrument is one that has

9815

cords stretched across a sounding board that are either plucked, strummed, bowed, or struck with hammers. The tighter the strings are stretched, the higher their musical pitch and the nearer to their breaking point. A person who reaches the breaking point more easily than most is said to be *high*-STRUNG. Also from Indo-European *strenk-* 'tight, narrow' are STRONG 'having great physical power; intense' [from Old English *strang*, from Germanic *strangaz*] and STRENGTH 'power; the ability to persevere' [from Old English *strengthu*, from Germanic *strangithō*]. Semantically, the connection is perhaps through the 'tightening' of the muscles caused by making a physical effort.

Greek cousins to these high-tension words are *stranx* 'a drop squeezed out,' *strangos* 'twisted,' and *strangalē* 'a rope, a cord, a halter.' *Strangalē* has a derivative verb, *strangalan* 'to put a halter on; to choke,' that was adopted into Latin as *strangulāre* 'to choke, to throttle,' whence Old French *estrangler*, whence English STRANGLE 'to kill by choking'; STRANGULATE 'to strangle; to twist so as to cut off the supply of blood'; and STRANGURY 'slow painful urination' [*stranx* 'a drop squeezed out' + *ouron* 'urine'].

Returning to Indo-European *streig-* 'to stroke, to rub, to press,' we find two other Latin words of this derivation. They are *striga* 'a furrow, a swath of grain; the flute of a column' and *stria* 'a furrow, flute of a column.' From these English has borrowed STRIGA 'a flute in a column'; STRIGOSE 'marked with fine, close-set grooves or streaks'; STRIA 'a minute groove or channel'; and STRIATION 'a series of parallel grooves.'

We are left with a few English/Germanic words that may or may not be related to the root *streig-* 'to stroke, to rub, to press.' They are STRIPE 'a long narrow band distinguishable from its surroundings' [from Middle Dutch *strīpe*]; STRIP 'a narrow piece of something' (land, cloth, etc.) [possibly a variant of STRIPE; related to Middle Low German *strippe* 'strap, thong']; and STRIPLING 'an adolescent boy' (slender as a STRIP). (Note that the verb to *strip* 'to remove the outer covering' is a different word.)

LI

Tigers Have Style

STYLE is more a matter of intuition than of ETIQUETTE. One can avoid the STIGMATA of a boor by STICKING to one's INSTINCTIVE reactions. This sense of STYLE 'the combination of manner, bearing, and deportment characterizing a particular person or group' seems far removed from the literal meaning, which is 'a sharply pointed instrument used by the ancient Greeks and Romans for writing on waxed tables' [from Latin *stilus* 'a pointed stake; a pointed instrument for writing']. The first figurative use of Latin *stilus* referred to a person's 'manner of writing; manner of expressing himself in writing,' and only later was the meaning expanded to cover the person's general behavior and demeanor. Now the figurative senses of STYLE are varied enough to fill more than two pages in the *OED*. Examples are ' "manner; fashion; a particular type of architecture; a general category based on similar characteristics," ' as well as nonabstract meanings like ' "an instrument for etching or engraving; a phonograph needle; (biology) any slender, tubular, or bristlelike process." ' The spelling of Old French, French, and English *style* with a -*y*- came about through an erroneous belief that Latin *stilus* 'writing instrument' was related to Greek *stulos, stylos* 'pillar' (Greek upsilon was transliterated into Latin as -*y*-, still called "y-Grecque" in French). The Italians knew better, and retained the -*i*- in Italian *stile, stilo* 'style, stylus; custom; knife.' The 'knife' meaning is of interest because it leads to STILETTO 'little knife; a slender dagger, a poniard.' STILETTO in its turn led, via French, to the medical STYLET 'a slender surgical probe.'

A 'pointed stake' made to be applied to the rear ends of reluctant cattle is known as a *goad*, called in Latin *stimulus* 'goad, prick; pointed stake; sting; spur, incentive.' The Latin word was first adopted into English in two medical terms with less vividly

9855

9860

9865

9870

9875

9880

graphic meanings, that is, STIMULUS 'anything that causes a response; something that incites or rouses to action; an incentive' and STIMULANT 'anything that temporarily arouses physiological activity.'

Some etymologists consider Latin *stilus* 'pointed stake; writing instrument' and *stimulus* 'pointed stake; goad' to be of obscure origin (*AHD*), but others see at least the possibility of a Latin root *sti- 'to prick' cognate with the root of English STICK, and therefore traceable to Indo-European *steig- 'to stick; pointed.' *Steig- is ancestor to English STICK 'to pierce with a pointed instrument; a long slender piece of wood' [from Old English *stician* 'to pierce, to stab' and *sticca* 'stick,' from Germanic *stik- and *stikkōn] and STITCH (originally) 'a thrust, a stab'; 'a sharp, sudden, local pain like that produced by the thrust of a pointed weapon; a single complete in-and-out movement of a threaded needle' [from Old English *stice* 'sting, prick,' from Germanic *stikiz]. Here is the origin of the phrase *in* STITCHES 'laughing uncontrollably,' or until one's sides hurt with stitches. *Steig- is also ancestor to English STEAK (originally) 'a piece of meat roasted on a stake'; ' "a small Slice of Meat to be broiled before or on the Fire when a Person cannot or will not stay till a regular Joint is boiled or roasted" ' (Dyche & Pardon, *A New General English Dictionary*, 1735.—*OED*). The connection between STEAK with STICK is that the meat is STUCK through with a spit before roasting. The word STEAK came into English from Old Norse *steik*, cognate with *steikja* 'to roast on a spit.'

While we're on the subject of beefsteak we shall mention an intriguing historical phrase dating back to 15th-century Scotland, to wit, STEAK *raid*. The phrase refers to ' "a custom among the Highlanders, that when a party drove any spoil of cattle through a Gentleman's land, they should give him a part of the spoil" ' (Lachlan Shaw). Sir Walter Scott says that a steak raid was a portion of the robber's booty paid by him to the laird through whose grounds the robber drove his prey. Whose cattle was being despoiled is not specified, although it was presumably the Lowlanders.

To get back to 'pointed sticks,' it would seem only reasonable to find the English word *stake* 'a piece of wood sharpened at one end' in this grouping. Indeed, several dictionaries do make cross-references to English STICK in their discussions of *stake*, indicating that the two words have a mutual ancestor. Others, however, trace *stake* to a different Indo-European root, *steg- 'pole, stick.' Semantically and phonologically, this seems quite close to Indo-European *steig- 'to stick; pointed.' (See Chapter XLIX, lines 9589ff.)

Another Germanic cognate of STICK is TICKET (originally) 'a little notice stuck to anything'; 'an identifying tag, a label; a paper slip indicating its holder is entitled to a specified service' [from French *etiquet(te)*, from Medieval/Old French *estiquet(te)*, from *estiqu(i)er* 'to attach, to stick,' from Middle Dutch *steken* 'to stick, to stab']. Note that the word went through the French form *etiquette*, modern English ETIQUETTE 'the body of prescribed social usages; any special code of behavior' (military ETIQUETTE). How this word meaning 'label, sticker' came to mean 'a code of behavior' is not historically clear. One suggested sequence is: "a label, a ticket, hence certain labels implying a certain order, a certain rank, hence Early French/French court ceremonial, hence formal good manners" (*EP*). The protocol problems of "who comes first?" = "which label outranks which?" may have prompted this semantic evolution.

Also from the Dutch *steken* 'to stick, to stab; to thrust' is English SNICKERSNEE 'a large knifelike sword; cut and thrust fighting with knives.' This word used to be *stick or snee* 'stab or cut,' from Middle Dutch *steken* 'to stab' + *snijden* 'to cut.' The *-t-* of Dutch *steken* became the *-n-* of English *snick-* by assimilation. (See line 9188.) Then there is the STICKLEBACK 'a small fish having erectile spines along the back' [from Middle English *styklbak* 'prickly back,' from Old English *sticel* 'prick, sting' + *baec* 'back']. (A word that is not a cognate is *stickler* 'one who insists on something unyieldingly,' which is related to *stair, stirrup,* and *stile*.)

When we look for Latin cognates derived from the Indo-European root **steig-* 'to stick; pointed' we come upon the combining form *-stīgāre*, seen in *instīgāre, instīgātus* 'to prod, to goad into doing; to incite,' whence English INSTIGATE 'to urge on, to goad; to foment, to stir up.' Latin *instīgāre, instīgātus* 'to incite, to goad' has a nasalized doublet in *instinguere, instinctus* 'to incite, to impel.' ("The problem of these forms is compounded by the appearance of the *-gu-*, which is irregular if they are derived from **steig-*." H. Craig Melchert.) The Latin past participle *instinctus* acquired a substantival meaning of 'incitement, impulse' and has been adapted into English as a semiscientific term and given the special meaning of INSTINCT 'innate, unlearned behavior.'

The 'goading' efficacy of the 'pointed stick' implied by Indo-European **steig-* 'to stick; pointed' is still apparent in INSTINCT, but it becomes less discernible in the Latin compound verb *distinguere, distinctus* 'to adorn, to decorate; to distinguish, to discriminate; to separate, to divide.' The connection with 'pointed' seems to be in the adornments, which are assumed to be of the nature of tattoos, or 'pricked marks' on the skin. (*Distinguere* is also a technical term meaning 'to punctuate.') *Distinguere* ' "to separate by means of pricked marks" ' (*EP*) leads to English DISTINGUISH 'to recognize as being different; to detect' [via Old French *distinguer*, *distinguiss(ant)*, from Latin *distinguere*, *distinctus* (*dis-* 'apart' + *-stinguere* (etymologically) 'to prick'].

The Latin past participle *distinctus* 'separated, marked off' gives us the English loanwords DISTINCT 'easily perceived; well defined'; DISTINCTIVE 'identifying; characteristic'; DISTINCTION 'differentiation; eminence.' The French past participle *distingué* is used in English with almost the same force as the English word DISTINGUISHED 'characterized by excellence; eminent, renowned.'

The accepted classical sense of Latin *stinguere* is not 'to goad, to prick' but 'to quench, to extinguish.' How this meaning was arrived at is a moot question (possibly because drops of water spattering on a fire 'prick it out'?). There are some etymologists who insist that *-stinguere* 'to goad' is "not to be confused with the self-contained, entirely distinct *stinguere* 'to quench' " (*EP*), which they associate rather with Latin *tinguere* 'to moisten.' Others however do make the connection with Latin *distinguere* and English *stick*, thus putting into the **steig-* group the English loanwords EXTINGUISH 'to quench, to put out (a fire, a light); to put an end to' [from Latin *ex(s)tinguere*, *ex(s)tinctus* 'to put out, to annihilate,' from *ex-* 'out' + *stinguere* 'to quench'] and EXTINCT 'no longer existing in living form; no longer in use; no longer active.'

In Greek, the Indo-European root **steig-* 'to stick; pointed' shows up in the word *stigma* 'prick, point; blemish, brandmark,' and the related verb *stizein* 'to prick, to tattoo.' *Stigma* was adopted into Latin with meanings of 'brand, mark of disgrace; cut' and, in the late 16th century, was borrowed into English as STIGMA 'a mark of disgrace or reproach'; (archaic) 'a mark burned into the skin of a criminal or slave.' These are not very flattering meanings, contrary to that of the plural STIGMATA 'marks resembling the crucifixion wounds of Jesus that sometimes appear on the bodies of persons in a state of religious ecstasy.' STIGMA also has a number of scientific meanings, mostly having to do with spots and small openings such as are made with a needle. In optics it seems to have the meaning of 'focal point,' inasmuch as STIGMATISM means 'a condition of the refractive media of the eye in which rays of light from a point are accurately brought to a point on the retina.' The opposite of this happy condition is ASTIGMATISM 'faulty vision caused by a defect in the lens, as a result of which light rays from a single point of an object fail to meet in a single focal point.' Camera lenses are often described as being ANASTIGMATIC, that is, having an ANASTIGMAT lens, or one that corrects for the aberrations of ASTIGMATISM.

Our next word is borrowed ultimately from Avestan, the eastern dialect of Old Iranian and oldest attested language of the Iranian branch of Indo-European. The dialect is called Avestan because it is the language of the *Avesta*, the sacred books of the ancient Persians, some of them perhaps written by Zoroaster (Zarathustra) himself. The English word is TIGER 'a large Asiatic feline' [via Old English *tigras* (plural) and Old French *tigre* from Latin *tigris*, *tigrem*, from Greek *tigris* 'tiger,' from Avestan *tigra* 'sharp, pointed.' (*AHD*)]. Related Avestan words are *tighra-* 'pointed' and *tighri-* 'arrow.' The semantic reference may be to the sharpness of a tiger's fangs or claws or, as others suggest, to its swiftness: "the tiger is arrow-swift" (*EP*). Similarly, the TIGRIS 'a river of Mesopotamia' is very rapid in its upper reaches. TIGER and TIGRIS come from a "reduced" form of Indo-European **steig* 'pointed,' that is, **tig-*, a form without the initial *s-* or the *-e-*.

We have already mentioned Indo-European **steg-* 'pole, stick,' ancestor of *stake* and many other words. There is yet another sticky Indo-European root, to wit, **stegh-* 'to prick.' In the nasalized form **stengh-*, this root shows up in Germanic as **stengjan-*, whence Old English *stingan*, whence English STING 'to pierce with a sharp pointed organ; to cause to feel a sharp smarting pain.' The adjective STINGY 'niggardly, tight-fisted' also comes from STING, by way of a dialectal pronunciation "stindge," and the notion that a STINGY person is 'sharp, acerb.'

Also from the root **stegh-* 'to prick' is English STAG 'the adult male of various deer; a man who attends a social affair without escorting a woman; an animal, especially a pig, castrated after reaching sexual maturity.' Originally, the word seems to have meant 'a male animal in its prime.'

10020

10025

10030

10035

10040

10045

LII

Typical Students

To the STUDENT, TOILING away at his desk, the road ahead
10050   sometimes seems impossibly STEEP. He sees himself as TYPIFY-
ING failure, as being hopelessly OBTUSE and STUPID, a STEPCHILD
of fortune. The situation is rarely as bad as all that, so before we
lose ourselves in pity for the unfortunate chap, let's go back and
examine some of the words that have been used, STUDENT, TOIL,
10055   STEEP, TYPIFY, OBTUSE, STUPID, and STEPCHILD.
The Indo-European root involved here is *steu- 'to push,
stick, knock, beat, pound; fragments and projecting objects.' This
root shows up with a figurative sense in the Latin verb *studēre*
(etymologically) 'to push forward,' hence 'to be zealous about; to
10060   pay attention to; to apply oneself to mentally; to study.' The
present participle of Latin *studēre* is *studēns* 'studying,' borrowed
into English as STUDENT 'one who zealously pushes forward; one
who seeks knowledge.' A related Latin noun is *studium*, which,
according to the *Langenscheidt Shorter Latin Dictionary* means
10065   'zeal, eagerness, application, enthusiasm, desire,' as well as 'favor,
inclination, attachment, devotion.' One is struck by the Roman
zest for what today may be looked upon as dry and boring, to wit,
STUDY 'a setting of the mind upon a subject to be learned; the
pursuit of knowledge' [from Middle English *studie*, from Old
10070   French *estudie*, from Latin *studium*]. Old French *estudie* also
becomes Modern French *étude* 'study,' a word adopted into
English as ÉTUDE 'a musical piece written for the practice and
development of some point of technique,' though the études of
Chopin, Prokofiev, et al., are also performed as concert pieces. In
10075   Late Latin the word *studium* developed the sense of 'a place of
study,' whence the Italian, whence English STUDIO 'an establishment where an art is taught and studied; an artist's workshop.'

On another tack, Latin *studēre* 'to pay attention to' is thought to have evolved into Vulgar Latin **(e)studiāre* 'to take care of,' which became Old French *estuier* 'to guard; to shut in,' with   10080
related noun *estui* 'prison; container.' Old French *estui* 'container' is the ancestor of Modern French *étui* 'case, box,' whence English ETUI, ETWEE 'a fancy case for small articles.' The plural of ETWEE is ETWEES, the antecedent of English TWEEZERS 'small pincers for plucking hairs and handling small objects,'   10085
because those instruments were carried about in small cases.

In STUPEFYING contrast to the STUDIOUS group of words descended from Indo-European *steu 'to push, knock, beat, pound' is another group typified by the Latin verb *stupēre* 'to be stunned, to be (knocked) senseless; to be amazed, to be sur-   10090
prised.' *Stupēre* and its relatives have given us the English loanwords STUPOR 'a state of reduced sensibility' [from Latin *stupor* 'senselessness; amazement']; STUPID 'slow to learn; slow to react; in a state of senselessness' [from Latin *stupidus* 'sense-less; amazed']; STUPEFY 'to dull the senses; to amaze, to astonish'   10095
[via Old French *stupefier* from Latin *stupefacere* 'to render senseless, to stun; to amaze']; and STUPENDOUS 'amazing, aston-ishing, wonderful; immense' [from Latin *stupendus* 'astonishing, to be wondered at']. The 'amazement' of the Latin words has vanished from English STUPOR and STUPID, but remains   10100
in STUPEFY and STUPENDOUS. So, a STUPID STUDENT is twice descended from Indo-European **steu-*.

If you cut off the initial *s-* of the Latin root *stup-* and add the suffix *-os* you will have Greek *tupos* 'a stroke, a blow; an impress, stamp, mark; a figure, image, statue; an outline, sketch, model,   10105
TYPE.' This is not what actually happened linguistically, of course: rather, the Indo-European extended root **steup-* had an aphetic, *s*-less variant **teup-*. (Compare HALF, line 9073.) The addition of the noun-forming suffix *-o-* caused the vocalism to change to zero-grade (without the *-e-*), which gives us **tupo-*,   10110
which with the nominative singular ending *-s* yields Greek *tupos*. Greek *tupos* was adapted into Latin as *typus* 'figure, image,' whence Late Latin *typus* 'pattern, model, symbol, type,' whence English TYPE 'a distinctive stamp; the general character common to a number of individuals; an example or model; a raised letter   10115
that leaves a printed impression; to write with a TYPEWRITER.' The following English derivatives and compounds are mostly self-explanatory: TYPICAL, TYPIST, TYPOGRAPHY, TYPIFY 'to serve as an example of; to represent by an image,' ARCHETYPE and PROTOTYPE 'an original model.'   10120

The Greek verb corresponding to the noun *tupos* 'a stroke, a blow' is *tuptein* 'to strike.' *Tuptein* has a nasalized relative, *tumpanizein* 'to beat a drum,' the drum being of course a *tumpanon*, or to use the Latin adaptation, a *tympanum*. In 10125 Medieval Latin the word *tympanum* is used to mean 'eardrum,' and it is still so used in anatomical and zoological parlance. The Italians, however, kept the musical significance of 'drum' in *timpano* 'kettledrum,' plural TIMPANI = TYMPANI 'a set of kettledrums; large, tunable, hemispherical drums with parchment 10130 heads.' The fellow who beats on TIMPANI, TYMPANI is a TIMPANIST, TYMPANIST, not to be confused with TYMPANITES 'distension of the abdomen caused by an accumulation of gas.' Other modern meanings of TYMPANUM are 'the diaphragm of a telephone'; (zoology) 'a thin, tight membrane'; (architecture) 'the 10135 panel formed by the cornices of a triangular pediment.' In printing, the word has a specialized meaning when shortened to TYMPAN 'a membrane placed between the paper and the impressing surfaces.' There are still other meanings when the word is further shortened to TYMP (metallurgy) 'the mouth of the 10140 hearth of a blast furnace'; (British mining) 'a horizontal timber for supporting the roof of a mine.'

Getting back to Greek *tumpanon* 'drum,' we take note of a Byzantine Greek descendant *tumbanon, timbanon* which was adopted into Vulgar Latin as *timbano* 'a drum.' Vulgar Latin 10145 *timbano* evolved into Old French *timbene, *timbne, *timbre* (originally) 'a kettledrum'; (later) 'a church bell struck with a hammer; a table bell.' The English speakers made *timbre* into the diminutive TIMBREL 'a small hand drum; a tambourine,' thus preserving the 'drum' meaning. However, the acoustical sense of 10150 TIMBRE 'the quality of a musical sound, including the human voice, that distinguishes it from other sounds of the same pitch' arose from the distinctive sounds made by bells, since this acoustical difference is "caused by the proportions in which the fundamental tone is combined with the overtones" (*OED*). This 10155 musical/acoustical meaning developed in French in the 17th century and was adopted into English in the 18th. (*Tymber* was used in Middle English to mean 'kettledrum.' Wyclif used it to translate Latin *tympanum* in his rendering of the Bible. In Modern French, *timbre* also means 'a bell,' which is struck, and 'a 10160 stamp, a postmark,' both of which are pounded.)

Strikingly similar in both form and sense to these Greek words are those that have come to English from the Persian, by way of Arabic, Spanish, Italian, and Old French. They are *tabor*, *tambour, tambourine*, and *taboret*, all meaning 'a drum' of one 10165 kind or another, with additional figurative senses. The original Persian word was *tabīr(āh)* or *tabūrāk* 'drum.' As if this did not provide us with enough words for 'drum,' there is yet another

similar enough to be mistaken for a cognate, that is *timbal* 'a kettledrum,' from French *timbale*, from Medieval French *tamballe*, from Spanish *atabal*, from Arabic *attabal*, for *al-tabl*   10170
'the drum.' This is as far as the experts carry the etymology of *timbal*, but it wouldn't surprise me to learn that Arabic *tabl* 'drum' was indeed related to Persian *tabīr(āh)* 'drum.' None of the above, however, from *tabor* to *timbal*, is held to be cognate with Greek *tumbanon, tupos, tuptein*, etc.   10175

Indo-European **steu-* 'to push, to knock, to beat, to pound' has a Latin descendant, nasalized and (like Greek *tupos, tumbanon*) without the initial s-, in the verb *tundere* 'to beat, to strike; to thresh, to pound.' *Tundere* sounds as if it might be related to English *thunder*, but it isn't. In fact, there is no longer any simple   10180
English loanword from this Latin verb, although English TUND 'to beat with a stick' is obsolete British schoolboy slang referring to whippings administered to younger boys by their officially appointed older fellows. ("To put a stick into the hand of a boy of sixteen and allow him to use it upon his schoolfellows . . . is   10185
neither fair on the tunder or the tunded." —Lord Sherbrooke in an 1876 letter quoted in the *OED*.) The Latin verb *tundere* 'to best, to strike' does live on in the English compounds CONTUSE 'to injure without breaking the skin; to bruise' [from Latin *contundere, contūsus* 'to crush, to bruise']; CONTUSION 'a bruise; an   10190
injury causing effusion of blood beneath the skin without the skin's breaking'; OBTUSE 'blunted; slow-witted; greater than a right angle' [from Latin *obtundere, obtūsus* 'to beat upon, to dull']; OBTUND 'to dull, to deaden'; RETUSE (botany) 'having a rounded apex, with a slight notch' [from Latin *retundere, retūsus*   10195
'to beat back']; PERTUSE 'punched; having holes; (of earlobes) pierced'; PIERCE 'to run through as with a sharp instrument; to make a hole in' [from Old French *percer, percier*, from Vulgar Latin **pertūsiāre*, from Latin *pertundere, pertūsus* 'to thrust through']. Backing up the unattested Vulgar Latin *pertūsiāre* are   10200
Provençal *pertusar* and Italian *pertugiare* 'to pierce.' (However, some etymologists trace Old French *percer* to Vulgar Latin **peritiāre* < Latin *peritus, perīre* 'to perish.')

Latin *tund(ere)* denasalized or *stud(ere)* with the initial s-dropped off would both yield *tud-* (< Indo-European **tud-* <   10205
Indo-European **steu-* 'to push, knock, beat, pound'). There is in fact a Latin noun with this root, *tudes* 'hammer, mallet,' as well as its diminutive *tudicula* 'a small hammer.' *Tudicula* was used colloquially for 'a machine for bruising olives, a mill for crushing olives.' This usage led to the development of a verb, *tudiculāre*   10210
'to stir about,' which evolved into Old French *tooillier* 'to stir, to agitate; to pull or drag about; to cause to roll or writhe.' From this

expressive verb came Norman French *toiler* 'to wrangle,' whence
Middle English *toilen* 'to struggle, to battle,' whence, much
10215 diminished in intensity, the Modern English word TOIL 'to make
one's way with difficulty; to labor continuously; exhausting labor.'
(*Toil(s)* 'entrapment, snare' comes from a different source via
French *toile* 'web, net.')

From Indo-European **tud-ti-*, suffixed variant zero-grade
10220 form of **steu-* 'to push, etc.' comes Latin *tussis* 'cough,' whence
English TUSSIS 'a cough'; TUSSIVE 'pertaining to a cough'; PER-
TUSSIS 'whooping cough'; and PERTUSSIN 'trade name for a cough
syrup.'

Except for the river STYX (which we shall save for the end,
10225 appropriately enough), that about finishes off the derivatives of
Indo-European **steu-* 'to push, to beat; fragments and projecting
objects' that have reached English as borrowings from the classical languages. However, there are many and various Germanic
derivatives to consider, and we shall find ourselves gradually
10230 getting away from the notions of 'pushing, knocking, beating,
pounding' and dealing more with the results and side effects of
such actions, as well as "fragments, projecting objects and certain
related expressive notions and qualities" (*AHD*).

We start off with STUNT 'to check the growth of' [from Old
10235 English *stunt* 'dull, stupid,' from Germanic **stuntaz*]. There is a
discernible semantic connection here with OBTUND 'to dull,' but
the modern sense of STUNT has been affected by the Old Norse
word *stuttr* 'short, dwarfish.' Note, also, STINT (originally) 'to cut
short; to stop'; 'to restrict; a limited amount; a fixed amount of
10240 work to be done' [from Old English *styntan* 'to blunt, to dull,'
from Germanic **stuntjan*]. Some etymologists see in English
STINT 'a fixed amount of work, a task' the source of the American
colloquialism *stunt* 'an unusual feat of skill.' But most label this
word as of obscure origin, while others suggest a derivation from
10245 *stump* 'a dare, a challenge.' Another Germanic derivative of Indo-
European **steu-* is STUB 'the short, blunt part of anything after the
larger part had been broken, torn or worn off; stump' [from Old
English *stub(b)*, *styb(b)*, from Germanic **stubbaz*, **stybbaz*].
However, *stump* 'the short part remaining after the larger part has
10250 broken away,' similar though it is to the **steu-* words, is ascribed
to a different root, related to *stamp*. Even more surprising is that
stubble is not related to STUB, but comes instead from Latin
stipula 'stalk, stem, stubble,' although the *OED* maintains, "it is
possible that [*stubble*] may have coalesced with a native word of
10255 similar meaning from the root of STUB." Furthermore, STUBBORN
'obstinate' [from Middle English *stoborne*, *stiborne*] is said by
many to be "probably," "perhaps," or "apparently" related to

STUB. The *ODEE* says this "connexion . . . cannot be proved," and the *AHD* lists Middle English *stoborne* as of obscure origin. Note, also, STUTTER ' "to push one's tongue too hard" ' (*EP*); 'to speak with a spasmodic repetition of consonants and syllables' [from Middle English *stutten*, from Germanic **staut-* 'to push, to force'], related to Middle Dutch *stotteren* and Middle Low German *stötern*. Germanic **staut-* is also the ancestor of STUD-DINGSAIL, STUNSAIL 'a sail set on an extension of the yardarm (thrusting out),' pronounced "stuns'l" even when spelled STUD-DINGSAIL. Yet another Germanic derivative of Indo-European **steu-* is STOCK (originally) 'a tree trunk'; 'a supporting structure; the more massive part of an instrument' (gunSTOCK); 'the original progenitor from which others have descended; lineage; family; a fund or store, as of money' (shares of STOCK, STOCKholders), 'animals' (liveSTOCK), 'raw materials' (paper STOCK, soup STOCK) [from Old English *stoc(c)* 'tree trunk,' from Germanic **stukkaz*]. The *OED* has sixty-five headings of listings trailing after the noun STOCK, while *MW3* has forty-nine. Included on both lists is STOCK (obsolete) 'a covering for the leg and foot,' originally differentiated into *nether-stocks* and *upper-stocks. Nether-stocks* became STOCKINGS 'close-fitting garments covering the foot and leg.' Some etymologists suggest as a source for STOCKINGS a humorous allusion to the STOCKS 'an instrument of punishment consisting of a heavy timber frame for confining the ankles, or ankles and wrists.'

Germanic **stukkaz* is evidenced in Modern German by the word *Stock* 'stick, walking cane.' English has adopted this German word in the compound ALPENSTOCK 'a long staff with an iron point used by mountain climbers.' (English *stick*, however, comes from a different root. See Chapter LI, lines 9891ff.)

Here we run into a difference of opinion among the experts concerning the English words STOKER, STOKE, and STUCCO, which are assigned by some to the Indo-European root **steu-* 'to push, knock, beat, pound,' but which, according to others, are related to *stick* and therefore to Indo-European **steig-* 'to stick; pointed.' Having pointed out the discrepancy, we'll take note of STOKER 'one that feeds and tends a furnace' [from Dutch *stoker*, from *stoken* 'to feed a fire']. The English verb to STOKE 'to feed, stir up and poke the fire in a furnace' is a back-formation from STOKER, but there is also an obsolete English verb to STOKE 'to pierce or stab a person; to make a thrust at' [from Old French *estoquier*, ultimately from Germanic **stukkaz*]. Note, also, STUCCO 'a kind of plaster for covering walls' [from Italian *stucco*, from Old High German *stucchi* 'crust'], akin to Old High German *stukki* 'fragment; crust, covering.' The semantic connection is presumably through the materials (lime, gypsum, sand, and marble) which have been pounded into a powder with larger fragments. (Compare German *Stück* 'piece, fragment.')

We get away from the 'knocking, beating, pounding' significations of *steu-* and back to the 'pushing' sense evidenced in *studium* when we come to the Germanic *stiup-* 'pushed out; deprived, bereft.' *Stiup-* evolved into the Old English prefix *steop-*, whence Modern English STEP-, denoting 'relationship by virtue of a remarriage,' as in STEPFATHER, STEPDAUGHTER, STEPSON. The original meaning of STEPCHILD = STEPBAIRN was 'a bereaved child, an orphan,' thus, etymologically speaking, a STEPMOTHER is ' "one who becomes mother to an orphan" ' (*OED*).

The next two words have to do with 'projecting objects': STEEP 'precipitous; having a slope approaching the perpendicular; having a high inclination; exorbitant' [from Old English *steap* 'lofty; deep; projecting,' from Germanic *staup-*] and STEEPLE 'a tall structure surmounting the tower of a church or other public edifice' [from Old English *stēpel, stȳpel*, from Germanic *staupilaz*]. A STEEPLECHASE was originally exactly that, i.e. 'a cross-country horse race with a steeple in view as the goal.' An ablaut relative of STEEP is STOOP 'to bow down, to descend' [from Old English *stūpian*, from Germanic *stūp-*]. *Stoop* 'a porch,' however, is from a different root, while *stoop* 'a holy water font' is from yet another.

Finally, from the Greek *Stux* by way of Latin *Styx* we get the STYX ' "the Hateful, the Horrible" ' (*L&S*); (in Greek mythology) 'the principal river of the lower world which had to be crossed to get to the regions of the dead.' The Greek word *stux* also means 'that which is hated' and is related to the verb *stugein* 'to hate,' the noun *stugos* 'hatred,' and the adjective *stugnos* 'hateful, gloomy.' Hence, via Latin *Stygius*, the English adjective STYGIAN 'gloomy, hellish,' as in the phrase STYGIAN *oath* 'inviolable oath,' since even the gods feared to break an oath sworn by the Styx. The semantic connection with *steu-* 'to push, knock, beat, pound' is obscure. In fact not everyone ascribes *stug-* 'hate' to *steu-* 'to push,' but rather to *stewə-* 'to condense, to congeal.'

LIII

Vasty Vacuous Wastes; Wanton Vanity

A VACUUM is a VOID is a VACUITY, and the whole nothingness 10340 sounds like a terrible WASTE, which in one sense it is, since one of the earliest meanings of the word WASTE is 'uninhabited, uncultivated land.' These words for the absence-of-anything are all thought to be related, and to stem from the Indo-European root *eu- 'lacking, empty,' which has extended forms *wā-, *was- and 10345 *wak-, among others. The extended form *wak- shows up in the intransitive Latin verb vacāre 'to be empty; to be free from duties,' whose present participle vacāns, vacant(em) has given us English VACANT 'unoccupied, containing nothing' [by way of Old French vacant]. The Latin past participle vacātus has given us 10350 the transitive English verb VACATE 'to give up the occupancy of,' and the associated Latin noun vacātiō, vacātiōn(em) leads to English VACATION 'a leave of absence for rest and relaxation' [via Old French vacation]. You stop 'occupying' your job, you give up your duties for a while, so that your post is VACANT. The meaning 10355 of VACATION fits in well with the 'free from duties' meaning of Latin vacāre. Latin vacātiō meant 'freedom from, immunity, exemption,' including 'exemption from military service.'

An adjectival derivative of Latin vacāre 'to be empty' is vacuus 'empty,' of which the neuter form was and is used as a 10360 noun, whence English VACUUM 'empty space.' Some secondary meanings of Latin vacuus are interesting, though irrelevant to English: for instance, 'free from care; heart-whole; single, unmarried, divorced; at leisure, quiet, calm.' Other Latin meanings ('worthless, useless, vain') are reflected in the English word 10365 VACUOUS 'devoid of serious occupation, spent in inanities and frivolity; lacking intelligence.' From the Latin adjective vacuus there developed the noun vacuitās, which was borrowed into English as VACUITY 'total absence of matter; emptiness; an

10370   unfilled cavity within a body.' Perversely, the French coined from Latin *vacuum* 'emptiness' the diminutive VACUOLE 'a little vacuum; a small cavity in the tissues of an organism containing air or fluid.' In this case the 'empty' sense is apparently interpreted as meaning 'empty of *solid* matter.'

10375   The archaic English verb, to *vacuate*, from Latin *vacuāre* 'to empty' has been replaced by the compound EVACUATE 'to make empty; to withdraw from' [from Latin *ēvacuāre* 'to empty out' (*e-* < *ex-* 'out')].

There were in Latin, living alongside *vacāre, vacuus, vacīvus*

10380   ('empty, void') two alternate forms in *-o-: vocāre* and *vocīvus*. *Vocīvus* 'empty, void' was dissimilated into Vulgar Latin **vocitus* 'completely empty,' while Old French, dropping the middle consonant as usual, changed **vocitus* into *vuit, vuide*. A dialectal variant, *voit, voide*, came into Middle English as *voide, void*,

10385   whence Modern English VOID 'containing no matter; ineffective, useless; having no legal force.' The Modern French is *vide* 'empty, void.' There are two English compounds: DEVOID 'completely lacking' [from Old French *desvuidier* (*des-* < Latin *dē-* (here) 'utterly,' or *dis-* 'utterly')] and AVOID (literally) 'to empty

10390   out'; (legal) 'to invalidate'; 'to shun' [via Norman-French *avoider* from Old French *esvuidier* 'to empty out' (*es-* < *ex-* 'out')]. (Some etymologists, however, credit the Norman French *a-* to Latin *ā-*, *ab-* 'away from.')

Another group of words descended from Indo-European **eu-*,

10395   **was-* 'empty' is typified by the Latin adjective *vāstus* 'empty, deserted, waste, desolate, uncultivated.' *Vāstus* evolved into Old French *guast*, Old Northern French *wast*, and Middle English *wast*. At this point the word ran into a synonymous Germanic cousin, Old English *wēste* 'uninhabited, uncultivated,' related to

10400   Modern German *wüst* 'desert, waste, uncultivated.' It seems to be the Romance cousin that won out, in the form of English WASTE 'wild, uncultivated, deserted; to use uneconomically; to squander; a worthless by-product.' The Old French spelling with *gu-* and the Northern French spelling with *w-* indicate a Germanic influ-

10405   ence somewhere along the line (Latin *v* does not usually change to French *gu*, but Germanic **w* does). The influence that led to the Romanic **wasto* representing Latin *vāstus* is found in Old High German *wuosti* or Old Frankish *wōsti* 'waste, desert.' The Modern French *gâté* 'spoiled' from Old French *guast* descended

10410   from Latin *vāstus*/Frankish *wōsti*.

WASTE as a verb, noun, and adjective has developed meanings of 'squandering' and 'worthlessness' that now predominate over the notion of 'emptiness.' Symptomatic of this semantic shift is the word WASTREL (originally) 'a tract of waste land'; (later) 'an article of imperfect workmanship'; 'a second'; 'an idler, a loafer.' 10415

Latin *vāstus* has a derivative verb, *vāstāre* 'to lay waste, to ravage,' with an intensive form *dēvāstāre* 'to ravage completely,' whence English DEVASTATE 'to lay utterly to waste.'

There is another Latin *vastus*, with a short *a*, that means 'immense, very extensive; barren, deserted land' (or seas, as in 10420 Shakespeare's "VASTY deep"). The obvious English loanword is VAST 'immense.'

Yet a third group of words descended from Indo-European *eu-*, *wā-* 'empty' is exemplified by Latin *vānus* 'empty, void, hollow; vain.' *Vānus* became Old French, whence English VAIN 10425 'empty; devoid of value; fruitless, futile; having undue pride in one's appearance.' The last meaning shows up in English VANITY 'excessive pride in one's appearance or accomplishments.' VAN- ITY traces back to Latin *vanitās*, where the primary meanings are 'emptiness; unreality; mere show,' meanings which are also 10430 shared by the English word. An expressive compound is VAIN- GLORY 'boastful and unwarranted celebration of one's accomplish- ments.' *Waynglori* first appears in English literature in 1300. It is a translation of Latin *vāna glōria*, a phrase used by Livy. (The old Romans also had the words *vāni-loquentia* 'boastful prating,' and 10435 *vāni-loquus* 'lying.')

Consistent with all this self-adulation is the Late Latin verb *vānitāre* 'to be vain,' attested by the gerund *vānitantes* 'vain people.' *Vānitāre* evolved into Old French *vanter* 'to be vain,' and developed an extended sense of 'to be boastful.' *Vanter* has 10440 come into English as VAUNT 'to brag, to brag about,' most often encountered in the past participle VAUNTED, as in "the VAUNTED Rumanian gymnastics team."

Another verb that developed on the base of Latin *vānus* 'empty' is *vānēscere* (etymologically) 'to begin to become empty; 10445 to fade away, to disappear.' (*-Escere* is an inceptive verb ending, that is, it indicates that the action expressed by the verb is beginning.) *Vānēscere* has an intensive form, *ēvānēscere* 'to disap- pear (out),' with the present participle *ēvānēscēns*, from which English has adopted EVANESCENT 'tending to dissipate like vapor; 10450 impermanent, transitory.' Old French adopted the Vulgar Latin equivalent of *ēvānēscere*, to wit, *exvānīre*, and changed it to *esvanir*, with the present stem *esvaniss(ant)*. Going over into Middle English the initial *es-* was dropped and the word became *vanissen*, *vanisshen*, whence Modern English VANISH 'to disap- 10455 pear; to become invisible.' An uncommon English form with the same meaning is EVANISH. (In Modern French the reflexive *s'évanouir* means 'to disappear, to fade away; to swoon.') Some

10460 etymologists suggest the possibility that Latin *inānis* 'empty, vain' and *ināne* 'empty space; vanity' may come from an older, unattested form, **invānus*, but the suggestion is not looked upon favorably by many. English borrowings from this Latin source are INANE 'empty space; the void; empty, silly, lacking substance' and INANITION 'exhaustion; emptiness.'

10465 On the subject of 'beginning to disappear,' that is exactly what happens to the moon when it is on the WANE 'a gradual diminishing' [from Middle English *wane* 'defect, shortage,' from Old English *wana* 'lack,' from Germanic **wanēn*]. The noun WANE has an interesting meaning for those concerned with

10470 lumber, since it refers to boards sawn from near the outside of the log that have imperfect edges: WANE 'the amount by which a plank falls short of being square; the defective edge of a plank that is not properly squared.' Some authorities see the possibility of a relationship between WANE and the adjective WAN (origi-

10475 nally) 'dark-hued; gloomy; sad, dismal'; (obsolete) 'of an unhealthy color; livid'; (of a heavenly body) 'partially obscured, faint; pale, faded.' These meanings show a progression from 'dark-hued' to 'pale,' aided, the *OED* suggests, by its application to 'heavenly bodies when obscured.'

10480 Undoubtedly derived from Indo-European **eu-*, **wā-* 'empty' is the once-prevalent English prefix *wan-* 'lacking,' still found in some Scottish and northern England dialects, and exemplified by words like *wanchancy* 'lacking in luck: dangerous,' *wandought* 'one who lacks strength; a puny creature,' *wangrace* 'lack of

10485 grace: wickedness,' *wanhope* 'despair; delusion,' *wanruly* 'unruly,' *wanweird* 'an unhappy fate,' and *wanworth* 'a bargain; anything worthless.'

Cognates survive in certain Modern German compounds with *Wahn-* (for *wan-*), like *Wahnwitz* 'lack of reason,' *Wahnsinn* 'lack

10490 of sense,' and *Wahnhoffung* 'vain hope.' However, the only current, universally used English word with the prefix WAN- 'lacking' is WANTON (etymologically) 'lacking in discipline; mindlessly brutal; unchaste, lewd' [from *wan-* 'lacking' + *towen* for *togen* 'drawn; brought up'], that is, 'lacking the proper bringing

10495 up.' The word dates back to the 13th century.

Finally there is WANT 'to lack; deficiency, shortage, lack; to desire, to wish for' [from Old Norse *vanta* 'to be lacking']. The meaning 'to desire, to wish for' did not arise until the early 18th century.

10500 Thus WASTE and WANT stem from the same root. The notions contrasted in the old saw "Waste not want not" are closer perhaps than the soothsayers knew—or than a *wantwit* 'a fool' could tell.

LIV

The Way of a Wag

The reason a quipster like Groucho Marx is called a WAG is not that his tongue WAGS so much (plus, in Groucho's case, WAGGLING eyebrows and cigar), but that jokers like him are apt to end their days WAGGLING from the end of a hangman's rope. In other words he's what was called in 16th-century England a WAGHALTER 'one who is likely to swing from a halter; a gallows bird.' This term of opprobrium was early shortened to WAG and applied humorously to mischievous boys and habitual pranksters. At least that's one theory advanced to explain the meaning of the noun WAG 'a jester; one full of sport and humor,' even though in the *OED* the earliest use of WAG 'a mischievous boy' (1553) antedates the earliest use of WAGHALTER (1570). More commonly used is the verb WAG 'to move briskly and repeatedly from side to side' [from Middle English *waggen*; from the root of Old English *wagian* 'to move about; to totter, to sway'], as a friendly or excited dog does his tail. WAGGLE 'to move back and forth or up and down repeatedly' is labeled by the authorities a "frequentative" of WAG, thus meaning 'to wag frequently' (though it strikes me as being a diminutive meaning 'to wag a little'). A WAGTAIL is 'one of a genus of birds characterized by long, constantly waggling tails.'

The source of all these words is Indo-European **wegh-* 'to move, to set in motion; to go, to transport in a vehicle.' The more specialized sense of 'to transport in a vehicle' hints at the fact that WAG, WAGGLE, WAGHALTER, and WAGTAIL are all first cousins to English WAGON 'a four-wheeled vehicle' [from Middle Dutch *wagen*], a vehicle in which things are transported. Wagons range all the way from children's go-carts through the homely VOLKS-WAGEN 'people's wagon' to that once luxurious mode of travel, the WAGON-LIT (literally) 'wagon-bed'; 'a continental European

10505

10510

10515

10520

10525

10530

railway sleeping car' [French *lit* 'bed']. The Old English words for four-wheeled vehicles were *wægen*, *wægn*, and *wæn*, predecessors of English WAIN 'a large horse-drawn farm wagon.' The very similar Dutch word *wagen* > WAGON was first adopted as a military term learned in the continental wars of the 16th century. Related words are WAINWRIGHT 'a builder of wagons' and WAINSCOT (etymologically) 'planking for wagons'; 'wood paneling applied to the walls of rooms' [from Middle Dutch or Middle Low German *wagenschot* (*schot* 'wooden partition')]. However, the identity of this Middle Dutch or Middle Low German *wagen* with *wagen* 'wagon' is doubted by some, who refer it to Old Frisian *wāch* = Old English *wāg* 'wall.'

A less easily recognized cognate of WAG 'to move to and fro' and WAGON 'a vehicle (for moving things)' is WEIGH (obsolete) 'to carry from one place to another'; 'to hoist; to raise a ship's anchor; to ascertain the heaviness (WEIGHT) of anything; to consider, to compare' [from Old English *wegan* 'to move, to carry, to weigh']. An Anglian (northern English) variant of Old English *wǣge* 'weight' was *wēg*, *wēge*, which became in northern Middle English *wei*, *we*, and was usually associated with the word 'little' so that 'a little wee' meant 'a little weight,' also 'a little bit (of anything).' Eventually the noun *wee* 'weight' came to be used as an adjective meaning 'very small': WEE 'tiny' (a WEE lad, a WEE drop, the WEE hours, the WEE folk).

The connection between WAGONING and WEIGHING is not hard to grasp, especially for a trucker, who would also appreciate the connection of both of these words with yet another cognate, that is, WAY 'a passage, road, street, track or path' [from Old English *weg*]. (In Modern German we have *Weg* 'way,' and *bewegen* 'to move.') Additional cognates are AWAY (originally) 'on the way'; 'from this place, from that place; at a little distance; in a different direction' [from Old English *aweg*, *onweg*; from *on weg* 'on the way, on one's way (from)']; ALWAYS 'in every way; at all times' [from Middle English *alle wei*, genitive *alles weis*, *alleweyes*, *alwayes*; from Old English *(e)alne weg* 'all way']; SIDEWAYS; LENGTHWAYS; WAYLAY 'to lie in waiting along the road; to ambush'; WAYFARER 'a traveler along the road'; and WAYWARD = AWAYWARD 'straying from the path.' Yet another cognate is WIGGLE 'to squirm; to move back and forth quickly; to move slightly to and fro,' described by some linguists as a "thinning" of WAGGLE, and certainly cuter.

The Latin word for 'way' is *via* 'way, road, street, route, highway; march, journey.' According to some etymologists, *via* traces back to Indo-European **wegh-* 'to move; to go' by way of Old Latin *veha* and Indo-European **wegh-ya-*. Others, however,

link Latin *via* to Indo-European **wei-* 'to go after something' or
associate it with Latin *vis, vim* 'force.' In English, the Latin word
via is used to mean 'by way of,' but *via* shows up in other English   10580
loanwords, like VIADUCT 'a bridge carrying a road over a valley or
other low-lying area' [from Latin *via* 'road' + *ductus* 'a leading']
(by analogy with *aqueduct*, from Latin *aquaeductus* 'an elevated
structure for supporting a water conduit over low-lying ground')
and VIATICUM 'supplies for a journey; an allowance for traveling   10585
expenses; the Eucharist given to a person in danger of death'
[from Latin *viāticum* 'money for a journey; a soldier's savings';
from *viāticus* 'of a journey' (*via* 'way' + *-āticus* 'pertaining to')].
Late Latin *viāticum* evolved into Old French *veiage, veage,*
viage, voiage, whence Anglo-French, whence Middle English   10590
veiage, viage, voiage, whence Modern English (and French)
VOYAGE 'a long journey to a distant land; a journey across the
open sea.' Thus, what started out as a road, then preparations for
taking to the road, now applies to trips across the trackless ocean,
or into outer space (and what started out as a day's trip, that is, a   10595
journey < *journée* 'a day's traveling' stretches out into years, and
what started out as a step, that is, a *trip* 'to step lightly' becomes a
journey).

The element *via* 'road' appears in many compound English
words, for example DEVIATE 'to turn aside from the path, to stray   10600
off the road; to digress' [from Late Latin *dēviāre, dēviātus* 'to go
off the road']. Late Latin *dēviāre* is based on the Latin adjective
devius 'out of the way; off the road,' which is also the ancestor of
English DEVIOUS 'roundabout, circuitous; not straightforward,
underhanded' and OBVIATE 'to remove from the way; to make   10605
unnecessary by anticipating or circumventing' [from Late Latin
obviāre, obviātus 'to meet, to encounter,' hence 'to prevent' (*ob*
'against, facing' + *via* '(in) the way')]. Here again the Late Latin
verb is based on an earlier Latin adjective, this one *obvius* (<
obviam) '(standing) in the way,' forerunner of English OBVIOUS   10610
(archaic) 'standing in the way'; 'easily perceived.'

In Latin a place where three roads meet is called a *trivium.*
One might expect the related adjective *triviālis* to have something
to do with forks in the road, but instead Latin *triviālis* means
'commonplace, ordinary; what can be met with anywhere, at any   10615
crossroads.' *Triviālis* has been borrowed into English as TRIVIAL
'ordinary, commonplace; of little importance.' The plural noun
TRIVIA 'insignificant matters, trifles' is a recent coinage, although
in Roman antiquity *trivia* meant 'a crossroads,' and capitalized,
'Diana as the three-faced goddess, Hecate.' Essentially a back   10620
formation from TRIVIAL, Modern English TRIVIA is not listed in
the *OED* nor the *OED Supplement* of 1933, but it is in *MW2,*

published 1934. In the Middle Ages a new meaning was assigned to the Latin word TRIVIUM 'the three liberal arts of grammar, rhetoric, and logic forming the elementary division of the seven liberal arts in medieval schools and required of all who would obtain a bachelor's degree.' The other four liberal arts were arithmetic, geometry, astronomy, and music. Together these were known as the QUADRIVIUM, which in Latin means 'crossroads; place where four roads meet.' According to Henry Hallam's *Introduction to the Literature of Europe*, the TRIVIUM and QUAD-RIVIUM were introduced into the halls of learning in the 6th century.

To go along with DEVIOUS and OBVIOUS we have PREVIOUS 'having gone that way before; existing or occurring before something else' [from Latin *praevius* 'going before, leading the way' (*prae* 'before')] and PERVIOUS 'open to passage, allowing passage through' [from Latin *pervius* 'passable, unobstructed' (*per* 'through')]. The last word is more often encountered in the negative IMPERVIOUS 'incapable of being penetrated.'

As already seen in the development of the word VOYAGE, Latin *via* 'way' changed to French *voy-*, or more correctly, to French *voie* 'way.' Similarly, Late Latin *inviāre* 'to send on a journey' became Old French *envoier* 'to send,' and has resulted in the two English words ENVOY 'a messenger sent on a mission; an emissary' and INVOICE 'a detailed list of goods shipped.' INVOICE is a variant spelling of the plural of French *envoi* 'parcel, package; goods forwarded,' i.e., *invois*, construed as a singular and respelled with *-ce* to conform with English usage. Also used in English literature is French ENVOI 'a short concluding stanza of certain verse forms; a parting word.'

Similar words are CONVOY 'to accompany on the way; to escort' [from Old French *conveier, convoier*, from Vulgar Latin **conviāre* (*con* < *cum* 'together with')] and CONVEY 'to carry from one place to another; to communicate, to make known' [from Old French *conveier, convoier* and Vulgar Latin **conviāre*].

The Classical Latin verb descended from Indo-European **wegh-* 'to move, to transport in a vehicle' is *vehere, vectus* 'to carry, to transport.' The most obvious English borrowing is VEHICLE 'any device for carrying passengers or goods; a medium of expression' [via French *véhicule* from Latin *vehiculum* 'convey-ance']. The Latin suffix *-iculum*, whence English *-icle*, usually indicates a diminutive, as in *particle* 'a little part,' *auricle* 'a little ear,' *versicle* 'a little verse,' and *article* 'a little joint, division,' but in this case it seems to be used as an instrumental suffix meaning 'means of (carrying).'

A word that is listed in some English dictionaries as foreign and not listed at all in others (although well known to members of the American Legion, especially the Forty-and-Eight Division), is French VOITURE 'a carriage; a railway coach; a railway car' [from Latin *vectūra* 'carrying; conveyance']. In the American Legion, a VOITURE is 'a local constituent unit of the Forty-and-Eight Division' (*MW3*), who took their name from the French railroad cars that were marked during World War I as capable of transporting forty men or (sardonically "and") eight horses 'voiture à quarante hommes ou huit chevaux.' 10670 10675

Latin *vehere, vectus* has many compounds, but only one that has been adopted into English as a verb, that is, INVEIGH (etymologically) 'to carry into; to sail into'; 'to assail with words; to give vent to a denunciation' [from Latin *invehere, invectus* 'to carry into,' passive *invehī* 'to burst into; to attack']. The past participle *invectus* yields Late Latin *invectīvus* 'vituperative' and Medieval Latin *invectīva* (*ōrātiō*) 'abusive (speech),' whence English INVECTIVE 'an abusive expression; a vehement denunciation.' 10680 10685

Speaking of *vehement* and VEHEMENCE 'forcefulness of expression; great or excessive ardor' [from Latin *vehemēns* = *vēmēns* 'violent, furious; forcible'], some etymologists suggest the possibility that these words may also derive from Latin *vehere* 'to carry, to transport.' (One speaks of an incensed person as being "transported" with rage.) The suffix *-ment* (< Latin *-mentum*) is used to express the result of an action (*fragment* 'what is left after something is broken') or the instrument of an action (*ornament* 'that which embellishes'). If *vehemence* stems from *vehere* that would make it either 'the product of being transported' or more likely 'the instrument of attacking' (*invehī* 'to attack'). However, other etymologists believe that the *vehe-* of Latin *vehemēns* = *vēmēns* is derived from Latin *vē-* 'lacking,' so that the etymological meaning would be 'lacking in or deprived of mind' (*mēns* 'mind'). 10690 10695 10700

Another English word based on the Latin past participle *vectus* 'carried, transported' is CONVECTION 'the process of transmitting or conveying' [from Late Latin *convectiō*, from Latin *convehere* 'to carry together']. CONVECTION is mostly restricted to scientific meanings in physics and meteorology (the fact that hot air rises is an example of *thermal convection* 'the transmitting of heat by motion of the hot materials'). In Latin, *convector* means 'fellow passenger.' 10705

A related term is Latin *convexus* 'vaulted, arched.' This is apparently an old past participle of *convehere, convectus* 'to carry together,' and the meaning arises because in forming an arch the 10710 extremities of the surface are "drawn together to a point" (*ODEE*). The English loanword from *convexus* is CONVEX 'curved like the outside of a circle or arch.'

10715   Other English borrowings from the past participle *vectus* are more abstruse; for example VECTOR (biology) 'an organism that carries pathogens from one host to another'; (mathematics) 'a quantity specified by a magnitude and a direction' [from Latin *vector* 'bearer, carrier']; ADVECTION 'a local change in a property

10720 of a system'; and EVECTION 'solar perturbation of the lunar orbit' [from Latin *ēvectiō* 'a carrying out; a raising up']. (A defaulting tenant's furniture is "carried out" when he is *evicted*, but this is a different word, from Latin *ēvincere*, *ēvictus* 'to conquer completely.') Note, also, PROVECTION 'the carrying forward of the final

10725 sound of a word to a following word.' Examples of provection are *a nickname* < *an ekename* ('an additional name'); *a newt* < *an ewt*; *the nonce* < *then ones*; *Nash* < *an ash*, *Powell* < *ap Howell*; and *Price* < *ap Rhys*. This linguistic phenomenon also takes place in the opposite direction. Examples are *an umpire* < *a nompere*;

10730 *an adder* < *a nadder*; *an apron* < *a napron* (compare *napery*); and *an orange* < *a narancia* (compare Spanish *naranja*). TRANS-VECTION, labeled rare in most modern dictionaries, refers to the 'transportation through the air of a witch by a devil,' fortunately a relatively uncommon occurrence these days.

10735   The Latin verb *vexāre* 'to agitate; to torment, to harass' is also thought to be related to Latin *vehere*, *vectus*, probably by way of the past participle. Since *vehere*, *vectus* 'to carry' implies transportation, and transportation in Roman days was by horseback, in springless vehicles, or on a boat or ship, one can see how the 'to

10740 agitate' meaning of *vexāre* arose, and the extended meanings of 'to torment, to harass.' (Compare the semantic progression of Vulgar Latin *tripāliāre* 'to torture' > Old French *travailler* 'to travail' > English *travel*.) Obvious English borrowings from Latin *vexāre* 'to harass' are VEX 'to irritate, to annoy' and its derivatives

10745 VEXATION and VEXATIOUS.

    Returning to Germanic derivatives of Indo-European **wegh-* 'to move, to set in motion; to go, to transport in a vehicle' that have come down to English, we are buoyed up by the English noun WAVE 'a swell moving along the surface of a body of water;

10750 oscillations' [from Middle English *wawe*, *waghe*; from Old English *wǣg* 'motion, wave']. This is the derivation given by some, but others trace the noun WAVE to the same source as the verb to *wave*, which comes from Indo-European **webh-* 'to weave.' What seems to have happened is that as the two forms approached each

10755 other phonetically, the one for 'moving the hand back and forth as a signal' (from **webh-* 'to weave') superseded the Middle English

waw 'a moving swell of water' (from **wegh-* 'to move, to go').
Note, also, VOGUE 'the prevailing fashion' [from French *vogue*
'rowing, sailing, going,' *voguer* 'to row (a boat)']. This elegant
word had a slangy origin, that is, to be in VOGUE was something   10760
like 'to be in the rowing, sailing, going.' (Compare *to be in the
swim.*) French *voguer* 'to row' has Italian, Portuguese, and Spanish counterparts, respectively *vogare*, *vogar*, and *bogar* 'to row.'
They all presumably come from a Germanic source related to
Middle High German *wogen* 'to float, to be borne by the waves'   10765
and descended from Indo-European **wegh-* 'to set in motion.'
Another derivative of Indo-European **wegh-* is EARWIG 'an insect
once thought to be able to penetrate a person's head through the
ear,' a creature known in German as *Ohrwurm* 'earworm.' The
-WIG of EARWIG comes from Old English *wicga* 'earwig; "thing   10770
that moves quickly"' (*AHD*), related to WIGGLE (although some
authorities tie the element -*wig* to *vetch*, which would make it a
descendant of Indo-European **wei-* 'to turn' or **weik-* 'to bend').
Still other derivatives of Indo-European **wegh-* are NORWAY
'northern way; northern region' [from Old Norse *Norvegr*] (the   10775
Modern Norwegian word is *Norge*); GRAYWACKE 'a kind of dark
gray sandstone' [from German *Grauwacke*, from *grau* 'gray' +
Wacke a German miners' word adopted as a geological term; from
Old High German *wacko*, *waggo* '"boulder rolling on a river
bed"' (*AHD*)]; and WALL-EYED 'having a light-colored, whitish   10780
eye or eyes; having one eye that turns out with a divergent
squint; having bulging eyes' [from Middle English *wawileghed*,
from Old Norse *vagleygr*]. The *wall-* element is thus traced to Old
Norse *vagl* 'wooden beam, roost, perch.' *Vagl* also survives in
Icelandic *vagl* 'a film over the eyes' and in Swedish *vagel* 'a sty in   10785
the eye.' However; the connection with 'to set in motion' is not
exactly obvious. *MW3* has Old Norse *vagl* 'beam, roost; beam in
the eye' akin to Old Norse *vega* 'to move, to carry, to lift,' so the
semantic connection may be by way of the notion of 'carrying.'

  English *wall-* < Middle English *wawil-* < Old Norse *vagl-*   10790
trace further back to Germanic **waglaz*, and thence to a "suffixed
o-grade form (of Indo-European **wegh-*) **wogh-lo-*" (*AHD*). From
this same **wogh-lo-* comes Greek *okhlos* 'disturbance, trouble;
populace, mob; moving mass.' Note that Greek drops the initial
digamma, or *w-*. *Okhlos* 'mob' gives us the English terms OCH-   10795
LOCRACY 'mob rule' and OCHLOPHOBIA 'morbid fear of crowds;
fear of mobs.'

LV

Wheeling Cyclones

If more people CULTIVATED BICYCLING instead of automobiling our modern CULTURE would have cleaner air. One can see the connection between CULTURE and CULTIVATION, but BICYCLING? The Indo-European root of all three words is *kwel- 'to revolve, move around, sojourn, dwell' (*AHD*). At first glance, there seem to be two contradictory meanings here, until one reflects that WHEELS can and often do 'revolve' or 'move around' and still stay in the same place, that is 'dwell, sojourn.'

First one of the 'revolving, moving around' words: CYCLE 'a recurrent period of time; an orbit in space; to ride a two- or three-wheeled vehicle' [via French *cycle* and Late Latin *cyclus* from Greek *kuklos* 'circle, wheel']. Greek *kuklos* represents a reduplication or doubling of *kwel-, a grammatical process in which all or part of the root is repeated. In this case the Indo-European form was *kwe-kwl-os, with reduplication of the root plus a suffix. (As we shall see below, other languages retain the *e* of the first syllable. Its nonappearance in Greek *kuklos* has not yet been satisfactorily explained.) *Kuklos* was transliterated into Latin as *cyclus*. (In Latin the *c-* is still pronounced as *k* and the *-y-* has the sound of *ü*.) Other English loanwords from Greek *kuklos* are CYCLONE 'a wind storm caused by air masses circulating rapidly around a low-pressure center' [via *kukloma* 'wheel' or *kuklon* 'circling, whirling']; CYCLOTRON 'an accelerator in which particles are propelled outward in a circular fashion' [-*tron* 'instrument']; CYCLOPS (literally) 'round-eyed'; 'one of a race of giants in Greek mythology with a single eye in the middle of the forehead' [via Latin *cyclōps* from Greek *kuklōps* (*kuklos* 'circle' + *ōps* 'eye')] (some authorities doubt this derivation); and CYCLOPEAN 'relating to prehistoric stone construction marked by the use of large irregular blocks or boulders laid upon one another, with the spaces between filled with small stones and the walls bound with a clay mortar.' Prehistoric walls of this construction standing in Greece were explained by the newly arrived Dorian Greeks, circa 1100 B.C., as having been built by the vanished one-eyed giants, who alone, they reasoned, would have been big enough and strong enough to erect such masonry. Similar work to which the term *cyclopean* has been extended is found in Etruria, as well as in China, Japan, and Peru. Still more English loanwords from Greek *kuklos* include CYCLORAMA 'a picture covering the interior walls of a large cylindrical room so as to be seen in perspective by a viewer standing in the center of the room' [*horama* 'view, sight']; CYCLIST 'one that rides a UNICYCLE, BICYCLE, TRICYCLE, or MOTORCYCLE'; and ENCYCLICAL 'intended for wide circulation; a circular letter, especially one issued by the Pope' [from Latin *encyclicus*, from Greek *enkuklios* 'circular']. The third -c- was inserted by Late Latin writers, who seem to have thought the Greek word should be *enkuklikos*. Two more in the same family are ENCYCLOPEDIA 'a comprehensive reference work' [from Medieval Latin *encyclopaedia* 'general education,' from spurious Greek *enkuklopaideiā*, a miscopying of *enkuklios paideiā* 'general (circular) education' (*paideiā* 'education,' from *pais, paidos* 'child')] and KU KLUX KLAN [supposedly from Greek *kuklos* 'circle' + *clan*]. ("The word *circle* appears in names of many secret societies supporting the Confederacy." *AHD*)

The English word *circle*, so similar in spelling and meaning to CYCLE, comes from an entirely different source. However, from the same suffixed, reduplicated Indo-European root form *kwekwlo-* 'circle' that yields Greek *kuklos*, with the *k* sounds replaced by aspirated *h*'s in Germanic *hwehula*, and with the second *h* sound replaced by a *g* in Old English *hweogol* 'wheel' and eliminated entirely in Old English *hwēol* 'wheel,' comes English WHEEL 'a disk with a hub in the center designed to turn on an axle.'

Like the denoted objects themselves, the root *kwel-* yields different forms in different areas. In Old Church Slavonic, for instance, *kwel* 'to revolve' gives us *kolo, koles-* 'wheel,' whence Czech *koleso*, plural *kolesa* '(something on) wheels,' whence German *Kalesche*, whence French *calèche*, whence English CALASH 'a light two-wheeled carriage with a collapsible top.' Also from Old Church Slavonic *kolo* 'wheel' is Czech *kolač* 'a wheel-shaped cake, whence English KOLACKY 'an east-European pastry.'

In Sanskrit, Indo-European *kw-* changes to *k-* or *c-*, thus the reduplicated root *kwkwl-* shows up in that language transmogrified into *çakra* 'wheel, circle,' whence Hindi *c(h)akkar* 'circle, turn,' and the polo-playing Englishman's CHUKKA, CHUKKAR,

CHUKKER 'a 7½-minute turn, or period of play, in a polo game' and CHUKKA 'boots; short, ankle-length boots with two pairs of eyelets.' Also from the Hindi is CHARKA, CHARKHA 'a spinning wheel' [from Hindi *carkha*, from Persian *charkha(h)* 'wheel'].

Besides the CYCLE, the WHEEL, and the CHARKHA, another thing that turns is one's head, and the axis that it turns upon is the neck, known in Latin by the word *collum*, another derivative from our Indo-European root **kwel-* 'to revolve, to move around; to dwell.' Latin *collum* 'neck' yields Latin *collāre* 'neckband,' whence English COLLAR 'something worn about the neck; a ringlike device that restrains, guides or secures a part' [via Middle English *coler* and Old French *col(i)er*] (the Modern English spelling having been influenced by the Latin spelling). In the general area of the neck is the COLLARBONE 'the clavicle; a bone linking the sternum to the scapula.'

In French, Latin *collum* 'neck' has become *col* 'neck,' a word the French also use in a topographical sense that has been adopted into English as COL 'a pass between two mountains; a saddlelike depression in a mountain ridge.' (*Col* is not related to the similar French word *colline* 'hill.') Other English loanwords from Latin *collum* 'neck' through the French are COLLET 'a metal collar or flange'; (glassmaking) 'the neck of glass left on the blowing iron after the removal of the finished article' (*OED*) [from French *collet* 'collar']; DÉCOLLETÉ 'having a low neckline' [from French *décolleter* 'to uncover the neck' (*de-* 'from; removal' + *collet* 'collar']; perhaps, CULLET 'refuse glass gathered for resmelting' [possibly an alteration and extension of *collet* 'the neck of glass left on the blowing iron,' but some suggest a derivation from Latin *collecta* 'things gathered,' by way of French *cueillette* 'gathering; crop; rags collected for making rage' (*ODEE*)]; ACCOLADE (literally) 'a hug around the neck'; 'the salutation given upon the bestowal of knighthood; the bestowal of praise' [via French from Provençal *acolada* or Italian *accollata*; from Vulgar Latin **accollāre* (*ac-* < *ad-* 'to, toward')] (the accolade given upon the bestowal of knighthood consisting of a kiss or an embrace or a tap on the shoulder with the flat of a sword); and TORTICOLLIS 'wryneck; an abnormal twisting of the neck' [New Latin, from *tortus* 'twisted,' past participle of *torquēre* 'to twist' + *collum* 'neck'].

The evolution of a word meaning 'neck' from Indo-European **kwel-* 'to revolve, to move around' also took place in Germanic, but here the Indo-European **kw-* is replaced by Germanic **hw-* (as in **hwehula* 'wheel'), so that the Germanic word corresponding to Latin *collum* is **hwalsaz* 'neck.' **Hwalsaz* has an Old Norse descendant in which the *w* sound has been lost, that is,

hals 'neck; ship's bow.' To see how a Norse word meaning 'neck' came to mean 'ship's bow' one has only to look at the Vikings' longships, whose high-rising prows were usually carved in the   10920
likeness of a dragon's or snake's head. Old Norse *hals* was adopted into Middle English as *halse*, whence phonetically spelled English HAWSE 'the space between the bow of a ship and her anchors; the part of a ship's bow that contains the HAWSE-
HOLES.' Now the HAWSEHOLES are 'the holes in the bow of a ship   10925
through which cables pass,' and another word for 'cable' is *hawser*, which certainly seems logical enough, except for the fact that this word *hawser* is not related etymologically to HAWSE 'the part of a ship where the HAWSEHOLES are located.' *Hawser* comes to English via Norman French *hauceor* and Old French *haucier*   10930
from Vulgar Latin **altiare* 'to raise, to lift up,' from Latin *altus* 'high.' (See Chapter XXXII, lines 6080ff.) Despite the difference in derivation the words are related in speakers' minds because "from an early period *hawser* has been associated by form and sense with HAWSE" (*OED*).   10935
    Other English words that trace back to Germanic **hwalsaz* are HAUBERK (literally) 'neck-protector'; 'a piece of defensive armor originally intended for the neck and shoulders; a long tunic made of chain mail' [from Old French *hauberc*, from Germanic **h(w)als-berg* (**bergan* 'to protect')] and RINGHALS (literally)   10940
'ring-necked'; 'a venomous African snake' [from Afrikaans, from Middle Dutch *ring* 'ring' + *hals* 'neck'].
    So much for the 'revolving, moving around' words derived from Indo-European **kwel-* 'to revolve, to move around; to sojourn, to dwell.' Turning to the 'sojourning, dwelling' words, we   10945
find a classic example in the Latin verb *colere* 'to farm; to abide.' A classic English borrowing from Latin *colere* 'to abide' is COLONY (obsolete) 'a farm; a country estate'; (Roman) 'a settle-ment in a hostile, newly conquered country'; 'a settlement, in a new country, subject to a parent state' [from Latin *colōnia* 'farm,   10950
settlement; colony,' from *colōnus* 'farmer, settler,' from *colere* 'to farm, to abide']. Many modern European cities were at one time Roman *coloniae*, that is, towns where Roman garrisons were established to provide the imperial governors with the necessary police force. For example, towns like London (Londinium), York   10955
(Eboracum), Bordeaux (Burdigala), Paris (Lutetia), and obviously COLOGNE, from *Colōnia*, earlier *Colōnia Agrippina*, after Agrip-pina, great-granddaughter of Augustus, sister of Caligula and mother of Nero. The lady was born at this distant outpost on the banks of the Rhine when it was still called Oppidum Ubiorum,   10960
whither her mother, also named Agrippina, wife of Germanicus Caesar, had accompanied her husband on a campaign.

COLOGNE water 'a kind of perfumed spirits; toilet water' was first manufactured in that city in 1709, and COLOGNE earth 'a 10965 brown pigment obtained from lignite' was first found near the city.

The past participle of Latin *colō, colere* is *cultus* 'farmed, tended to,' from which is derived the Latin noun *cultus* 'labor, care; culture; worship.' (This semantic progression gives us a hint 10970 about the foundations of Roman religion.) Latin *cultus* leads to English CULT 'worship; a particular system of religious worship; excessive devotion to an ideal' [via French *culte*]; CULTURE (obsolete) 'worship'; 'tilling of the soil; growing of plants; breeding of animals; the growing of microorganisms in a nutritious 10975 soup; socially transmitted behavior patterns; acquaintance with the fine arts, the humanities, and broad aspects of science' [via French from Latin *cultūra* 'cultivation, labor']; and CULTIVATE 'to bestow labor upon (land, plants) in order to promote growth; to improve by training; to court the friendship of' [from Medieval 10980 Latin *cultīvāre*, from Late Latin *cultīva (terra)* 'tilled (land),' from *cultīvus* 'tilled,' from Latin *cultus* 'farmed']. Also derived from Latin *colere* 'to dwell in a place' is the suffix *-colous*, used by biologists to indicate habitat, that is 'dwelling on or amongst,' as in MARICOLOUS 'living in the sea' [*mare* 'sea']; ARENICOLOUS 10985 'sand-inhabiting' [*arena* 'sand']; SAXICOLOUS 'dwelling among rocks' [*saxum* 'rock'], etc.

A Greek element similar to Latin-derived *-colous* 'dwelling amongst' is found in the *-kolos* of Greek *boukolos* 'cowherd, herdsman.' (For *bous* 'ox,' see line 1726.) The associated Greek 10990 adjective *boukolikos* 'pertaining to a cowherd' leads to English BUCOLIC 'pastoral, rustic' [via Latin *būcolicus*].

Usually, however, Indo-European **kw* does not become *k* in Greek, but changes to *p* or (in most Greek dialects) to *t* when followed by *e*. A Greek derivative of Indo-European **kwel-* 'to 10995 revolve; to dwell' is *polos* (for **kwolos*) 'axis of a sphere; pivot.' (Note that both axes and pivots both 'revolve' and 'dwell,' that is 'stay in the same place.') Greek *polos* was adapted into Latin as *polus* 'the pole of the earth,' source of English POLE 'the extremities of an axis through a sphere; either of two opposing regions on 11000 a magnet at which the field is most intense'; POLAR 'located near the North or South Pole; characterized by opposite extremes; pivotal'; and POLARIZE 'to cause to concentrate around two contrasting positions.'

Greek *polos* 'axis' had a Late Greek diminutive **polidion* 11005 which was adapted into Vulgar Latin as **polidium*. **Polidium* evolved into Old French *po(u)lie*, whence Middle English *po(u)ley*, whence English PULLEY 'a grooved wheel with a cord

passing over it used for changing the direction of power, especially for raising an object by pulling downward on the cord.' Despite the spelling and the sense, there is no etymological   11010
connection between PULLEY and *pull*.

Another Greek word descended from Indo-European **kwel-* 'to revolve; to dwell' is the adverb *palin* 'back; again, once more' (a stationary wheel keeps coming 'back again' to the same spot). Greek *palin* is found in some fairly abstruse English words, the   11015
best known of which are PALINDROME (literally) 'a running back again'; 'a word or phrase that reads the same backward as forward' (see line 3372.) [Greek *dromos* 'a running']; PALINGENESIS 'the doctrine of the transmigration of souls; reincarnation; the recapitulation by an embryo of various stages in the evolution of the   11020
species' [*genesis* 'origin']; PALIMPSEST 'writing material, such as parchment, that has been used two or three times after the earlier writing has been erased' [from Greek *palimpsēstos* via Latin *palimpsēstus* (*psēstos* 'rubbed, scraped')]; and PALINODE 'a poem written in retraction of an earlier poem; a formal retraction' [*ōidē*   11025
'song'].

Lastly, there are two other Greek words derived from Indo-European **kwel-* 'to revolve, to dwell,' but these begin with *t-* because they are followed by *-e-*. They are the noun *telos* 'completion of a cycle; consummation; end' and the adjective   11030
teleos 'complete, finished.' *Telos* and *teleos* are represented in English mostly by scientific and philosophical terms, like TELEOST (literally) 'completely bony'; 'belonging to a group of fish with completely bony skeletons and rayed fins' [*osteon* 'bone'] and TELEOLOGY 'the doctrine that ends and purposes are imma-   11035
nent in nature.' One nonscientific, nonphilosophical English word containing the Greek element *telos* 'fulfillment, result' is TALISMAN 'a stone, ring, statuette or other object engraved with characters to which occult powers are attributed; any object held to be endowed with magical charms.' The 'completion' or 'fulfillment'   11040
implied here is of the preliminary course of instruction necessary to acquire mastery over the magical charm. TALISMAN comes to English via French *talisman*, or Spanish *talismán*, or Italian *talismano*, from the Arabic *tilsām*, an adaptation of Medieval Greek *telesma* 'a sanctified object,' from Late Greek *telesma* 'a   11045
completion; an initiatory rite,' from Greek *telein* 'to bring to an end; to initiate into the mysteries.'

LVI

Who, What, Where, When, Why

The fact that the Indo-European languages are related by descent from one ancestral language is often illustrated by point-

11050 ing out the similarities between words that stand for basic concepts, such as FATHER, *fader, fæder, fadar, fater; Vater, vader; pater, patēr, pitar, padre, père, pācar; athir, athair; hayr* [Indo-European **p-* > Greek, Latin, Romance, Sanskrit, Tocharian *p-;* Germanic **f-;* German *v* (pronounced *f*); Dutch *v-;* Celtic

11055 (disappeared); Armenian *h(w)-*] or THREE, *thrie, thrē, thrir, thrija; trēs, tres, treis, tria, trei, trois, trayas, trys; drī, drie, drei* [Indo-European **t-* > Greek, Latin, Sanskrit, Celtic, Lithuanian *t-;* Germanic **th-;* Dutch and German *d-*]. Some of the relative/ interrogative pronouns and adverbs are also noticeably similar, for

11060 example WHO, Old English *hwā*, Old High German *hwer*, German *wer*, Latin *qui(s)*; WHAT, Old English *hwæt*, Old High German *hwaz*, German *was*, Latin *quod*; WHERE, Old English *hwǣr*, Old High German *hwār*, German *wo*, Latin *quō*; and WHEN, Old English *hwenne*, Old High German *(h)wanne*, Ger-

11065 man *wenn, wann*, Latin *quando, quom* [Indo-European **kw-* > Germanic **hw-*, English *wh-*, German *w-* (pronounced *v*), Latin *qu-*]. The Indo-European root is **kwo-*, **kwi-*, identified simply as a "stem of relative and interrogative pronouns" (*AHD*). The English form WHOSE 'of whom; belonging to whom' [from Old

11070 English *hwæs*] exemplifies the possessive *-s*, parallel with *his, hers, its, ours, yours, theirs, John's* and, just as WHOM, the objective/dative case of *who* [from Old English *hwām, hwæm*] exemplifies the accusative/dative *-m*, parallel with *him* and *them*. WHY 'for what reason' [from Old English *hwī, hwȳ*] was originally

11075 the instrumental case of *hwæt*, whence WHAT ('by what'), and HOW 'in what manner' comes from Old English *hū*, from Germanic **hwō*. Note, also, WHICH (originally) 'who-like' [from Old

English *hwilc*, from Germanic **hwa-līk-*]. WHENCE 'from where'
[from Middle English *whennes*, from Old English *hwanon(e)*]
looks as if it should mean 'from when' or 'of when,' but it doesn't.   11080
Middle English *whenne*, of which *whennes* > WHENCE is the
genitive, as well as Old English *hwanone*, all meant 'from where.'
Another interrogative adverb is WHITHER 'where to' [from Old
English *hwider*, from Germanic **hwithrē*]. The *-ther* < *-der* suffix,
also found in *hither* and *thither*, here means 'toward.' It can also   11085
mean 'of two,' as in WHETHER (originally) 'which of two'; 'if it is
true that; if it should happen that' [from Old English *hwæther*,
from Germanic **hwatharaz*]. Old English *hwæther* is also lurking in English EITHER 'each of two; both; one of two' [from Old
English *ægther*, whence *æghwaether*, from Germanic **aiwo*   11090
giwatharaz 'ever each of two']. NEITHER 'not one nor the other,'
the negative of EITHER, is historically a compound of *no* 'not' +
hwæther 'which of two.' This *-ther* corresponds to Latin *-ter*
found in *uter* 'which of two; either' (based on Latin *ut* 'how; that,'
which is a descendant of our Indo-European root **kwo-*, though   11095
the *k* sound has disappeared). *Uter* is not an English loanword,
but its negative, *ne uter*, whence *neuter*, whence English NEUTER,
is: 'neither of the two; of neither sex or gender; a castrated
animal; a sexually undeveloped female insect; a plant without
pistils or stamens; one who does not take sides.'   11100
    The Latin relative/interrogative pronouns *qui, quae, quod*
'who, what' and their derivatives have contributed these English
loanwords: QUA 'by what way; in what manner; in the capacity of'
[the ablative feminine singular of *qui*]; QUALITY 'the natural
characteristics of something' [via Old French *qualité* from Latin   11105
qualitās, from *quālis* 'of what kind']; QUALIFY 'to characterize; to
modify; to achieve a certain standard' [via Old French *qualifier*
from Medieval Latin *qualificāre* 'to attribute a quality to' (*quālis*
'of what kind' + *facere* 'to make')]; QUANTITY 'amount' [via Old
French *quantité* from Latin *quantitās*, from *quantus* 'how much'];   11110
and QUORUM (literally) 'of whom'; 'the number of members of a
body necessary to transact business legally' [genitive plural of
qui]. QUORUM comes from the first word of the Medieval Latin
phrase *quorum vos . . . unum esse volumus*, used in 15th-century
England to commission justices of the peace ('of whom we will   11115
that you be one'). More English loanwords include QUOTA 'an
allotted share' [from Latin *quotus, quota, quotum* 'of what
number,' from *quot* 'how many']; QUOTIENT 'the result of dividing
one number by another' [from Latin *quotiēns* 'how often']; QUOTE
(originally) 'to mark a book with numbers for reference'; 'to repeat   11120
the words of another' [from Medieval Latin *quotāre* 'to number,'
from Latin *quotus* 'of what number'] (English *quoth* as in "quoth

he" or "quoth the raven" is not an archaic third person singular of
QUOTE, but comes from Old English *cwethan* 'to speak,' from
11125 Indo-European **gwet-* 'to say'); QUOTIDIAN 'daily' [from Latin
quotīdiē 'each day,' from *quot* 'how many' + *diēs* 'day']; QUASI
(literally) 'as if'; 'resembling but not being the thing in question'
[from Latin *quasi* 'as if,' from *quam* 'as' + *si* 'if']; QUONDAM
'former' [from Latin *quondam* 'at one time,' from *quom* 'when'];
11130 and QUIBBLE 'to raise· trivial objections' [probably from Latin
quibus 'to whom, by whom,' dative and ablative plural of *qui*].
Quibus 'to whom, by whom' appeared frequently in legal briefs
written in Latin, and was thus associated with finicky, legalistic
distinctions. The English word QUIBBLE first appeared in writing
11135 in 1611, but the *OED* suggests that QUIBBLE may be a diminutive
of the now obsolete *quib* 'a pun,' also based on Latin *quibus*. A
1592 quotation reads: "These lawiers haue . . . such quibs and
quiddits, that beggering their clients they purchase to themselves
whole lordships." There is yet another obsolete English *quib*,
11140 said to be a variant of QUIP 'a clever remark' [from Latin *quippe*
'indeed, of course, to be sure' (with sarcastic force), from *quid*
'what']. Some writers also attribute QUIBBLE to this source, rather
than to *quibus*. Note, also, UBIQUITY 'omnipresence' [from Modern Latin *ubīquitās*, from Latin *ubique* 'everywhere']. Here the
11145 element that is descended from Indo-European **kwo-* is Latin *ubī*
'where' (for **quubi*. As in *ut*, the *k* sound has disappeared.). The
-quity comes from the Latin *-que*, an enclitic (leaning on the
preceding word) form meaning 'and.' Latin *ubī* 'where' has
a counterpart in Latin *ibī* 'there,' found in the English loanword
11150 ALIBI (literally) 'elsewhere'; 'proof that a person was elsewhere
when a crime was committed' [from Latin *alibī* 'elsewhere,' from
alius 'other' + *ibī* 'there'].
　　A related *quid* word is the Spanish term HIDALGO 'a member
of the minor nobility' [from Old Spanish *hijo dalgo* from *hijo de*
11155 *algo* 'son of something' from Latin *filius de aliquid* (*aliquid*
'something,' from *alius* 'some, other' + *quid* 'what')]. In Old
Spanish, *algo* 'something' was used to mean 'possession,' thus a
hijo dalgo was a 'man of property.' But the Spanish 'son of
something' is small potatoes compared to a Hindu *chīz* 'thing,'
11160 whence English CHEESE 'very important person; something first
rate; the correct thing' [from Hindi or Urdu *chīz* 'thing,' from
Persian *chīz* 'thing,' from Indo-European **kwo-*] (*AHD*). (This
is not related either to edible cheese or to *Cheese it! the cops!*)

LVII

Wise Historians, Idealistic Visionaries

Much of the HISTORY that has been written is IDEALIZED, that is, slanted to favor the culture or nationality of the writer and sometimes including fictitious STORIES that enhance the reputation for WISDOM of national heroes, like Parson Weems's stories about George Washington. What interests us most in the preceding sentence is that the words HISTORY, STORY, IDEALIZE, and WISDOM all spring from the Indo-European root *weid- 'to see,' having reached us variously by way of Old Greek *widein (later idein) 'to see,' *weidenai (later eidenai) 'to know,' *widtōr (later histōr) 'wise, learned,' and Old English wīs 'wise.'

The semantic development from 'see' to 'know' probably took place early in the evolution of the Indo-European languages, evidenced by Sanskrit, Celtic, Latin, Greek, Germanic, and other groups. Thus the progression from Greek idein 'to see' to Greek idea 'semblance, form, pattern; notion, concept' is not hard to comprehend, or "visualize." The semantic sequence probably went something like the following: 'to see > to see truly > to see with the mind's eye > to know.' The later senses, influenced by Plato's definition of idea as "an eternal pattern of which individual things are imperfect copies" led to the Latin idea 'a Platonic idea, an archetype' and English IDEA 'a thought; something that exists in the mind.' Latin idea begat the Late Latin adjective ideālis, which led to French idéal and English IDEAL 'ultimately perfect; existing as an archetype; a standard of perfection; that which exists only in the mind.' A number of related words include IDEALIZE 'to attribute perfection to'; IDEALISM 'the practice of envisioning reality in terms of perfection; a conviction that the highest standards of morality and ethics shall ultimately prevail; a philosophical theory that objects of external perception

11165

11170

11175

11180

11185

11190

consist of ideas'; IDEATE 'to think; to imagine'; and IDÉE FIXE 'fixed idea; an obsession.'

11195   From the Greek *idea* 'concept' the French devised the combining form *ideo-*, notably in *idéologie*, whence English IDEOLOGY 'the manner of thinking characteristic of an individual or group' and IDEOGRAM 'a symbol representing an idea or a thing without expressing a particular word for it,' such as Chinese
11200   characters, the Arabic numerals, and the schematic devices on highway signs.

      Related to Greek *idein* 'to see' and *idea* 'form, semblance' by common descent from Indo-European **weid-* 'to see' is Greek *eidos* (< **weid-os-*) 'act of seeing; shape, form,' with derivative
11205   *eidōlon* 'image, vision; shape.' *Eidōlon* leads us away from abstract thought and the quicksands of philosophical dialectic to such good, solid, objective objects as those denoted by its descendants, Late Latin *īdōlum*, whence French *idole*, yielding English IDOL 'an image of a false god; one that is adored or greatly
11210   admired' (matinee IDOL); IDOLATRY 'worship of images; blind devotion'; and IDOLIZE 'to make an object of worship of; to regard with blind devotion.' A diminutive of Greek *eidos* 'shape, picture,' *eidullion* 'a small image; a short descriptive poem,' leads us not to graven images but to graphic verse in Latin *īdyllium*,
11215   whence English IDYLL 'a short poem descriptive of a picturesque scene, especially of rural life; any simple description of rural life; a carefree episode' and IDYLLIC.

      Greek *eidos* 'act of seeing; form; picture' is also the source of the suffix *-oid* [<· Latin *-oides* < Greek *-oeidēs*] '-like; having the
11220   shape of; having the nature of,' as in ANTHROPOID 'manlike, resembling man'; OVOID 'egg-shaped'; CRYSTALLOID 'resembling crystal'; ADENOID 'glandlike'; (plural) 'lymphoid tissue growth in the nose or upper pharynx' [Greek *adēn* 'gland; acorn']; LYMPH-OID 'pertaining to lymph, a pale coagulable fluid that bathes
11225   the tissues'; PLANETOID 'a small celestial object orbiting the sun'; ASTEROID 'starlike; a planetoid'; and KALEIDOSCOPE (literally) 'viewer of beautiful forms'; 'a tube in which mirrors reflect light transmitted through bits of loose colored glass, causing them to appear in symmetric designs that change constantly as the tube is
11230   turned' [*kalos* 'beautiful' + *eidos* 'form' + *skopein* 'to see']. From a contracted form of Greek *-oiedēs*, *-ōdēs*, come Modern Latin *-ōdium* and English *-ode* '-like, resembling,' as in GEODE (literally) 'earthlike'; 'a small hollow rock with crystals lining the inside wall' [*gē* 'earth']; NEMATODE 'threadlike; worms having
11235   threadlike unsegmented bodies' [*nēma* 'thread']; and SARCODE 'fleshlike; protoplasm' [*sarx* 'flesh'].

There is a possibility (*AHD*) that HADES 'the god of the nether regions; the dwelling place of the dead; Hell,' from the Greek proper noun *Aidēs*, *Haidēs* 'Hades' may stand for 'the invisible,' from *a-* 'not' + *-idēs* 'seen.'   11240

"Seeing is believing" and 'believing' comes very close to 'knowing,' even if the beliefs are wrong, since when you believe something you think you know it. An agent-noun closely related to (**w*)*idein* 'to see' and (**w*)*eidenai* 'to know' started out as **widtōr*, then dropped the digamma (*w*) and evolved further into   11245 *histōr* 'one who has seen, a seer; one who knows; knowing, judge.' *Histōr* led to *historia* 'inquiry, information, knowledge; narration,' whence English HISTORY 'an account of what is known about past events' [via Latin *historia*]. Those past events can be real, legendary, or fictitious. In English a common word for a   11250 narration is a truncated form of HISTORY, that is, STORY 'any type of fictitious composition; the narration of any event, whether real or fictitious; one of the horizontal levels of a building, a floor' [from Norman French (*e*)*storie*, from Old French *estoire*, from Latin *historia*]. However, a Late Latin shortened form, *storia*, had   11255 already developed by the 5th century (*EP*). The 'floor of a building' meaning of STORY apparently comes from the medieval practice of painting the windows and setting up statuary along the tiers of a building to depict different narratives, so that each floor told a *historia* or STORY. [Anglo-Latin *historia* ' "picture decorat-   11260 ing a building [hence] a part of the building so decorated" ' (*RHD*).] However, not all writers agree with this etymology.

The Latin cognate and equivalent of Greek (**w*)*idein* 'to see' is *vidēre* 'to see.' *Videō*, *vidēre*, *vīsus* has a host of compounds and an array of English loanwords. For example, VIDEO 'the   11265 pictures of a television broadcast' [Latin *videō* 'I see']; VIDE 'see!' (as in a bibliographic reference); and VIDELICET 'namely; that is' [Latin: 'it is permissible (i.e., easy) to see']. VIDELICET is abbreviated to *viz.*, and used before giving an example, or listing items that illustrate what has just been stated. The *-z* of *viz.* "represents   11270 the ordinary Medieval Latin symbol of contraction for *et* or *-et*" (*OED*), superseded in part by the ampersand (&) which also stands for Latin *et*. From the participial stem *vis-* come English VISION; VISIONARY; VISIBLE; VISUAL; VISA 'an endorsement added to a passport' [Latin: 'things seen']; VISAGE 'face' [from Old   11275 French *visage*, from Old French *vis* 'face,' from Latin *vīsus* 'seen; thing seen; appearance']; ENVISAGE (archaic) 'to look into the face of; to confront'; 'to form a mental image of; to ENVISION; to foretell'; VIS-À-VIS 'face to face; compared with; one of two things that are opposites; one of two things that correspond to each   11280 other' [French]; and VISOR, VIZOR 'the movable face-covering of the helmet of a suit of armor; an eyeshade' [from Norman French *viser*, from Old French *vis* 'face'].

In Italian, Latin *vidēre* becomes *vedere* 'to see,' and the past participle *vīsus* is replaced by *veduto* or *visto* 'seen.' The feminine past participle *vista* has substantive meanings of 'sight, eyesight; prospect.' English has borrowed the last meaning in the word VISTA 'a view, a prospect; especially one seen through a long, narrow opening; an extensive mental view.' Something similar has happened to Old French *veue*, feminine past participle of *veoir* 'to see' (from Latin *vidēre* 'to see'), which has been adapted into English as VIEW 'an act of looking; a vista, a prospect; an aspect of something seen from a specific vantage point.' Old French *veoir* is the ancestor of Modern French *voir* 'to see,' as well as of the following derivatives that have found their way into English: VOYEUR (literally) 'viewer; one who sees'; 'a Peeping Tom' and CLAIRVOYANCE (literally) 'clear seeing'; 'the professed power of seeing objects that are hidden from view, or that are at a great distance.'

Latin *vidēre*, *vīsus* 'to see' has an intensive form *vīsere*, *vīsāre* 'to look at carefully; to go to see,' with frequentative *vīsitāre* 'to see often; to go to see often,' whence English VISIT 'to go to see; to stay with as a guest' and VISITATION 'the apparition of a supernatural being; the infliction of divine wrath as punishment, or bestowal of divine beneficence as reward; the right to visit; a visit.'

Prefixed compounds borrowed from the Latin are REVISE (literally) 'to look at again'; 'to modify' [from Latin *revīsere* 'to go again to see']; REVIEW (literally) 'to see again'; 'to examine again' [from Old French *rev(e)ue*, from *rev(e)oir*; from Latin *revidēre* 'to see again; to go back to see']; and REVUE 'a musical show that satirizes current events and topics' [from French *revue* 'review; a magazine']. A REVUE passes the contemporary scene in REVIEW. As long as we're talking about a French compound that includes the element *vue* 'seen; sight, view,' we may as well mention the ubiquitous place-name BELLEVUE 'beautiful view' [from Latin *bellus*, French *belle* 'pretty'] and its Italian equivalent BELVEDERE (literally) 'beautiful to see; beautiful view'; 'a structure commanding a fine prospect.'

Continuing with our English loanwords we come to INTERVIEW 'a face-to-face meeting; a conversation between a reporter and a person from whom he seeks facts or statements' (*AHD*) [from Old French *entrevue*, from *s'entrevoir* 'to see each other,' from *entrevoir* 'to see imperfectly, to catch a glimpse of']. English INTERVIEW has been borrowed back into French (or Franglais) as a word for the journalistic encounter. Yet more English loanwords

are SUPERVISE 'to oversee' [from Medieval Latin *supervidēre,*
supervīsus]; PROVIDE (literally) 'to see ahead, to foresee'; 'to
furnish, to supply; to set down as a stipulation' [from Latin
prōvidēre, prōvīsus 'to see beforehand; to provide']; PROVISION(S)   11330
'supplies; stipulation' [via Old French from Latin *prōvīsiō* 'foresight']; PROVIDENT 'foreseeing; frugal, economical, prudent' [from
Latin *prōvidēns* 'foreseeing']; and PROVIDENCE 'preparation in
advance; prudent management; divine direction'; (capitalized)
'God' [from Latin *prōvidentia* 'foresight']. *Divine Providence,*   11335
signifying 'the will of God,' was already a catch phrase in the 15th
century, and PROVIDENCE was personified as 'God' by the 17th.

The ancient Latin speakers themselves shortened the present
participle *prōvidēns* 'foreseeing' into the compressed form
prūdēns 'experienced, wise, discreet' that led to English PRU-   11340
DENT 'careful in handling practical matters.' (The word *prude*
'one overconcerned with propriety' is not from PRUDENT but from
Old French *preu* 'virtuous.' See line 8615.) Other words involving
prevision or the lack of it are PROVISO 'a conditional stipulation'
[from the Medieval Latin phrase *prōvīsō quod* 'provided that']   11345
and IMPROVISE(D) (literally) 'not prepared in advance'; 'to invent
something offhand' [via French *improviser* from Italian
improv(v)isare, from *improv(v)iso* 'unforeseen'].

In some French derivatives of Latin *prōvidēre* 'to foresee; to
provide' the prefix *prō-* has been metathesized into *por-* > *pour-*,   11350
yielding English *pur-*, as in PURVEY (obsolete) 'to see in advance';
'to supply, to dispense' [from Old French *porveeir, porve(i)oir* 'to
foresee, to provide'] and PURVIEW (obsolete) 'a proviso'; 'the body
of a statute; area of competence; range of authority.' Like PRO-
VISO, PURVIEW was originally a legal term, used to introduce the   11355
various clauses of a statute in Anglo-Norman days in the phrases
purveu est 'it is provided' and *purveu que* 'provided that,'
followed by stipulations. The form *-vey* is also found in English
SURVEY 'to look at in an all-inclusive way; to determine the
boundaries of' [from Old French *so(u)rveeir,* from Medieval Latin   11360
supervidēre 'to look over'].

Remaining to be mentioned as loanwords based on Latin
vidēre 'to see' are EVIDENT 'easily seen' [from Latin *ēvidēns*
'making itself seen'; 'clear, plain, manifest' (*ē* < *ex* 'completely' +
vidēns 'seeing')] and EVIDENCE 'testimony'; (literally) 'what can   11365
be seen' [from Latin *ēvidentia* 'clearness, distinctness']. There is,
however, no Latin verb *ēvidēre. Evidens* and *ēvidentia* are
Ciceronian translations of Greek philosophical terms (*EP*). Note,
also, ADVISE (obsolete) 'to look at'; 'to take counsel together; to
offer counsel' [from Old French *aviser,* from Vulgar Latin   11370
advisāre, from *advīsum* 'a look at; a view, an opinion']; ADVICE;

and INVIDIOUS (obsolete) 'envious'; 'discriminatory; arousing ill will' [from Latin *invidiōsus* 'envious, hateful,' from *invidia* 'envy, ill will; odium,' related to *invidēre* 'to look askance at; to envy'].

11375 Etymologically, all that Latin *invidēre* means is 'to look into or upon,' but it early acquired opprobrious denotations, reflecting the darker side of human nature epitomized by "evil-eye" superstitions. Latin *invidia* evolved into Vulgar Latin **inveia* (*EP*) and Old French *envie*, whence English ENVY 'resentment of another's

11380 possessions, usually with a strong desire to have them for oneself.' *Envie* in Modern French also has the milder meaning of 'want, desire,' as in J'ai *envie* d'y aller 'I want to go there.'

"God WOT, I don't want to be known as a WISEACRE, nor as a WIZARD either, nor would I WITTINGLY bear false WITNESS," he

11385 said self-RIGHTEOUSLY. The Indo-European **weid-* 'to see' that gave rise to Latin *vidēre* 'to see,' Greek *idein* 'to see,' and Greek *eidenai* 'to know' also led to the Old English verb *witan* 'to know,' which survives in English to WIT (literally) 'to know'; 'namely, that is to say, videlicet, scilicet'; God WOT 'God knows';

11390 WITTINGLY 'knowingly'; UNWITTINGLY 'unknowingly'; WITNESS 'one who has seen; one who knows; anything that serves as evidence' [from Old English *witnes* 'knowledge']; and WIT 'the ability to know; understanding' (He has his WITS about him; He's out of his WITS); 'the ability to see and express relationships in a

11395 humorous manner'; (archaic) 'an informed, knowing person'; 'one capable of quick, humorous remarks.' When 18th-century authors wrote about the WITS who gathered in contemporary London coffeehouses to argue politics and dispose of weighty intellectual problems, they were not speaking of quipsters or "persons of

11400 fancy who have the faculty for saying smart or brilliant things" (*OED*), but of informed, intelligent men, "persons of great mental ability" (*OED*).

Closely related to these knowing, WITTY words are WISE 'knowing, sagacious' [from Old English *wīs*, from Germanic

11405 *wissaz* 'known']; WISDOM 'capacity of judging rightly; understanding of what is true' [from Old English *wīsdōm*]; and WISEACRE 'a soothsayer; a pretender to wisdom; an offensively self-assertive person' [from Middle Dutch *wijssegger* 'soothsayer' (*segghen* 'to say'); from Old High German *wīssago*, a folk-etymological altera-

11410 tion of *wizago*, *wiʒago* 'seer, prophet']. The Old English equivalent of Old High German *wizago*, *wiʒago* was *wītega* 'prophet,' and both -*ago* and -*ega* are noun-forming suffixes. However, in Old High German *wizago* > *wissago*, the -*sago* combination was associated with *sagen* 'to say,' so that the word was interpreted to

11415 mean 'one who says wise things.' The alteration of -*sago* to Middle Dutch -*seggher* to English -(*se*)*acre* is unexplained. Nowa-

days, a WISEACRE is a WISENHEIMER is a WISE guy who is
continually making WISECRACKS and should be told to WISE up.
Note, also, WIZARD 'a wise man; a sorcerer' [from Middle English
wysard, wise(e)ard, from Old English *wīs* 'wise' + *-ard* 'bold,   11420
hardy']. The suffix *-ard* 'bold, hardy' is mostly used in proper
names like *Bernard* 'bold bear' and *Gerard* 'spear-hardy,' or in
common nouns with the sense of 'one who does (something)
conspicuously or to excess,' like *drunkard, dullard,* and *sluggard.*
WIZARD could thus be interpreted as 'one who is conspicuously   11425
wise.' WIZARD is sometimes used as the masculine of *witch*
(though the preferred term is *warlock*), but *witch* itself does not
derive from *witan* 'to know' or from **weid-* 'to see,' but from
*weik-, a root associated with words of magical or religious
content (*AHD*). The etymology of *witch* is considered uncertain   11430
by many etymologists.

Related to the adjective *wise* 'sagacious' is the English noun
WISE 'manner, way' (in such WISE as; in no WISE different).
Related to this noun is the suffix -WISE, which when added to a
noun or adjective forms an adverb indicating manner, direction,   11435
or position, as in LIKEWISE; OTHERWISE; CLOCKWISE, ANTICLOCK-
WISE, and COUNTERCLOCKWISE. This formation has been over-
worked in recent years by the creation of such nonce
monstrosities as *inflationwise, educationwise, dictionarywise,* etc.
However, a similar creation originated in Anglo-Saxon days in the   11440
Old English form *rihtwīs* 'in the right manner,' and evolved into
Middle English *rightwise,* whence Modern English RIGHTEOUS
'just, virtuous; morally conforming' and SELF-RIGHTEOUS 'indignantly virtuous; self-satisfied, self-serving.'

Other less easily recognizable descendants of Indo-European   11445
*weid- 'to see' are GUIDE 'one who shows the way' [from Old
French *guide(r),* from Old Provençal *guidar* 'to show the way,'
from Common Romanic **widare,* from Germanic **witan* 'to show
the direction to']; GUISE 'outward appearance; false appearance'
[from Old French *guise,* from Romanic **wisa* 'style, manner,' from   11450
Germanic **wis(s)on*]; and TWIT 'to find fault with in a teasing
way' [from Old English *ætwītan* 'to reproach' (*æt* 'at' + *wītan* 'to
reproach')]. Old English *wītan* 'to reproach' is not the same word
as *witan* 'to know,' but a parallel development from the same root,
*weid- 'to see.' The development in this case went something like   11455
the following: 'to see > to observe > to observe what is wrong >
to reproach.' Also belonging to this group, according to some
etymologists, is GUY 'a rope or cable used to steady something'
[from Old French *guier* 'to guide'], although others trace this *guy*
to a Low German source that is also the source of Dutch *gei* 'a   11460
line used to furl sails,' of obscure origin.

There remains a handful of loanwords derived from Indo-
European *weid- 'to see' that have reached English by routes
other than Greek, Latin, or Germanic. Among them are VEDA 'old
11465   sacred writings of Hinduism' [from Sanskrit vēda 'knowledge,
sacred knowledge,' related to Sanskrit veda 'I know; I have seen']
and DRUID (etymologically) either 'soothsayer' or 'knower of
trees'; 'one of an order of priests in ancient Britain and Gaul'
[from either Old Celtic *derwos 'true' or *dru- '(oak) tree' + *wid-
11470   'to know']. This etymological information is in accord with speculations of some Celtic scholars, but recent developments have
ousted the "tree" etymology and probably also the true explanation as well, so that what it is the DRUIDS saw or knew is still a
mystery. Note, also, PENGUIN (literally) 'whitehead' [from Welsh
11475   pen 'head' + gwyn 'white' ('clearly visible'); from the Indo-
European "suffixed nasalized zero-grade form *wi-n-d-no-"
(AHD)]. The name PENGUIN 'whitehead' was originally applied to
the great auk, an extinct, flightless bird of the northern hemisphere, but when explorers of the 16th century came upon the
11480   flightless birds of the southern seas they were so reminded of the
penguins 'great auks' of Iceland, Greenland, etc., that they transferred the Welsh or Breton name without a second thought,
although the two kinds of birds are not related. Actually neither
the penguins nor the great auks have white heads, although the
11485   latter did have a large white spot on each side of the head. Some
etymologists believe that the word penguin 'whitehead' was first
used to describe a "white promontory on an island near New-
foundland [probably Funk Island] where great auks were found in
large numbers" (MW3), and later came to be applied to the birds
11490   themselves. In French the word pingouin is still applied to the
great auk, while the southern birds are known as manchot(s).

LVIII

They Work
the Boulevards

The one thing that SHIPWRIGHTS, WAINWRIGHTS, WHEEL-
WRIGHTS, MILLWRIGHTS, and PLAYWRIGHTS have in common is
that they all WORK at making something: ships, wagons, wheels,
mills—or at least MILLWRIGHTS used to make mills. Nowadays a   11495
MILLWRIGHT is 'a high-class mechanic who sets precision machinery to very fine tolerances' and PLAYWRIGHTS 'make, or write
plays.' The word WRIGHT 'an artificer, a constructive workman; a
carpenter, a joiner'; (obsolete) 'to construct'; (Scottish) 'to work as
a carpenter' [from Old English *wyrhta, wryhta*] has nothing to do   11500
with any of its homonyms, *write, right,* or *rite.* WRIGHT is closely
related to the Old English verb *wyrcan* 'to work' and noun *weorc,
werc, worc* 'work,' ancestors of Modern English WORK 'what is
done; what is to be done; labor; to do, to perform' (to WORK a
miracle); 'to labor'; 'to fashion' (to WORK metal). Note that the   11505
word WROUGHT 'fashioned, beaten into shape' is identified by
lexicographers as a past participle of WORK, although it looks
more like a past participle of obsolete *wright* 'to construct.'
    The people one sees strolling along the BOULEVARDS of Paris
may or may not be BULWARKS of society, but the *boulevards*   11510
'broad city streets' they are treading used to be BULWARKS.
BOULEVARD 'the promenade or avenue laid out on a demolished
fortification' meant (originally) 'the horizontal portion of a rampart' [from Early Modern French *boullewerc,* from Middle Dutch
boliverc or Middle High German *bolwerc* or Middle Low German   11515
bolwerk (*bole* 'plank' + *werc, werk* 'work')]. When the protective
walls or BULWARKS were torn down, the broad empty corridors
left where the walls' bases had been were converted into thor-
oughfares. BOULEVARD is thus the etymological equivalent of
English BULWARK 'a wall or wall-like structure raised as a   11520
defensive fortification.' Both words are ultimately compounds of

words meaning *bole* 'trunk of a tree' and *works* 'engineering structures,' and therefore 'works constructed of tree trunks.'

11525   If you are among those who find WORK IRKSOME you may have the wisdom of language on your side, for there is a distinct possibility that the two words are related. The verb IRK 'to weary; to vex, to irritate' [from Middle English *irken, yrken* 'to weary; to become weary'] is related to the dialectal adjective IRK 'weary, tired; bored' and the rare noun IRK 'a source of annoyance.' The
11530   definite etymological trail stops with Middle English, but since the words originated in the northern parts of "Scandinavianized areas" (*ODEE*) of Britain, antecedents are looked for in Old Norse. A candidate found in Old Norse is *yrkja* 'to work,' a cognate of Old English *wyrcan* 'to work.'
11535   The Indo-European root of the words we have been discussing is **werg-* 'to do, to work.' A large number of English words stemming from this root came into the language not by way of French or German or Old English or Old Norse, but by way of the Greek *ergon* 'work, deed, action' (Greek loses the Indo-European
11540   **w-*). The simplest of these Greek loanwords (though not the oldest, since it was coined in 1873) is the physics term ERG ' "the unit of work according to the centimetre-gramme-second system; the quantity of work done by a force which, acting for one second upon a mass of one gramme produces a velocity of one centimetre
11545   per second" ' (*OED*).

The physicist's definition of WORK is 'the transfer of energy from one physical system to another,' and if you look twice you will notice the syllable *-erg-* in the word ENERGY 'the capacity for action' [via Late Latin *energīa* from Greek *energeia* 'activity,
11550   efficacy, effect,' from *energēs, energos* 'in work, at work; active, working']. The Greek term *energeia* was coined by Aristotle to express one of his philosophical concepts, 'exercise of power, actual working,' as contrasted with *dynamis* 'latent power; the ability or capacity to produce an effect.' Today we use the word
11555   ENERGY with both the 'latent' and the 'working' meanings.

The ending *-ergy* 'worker, working' is also found in ALLERGY (literally) 'working otherwise'; 'altered reaction; an abnormal reaction to environmental substances' [*allos* 'other'] and SYNERGY 'working together; the combined effective action of two or more
11560   muscles to achieve an effect of which each is individually incapable' (*syn-* < *sun* 'together'), also used of the combined effective action of two or more drugs. Note, also, SYNERGISM 'the doctrine that spiritual regeneration is effected by a combination of human will and divine grace.' There is also, as a variant of *-ergy*, the
11565   ending *-urgy*, found in DRAMATURGY 'the composition and presentation of plays; the workings of the theater' [from Greek

drāmatourgia; drāma 'deed, action; action on the stage']; METAL-
LURGY 'the science of extracting, purifying, and working metals'
[from Greek *metallourgos* 'miner'; *metallon* 'pit, mine, quarry'];
THAUMATURGY 'the working of miracles; magic' [*thauma, thau-*   11570
matos 'wonder, marvel; astonishment'] and LITURGY 'rites prescribed for public worship; formal religious worship conducted by
authorized officiants for the benefit of the laity' [via Late Latin
lītūrgia from Greek *leitourgia* 'public service; divine service,'
from **leitos* 'belonging to the public, lay,' from *leōs, laos* 'people'   11575
+ *ergon* 'work']. The word THAUMATURGE was formerly applied
to saints who possessed miraculous powers. It is now used more
often to refer to magicians, conjurers, and illusionists.

If a DRAMATURGE writes plays, a METALLURGIST works with
metals, and a THAUMATURGE works miracles, what does a DEMI-   11580
URGE do? The word *dēmiourgos* in ancient Greece meant '(one)
working for the commonweal; a craftsman, workman, artist;
maker, creator' [Greek *dēmios* 'public' from *dēmos* 'common
people' + *ergon* 'work']. Plato used *Dēmiourgos*, capitalized, to
mean 'the Creator of the material world' > Late Latin *dēmiūrgus*   11585
> English DEMIURGE 'a public official in certain ancient Greek
states'; (Gnosticism) 'the creator of the material world.' In the
Platonic system the material, sensible world is vastly inferior to
the ideal world of transcendental universals, and so the DEMI-
URGE is inferior to the Supreme Being.   11590

The Greek element *ergon* 'work' also lurks in the English
word SURGERY (etymologically) 'manual labor; handwork'; 'the
medical treatment of injury, deformity, or disease by manual and
instrumental operations' [from Medieval French *surgerie,*
serurg(er)ie, from Old French *cirurg(er)ie;* from Latin *chīrūrgia;*   11595
from Greek *kheirourgia* 'a working with the hands' < *kheir*
'hand,' as in *chiropractic* 'manipulation' and *chiromancy* 'palm-
reading']. Nowadays, a manual laborer is at the opposite end of
the scale from a surgeon when it comes to skill, prestige, and
emoluments, but the high social position of surgeons is a compar-   11600
atively recent development. Consider that in the Middle Ages and
later the local surgeon was also the local barber (a situation
reported to prevail still in parts of North Africa), and that the red
twist in a barber pole represents blood and bloodletting.

The Modern French word for 'surgery' is the reconstructed   11605
chirurgie. When surgeons want to put on airs they apply to
themselves the adjective CHIRURGICAL 'surgical' (The Medical
and Chirurgical Faculty).

There are men named GEORGE in all walks of life, from
George Bernard Shaw, the eminent dramaturge, to Gorgeous   11610
George, the resplendent wrestler, but the original GEORGE was 'a

farmer, a worker of the soil' [from Greek *geōrgos* 'farmer,' from *gē* 'earth, land, soil' (as in *geology, geography*) + *-ōrgos* 'worker']. Thus a GEORGIC is 'a poem concerning farming or rural life' [via Latin *Georgica* from Greek *geōrgika* 'cultivated lands'].

Other English words containing the Greek element *ergon* 'work' are ARGON 'an inert gas constituting approximately 1% of the earth's atmosphere' [from Greek *argos, argon* 'not working, lazy, idle' (*a-* 'not, without' + *ergon* 'work')]; ERGOPHOBIA 'a dread of work'; ERGOLATRY 'idolatrous devotion to work'; and ERGATOCRACY 'government by the workers.'

Also derived from Indo-European **werg-* 'to do, to work' is the Greek word *orgia* 'secret rites, worship; the celebration of religious mysteries whose inner workings are revealed only to the initiates.' Among the most widespread 'secret rites, inner workings' of the ancient world were those in honor of Dionysus/Bacchus, god of wine, god of the power and fertility of nature. These ORGIASTIC celebrations naturally involved the drinking of wine and came to resemble what would today be called a "wild party" or an ORGY 'a revel involving unrestrained indulgence, especially sexual excesses' [via French *orgies* from Latin *orgia* 'secret frantic revels' (*OED*), from Greek *orgia*]. The English singular ORGY and French *orgie* are back formations, since all the antecedent forms were in the plural, including the earliest English use (1589). The Bacchanalia, or Roman *orgia* in honor of Bacchus, became so unrestrained that they were forbidden by law in 186 B.C.

Speaking of sexual indulgence, the word ORGASM 'a paroxysmal climax,' associated with sexual intercourse, is not a member of this group, despite the resemblance to ORGY. *Orgasm, orgasmic,* and *orgastic* are the lone English representatives of another Indo-European **werg-, *uerg-,* this one meaning something like 'to swell' (*EP*). **Werg-, *uerg-* is the source of the Greek verb *organ, orgaein* 'to grow ripe, to swell, to be lustful,' whence Greek *orgasmos* > English *orgasm,* as well as Greek *orge* 'impulse, passion, anger' and Sanskrit *ūrjā* 'sap; vigor, power.'

Lastly, descended from our first Indo-European **werg-* 'to do, to work' is the Greek noun *organon* 'instrument, implement, tool' (something that one works with), adapted into Latin as *organum* 'instrument; engine; musical instrument' > Late Latin 'church organ.' *Organon* > *organum* is the base of English ORGANISM 'an interdependent assemblage of specialized parts, each adapted to a particular function'; ORGANIZE 'to put together into an orderly, functional whole'; ORGANIZATION 'a structural working whole'; ORGAN (obsolete) 'a musical instrument in general'; 'a musical instrument consisting of a number of pipes that are supplied with wind by means of bellows and stops operated by keys; a part of an animal or plant that has become adapted for the performance of some specific function; a periodical published by an institution or business firm' [via Old English *organa* and Old French *organe*]. In Latin, an *organicus* is 'a musician,' and the earliest meaning of ORGAN in (10th-century) English was '(any kind of) musical instrument.' The sense of 'a member of an animal or plant body' did not appear until the 14th century.

11660

LIX

Worldly Virtues

11665 Today's WORLDLY-wise reject anthropomorphism, the assumption that man is the most significant fact of the universe, but to our linguistic forebears who coined the word WORLD, this assumption just came naturally. The first meaning given in *MW2* for WORLD is ' "the earth and the heavens and universe of which 11670 it was once believed to be the center." ' An earlier meaning is simply ' "human existence," ' as can readily be seen in this etymology: WORLD comes from Old English *worold*, *weorold*, from Germanic **werald-*, from **wer(az)* 'man' + **ald-* 'age.' The etymological meaning is 'man-era; the age of man.' Because his 11675 own existence was of the first importance to him, English-speaking man soon extended this early meaning of WORLD to the all-inclusive sense, 'universe.'

The Germanic **werald-* has become even more contracted than English *world* in German *Welt* 'world,' encountered in 11680 English in the compound loanwords WELTSCHMERZ (literally) 'world-pain'; 'mental depression caused by contemplating the state of the world'; WELTANSCHAUUNG (literally) 'looking at the world'; 'world outlook; comprehensive view of the universe and man's place in it'; and WELTPOLITIK 'international politics.'

11685 The Old English word *wer(e)* 'man, a male human being' was current until the 13th century when its use died out in favor of the word *man*, which before that meant simply 'human being' (a meaning it still retains, though women's liberationists choose to ignore that fact). *Wer(e)* survives only in Germanic law in the 11690 compounds WERGILD, WERGELD, WEREGILD 'the monetary value of a man,' that is, 'the amount that must be paid to his kindred or his lord in the event of his being killed, or by himself as a fine for certain crimes, or by his family and friends as a ransom.' A man's *wergild* varied according to his social status. "The price of the

king's head ... was 30,000 thrimsas" (David Hume, *History of* 11695
England, 1762), whereas a bishop's and an alderman's *wergild*
was only 8,000 thrimsas (< Latin *tremis* 'the third part of an
aureus,' a coin of whose value historians are uncertain). The
ransom or *wergild* of a thief throughout Scotland was thirty cows
and one heifer. (This *-gild* or *-geld* does not mean 'gold,' but is 11700
related to *yield* and to the German *Geld* 'money'; it has a meaning
of 'payment, tax.') Note, also, WEREWOLF (literally) 'man-wolf'; 'a
person who has been transformed into a wolf; a person who can
assume the form of a wolf at will' [from Old English *werewulf*].
Werewolves are the classic European examples of such magical 11705
transformations, but belief in lycanthropy is worldwide. In the
19th century, English-speaking anthropologists started using *wer-*
as a prefix to be attached to the names of other animals into which
men had reputedly transformed themselves, or been transformed
by witchcraft like the *wer-bear* in Scotland, the *wer-tiger* in 11710
Malay, the *wer-fox* in Japan, the *wer-hyena* in Nigeria, and the
wer-leopard in Africa.

In French, a WEREWOLF is known as a *loup-garou* (literally)
'wolf-man-wolf,' from *loup* 'wolf' + *-garou*. The *-garou* element
comes from Old French *garoul*, *garulf*, from Frankish **werwulf* 11715
(Germanic **w-* > French *g-*).

These considerations throw light upon another word, WORM-
WOOD 'an aromatic plant of the genus *Artemisia*,' especially
Artemisia absinthium, which yields a bitter extract formerly used
in making absinthe. The linguistic ancestry of *wormwood* has 11720
nothing to do with either *worms* or *wood*, for the word is a folk-
etymological distortion of Old English *wermōd*, which is in turn
derived from Germanic **wer-mōd-* and is, according to most
authorities, of obscure origin. However, some of them (*EP, M.
O'C., Walshe*) see in it 'man-courage.' The German cognate is 11725
Wermuth 'wormwood,' possibly from *wer* 'man' + *mut* 'courage.'
It is possible that the appellation *wermōd* 'man-courage' was
given to the herb because it was used as an aphrodisiac, but if so
this lore has been forgotten. The *worl-* form evolved "due to the
use of Artemisia as a remedy for worms in the body" (*ODEE*). 11730
Germanic *wermut(h)* 'wormwood' is the source of French
vermout 'bitters,' which became the English VERMOUTH 'a wine
flavored with aromatic herbs.' Because of the toxicity of absinthe,
owing to the wormwood ingredient (*Artemisia absinthium*), its
manufacture and consumption have been forbidden in France 11735
since 1912.

Old English *wer(e)* traces back through Germanic **weraz*
'man' to the Indo-European root **wiros* 'man,' which also has the
Latin descendant *vir* 'man, adult male human being.' Latin *vir* is

11740   the ultimate source of the English loanwords VIRILE 'having masculine strength and vigor' [from Latin *virīlis* 'manly'] and VIRAGO (archaic) 'a heroic woman, strong and brave as a man'; 'a noisy, domineering woman' [from Latin *virāgō* 'a warlike woman; a female warrior'], *-āgō* being a "suffix expressing association of

11745   some kind, here resemblance" (*RHD*). Women coming under the first definition would include Joan of Arc and Molly Pitcher. In the Vulgate translation of the Bible the word *virāgō* is used to describe the newly created Eve (*Genesis* ii, 23), *quoniam de viro sumpta est* 'because she was taken out of man.' Going back to the

11750   same root is VIRTUE (obsolete) 'manly courage'; 'moral excellence; chastity, especially on the part of women' [from Latin *virtūs* 'manly strength; worth, excellence; moral perfection']. The sequence of meanings here shows that male chauvinism is not new. Still more English loanwords from Latin *vir* include VIRTU-

11755   OSO (archaic) 'a connoisseur of the arts'; 'one who has complete mastery over the technique of his art' [Italian, from Late Latin *virtuōsus* 'skillful,' from Latin *virtūs* 'excellence']; VIRTUAL (obsolete) 'having the power of producing a certain effect'; 'being (something) in effect, but not in fact' (to him, coffee is a VIRTUAL

11760   necessity) [from Medieval Latin *virtuālis*, from Latin *virtūs* 'worth']; and TRIUMVIRATE 'a partnership of three men' [from Latin *triumvirātus*, from *triumvir(i)*, from *triumvirōrum* '(one) of three men,' from *trēs virī* 'three men']. The two most famous of the Roman triumvirates were those of Julius Caesar, Pompey, and

11765   Crassus, and of Octavian Caesar, Marc Antony, and Lepidus. Less frequent is DUUMVIRATE 'a partnership of two men.' Both words were probably formed by analogy with DECEMVIRATE 'a body of ten Roman magistrates appointed in 451 B.C. to formulate a code of laws [*decem* 'ten']. Then there is the Roman CURIA (originally)

11770   'one of the primitive subdivisions of a tribe'; 'the place of assembly of a Roman tribal subdivision; the Roman senate house; the governing central administration of the Roman Catholic Church' [Latin *cūria* from Old Latin **coviria*, for **kowiriyā* 'men together' (**ko-* 'together' + **wiro* 'man')].

11775   The stereotype of the VIRILE man is that he is full of VIM, sometimes VIOLENT, and not above VIOLATING laws or women as the occasion presents itself. There a possibility that Indo-European **wiros* 'man' is an extended form of the Indo-European root **wei-* 'vital force,' ancestor via Latin of the English loan-

11780   words VIM 'energy, vitality' [supposedly from Latin *vīs*, *vim* 'force, power, strength']; VIOLENT 'manifesting extreme physical force' [via Old French from Latin *violentus* 'impetuous, boisterous']; and VIOLATE 'to break (a law or regulation); to do harm to; to rape; to invade the privacy of' [from Latin *violāre, violātus* 'to maltreat, to dishonor'].

LX

The Adjustable Yoke

In some CONJUGAL arrangements, one member of the YOKE becomes more SUBJUGATED than CONJUGATED and may end up slashing the other's JUGULAR or turning for peace of mind to YOGA. The capitalized words all have meanings that imply a
11790   JOINING or JUNCTION, words that derive from the Indo-European root *yeug- 'to join, to bind together.'

The literal meaning in Sanskrit of the word YOGA is 'union,' but this meaning has been enlarged in Hindu philosophy to 'union of the self with the universal spirit,' hence 'a system of
11795   physical exercise and mental discipline aimed at achieving union of the self with Brahma, the supreme essence of the universe; immaterial, uncreated, illimitable, timeless.' One who practices this exercise and discipline is a YOGI.

A related Sanskrit word, less familiar to westerners, is YUGA,
11800   YUG (literally) 'yoke'; 'one of the four Ages of the World that constitute the cycle of history.' According to Hindu cosmologists the world goes through mathematically regular cycles of ages. Each cycle, or MAHAYUGA 'Great Yoke,' lasts 4,320,000 years and is divided into four YUGAS of 1,728,000, 1,296,000, 864,000 and
11805   432,000 years (the ratios of these numbers to each other is 4, 3, 2, 1, which adds up to 10).

In Old English, Indo-European *yeug- 'to join' shows up in the guise of geoc 'yoke' > Middle English yok > English YOKE 'a device that joins two things together; a crosspiece attached to
11810   necks or heads of draft animals, especially oxen; a band fitted around the neck and shoulders, or at the hips, to support the suspended part of a garment; an arch of spears' [from Germanic *yukam]. (See Latin iugum, below.) Probably related to YOKE is YOGH 'the Middle English letter ȝ, used to represent voiced or
11815   voiceless palatal or velar fricatives; replaced in Modern English

spelling by *g*, *gh*, or *y*, possibly from Middle English *yok* 'yoke,' so called because its shape resembles a yoke. (Some versions of the yogh look like ȝ, which could be a yoke standing on end. The Latin word used to denote this letter was *jugum* 'yoke.') Some words once spelled with a yogh are *yoke* < Middle English ȝeoc, *yok* < Old English *geoc*; *yogh* < Middle English ȝok, ȝoch; *yclept* < Middle English ȝeclypod < Old English *geclypod*; *straight* < Middle English strei ȝet; *rough* < Middle English ruȝ, rowȝ < Old English *rūh*; and *give* < Middle English ȝiofan < Old English *giefan*. In the International Phonetic Alphabet, ȝ (yogh) is used to indicate the sound of -*s*- in *measure*, -*si*- in *vision*, -*z*- in *azure*, *g*- in *genre*, *j*- in the French pronunciation of *jabot*, *jalousie*, etc. These sounds are indicated in other phonetic systems by -*zh*-, -*z*-, and by various other symbols.

Indo-European **yeug*- 'to join' is exemplified in Latin by the word *iugum* 'yoke; yoke of slavery, yoke of matrimony; a rowers' bench (to which the galley slaves were chained); an arch made of two upright spears, with a third spear laid across the top,' under which the conquered foes of the Roman legions were required to walk, in single file, as an acknowledgment of their SUBJUGATION. *Iugum* < *jugum* is an English technical term in biology, JUGUM 'a paired structure.' The corresponding adjective is JUGATE 'joined in pairs.' Latin *iugum* 'yoke' has the diminutive *iugulum* 'collarbone' (joining the shoulders and chest); 'base of the throat, throat, neck.' The adjective for *iugulum* is *iugulāris*, whence English JUGULAR 'situated in the throat or neck; a large vein in the neck.' The Latin verb based on *iugulum* is *iugulāre* 'to cut the throat, to murder; to destroy,' but the verb based on *iugum* 'yoke,' to wit, *iugāre*, *iugātum*, has the nonsanguinary meanings of 'to connect, to bind; to marry.' Simple *iugāre* has not been borrowed by English but some of its compounds have. For example, CONJUGATE 'joined together, especially in pairs; to join together, to unite; to list in order the forms of a verb' [from Latin *coniu(n)gare*, *coniu(n)gatus* 'to join together']; CONJUGAL 'of marriage' [from Latin *coniugālis*, from *coniu(n)x* 'spouse']; and SUBJUGATE (literally) 'to put under the yoke'; 'to conquer, to subdue; to enslave' [from Latin *subiugāre*, *subiugātus* 'to place under a yoke'].

Latin *iugo*, *iugare*, *iugatus* 'to join, to bind together; to marry' has a nasalized counterpart in the verb *iungo*, *iungere*, *iūnctus* 'to join, to yoke, to harness.' *Iungere* is in fact more widespread in its uses and in the number of English loanwords ascribable to it than the nonnasalized *iugāre*. From the past participle *iūnctus* come English JUNCTION 'a place where two things meet' [from Latin *iūnctiō(nem)* 'a joining'] and JUNCTURE 'the act of joining; a point

11820

11825

11830

11835

11840

11845

11850

11855

11860

in time; a crisis' [from Latin *iunctūra* 'a joining, a joint']. The feminine of Latin *iūnctus* 'joined,' *iūncta*, shows up in Spanish JUNTA 'a meeting, an assembly; a small legislative body; a group of military officers who seize the reins of government by a coup

11865   d'état.' An English variant of JUNTA, popular during the 17th and 18th centuries but since fallen into disuse, is JUNTO 'a small group of persons combined for a special purpose; a clique, a cabal.' (In Spanish, *junto* is an adjective meaning 'joined, united,' used with prepositional effect in the phrases *junto a* 'next to' and *junto con*

11870   'together with.')

Compounds of Latin *iungo, iungere, iūnctus* 'to join, to yoke' that have been adapted into English are ADJUNCT 'something joined on to something else in a subordinate position' [from Latin *adiungere, adiūnctus* 'to yoke to']; CONJUNCTION 'the act of

11875   joining together; a simultaneous happening, a coincidence; a connective word' [from Latin *coniunctiōnem*, from *coniungere, coniūnctus* 'to join together, to connect']; CONJUNCTIVA 'the mucous membrane of the inner surface of the eyelid' [from Medieval Latin *membrāna conjunctīva* '(the) connective mem-

11880   brane']; DISJUNCTIVE 'serving to separate' [from Latin *disiungere* 'to unyoke']; and SUBJUNCTIVE (literally) 'joining under'; 'the verbal form used to indicate hypothetical or contingent actions or states' [from Late Latin *mōdus subiunctīvus* 'subjoined mood']. *Mōdus subiunctīvus* is a translation of Greek *hupotaktikē enklisis*

11885   'subordinated mood,' and the name arises because the subjunctive is usually used in a subordinate clause, though also in independent clauses expressing wishes and exhortations such as "Long live the king!" and "Have a good day!" Not as easy to follow, semantically, is INJUNCTION, ENJOINMENT, ENJOINDER 'an authori-

11890   tative order; a judicial order prohibiting a specified act' [from Latin *iniungere* 'to join into, to attach to; to impose (a penalty, a duty) upon; to enjoin'].

In transmigrating to Old French, Latin *iungere* (> Medieval Latin *jungere*) was transmogrified into *joindre*, with present

11895   participle *joignant*, and 3rd person plural *joignent*. These forms gave rise to Middle English *joignen* > *joinen*, whence Modern English JOIN 'to unite, to put together, to connect; to participate.' From the Old French past participle *joint* comes English JOINT 'a place where two or more things are connected; shared by two or

11900   more'; (slang) 'a gathering place'; (slang) 'a marijuana cigarette.'

The compound forms of *-join-* display the full complement of prefixes already seen with *-juga-* and *-junct-*, that is, *ad-, con-, dis-, en-* (for *in-*), *sub-*, and in addition, *re-*. The words in *-join-* all include verbs, lacking in the *-junct-* words, which are all nouns

11905   and adjectives. Otherwise, the *-join-* words show a parallelism

with those in -*junct*-, often with only slight differences in meaning. Consider JOINTURE, JOINT, JUNCTURE (legal) 'the holding of property for the joint use of a husband for the lifetime of the survivor; property set aside by a husband for the support of his widow'; ADJOIN 'to unite; to be next to; to be an ADJUNCT to';   11910
CONJOIN 'to join together; to be in CONJUNCTION with'; CONJOINT, CONJUNCT 'joined together'; DISJOIN 'to undo a union, to separate; to effect a DISJUNCTION'; DISJOINT 'to dislocate; to take apart at the joints; to destroy the coherence of' (He spoke in DISJOINTED sentences); ENJOIN 'to command; to prohibit'; ENJOINDER, ENJOIN-   11915
MENT, INJUNCTION 'prohibition'; and SUBJOIN 'to add at the end; to attach' [from Latin *subiungere* 'to add']. The prefix *sub*-, which usually has meanings of 'under, below, inferior to, up from under, up,' in this instance means 'in addition to' or 'very soon after.' Compare the *sub*- in *subapostolic*, designating 'the age immedi-   11920
ately after that of the apostles.' Note, also, REJOIN 'to join again; to answer a reply.' These two meanings are treated by some dictionaries as two different words, although they both trace back to Old French *rejoindre* 'to join again,' but the sense 'to answer' is not found in either Old or Modern French. The reason for the   11925
distinction is that English REJOIN 'to answer, to say in reply' is really a back formation from the English noun REJOINDER 'an answer in response to a reply.' A rejoinder is therefore the second time the person making the rejoinder has spoken. The first time this person spoke is a JOINDER (legal) 'the formal acceptance of a   11930
suit offered; the joining of parties in a suit'; 'the act of joining.' What happened linguistically is that the English speakers took over the Old French infinitive *joindre* 'to join' and used it as a noun, JOINDER 'a joining.' What takes place in a lawsuit is that (1) the plaintiff makes a complaint against the defendant who (2)   11935
joins the issue by making a JOINDER 'an acceptance of the suit offered.' (3) The plaintiff makes a *replication* 'a response to the defendant's plea,' whereupon (4) the defendant makes a REJOIN-DER 'an answer to the reply.' Hence the verb to REJOIN (in lieu of *rejoind*). REJOINDER is also used loosely to mean simply 'a   11940
reply.'

Following the lead given by JOINDER and REJOINDER English speakers have also coined the words SUBJOINDER 'an additional remark' [from *subjoin* 'to add on'] and ENJOINDER 'an order; an injunction' [from *enjoin* 'to order; to prohibit'].   11945

The JUXTAPOSING of lances that takes place in a JOUST creates a fearsome JOSTLING that requires the knights involved to make skillful ADJUSTMENTS or find themselves READJUSTING from a prostrate position. The verb to JOIN has shades of meaning that taper down from the perfection of 'to unite' to the loose associa-   11950 tion of 'to take part in; to be near.' A Latin word that expresses this 'nearness' is *iuxtā* 'near, close, hard by' (from earlier **iugstā* or **iugistā*, related to the root of Latin *iugum* 'yoke' and *iugāre* 'to join' by common descent from Indo-European **yeug-* 'to join').

11955   *Iuxtā* > *juxtā* is evident in English JUXTAPOSITION 'the state of being placed side by side,' a Modern (17th-century) French coinage combining Medieval Latin *juxtā* 'very close to' with *position*. The verb JUXTAPOSE is a back formation from JUXTAPO-SITION. The noun appears in English writing in 1665, the verb in

11960   1851. Also from Latin *iuxtā* 'near' is English JOUST, JUST 'to join in battle; a combat in which two mounted knights encounter each other with lances; a sporting encounter as above; a tilting match' [from Old French *joster, juster*, from Vulgar Latin **juxtāre* 'to approach, to come together, to meet']. The historically correct

11965   spelling and pronunciation of this word is JUST. Diminutive or frequentative forms of *just/joust* that were bandied about on the tournament field were *justle/joustle*, meaning 'to come into colli-sion with.' These led eventually to English JOSTLE 'to collide with, to knock against with one's body; to force one's way by

11970   pushing and elbowing.'

Another word that is, according to some, derived from Latin *iuxtā* 'near' is English ADJUST 'to rearrange; to harmonize; to adapt to conditions' [from Old French *ajoster*, from Medieval Latin *adjustāre*, from Vulgar Latin **adjuxtāre* 'to place close to'].

11975   Others, however, derive *adjust* from Latin *ad-* 'toward' + *iustus* 'just, right.' This, says the *OED*, is a natural but erroneous view of the derivation of Medieval Latin *adjustāre*, and because of this high-level error the English word ADJUST was and is consciously used by many speakers and writers as though derived from Latin

11980   *iustus* 'right.'

There is no doubting the Greek descendants of Indo-Euro-pean **yeug-* 'to join,' though the ancestral **y-* has become Greek *z-*, as in *zeugma* 'band, bond, bar, bridge; yoke, a yoking, a joining.' (Indo-European **y-* to Greek *z-* is a regular sound

11985   correspondence. See line 000.) *Zeugma* is also used figuratively in ZEUGMA 'a rhetorical figure in which a word modifies two incongruously coupled words' ("He left in a high dudgeon and hat." "See Pan with flocks, with fruits Pomona crowned."—A. Pope). From the zero-grade, *e*-less Indo-European form **yug-* 'to

11990   join' comes Greek *zugon* 'yoke, cross bar; a pair, a team,' which, together with the related verb *zugoun* 'to yoke, to join' gives rise to English ZYGOTE 'the cell formed by the union of two germ cells (ovum and sperm)' [from Greek *zugōtos* 'joined, yoked']; ZYGOMA 'the cheekbone'; ZYGOMATIC arch 'the arch of bone

11995   along the side or front of the skull beneath the eye socket' [from

Greek *zugōma* 'bolt, bar, yoke']; ZYGODACTYL 'having two toes projecting forward and two backward, like a parrot' [*daktulos* 'finger, toe']; AZYGOUS 'unpaired' [New Latin, from Greek *azugos* 'not yoked, not one of a pair']; and SYZYGY 'points in the orbit of a celestial body where it is in conjunction with or opposition to the   12000
sun' (as the moon at new and full moon); 'the configuration of the sun, earth, and moon all lying in a straight line' (as during solar and lunar eclipses); (in classical prosody) 'two feet combined into a metrical unit' [from Greek *suzugia* via Late Latin *syzygia* (*sun* 'together' + *zugon* 'yoke')].   12005

Index

achever, 2316
ACHIEVE, 2315
'achievement', 4239
'acknowledge', 4740
acolada, 10905
ACOLYTE, 9411
acolytus, 9413
'acorn', 11223
'acorn cup', 8943
'acquire', 7986, 8150
'acquire again', 8066
'acquire from', 3257
'acquisition from', 3257
'acquit', 7216
ACROPHOBIA, 5680
'across', 3462
'act', 101, 4494
ACT, 103
'acting, way of', 7547
'action', 105, 11539, 11567
ACTION, 108
'action, capacity for',
   11548
ACTIVATE, 108
'active', 11550
ACTIVE, 108
'activity', 11549
ACTIVITY, 108
'activity, physiological',
   9884
'act of', 9734
'actor', 92
ACTOR, 109
'act or move, unable to',
   463
ACTORS, 115
'act together secretly', 3876
'actual', 8729
ACTUAL, 111
ACTUALITY, 111
āctuārius, 113
ACTUARY, 111
ACTUATE, 111
āctum, 100
āctus, 105
'acute', 5291, 8764
'acuteness, mental', 6589
ad, 533, 4136, 4263, 5999,
   7213, 8095, 8245, 9795
ad-, 663, 3873, 4696, 5309,
   9175, 9223, 10906,
   11902, 11975
'adapt', 11973

ad collectām, 6561
'add', 11917
'add at the end', 11916
'added word', 4581
addīcere, 6153
ADDICT, 6155
addictus, 6156
'adding', 4603
'add on', 11944
'adduce', 7213
ADDUCE, 3482
addūcere, 3483
ADELPHOGAMY, 9417
adelphos, 9415
-ADELPHOUS, 9419
adēn, 11223
ADENOID, 11222
'adequate', 3272, 4311
adesse, 8640
'adhere', 7086, 7113
adiūnctus, 11874
adiungere, 11874
ADJOIN, 11910
'adjudge', 6154
ADJUNCT, 11872, 11910
adjust, 11975
'adjust', 4028
ADJUST, 11972
adjustāre, 11974
ADJUSTMENTS, 11948
*adjuxtāre, 11974
ad legem, 7223
adlēgiāre, 7223
'administrative official',
   4301
'admiration, power to
   command', 9798
'admired', 11210
'admission', 5605
'admission of a wrong',
   6868
'admit', 4743
ADO, 4489
adobar, 4021
adobāre, 4023
adobe, 4025
ADOBE, 4021
adolere, 6059
adolēscēns, 6000
ADOLESCENT, 6001
'adolescent boy', 9850
ADOLESCENTS, 5953
adolēscere, 5999

adōnāi, 2807
'adored', 11209
'adorn', 3283, 3733, 4023,
   6263, 8009, 8060, 9969
ADORN, 635
adōrnāre, 636
'adornment', 8010
adouber, 4020
*ad partem, 8210
*adrationāre, 663
'adroit', 3289, 5810
'adroit move', 7770
'adroitness', 3296
adsimilāre, 9193
ADSUM, 8640
'adult', 6088
ADULT, 6002
adulterate, 6018
adultery, 6018
ADULTS, 5953
adultus, 6001
'advance', 4303
'advance, not prepared in',
   11346
'advancing toward
   perfection', 4305
'advantage', 8630
'advantageous', 8593, 8628
'advantageous combination',
   8402
ADVECTION, 10719
'adventure', 2224
'adventurer', 8470
'adversary', 96
'advice', 681
ADVICE, 11371
'advice, give', 679
'advisable, praise as', 7622
*advisāre, 11371
'advise', 695
ADVISE, 11369
*advīsum, 11371
'advocate', 92
aedēs, 4065, 4373
aedificāre, 4068
AEDILE, 4074
aedīlis, 4074
aedis, 4065
aeghwaether, 11090
aegther, 11090
ǣlan, 4134
aelf, 690, 3903, 3953

Aelfhere, 3911
aelfr, 3951
Aelfraed, 3904
*aelfrīce, 3934
AERODROME, 3367
AEROPHYTE, 1675
aestās, 4111
aestātem, 4111
AESTIVAL, 4119
aestivāre, 4115
AESTIVATE, 4115
aestīvus, 4120
*aestotātem, 4111
aestuārium, 4125
aestus, 4125
aet, 11452
aeternus, 9250
aethele, 691
aether, 4090
aetwītan, 11452
af-, 4696, 5309
afaire, 4272
afere, 4274
affābilis, 4696
AFFABLE, 4695
AFFAIR, 4275
AFFAIRS, 4276
'affairs, human', 6098
affārī, 4696
AFFECT, 4264
affectāre, 4268
AFFECTATION, 4270
AFFECTION, 4265
affectus, 4262
AFFETTUOSO, 4266
afficere, 4262
'affinity', 8360
'affinity, emotional', 8363
'affirm as an attribute',
    6213
'affliction', 340
AFFLUENCE, 5308
'after', 1652, 4583, 6805
*ag-, 6, 71, 99, 160, 222,
    290
'again', 154, 1194, 2799,
    8039, 8366, 11013
'against', 96, 197, 2051,
    3898, 4828, 7995, 8073,
    10608
'against life', 8863
'age', 9457, 11673
'age, having a specified',
    6091

agein, 5, 55, 179, 297
agenda, 164
AGENDA, 158
agendum, 163
agens, 161
'agent', 4151, 7179
AGENT, 157
'age of man', 6099, 11674
ager, 3636
agere, 100, 159, 187, 215,
    286
AGILE, 157
agilis, 165
agitāre, 174
'agitate', 798, 10212, 10735
AGITATE, 157
'agitated', 789
agnail, 2571
AGNAIL, 315
agō, 100
-ago, 11412, 11744
agog, 58
agōgos, 4, 46
-agogue, 3
-AGOGUE, 40, 70
-AGOGUERY, 3
agōn, 67
agōnia, 66
AGONIST, 94
agōnistēs, 91
'agony', 66
AGONY, 61, 88
agora, 5682
AGORA, 5684
AGORAPHOBIA, 5682
agos, 47
agra, 308
agraphia, 6758
'agree', 2052, 5062, 6175
'agreeability', 9273
'agreeable', 9270
'agreeing with', 8712
'agreement', 6175, 6851
'agreement of sentiment',
    552
'agreement, point of', 6176
'agreement, secret', 3877
*agtios, 290
'ahead of', 7997
'aid', 2033
Aidēs, 11239
*aidh-, 4069, 4110

*aidh-lo-, 4131
*aidh-sto-, 4110
*ail-, 4132
ailp, 4044
'aim at', 4268, 5052
-aimiā, 7397
*ainlif, 1056
*ainlif-, 7071
aire, 3635
'airport', 3368
'air, upper', 4085
*aistaz, 4130
aithein, 4084
aithēr, 4085
*aiwo giwatharaz, 11090
ajoster, 11973
akantha, 5475
akolouthos, 9413
akros, 5680
akvavit, 8921
āl, 4132
al-, 3873, 5996
-al-, 5957
*al-, 5958, 6114
ala, 6089
alan, 6089
ALARM, 530
ALARUM, 534
alb, 3924
ALB, 3960, 4003
*alb-, 4031
alba, 4005, 4037
*alba, 4004
albada, 4008
albalux, 4006
Albanus, 4039
albāre, 4018
*albaz, 3921, 3955
albe, 3961
albellus, 4001
Alberich, 3925
*albho-, 4049
albino, 3985
ALBINO, 3984
Albion, 4038
ALBION, 4029
albiz, 3956
albo, 3986
alborne, 3989
album, 3976
ALBUM, 3977
albūmen, 3983

ALBUMEN, 3982
ALBURNUM, 3997
alburnus, 3988
albus, 3958, 4002
'alcohol', 8918
ald, 6091
*ald-, 11673
*aldaz, 6088
ALDERMAN, 6093
alegier, 7214
'alehouse', 8318
āleph, 2690
alere, 5960, 6027
'alert', 8844
alēscere, 5996
'Alexander the Great, war-
   horse of', 1773
ALEXIA, 6754
ALFRED, 690, 3899
algo, 11157
alibī, 11151
ALIBI, 11150
alibilis, 6015
ALIBLE, 6015
'alien', 5505
'alike', 9167
ALIMENT, 5960
ALIMENTARY, 5961
alimentum, 5960
alimōnia, 5964
ALIMONY, 5962
aliquid, 11155
alitus, 6041
alius, 11152
'alive', 8771, 8874
'alive, almost', 8780
'alive, as if', 8780
'alive, remain', 8797
'all', 855, 7724
all-arm, 536
all'arme, 532
*alleague, 7233
allēgāre, 7212
allēgātiō, 7211
ALLEGATION, 7203
ALLEGATIONS, 7134
allēgātus, 7212
allege, 7229
'allege', 7213
ALLEGE, 7203, 7231
alleguer, 7232
ALLERGY, 11556
alles weis, 10566

alle wei, 10566
alleweyes, 10567
'alliance', 6006
'all-inclusive', 864
'all in one piece', 751
'all of time', 9241
allos, 11558
'allot', 7991, 8110, 8155
ALLOT, 2679
'allot a share to', 8244
ALLOTMENT, 2679
'allotted', 8156
'allowance', 10585
'allowing passage through',
   10637
'allow to remain behind',
   7104
ALLUDE, 3843, 3870
allūdere, 3872
'all way', 10567
alma, 5966
alma mater, 5968
ALMA MATER, 5973
almarie, 525
almārium, 526
almerie, 525
almum, 5967
almus, 5966
'alone', 6810, 9227
'aloofness', 9628
aloter, 2678
Alp, 3922, 4044
ALP, 4040
alpa, 4044
alpas, 4051
Alpeis, 4043
ALPENSTOCK, 10285
Alpēs, 4043
alpha, 2688
'alphabetical listing', 6192
alphos, 4050
Alps, 4041
al-tabl, 10170
'altar', 5406, 6058
ALTAR, 6052
altare, 6054
altaria, 6054
alter, 6019, 9376
*al-tero, 9377
althaia, 6113
ALTHEA, 6111
althein, 6114
*altiāre, 6080, 10931

ALTIMETER, 6048
ALTITUDE, 6047
altitūdō, 6047
ALTO, 6049
al-ṭōba, 4025
ALTRICIAL, 6015
altrīcis, 6017
altrīx, 6017
altum, 6043
altus, 6041, 6080, 10931
alumna, 5977
ALUMNA, 5978
alumnus, 5976
ALUMNUS, 5978
alusson, 7403
alwayes, 10567
'always', 9238
ALWAYS, 10565
ALYSSUM, 7402
am, 1561, 8494
AM, 8478
*a man, a plan, a canal,
   Panama!*, 3375
ā manū, 7554
āmanuēnsis, 7553
AMANUENSIS, 7552
'amaze', 10095
'amazed', 10090
'amazement', 10093
'amazing', 10097
ambactia, 228
*ambactiāre, 229
*ambactiator(em), 230
*ambactos, 224
ambactus, 226
AMBAGE, 240
ambages, 241
AMBAGES, 245
*ambagto-, 223
ambasciator, 233
ambassadeur, 232
AMBASSADOR, 231
*ambhi-, 219
ambi, 1564
ambi-, 215, 937, 3298
*ambi-, 220
AMBIDEXTROUS, 217, 3297
AMBIENCE, 217
ambigere, 214
'ambiguous', 4434
AMBIGUOUS, 212, 244
ambiguus, 213

AMBIVALENCE, 936
AMBIVALENT, 217, 934
Ambivalenz, 937
AMBRY, 523
'ambush', 10569
âme, 5990
'amiable', 4695
'amid', 9530
'amiss', 2321, 6912
'amnesty', 6011
'among', 1652, 6592
'amount', 717, 11109
'amount, fixed', 10239
amparar, 8040
amphi, 1564, 8863
amphi-, 218
AMPHIBIOUS, 218, 8862
AMPHITHEATER, 218
'ample', 4371
AMPLIFY, 4370
amplus, 4370
'amuse oneself', 8374
'a musical sound, quality
    of', 10150
an, 408
an-, 9361, 9423
ana, 4541, 6849
ana-, 2798, 6719
Anacreon in Heaven, 4842
a nadder, 10730
ANADROMOUS, 3377
ANAGRAM, 2796
anagramma, 2797
anagrammatizein, 2798
analecta, 6720
ANALECTS, 6716
analegein, 6719
analekta, 6718
analogia, 6848, 8240
ANALOGIES, 6859
ana logon, 8239
ANALOGUE, 6863
ANALOGUES, 6860
analogy, 8240
ANALOGY, 6847
An Apology for the Bible,
    6875
an apron, 10730
a narancia, 10731
ANARTHOUS, 398
an ash, 10727
ANASTIGMAT, 10018
ANASTIGMATIC, 10018

anathema, 4537
ANATHEMA, 4535
anatithenai, 4540
'ancestry, persons of
    common', 701
'anchor', 3088
'ancient', 6832
'ancient Greece, political
    subdivision of', 1686
'and', 992, 11148
'and also', 992
'and moreover', 992
an ekename, 10726
an ewt, 10726
ang-, 335
*ang-, 324
'anger', 8410, 11646
ANGER, 314
angere, 353
ANGER-NAIL, 334
*angh-, 317, 354
angina, 367
ANGINA, 365
'angle', 6376, 6416, 9402
'angled', 6375
'angles, science of
    measuring', 6385
ANGLO-, 5697
ANGLOPHONE, 4865
angnaegl, 321
angosto, 358
angostura, 358
ANGOSTURA, 361
angr, 340
ANGRY, 335
ANGST, 350
ANGUISH, 315, 355
anguisse, 356
angustia, 356
angustus, 357
a nickname, 10726
anima, 5991
'animal', 5717, 8875, 8903,
    9349
'animal, castrated', 11098
'animal, chimerical', 8135
'animal life, science of',
    8883
'animals', 10272
'animals, dread of', 5717
'animated', 7115, 8786
'animosity, intense', 5676
ankhein, 368

ankhonē, 367
ANNEAL, 4133
'annihilate', 9996
an notch, 9560
annoy, 9286
'annoy', 798, 1831, 10744
'annoyance', 1831
'annoyance, source of',
    11529
'annoyed, become', 4385
'annoying', 9285
'annual', 818
'annul', 4492, 6008
'annulment', 6010
annus, 820
ANOMALOUS, 9360
a nompere, 10729
an orange, 10731
a + noumpere, 7908
-āns, 8548
'answer', 11924
'answer a reply', 11922
'answer in response to a
    reply', 11928
ANTAGONIST, 95
antef(a)na, 4832
antefn(e), 4833
antem(ne), 4833
antempne, 4833
*anteparāre, 8041
*an-tero-, 9377
ANTHEM, 4834
anthologia, 6826
ANTHOLOGY, 6821
ANTHROPOID, 11220
anthymne, 4836
anti, 4828
anti-, 96
ANTIBIOSIS, 8864
ANTIBIOTIC, 8863
ANTICLOCKWISE, 11436
'anti-hymn', 4837
antilegein, 6905
antilogein, 6905
antilogia, 6905
ANTILOGISM, 6908
antilogos, 6904
ANTILOGY, 6907
ANTIPHON, 4829
antiphōna, 4830
antiphōnos, 4830
ANTIPHONY, 4827

-antis, 8549
ANTITHESES, 4554
antithesis, 4562
antitithenai, 4562
antparar, 8040
an umpire, 10729
anxi, 353
anxietās, 351
'anxiety', 795
ANXIETY, 314, 350
'anxiety, feeling of', 350
'anxious', 793
ANXIOUS, 351
anxius, 352
apareil, 8096
a part, 8209
'apart', 2359, 2626, 3460,
    4426, 6543, 6609, 8100,
    9625, 9977
APART, 8207
ā parte, 8211
'apart, existing', 8104
'apart from', 8374
'apart from others', 7811
apartheid, 8220
APARTHEID, 8218
'apart-hood', 8218
APARTMENT, 8213
apetit, 5060
'apex, having a rounded',
    10194
APHASIA, 4861
'aphonia', 4862
APHONIA, 4859
APHONIC, 4861
ap Howell, 10727
apo, 5616, 6341, 6872
apodeiknunai, 6340
apodeixis, 6340
apodissa, 6339
apodixa, 6339
apodixis, 6339
apologia, 6871
Apologia pro Vita Sua,
    6876
Apologie of Syr Thomas
    More, Knyght, 6874
Apologie or Defence of our
    Dayes, 6873
APOLOGY, 6868
apophugē, 5616
APOPHYGE, 5614
apothēca, 4617

apothēcārius, 4617
APOTHECARY, 4613
apothēkē, 4618
apotithenai, 4618
apparāre, 8095
apparātus, 8094
APPARATUS, 8092
APPAREL, 8096
'apparent', 7500
*appariculāre, 8097
'apparition', 3922, 3956,
    11303
appartare, 8215
appartement, 8214
appartemento, 8215
appartīmentum, 8217
appartīre, 8217
'appear', 4402
'appearance', 4240, 4395,
    11277
'appearance, false', 11449
'appearance, on first', 4406
'appearance, outward',
    9214, 11449
'appear to be', 3222
'appeases', 5101
appetere, 5057
APPETITE, 5059
appetītiō, 5058
appetītus, 5058
'appetizer', 5573, 7758
'apple, wild', 2856
'application', 6604, 10065
'applying to a prior
    period', 155
'apply oneself to mentally',
    10060
'appoint', 4300
'appoint a deputy', 7179
apportāre, 8366
'apportion', 2679, 8217
APPORTION, 8244
apportionner, 8245
'apprehension, feeling of',
    531
'approach', 11964
'approach by stealth', 3872
'appropriate', 8400
approve, 8633
ap Rhys, 10728
'apse', 2324
APTERYX, 5109
'aptitude', 4336, 5850

'apt, sufficiently', 5063
aqua, 3549
aquae-ductus, 3549, 10583
AQUAVIT, 8921
AQUA VITAE, 8918
aqueduct, 10583
AQUEDUCT, 3547
*ar-, 384, 414, 473, 557,
    631, 669, 715
araisnier, 662
'arbiter', 6118
'arcade', 8277
ARCHAEOLOGY, 6831
ARCHAEOPTERYX, 5110
'arched', 10709
'archetype', 11184
ARCHETYPE, 10119
'architecture, type of',
    9865
-ard, 11420
*ar-dhro-, 387
ardor, 5456
'ardor, excessive', 10687
'ardor, great', 10687
are, 1561
'are', 8709
ARE, 8503
'area of competence',
    11354
arena, 10985
ARENICOLOUS, 10984
Arenwald, 985
argon, 11618
ARGON, 11617
argos, 11618
'argumentation, legal', 5533
*(a)rī-, 716
'Arian', 8663
Aries, 8905
*aristo-, 732
ARISTOCRACY, 734
aristos, 733
arithmein, 720
ARITHMETIC, 717
arithmētikē, 719
arithmētikos, 719
arithmos, 716, 6774
arkhaios, 6832
arkhē, 6832
àrm, 546
'arm', 484
ARM, 470

arma, 476, 522
armada, 492
ARMADA, 490
ARMADILLO, 377, 495
armado, 497
armaire, 520
ARMAMENT, 487
armāmenta, 488
armāre, 483
armārium, 520
armāta, 483
armāti, 485
armātūra, 499
ARMATURE, 377, 500
*armaz, 473
'armed one', 483
armee, 482
armëure, 499
armiger, 517
ARMIGER, 516
armilla, 538
armillaire, 541
armillaris, 541
ARMILLARY, 542
ARMISTICE, 528
armistitium, 529
'armlet', 539
armoire, 519
ARMOIRE, 519
armoirie, 507
'armor', 476
ARMOR, 498
'armorbearer', 516
'armor collectively', 505
'armor, defensive', 9046
'armored', 497
'armored one, little', 495
ARMORIAL, 508
'armorial insignia, specialist in', 976
'armorlike jointed bony plates, protected by', 495
ARMORY, 505
ARMS, 475, 510
'arms, coats of', 509
'arms factory', 506
'arms, heraldic', 509
'arms, summons to', 4937
'arms!, to', 530
'arm, upper', 469
armure, 499
armurie, 507

armus, 469, 538
'army', 49, 486, 970, 3576, 3911, 6526
ARMY, 481
'army, leader of an', 48
'army, one who serves in an', 841
'army pay', 839
arn, 985
ARNOLD, 984
'around', 215, 7995
ARRAIGN, 661
'arrange', 587, 625, 716, 6264
'arranged', 625
'arrange in a pile', 9600
'arrangement, systematic', 571
'arrange systematically', 574
'arranging', 589
'array', 570
'arrest', 9611
'arrogance', 6067
'arrogant', 6068, 8599
'arrow', 5717, 8034, 10029
'arrow poison', 5716
ars, 415, 459
arse, 2046
'arsenal', 505
*ar-smo-, 549
'arsonist', 5474
'art', 4341
ART, 417, 448, 8503
arte, 4205
ARTEFACT, 4204
artefatto, 4207
artem, 416
Artemisia, 11718
Artemisia absinthium, 11719
ARTFUL, 448
'artful contrivance', 4208
arthr-, 389
ARTHRITIC, 379
ARTHRITIS, 390
arthritis nosos, 393
arthro-, 389
arthron, 386
ARTHROPOD, 394
ARTHROSIS, 396
article, 10664
ARTICLE, 403

'article, used without an', 398
articulāre, 410
ARTICULATE, 381
ARTICULATED, 377, 410
articulō, 383
articulus, 400
ARTIFACT, 454, 4204
artifex, 453, 4210, 4345
artifex carpentārius, 1984
ARTIFICE, 450, 4208
'artificer', 4345, 11498
'artificial', 4207
ARTIFICIAL, 453, 4204
artificium, 452, 4209
artigiano, 456
artillery, 597
'artillery', 594
'artillery, timed discharge of', 771
artīre, 458
artis, 415, 459
ARTISAN, 455
artist, 444
'artist', 4210, 4345, 11582
ARTIST, 436
ARTISTE, 440
'artist's workshop', 10077
*artitiānus, 457
artītus, 457
ARTLESS, 449
'art of calculation', 6777
'arts', 432
ARTS, 420
'arts, fine', 3722
'arts, instruct in', 458
'arts, skilled in', 457
*ar-tu-, 387
artus, 386
as, 8691
'as', 11128
as-, 8675
'ascertain the nature of something', 676
(a)sconsa, 4467
'ascribe', 8361
'aside', 3460
'as if', 11127
'ask', 7605
'ask for', 7608
'ask for peremptorily', 7604
'aspect', 4395, 11293

avētō, 988
aviser, 11370
'avoid', 3874
AVOID, 10389
'avoid by adroitness', 3873
'avoid disaster', 2217
avoider, 10390
avoir, 5743
avoir-de-pois, 5749
AVOIRDUPOIS, 5745
'avow', 4741
'avowal', 4768
'award', 6154
'away', 285, 5616, 8551
AWAY, 10562
'away from', 3474, 4225,
    4428, 6207, 6872, 10393
AWAYWARD, 10570
aweg, 10564
'awe, inspiring', 9282
*awes-, 3795, 3822
'awesome', 1173
AWESOME, 9282
awe-struck, 9700
AXIOLOGY, 305
AXIOM, 304
axiōma, 300
axios, 290
axioun, 299
'axis', 11004
'axis of a sphere', 10995
azo-, 8885
AZOIC, 8890
AZOTE, 8886
azugos, 11998
azure, 11826
AZYGOUS, 11998

B

b-, 1184
-b, 1597
-b-, 5902
*b-, 4788, 5262
babble, 3744
baby, 3744
babyll, 3745
Bach, 5728
'bachelor', 6169
'back', 154, 2798, 3374,
    8366, 9950, 11013
'back again', 11014
'back-and-forth motion',
    9437

'backgammon, exposed
    piece in', 5360
'back, prickly', 9949
'backwards', 156, 3374
'bad', 2829, 3677, 4244,
    4799, 4849, 6753, 8700
*badjan, 2500
'badly', 4797, 5893
'bad-tempered', 606
baec, 9949
'baffle', 3849
'bag', 6485
baggatiway, 2971
bainīth, 3669
*bakjaz, 5728
'balance', 133
BALANCE, 1263
ban, 4900
BAN, 4894
*ban, 4911
'ban, against the', 4944
BANAL, 4883
band, 1484
'band', 9360, 11983
'bandage, cap-shaped', 2281
bandetto, 4934
bandire, 4930
BANDIT, 4933
banditi, 4935
bandito, 4931
banditti, 4934
bando, 4942
bandon, 4923
'band together', 4939
bandum, 4914, 4943
'bandy words', 8014
banir, 4926
'banish', 4930, 7182
BANISH, 4927
BANISHED BANDITS, 4883
banishen, 4926
'banishment', 4901
baniss (ant), 4926
BANLIEU, 4917
BANLIEUS, 4884
banna, 4907
bannan, 4898
*bannan, 4791, 4888, 4938
BANNED, 4884
bannīre, 4929
*bannīre, 4925
BANNS, 4895

bannum, 4902, 4942
'banquet', 8802
bār, 5605
'bar', 2563, 5697, 11983
-bar, 1089
bārak, 1378
-bard-, 8457
bard/berd, 8467
bare, 9348
'bargain', 10486
'bark', 5384
barm, 3041
'barn', 1453
'barrage against, lay down
    a', 6227
'barrel, little', 1582
'barren', 10420
'barrier', 9590
'barrier, protective', 8038
'barriers', 2652
'bartering', 7999
'bar the way', 5873
'basis, logical', 653
'basket', 3146
'bat', 2983
BATHOPHOBIA, 5681
bathos, 5681
'battle', 6796, 10214
'battle-ax', 9481
'battle-ax with two cutting
    edges', 1064
'battlement', 4972
'battlement, small', 4979
'battle, trial by wager of',
    1187
baubel, 3741
BAUBLE, 3739
Bauer, 1446
Baum, 1568
BAUM, 1583
*baumaz, 1567
Baummarder, 1585
'bay', 3061
be, 881, 8501, 8708
'be', 1554, 1587, 1621,
    1708, 8481, 8507, 8542,
    8639, 8675, 8701, 8731
BE, 1556, 8505
be-, 1050, 1562, 2330
-bē, 1824
'be able', 3518
'beads, prayer', 2242

bealte, 3732
bēam, 1572
'beam', 10787
BEAM, 1568
'beam, wooden', 10784
'beans', 6528
bear, 9349
'bear', 1090, 6033
beāre, 3746
'bearer', 10719
'bearing', 518, 7877, 8122, 8345, 9855
'bearing arms', 517
'beat', 9596, 10057, 10088, 10176, 10206, 10291, 10337
'beat a drum', 10123
'beat back', 10196
'beaten into shape', 11506
beātificāre, 3754
BEATIFY, 3752, 4371
'beating', 10230, 10306
BEATITUDE, 3749
beātitūdo, 3751
*beator, 3756
BEATRICE, 3755
BEATRIX, 3755
'beat upon', 10193
beātus, 3746, 4371
'beat with a club', 191
'beat with a stick', 10182
beau, 3718
BEAU, 3719
beau-, 3714
beaute, 3732
'beautiful', 3275, 3609, 3712, 11230, 11318
BEAUTIFY, 4372
'beautify, anything used to', 633
'beauty', 2828, 3338, 3721
BEAUTY, 3731
BEAUX, 3722
beaux arts, 431
'be before', 8545
bêche, 2335
bêche de mer, 2343
bechevet, 2329
BECK, 5726
become, 1562
'become', 1556, 1613, 8505
'become weary', 11527
'becoming', 3268, 7528

'becoming ill', 2994
'becoming one's own', 7528
'bed', 10533
BED, 2500
'bed, child's', 3145
'bedeck', 8061
'bedhead, double', 2329
bedight, 6262
'beds, four-poster', 947
BEEF, 1730
'beef, slice of', 1733
BEEFSTEAK, 1733
BEEN, 1560, 8505
'beer, dark', 8307
'beetles having club-shaped antennae', 2593
'before', 3480, 5887, 6803, 7709, 7989, 9321, 10637
befriend, 1562
'beg', 5053
'beget', 6406, 8112, 8148
'begin', 615
'beginner', 1680
'beginning', 618, 6832, 7527
'beginning, existing at', 619
'beginning, first', 621
'beginning, from the', 2382
'beginning to', 939, 5997
'behave', 104, 3486, 8346
'behave (oneself)', 8343
'behavior', 3487, 8345
'behavior, artificial', 4270
'behavior, code of', 9934
'behavior, insolent', 5078
'behavior patterns', 10975
'behavior, seemly', 3277
'behavior, unlearned', 9965
'beheading', 2138
'be healthy', 748, 876
'being', 8508, 8538, 8644, 8670, 8730
BEING, 1559, 8505
'be in good health!', 880
'being seated, a', 1710
'being, state of', 6177
be in the swim, 10761
bekkr, 5727
bel, 3718
bel-, 3711
belbel, 3737
beldam, 3710
BELDAME, 3602, 3709

'belief', 3199
'belief, basis for', 649
'beliefs, traditional', 3243
'believing', 11241
'belittle', 7970
'bell', 10159
bel(la), 3607, 3697
bella donna, 3700
BELLADONNA, 3601, 3698
BELLA VISTA, 3735
bel(le), 3712, 11317
BELLE, 3728
belle-, 3714
belle-dame, 3713
belle-mère, 3716
BELLES, 3730
BELLEVUE, 3734, 11316
*bellitātem, 3732
bellum, 1184, 3608, 3698
bellus, 3608, 3697, 3732, 3765, 11317
'belonging to', 7555
'below', 5645, 11918
BELVEDERE, 3734, 11317
bend, 6973
'bend', 1378, 3062, 6397, 7387, 10773
'bend frequently', 3002
'bending', 2993
'bending over', 3056
'bend the knee', 1378, 6398
bene, 3622, 3686, 3748
benedīcere, 1372, 6159
Benedick, 6163
BENEDICT, 6163
benedicta, 3695
BENEDICTION, 3688, 6160
benedictus, 3693
bene facere, 4169
benefactiō, 4168
BENEFACTOR, 3688, 4165
benefactum, 4223
benefactus, 4169
BENEFIC, 4217
BENEFICE, 4218
'beneficent', 4218
BENEFICENT, 4217
beneficere, 4169, 4215
'beneficial', 8583
BENEFICIAL, 4216
'beneficial!, may it be', 8584

'benefit', 4305, 8564
BENEFIT, 3688, 4222
'benefit, gratuitous', 4954
beneit, 3694
beneite, 3695
BENEVOLENT, 3689
benfet, 4223
*benigenus, 3691
BENIGN, 3689
benignus, 3691
benn, 5038
BENNET, 3693
BENNET(T), 3692
benoite, 3695
'bent', 2892
'bent at abrupt angle',
    6401
'be of concern', 8559
bēon, 1557, 1614
'be on hand', 8545
'bequeath', 7174
*beran, 1089
-berd-, 8457
'bereft', 10309
*bergan, 10940
Bernard, 11422
bescuit, 1234
BESEEM, 9268
'beside', 4575
'best', 733, 7703, 10187
'bestow', 5938
'bet', 7947, 9585
beta, 2690
'betake oneself', 8067
bēth, 2690
bethad, 8927
bethu, 8927
'betrayer', 6193
between, 1563
'between', 6592, 6808,
    8559
BETWEEN, 1049
BETWIXT, 1049
beubelot, 3737
bewegen, 10562
'be well!', 911
'be worth', 295
'beyond', 1654, 3249, 4262,
    5507
*bh-, 1601, 4787, 4885,
    5250
*bhā-, 4786, 4886, 4951
*bhā-ni-, 4952

*bhegw-, 5673, 5725
*bhel-, 1847, 5171, 5218,
    5259, 5285, 5349, 5385
*bhendh-, 1494
*bheu-, 1158, 1552, 1595,
    1621, 1708, 8504
bheug-, 5666
*bheug-, 5610
*bhlei-, 5370
*bhleu-, 5348, 5380
*bhlō-, 5260
*bhol-yo, 5250
*bhol-yo-, 5219
*bhrāter-, 1881
*-bhw-io-, 1596
*-bhw-o-, 1596
bi-, 1039, 1195, 1232, 1280
BIANNUAL, 1273
BIAXIAL, 1291
bib and tucker, 3589
BIBELOT, 3736
biblion, 4628
BIBLIOTHECA, 4627
BICAMERAL, 1292
BICARBONATE, 1292
BICENTENNIAL, 1292
biceps, 2176
BICEPS, 1206, 2173
bicho, 2346
BICORN, 1292
BICUSPID, 1207
BICYCLE, 1196, 1233,
    10839
BICYCLING, 10800
biddikil, 5881
BIENNIAL, 1271
biennium, 1272
BIFARIOUS, 4433
BIFOCAL, 1200
bifteck, 1734
bifteck d'ours, 1740
BIFURCATE, 1258
bifurcus, 1259
bigamus, 1261
BIGAMY, 1259
BIKE, 1233
BILABIAL, 1203
*bilancia, 1266
bilanx, 1266
BILINGUAL, 1205
-bilis, 5817
bilix, 1038
BILLION, 1275

BIMONTHLY, 1270
bin, 5882
bin-, 1195
bīnārius, 1214
BINARY, 1213
BINAURAL, 1202
bind, 1484, 1519
'bind', 1494, 7200, 11845
'bind back', 9776
'binding', 9733
'binding, rigorously', 9739
'bind (the eyes)', 6309,
    9802
'bind together', 9780,
    11791, 11854
'bind within limits', 9793
bīnī, 1214
BINNACLE, 5876
BINOCULAR, 1199
BINOMIAL, 1215
BIOCHEMISTRY, 8872
BIODEGRADABLE, 8872
'biographies of saints', 6678
BIOGRAPHY, 8859
'biography of a saint', 6672
'biological development',
    8672
BIOLOGY, 6833, 8860
BIONICS, 8872
BIOPHYSICS, 8872
BIOPSY, 8861
bios, 6833, 8852
-bious, 1158
BIPARTISAN, 1211
BIPARTITE, 1210
BIPED, 1197
BIPOD, 1198
bird, 4586
'birth', 1624, 3692, 6405,
    8673
'birth, give', 6407, 8792
bis, 1191, 1234, 2330
bis-, 1194
biscuit, 1238
BISCUIT, 1233
biscuits, 1244
BISECT, 1209, 9529
bishop, 1805
'bishop', 4361
bisket, 1237
BISQUE, 1254
BISSEXTILE, 1216

'bit', 10553
bitácola, 5878
bitácora, 5878
bitácula, 5878
bitakle, 5877
'bite', 6485
biticle, 5877
bittacle, 5877
'bitters', 11732
-bius, 1157, 1588
BIWEEKLY, 1268
*biwos, 8855
BIYEARLY, 1271
BLADE, 5283
blæd, 5284
BLAIN, 5372
*blajinōn, 5374
BLAME, 4810
blamen, 4810
blâmer, 4810
blanc, 3981
'blandish', 8717
'blank', 3976
blapsis, 4804
blaptein, 4805
blas-, 4802
blasmer, 4809
blasphēmāre, 4806
'blaspheme', 4807
blasphēmein, 4805
blasphēmia, 4801
blasphēmos, 4801
BLASPHEMY, 4800
*blastēmāre, 4808
blat, 5365
*blaut-, 5356
blautr, 5356
blǣdsian, 1356
-ble, 5813
BLEED, 1418
'bleeding', 1412
blegen, 5373
'blemish', 6322, 10000
'bless', 1354, 3747
BLESS, 1358
'blessed', 3693, 4372
BLESSED, 1352
'blessedly happy, make',
    4371
'blessedness', 3749
'blessing', 6160
BLESSING, 1370
blestre, 5372

blētsian, 1356
blettr, 5364
'blind', 9802
'blindfold', 9801
bliss, 1384
'blister', 5373
BLISTER, 5370
blithe, 1388
'blithe', 1388
*blīthiz, 1387
BLOAT, 5355
'block, psychic', 5864
blōd, 1394
blōm, 5263
blōma, 5265
*blō-mōn, 5261
'blond', 3990
blood, 1409
'blood', 1358, 1391, 7127,
    7397
BLOOD, 1352, 1392
'blood corpuscle, white',
    7394
'blood, emit', 1418
'blood feud, hereditary',
    6245
'bloodstained', 1394
'blood vessels, minute',
    2352
'bloody', 1406
BLOODY, 1394
'bloody drunk', 1404
'bloom', 5171, 5218, 5259,
    5286
BLOOM, 5170, 5262
BLOOMER, 5267
'blooming', 5195
bloot, 5358
'blossom', 5174
BLOSSOM, 5170, 5281
'blossoming', 5181
blōstm, 5281
blōs(t)ma, 5281
blost(r)e, 5366
'blot', 5364
BLOT, 5360
'blotch', 5373
BLOTCH, 5376
*blōtham, 1357, 1391,
    1420
*blōthisōjan, 1357
blotte, 5366
'blow', 5370, 9665, 10104

BLOW, 5275
'blow, deal a', 9674
'blow, hard', 6470
'blow, sharp', 6468
'blunt', 10240
'blunted', 10192
'blunt part', 10246
blush, 5341
'blush', 5336
Blut, 1394
bluten, 1419
blutig, 1395
bluyster, 5372
*bō-, 1506, 1551
bōa, 1499
bōandi, 1499
'board', 6361, 9047
'boastful', 10440
bod, 1709
BODEGA, 4623
bodeguero, 4625
bōdel, 1528
bodhar, 1834
bodhraim, 1835
'bodily processes, study of',
    1638
'body', 5761
'body and its diseases',
    1632
'body, dead', 5127
'body, fallen', 5122
'body (of men)', 2369
'body, of the', 1634
'body, treatment of', 1639
boedel, 1529
boef, 1731
boeiai (dorai), 1870
boer, 1428
BOER, 1429
boeuf, 1732
bogar, 10763
boiae, 1872
'boil', 5373, 9307
'boil over', 5382
'boisterous', 11782
bold, 1525
'bold', 11420
'bold bear', 11422
bole, 11516
boliverc, 11515
'bolster', 2326
'bolt', 2556, 5697, 11996

bolwerc, 11515
bolwerk, 11516
bommekijn, 1582
bon, 3632, 4952, 8761
BON, 3648
bona, 3619, 3661
BONA, 3684
bonacia, 3679
*bonacia, 3675
BONANZA, 3673
BONBON, 3640
'bonbons', 4282
bond, 1484
'bond', 6450, 11983
BOND-, 1489
bōnda, 1472
BONDAGE, 1467, 1495
bondāgium, 1471
bōndi, 1472, 1499
BONDMAID, 1489
BONDMAN, 1489
BONDSERVANT, 1489
BONDSLAVE, 1490
bondsman, 1492
'bondsman', 6157
BONDSMAN, 1490
'bond, unsecured', 5909
bone, 3653
'bone', 11034
bonhomie, 3642
BONHOMIE, 3641
bonhomme, 3643
bonita, 3662
bonitātem, 3659
bonito, 3662
BONITO, 3665
*bōniz, 4952
bonne, 3639
BONNE, 3638
BONNY, 3630
bonte(t), 3659
bonum, 3619
bonus, 3619, 3660, 3748, 4958
BONUS, 3624
bon(us + mal)acia, 3679
bon vivant, 8757
'bony, completely', 11033
BOODLE, 1530
'book', 4628
'book of diction', 6727
'book of words', 6727
'book storehouse', 4627
boom, 1575

BOOM, 1572
'boom, device resembling a ship's', 1574
boomken, 1576
'boom, little', 1577
boon, 3655, 4957
BOON, 3652, 4953
BOOR, 1426, 1496
BOORS, 1425
BOOTH, 1521
'boots', 10874
'booty', 8187
boreās, 3828
'bored', 4525, 11529
BOREDOM, 4525
'born', 9339
'borne by the waves', 10765
'borrow', 6958, 7097
bōs, 1726, 1829, 1858
BOS, 1728
'Bos, animal of the genus', 1741
boskein, 1856
BOSP(H)ORUS, 1778
Bosporos, 1781
botanē, 1856
botanicus, 1861
botanikos, 1861
'botany', 1670
BOTANY, 1851
botch, 5377
bōth, 1522
'both', 1097, 11089
BOTHER, 1831
*bōthla, 1528
'both sides, on', 937
botica, 4620
botl, 1525
boubalos, 1751
'boudoir', 1444
'bough, green', 5257
boukolikos, 1771, 10990
boukolos, 1771, 10988
boulevard, 11510
BOULEVARD, 11509
boulimia, 1827
boullewerc, 11514
boun, 1513
bound, 1484, 1518
BOUND, 1515
'boundaries of, determine', 11359

'bounded area', 2550
'bountiful', 5967
BOUNTY, 3656
bous, 1721, 1748, 1794, 1824, 10989
boustrophedon, 6514
BOUSTROPHEDON, 1774
BOUTIQUE, 4621
boutiquier, 4625
bouturon, 1783
bouwen, 1450
bouwerij, 1450
bovem, 1732
BOVINE, 1741, 1850
'bovine family', 1723
'bovines', 2199, 7800
BOVINES, 1844
bovīnus, 1742
bovis, 1726
bow, 9345
'bow down', 10324
BOWER, 1444, 1495
BOWERY, 1424, 1508
'bowl', 7456, 9006
'bow, ship's', 10918
'box', 10082
'boxing, practice', 8014
boy, 1879
'boy', 7859
BOY, 1867
boye, 1877
'boy, mischievous', 10513
'boy, young', 2125
'bracelet', 539
'bracket, wall', 4461
'brag', 10441
'brains', 2181
'branch', 1048
'branch of an organization', 2188
'branch, small', 1047
'brand', 10002
'brandish', 5175
'brandmark', 10000
'brandy', 8919
'brave', 932, 3824, 8596, 8629, 8740, 11742
'bravery', 931
'bravery, distinguished', 8625
'bravest', 733

'bread', 2498
'bread, light', 3035
'bread, particle of', 3124
'break', 9514
'breakable', 5836
'breaking loose', 2223
'break into small pieces',
  3125
'breath', 5991
'breeding', 10973
'breeze', 5991
Brewer, 4685
'bribe money', 1530
'bribery', 2706
'brick', 4026
brid(d), 4586
'bridge', 4348, 10581,
  11983
'bridgebuilder', 4347
'bridgemaker', 4347
'bright', 7293, 7329, 7392
'bright-beautiful', 3604
'brighten', 7362
'brightening', 7328
'brightness', 7253, 7322,
  7364, 7406
'brilliant', 7329
'bring', 7283
'bring about', 4290
'bring back', 153, 3470, 8361
'bring forth', 3478
'bring forward', 3482
'bringing forward', 7212
'bringing up, lacking
  proper', 10494
'bring to', 8366
'bring to an end', 11046
'bring together', 6562, 9221
'bring under control', 3522
'bring up', 3466, 3595,
  6041, 8371
'bring upon oneself', 2049
'bring up (out of
  ignorance)', 3465
'brisk', 8764
'briskly', 8788
'bristle', 4374
'brocade used in trimming',
  9547
'brook', 5729
'brook, small', 5727
Brot, 2498

Brötchen, 2498
'brothel', 4780
'brother', 9415
BROTHER, 1881
'brother, younger', 2116
'brought up', 10494
'bruise', 10189
'brutal, mindlessly', 10492
bu-, 1845
*bū-, 1435, 1506, 1551
būa, 1473, 1509
buadhrim, 1836
buadrim, 1835
būandi, 1472, 1499
būbalus, 1751
Bube, 1882
BUCEPHALUS, 1773
'bucket', 1091
BUCOLIC, 1712, 1770, 10991
būcolicus, 1770, 10991
būculus, 1716, 1745
buena, 3661
bueno, 3661
búfalo, 1749
būfalus, 1750
bufaro, 1750
BUFF, 1763
'buffalo', 1743
BUFFALO, 1748
buffle, 1761
bugle, 1745
BUGLE, 1714, 1742
'bugle-horn', 1743
'build', 4057, 4373
BUILD, 1524
'build houses', 4068
'building', 4053
būinn, 1511
BULIMIA, 1825
BULIMY, 1825
bull, 1845
'bull', 1718, 1748, 1839,
  1867, 8906
'bullfight', 2089
BULWARK, 11510
BUMKIN, 1579
'bump', 6462
BUMPKIN, 1548, 1579
'bunch', 3101, 8180
'bunch of grapes', 3078
Bundesrat, 3906
'bundle', 7451

būr, 1442
'burden', 1955
BURDENSOME, 9282
'burden, tending to be a',
  9282
*burgs, 5587
burgus, 5580
'burial place', 5465
*būrjam, 1454
'burl on a tree', 6463
'burn', 4069, 4110
'burn brightly', 4084
'burnt', 859
'burnt whole', 859
'burst into', 10681
'bury', 4451
BUS, 7729
-bus, 1588, 1800
'business, wind up a', 7014
'bus, sight-seeing', 1888
*buthla(m), 1526
BUTTER, 1782
BUTTERCUP, 1784
BUTTERCUPS, 1713
'butter firkin', 1086
BUTTERFLOWER, 1786
BUTTERFLY, 1788
būtȳrum, 1782
'buy', 7986
bwey, 1876
by, 1465, 1563
BY, 220
BY-, 1463
-by, 1456
bye, 1876
'by hand', 7428
BYLAW, 1459, 1508
byldan, 1525
'by means of', 2714
'by-product, worthless',
  10403
bȳr, 1454
bȳre, 1453
BYRE, 1452, 1508
BYRLAW, 1459
'by way of', 10580

C

ca-, 1542, 1929
'cabal', 11867

caballus, 2185
'cabbage', 5215
'cabbage flower', 5214
cabeza, 2387
CABEZON, 2386
'cabinet or wardrobe', 519
'cable', 10926, 11458
CABOODLE, 1425, 1540
CACHE, 255
cacher, 256
CACHET, 267
CACOGRAPHY, 2828
CACOPHEMISM, 4798
CACOPHONY, 4848
CAD, 2101
CADDIE, 2107
cadet, 2115
CADET, 2117
'cage', 2652
'cajole', 8717
cake, 3045
'cake', 10868
çakra, 10871
CALASH, 10866
'calculate', 646, 6779
'calculated', 658
'calculation', 647, 709
'calculation, skilled in',
    6777
'calculator', 6779
calèche, 10865
calefacere, 4387
*cal(e)fāre, 4387
calere, 4387
'call before a court', 661
CALLIGRAPHY, 2827
'call to account', 662
'calm', 10364
'calmness', 3676
'camel', 2691
'camel, Arabian', 3343
'camel, running', 3346
camēlus dromedārius, 3346
can, 3518
Cancer, 8906
Candide, 7713
'candies', 4282
'candy', 3641, 4281
'cantankerous', 606
cantelcāp, 2227
caoli fiori, 5214
cap, 2381
CAP, 2201

-cāp, 2227
capa, 2215, 2294
capabilis, 5830
capable, 2409
'capable', 5842
CAPABLE, 5829
'capable of being relied
    upon', 5831
'capable of retaining
    knowledge', 5825
'capacious', 5829
'capacity', 941, 4339
'capacity for knowledge
    and understanding', 6588
'capacity of, in the', 11103
CAP-À-PIE, 2307
caparasso, 2294
caparasson, 2293
caparazón, 2293
CAPARISON, 2291
CAPARISONED, 2296
capdet, 2126
cape, 2214
'cape', 2381
CAPE, 2213, 2380
capelan, 2269
CAPELAN, 2274
CAPELIN, 2274
capelina, 2284
capeline, 2283
CAPELINE, 2280
'cape, little', 2250
capere, 2409, 5830, 7510,
    7581, 8196
'cap, French military',
    2305
CAPILLARY, 2352
capillātūra, 2356
capillus, 2311, 2348
capit-, 2164
CAPITA, 2161
capitain(e), 2133
CAPITAL, 2133
capitale, 2141, 2193
capitālis, 2137
'capital of a column', 2189
capitāneus, 2133
capitellum, 2127, 2385
*capitia, 2388
capitium, 2327
CAPITOL, 2150
CAPITOLINE, 2155

Capitōlium, 2153
capitulāre, 2159
CAPITULATE, 2156
capitulum, 2159, 2186
CAPLIN, 2274
CAPLING, 2274
capo, 2374
CAPO, 2382
capo corporalis, 2376
caporal, 2375
CAPORAL, 2361
caporale, 2363
capote, 2230
CAPOTE, 2229
cappa, 2202, 2228, 2285
cappella, 2249
CAPPELLA, 2263
cappellan, 2269
cappellāni, 2261
cappellānus, 2270
cappellus, 2238
*cappellus, 2237
cappuccino, 2301
cappuccio, 2302
capra, 2184, 2310, 2394
capriccio, 2392
CAPRICCIO, 2390
CAPRICCIOSO, 2388
CAPRICE, 2389
Capricorn, 8907
capr(o), 2395
CAPSTONES, 2233
'captain', 47, 2127, 3451,
    3498
CAPTAIN, 2132
'caption', 6663
'captivity', 1471
capture, 2409
CAPUCHE, 2300
CAPUCHIN, 2301
*capum, 2312
caput, 1207, 2128, 2156,
    2191, 2286, 2312, 2342,
    2379
car, 3162
'car', 1932
CAR, 1898, 1924
'carbon', 2814
CARDIOGRAM, 2785
CARDIOGRAPH, 2785
'care', 809, 7133, 7482,
    10969

'care, anxious', 813
'care, attentive', 795
'career', 1914
CAREER, 1911
'carefree', 813, 1388, 3634,
  11217
'careful', 11341
'carefulness', 6606
'careless', 811, 6581
'caress', 9663
carete, 1927, 3162
'care, without', 814
cargo, 1973
CARGO, 1972
cariage, 1910
caricare, 1975
caricatura, 1978
CARICATURE, 1978
carier, 1901
CARIOLE, 1916
carkha, 10876
carnelevare, 4588
carnevale, 4587
carnival, 4587
CAROCHE, 1918
carpentārius, 1984
'carpenter', 11499
CARPENTER, 1986
carpentier, 1985
*carpentom, 1983
carpentum, 1982
carra, 1896
carre, 1896, 1927
carri, 1917
'carriage', 1925, 3160,
  10670
CARRIAGE, 1906
'carriage entrance', 8281
'carriage-maker', 1984
'carriage, one-horse', 1916
'carriage road', 1915
CARRIAGES, 1884
'carriages, for', 8284
'carriage, two-wheeled',
  1982, 10866
'carriage with benches',
  1888
carricāre, 1956
'carried', 10702
'carried away', 8375
'carrier', 518, 8309, 10719
CARRIER, 1905
carriera, 1914

carrière, 1914
'carrier of baggage', 8306
carriola, 1917
*carrium, 1918
carro, 1922
carroccio, 1920
carroche, 1920
carros, 1894
carrosse de diligence, 6620
carrus, 1895, 1922, 1956
'carry', 518, 1089, 2542,
  8259, 8303, 8353, 8391,
  8436, 9349, 10547,
  10654, 10690, 10737,
  10788
CARRY, 1900
'carry away', 8346
'carry back', 8356
'carry back to', 8365
'carry-cloak', 8298
'carry forward', 8340
'carry from underneath',
  8368
'carrying', 8327, 10671,
  10789
'carrying, act of', 1906
'carrying boats overland',
  8304
'carrying, means of', 10666
'carrying out', 10721
'carry into', 8337, 10679
'carry off', 3457
'carry on', 7544
'carry over', 8355
'carry through', 116
'carry together', 8349,
  10704
'carry up toward', 8371
CARS, 1883
cart, 1923
'cart', 1895, 1925
CART, 3159
'cart-load', 8438
'carve', 9106
CARVE, 2839
'carved figures', 9111
'case', 4605, 10082
'case, fancy', 10083
'cash', 832
'cash, convert into', 7014
'cast down headlong', 2168
CASTE, 203
castellum, 2186

'cast figures', 9111
castīgāre, 199
CASTIGATE, 198
'castle', 2186
CASTRATE, 203
'castrated animal', 10046
castus, 200
'casual', 6582
CAT, 2501
CATADROMOUS, 3378
CATALOGUE, 6817
catalogus, 6819
'cataloque', 8151
catch, 2409
'catch a glimpse of', 11324
'catching', 308
'category', 6218
catel, 2198
'cathartic', 1632
CATHOLIC, 863
catir, 272
'cats, wild', 7410
cattle, 7799
'cattle', 7796, 7832
CATTLE, 2194
'cattle-property', 7848
caudillo, 2385
CAUDILLO, 2383
caught, 6071
CAULIFLOWER, 5213
caulis, 5215
'cause to grow', 1553
'causing death', 4704
caustic, 859
'cavalryman', 2012
'cavity', 10372
'cavity, unfilled', 10370
cavolfiore, 5214
-ce, 1052, 10649
ceald, 2476
cēlan, 2487
'celebrate', 72, 178
'celebration, boastful and
  unwarranted', 10432
'cell', 7394, 11992
'cellar, town-hall', 683
CENOBITE, 8868
'censure', 4811
'center, toward the', 5094
CENTRIFUGAL, 5654
CENTRIFUGE, 5653
CENTRIPETAL, 5094

'come to be', 1557
'come together', 9221,
  11964
'come to terms', 2158
COMFIT, 4284
'command', 588, 6817,
  7599, 8074, 11915
COMMAND, 7423, 7585
commandāre, 7596
'command, authoritative',
  7591
COMMANDEER, 7598
commander, 7599
'commander', 973, 3453,
  3575
'commander, army', 968
commando, 7602
COMMANDO, 7599
'commence', 615
'commend', 1354, 6159
COMMEND, 7621
commendāre, 7619
'commerce', 3396
'commission', 7174
'commissioned together',
  7185
'commit a crime', 5568,
  6975
'commit to the care of',
  7619
'common', 605, 2035, 8870
'common people', 8
'commonplace', 599, 4908,
  10615
'commotion', 1842, 4489
'communicate', 10655
'communicate knowledge',
  6314
'communicate (to)', 8230
'communication', 2032,
  8360
'companion, table', 8805
compār, 7959
comparāre, 7962
'compare', 10549
COMPARE, 7963
compared, 8002
'compared with', 11279
comparer, 7965
'comparison', 9171
compartiment, 8221
compartimento, 8222
compartire, 8222

compartīri, 8223
COMPARTMENT, 8220
'compartment, enclosed',
  1522
'compass, housing of a',
  5876
compater, 7961
COMPEER, 7957
'compel', 9777
'compelling', 169
'compensation', 8564
'compensation for
  damages', 8561
comper, 7959
compère, 7961
COMPETE, 5068
'competence', 5849
'competent', 5829
COMPETENT, 5063
competere, 5061
COMPETITIVE, 5065
'complete', 854, 4296,
  11031
'completely', 4018, 6992,
  7306, 11364
'completion', 11040
'completion of a cycle',
  11030
'complexion, ruddy', 5184
'compliant', 3638
COMPORT, 8348
comportāre, 8349
COMPORTMENT, 8348
'compose', 4441, 6187,
  6252
'composed', 6257
'composition', 6258, 7656
'composition, fictitious',
  11252
'compost', 7498
'compounding', 4280
'comprehending', 6601
'compress', 256
'compressed', 324, 3015
'compress into a ball', 6430
'compromise', 8841
'comrade', 7958
con, 3517, 10654
con-, 939, 2422, 3334,
  11902
'conceal', 4453
'concealed', 4456
'concealed place', 1176

'conceal intentions', 9203
'concealment', 5642
'concept', 11178
'concern', 8564
'concerned', 809, 8570
'concern, fill with', 801
'concern, full of', 793
'concerning', 866
conclāve, 2549
CONCLAVE, 2503, 2545
CONCLUDE, 2623
concludere, 2624
'conclusion', 2602
CONCLUSION, 2505
'conclusion, draw a', 3472
'conclusion, unfortunate',
  2319
'concord', 550
CONCOURSE, 2030
CONCUR, 2051
cond, 3513
'condense', 2169, 10339
condere, 4441, 7587
'condescend', 3327
condīcere, 6174
condiciō, 6175
condie, 3513
CONDIGN, 3330
condīgnus, 3333
CONDIMENT, 4449
condimentum, 4448
condire, 4445
condite, 4447
'condition', 398, 697, 4523,
  5780, 5894, 9392
CONDITION, 6176
'condition, in poor', 5893
'condition, specific', 6219
conditum, 4445
CONDOTTIERE, 3497
condotto, 3502
CONDUCE, 3483
condūcere, 3484
'conduct', 3455, 3514, 8345
CONDUCT, 3485
'conduct, code of social',
  7547
conducti, 3506
CONDUCTING, 3446, 3568
conductor, 3504
CONDUCTOR, 3492
conductorum, 3506

conductus, 3484
condue, 3513
conduire, 3507
conduit, 3488
'conduit', 3547
CONDUIT, 3490
conduttore, 3496
conduyt, 3488
CONFAB, 4693
confābulārī, 4694
CONFABULATE, 4692
CONFECT, 4279
CONFECTION, 4280
confectus, 4278
'confer a medal', 3283
'confess', 4740
CONFESS, 4743
confessāre, 4742
CONFESSED, 4744
confesser, 4743
CONFESSER, 4747
'confession, one who makes a', 4746
'confessions, one who hears', 4747
CONFESSOR, 4745
confessus, 4742
CONFETTI, 4282
conficere, 4278
'confine', 5007, 5041
'confined spaces, fear of', 2654
CONFITEOR, 4757
confitērī, 4741
CONFITURE, 4284
'conflagration', 858
'conflicting attitudes, coexistence of', 936
'conflicting feelings of love and hate', 934
'conflicts, one beset by', 95
CONFLUENCE, 5311
'conforming', 3269
'conforming, rigidly', 9740
'conformity to social conventions', 3279
'conform (to)', 3171, 3231, 3264, 9269
'confront', 11278
con fuoco, 5450
'congeal', 10339
CONGEAL, 2413
congelāre, 2422

congeler, 2421
'congregation', 5691
'congruity', 9273
coniugālis, 11850
coniunctiōnem, 11876
coniūnctus, 11877
coniu(n)gare, 11849
coniu(n)gatus, 11849
coniungere, 11876
coniu(n)x, 11850
'conjecture', 4568
CONJOIN, 11911
CONJOINT, 11911
CONJUGAL, 11786, 11849
CONJUGATE, 11847
CONJUGATED, 11787
CONJUNCT, 11912
CONJUNCTION, 11874, 11911
CONJUNCTIVA, 11877
'conjurer', 6308
'conjuring tricks', 9805
'conjuror', 9811
CON(N), 3511
'connect', 9610, 11845, 11877
'connection between bones', 396
'connective membrane', 11879
CONNING, 3514
'connive', 3876
'connoisseur of the arts', 11755
'conquer', 11851
'conquer completely', 10723
conscience-stricken, 9702
'consecrate', 6208
'consecrated gift', 4539
'consecrate with blood', 1356
'consider', 179, 4513, 10548
'consideration', 128
'consign', 7181
'consonance', 550
CONSTRAIN, 9777
'constraint, freedom from', 4920
CONSTRICT, 9777
'constrictive', 9738
constrictum, 9779

CONSTRINGE, 9778
constringere, 9779
'construct', 1524, 4058, 11499
'consummation', 11030
'contain', 2409, 2621, 8340
'container', 2893, 3136, 4605, 10081
'contempt', 3320
'contempt, term of', 4579
'contemptible', 3133
'contend with physically', 7883
'contention', 66, 195, 6905
'contest', 68
'continue, cause to', 5087
contra, 4253, 7612, 8229
CONTRABAND, 4883, 4945
contrabando, 4944
'contract', 3004, 9728, 9765
'contract, cause to', 9778
'contract for', 3504
'contracting', 3056
contrādīcere, 6183
CONTRADICT, 6183
'contradiction in terms', 6907
'contradictory', 6904
CONTRALTO, 6050
contrebande, 4947
'contributions, person who seeks', 803
'contrivance', 4276, 7768
'control, exert', 7514
'control over other nations', 8090
'control, parental', 7512
'controversy', 6905
contundere, 10189
CONTUSE, 10188
CONTUSION, 10190
contūsus, 10190
CONVALESCE, 938
convectiō, 10703
CONVECTION, 10702
convector, 10707
convectus, 10710
convehere, 10704
conveier, 10653
'convenience', 4336
'convenient', 9290

coutelier, 9130
coutel(l)erie, 9134
couvrechef, 2314
couvrir, 2315
'cove', 3063
'covenant', 6929
'cover', 2315, 4605
'cover-head', 2314
'covering', 2235, 2341,
   4606, 10302
'covering, defensive', 498
'covering for the head',
   2201
'covering, hard', 8941
'cover of a pillow or
   mattress', 4611
'cover, protective', 9054
*coviria, 11773
covrefeu, 5436
cow, 2045
'cow', 1718, 1748, 1794,
   1839, 1867
COW, 1712
cowarce, 2045
'cow-cheese', 1783
'cower', 2999
'cowherd', 1771, 10988
'cowl', 2302
'cowshed', 1453
COWSLIP, 1848
'cow, wild', 7274
'cozening tricks', 9807
cr-, 3056
'crab', 2868, 8906
CRAB, 2846
crabba, 2846
CRABBED, 2853
CRABBY, 2853
Crabs, 2859
CRABS, 2859
'crack', 6484
crackers, 1244
'cracking', 6471
CRADLE, 2883, 3154
cradol, 3155
craet, 1925, 3160
'craftsman', 453, 4345,
   11582
'crafty', 449
'cramp', 3010
CRAMP, 3008
crampe, 3009
CRAMPED, 3015

crampon, 3018
CRAMPON, 3016
CRAMPS, 3013
cranc, 2996
'crane, mast of a mobile',
   1573
crang, 2997
'cranium', 8966
'cranium, upper half of',
   2180
CRANK, 2884, 2986
CRANKY, 2990
CRAP, 2862
crape, 3078
craper, 3077
craps, 2865
CRAPS, 2858
'craving, compulsory', 6155
'craving, instinctive', 5059
'craw', 3103
CRAWFISH, 2871
'crawl', 2877
CRAWL, 2876
CRAYFISH, 2871
create, 9254
'created, artificially', 4565
'creator', 11583
CRÈCHE, 3151
creek, 3072
'creek', 3063
CREEK, 3060
'creep', 2877
CREEP, 2885, 3057
crēopan, 3058
crescent, 9254
'crescent-shaped', 7358
'crest', 4968
crevice, 2870
crevis(e), 2870
'crib', 3152
CRIB, 2883, 3143
crib(b), 3148
CRIBBAGE, 3148
CRICKET, 2973
'crime', 4731
'crime, commit', 4261
'criminal', 4166, 4732, 8705
CRIMP, 3019
crincan, 2996
cringan, 2997
CRINGE, 2885, 2999
CRINGLE, 3004
CRINGLES, 3007

CRINKLE, 3001
'cripple', 5844
CRIPPLE, 3058
crique, 3063
criquer, 2984
criquet, 2978
'crisis', 401, 11861
'criticize severely', 199
croc, 2899, 2926
crocc(a), 3138
croccia, 2942
croce, 2943
croche, 2899, 2933
CROCHE, 2900
crochen, 2928
crochet, 2903
CROCHET, 2902
crochir, 2927
crocier, 2943
CROCK, 3137
CROCKET, 2901
CROFT, 3164
croisier, 2960
croiz, 2958
crōk, 2897
croll(e), 3053
crollid, 3052
crompid, 3045
'crony', 7961
'crook', 2899, 2933
CROOK, 2895, 2982
'crook-bearer', 2961
'crooked', 2892, 3022
'crook, shepherd's', 2911
'crop', 10902
CROP, 3100
crop(p), 3101
croquer, 2925
croquet, 2909
CROQUET, 2884
croquette, 2924
'crosier', 2933
CROSIER, 2947
'crosier, bishop's', 2896
cross, 2956
'cross', 2953
'cross bar', 11990
'cross-bearer', 2960
crosse, 2943
crossier, 2943
'cross, processional', 2950
'crossroads', 10619

'curule chair', 2081
'curule chair, privileged to sit in', 2079
curulis, 2081
'curved', 2892, 3027, 3167, 10713
cuspis, 1209
'custom', 4191, 7780, 9874
'customary', 2041
'customs, local', 1460
cut, 2842, 9136
'cut', 1210, 1348, 2839, 8795, 8936, 9023, 9075, 9106, 9146, 9429, 9456, 9505, 9544, 9574, 9945, 10002
'cut across', 9530
'cut and thrust', 9943
'cut apart', 9529
'cut a part of', 9532·
'cut back', 9531
cute, 9139
'cut into', 9427, 9533
'cut into shapes', 2840
'cut in two', 9074, 9529
cutlash, 9125
cutlass, 9127
CUTLASS, 9126
CUTLASSES, 9135
CUTLER, 9131
CUTLERS, 9135
CUTLERY, 9132
'cut off', 8103, 9554
'cut off by firepower', 6227
'cut off from', 200
'cut off part of', 9531
'cut short', 3105, 10238
'cuttable', 9545
cutte, 9139
cutten, 9139
'cutter', 9542
'cut the throat', 11842
'cut through', 9529
'cutting', 9540
'cutting, act of', 9539
'cutting instruments and tools', 9132
'cutting tool', 9432
cuttleax, 9125
cw-, 8851
cwethan, 11124
cwic, 8768
cwic(u), 8765, 8851

cycle, 10808
CYCLE, 10806, 10853
CYCLIST, 10839
CYCLONE, 10818
cyclopean, 10834
CYCLOPEAN, 10825
cyclōps, 10824
CYCLOPS, 10822
CYCLORAMA, 10836
CYCLOTRON, 10820
cyclus, 10808
cȳ(e), 1722
cȳna, 1724
-cyte, 7394

D

d-, 11058
-d, 1514
-d-, 6125
*-d-, 4439
DACTYL, 6288
dactyl(us), 6287
dǣd, 4495
'dagger', 9481
'dagger, slender', 9875
dáil, 4646
DAIL, 4643
DÁIL ÉIREANN, 4644
'daily', 11125
'dainty', 4105
DAINTY, 3336
DAIS, 6368
*dak-, 6285
daktulon, 1112
daktulos, 5114, 6281, 11997
dāl, 4646
dāleth, 2691
'dalliance, amorous', 8379
dam, 3711
'damage', 2317, 8565
'damage the surface of', 4425
dame, 3712
'damnation', 4537
'dance, French', 2066
'dancer', 3864
'dance, war', 5489
DANDIFY, 4372
'dandy', 3719
'danger', 9551
'dangerous', 10483

'danger, run into', 9552
dans, 5501
dar, 5605
darbār, 5604
dāre, 7583
'dare', 10245
-dāre, 7586
'dark-hued', 10475
'darkness, opposite of', 7255
'dash', 4964
DATE, 6293
datil, 6296
dau, 1018
DAUB, 4015
dauber, 4019
'dawn', 3788, 3827, 4003
'dawn horse', 3832
'dawn, new', 3830
'dawn stones, of the', 3835
'day', 11126
'day, each', 11126
'daylight', 7276, 7319
'daystar', 7286
'dazzle', 6310, 9802
dē, 3474, 5752, 7484
dē-, 4018, 4225, 4426, 6209, 6991, 10388, 10897
-de-, 5754
'dead, dwelling of the', 11237
'deaden', 10194
'dead hand', 7558
'deadly nightshade', 3698
'deaf', 1835
'deafen', 1835
dēalbāre, 4017
'dealt with', 715
'death', 4503, 8747
'death penalty', 2135
'debate', 180, 5533
debentur, 5910
DEBENTURE, 5909
dēbēre, 5896
DEBIT, 5898
*dēbita, 5901
*debitas, 5933
debitatem, 5933
dēbitum, 5900
DE BOIS, 2071
debonair, 3635

DEBONAIR, 3633
débonnaire, 3637
de bon(ne) aire, 3635
'debt', 5900
DEBT, 5731, 5906
'debt, certificate
  acknowledging', 5909
'debtor', 6157
'debt, settle a', 7014
*débūtum, 5921
DECAGON, 6381
DECALOGUE, 6816
de cap a pe, 2308
DECAPITATION, 2138
'deceit', 451
'deceitful', 449, 3297
'deceits', 9807
'deceive', 3875
decem, 1105, 11769
DECEMVIRATE, 11767
DECENT, 3268
decēnt-, 3268
'deceptions', 6309, 9806
'deceptiveness', 1140
decēre, 3267
'decide', 696
decies centena milia, 1284
deciple, 3206
'decision, premature', 6249
'declaration, public', 7504
'declare', 6690
'declare publicly', 4764
*decnos, 3313
DÉCOLLETÉ, 10896
décolleter, 10897
decor, 3279
DECOR, 3281
decorāre, 3284
'decorate', 627, 9969
DECORATE, 3283
'decorated, elaborately',
  634
'decorate in color', 7341
'decoration', 634
'decorative object', 3736
decōris, 3280
DECOROUS, 3277
DECORUM, 3278
decōrus, 3278
'decree', 584, 3217, 4501,
  4530, 4643, 6185, 7647
'decreeing', 4498
decus, 3280

dēdicāre, 6209
'dedicate', 4541, 6209
DEDICATE, 6207
dēdignāri, 3321
*dēdiz, 4496
'deduce', 6517
DEDUCE, 3471
dēdūcere, 3473
DEDUCT, 3474
dēductus, 3473
'deed', 103, 455, 4237,
  4496, 11539, 11567
DEED, 4144, 4493
'deed of honor', 3280
'deed, outstanding', 4239
DEEM, 4144, 4513
'deep', 5316, 10319
DEFACE, 4425
*dēfactus, 4231
DEFAMATORY, 4648
DEFAME, 4783
DEFEAT, 4250
'defeat utterly', 4285
'defect', 7047, 10467
DEFECT, 4233
'defective', 7565
'defect of vision', 1814
dēfectus, 4227
'defend', 6234, 8024, 8060
'defending', 8022
'defense', 6877, 8023
'defense against rain', 8026
'defensive fortification,
  small', 1174
dēficere, 4227
'deficiency', 7047, 10496
dēficiens, 4227
'deficient', 7055
DEFICIENT, 4226
déficit, 4229
DEFICIT, 4228
'defined, well', 9979
DEFOLIATE, 5243
'deformed child', 3950
'degrade', 7969
dehibēre, 5896
*deig-, 6272
DEIGN, 3326
deignier, 3324
deik-, 6285
*deik-, 6267, 6311, 6343
deiknumi, 6285
deiknunai, 6329

deintie, 3338
dē intus, 5499
deinz, 5499
de(i)nzein, 5497
De(i)nzen, 5498
deis, 6365
*dek-, 3171, 3230, 3264,
  3294, 9644
deka, 1112, 6816, 9401
dekesthai, 3258
*dek-no, 3314
*dekos, 3292
*deks-, 3290
'delay', 8504
dēlēgāre, 7180
DELEGATE, 7178
dēlēgātus, 7180
'deliberate', 179
'deliberation', 6697
'delicacy, lacking in', 2036
'delicate', 4105
'delicious', 3336
'delimit', 4377
dēlinquēns, 6976
DELINQUENT, 6944, 6977
dēlinquere, 6975
delphus, 9415
delta, 2691
DELUDE, 3874
dēlūdere, 3875
'delusion', 10485
DELUSION, 3838
'delusions', 9807
DEM-, 8
dēmagōgos, 9
DEMAGOGUE, 1
dēman, 4515
'demand', 119, 7611
DEMAND, 7604
dēmandāre, 7605
demander, 7604
'demand, excessive', 9771
'demanding', 142
'demeanor', 8345
dēmios, 11583
dēmiourgos, 11581
DEMIURGE, 11580
dēmiūrgus, 11585
'demonstration', 6340
dēmos, 8
denizen, 5500
'dense', 826

'diamonds, set of', 8011
'Diana', 10620
DIAPHONY, 4825
'diaphragm', 10133
-diare, 7517
dicāre, 6203, 6230
'dice, pair of', 7956
dīcere, 6121, 6152, 6203, 6230
DICHOTOMY, 1346
dichten, 6264
Dichter, 6265
dict, 6131
dictāre, 6252
'dictate', 6253
DICTATE, 6253
'dictation, one who takes', 7552
dictator, 6254
DICTATOR, 6253
dictatum, 6252
dictiō, 6145
'diction', 6724
DICTION, 6147
Dictionarie of the French and English Tongues, 9808
dictiōnārium, 6150
dictiōnārius, 6148
'dictionary', 6728
DICTIONARY, 6116, 6151
Dictionary of the Arts and Sciences, 4093
dictionarywise, 11439
dictiōn(em), 6145
dictum, 6127
DICTUM, 6128
dictus, 6127
DID, 4493
diēs, 11126
dies bissextus ante Calends Martias, 1229
'diet-deficiency disease', 311
dif-, 4343
'difference in substance', 8661
'differentiation', 9981
'differing in opinion', 3244
difficilis, 4343
difficul, 4343
'difficult', 4877
difficultās, 4343

'difficulty', 356
DIFFICULTY, 4342
'difficulty, position of', 9749
DIGHT, 6263
DIGIT, 6274
DIGITAL, 6320
digitālis, 6280
DIGITALIS, 6278
digitorum, 1110
digitus, 6272, 6300
dīgnāri, 3324
dignete, 3311
DIGNIFIED, 3316
DIGNITARY, 3317
dīgnitās, 3311
dignitātem, 3338
'dignity', 3339
DIGNITY, 3310
dīgnus, 3312
'digress', 10601
'digression', 7762
dihtan, 6263
*dik-, 6347
dikein, 6342
dikha, 1347
dikhotimia, 1347
dikhotomein, 1347
*dikskos, 6352
dīlectus, 6607
DILEMMA, 1348
DILIGENCE, 6603
diligencia, 6622
diligentia, 6606
diligenza, 6622
dīligere, 6607
'dimensions, comparative', 8244
'diminish', 3470, 8069
'diminishing', 10467
DIMITY, 1342
'dining room', 4310
'diphtheria', 366
DIPHTHONG, 1344
DIPLOID, 1340
diplōma, 1299, 1334
DIPLOMA, 1296
DIPLOMACY, 1332
DIPLOMAT, 1314
DIPLOMATIC, 1333
'diplomatic official', 231
diplōmaticus, 1321
diporto, 8384

DIPTYCH, 1340
'direct', 6313, 8361
'direction, divine', 11333
'direction, in a different', 10563
'direction of running', 1994
'direct one's course', 192
'direct things be done', 574
'direct with authority', 7594
dis-, 2028, 2359, 4343, 4426, 5796, 6609, 7971, 8374, 9175, 9977, 10389, 11902
DISABLE, 5844
'disabled', 5577
'disappear', 6009, 10446
'disappear, cause to', 4427
'disappearing', 7034
'disarranged', 2357
'disaster', 5122
'disbelieve, tend to', 1165
disc, 6356
DISC, 6355
'discards', 3149
discēre, 3170, 3203, 3229
'discerning', 9094
'discernment', 6595, 9092
discipilus, 3206
DISCIPLE, 3203
disciplīna, 3210
DISCIPLINARIAN, 3211
DISCIPLINE, 3206
'disciplined', 487
'discipline, enforcing', 9740
'discipline, lacking in', 10492
discipul, 3205
'disclaim', 6205
disclaudere, 2617
'disclose', 6197
DISCLOSE, 2616
'discoloration of the skin', 5376
DISCOMFIT, 4285
*disconfecere, 4287
*disconfectus, 4287
'disconnect', 9623
'discord', 1034
'discourse', 4816, 6696, 6732, 6765, 7143, 8860

DISCOURSE, 2028
'discourse, amorous', 5163
'discourse, of', 6737
'discreet', 11340
'discriminate', 9970
'discriminatory', 11372
DISCURSIVE, 2027
discursīvus, 2027
discursus, 2029
discus, 6352
'discus', 6352
DISCUS, 6350
'discuss', 180
'discussion, topic of', 4533
DISDAIN, 3320
*disdignāre, 3322
'disease', 392
'diseased', 6753
'disease of the joints', 393
disfacere, 4249
'disgrace, mark of', 10002
'disguise', 9204
'disguise the nature of',
    9205
'disgust', 1838
DISH, 6356
DISHABILLE, 5795
DISHEVELED, 2356
'dishonor', 11785
DISINFECTANT, 4295
disinterested, 8573
'disinterested', 8164
DISINTERESTED, 8571
disiungere, 11880
DISJOIN, 11912
DISJOINT, 11913
'disjointed', 7386
DISJOINTED, 11914
DISJUNCTION, 11913
DISJUNCTIVE, 11880
DISK, 6355
diskos, 6352
'dislike, violent', 698
'dislocate', 7386, 11913
'dismal', 10475
'Disneyesque cow', 3604
'disorder', 5141
'disown', 6205
DISPARAGE, 7968
disparāre, 7935
DISPARATE, 7934
'disparate, state of being',
    7934

DISPARITY, 7934
'dispatch', 7182
'dispense', 11352
'dispirited', 4292
'display', 5866, 6341, 8061
'displeasure, hot', 339
DISPORT, 8372
'disputation', 9087
'dispute', 195
'disquiet', 795
'disregard', 6578
DISSECT, 9529
DISSEMBLE, 9205
dissembler, 9207
'dissension, giving rise to',
    4184
'dissertation', 4552
DISSIMILAR, 9156
dissimilāre, 9201
'dissimilarity', 6852
DISSIMILATE, 9193
DISSIMILATION, 9194
dissimulāre, 9203
DISSIMULATE, 9202
'dissipate', 10450
'dissolve', 6996
distaccare, 9629
distaccato, 9630
'distance, at a', 4815
'distance, at a little', 10563
'distillation', 8536
DISTINCT, 9979
DISTINCTION, 9980
DISTINCTIVE, 9980
'distinctness', 11366
distinctus, 9969
distingué, 9981
distinguer, 9976
distinguere, 9969
'distinguish', 9093, 9969
DISTINGUISH, 9975
DISTINGUISHED, 9983
distinguiss(ant), 9976
'distortion', 1979
DISTRAIN, 9781
'distress', 356, 9758
DISTRESS, 9760
DISTRICT, 9792
*districtia, 9787
districtum, 9780
districtus, 9788
distringere, 9780
'distrust', 1165

'disturb', 798
'disturbance', 10793
'disunion', 1033
ditie, 6257
ditto, 6141
DITTO, 6143
ditton, 6131
DITTY, 6258
'diversity', 4435
'divert', 8373
'divert oneself', 8372
'divide', 8100, 8161, 8217,
    9970
'divide by cutting', 2839
'divide by force', 2581
'divided', 8247, 9074
'divided into different
    colors', 8248
'divided in two', 1047
'divide into allotments',
    8178
'divide into parts', 8103
'divide in two', 1032
'dividend, extra', 3625
'dividing', 411
'dividing into parts', 8184
'divine law', 4730
'divine power, associated
    with a', 895
Divine Providence, 11335
'divine will', 4701, 4729
division, 9078
'division', 401, 1216, 8157,
    8185, 8224, 9076
'division into two parts',
    1346
'division, little', 10664
'division of land', 8177
'division of time', 401
'divisive', 4184
'divorced', 10364
d-k-, 6282
*dkm-tom, 713
do, 1018, 7586
'do', 101, 3762, 4140,
    4245, 4273, 4316, 4363,
    4395, 4481, 7737, 9315,
    11504, 11536, 11622
DO, 4143, 4480
dō-, 1111
*dō-, 4476
'doable', 4246, 4333, 5839

'do again', 5085
'do away with', 6007
doble, 1120
doblón, 1120
doccia, 3552
doccione, 3553
Docent, 3189
DOCENT, 3185
docent-, 3188
docēre, 3169, 3229
DOCILE, 3194
docilis, 3195
DOCK, 3554
docke, 3557
doctor, 3180
DOCTOR, 3177
doctrīna, 3196
DOCTRINAIRE, 3197
'doctrine', 3218
DOCTRINE, 3195
doctum, 3177
doctus, 3182
DOCUMENT, 3199
'document, official', 1297
documentum, 3202
dōdekadaktulon, 1111
'dodge', 6466
'doer', 4152
'Do everything!', 4320
DOFF, 4486
'dog', 371
'dog collar', 370
doge, 3546
DOGE, 3544
dogma, 3214, 3315
'dogma', 3196
DOGMA, 3214
'dog of an ancient breed',
  7532
'do good (to)', 4169
'dog throttle', 371
'do honor', 3767
'doing', 4172, 4245, 4431,
  4495
'doing away', 4226
dokein, 3221, 3315
'dolt', 3950
dōm, 4501
-DOM, 4523
dōmaz, 4515
*dōmaz, 4500
DOMESDAY, 4504
'domineering', 8089

'dominion', 736, 8086
dominus factotum, 4322
*dōmjan, 4515
dōms, 4522
dōn, 4481
DON, 4484
*dōn, 4481
dōnāre, 5947
'done', 105, 4149, 4236,
  4275
'done, something', 4497
'done with little effort',
  4335
DO OFF, 4486
'doom', 4514, 4702
DOOM, 4144, 4501, 4530,
  4642
DOOMBOOKS, 4509
DOOMS, 4512
DOOMSDAY, 4504
DO ON, 4485
'door', 5512, 5597, 8256,
  8283
DOOR, 5514
'door, belonging to a',
  8281
'doorkeeper', 8280
'doorman', 8306
'door-shaped', 5600
'door, sliding', 8286
'doorway', 5513, 8253
DO OUT, 4487
dor, 5516
dora, 5709
DORAPHOBIA, 5709
dos, 1018
-dōs, 4472
'dose', 5943
dosis, 5943
'do something', 104
-dōtis, 4472
'do to', 4273
doua, 1019
'double', 1113, 1139, 1340
DOUBLE, 1115
'double-dealing', 1139
'doubleheader in the late
  afternoon', 1067
doublet, 1119, 9231
DOUBLET, 1116
'double thread, with a',
  1039
DOUBLOON, 1119

doubt, 5908
'doubt', 214, 1162
DOUBT, 1095, 1164, 1593
'doubtful', 1593
'doubt, subject to', 1168
douche, 3552
DOUCHE, 3551
'doughty', 8620
doui, 1019
DO UP, 4488
DOUT, 4487
douten, 1164
douter, 1163
douzepers, 7921
'down', 6820
'downbeat', 4552
'down to the bottom', 6992
'down to the dregs', 6992
doxa, 3240, 9390
DOXY, 3241
doze, 1152
dozeine, 1152
DOZEN, 1151
Dozent, 3189
'drag', 2876, 3454, 3570
'drag about', 10212
drāma, 11567
drāmatourgia, 11567
DRAMATURGE, 11579
DRAMATURGY, 11565
'draperies, short
  ornamental', 946
'draw', 2684, 3454, 3535,
  3562, 3600, 7340
'draw a line through', 9693
'draw asunder', 9781
'drawing', 2685, 2714, 3569
'drawing tight', 9740
'drawing together', 3000
'drawn', 10494
'draw out', 3462
'draw tight', 9727, 9765
'draw together', 3004,
  6452, 9795
'dread', 1174
'dread, irrational', 5676
'dream, interpret a', 674
drei, 11056
'dress', 5780, 6263
'dress, distinctive', 5779
'dressing gown', 7870
'dressing gown, woman's
  loose', 6584

'dress with a trowel', 9673
drī, 11056
drie, 11056
drill, 1040
drillich, 1040
'drill, military', 7768
'Drink-hail!', 885
'drinking bowl', 9004
'drinking festivity', 878
'drinking vessel', 9011
'drink, spiced', 879
'drive', 5, 71, 99, 159, 188,
 222, 290, 3508
'drive away', 5652
'drive forth', 284
'drive out', 118
'driver', 109
'driver, professional', 4392
'drive through', 211
'drive together', 167, 253
'driving', 106, 293
-drom-, 3369
dromados, 3345
dromas, 3344
dromedārius, 3345
DROMEDARY, 3343
dromos, 3357, 11018
'drop', 9829
'droppings, cow', 1849
*dru-, 11469
'drug', 1632, 7748
'druggist', 4614
DRUID, 11467
'drum', 10127, 10164
drunkard, 11424
'drunk as a blood', 1405
'drunk as a lord', 1405
drus, 9367
du, 1017
dû, 5923
du-, 1156, 1183, 3611,
 3758
-du-, 5753
DUAL, 1113
duālis, 1114
DUALITY, 1011
dubāre, 1161
DUBIETY, 1095, 1169
DUBIOSITY, 1095
DUBIOUS, 1094, 1156, 1549,
 1593
DUBIOUSNESS, 1095
DUBITABLE, 1168
DUBITANCY, 1095

dubitāre, 1162, 3532
DUBITATION, 1095
dubius, 1155, 1592
duca, 3447
DUCAT, 3536
ducato, 3538
ducātus, 3538
duce, 3450, 3546
-duce, 3456
Duce, Il, 3445
dūcere, 3454, 3522, 3570
'duchy', 3538
DUCHY, 3535
*ducs, 3453
'duct', 3491
DUCT, 3546
-duct, 3456
*ductia, 3559
ductiō, 3553
ductum, 3454
ductus, 3547, 10582
due, 1016, 1101, 5923
'due', 5900
DUE, 5923
DUEL, 1177
DUELING, 994
duello, 1189
duellum, 1182, 3612
duene, 3621, 3764
duenelos, 3616, 3765
duenos, 3617, 3763
'due, not', 5926
'duet', 1101
DUET, 1100
dueté, 5932
duetto, 1101
dui-, 1253
duis, 1192
'duke', 3575
DUKE, 3448
'dukedom', 3535
'dull', 10194, 10235
dullard, 11424
'dull the senses', 10095
duma, 4522, 4643
DUMA, 4520
'dumpling', 6481
'dumpling of forcemeat',
 6476
'dumplings', 6474
dun-, 3769
dunamikos, 3776
dunamis, 3774

dunasteia, 3782
dunastēs, 3782
dunasthai, 3769
'dung', 1838, 7777
'dung or compost, enrich
 the earth with', 7497
duo, 1015, 1097, 1138,
 1181, 1294, 6814
DUO, 1099
duodecim, 1105, 1153
DUODECIMAL, 1104
DUODECIMO, 1102
duodeni, 1110
DUODENUM, 1106
DUOLOGUE, 6813
duonos, 3618
duos, 1141
DUP, 4488
DUPLE, 1114
duplex, 1138
DUPLEX, 1137
'duplicate', 7698
DUPLICATE, 1138
duplicis, 1138
DUPLICITY, 1139
duplus, 1114
DURBAR, 5603
'during', 9240
duru, 5516
dus-, 4797, 6752
dusphēmein, 4797
'Dutchman', 1580
DUTIES, 5734
'duty', 5913, 7735
DUTY, 5732, 5930
'duty, disregard of', 6576
'duty, performance of',
 4315
DUUMVIRATE, 11766
duus, 1148
*duwō, 1020
*d(u)wō, 1097
dux, 3453, 3534
dva, 1016
dve, 1016
dvi, 1019
dvis, 1192
'dwarfish', 10238
'dwell', 1435, 1474, 1510,
 1537, 5764, 6786, 7110,
 8504, 9523, 10802,
 10881, 10945, 10982,
 11013

'dweller', 1441
'dweller on the land', 1468
'dwell in', 5769
'dwelling', 1442, 1526,
   4066, 6786, 10945
'dwelling among rocks',
   10985
'dwelling, construct a',
   1525
'dwelling place', 8213
'dwelling, small', 5879
'dwelling, temporary', 1521
*dwene, 3764
*dwenelos, 3765
*dwenos, 3763
*dwō, 1020, 1111
dyn-, 3771
DYNAMIC, 3774
dynamique, 3775
dynamis, 11553
DYNAMITE, 3778
DYNAMO, 3776
Dynamoelektrischemas-
   chine, 3777
dynastia, 3781
dynastie, 3781
DYNASTY, 3780
DYNE, 3771
dyo, 1015, 1294
dys-, 4877, 6752
DYSLEXIA, 6751
DYSPHASIA, 4876
DYSPHEMISM, 4795

E

ē, 11364
ē-, 3463, 6544, 7305, 10377
ēad, 7644
'eagerness', 10065
'eagle', 985
'eagle power', 984
eald, 6091
(e)alne weg, 10567
eam, 8494
'ear', 1203
'eardrum', 10125
'ear, little', 10664
'early', 7995
earm, 474
'earth', 6098, 11234, 11613
'earthernware vessel', 3137
'earthlike', 11233

'earthly', 7354
'earthquake', 2827
'earwig', 10770
EARWIG, 10767
'earworm', 10769
'ease', 4336, 8718
'easily', 4337
'easily borne', 8746
'easily moved', 165
'east', 3805
EAST, 3784
EASTER, 3785
Ēastre, 3787
'East Saxony', 9497
'easy', 4333, 9234
'easy death, painless', 8746
'easy to handle', 9287
'eat', 1674, 6485
eatable, 5814
'eat together', 8804
eau de vie, 8920
écacher, 266
écaille, 8952, 9040
écale, 8954
'eccentric', 2991, 7811
'eccentricities, full of',
   2905
'ecclesiastical living', 4220
ECLECTIC, 6713
eclipse, 7035
ECLIPSE, 7031
ECLIPSED, 7033
eclīpsis, 7035
ECLIPTIC, 7036
éclosion, 2635
ECLOSION, 2634
eclypod, 11822
'economical', 11332
écrevisse, 2870
edel, 692
edi-, 4064
ēdīcere, 6184
EDICT, 6185
EDIFICE, 4052
EDIFY, 4054, 4372
EDIFYING, 4052
'edit', 152
'editor', 154
EDMUND, 7644
ēducāre, 3465, 3595
'educate', 3467
EDUCATE, 3464
'education', 10848

'education, general', 10846
educationwise, 11439
ēducātus, 3465
EDUCE, 3462
ēdūcere, 3463, 3595
-ee-, 2494, 4517
'eerie', 3937
ef-, 4428, 4698, 5310
EFFACE, 4426
effacer, 4428
effārī, 4698
'effect', 4290, 11550
EFFECT, 4264, 4290
'effect, desired', 7666
'effect, having a good',
   4216
EFFECTIVE, 4291
'effectless', 4292
'effects', 1529
EFFECTUAL, 4291
effectus, 4289
'efficacious', 930
EFFICACIOUS, 4291
'efficacy', 11550
efficere, 4289
'efficient', 5829
EFFICIENT, 4291
EFFLUENT, 5310
EFFLUVIUM, 5311
EFFLUX, 5311
'effort', 7658
'effort to finish
   architectural project,
   intensive', 1947
-ega, 11412
'eggs', 8123
'egg-shaped', 11221
'eggs, producing', 8793
ēgi, 100
-ēgos, 49
eidenai, 11172, 11387
eidōlon, 11205
eidos, 9408, 11204, 11230
eidullion, 11213
Eimer, 1090
eimi, 8495, 8643
ein-, 1091
einbar, 1092
EISTEDDFOD, 1710
'either', 11094
EITHER, 11089
ek-, 3258, 6716

ekdekhesthai, 3257
ekdokhē, 3256
eklegein, 6716
ekleipein, 7035
ekleipsis, 7034
eklektikos, 6715
eklektos, 6715
el-, 7048
'elbowing', 11970
elder, 1805
'elder', 1796, 6096
ELDER, 6092
'elder in church', 1795
ELDRITCH, 3937
ELECT, 6543
ēlecta, 6550
'electromagnetic rays', 1570
ēlectus, 6544
'elegance', 3280
ēlegāns, 6554
'elegant', 4415
ELEGANT, 6553
ēlegāntis, 6554
*ēlegāre, 6556
elegeion, 6891
elegos, 6892
Elegy, 5447
ELEGY, 6891
'elevation, artificial, of
    earth', 7638
eleven, 1056
ELEVEN, 7061, 7095
elf, 7074
'elf', 690, 3903, 3951
'elf army', 3911
'elf council', 3904
'elf counsel', 690
ELFISH, 3906
'elf-kingdom', 3934
'elicit', 3463
ēligere, 6544
ēligibilis, 6552
ELIGIBLE, 6551
élite, 6548
ELITE, 6546
elleipein, 7048
elleipsis, 7047
ellerkonge, 3944
ELLIPSE, 7051
ellīpsis, 7047
ELLIPSIS, 7045
éloge, 6888
ēlogium, 6886

elogy, 6888
Elōhim, 2807
elphrish, 3939
'elsewhere', 11150
ēlūcidāre, 7304
ELUCIDATE, 7305
ELUDE, 3842, 3873
'elude capture', 2216
ēlūdere, 3874
elverkonge, 3944
ELVES, 3901
'elves, ruler of', 3925
em, 8494
EMANCIPATE, 7511, 7581
EMANCIPATION, 7420
embassador, 236
embassadour, 236
embassiator, 236
EMBASSY, 234
embel(l)ir, 3734
'embellish', 628, 3284,
    8009
EMBELLISH, 3733
embelliss(ant), 3734
'embezzlement', 7821
'emblem', 6794
'emblem, symbolic', 515
'embody', 8340
*embuié, 1875
embuier, 1874
-emia, 7396
'eminence', 9981
'eminent', 9983
'emissary', 7176, 10646
ēmittere, 7508, 7580
-emnis, 822
emparer, 8040
empereor, 8084
EMPEROR, 8082
'emphasis', 9759
emphuein, 1697
emphutos, 1698
EMPIRE, 8085
'employment', 4328
'employment domestic',
    4328
'employment, place of',
    4329
emporion, 8444
EMPORIUM, 8445
emporos, 8443
emprouer, 8631
emprower, 8632

'emptiness', 10369, 10413,
    10464
'empty', 10345, 10373,
    10424, 10459
'empty, make', 10376
'empty out', 10377
'empty space', 10361,
    10460
EMPYREAN, 5477
en, 4575, 7048
en-, 7338, 11903
ENABLE, 5843
ENACT, 114
'enchantment', 2765, 4715
ENCLAVE, 2502, 2550
enclaver, 2552
encloer, 2590
enclore, 2614
enclos(e), 2614
'enclose', 2552
ENCLOSE, 2613
'enclosed places, dread of',
    5696
'enclosure', 2610, 2650,
    5041
'enclosure for livestock',
    2090
'enclosure for vehicles',
    2094
'Encore!', 1194
'encounter', 10607
ENCROACH, 2932
ENCROACHERS, 2884
encrochier, 2931
ENCYCLICAL, 10840
encyclicus, 10842
encyclopaedia, 10846
Encyclopaedia Britannica,
    2915
ENCYCLOPEDIA, 10845
'end', 2320, 2606, 11030
ENDEAVOR, 5917
enditer, 6188
'endocrine gland', 5599
energeia, 11549
energēs, 11550
energīa, 11549
energos, 11550
'energy', 8825, 11780
ENERGY, 11548
'energy, pertaining to',
    3774

enewren, 7784
enfant, 4662
enfaunt, 4662
eng, 348
engen, 348
'engender', 1626, 1688
'engine', 8094, 11650
'English, aversion toward anything', 5698
'English Channel', 7578
en gogues, 59
'engraft', 1700
'engrafted', 1698
'engrave', 2684
'engraving instrument', 9867
enhalcier, 6085
ENHANCE, 6083
enhaucer, 6085
enhauncer, 6084
enjoin, 11945
'enjoin', 11892
ENJOIN, 11915
ENJOINDER, 11889, 11915, 11944
ENJOINMENT, 11889, 11915
*enkuklikos, 10844
enkuklios, 10842
enkuklios paideiā, 10847
enkuklopaideiā, 10847
'enlarge', 4370
ENLIGHTEN, 7262
enluminen, 7338
enluminer, 7337
-ennis, 822
'enough', 4380
'enrapture', 8354
'enroll for military service', 3478
ENS, 8538
-ēns, 8548
ensconce, 4469
ENSEMBLE, 9218
-ēnsis, 7555, 8205
'enslave', 1873, 7509, 11852
'enter into an alliance with', 7199
'enthusiasm', 10065
'enthusiast', 1768
ENTIA, 8538
'entice', 3458
'entire', 788, 817, 855

'entirely', 6821
-entis, 8548
ENTITY, 8554
entoma, 9536
entomon, 9537
entos, 8896
ENTOZOA, 8895
'entrance', 8255
'entrance, covered', 8277
'entrance hall', 5393
'entranceway', 5515
'entrapment', 10217
'entreat', 802
entredit, 6228
entrevoir, 11324
entrevue, 11323
'entrust', 7181, 7605
'entrust to another', 7179
'entrust (to someone) by law', 7173
'entwine thread', 1007
enui, 9286
'enumerate', 6821
'enumerating', 6829
'enunciation', 6147
'envelope', 4607
envie, 11379
'envious', 11372
'environment', 5762
ENVISAGE, 11277
ENVISION, 11278
envoi, 10647
ENVOI, 10650
envoier, 10644
'envoy', 226
ENVOY, 10645
'envy', 11373
ENVY, 11379
eoc, 11820
EOCENE, 3830
EOHIPPUS, 3832
EOLITHIC, 3835
ēōs, 3788, 3831
Ēostre, 3787
EP, 3891, 4006, 5934, 6101, 7114, 7817, 8008, 8257, 8855, 8989, 9939, 9974, 10031, 10260, 11256, 11368, 11643, 11724
epi, 1677, 2733, 6805
'epidermis', 9466
EPIGRAM, 2733

epigramma, 2735
EPIGRAMMATIC, 2683
'epigrams', 6823
'epigraph', 2733
EPIGRAPH, 2730
epigraphē, 2732
epigraphos, 2733
EPILOGUE, 6804
EPIPHYTE, 1676
'episode', 7762
'episode, intervening', 3888
'epitaph', 6887
EPITHET, 4575
epitheton, 4580
'equal', 7903, 7929, 7957
'equal footing', 7930
'equality', 7932
'equal, make', 7948
'equal rank, person of', 7958
'equals', 7940
'equals, bring together as', 7962
'equip', 627, 7979, 8095
'equipment', 634, 8093
'equivalence', 7933
'equivalent', 291
EQUIVALENT, 933
equus, 3306
*er-, 8503
'erase', 4427
'erect', 1524
ERG, 11541
-erg-, 11548
ERGATOCRACY, 11621
ERGOLATRY, 11620
ergon, 11539, 11576, 11616
ERGOPHOBIA, 11619
-ergy, 11556
ERLKING, 3940
Erlkönig, 3943
es-, 271, 10391
-es, 1053
*es, 8734
*es-, 8481, 8675, 8701, 8732
escale, 8950
ESCALLOP, 8957
escalope, 8956
ESCAPADE, 2222
'escape', 5616, 5642
ESCAPE, 2215

ESCAPEE, 2219
ESCAPEMENT, 2219
escaper, 2217
-esce, 938
-escent, 5191
-ēscere, 5997, 7527, 10446
esconse, 4467
'escort', 10653
*-ēse, 8205
*esem, 8496
esligier, 7215
eslire, 6549
eslite, 6548
*es-mi, 8482
esquatir, 270
essai, 138
essaier, 137
ESSAY, 138
'essay, introductory', 3893
esse, 8507, 8541, 8639,
    8706
essence, 8533
'essence', 8514, 8645
ESSENCE, 8510
'essence of the universe',
    11796
ESSENCES, 8533
*essens, 8508, 8541
essentia, 8510
ESSENTIAL, 8516
ESSEX, 9496
est, 8486
estaca, 9592
estacada, 9591
estacade, 9591
*estacare, 9614
estache, 9612, 9642
estachier, 9611
estado, 4596
estat, 4596
'estate', 1529, 4329, 10948
ESTATE, 4597
'estate in land', 7850
'estate, landed', 7838
'esteem highly', 6608
esti, 8486
*es-ti, 8482
'estimate', 298
'estimation', 301
estiquet(te), 9930
estiqu(i)er, 9931
ESTIVAL, 4119
ESTIVATE, 4114
estocade, 9590

estoire, 11254
estoquier, 10299
(e)storie, 11254
estrangler, 9833
estrece, 9756
estreindre, 9769
estreit, 9745
estresse, 9756
estrique, 9709
estriquer, 150, 9710
estroit, 9745
ESTUARY, 4123
*(e)studiāre, 10079
estudie, 10070
estui, 10081
estuier, 10080
*esu-, 8739
esvanir, 10453
esvaniss(ant), 10453
esvuidier, 10391
eszi, 8486
et, 11271
-et, 2612, 11271
et alii, 4690
état, 4596
'etching instrument', 9867
été, 4112
eteos, 8729
'eternal', 5094, 9250
ETHELRED, 691
ETHER, 4090
ETHEREAL, 4105
ETHYL, 4102
etiquet(te), 9930
ETIQUETTE, 9852, 9933
étriqué, 149, 9718
étroit, 9745
-ette, 2612
étude, 10071
ÉTUDE, 10072
étui, 1079, 10082
ETUI, 10083
etuis, 1079
etumon, 8727
etumos, 8729
ETWEE, 10083
ETYMOLOGY, 8726
eu, 4795, 6884, 8740
eu-, 1690, 8451, 8740
*eu-, 10345, 10394, 10424,
    10480
'Eucharist for a dying
    person', 10586

'eucharist, preparation of
    the', 4599
eugenēs, 8743
EUGENICS, 8742
eulogein, 1372
eulogia, 6883, 8745
eulogium, 6883
'eulogize', 1374
EULOGY, 6881, 8744
euphēmein, 4794
euphemism, 1695
EUPHEMISM, 4792
euphōnia, 4846
EUPHONIOUS, 4842
EUPHONIOUSLY, 4840
EUPHONIUM, 4847
euphōnos, 4846, 8744
EUPHONY, 4844, 8744
EUPHORIA, 8745
euphoros, 8746
EUPHRATES, 8449, 8756
euphuēs, 1689
EUPHUISM, 1694
eus, 4794, 8739
EUTHANASIA, 8746
ēvacuāre, 10377
EVACUATE, 10376
ēvānēscēns, 10449
'evanescent', 5647
EVANESCENT, 10450
ēvānēscere, 10448
EVANISH, 10457
ēvectiō, 10721
EVECTION, 10720
'even', 7944, 9355
'even (opposed to *odd*)',
    7943
'event', 4237
'ever', 9237
'everywhere', 11144
evicted, 10722
ēvictus, 10723
'evidence', 8359, 11392
EVIDENCE, 11365
ēvidēns, 11363
EVIDENT, 11363
ēvidentia, 11366
*ēvidēre, 11367
'evil', 4733
'evil-doer', 4166
'evil, doing', 4217

'evil-speaking', 4801
ēvincere, 10723
'ewe', 7827
ex, 7306, 8016, 11364
ex-, 271, 2219, 3463, 4428,
  4698, 5310, 6544, 7216,
  9996, 10378
'exact', 9740
EXACT, 118
'exacting', 143
EXACTING, 122
exāctum, 120
'exact weight', 147
*exagere, 120
'exaggerate', 1976
'exaggeration', 1977
'exaggeration', 1978
*exagiare, 136
exagion, 134
exagium, 132
*exagmen, 295
*exag(s)men, 127
EXALT, 6050
exaltāre, 6051
'exalted', 6069
EXALTED, 5954
exāmen, 126, 296
exāmināre, 129
'examination', 128, 296
'examine', 121, 295, 3518
EXAMINE, 130
'examine again', 11309
EXAMINING, 123
'example', 6330, 10115
*excappāre, 2218
'excellence', 9983, 11752
'excellent', 1589
'excess', 7384
'excesses, sexual', 11630
'excessive', 608, 5928
excite, 792
'excite the mind', 176
*exclaudere, 2635
EXCLUDE, 2622
excludere, 2622
EXCLUSION, 2633
EXCLUSIVE, 2633
'excommunication', 4896
'excrescence', 3102
EXCURSION, 2033
'excursion, hostile', 2003
'execration', 4537
'execute', 4480

'exemption', 10358
'exemption from military
  service', 10358
'exercise, military', 7495
'exercise, preliminary', 3893
exercitus, 487
'exert', 9770
'exertion', 7658
EXFOLIATE, 5244
'exhaustion', 10464
exhibēre, 5866
'exhibit', 6334
EXHIBIT, 5865
'exhibition', 4600
exigens, 143
EXIGENT, 142
exigere, 120
EXIGUOUS, 143
exiguus, 145
'exile', 8353
'exist', 1554, 1621, 8505
'existence', 8538
'existence, human', 6097,
  11671
'existence, maintain a
  separate', 8833
'existing', 8692, 8730
'exists', 8693
*exlegere, 6549
*exlītigāre, 7216
'exorbitant', 10317
exōrdior, 616
exōrdiri, 616
EXORDIUM, 618
'expectation', 3240
'expectation, joint', 3255
'expel from a country',
  8343
'experienced', 11340
'explain', 7305
'exploit', 455, 3281
'explosive', 3778
'exponent', 6771
EXPORT, 8330
'exposed', 5359
'exposition', 6642
'express', 6690
'expression, abusive', 10684
'exquisite', 3336, 4105
ex(s)tinctus, 9995
ex(s)tinguere, 9995
'extended', 7024
'extensive', 10420

EXTINCT, 9996
'extinguish', 9986
EXTINGUISH, 9994
'extract', 8531
'extraordinary', 9229
EXTRAORDINARY, 607
'extravagance', 7382
'extremes, opposite', 11001
'exuberance', 8825
*exvānīre, 10452
'eye', 1200, 1815, 7319,
  10824
'eyeglasses', 7359
'eye, of the', 1199
'eyes, bulging', 10780
'eyeshade', 11282
'eyesight', 11286
-ezan, 8204

F

f-, 5260
-f, 1598
fable, 4686
FABLE, 4684
'fabricate', 4156
'fabric, rugged woolen',
  1042
'fabric with diagonal
  parallel ribs', 1037
fābula, 4683
FABULISTS, 4689
FABULOUS, 4690
fac!, 4318
*fac-, 4401
FAÇADE, 4411
faccia, 4412
facciata, 4412
'face', 4396, 11275
FACE, 4409
'face-covering', 11281
'face, little', 4413
'face of a building', 4411
'face of it, on the', 4406
facere, 453, 661, 4063,
  4140, 4214, 4245, 4302,
  4332, 4363, 4394, 4432,
  6031, 7737, 11109
'face, remove the', 4428
facēs, 4401
FACET, 4413
facētia, 4417

FATE, 4701
'fated', 1518
FATEFUL, 4704
fater, 11051
fatēri, 4739, 4765
'Fates', 4708
'father', 8114
FATHER, 11051
'fat in the blood', 7126
'fatty', 7124
fātum, 4700, 4729
fātus, 4681, 4728, 4887
fau-, 5581
faubourg, 5579
FAUBOURG, 5578
'fault', 6322
'faulty', 6753
faunt, 4671
fauntekin, 4672
fauntelet, 4672
FAUNTLEROY, 4673
faux, 5579
fauxbourg, 5582
'favor', 3655, 4953, 10065
'favorable', 3287, 5095,
  8400
'favoring', 8163
'favors, person who seeks',
  803
'favourable', 3293
fax, 4401
'fay', 4720
FAY, 4711
'fays', 4715
'fays, land of the', 4715
FAZENDA, 4330
fazon, 4187
fe, 7841
'fear', 66, 1171, 5675
'fear, dread of', 5721
'feared', 1173, 3532
fearn, 8474
FEASANCE, 4242
feasible, 5839
FEASIBLE, 4246
'feast together', 8805
FEAT, 4238
'feather', 4970, 5000, 5046,
  5106, 8476
FEATHER, 5152
'feathered', 5004
'feather, huge', 4992
'feather, little', 4969

'feather, resembling a',
  5005
'feathers, tuft of', 4968
'feat, unusual', 10243
FEATURE, 4240
FEBRIFUGE, 5661
febrifugia, 5665
febris, 5662
FECKLESS, 4292
-fect, 4142
-fectus, 4251
Feder, 5152
'Federal Council', 3906
fee, 7836
'fee', 7843
FEE, 7792, 7838
'feed', 1865, 10295
'feedbag', 2299
'feeder', 3144
*feht-, 7882
fehu, 7832
*fehu, 7832
*fehu-, 7830
*fehu-ōd, 7848
'feign', 4253, 9177, 9205
-feit, 4142, 4252
feitiço, 4195
fēlagi, 7856
felawe, 7858
'feline, Asiatic', 10025
'fellow', 1442, 7941
FELLOW, 7858
'fellow-dweller, near', 1439
'fellow member', 7186
'female warrior', 11743
'fence, on the', 934
feodum, 7842
feoh, 7833
feohtan, 7883
fēolaga, 7857
fer-, 8418
FERDINAND, 8469
*fer-giban, 5945
ferian, 8424
ferja, 8425
'fern', 5118
FERN, 8472
'ferns, science of', 5119
ferre, 6033, 7283
'ferry', 8426
FERRY, 8423
'ferryboat', 8425
*ferthuz, 8428

'fertile', 6030
'fertilizer, organic', 7776
'festival, keep a', 72, 178
'festive celebrations, place
  of', 69
-festus, 7502
fet, 4238
fether, 5151
*fethrō, 5151
fétiche, 4198
FETISH, 4138, 4198
'fetter', 1873
'fettered', 1875
'fettered, condition of
  being', 1486
'fetters', 1872
'fetus, first movement of',
  8778
feu, 5433
feud, 7846
'feudal estate', 7842
FEUDALISM, 7843
'feudal jurisdiction', 4911
feudum, 7842
feuel, 5418
Feuer, 5457
FEUILLETON, 5247
'fever-chaser', 5664
FEVERFEW, 5664
'few', 8105
fewaile, 5418
-fex, 453, 4344
fi-, 5198
fiat, 1615
'fibula', 9638
-fic, 4318
-fic-, 4215
-ficāre, 661, 4062, 4365
-fice, 4061
-ficere, 4063, 4214, 4302,
  4366
-ficient, 4142
'fiction', 4684
-ficus, 6031
fiddle, 1005
fide, 3684
'fief', 4218
FIEF, 7843
'field', 3165, 3636, 7269
'field hand', 1868
-fier, 4062, 4365
fieri, 1613

'fifth essence', 8521
fight, 7887
'fight', 6797, 7882
FIGHT, 7883
'fight, out of the', 5577
'figure', 2714, 8903, 10105
'figures, circle of', 8902
'figure, sculptured', 8902
'figwort', 6279
filius de aliquid, 11155
'fill', 7450
'filled', 5337
'fillet (of meat)', 8962
'film over the eyes', 10785
'filter', 9771
'fin', 4974, 5019
FIN, 5017
'financial aid, one who
    gives', 4165
'find fault with', 11451
'fine', 2352, 3609, 3719,
    6554
'fine arts, practitioner of',
    436
'finely made', 4415
'fineness, lacking in', 2036
'finery', 8010
finger, 6194
'finger', 1112, 5114, 6273,
    6300, 11998
'finger or toe', 6274
'finger's breadth', 1112
'finished', 11031
finn, 5024
finne, 5024
fioh, 7833
fiore, 5198
Fiorello, 5201
Fiorenza, 5200
fiorino, 5197
fir-, 8418
fire, 5455
'fire', 4126, 5416, 5449
FIRE, 5461
'firearms, discharge of',
    5424
'firebox', 5404
'firebug', 5473
'fire-colored', 5485
'fire condition', 5477
'fire, dread of', 5710
'fire enthusiast', 1766
'fire-grate', 5404, 5458

'fire, land of the', 5451
'fireman', 4392
Firenze, 5200
'fire-pan', 5406
'fireplace', 1201, 5392,
    5430
'fire-stone', 5468
'fire thorn', 5475
'firewood', 6532
'fireworks', 5474
'first', 97, 620, 2135, 2172,
    7995, 8893
'first-class', 2135
'"first" man, of the', 2144
'first rate', 11160
FIRTH, 8426
FIRTHS, 8431
-FISH, 2873
'Fishes', 8907
'fish scale', 8951
'fish with venomous
    spines', 8137
'fist', 7887
'fit', 5799
'fitness', 5850
'fit out', 627, 8098
'fit, render', 5851
'fitter-together', 641
'fitting', 3267, 3312, 9269
'fitting things together',
    411
'fitting together', 468, 546
'fit to be eaten', 5816
'fit together', 384, 414,
    473, 550, 578, 631, 669,
    715
fu, 7841
'five', 6375
'five-centime piece', 845
'five-leaf', 5239
'fixed', 658
'fix in a habit', 5791
fjor-, 8418
FJORD, 8426
fjördhr, 8428
FJORDS, 8431
fjörthr, 8428
fl-, 5198
'flag, triangular', 4988
'flamboyance', 4965
'flange', 10894
flash, 5341
'flash', 7257

'flashing', 7257
'flask', 3139
'flat', 9066
'flatten thoroughly', 271
'flawless', 4297
'flay', 9466
flèche, 8034
flectere, 6397
'flee', 5611, 5651
'flee back', 5640
'flee, cause to', 5652
'fleeing', 5648
'flee in terror', 5674
'flee secretly', 5644
fleet, 5350
'fleet', 490, 3345
'fleet, armed', 494
'fleeting', 5632
'fleet, war', 493
'flee under', 5644
'flesh', 11236
'flesh as food', 8810
'fleshlike', 11236
'flesh, raw exposed', 8764
fleur de lis, 5203
FLEURET, 5206
fleureter, 5161
fleurette, 5163
'flight', 5616, 5651
'flight feather', 5005
'flight, put to', 5613
'fling out the feet', 8017
'flintlock musket', 5426
'flippant', 4419
FLIRT, 5155
flirter, 5165
flirteur, 5166
flirteuse, 5166
FLO, 5182
'float', 10765
'flocks', 7802
'floor', 11253
flora, 3791
FLORA, 5180
Flore Homoecop, 3702
flōrem, 5210
FLORENCE, 5179
flōrens, 5195
flōrentia, 5195
'Florentine', 5196
flōrēre, 5177
FLORESCENT, 5191

FLORID, 5156, 5183
FLORIDA, 5156, 5186
floride, 5185
flōridus, 5185
FLORIN, 5179
florir, 5176
*flōrīre, 5177
floris, 3791, 5168, 5194
floriss(ant), 5176
FLORRIE, 5182
flos, 3791, 5168, 5260
flōs farinae, 5212
FLOSSIE, 5183
flo(u)r, 5210
FLOUR, 5210
flour de farine, 5211
FLOURISH, 5155
'flourishing', 5200
FLOURISHING, 5178
flow, 5344
'flow', 5306, 5345, 6800,
    6994, 7023
'flow, beginning to', 5193
'flower', 5180, 5260
FLOWER, 5158, 5209
'flower-gathering', 6825
'flowering', 5195
'flower, little', 5197
FLOWERS, 5216
'flowers, collection of',
    6826
'Flowers Feast of', 5190
'flower, small', 5163
'flowers, Roman goddess
    of', 5181
'flowery', 5184
FLOWERY, 5156
'flow in', 5300
'flowing', 2025, 5287, 5321,
    6800
'flowing out', 5310
'flowing together of
    streams', 5311
'flowing toward', 5309
'flow, steady', 2057
fluctuāre, 5328
FLUCTUATE, 5329
fluctus, 5327
FLUENT, 5312
fluere, 5306, 5345
'fluid', 7005
FLUID, 5288
'fluidity', 7008

flum, 5317
FLUME, 5316
flūmen, 5315
fluor, 5321
FLUOR, 5322
FLUORESCENCE, 5323
FLUORIDE, 5323
FLUORINE, 5322
FLUORITE, 5323
FLUOROMETER, 5323
FLUOROSCOPE, 5323
flus, 5331
flush, 5334
FLUSH, 5332
flushed, 5342
'flush (in playing cards)',
    5331
'flute of a column', 9839
FLUVIAL, 5318
fluviālis, 5320
fluvius, 5318
flux, 5331
'flux', 5331
FLUX, 5325
'flux, unit of luminous',
    7323
fluxus, 5325
fly, 5350
'fly', 5047, 5104
'fly away, tending to', 5840
'flying up suddenly', 5342
FOCAL, 5414
focalia, 5416
focārium, 5394
*focile, 5429
focus, 1201, 5393, 5430
'focus', 5405
FOCUS, 5411
FOCUSED, 5388
-fod, 1709
'fodder', 1856, 5884
foedus ferire, 9690
fogli, 8297
foglio, 8297
foil, 5232
FOIL, 5227
'foil, fencing', 5206
foillage, 5220
foille, 5220
foisil, 5429
'fold', 1342, 4431, 9408
'folded', 1138, 9235
'folder for paper', 8295

'foliage', 5256
FOLIAGE, 5216
FOLIO, 5225
folium, 5219, 8297
FOLIUM, 5223
'folklore, Germanic', 3941
'follow', 9567
'follower', 9412
'foment', 9957
'fondness, feeling of', 4266
'food', 5883, 5960, 8807
'food and drink', 8421
'food elements, essential',
    8826
'food for livestock', 5883
'food, giving', 5967
'food, insatiable appetite
    for', 1826
'fool', 3951, 10502
'foot', 31, 311, 1198, 2308
'foot, jointed', 394
'foot, metrical, of three
    syllables', 6289
'foot, seizure of the', 310
'foot, unstressed', 4553
for, 4681
'for', 5947
for-, 5588
forain, 5501
'for all', 7730
forānus, 5502
forās, 5503
'forbid', 5867, 6225
'force', 294, 982, 10263,
    10579, 11780
'force, driving', 5072
'forcefulness of expression',
    10686
'forceful person', 3777
'force into service', 7598
'force, military', 6526
'force out', 118, 294
'force, physical', 11781
'force, vital', 11779
'forcible', 10688
forclore, 5571
forclos, 5570
ford, 8430
'ford', 1778
FORD, 8429
FORDS, 8432
for(e), 5562

FORECLOSE, 5569
'forefinger', 6192
FOREIGN, 5503
FOREIGNER, 5522
'foreign relations', 1318
forein, 5498
'foreleg', 7439
FORENSIC, 5532
forēnsis, 5534
'forerunner', 2023, 3371
'foresee', 11328
'foreseeing', 11332
'foreshadows, one that',
 977
'foresight', 11331
forest, 5560
FOREST, 5536
forestem silvam, 5539
FORESTER, 5554
forestis, 5544
forestis silva, 5540
'foretell', 675, 6211, 11279
'foreteller', 4881
'forever', 5093
FORFEIT, 4258, 5564
forfet, 4260, 5567
forgeben, 5951
forgiefan, 5945
FORGIVE, 5944
forīs, 4261, 5502, 5563
forisfacere, 4261, 5568
'fork', 1048, 1258, 2935
'forked, something', 1047
'forked tongue, speaking
 with', 1140
'fork-shaped timber', 2938
'form', 6897, 11178, 11204,
 11230
'formation', 4241
'former', 11129
'formidable', 1172
'form in a certain way',
 4191
fors, 5575
'forsake', 4920, 6954
'forsake completely', 6988
'forsaking', 7034
forsborc, 5580
forsbourg, 5585
for(s)faire, 4260, 5568
FORSOOTH, 8714
'forth', 285, 6028
'fortification', 3527

'fortified place', 5581
'fortify', 8039
'fort, small', 4470
'fortune', 8678
'fortune, good', 3674
'forty-all', 1145
'Forty-and-Eight Division',
 10672
forum, 5545
'forum', 5535
FORUM, 5525
'forward', 5079, 5868,
 6028, 7993, 8415
'for what reason', 11074
'fossil, living', 6986
'foster mother', 5973, 6017
fouaille, 5417
'foundling hospital', 3153
'four', 6840
'four letters, consisting of',
 2801
'four, series of', 6839
'foxglove, dried leaf of',
 6277
foyer, 5395, 5458
FOYER, 5387
'fraction', 8157
frāctum, 9514
fragile, 5838
'fragile', 5835
fragment, 10692
'fragment', 3124, 10302
'fragments', 6982, 10057,
 10226
'framework', 3146
FRANCO-, 5697
FRANCOPHONE, 4864
frangere, 9514
frangible, 5838
FRANGIBLE, 5835
'fraternity', 7191
'free', 7506
FREEDOM, 4524
'freedom from', 10357
'free from care', 10363
'free from duties', 10347
'freeing of a slave', 6243
'free man', 1478
'freeze', 2415, 2448, 2474
'freeze solid', 2422
frēgī, 9514
'freight', 1972
'French-speaking', 4865

'frenzy', 6799
'frequent', 5788
'frequenter', 5787
'frequently', 7785
'friction match', 7282
'frighten', 4380
'frightening', 1172
'fringe', 9644
'frisky', 2394
'frolic', 8372
'from', 6341, 10897
'front', 4411
'front, in', 5887
'frost', 2417
'frozen', 2419, 2477
'frozen dessert', 4297
'frugal', 11332
'frugality', 6607
'fruitless', 10426
'fruit, producing', 6030
'frustrated', 7565
fuego, 5451
FUEL, 5419
FUELS, 5387
fueram, 1606
fuerās, 1606
fuerō, 1607
fuga, 5613, 5651
FUGACIOUS, 5609, 5647
fugacis, 5648
fugare, 5613, 5652
fugāx, 5648
fuge, 5626
fugere, 5612, 5651
FUGIO, 5669
fugitive, 5633
FUGITIVE, 5608
fugitīvus, 5633
fugitum, 5634
fugue, 5625
FUGUE, 5620
FUGUES, 5607
führ, 8418
Fuhre, 8437
führen, 8436
FUHRER, 8435
fuī, 1605
fuier, 5395
fu(i)sil, 5429
fuisse, 1608
fuistī, 1605
fuit, 1605

'fulfillment', 11037
FULL-BLOWN, 5279
'fuller', 3585
'full-figured', 3135
'full of light', 7367
fūmigāre, 190
FUMIGATE, 190
fūmus, 190
'function, cause to', 7665
'function, having the same', 9352
'functions, arithmetical', 721
'fund', 10271
'funeral pile', 5407, 5465
'funeral pyre', 4136
'funnel', 9606
f(u)oco, 5450
furca, 1259
**furduz*, 8431
'furious', 10688
'furnish', 7987, 8065, 8112, 11329
'furnish ahead of time', 7988
'furnishings', 8097
'furrow', 9839
'furs, dread of', 5709
'fury', 3603, 7404
fuse, 5430
fusee, 5431
FUSIL, 5426
FUSILLADE, 5421
'fuss', 4489
fūstigāre, 192
FUSTIGATE, 191
fūstis, 192
'futile', 4803, 10426
futur, 1611
FUTURE, 1611
futūrus, 1609
-*fy*, 4061, 4142, 4364

G

**g-*, 2475, 2837
ga, 8467
gabardina, 8454
GABARDINE, 8451
GABERDINE, 8451
'gain', 4306
'gainsay', 6906
'gallant', 8596, 8629

gallevardine, 8454
GALLO-, 5697
'gallows bird', 10508
galvardine, 8454
'game', 3847, 8379
'games, public', 3860
'gamester's assistant', 3112
'gamete, fertilizing, of a male', 8894
gamma, 2690
gamos, 1261, 9418
'garment, ceremonial', 2226
'garment of white', 3963
'garments', 8096
'garment, unlined woolen', 9230
-*garou*, 11714
garoul, 11715
garulf, 11715
'gash', 9137
'gasoline', 8534
gâté, 10409
'gate', 5512, 8252, 8312, 8391
'gatekeeper', 8307
'gates', 2652
'gateway', 8273
gather, 6516
'gather', 6500, 6566, 6610, 6636, 6687, 6926, 7195
'gather apart', 6542, 6609
'gathered', 6524
'gathered together', 257
'gathering', 6631, 10902
'gathering place', 11900
'gather together', 6560
gauvard(ine), 8463
GAVE, 5938
'gay', 1388
gē, 11234, 11612
ge-, 1442
-*ge*, 7518
geaf, 5939
'gear', 8093
gēa sī, 8723
gēa swā, 8724
gebann, 4907
gebūr, 1441
geclypod, 11822
gecrympan, 3021
GEESE, 2500
gei, 11460
GEL, 2431

**gel-*, 2415, 2454
gelāre, 2416
gelata, 2427
GELATIN, 2432
gelatina, 2426
GELATIN(E), 2424
gelatus, 2478
Geld, 11701
-*geld*, 11700
gelee, 2431
geli, 2430
GELID, 2419
gelidus, 2420
gelū, 2417
gelum, 2417
gelus, 2417
gely, 2430
**g(e)n-*, 6390, 6430
genea, 8673
genera, 3792
'general', 48, 864, 8870
'generalship', 52
'generation', 8673, 9457
'generator', 3776
genere, 6406
generis, 3792
'generosity', 3657
'generous', 3271, 3653, 9288
-*genēs*, 9338
genesis, 11021, 11748
GENICULATE, 6400
geniculātus, 6401
geniculum, 6402
genre, 11827
'gentle', 1387, 3689
'gentleness', 7523
genū, 6395
**genu-*, 6389, 6415
GENUFLECT, 6399
genuflectere, 6398
'genuine', 3685, 7170, 8690
GENUINE, 6403
'genuineness, lacking', 4193
genuīnus, 6404
genus, 3691, 3791, 6405
geoc, 11808
GEODE, 11232
'geography', 11613
GEOGRAPHY, 2831
'geologic era', 3830
geology, 11613

GEORGE, 11609
GEORGIC, 11614
Georgica, 11615
geōrgika, 11615
geōrgos, 11612
gēr, 980
-*ger*, 518
*ger-, 2888, 3074
GERALD, 979
Gerard, 11422
*gerebh-, 2835, 2875
gerere, 518, 2544
GERMANO-, 5697
Gēr(w)ald, 980
gēse, 8723
'gestures, expressive', 5175
'get', 7979, 8111
'get along', 8420
'get back', 8066
'get better', 8634
'get in return', 8110, 8155
'get out of', 2218
-*ggiare*, 7517
gh, 6072
-*gh*-, 6070
*ghabh-, 5735, 5812, 5935
*ghebh-, 5937
*ghel-, 2455
'ghostwriter', 7556
*giban, 5939
giefan, 5939, 11825
gift, 5940
'gift', 5942, 8552
GIFT, 5731, 5939
'gift, additional', 3625
*giftiz, 5941
'gift, temporary', 6950
-*gild*, 11700
gimel, 2691
gipt, 5940
Giraut, 980
'girl', 2499
'girl, beautiful', 3728
'gist', 6446
give, 11824
'give', 4476, 5735, 5812, 5935, 7583
GIVE, 5938
'give a gift', 8553
'give birth', 8112
'given', 7504
'give oneself up to', 6158
'give temporarily', 6949

'give up', 6980
'giving', 5943
GIVING, 5731
*gl-, 2439
glace, 2441
GLACÉ, 2450
*glace, 2463
glacer, 2450
glacia, 2444
GLACIAL, 2445
glaciālis, 2446
glaciāre, 2448
GLACIATE, 2447
GLACIATED, 2414
glacier, 2443
GLACIER, 2411, 2441
'glaciers, pertaining to', 2445
glaciēs, 2437
glacis, 2460
GLACIS, 2458
glad, 2455
'gladiatorial school', 3863
'gladiator's wife', 3864
gladiolus, 9475
glamer, 2765
glammar, 2765
GLAMOR, 2765
glamour, 2767
GLANCE, 2461
'gland', 11223
'glandlike', 11222
glanss, 2468
glass, 2452
'glass bottle, small', 3138
glaunce, 2469
glaunche, 2468
glaunse, 2468
glawnse, 2468
glaze, 2452
'glaze', 2450
'glazed', 2449
glazier, 2453
gleam, 2454
'gleanings, literary', 6717
glence, 2468
glench, 2468
glens, 2468
glenten, 2470
'glide from tone to tone', 8326
glint, 2454
'glint', 2470

glitter, 2454
'gloomy', 10334, 10475
GLORIFY, 4374
gloss, 2452
'glossary', 2540
'glut', 2587
GNARLED, 6464
gnath-, 6419
GNATHIDIUM, 6421
GNATHOMETER, 6422
GNATHOPODITE, 6421
gnathos, 6418
GNATHOSTEGITE, 6422
*gneu-, 6389
GNOCCHI, 6474
gnōmōn, 1642
'go', 1802, 9685, 10525, 10576, 10747
goad, 9879
'goad', 9879, 9956, 9986
'goading', 9966
'go after something', 10578
'goat', 2394
'Goat (horned)', 8907
'go away from', 7087, 7131
'go back to see', 11311
'goblin child', 3949
'god', 9401, 11335
'God be with ye', 742
'godfather', 7961
'God give you a good morning', 741
'God knows', 11389
'god, one supreme', 9400
'God, reviling', 4800
'gods', 984
God's blood, 1410
'go forward', 5090
'going', 10759
'going before', 10636
'going in front', 1803
'going on foot', 32
'going toward', 1515
'gold', 3673, 11700
gold-cup, 1787
'Golden Legend', 6682
'gold, fool's', 5466
'golf-player's attendant', 2110
-*gon*, 6383
*gōn-, 6389
gōnia, 6376, 9402

'guard', 10080
'guardian', 20
guast, 10397
guidar, 11447
'guide', 47, 3451, 11459
GUIDE, 11446
guide(r), 11447
'guiding', 3486
'guiding hand', 7636
guier, 11459
'guild', 7191
'guile, without', 449
'guilty', 4259, 8704
guise, 11450
GUISE, 11449
*guiuos, 8855
guivre, 8133
gush, 5341
guy, 11459
GUY, 11458
*gw-, 1718, 8850, 8876,
   8908
*gwā-, 1802
*gwei-, 8766, 8823, 8850,
   8878, 8909
*gwet-, 11125
*gwiy-o-, 8856
*gwou-, 1718, 1837, 1867
gwyn, 11475

H

ha-, 9404
habeas, 5760
HABEAS, 5757
*habēn, 5741
habenda, 5887
habēre, 5737, 5768, 5859,
   5888, 5936
habile, 5809
HABILE, 5810, 5840
HABILIMENT(s), 5803
habilis, 5798, 5847
habilitar, 5853
habilitāre, 5851
habilitās, 5848
HABILITATE, 5852
(h)abilite, 5849
habilitieren, 5854
habiller, 5792
HABIT, 5777
habitāculum, 5879
habitant, 5776

HABITANTS, 5774
habitāre, 5764, 5879
HABITAT, 5762
'habitation, little', 5876
HABITUALLY, 5767
habituāre, 5788
HABITUATE, 5790
HABITUÉ, 5787
habituer, 5788
habitus, 5780, 5893
hacienda, 4328
HACIENDA, 4325
'hacienda, Brazilian', 4330
'Hades', 11239
HADES, 11237
'hag', 3603
Haidēs, 11239
'hail!', 754, 986
HAIL!, 871, 905
*hail-, 873
'hail and farewell', 992
*hailaz, 874
'Hail! Farewell!', 988
'Hail! Mary', 986
haima, 7127, 7397
'hair', 2351
'hair, concerning or
   resembling a', 2352
'hair in disarray', 2357
'hair of the beard', 2348
'hair of the head', 2311,
   2347
Hakenkreuz, das, 8683
hāl, 890
*halbaz, 9074
hal beo thu, 904
HALE, 886
'half', 1062, 2182
HALF, 9073, 10108
'half-light', 1063
'half-wit', 3950
hālig, 896
Hallo, 907
Halloo, 907
HALLOW, 898
'hallucination induced by
   drugs', 3429
'hallway', 2086
hals, 10918
halse, 10922
'halt', 910
'halter', 9831
hama, 9364

hamadruas, 9366
HAMADRYAD, 9365
HAMADRYAS, 9369
'hammer', 10207
'hammer, small', 10208
'hand', 4159, 7426, 7484,
   7510, 7552, 7579, 7634,
   11597
'hand, accustom to the',
   7524
'handbook', 7429
'hand, by', 7522
'handcuff', 7441
'hand drum', 10148
'handful', 7448
'hand, hold in the hand',
   7545
'handiwork', 7434
'handle', 3104, 7514
'handle (a horse)', 7515
'handle an ax', 965
'handle a sword', 965
'handled', 1089
'handle, easy to', 5841
'handling', 7425
'handling, way of', 7548
'hand, little', 7442
handmade, 7437
'handmade', 7435
'hand, make by', 7433
'hand, of the', 7430, 7550
'hand over', 7605
'hands', 7425, 7481
'hands and fingernails, care
   of the', 7482
'hand, seized by the', 7502
'hands, having four', 7485
'handsome', 3274, 3608,
   3719, 9275
HANDSOME, 9287
'hands, working with the',
   11596
'hand, take into', 7509
'handwork', 7491, 11592
'hand, work by', 7490
'hand, work the soil by',
   7496
'handwriting, bad', 2828
'handwriting, beautiful',
   2827
'handwriting, study of',
   2817

'handwritten', 7431
'handwritten document',
  860
'handy', 5805, 9290
'hanging', 336, 4993
'hanging piece', 9646
'hangnail', 320
HANGNAIL, 313
HAPLOID, 9406
haploidēs, 9408
HAPLOSIS, 9409
haplous, 9405
'happen', 2050, 5137
'happen again', 2051
'happen at the same time',
  2051
'happening together', 5138
'happiness', 3752
'happiness, serene', 1384
'happiness, supreme', 3749
Haraldr, 972
'harass', 10735
'harbor', 8251
'harbors, god of', 8397
'hard', 326, 826
'hard by', 11952
'harden', 2422
hard liquor, 7010
'hardship', 9758
'hardy', 11421
hari, 970
Harja-waldan, 973
harja-waldaz, 972
harjaz, 973
'harm', 4805, 11783
'harm, free from', 757
'harmful', 9285
'harming', 4804
'harm, keep from', 757
harmonia, 550
HARMONICA, 554
HARMONICS, 554
HARMONIOUS, 378, 554
HARMONIUM, 555
'harmonize', 610, 11972
HARMONIZE, 554
'harmony', 4848, 8360
HARMONY, 551
harmos, 549
harmozein, 550
'harness', 11856
HAROLD, 971
'harp', 2537

'harrow in', 9564
'harsh', 4848
'harvest', 3100
'harvest, goddess or the',
  7683
'harvest grapes (with a
  hook)', 3077
'haste', 6617
'hasten', 2171
'hast, (that) thou', 5760
'hasty', 2023
'hat', 2238
'hatch', 2623
'hate', 699, 10332
'hated', 10332
'hateful', 10333, 11373
'Hateful, the', 10329
hatereden, 698
hateros, 9374
'hat, little', 2284
'hatred', 10333
HATRED, 698
'hatred, in', 9287
'hat with a small crown
  and wide brim', 2282
hauberc, 10939
HAUBERK, 10937
haubid-, 2403
haubidam, 2401
haubitham, 2401
haubudam, 2401
haubutham, 2401
hauceor, 10930
haucier, 6080, 10930
haught, 6068
'haughtiness', 6067
'haughty', 8599
HAUGHTY, 6068
hauh(az), 6063
Haupt, 2406
Hauptmann, 2406
Haus, 2497
Häuser, 2497
haut, 6065
hautbois, 6077
HAUTBOY, 6075
haute, 6069
hauteur, 6067
HAUTEUR, 6066
have, 5740
'have', 5737, 5768, 5859
'have been', 1605
'haven', 8257

'have the strength to',
  3770
'have, thou shalt', 5760
'having holes', 10196
'having two peaks', 2176
hawse, 6081
HAWSE, 10923
hawsehole, 6081
HAWSEHOLES, 10924
hawser, 10927
HAWSER, 6078
hayr, 11052
'haystack', 9600
'hazard', 9551
head, 2340, 3260
'head', 1207, 1774, 2128,
  2156, 2200, 2286, 2316,
  2350, 2380, 6439, 11475
HEAD, 2399
'head against foot', 2337
'head, big', 2386
'head, bring to a', 2315
'head city', 2134
'head cook', 2313
'head covering', 2239,
  2285, 2324
'headed for', 1515
'headfirst', 2167
'headings, list again under',
  2160
'headings, list under', 2157
'head, little', 2127
'headlong', 2167
'head man', 2132, 2313,
  2370, 6093
'head man, of the', 2145
'head (of a bed)', 2326
'head of a pillar', 2148
'head of hair', 2355
'head of land', 2380
'head, of the', 2137
'head (of the family),
  little', 2124
'head, opening for the',
  2324
'head, small', 2160, 2187,
  2385
'head to foot, from', 2307
hēafod, 2400
HEAL, 887
'healer', 6113
healf, 9072

'healing plant', 764
'health', 746
HEALTH, 871
'health and well-being,
  conducive to', 766
'health!, be in good', 753
'healthful', 767
'health, goddess of', 8911
'health, good', 914, 8910
'health, in good', 886, 922
'health, of sound', 929
'health, poor', 914
'health, restore to', 887
'health, state of', 913
'healthy', 751, 875, 3631,
  8913
'healthy!, be', 748
'heap', 3127
hear, 9342
'hearing with two ears',
  1202
'heart', 2787
'heartburn', 5477
'hearth', 4066, 5394
'heart of a problem', 6446
'heart-whole', 10363
'heat', 4385
'heat by rubbing', 4384
'heavenly bodies, obscured',
  10479
'heavens', 4091
'heavy, not', 7260
HECATOMB, 1822
'hedgehog', 2392
'heedless', 811
Heer, 3576, 3911
height, 6072
'height', 6043
heill, 875
'heir, joint', 8189
heis, 9396
hekatombē, 1824
hekaton, 1824
hêlēl, 7286
*helfe, 9071
helga, 900
HELIOPHOBIA, 5718
helios, 5718
'Hell', 11237
'hellish', 10335
Hello, 902
hē logikē tekhnē, 6768
'hem in', 2552
*hems, 9397

hen, 9396
HENDECAGON, 9401
HENOTHEISM, 9399
*hens, 9397
heōs, 3789
HEPTAGON, 6380
her, 11071
HERALD, 974
HERALDRY, 977
herb, 3694
'herb', 1856
herba, 3695, 9513
herbe, 3695
'herb, kind of', 3694
'herd, leader of', 1801
'herds', 7802
'herdsman', 10988
'herdsmen', 1770
here, 9343
'hereditary improvement',
  8742
HERESYPHOBIA, 5709
Herzog, 3575
'hesitate', 1163
hete, 699
HETERO-, 9381
HETERODOX, 3244, 9389
HETEROGENEOUS, 9383
HETEROLOGOUS, 6867
HETEROLOGY, 6852
HETERONYM, 9386
HETEROOUSIA, 8661
HETEROOUSIAN, 8661, 9385
heteros, 3245, 6853, 8662,
  9375
HETEROSEXUAL, 9384
HETEROSIS, 9391
hetman, 2407
HEXAGON, 6380
-hibere, 5860
hibernate, 4119
HIDALGO, 11153
'hidden', 4455
'hidden goods, store of',
  255
'hide', 256, 4451, 5709,
  9203, 9466
'hide away', 4458
'hides, ox', 1870
'hiding place', 255, 4467
high, 6064, 9822
'high', 4032, 6042, 6068,
  10932

'high office, give up', 6205
'high-pitched', 6076
'high place', 6055
'high places, dread of',
  5680
'high rank, man of', 7928
'high-shield', 9053
'highway', 1914, 10575
'high-wood', 6075
hijo dalgo, 11154
hijo de algo, 11154
'hill', 10892
'hill-fort', 5587
'hillock', 3127
him, 11073
'hindquarters', 3109
'Hinduism, sacred writings
  of', 11465
Hippodrome, 3358
HIPPODROME, 3355
hippodromos, 3356
HIPPOPOTAMUS, 5149
hippos, 3357, 3834
'hire', 3484
his, 11070
HISPANO-, 5697
histōr, 11173, 11246
historia, 11247
HISTORY, 11164, 11248
History of England, 11695
'hit a crushing blow', 276
'hit at', 277
hither, 11085
'hit in baseball', 277
'Hitler', 8435
'hit sharply', 9663
hlot, 2665
*hluta-, 2661
ho, 910
'hoard', 4453
'hobo', 3431
HOBO, 3722
hoch, 6064
HOCHSCHILD, 9053
'hockey stick', 2912, 2964
'hoist', 10547
hol-, 852
holà, 909
'hold', 5737, 5831, 5859,
  5888, 5936, 7581
'holdable', 5799

'hurting', 4804
hūs, 1498
*husam, 1498
husar, 2010
HUSBAND, 1496
'husbandman', 1483
HUSBANDMAN, 1503
HUSBANDRY, 1502
hūsbonda, 1497
hūsbōndi, 1498
'husk', 8950, 9026
'husk (of nuts)', 8954
HUSSAR, 2017
hussard, 2016
huszar, 2011
'hut', 1453
h(w)-, 11055
*hw-, 10914, 11066
hwā, 11060
hwaem, 11072
hwǣr, 11063
hwaes, 11070
hwaet, 11061
hwaether, 11087
*hwa-līk-, 11078
*hwalsaz, 10916
*h(w)als-berg, 10940
hwām, 11072
(h)wanne, 11064
hwanon(e), 11079
hwār, 11063
*hwatharaz, 11088
hwaz, 11062
*hwehula, 10856, 10915
hwenne, 11064
hweogol, 10857
hwēol, 10858
hwer, 11060
hwī, 11074
hwider, 11084
hwilc, 11078
*hwithrē, 11084
*hwō, 11077
hwy, 991, 11074
HYDROPHOBIA, 5700
HYDROPHYTE, 1678
Hygeia, 8911
HYGIENE, 8756, 8914
hymn, 4838
'hymn of praise', 4835
hyperopia, 1818
HYPNAGOGIC, 43
'hypocritical', 3298

hypothēca, 4630
hypothēcāre, 4630
HYPOTHECATE, 4628
HYPOTHESIS, 4566

I

(I) am, 8643
*-iano, 8205
-iānus, 8205
ibī, 11149
ibid., 5557
-ible, 5813
'ice', 2417
'iced', 2449
'ice, field or river of', 2442
'ice, hard as', 2446
'ice or snow, cover with', 2447
-icle, 10662
-iculum, 10662
'icy', 2419, 2447
'icy cold', 2420, 2446
idea, 6897, 11178
'idea', 6897
IDEA, 11184
'idea, fixed', 11194
idéal, 11186
IDEAL, 11186
ideālis, 11186
IDEALISM, 11189
IDEALIZE, 11169
IDEALIZED, 11164
'idea, Platonic', 11183
'ideas, origin of', 6896
IDEATE, 11193
IDÉE FIXE, 11193
idein, 11172, 11202, 11386
idem, 4375
'identical', 9261
'identify', 3481
IDENTIFY, 4374
'identifying', 9980
'identity in substance', 8655
ideo-, 11196
IDEOGRAM, 2788, 11198
ideologia, 6897
idéologie, 11196
IDEOLOGY, 6895, 11197
-idēs, 11240
-idion, 7879
-idium, 7878

'idle', 11619
'idler', 10415
IDOL, 11209
IDOLATRY, 11210
idole, 11208
IDOLIZE, 11211
īdōlum, 11208
IDYLL, 11215
IDYLLIC, 11217
īdyllium, 11214
-iere, 3502
'if', 11086, 11128
-if, 7536
-igere, 188, 215, 285
-igiano, 8204
ignis, 5455
ignite, 5455
ignoscere, 5948
il-, 3897, 7335
ilē, 9360
-ile, 5837
-ilis, 165, 5837
'ill', 2321, 2992, 4797
illa, 533
'illegal', 5928
ILLEGITIMACY, 7134
'ill humor', 5077
'illimitable', 11797
-illion, 1280
'illness, (a person) disabled by injury or', 917
-illo, 498
'ill-tempered', 2990
illūdere, 3897
ILLUME, 7330
illūmināre, 7334
'illuminate', 7263, 7331, 7362
ILLUMINATE, 7331
'illuminate books', 7336
ILLUMINATES, 7250
'illumination, international unit of', 7277
'illumine', 7331
ILLUMINE, 7331
ILLUSION, 3837, 3894
illusiō(nem), 3896
'illusions', 6308, 9805
ILLUSTRATE, 7367
ILLUSTRIOUS, 7366
illūstris, 7367
'ill will', 11372

im, 8494
'image', 9178, 10105, 11205
'image of, mental', 11278
'image, small', 11213
'images, worship of', 11210
'imagine', 11193
imbassator, 236
*imboiāre, 1873
'imbue with opinions', 3198
'imitate', 7699, 9177
'imitation', 4868
'imitation, fraudulent', 4252
'immaterial', 11797
'immense', 10098, 10420
'immoderate', 609
'immunity', 10357
IMP, 1548, 1702
impa, 1702
impair, 7944, 8069
IMPARITY, 7933
IMPART, 8229
'impartial', 7911, 8572
IMPARTIAL, 8164
impartīre, 8230
IMPECUNIOUS, 7809
IMPECUNIOUS FELLOW, 7791
'impel', 9959
imperāre, 8073
IMPERATIVE, 8087
imperātor, 8076
'imperfection', 4234
IMPERIALIST, 8090
IMPERIOUS, 8089
imperium, 8085
'impermanent', 10451
IMPERVIOUS, 10640
impetere, 5070
impetīgō, 5076
IMPETIGO, 5075
impetuōsus, 5073
'impetuous', 11782
IMPETUOUS, 5074
impetus, 5070
IMPETUS, 5072
impian, 1701
impious, 1707
'implant', 1697
'implanted', 1698
'implement', 11648
'implements, furnish with', 484

'imply', 8333
IMPORT, 8331
'importance, of little', 10617
importāns, 8335
IMPORTANT, 8334
importāre, 8336
IMPORTUNATE, 8411
'importune', 802
IMPORTUNE, 8410
importūnus, 8406
'impose', 6191
'impose upon', 11891
'impostures', 9807
*impotare, 1700
impotus, 1699
'impress', 10104
'impression', 6795
'impression, make an', 9692
'impression, making a strong', 8773
'impression of, give the', 9267
'improve', 4054
IMPROVE, 8634
'improve by training', 10979
IMPROVISE(D), 11346
improviser, 11347
improv(v)isare, 11348
improv(v)iso, 11348
'impulse', 9963, 11646
'impulse, violent', 5071
'in', 4575, 7049
in-, 210, 464, 919, 3897, 4680, 6086, 7335, 8072, 11903
'in behalf of', 8585
'in accordance with facts', 119
'inactive', 463
'in addition', 6805
'in addition to', 4603, 11919
*inaltiare, 6085
ināne, 10460
INANE, 10463
inānis, 10459
INANITION, 10464
in articulo mortis, 406
'in back of', 2180
inbassetour, 237
'incapable of being used', 7671

incendiary, 5456
incendium, 5456
'incentive', 9880
incite, 792
'incite', 799, 9956
'incitement', 9962
*inclaudere, 2615
inclāvāre, 2590
*inclāvāre, 2553
'inclination', 10066
'inclination, compulsive', 5777
'incline', 2458
'inclined (to)', 5098
'inclined to both sides', 213
INCLUDE, 2621
inclūdere, 2615
INCLUSION, 2632
INCLUSIVE, 2633
'incomplete', 8163
'increase', 6084
'increase the value of', 8634
'incredible', 3249
INCUR, 2049
INCURSION, 2034
'indeed', 8715, 11141
'independent, eccentrically', 606
index, 6193
INDEX, 6192
indicāre, 6197
'indicate', 6189
INDICATE, 6198
indīcere, 6190
indicis, 6193
INDICT, 6185
*indictāre, 6189
indictus, 6190
'indifferent, blithely', 812
INDIGNATION, 3328
'indirect pathway', 240
INDITE, 6187
'individual', 7238, 8104
INDOCTRINATE, 3198
INDUBITABLE, 1169
INDUCE, 3475
indūcere, 3476
'induce (someone) to do something unlawful', 637

'jesting', 8379
(je) suis, 8499
'jet of water or air', 3551
(jeu de) la crosse, 2970
'jewelry, matched', 8011
'Jewish congregation', 33
J-H-V-H, 2810
'JHVH', 2802
'jogging', 3406
Johannes factotum, 4323
John, 7626, 11071
'John Do-everything', 4323
joignant, 11895
joignen, 11896
joignent, 11895
'join', 11791, 11830, 11856,
   11933, 11982
JOIN, 11897, 11949
-join-, 11901
'join again', 11921
'join battle', 9617
JOINDER, 11930
joindre, 11894, 11933
'joined', 11862, 11993
'joined in pairs', 11837
joinen, 11896
'joiner', 11499
'join in battle', 11960
'joining', 468, 11860,
   11931, 11984
JOINING, 11790
'joining together', 11875
'joining under', 11881
'join into', 11891
joint, 11898
'joint', 385, 549, 11861
JOINT, 11898
'joint connecting two parts
   of the body', 403
'joint, degenerative process
   in a', 397
'jointed limbs, invertebrates
   with', 395
'joint, little', 10664
'join together', 11847,
   11877, 11911
'joints', 545
'joints, lacking', 398
'joint, small', 400
JOINTURE, 11907
JOLLIFY, 4375
'jolly', 3652
joster, 11963

JOSTLE, 11968
JOSTLING, 11947
jot, 8666
jot or tittle, 8666
journée, 10596
journey, 10596
'journey', 3428, 8422, 8458,
   10575
'journey across the sea',
   10592
'journey long', 10592
'journey, of a', 10588
'journey, wondering', 8468
joust, 11966
JOUST, 11946
joustle, 11967
'joy', 9295
'joyous', 3852, 9294
jūdex, 6122
'judge', 646, 1642, 4513,
   6123, 6250, 11247
JUDGE, 6117
'judge beforehand', 6247
'judging by features', 1644
'judging of nature', 1644
'judging rightly, capacity
   of', 11405
'judgment', 4501, 6132
'judgment, preconceived',
   6248
'judgment, pronounce',
   4514
jūdicāre, 6123
JUDICIARY, 6135
'judicious', 6122
jūdicus, 6122
-juga-, 11902
JUGATE, 11837
juge, 6124
'juggler', 6308
'juggling tricks', 9807
JUGULAR, 11788, 11841
jugum, 11819
JUGUM, 11836
-junct-, 11902
JUNCTION, 11790, 11859
JUNCTURE, 11860, 11907
'juncture in time', 405
jungere, 11894
JUNTA, 11863
junto, 11868
JUNTO, 11866
junto a, 11869

junto con, 11869
'jurisdiction', 4524, 4919
'jurisdiction, area of', 9791
'jurisdiction, feudal', 4911
just, 11966
'just', 11443, 11976 .
JUST, 11960
juster, 11963
'justification', 6233, 6877
justle, 11967
juxtā, 11955
JUXTAPOSE, 11958
JUXTAPOSING, 11946
'juxtaposition', 4561
JUXTAPOSITION, 11955
*juxtāre, 11963
juzgado, 6137
juzgar, 6138

K

k-, 2475
*k-, 2837
-ka, 8679
*kailo-, 872
kainos, 3832
kakos, 2829, 4799, 4849
*kaldaz, 2477
KALEIDOSCOPE, 11226
Kalesche, 10865
*kaliz, 2483
kallos, 2828
kalos, 11230
*kamelodrome, 3353
*kap-, 2408, 5741
Kappe, 2306
käppi, 2305
*kaput, 2129, 2399
kardia, 2787
*karros, 1893
kartr, 1925, 3160
kata, 866, 6820, 9146
katalegein, 6820
katalogos, 6819
katholou, 866
kaustos, 859
KEEL, 2484
'keep in check', 5868
'keep up', 7544
'keep within bounds', 4376,
   9777
'keep within limits', 9775

'language, regional variety of', 6731
'languages, related', 1683
'languages, speaking two', 1205
'lantern', 4467
lanterna, 4465
lanterna absconsa, 4464
'lantern, hidden', 4465
lanx, 1266
laos, 11575
laque en écailles, 9040
larboard, 8264
'large', 4371, 7532
'largeness', 4991
'large number', 6526
'lark', 2223
last, 1226
'latent', 11555
'laughing uncontrollably', 9899
*lauhaz, 7268
laūkas, 7269
'launch', 2471
'laurel family', 9522
lavāre, 7378
'lavish', 7686
law, 3261
'law', 198, 4501, 6120, 6929, 7137, 7166, 7234
LAW, 7244
'law, break a', 11783
'lawful', 7170
'lawmaker', 7169
'law officer', 805
'law of the act', 7150
'law of the forum', 7151
'law of the merchants', 7153
'law of the place', 7147
'law of the site', 7149
'law, private', 7235
'law, proposer of', 7169
'law, Salic', 7155
'laws, codes of Old Teutonic', 4509
'lawsuit', 195
'lawsuit, bring a', 197
'lawsuit, carry on a', 7216
'lawsuit, subject to', 194
'law, unwritten', 7154
'law, written', 7153
'lay', 7247, 11575

'layer of metal', 5229
'lay flat with a blow', 275
'laying down', 4498, 7855
'lay waste', 10416
'laziness', 465
'lazy', 605, 11619
-LD, 6097
LEA, 7272
'lead', 5, 55, 100, 159, 215, 297, 2814, 3454, 3492, 3522, 3562, 8414, 8448
'lead aside', 3459
'lead astray', 3458
'lead away', 3458, 3524
'lead back', 3471, 3530
'leader', 4, 40, 2132, 2385, 3445, 3534, 3575, 8435
'leader, Cossack', 2407
'leader, military', 2384, 3451
'leader of a Greek chorus', 56
'leadership', 3502
'lead forth', 3472
'lead in', 3477
'leading', 3486, 3547, 10582
'leading around', 212
'leading the way', 10636
'lead inside', 3481
'lead into', 3475
'lead over', 3461
'lead to', 3483
'lead together', 35, 3483
'leaf', 5219, 8297, 8476
'leafage', 5220
'leaflike design', 5227
'leaf, little', 5249
league, 7201
lēah, 7271
'leap year, pertaining to', 1217
learn, 3174
'learn', 3170, 3203
'learned', 11173
'learned man', 3178
'learn from', 3258
'learning, branch of', 4338
'learning, formal branch of', 419
'learning, leisure devoted to', 9086
leave, 7128

'leave', 6954, 6999, 7029, 7061, 7088, 8162, 8227
LEAVE, 7082, 7130
'leave behind', 6978, 7048
'leave in', 7048
'leaven', 3042
'leave out', 7036
'leaves', 5216, 8297
LEAVES, 7131
'leaves and shoots, throw out', 5174
'leaves, arrangement of', 5253
'leave secretly', 4459
'leaves, five-lobed', 5237
'leave undone', 6975
'leaving', 7090
'leaving, act of', 8225
LEBENSRAUM, 7120
leccion, 6660
lecon, 6659
LECTERN, 6650
lectiō, 6659
LECTION, 6661
lectiōnem, 6659
lēctor, 6650
LECTOR, 6648
lect(ō)rīnum, 6653
*lectorium, 6654
lectrum, 6653
lectum, 6499
lectūra, 6644
'lecture', 9357
LECTURE, 6496, 6641
lectus, 6540, 6638, 6686
LEECH, 6936
LEFT, 7104
'left behind', 6981
'left over', 7077, 7763
'leftovers', 6716
'left side of a ship', 8260
-*lēg*-, 7193
*leg-, 6928, 7141
legacie, 7178
LEGACY, 7176
'legacy, one who has inherited a', 7176
'legal', 7242
LEGAL, 7166
'legal entanglement, get out of', 7218
'legal force, having no', 10386

'legal instrument', 4493
lēgālis, 7168, 7240
LEGALISTS, 7144
'leg and foot covering',
    10276
lēgāre, 7173, 7213
LEGATE, 7175
LEGATEE, 7176
lēgātia, 7178
legato, 7201
lēgātus, 7175
legein, 6686, 6712, 6759,
    6821, 6894, 6921
LEGEND, 6498, 6663, 7197
legenda, 6669
Legenda Aurea, 6682
LEGENDARY, 6495
legende, 6668
leger, 7484
LEGERDEMAIN, 7482
legere, 6499, 6536, 6609,
    6636, 6686, 6748, 6926,
    7195
legereoculis, 6505
legesthai, 6734
*legh-, 7246
legibilis, 5818, 6641
LEGIBLE, 6640
legiō, 6520
legion, 6525
LEGION, 6495, 6526, 7197
legiōnem, 6520
'legion, Roman', 6520
'legion subdivision', 7454
lēgis, 6929, 7136, 7166,
    7234
LEGISLATE, 6930, 7168
LEGISLATIVE, 7135
'legislative body', 11863
lēgis lātor, 7169
'legislator', 6096
LEGISLATOR, 7168
LEGISLATORS, 7144
lēgitimāre, 7171
LEGITIMATE, 7170
lēgitimātus, 7170
lēgitimus, 7171
*legnom, 6532
le grand chariot, 1951
*legsis, 6724
légume, 6528
LEGUME, 6529
legūmen, 6527

leial, 7242
*leid-, 3854
*leig-, 7200
leihen, 6957, 7096
*leikw-, 6955, 6999, 7029,
    7061
*leip-, 7076, 7111
leipein, 6953, 7030, 7088
'leisure, at', 10364
'leisure, work of', 9087
*leitos, 11575
leitourgia, 11574
*lekjaz, 6938
lektos, 6686, 6723
lēmma, 1350
lend, 6959
'lend', 6958, 7096
LEND, 6949
LENDING, 6945
LENGTHWAYS, 10568
'lenses for nearsightedness,
    farsightedness', 1200
Leo, 8906
lēoht, 7265
'leopard, snow', 7418
leōs, 11575
le petit chariot, 1951
'leprosy, dull white', 4050
'less', 2322
'less heavy', 7261
'lesson', 3202, 6675
LESSON, 6656
'let go', 7508, 7580
'let it be (done)', 1615
'letter', 2799, 6792
'letter, circular', 10841
'letter of the alphabet',
    2686, 2740
'letter, raised', 10115
'letters, fine', 3730
let(t)run, 6652
*leubh-, 7133
LEUCITE, 7397
leuco-, 7391
LEUCOCYTE, 7394
LEUCOMA, 7399
*leug-, 7387
*leuhtam, 7266
leuk-, 7391
*leuk-, 7253, 7321, 7388
LEUKEMIA, 7395
leuko-, 7391
leukos, 7392

*leuksna, 7348
*leut-, 3852
'level', 9355, 9671
'level, not', 9360
'lever attached to a pivot',
    1568
'lewd', 10493
lēx, 6929, 7136, 7166, 7234
lex actus, 7150
lex fori, 7151
-lexia, 6753
LEXICON, 6728
lexikon, 6725
lexikon biblion, 6727
lexikos, 6725
lexis, 6724, 6753
lex loci, 7147
lex mercatorum, 7152
lex non scripta, 7154
lex Salica, 7155
lex scripta, 7153
lex situs, 7149
*lībam, 7108
libban, 7110
*līben, 7111
'liberality', 3657
liber dictiōnārius, 6149
'library', 4627
līcium, 1039
licour, 7007
'lie', 7247
'lie in waiting', 10568
lieu, 4919
līf, 7108
*-lif, 7075
'life', 6833, 8823, 8853,
    8887, 8927
LIFE, 7105
'life, bring back to', 8774
'life, come to', 8779
'life, communal', 8870
'lifeless', 8885
LIFELESS, 7115
'lifelike', 8773
LIFELIKE, 7115
'life, minute form of', 8871
'life, necessary to', 8824
lifer, 7118
'life, rural, description of',
    11216
'life, science of', 8860
'life, water of', 8918

'life, way of', 8841
'life, without', 8890
lifian, 7110
'lift', 6080, 10788
'lifter', 6079
'lift up', 10931
-*ligere*, 6540
light, 7260
'light', 5650, 5719, 7253, 7279, 7307, 7383, 7484
LIGHT, 7252
'light, admitting', 7302
'light, avoiding', 5649
'light, bearer of', 7281
'light between night and day', 1063
'light-bringer', 7281
'light-bringing', 7282
'light, bringing to', 7347
lighten, 7260
LIGHTEN, 7256
LIGHTENING, 7258
LIGHTENS, 7250
'light, giving off', 7295
LIGHTNING, 7258
'light of hand', 7483
'light, ray of', 1570
'light, shining with reflected', 7365
'light up', 7335, 7362
LIGNIFY, 6534
LIGNITE, 6534
lignum, 6532
LIGNUM, 6534
līht, 7265
-*lika*, 7078
'like', 7914, 7959, 8660, 9168, 9261, 11219
'-like', 11232
'liken', 7963
'likeness', 9180, 9279
'likenesses in structure', 6861
'like premolar tooth', 1208
'likewise', 9264
LIKEWISE, 11436
likvidirovat, 7018
'lily', 5204
'limb, artificial', 4602
'limb, upper', 470
'limited', 10239
LIMN, 7340
limnen, 7340

limos, 1827
'line', 11461
'lineage', 10270
'lined up', 5337
lingua, 1205
'lingua franca', 2344
'linking', 9327
*linkw-, 6964
linquere, 6953
'Lion', 8906
'lions, company of', 8606
'lip', 1205
lip-, 7077
LIPAROID, 7127
liparos, 7124
LIPEMIA, 7126
LIPOMA, 7125
lipos, 7124
'lips, having two', 1204
'lips, pronounced with both', 1204
liquāre, 6996
liquefacere, 7021
liquefier, 7020
LIQUEFY, 4375, 7019
liquēre, 6995, 7022
liqui, 6995
'liquid', 6996, 7022
LIQUID, 7003
liquidāre, 7015
LIQUIDATE, 7013
liquide, 7004
liquidus, 7004
liquor, 7007
LIQUOR, 7005
'liquor, strong', 8918
līs, 195
'list', 6820
'list, cargo or passenger', 7501
'listing', 8151
'listing, alphabetical', 6199
'listing, systematic', 6817
'list terms (of surrender)', 2157
'list verb forms', 11848
lit, 10533
'literature', 3730
LITHOGRAPHY, 2832
lithos, 3836
lītigāre, 195, 7216
LITIGATE, 194
lītis, 195

'little', 8140, 10552
'little white', 4001
lītūrgia, 11574
LITURGY, 11571
*liuhtam, 7266
'Live!', 991, 1510, 7114, 8762, 8791, 8823, 8850, 8878, 8909
LIVE, 7109
'live, capacity to', 8825
LIVELIHOOD, 7116
'lively', 8764
LIVELY, 7115
LIVER¹, 7116
'lives, he', 8879
'livestock', 2194, 7836
'livestock, raising of', 1502
'live together', 8803
'live with', 8868
'livid', 10476
'living', 3650, 8761, 8851, 8879
LIVING, 7112
'living being', 8874
'living, capable of', 8833
'living, means of', 8815
'living, mode of', 8841
'living on land in water', 8862
'living, riotous', 7382
'living together', 9358
*lixus, 7023
'lizard, winged', 5115
'load', 1953
'load a gun', 1953
'load a wagon', 1956
'loading', 1971
'loading side', 8264
'loads, one that', 1965
'loafer', 10415
loan, 6959
LOAN, 6945
'lobby', 5392
loc, 7148
'lock', 2507, 2597
'locked in', 2550
'lock in', 2553
'lock of hair', 9644
'locks', 2652
locus, 4920⁻
lodge, 6787
lodging, 6787

LUNATIC, 7251, 7350
*luncia, 7414
LUNETTE, 7358
lunx, 7411
Lusitania, 8270
lussa, 7403
LUSTER, 7249, 7365
'lustful', 11644
lūstrāre, 7361
lustre, 7364
lustro, 7364
lūstrum, 7377
LUSTRUM, 7371
*lut-, 3852
lux, 5650, 7275, 7307, 7383
LUX, 7276
*lux, 7411
luxāre, 7386
luxuria, 7382
luxurie, 7382
'luxurious', 7686
LUXURY, 7380
luxus, 7384
'lying', 10436
'lymph', 11224
LYMPHOID, 11223
lyncis, 7410
lynx, 7410
LYNX, 7410

M

-m, 11073
'machine', 8093
'machine, made by', 7435
'mad', 6324
madam, 3375
Mädchen, 2498
'made', 4148, 4206, 4236
'made before', 9318
'made by art', 4194
'made consistently', 9338
'made in contrast to', 4254
'madness', 6798, 7405
'madwort', 7402
'magazine', 11313
Magd, 2498
'magic', 2765, 11570
'magical art', 4197
'magical power of
   inanimate object', 4198
'magic spell', 9810

magistral, 7749
'magnet piece', 501
MAHAYUGA, 11803
'maid', 2498
'maimed', 7567
main, 7484, 7552
'maintain', 8369
MAINTAIN, 7422, 7544, 7582
'maintenance', 5962
maintenir, 7545
'make', 453, 661, 4063, 4140, 4318, 4363, 4395, 4481, 6031, 7737, 9315, 11109
'make a profit in', 8632
'make better', 8634
'make by hand', 4157
'make chaste', 198
'make fit', 8098
'make fixed', 660
'make for', 5051
'make game of', 3870
'make in excess', 4254
'Make it similar!', 4319
'make known', 6341
'make lawful', 7171
'make like', 9177, 9217
'make love', 5162
'make out', 4289
'make progress', 4303
'make pure', 198
'maker', 453, 4152, 4344, 11583
'maker by art', 4345
'make ready', 4279, 8098
'make solid', 849
'make thoroughly', 4296
'make unlike', 9193
'make whole', 887
makhē, 6796
'making', 4061, 4171, 4241
'making off', 4226
mal-, 4244
malacia, 3676
malade, 5892
maladie, 5892
MALADY, 5891
malakia, 3680
'Malay Archipelago', 3821
male, 5893
'male', 1497, 1868, 11685
'male, adult', 11739

'male animal in its prime', 10048
maledīcere, 6231
maledictiō, 6231
MALEDICTION, 6230
MALEFACTOR, 4166
MALEFICENT, 4217
male habitus, 5893
'male of deer', 10045
MALFEASANCE, 4243
'malicious behavior', 2317
'mallet', 10207
MALOCCLUSION, 2631
'maltreat', 11785
malus, 3677
'mammal of sub-tropical
   America', 495
man, 3375, 11687
'man', 2497, 6100, 7859, 11673, 11726, 11774
*man-, 7426, 7634
MANACLE, 7441
MANACLES, 7421
'manage', 101
MANAGE, 7421, 7514
'manageable', 5804
'management, prudent', 11333
'manager', 110
'manage shrewdly', 7447
mancare, 7566
manche, 7577
Manche, la, 7578
manchot(s), 11491
mancipāre, 7510
MANCIPATE, 7508
manco, 7566
'man-courage', 11725
mancus, 7567
MANDAMUS, 7589
mandāre, 7583, 7610
MANDATE, 7591
'Mandate Thursday', 7624
MANDATORY, 7593
mandātum, 7592, 7631
mandātum novum, 7627
Mande, 7632
manège, 7520
MANÈGE, 7519
maneggiare, 7515
maneggio, 7520
'man-era', 6099, 11674

'Nativity scene', 3152
'natural', 1627, 6404, 9318
'natural science', 1629
'nature', 1624
'nature, good', 3642
'nature of, having the',
11220
'naughty', 1589
'naval exercise', 7770
nāvigāre, 193
NAVIGATE, 192
nāvis, 194
'navy', 492
ne, 6578
nēah, 1441
nēahgebūr, 1441
'near', 1441, 7995, 11951
'nearby, one who lives',
1440
'nearness', 11952
'neat', 3664, 3766
nec-, 6578
'neck', 10881, 10911,
10942, 11839
'neck armor', 10937
'neckband', 10881
'neckline, having a low',
10896
'neck-protector', 10937
'needlework', 2902
NEFARIOUS, 4732
nefārius, 4732
nefās, 4731
neg-, 6578
NEGLECT, 6576
'neglected', 6585
'neglectful of duty, grossly',
6989
neglēctus, 6577
neglegere, 6578
NEGLIGEE, 6581
NEGLIGENT, 6581
negligere, 6578
NEGLIGIBLE, 6580
NEIGHBOR, 1439, 1495
NEIGHBORS, 1424
NEITHER, 11091
'neither of the two', 11098
'neither sex or gender',
11098
nēma, 11235
NEMATODE, 11234
nemel, 705

NEOPHYTE, 1680
'nervous agitation, state of',
1842
'net', 10218
nether-stocks, 10277
neuter, 11097
NEUTER, 11097
'new', 3832
*New General English
Dictionary*, 9903
'New Zealand', 3820
'next to', 11869, 11910
'nibble', 6486
'nick of time', 404
'niggardly', 10041
'nigh, one who lives', 1440
'night', 7317
'night light', 7316
'nightmare', 3923
'nightshade, deadly', 3601
'night, work by', 7309
nimble, 705
'nimble', 164, 6298
'nip as with pincers', 1073
'nitrogen', 8886
nn, 5880
no, 11092
NOB, 6440
nobis interest, 8560
'noble', 691, 8740
'nobleman', 7929
'noblest', 733
nocchio, 6475
noctilūca, 7316
NOCTILUCA, 7314
noctis, 7317
'nocturnal study', 7311
'node', 6449
'noise, explosive', 8356
NOISOME, 9285
'noisy', 11743
'no longer active', 9997
'no longer existing', 9997
'no longer in use', 9997
nombre, 9212
nómos, 1215
nomper, 7907
NONAGON, 6380
'noncommissioned officer,
lowest rank of', 2367
'noncompromisers', 209
NONENTITY, 8555
'none other', 9261

'nonesuch', 7893
'nonored', 3317
nonpareil, 7914
NONPAREIL, 7892
nonper, 7905
NOODLE, 6479
'nook', 3062
Norge, 10776
'normal', 7931
'normal, departure from',
5141
'north', 3828
'northern region', 10775
'northern way', 10775
Norvegr, 10775
NORWAY, 10774
nosos, 392
not, 1336, 1488
'not', 210, 399, 464, 920,
4343, 4680, 4861, 6579,
6755, 7403, 8887, 9324,
9361, 11092, 11240,
11619
NOTCH, 9560
'notch made by cutting',
2845
'notch, make a', 9561
'not chosen', 6577
'note, quarter', 2904
'not favoring', 8164
'nothing, containing', 10349
'notice, give', 4378
'notice, little', 9928
NOTIFY, 4378
'notion', 3240, 11178
'not one nor the other',
11091
'not transacting', 207
'not universal', 8171
'nourish', 5958, 6027, 6089
'nourished', 6045
'nourishing', 5967, 6015
'nourishment', 5960, 8816
'now', 8552
nox, 7317
noy, 9286
NUB, 6445
NUBBIN, 6447
NUBBLE, 6447
Nudel, 6480
'null', 918
number, 9212

'number', 710, 6774, 11121
'number, certain', 9267
'number, indefinite', 9265
'number, map', 609
'number ratio', 6773
'number reckoning', 6773
'numbers, science of', 718
Number Words and Number Symbols, 1085, 7070
'numerals, Arabic', 6274
numerus, 9212
nummi, 833
nummus, 832
'nurse', 6017
'nurseling', 5977
'nursemaid, French', 3639
'nutrition', 5961

O

OAF, 3949
'oak', 11469
OAST, 4129
oath, 10335
'oath, inviolable', 10335
ob, 7709, 8396, 10607
ob-, 197, 2050, 2180, 2630
OBERON, 3930
obiūr(i)gāre, 196
'object', 4276
'object, magical', 11039
'object produced by human workmanship', 454
'object, sanctified', 11045
'objects, projecting', 10316
OBJURGATE, 195
'obligation', 7735
'obligation, moral', 5930
'obligation, written', 1493
'obligatory', 7594
'obliging', 7745
OBOE, 6076
'obscured, partially', 10476
'observe', 11456
'obsession', 11194
'obstinate', 10256
'obstruct', 3019
'obtain', 7979, 8064
'obtaining', 7984
OBTUND, 10194, 10236
obtundere, 10193
OBTUSE, 10051, 10192

obtūsus, 10193
obviam, 10610
obviāre, 10607
OBVIATE, 10605
obviātus, 10607
'obvious', 7500
OBVIOUS, 10610
obvius, 10609
oc-, 2050, 2180, 2630
occiput, 2180
OCCIPUT, 2179
OCCLUDE, 2628
occludere, 2630
'occupation', 3398, 4341
'occupation requiring specialized study', 4769
'occupy', 1556, 5771
'occupying', 10354
OCCUR, 2049
'occurrence', 5138
'occurring every year', 820
'Oceania', 3819
OCEANOGRAPHY, 2831
och, 11821
OCHLOCRACY, 10795
OCHLOPHOBIA, 5695, 10796
OCTAGON, 6380
oculāris, 1199
oculus, 1200
odd, 7943
'odd', 7944
'odd-job-man', 2109
'odd notion', 2905
-ode, 11232
ODEE, 2644, 3702, 4283, 5881, 6059, 7059, 8205, 8831, 8998, 9563, 10258, 10713, 10903, 11532, 11730
-ōdēs, 11231
'odium', 11374
-ōdium, 11232
-oeidēs, 11219
oeuvre, 7756
OEUVRE, 7757
OEUVRES, 7652
oevre, 7755
'of', 4225, 7484
'of consequence', 8333
of course, 2041
'of course', 11141
'off', 4225, 6341
'offense, serious', 8698

'offensive', 9286
'offer counsel', 11370
'offering, burnt', 857
'offerings, burnt', 6058
'offerings, propitiatory', 4356
'office', 4524
OFFICE, 4313, 7739
OFFICER, 7740
OFFICIAL, 7742
'official, public', 11586
OFFICIATE, 7742
officīna, 7750
OFFICINAL, 7748
officiōsus, 7744
OFFICIOUS, 7743
officium, 4315, 7735
'offspring', 4317, 6026
'offspring, giving birth to living', 8792
'offspring, making', 6031
*oft-, 7789
OFTEN, 7650, 7785
'of the', 8464
'of uncertain nature', 214
'of what kind', 4379
Ohrwurm, 10769
-oid, 11219
ōidē, 11025
-oidēs, 11219
-oiedēs, 11231
'oil-lamp', 7308
'oil-press', 4160
'oil-presser', 4153
'oily', 7124
*oino-, 9157
'ointment, medical', 784
ok, 11821
okhlos, 5695, 10793
-ol-, 5957
OLD, 5955, 6091
'old age', 1814
'older', 6092
Old French and Modern English Idiom, 1410
'old man', 1797, 6095
olere, 6059
OLGA, 900
OLIVER, 3912
olivier, 3908
OLIVIER, 3899
-oma, 7126, 7400

omelie, 9357
'omission of words', 7046
omni-, 7721
OMNIBENEVOLENT, 7722
omnibus, 7730
OMNIFARIOUS, 4435
OMNIPOTENT, 7721
'omnipresence', 11143
omnis, 7724
OMNISCIENT, 7721
on, 4134, 8542, 8644
'on', 1677, 2733, 4485
-on, 4991
onǣlan, 4134
'on all sides', 8863
'on both sides', 215, 8863
once, 1053, 7415
'once for always', 9238
one, 9157, 9278
'one', 1053, 1091, 9156,
    9225, 9251, 9305, 9332,
    9363, 9394
-one, 1283
'one and the same', 9334
'one-during', 9241
'one each', 9226
'one entrusted with
    education of children',
    17
'one-fold', 9232, 9405
'one leave', 7063
'one left over', 7063
'oneness', 9162, 9238, 9423
'one of a number', 9265
'one of two', 9374
ONERY, 605
'one's own', 7527
'one twentieth of a franc',
    846
'one who saves another',
    761
'one with another', 6808
'only', 6810
onoma, 9342
*On the Properties of
    Things*, 9476
on the qui vive, 8849
ONTOGENY, 8672
ONTOLOGY, 8674
onto(s), 8670
on weg, 10564
op-, 8396
*op-, 7653, 7680, 7707,
    7734, 7788

'open', 1082, 2617, 2646
'opening', 7320, 9137
'opening, minute', 8440
'open space', 5689
'open spaces, dread of',
    5682
'open to passage', 10637
opera, 7657, 7755
OPERA, 7660
'opera, little', 7661
operārī, 7579, 7666
'operate', 7447
OPERATE, 7648
operātus, 7666
OPERETTA, 7661
opēs, 7684
-ōpia, 7687
*opificium, 7736
'opinion', 3217, 9391,
    11371
'opinion, have an', 4513
'opinion, public', 4775
'opinion, religious', 3241
opis, 7680, 7790
*op-ni-, 7725
o porto, 8265
OPPORTUNE, 8401
OPPORTUNIST, 8403
OPPORTUNITY, 8402
opportūnus, 8396
'opposite', 4253, 4561,
    4828, 8229
'opposite to', 7613, 9324
'opposition', 4562
'oppression', 9757
ōps, 1815, 10824
OPS, 7682
*ops, 7680, 7790
opsis, 8861
OPTIMISM, 7713
optimum, 7703
OPTIMUM, 7648, 7705
OPULENT, 7685
OPULENT OFFICE, 7649
opulentus, 7685
opus, 4315, 7656, 7737,
    7790
OPUS, 7655
oracle, 7443
'oral', 8843
ōrātiō, 10683
'oration honoring dead',
    6881

oratories, 2259
'oratory', 5533
'orbit', 10807
'orchestra', 4853
ōrd-, 576
ORDAIN, 584
ordeiner, 586
ord(e)ne, 575
ordener, 586
'order', 576, 625, 1953,
    5253, 6816, 7593, 8086,
    11944
ORDER, 571
'order, arbitrary', 1616
'order, authoritative', 11889
'order back', 7613
'order, judicial', 11889
'order, reverse an', 7612
'orders against, give', 8074
'orders, give', 7595
'order, we', 7589
*ōr-dh-, 579
'ordinance', 7235
ORDINANCE, 587
ōrdināns, 589
ōrdināre, 587, 625
ōrdinārius, 600
'ordinary', 2035, 10615
ORDINARY, 598
ORDINATE, 608
ōrdinātus, 624
ōrdinem, 567, 613
ōrdior, 614
ōrdiri, 614
ORDNANCE, 590
ōrdō, 566, 613
ordre, 575
orgaein, 11644
organ, 11644
ORGAN, 11655
organa, 11660
'organ, church', 11650
organe, 11660
organicus, 11661
ORGANISM, 11651
'organisms', 8892
'organisms, single-celled',
    8893
ORGANIZATION, 11654
ORGANIZE, 11653
organon, 11648

'organ stop', 3605
organum, 11649
'organum', 4826
ORGASM, 11638
orgasmic, 11640
orgasmos, 11645
orgastic, 11641
orge, 11645
orgia, 11623
ORGIASTIC, 11628
orgie, 11633
orgies, 11631
-ōrgos, 11613
ORGY, 11630
oriens, 3805
'origin', 3692, 11021
'original', 620, 9318
'origin, place of', 3636
Origins, 3291, 5160, 9639
orloge, 6922
ornament, 10693
'ornament', 3280, 8010
ORNAMENT, 633
'ornaments, put on', 635
ōrnāmentum, 634
ōrnāre, 627
ORNATE, 634
ōrnātrīx, 637
ORNERY, 605
'orphan', 10313
orthodox, 9390
ORTHODOX, 3242
ORTHOGRAPHY, 2829
orthos, 2830, 3243
-os, 10104
o(s)che, 9561
o(s)chier, 9561
'oscillate', 3745
'oscillations', 10750
-osis, 397, 9392
OSSIFY, 4378
Ost, 3800
ostaricchi, 3803
osteon, 11034
Ostern, 3801
Österreich, 3801
OSTMARK, 3825
OSTROGOTH, 3823
other, 9377
'other', 3245, 6019, 6853,
    8662, 9374, 11152,
    11558
'other of two', 9377
OTHERWISE, 11436

OUNCE, 7418
ouph, 3952
our, 11071
ouron, 9836
ousia, 8514, 8644
'out', 4698, 5310, 5506,
    6544, 7306, 9996, 10378
'outbuilding', 7761
'outcast, social', 6991
'outermost layer', 4421
'outing', 2033
'outlaw', 4931
'outlawry', 4901
'outlaws', 4935
'outline', 10105
'outlive', 8797
'outlook, world', 11683
'out of', 2219, 3258, 4428,
    6716
'out of doors', 5503, 5530,
    5563
'out of the way', 5870
'outside', 4261, 5505, 5563
'outside one's country',
    5505
'oval figure', 7051
'over', 3462, 4828
'over against', 4253
'overbearing', 8090
'overdo', 4254
'overembellished', 5184
'overflow', 5348
'overflowing', 5287, 5313
'overload', 1975
'overlook', 5948, 6578
'overlooked, safely', 6580
'oversee', 11327
'overseer', 4301
'overstep the bounds', 5566
OVIBOS, 1828
OVIPAROUS, 8123
ovis, 1829
OVOID, 11221
OVOVIVIPAROUS, 8125,
    8792
'owe', 5897
'owed', 5898, 5933
'owed, that which is', 5906
'owing', 5924
'ox', 1718, 1748, 1794,
    1824, 1859, 2690, 10989
'oxen (in plowing), turning
    like', 1775

'oxen, species of', 1749
Oxford Dictionary of
    English Etymology,
    1407, 2042, 6057, 7000
Oxford English Dictionary,
    1361
'ox-headed', 1773
'ox, little', 1716, 1745
'ox river', 1778
'ox, wild', 1743

P

*p-, 8440
pācar, 11052
'package', 8178, 10647
padre, 11052
paedagōgāntem, 24
paedagōgāre, 23
paedagōgus, 19
'page size', 1102
paidagōgos, 15
paideiā, 10848
paidos, 18, 10848
'pail', 1091
'pain', 65, 8718, 9895
'pain, agonizing', 355
'pain, cause of', 341
'pain, cause to feel', 10040
'pain, feel', 353
'painful', 317, 343
'pains', 7658
'pains or afflicts, that
    which', 337
'pains, take', 1831
'pain, suffering of intense',
    89
'paint', 4015, 7340
'painter', 437
pair, 7919
'pair', 7942, 7999, 11990
PAIR, 7936
-pair, 8070
paire, 7939
'pair of inverted stamps',
    2338
'pair of similar things',
    1117
'pair, one of a', 1117
pais, 18, 10848
'pale', 5590, 10477

PALIMPSEST, 11021
palimpsēstos, 11023
palimpsēstus, 11024
palin, 3374, 11013
PALINDROME, 3372, 11016
PALINGENESIS, 11018
PALINODE, 11024
'palm-reading', 11597
'palpable', 7502
panache, 4967
PANACHE, 4960
'paneling, wood', 10539
'panic', 5675
panic-stricken, 9702
par, 7902, 7929, 7967
'par', 7941
PAR, 7930
para, 3249, 4575, 6912,
    8024
para-, 8023
-para, 8121
PARACHUTE, 8027
parada, 8047
PARADE, 8050
paradeigma, 6333
paradeiknunai, 6334
PARADIGM, 6330
PARADOX, 3245
paradoxos, 3248
parage, 7971
'paragon', 7893
PARAGRAPH, 2818
paragraphos, 2821
paragraphus, 2820
PARALOGISM, 6911
PARAPET, 8028
parapetto, 8030
parapluie, 8026
parar, 8044
parāre, 7979, 8007, 8043,
    8072, 8111
PARASOL, 8024, 8060
parasole, 8025
'parcel', 10647
PARCEL, 8177
parcelle, 8175
PARCENER, 8189
parçon, 8187
parçonier, 8188
pardon, 5948
'pardon', 5944
pare, 8008
PARE, 8005

'pare down', 9531
pareil, 7913
parēns, 8113
PARENT, 8115
parentēs, 8114
parenthesis, 4574
PARENTHESIS, 4571
parer, 8006, 8034
parere, 8112, 8148, 8792
parfait, 4299
PARFAIT, 4297
PARFLECHE, 8032
pari, 7947
PARI, 7950
paria, 7940, 7981
*paria, 7999
*pariāre, 7948
*pariculus, 7912
parier, 7947
paritās, 7933
PARITY, 7932
PARLAY, 7953
par le sang Dieu, 1414
'parliament', 4643
'parliament, Russian', 4521
paro, 7956
paroli, 7955
-parous, 8121
'parry', 3874, 8044
PARRY, 8022, 8060
pars, 1211, 8159, 8195,
    8234
PARSE, 8181
pars ōrātiōnis, 8182
'part', 401, 1211, 8159,
    8186, 8213
PART, 8161, 8191
PARTAKE, 8192
'partaker', 8195
PARTAKER, 8197
partaking, 8193
PARTED, 8161
partem, 8159, 8198
partezan, 8204
parti, 8247
PARTIAL, 8163
partiālis, 8164
*particella, 8174
particeps, 8195
PARTICIPANT, 8197
'participate', 11897
PARTICIPATE, 8192
participātiō, 8194

'participation', 8194
'participation in', 8567
participe, 8201
participium, 8201
participle, 8201
PARTICIPLE, 8198
particle, 10663
PARTICLE, 8170
'particles, consisting of
    large', 2036
PARTICOLORED, 8249
particula, 8171
PARTICULAR, 8171
particulāris, 8173
partie, 8169
PARTIES, 8167
partigiano, 1212, 8203
PARTING, 8162
'parting from', 8225
'parting word', 10651
partir, 8169
partīre, 8170
partis, 1211, 8195, 8234
'partisan', 4185
PARTISAN, 8202
partisano, 8203
partītiō, 8186
'partition', 2658
PARTITION, 8183
'partitioned', 2655
partītiō(nem), 8185
'partition, wooden', 10541
partitus, 8185
'part, little', 10663
'partner', 1497, 7857
PARTNER, 8191
'partner in office', 7187
'partnership of three men',
    11761
'partnership of two men',
    11766
'part of speech', 408, 8182
PART(s), 8157
'part singing', 4825
'part, small', 8170
'parts, one of two equal',
    9073
PART TAKER, 8197
part taking, 8194
partum, 8116
PARTURIENT, 8120
parturīre, 8119

PARTURITION, 8120
parturus, 8118
party, 8248
'party', 4173
PARTY, 8163
parure, 8010
PARURE, 8011, 8061
parure de diamants, 8010
-*parus*, 8121
Pascua Florida, 5190
'pass a bill', 114
'passable', 10638
'passage', 1778, 8257,
10560
'passage money', 8419
'passage, narrow', 9786
'passage, narrow, of water',
9747
'passageway', 2086, 8255,
8442
'passageway, minute', 8441
PASSEL, 8180
'passenger, fellow', 10708
'passenger, paying', 8419
'passing quickly', 5632
'passion', 11646
'pass laws', 7168
'pass, mountain', 8256
'passport endorsement',
11274
'pass the summer', 4115
'pass through', 8414, 8448
'pasta shaped like sleeves',
7573
'pastime', 3848, 8379
'pastoral', 1770, 10991
'pastroal crook', 2942
'pastry', 10868
'pasture', 1856
pater, 11052
'path', 1912, 3395, 8442,
9414, 9566, 10560
'pathfinder', 4354
'path of running', 1994
pathos, 9351
'patronage, deserving of',
7622
'pattern', 10113, 11178
pau(cus), 8140
pauper, 8139
PAUPER, 8142
paupertās, 8146
'pay', 838

'payable', 5924
'payable, not yet', 5926
'pay attention to', 10060
'payment', 11702
'payment, compensatory',
8561
'payment, demand and
obtain', 6560
'payment, have by
withholding', 5897
'peak', 5038
'peas', 6528
'peasant', 1427
pecora, 7827
PECORINO, 7827
pecten, 7866
PECTEN, 7867
pectināre, 7871
PECTINATE, 7868
pectus, 8031
pecū, 7802
pecūlārī, 7820
PECULATION, 7793, 7822
pecūlātus, 7821
PECULIAR, 7793
pecūliāris, 7813
pecūlium, 7814
pecūnārius, 7806
pecūnia, 7806
PECUNIARY, 7793
pecūniōsus, 7807
PECUNIOUS, 7807
ped-, 31
PEDAGOGUE, 2
'pedal', 3386
pedant, 28
PEDANT, 26
pedante, 25
'pedantry in speech and
writing', 7313
pedis, 1197
'peel', 5244
'Peeping Tom', 11297
peer, 7919
'peer', 7905, 7941, 7972
PEER, 7918
peer group, 7919
PEERLESS, 7899, 7930
'peevish', 2990, 6321
'peevishness', 5083
'peg', 2509, 2556, 2661,
5032
peigne, 5013

peigner, 7870
PEIGNOIR, 7868
peior, 8071
peis, 5752
peitiō(nem), 5055
*pek-, 7861
*peku, 7835
*peku-, 7797, 7829
pel-, 7302
pelegrīnus, 9199
PELLAGRA, 311
pellis, 312
PELLUCID, 7301
'pelt', 9465
pemptē ousia, 8521
pen, 11475
'pen', 5000
PEN, 4999, 5041
pendant, 4993
'penetrated, incapable of
being', 10640
'penetrate with a sharp
edge', 9137
penguin, 11481
PENGUIN, 11474
PENKNIFE, 5002
penna, 4971, 5021, 5048,
5153
pennachio, 4967
PENNANT, 4959, 4994
PENNATE, 5004
pen(n)e, 4989
'penniless', 7809
pen(n)on, 4989
PENNON, 4987
PENS, 5044
pēnsum, 5753
PENT, 5042
PENTAGON, 6371
pentagōnon, 6375
pentagōnum, 6374
pentaphullon, 5240
pente, 6375
'people', 11575
'people, group of related',
699
'peoples, extinct or
prehistoric', 6831
'people under the same
discipline', 581
'people, vain', 10438
per, 5947, 7904, 7972,
10638

*perə, 0799
per-, 5088, 7303, 7992
-per, 9239
*per, 8155
*per-, 7996, 8155, 8414, 8448, 9240
'perceive', 6591
'perceived, easily', 9979, 10611
'perceptible', 5826
'perception', 3518, 6594
percer, 10198
'perch', 10784
percier, 10198
perdōnāre, 5946
père, 11052
*per(e)-, 8110
peregrine, 9200
peregrīnus, 9199
'perfect', 4298, 11187
PERFECT, 4297
'perfection, standard of', 11187
'perfection to, attribute', 11189
perfectus, 4296
perficere, 4295
'perform', 101, 3762, 4480, 11504
'performance', 105, 4242
'performance between acts', 3889
'performance, introductory', 3883
'performance, trial', 3893
'perform another time', 116
'perform efficiently', 3765
'performer', 4478
'performer in a play', 110
'perform well', 3766
'periodic', 818
'periodical', 11659
'period of time, recurrent', 10807
perīre, 10203
'perish', 10203
perishable, 5814
'perish, tending to', 5816
*peritiāre, 10203
peritus, 10203
'permission', 7129
'permissive, not', 9740
perpes, 5091

perpetis, 5091
'perpetual', 9249
PERPETUAL, 5093
perpetuālis, 5093
perpetuāre, 5088
PERPETUATE, 5087
perpetuus, 5093
per se, 8557
'perseverance', 6603
'persevere, ability to', 9825
'persist irksomely', 8411
'personal worth', 3310
'person, notable', 7330
'person or thing', 9266
'person, per', 2161
'person, rude', 1427
'person, unrefined', 1427
'person, very important', 11160
'persuade', 3475
'pertaining to', 10588
pertugiare, 10201
pertundere, 10199
'perturb', 176
pertusar, 10201
PERTUSE, 10196
pertūsiāre, 10200
*pertūsiāre, 10199
PERTUSSIN, 10222
PERTUSSIS, 10222
pertūsus, 10199
'peruse', 678
PERVIOUS, 10637
pervius, 10638
pes, 1197, 2308
'pester', 1831
pet, 5083
*pet-, 5047, 5104, 5146
petere, 5050, 5081
'petition', 808
PETITION, 5054
PETRIFY, 4378
*pet(s)na, 5048, 5153
petto, 8030
-petuare, 5089
PETULANCE, 5077
petulāns, 5079
*petulāre, 5080
pfinn, 5025
ph-, 1618, 4788, 5251
-ph-, 1619
phagein, 1674
phalburgensis, 5592

phanai, 4790, 4873
'pharmacist', 4614
pharmakon, 5716
phasis, 4874
phatos, 4874
phebesthai, 5674
phēmē, 4789
'phenomenon', 5139
PHILADELPHIA, 9421
philos, 9422
PHIZ, 1643
PHLOEM, 5383
phloos, 5384
phluktaina, 5382
phlu(z)ein, 5382
PHLYCTENA, 5381
PHOBIA, 5676, 5708
-PHOBIA, 5698
PHOBIAC, 5677
PHOBIC, 5677
PHOBISM, 5677
PHOBOPHOBIA, 5721
phobos, 5674
Phoenix dactylifera, 6294
phōnē, 2775, 4790, 4828, 4859
phōnēma, 4819
PHONEME, 4817
PHONETIC, 4816
phōnētikos, 4817
phoney, 4868
PHONOGRAM, 2778
PHONOGRAPH, 2773, 4821
'phonograph needle', 9867
'phonograph records', 3979
PHONOLOGY, 4815
phony, 4868
-phore, 7877
phōs, 5719
phōsphoros, 7284
PHOTOPHOBIA, 5719
phōtos, 5719
'phrase', 6724
phthoggē, 1345
phthongē, 1345
phuein, 1625, 1688
phugē, 5616
phullon, 5251
phulon, 1625, 1682
phusikos, 1627
phusiognōmonia, 1644
phusis, 1624, 1665

phuton, 1624, 1667
PHYLE, 1686
-phyll, 5252
PHYLLIS, 5256
phyllo-, 5252
PHYLLOTAXY, 5253
PHYLON, 1682
PHYLUM, 1683
PHYSIC, 1631
physica, 1629
'physical', 1637
PHYSICAL, 1634
'physical power, having
   great', 9823
'physician', 3182, 6937
PHYSICIAN, 1633
'physics', 1631
PHYSICS, 1628
'physics, after', 1649
'physics, (studies) beyond',
   1655
physio-, 1637
PHYSIOGNOMY, 1548, 1640,
   1672
PHYSIOLOGY, 1638
PHYSIOTHERAPY, 1638
physique, 1636
PHYSIQUE, 1549, 1635
-phyte, 1674
phyto-, 1669
PHYTOGNOMY, 1670
PHYTOLOGY, 1670
PHYTON, 1667
PHYTOPHAGOUS, 1673
PHYTOPSYCHE, 1672
'piano', 2524
pianoforte, 2533
'pick', 6566
'picked out', 6546
'pickle', 4445
'pick out', 6542, 6687,
   6716, 6820
'pick up', 6636, 6719
PICTOGRAPHS, 2688
'pictorial', 2718
'picture', 2685, 2716, 8903,
   11212
'piece', 8157, 9539, 10305
'piece broken off', 9507
'piece cut off', 8939, 9547
'piece, narrow', 9847
'pieces', 8208
'pied', 8250

piede, 31
'pier', 3555
'pierce', 9891, 10040,
   10201
PIERCE, 10197
'pierced, (of earlobes)',
   10196
'pig, female', 9389
'pigment, brown', 10965
pignon, 5008
'pile', 9599
pilgrim, 9199
'pilgrimage', 8455
'pillar', 9871
'pillow', 2326
'pilothouse', 3515
pilus, 2351
'pin', 2556
PIN, 5019
'pin, belaying', 2561
'pincers, small', 10085
'pinch', 348, 1073
'pinch sharply', 1069
pīnea, 5014
'pine-cone', 5014
'pine marten', 1586
'pine marten, fur of the',
   1584
'pine nut', 5015
pingouin, 11490
PINION, 5005
pin(n), 5031
pinna, 4969, 5009, 5037
PINNACLE, 4961
pinnāculum, 4968
PINNATE, 5005
*pinniō(nem), 5008
PINS, 5045
'pipe', 3490
'pipe, bowl', 5404
piptein, 5131
'pirate', 1999
Pisces, 8907
pistole, 1127
pistolet, 1129
'pit', 11569
pitar, 11052
'pitcher', 3140
'pitch of baseball', 9686
'pivot', 10995
'pivotal', 11002
*pkt-, 7872
*pktenos, 7874

'placate', 8718
'place', 3636, 4542, 4919
'place close to', 11974
'place for keeping things',
   523
'place in a high position',
   6050
'place of work', 7739
'place under', 4629
'placing', 4549
'placing before', 4591
'placing together', 9327
'plagiarize', 3147
'plain', 11364
'plan, artfully contrived',
   7494
'planetoid', 11226
PLANETOID, 11225
'plank', 11516
'plant', 1625, 1667
'plant, air', 1676
'plantation', 4327
'plantation, coffee', 4331
'planted, newly', 1680
'plant life, science of',
   1860
'plant, minutely small',
   1677
'plant, nonparasitic', 1676
'plant or tree, young shoot
   of', 1702
'plants collectively', 5180
'plants, cultivation of',
   1502
'plants, feeding on', 1674
'plants, properties of', 1671
'plants, study of', 1670
'plant structure, unit of',
   1667
'plant that flowers', 5267
'plant that grows in water',
   1678
'plant that likes high
   temperatures', 1679
'plant, three-leafed', 5237
'plaster', 4018, 10300
'plate', 1267
'platform for cargo', 3556
'platform, raised', 6366
'play', 3847, 8372
'play at courtship', 5158
'playful', 3845

'portion, fixed', 652
portiōnis, 8235
portionner, 8246
'portion of land', 8178
'portion out', 8246
PORTLY, 8294
PORTMANTEAU, 8298
'port, not toward', 8407
Porto, 8267
'port of Cale', 8268
'port, toward', 8396
Portucale, 8269
PORTUGAL, 8269
Portūnus, 8397
portus, 8256, 8326, 8367, 8397
Portus Cale, 8268
'port, without a', 8407
porus, 8441
porveeir, 11352
porve(i)oir, 11352
position, 11958
'position, commanding', 9799
'position of authority', 7739
'possess', 5737, 5768, 5859
'possession', 11157
'possession, movable', 2195
'possessions', 1533, 7644
'possible, make', 5843
'post', 1572, 9580
'postmark', 10160
POSTPARTUM, 8117
'posture', 1906
'pot', 2341, 3140
*pot-, 5147
potamos, 5147
'potassium aluminum silicate', 7398
POTHER, 1842
po(u)ley, 11007
po(u)lie, 11006
'pound', 10057, 10089, 10176, 10206, 10291, 10337
'pounding', 10231, 10306
pour-, 11350
poure, 8144
'poured forth', 7023
pous, 311, 1198
poverte, 8146
POVERTY, 8146
povre, 8144

Powell, 10727
'power', 735, 982, 3774, 4338, 6237, 9825, 11646, 11781
'power, exercise of', 11552
'power, exert', 964
'powerful', 926, 3775
'power, having sufficient', 5842
'power, latent', 11553
'powers, decreeing', 983
'power, wielder of', 981
'practice', 7782
'practitioners', 4770
prae, 5887, 10637
prae-, 2172, 2627, 5885, 7989
praebenda, 5885
praeceps, 2166
praecipitāre, 2170
praecipitis, 2166
praecipitium, 2166
praecludere, 2627
praecursor, 2022
praedicare, 6214
praedīcere, 6212
praedīlectus, 6624
praedīligere, 6624
praeësse, 8545
praefārī, 4738
praefātiō, 4737
praefectus, 4300
praeficere, 4299
praehibenda, 5886
praeiūdicāre, 6247
praeiūdicium, 6249
praelūdere, 3883
praeparāre, 7988
praesens, 8544
praesentem, 8550
praesentis, 8544
praestigiae, 6308, 9805
praesto, 6300
*praestrigiae, 6309, 9805
praestringere, 6309
praestringere oculos, 9801
praevius, 10636
'praise', 1374, 6881, 7621, 8745
'praise God', 1378
'praise, great', 8745
Prakrit, 9317
prakrta, 9318

'prank', 2223
'pranks', 2317
'prating, boastful', 10435
'prayer', 4952
pre-, 7996
PREACH, 6222
PREBEND, 5889
prechier, 6223
'precipice', 2166
PRECIPICE, 2165
PRECIPITATE, 2167
'precipitous', 10317
'precise', 2607, 9740
PRECLUDE, 2626
PRECURSOR, 2022
PREDICAMENT, 6216
PREDICATE, 6212
PREDICT, 6211
'prediction', 4878
PREDILECTION, 6627
'predisposition', 6628
'predominant', 933
pref, 1598
'preface', 3884
PREFACE, 4737
PREFECT, 4301
'prefer', 6625
'preference', 6628
PREJUDICE, 6248
PRELUDE, 3843, 3882
'premium', 3658
prēost, 1811
'preparation', 8097
'preparation in advance', 11333
prepare, 7997
'prepare', 1511, 4279, 8004, 8064, 8095
PREPARE, 7987
'prepare against', 8073
'prepare apart from', 8099
'prepare before', 8041
'prepared', 1512
'prepossession, favorable', 6627
pres-, 1800
presbus, 1797
presbuteros, 1797
presby-, 1813
PRESBYOPIA, 1814
presbyter, 1808
PRESBYTER, 1795

PRESBYTERIAN, 1804
'present', 3481, 5940, 8545, 8641
PRESENT, 8552
'present again', 8636
'present in the place of', 8637
'present, make a', 5938
'preservation', 760
'preserve', 4446
'preserved', 752
'preserves', 4281
'press', 265, 3019, 9659, 9723, 9838
'press flat', 272
'press together', 272
preste, 6298
prēster, 1809
*prester, 1808
prestidigitateur, 6303
prestidigitator, 9812
PRESTIDIGITATOR, 6297
prestige, 9807
'prestige', 9810
PRESTIGE, 9798
prestigiator, 6308, 9738, 9811
presto, 6299
presto digiti, 6305
prestre, 1810
'pretaste food or drink', 779
'pretend', 4761
'pretended', 4212, 9185
'pretender to wisdom', 11407
'pretense, put on a', 4269
prêtre, 1810
PRETTIFY, 4368
'pretty', 3135, 3608, 3664, 3733, 3766, 11317
'pretty, make', 4369
'pretty-pretty', 3737
preu, 8623, 11343
preux, 8619
PREUX, 8621
PREVAIL, 932
preve, 1598
'prevent', 5867, 10607
'prevention of, order the', 5871
'prevent the passage of', 2628

PREVIOUS, 10634
Price, 10728
'prick', 9880, 9949, 9977, 10037
'prick it out', 9988
PRIDE, 8605
'pride, undue', 10426
'priest', 1796, 4347, 4474
PRIEST, 1811
'priest, beggarly (needy)', 2277
Priester, 1809
'priests, pertaining to', 4473
prima FACIE, 4405
'primitive', 6832
PRIMORDIAL, 619
prīmōrdiālis, 620
prīmōrdium, 621
'primrose', 1848
prīmus, 621
'prince', 4669
'prince, of the', 2144
principal, 2143
'principal', 2143
principe, 4669
'principle, philosophic', 3215
'principle, self-evident', 304
'principles, guiding', 6336
'principle, valid', 3218
'prison', 10081
Privatdozent, 3190
'private', 7238
'privateer', 1999
PRIVILEGE, 6930, 7235
prīvilēgium, 7237
prīvus, 7238
'prize', 77, 2667, 6608
'prize, contending for a', 91
'prize, for a', 76
prō, 3480, 6803, 8585
prō-, 285, 1865, 4764, 5885, 6028, 8589, 11350
*prōales, 6026
proba, 1599
PROBABLE, 1591
PROBATION, 1592
PROBE, 1591
prōbenda, 5884
'probe, surgical', 9877
PROBITY, 1591

PROBOSCIS, 1851
proboskis, 1864
probus, 1590
'proceed', 9685
'process', 397
'process, bristlelike', 9868
'procession', 8058
'process of', 9734
'process raw materials', 4157
'process, tubular', 9868
'proclaim', 4888, 4929, 6184, 6215
'proclaimed', 4931
'proclaim openly', 4760
'proclamation', 4900, 4942
'procure', 8148
prod, 8595
'prod', 9954
prōd-, 285
prōde, 8592, 8627
prōde est, 8592
prōdesse, 8583
prōdest, 8591
PRODIGAL, 282
prōdigālitās, 283
PRODIGALITY, 283
prōdigere, 284
prodigious, 288
prōdigus, 284
prodigy, 287
PRODROME, 3371
'produce', 4290, 8148, 8361
PRODUCE, 3478
'produce an effect upon', 4264
'produced', 9339
'produced, artificially', 4192
'produce in abundance', 7653, 7788
prōducere, 3479
'producing', 8122
'producing in abundance', 4316
'producing little', 8139
'producing young', 8113
PRODUCT, 3479
'product of', 489
prōductum, 3479
proesse, 8623
proeve, 1599
prof, 1598

prōfectus, 4303
PROFESS, 4760
'profession', 416, 4341
PROFESSION, 4768
PROFESSIONAL, 4771
PROFESSOR, 4765
'profess outwardly', 8338
professus, 4759
prōficere, 4303
'proficiency', 9091
PROFICIENT, 4304
'profit', 8630
PROFIT, 4305
profitērī, 4759
'progenitor', 8115, 10270
PROGNATHOUS, 6419
'prognosticator', 8714
PROGRAM, 2791
programma, 2794
PROGRAMME, 2791
prographein, 2795
'progress', 4306
'progress through a
  profession', 1913
prōhibēre, 5868
'prohibit', 4896, 11915,
  11945
PROHIBIT, 5867
'prohibition', 4896, 11916
'projecting', 10319
PROLAN, 6037
prōlēs, 4317, 6026
PROLETARIAT, 6022
proletarii, 6025
prōlifer, 6032
PROLIFERATE, 6031
PROLIFERATING, 6023
PROLIFIC, 4316, 6022
prolificus, 6031
PROLIX, 7024
prōlixus, 7023
PROLOGUE, 6802
PROLUSION, 3892
'promenade', 11512
Promethean, 7291
'promiscuous woman', 3433
'promise to pay', 6956
'pronouncement,
  authoritative', 6128
'proof', 6340
PROOF, 1550, 1591
prōoles, 6026
prō partiōne, 8238

'properly', 8740
'property', 1528, 2143,
  2193, 7645, 7853
'property in cattle', 7806
'property, movable', 7798,
  7850
'property, personal', 7812
'property, private', 7813
propetēs, 5097
PROPHECY, 4878
PROPHESY, 4882
'prophet', 11410
PROPHET, 4882
prophēteia, 4881
prophētēs, 4881
'prophetic declaration',
  4701
'prophetic utterances', 4729
propicius, 5096
PROPITIATES, 5100
'propitious', 3286
PROPITIOUS, 5095
propitius, 5096
prōportāre, 8340
prōportiō, 8241
'proportion', 551, 724,
  6698, 6764, 6848, 8240
PROPORTION, 8243
'proportionally', 8237
'proportionate', 8239
prō portiōne, 8236
'proposition', 1350, 4532
'proposition taken for
  granted', 304
'propriety, overconcerned
  with', 11342
PROPTOSIS, 5145
pros, 4603
'proscribe', 4929
'proscribed', 4931
'proscription', 4900, 4942
prōsit, 8590
PROSIT, 8584
'prospect', 11286
'prosperity', 3673
'prosperous', 4372, 5178
prosthesis, 4603
PROSTHESIS, 4602
'prostrate', 5103
PROTAGONIST, 96
'protect', 10940
'protection', 5639, 7636
'protective structure', 500

'protector', 6235, 7636
'protector of property',
  7644
PROTHESIS, 4591
proto-, 97
'protoplasm', 11236
protos, 8893
PROTOTYPE, 10120
PROTOZOA, 8893
'protuberance', 3102, 4045
'protuberance, rounded',
  6437
prou, 8623
PROUD, 8601
prove, 8633
PROVE, 1591
PROVECTION, 10724
PROVENDER, 5883
provend(r)e, 5884
'proverb', 6765
'provide', 7987, 11330
PROVIDE, 11328
'provided', 11357
'provided that', 11345
PROVIDENCE, 11333
prōvidēns, 11333
PROVIDENT, 11332
prōvidentia, 11335
prōvidēre, 11330
prōvīsiō, 11331
PROVISION(S), 11330
'proviso', 11353
PROVISO, 11344
prōvīsō quod, 11345
prōvīsus, 11330
PROW, 8624
PROWESS, 8625
proz, 8595
prud, 8595
prude, 8611, 11341
PRUDE, 8613
prudefemme, 8609
prudence, 8618
prūdēns, 11340
'prudent', 11332
PRUDENT, 11340
prud'homme, 8609
PRUDISH, 8616
prueve, 1599
prūt, 8598
pruz, 8595
prȳde, 8605

prȳte, 8605
psēstos, 11024
-*pt*, 2191
PTERIDOLOGY, 5118
PTERIDOPHYTE, 5119
pteridos, 5118
pteris, 5118
**pt-ero*-, 5105
PTERODACTYL, 5112
'pterodactyls', 5115
pteron, 5106, 5153
PTEROSAUR, 5115
pterux, 5106
ptōma, 5122
PTOMAINE, 5127
ptōmat-, 5129
ptomatine, 5130
PTOSIS, 5143
ptukhē, 1342
'public', 5511, 11575
'publication', 4900
'public building official',
  4074
'public declaration, one
  who makes', 4766
'public domain, outside
  the', 5542
'public games', 8386
'public position', 4314
'public works', 4075
pugnus, 7887
pull, 11011
'pull', 3454, 3572, 9770
'pull about', 10212
'pull along', 3577
'pull at', 3567
'pulled tight', 3579
PULLEY, 11007
'pulling', 3569
'pull into a fold', 3581
'pull together and knot',
  3591
-*pulus*, 7449
'pun', 11136
'punched', 10196
'punctuate', 9973
'punish', 199, 3582
'punishment, divine wrath
  as', 11303
'punishment fit the crime',
  3332
puntis, 4356
'puny creature', 10484

'pupa covering', 4608
'pupil', 3206, 5977
pur, 5463, 5710
pur-, 11351
**pur*-, 5462
pura, 5465, 5492
'purchases, person who
  seeks', 803
'pure', 201, 250, 6404,
  9252
pūrgāre, 249
PURGE, 249
purger, 249
'purification, ceremonial',
  7371
'purify', 249, 7375
'purify by expiation', 7370
pūrigāre, 250
puritēs lithos, 5467
'purloining', 6632
PURPORT, 8338
purporter, 8339
purr(h)ikhē, 5489
**purr(h)ikhē*, 5492
**Purr(h)ikhos*, 5490
*purr(h)os**, 5485
'pursue', 1996, 5052
pūrus, 250
purveu est, 11357
purveu que, 11357
PURVEY, 11351
PURVIEW, 11353
'push', 5073, 9596, 9651,
  10056, 10088, 10176,
  10206, 10262, 10291,
  10337
'pushed out', 10308
'push forward', 10059
'pushing', 10230, 10307,
  11970
'put', 4145, 4432, 4471,
  4541, 4575, 4735, 7587
'put against', 4562
'put an end to', 9995
'put away', 4618
'put back together with',
  4453
'put in', 4294
'put in a secure place',
  4469
'put in front', 4300
'put into a snug place',
  3581

'put into one's hand', 7588
'put off', 4487
'put on', 4485, 4580
'put on (a garment)', 4484
put oneself in dever, 5918
'put out', 4487, 9995
'put out a fire', 9994
'put out of the way', 4454
'puts together', 4444
'putting after', 4582
'putting in beside', 4574
'putting together', 4281,
  4566
'putting under', 4569
'put together', 4278, 4441,
  7587, 9314, 11897
'put under', 3527, 4310,
  4570
PYRACANTHA, 5474
PYRE, 5463
PYRES, 5494
PYREX, 5476
PYRITE, 5466
PYROMANIAC, 5473
PYROPHOBIA, 5710
PYROSIS, 5477
PYROTECHNICS, 5474
PYRRHIC, 5480
Pyrrhus, 5482

Q

qu-, 8768
-*qu*-, 7009
QUA, 11103
QUADRIVIUM, 10629
QUADRUMANA, 7486
QUADRUMANOUS, 7485
'quadrupeds, ruminant',
  1728
quae, 11101
qualificāre, 11108
'qualified', 6551
qualifier, 11107
'qualify', 5851
QUALIFY, 4379, 11106
qualis, 4379, 11106
qualitās, 11106
qualité, 11105
QUALITY, 11104
'quality, of inferior', 2035
'quality to, attribute a',
  11108

quam, 11128
quando, 11065
quantitās, 11110
'quantitative measurement',
656
quantité, 11110
'quantity', 717, 10718
QUANTITY, 11109
quantus, 11110
'quarrel', 1034
'quarrel between two
families', 7846
'quarry', 11569
quartermaster, 6786
'quarters', 6786
quasi, 11128
QUASI, 11126
quatir, 271
-que, 11147
'quench', 9986
QUENELLE, 6476
'questionable', 1156
qui, 11101, 11131
quib, 11136
QUIBBLE, 11130
quibus, 11131
'quick', 165
QUICK, 8758
QUICKEN, 8779
QUICKENING, 8777
QUICKSAND, 8758
QUICKSILVER, 8783
quid, 11141
'quiet', 10364
quinancia, 373
quinencie, 374
quinesye, 375
quīnquefolium, 5239
'quinsy', 367
QUINSY, 375
quinta essentia, 8521
QUINTESSENCE, 8521
'quip', 3648
QUIP, 11140
quippe, 11140
qui(s), 11061
'quit', 6954
-quity, 11147
quō, 11063
quod, 11062, 11101
'quoit', 6352
quom, 11065, 11129
quondam, 11129

QUONDAM, 11128
*quoniam de viro sumpta
est,* 11748
QUORUM, 11111
*quorum vos   unum esse
volumus,* 11114
quot, 11118
quota, 11117
QUOTA, 11116
quotāre, 11121
'quotation', 2731
'quote', 8361
QUOTE, 11119
quoth, 11122
QUOTIDIAN, 11125
quotīdiē, 11126
quotiēns, 11119
QUOTIENT, 11118
quotum, 11117
quotus, 11117
**quubi,* 11146

R

-r-, 6106
'rabble rouser', 10
'rabies', 5700, 7403
'race', 1625, 1682, 6406
'race-chariot', 2076
'racecourse', 1911, 2076,
3363
Races of Man, 4864
'racetrack', 3357
'racetrack, horse', 3356
'rack of bombs,
simultaneous release of
a', 771
radh, 692
radhulfr, 694
'radio signal, directional',
1571
radulf, 694
rǣd, 690
-raed, 3905
rǣdan, 674
rǣden, 697
'rage', 7403
**ragin,* 7646
Raginmund, 7646
'rags', 10902
raid, 9910
'railway car', 10670
'railway coach', 10670

Raimund, 7646
'rain', 8027
'raise', 6086, 10931
'raise anchor', 10547
'raised structure', 6053
'raise high', 6051
raisin, 3081
raisin de corauntz, 2063
'raising up', 10721
'raisins of Corinth', 2064
RALPH, 693
'Ram', 8905
'rambling', 2027
ramparer, 8039
'rampart', 11513
RAMPART, 8037
'ranching', 4326
'range of authority', 11354
'rank', 571, 7966
'rank, deprive of', 7968
'rank, equality of', 7972
'rankness', 7382
'rank, of superior', 2079
'rap', 6486
'rape', 11784
'rapid, become more', 8779
rapport, 8358
RAPPORT, 8363
rapporter, 8358
Rat, 681, 3905
rata, 658
RATE, 656
**rath,* 710
Rathaus, 682
RAT(H)SKELLER, 682
ratificāre, 660
RATIFY, 659
ratiō, 647, 709
'ratio', 724, 6698, 6765,
6849, 8360
RATIO, 651
RATION, 652
'rational', 6769
RATIONAL, 652
RATIONALE, 653
RATIONALIZE, 653
ratiōnem, 647
'ratio-number', 721
ratum, 645
'ravage', 10417
'ravine, narrow', 5316
'rawhide', 8032

'raw materials', 10272
RAYMOND, 7645
'razor', 9114
re-, 154, 2643, 8039, 8366, 11903
*rē-, 645, 672
'reach an agreement', 9688
REACT, 116
'reaction, abnormal', 11557
'reaction, altered', 11557
'read', 686, 6502, 6639, 6687, 6760, 6926
READ, 674
'readable', 5818, 6641
'read aloud', 6502, 6639
'read, capable of being', 6640
'reader', 6650
Reader's Encyclopedia, 6167
'reading', 6641, 6748
READING, 665
'reading aloud', 6642
'reading desk', 6650
'reading, place for', 6654
READJUSTING, 11948
READS, 677
'ready', 1512, 5804, 6299, 7988
'ready, always', 9245
'ready, make', 5801
'ready to go', 1513
'real', 6404, 8693, 8729
'realm', 3935
'rear', 3467, 3596, 6027
'reared', 6045
'rearrange', 11972
'reason', 4816, 6697, 6765
REASON, 642
'reasoned, correctly', 930
'reasoning', 647, 6927
'reasoning, art of', 6768
'reasoning, deductive', 6900
'reasoning, fallacious or illogical', 6911
'reasoning, principles of', 6767
'reason, lack of', 10489
'reason, manifestation of', 6699
'rebelling', 612
'rebuke sharply', 196
RECAPITULATE, 2160

receive, 2410
'receive', 3258, 5735, 5812, 5935, 6501
'receptacle', 4618, 5882
'recess for sacramental objects', 524
'recite', 6502, 6639, 6687
'reckoning', 647, 709, 6693, 6764, 6903, 8239
'reckoning together', 6902
recludere, 2640
reclure, 2640
reclus(e), 2640
RECLUSE, 2638
reclūsus, 2641
'recommend', 7619
RECOMMEND, 7621
recommendāre, 7623
recondere, 4453
RECONDITE, 4455
reconditus, 4453
'recount', 6690
RECOURSE, 2032
RECTIFY, 4379
rectus, 4379
RECUR, 2051
'red', 5486
red-, 154
-red, 689
REDACT, 152
REDACTOR, 154
redactum, 153
*rēdan, 673
'redden', 5336
REDE, 679
*rē-dh-, 673
redigere, 153
REDOUBT, 1174, 3527
redoubtable, 3532
REDOUBTABLE, 1173, 1594
redoutable, 1172
redoute, 3528
redouter, 1171
'red-shield', 9053
REDUCE, 3470
redūcere, 3471, 3530
reductus, 1176, 3529
REFECTION, 4308
refectōrium, 4310
REFECTORY, 4308
refectum, 4307
'reference work', 10845
reficere, 4306

'refined', 3336, 4105, 9314
'reflection', 6697
'reflect upon', 184
'refresh', 4307
'refreshment', 4308
'refuge', 3529, 8258
REFUGE, 5609, 5638
REFUGEE, 5641
refugere, 5640
refugium, 5640
'refusing to compromise', 207
regen, 982
Regenweald, 982
REGINALD, 981
'region', 8159
'region, geographic', 8157
'registrar of documents', 113
'regularity', 571
'regulation', 1462
'regulation, break a', 11783
REHABILITATE, 5855
reign, 5509
'reimburse', 8361
'reincarnation', 11019
'reinstate', 5856
reisun, 650
'reject', 6206
'rejecting', 6568
REJOIN, 11921
*rejoind, 11940
REJOINDER, 11927
rejoindre, 11924
'relation', 6697, 6854, 8360
'relation, numerical', 651
'relationship by remarriage', 10310
relēgāre, 7182
RELEGATE, 7181
relēgīus, 7182
RELIABLE, 5831
RELIC, 6983, 7095
RELICT, 6985
relictus, 6978
'relieve pain', 8718
'religion, new convert to a', 1680
'religious functionary', 1811
'religious law', 7137
'religious organization, member of a', 4766

REVUE, 11311
'revulsion', 935
'reward', 9584
'reward, divine beneficence
  as', 11305
rex, 3926
rhein, 6800
rhiza, 9558
*rī-, 715
Ribes, 2062
riccio, 2392
rīce, 3935
rich, 3926
'rich', 7808
'riches', 1529, 7644, 7684,
  7806
RIDDLE, 687
'riddle, interpret a', 675
'ridicule', 3462, 3849
'ridiculous', 3845
ridotto, 3528
'rigging', 8093
right, 9343, 11501
'right', 3243, 3286, 11976
'right angle, greater than
  a', 10192
RIGHTEOUS, 11442
RIGHTEOUSLY, 11385
'right granted', 7236
'right hand', 3295
'right hand, on the', 3286
'right moment', 8403
'right side', 3288
'right to visit', 11305
rightwise, 11442
'rigorous', 9740
rihtwīs, 11441
'rind', 8943
ring, 10942
'ring', 2093, 3006, 10942,
  11038
'ring, arm', 539
'ring, finger', 4871
RINGHALS, 10940
'ring, metal', 540
'ring-necked', 10941
'rings, iron', 542
'rise and fall', 5329
risicare, 9552
risico, 9552
'rising', 3806
'risk', 8471
RISK, 9551
'risk at sea', 9553

risque, 9552
rite, 9343, 11501
RITE, 728
'rite, initiatory', 11046
'rites', 11571
'rites, secret', 11623
RITUAL, 729
rītuālis, 730
rītus, 727
'rivalry', 5065
'river', 1781, 5147, 5318
'river-horse', 5149
'river of Mesopotamia',
  10032
'rivers, land between', 5150
'road', 1914, 3551, 8838,
  10560, 10599
'road, off the', 10603
'roast', 10784
'roast on a spit', 9907
'robber, highway', 2011
'robbery of temple', 6634
'robust', 3631
'rock', 9504, 10986
'rock, easily split', 9025
'rock fragment', 9503
'rocks, growing on', 9523
'rocks, living among', 9523
'rock, thin layer of', 5224
rögn, 983
Rögnvaldr, 983
'roll', 2498
'roll, cause to', 10212
'Roman senate house',
  11771
RONALD, 982
'room', 4065, 4373
'room, arrangement and
  embellishment of', 3282
'room, heated', 5395
'rooms, suite of', 8215
'room that can be locked
  with a key', 2549
'roomy', 5830
'roost', 10787
'root', 9558
'rope', 3592, 9830, 11458
rosaries, 2247
rosārium, 2248
'rose garden', 2247
'rose of Sharon', 6112
'rotate without purpose',
  1004

ROTHSCHILD, 9053
rough, 11823
'rough breathing', 547
'round', 1082
'roundabout', 10604
'roundabout way', 242
'rounded', 3167
'rounded object', 2893
'round-eyed', 10822
'round-headed excrescence',
  326
'round object', 3136
'round up (livestock).',
  2090
'route', 10574
row, 11823
'row', 10762
'row (a boat)', 10759
'row backwards', 5862
'rowers' bench', 11831
'rowing', 10759
'rowing, in the', 10761
'row of threads in a loom',
  583
'rows, arranged in', 608
-rrhoia, 6800
ru, 11823
'rub', 9659, 9722, 9837
'rubbed', 11024
'rub lightly', 9663
RUGBY, 1457
rūh, 11824
'ruin', 2171, 4503, 5122
'rule', 571, 696, 962, 5509
'rule by the best', 734
'ruler', 984, 3453, 3783,
  3926
'ruler, absolute', 4322
'ruler of the gods', 982
'rulers, succession of', 3780
'rules, code of', 7244
'rules, collection of', 6932,
  7142
'ruling class, hereditary',
  734
'rumor', 4775
'run', 1893, 1988, 2048,
  2093, 3382, 3444, 6994
'run against', 2050
'run away', 5673, 5725
'run, brief', 9696

'saving', 759
SAVIOR, 761
'savory', 4445
'saw', 9433
SAW, 9425, 9572
-SAW, 9440
sawdyour, 842
sawgeour, 842
SAWYER, 9436
SAX, 9498
SAXICOLOUS, 9522, 10985
saxifraga, 9513
SAXIFRAGE, 9512
saxifrax, 9520
Saxō, 9493
SAXON, 9490
Saxōnes, 9493
SAXONS, 9482
saxum, 9503, 10986
'say', 4682, 6153, 6690,
   11125, 11409
'say again', 5085
'say between', 6225
'say in advance', 4738,
   6212
'saying', 2733, 4813, 6129,
   6350, 6695, 6927
'say in reply', 11926
'say loudly', 6252
'say often', 6252
'say the opposite to', 6183
sblood, 1409
scala, 8991, 9021
scale, 9019
'scale', 1267, 8943, 9040
SCALE, 8949, 9011
'scale (of a balance)', 9006
SCALES, 8932, 9004
SCALLOP, 8957
SCALLOPED, 8961
SCALLOPINI, 8965
SCALLOPS, 8930
scaloppa, 8962
SCALOPPINE, 8965
SCALP, 8932, 8966
'scalpel', 9104
SCALPEL, 9102
scalpellum, 9104
scalper, 9104
SCALPER, 8974
scalpere, 9105
scalprum, 9104
'scanty', 144, 2831, 9718

'scatter seed', 9389
sc(e)alu, 9026
sceld, 9046
scell, 8940
Schale, 8943
'scheduled', 5925
schel, 8942
schelf, 9065
schelp, 8971
Schild, 9052
sc(h)ola, 9086
'scholar', 3206
schōle, 9079
school, 9085
'school', 9087
SCHOOL, 9082
'school, elementary', 3858
'schoolmaster', 26
'school of higher learning',
   7190
'schoolteacher', 17
schot, 10541
schulle, 8984
scield, 9046
scieldtruma, 9057
sciell, 8940
science, 9096
'science', 416
'science of life', 6833
scild, 9046
'scilicet', 11389
scindere, 9448
scinn, 9466
'scion', 1049, 1703
scīre, 9095
scissors, 9008
'scold', 196
'scolding', 6643
scole, 9084
scolle, 8984
scolu, 9079
sconce, 4469
SCONCE, 4461
Scorpio, 8906
'Scorpion', 8906
'Scottish', 4039
'scourge, leather, for
   flogging', 6454
'scout', 2023
'scraped', 11024
'scratch', 2684, 2711, 2834,
   2876, 9106
scripta cursiva, 2025

'script, flowing', 2025
'Scripture read aloud', 6656
'scrutinize', 131
'scuffle', 7886
sculpere, 9106
sculptor, 9109
'sculptor', 437, 9110
SCULPTOR, 9108
sculptum, 9107
sculptūra, 9112
SCULPTURE, 9111
'scutcheon bearer', 516
SCYTHE, 9425, 9573
se-, 2625, 3459, 6543, 8100
'sea', 7008, 10984
se abdicāre, 6206
-(se)acre, 11416
'sea-cucumber', 2343
se addīcere, 6158
'sea, living in the', 10984
'seal on a letter or
   document', 267
'seashell', 8944, 8991
'seasoning', 4448
seax, 9480
secāns, 9543
SECANT, 9542
secānt(em), 9543
secāre, 1210, 8795, 9456,
   9525, 9565
secg, 9470
SECLUDE, 2624
secludere, 2625
(se) comporter, 8348
'second', 10415
'secret', 2788
'secretary', 7553
'secret code, in a', 2787
'secret, in', 5645
'secretive', 2606
sect, 9564
'sect', 4173, 9566
-sect, 9528
secta, 9566
SECTILE, 9544
sectilis, 9545
'section', 8235
SECTION, 9425, 9539
sectiōn(em), 9540
sector, 9542
SECTOR, 9541
sectum, 9525

sic semper tyrannis, 9246
'side', 4413, 8166, 9072
'side by side', 11956
'sided', 4431
'side dish', 7758
'side, on the', 8211
'side, opposing', 8167
'sides, on both', 3298
'side, to the', 8209
SIDEWAYS, 10568
'sieve', 8288
'sight', 10839, 11286, 11315
'sign', 6315
'significant', 8333
'signs, circle of', 8902
si(g)the, 9445
'silly', 10463
'silver', 3674
similaire, 9168
'similar', 7943, 8660, 9261, 9336
SIMILAR, 9167
similāre, 9192
'similarity', 9215, 9279
SIMILARITY, 9186
'similarity between things otherwise dissimilar', 6847
'similarity in substance', 8658
simile, 9171, 9224
SIMILE, 9168
similis, 9168, 9224
SIMILITUDE, 9186
'simple', 9232, 9405
SIMPLE, 9153, 9233
SIMPLETON, 9256
simplex, 9235
simplicis, 9235
simplicitās, 9236
SIMPLICITY, 9236
simplus, 9232
simul, 9173, 9223
simulācrum, 9179
SIMULACRUM, 9178
simulāre, 9178, 9213
SIMULATE, 9177
'simulated', 9184
simultané, 9183
SIMULTANEOUS, 9180
'simultaneous happening', 11875

simultāneus, 9184
'sin', 4731, 5567, 8699
SIN, 8698
SINCERE, 9254
SINCERITY, 9256
sincērus, 9251
sinciput, 2181
SINCIPUT, 2180
sind, 8708
'sinful', 4732
'singing in responses', 4827
'singing without accompaniment', 2263
'single', 9226, 9406, 10363
SINGLE, 9227
SINGLET, 9229
SINGULAR, 9228
singulāris, 9229
singulus, 9226
'sinner', 8705
SINO-, 5698
sistere, 529
sithe, 9450
'sit on one's heels', 270
'sitting', 1710
situ, 7150
'situation, troublesome', 6217
sixth, 1227
sk, 9069
sk-, 9468
skaal!, 9012
skāl, 9005
*skāla, 8951
*skaljō, 8939
*skalō, 8948, 9026
skalp, 8970
skālpr, 8970
*skei-, 9098
skel, 8944, 8991
*skel, 9038
*skel-, 8936, 9023, 9075
*skelduz, 9047
*skelf-, 9065·
*skeli-, 9092
*skēlō, 9007
'sketch', 10105
skholē, 9087
skil, 9091
skilja, 9093
'skill', 416, 452, 4208, 5849
SKILL, 9091
'skilled', 4304, 5806

'skilled in calculation', 6778
'skillful', 448, 3286, 5809, 5840, 11757
SKILLFUL, 9093
'skillfulness', 3296
'skill in dealing with others, one who possesses', 1315
'skill, lacking', 449
'skills, without', 463
'skin', 312, 5709, 8943
SKIN, 9427, 9464
'skin, bare human', 1766
'skin disease', 5075
skinn, 9467
'skin seizure', 311
*skinth-, 9467
'skip', 3422
skoal!, 9014
SKOAL, 9012
skol, 8987
skolt, 8986
skoltr, 8985
skopein, 11230
skrabba, 2856
skul, 8987
'skull', 2341, 8987
SKULL, 8981
'skull, back of the', 2179
'skullcap', 2280
skulle, 8985
*skulō, 9076
skult, 8986
'sky, clear', 4085
'slander', 3461, 4783, 6230
'slave', 15, 2195, 6157
'slave at hand', 7555
'slave collar', 1872
'slave in charge of children', 20
'slave, runaway', 5635
'slavery', 1471
'sleep', 44
'sleep, inducing', 44
'sleeping car', 10533
'sleeve', 7570
'sleeve, like a', 7573
'sleight of hand', 7483
'sleight-of-hand artist', 6298, 9812
'slender', 2352
'slide', 2460, 8287

'slip, paper', 9928
'slogan', 6794
'slope, gentle', 2458
'slovenly', 6582
'slow-moving', 2446
'slow to learn', 10093
'slow to react', 10093
'slow-witted', 10192
sluggard, 11424
sm̊-, 9404
'small', 8871, 9159, 10555
'small blister', 5381
'smaller, make', 9778
'small intestine, first
  portion of', 1106
'smell', 6059
'smelts', 2274
'smitten', 9699
smma, 9364
'smoke', 191
SMOKESTACK, 9606
'smooth', 9671
'smooth and sweet', 5314
sm̊-tero-, 9374
sm̊-tero-s, 9380
'snake, venomous', 8128,
  8811, 10941
'snap', 6486
'snare', 3414, 10217
snick-, 9946
SNICKERSNEE, 9943
snijden, 9945
'snout, long animal's', 1862
'so', 8724
'soaked', 5357
'social duty', 5914
'social position', 7966
'social usages', 9934
sodger, 843
soema, 9269
soemr, 9269
'soft', 3681, 5357
soft liquor, 7011
'softness', 3681
'soil', 11613
sojor, 843
'sojourn', 10802, 10945
'sojourning', 10945
sol, 845
sol-, 750, 787, 825, 851,
  9270
solder, 849
'solder', 850
SOLDER, 829

SOLDIER, 829
'soldier, foot', 4651
'soldiers', 486
'soldiers, armed', 499
'soldier's savings', 10587
soldus, 837
'sole', 9227
'solemn', 819
SOLEMN, 823
solem(p)ne, 824
'solicit', 807
SOLICIT, 801
'solicitation', 5055
SOLICITOR, 803
SOLICITOUS, 793
SOLICITUDE, 744, 794
solid, 10374
'solid', 826
SOLID, 827
solidāre, 848
'solid, make', 848
'solid mass, become a', 250
sol-ido-, 825
solidus, 826
solidus nummus, 831
'soliloquy', 6808
sol(l)emnis, 818
sol(l)ennis, 818
sollicitāre, 797
solliciter, 800
sollicitūdō, 796
sollicitus, 789
sollo-, 787
sollus, 788, 817
sol-o-, 9335
'some', 11156
SOME, 9264
-SOME, 9279
'something', 11156
'something demonstrably
  true', 4151
'something done', 4150
som-o-s, 9379
'song', 3851, 11026
'song, simple', 6259
sōns, 8704
sontis, 8704
'son, younger', 2116
'soon after', 11919
sooth, 8712
SOOTHE, 8716
'soothes, something that',
  784

'soothsayer', 11407, 11467
SOOTHSAYER, 8713
'sorcerer', 11419
'sorcery', 4196
'sore', 5372
'sore throat', 372
'sorrow', 340, 6108
'sorrow, song or poem of',
  6891
sōth, 8711
SOU, 829
souci, 813
souder, 850
so(u)duire, 3523
soul, 845
'soul', 5991
soulde, 838
souldeour, 840
'sound', 875, 1346, 2775,
  4790, 4819, 4859
'sound, agreeable', 4844,
  8744
'sound from two sources',
  1202
'sound, same', 9347
'sounds, disagreeable', 4849
'sounds, discordant', 4848
'sounds in speaking', 4817
'sounds, transposition of',
  4581
'sound-writing', 2774
'sound, written', 2775
so(u)rveeir, 11360
sourvivre, 8798
sous, 845
'south', 3804, 3830
'southern land', 3816
'South Saxony', 9497
soux, 845
sovereign, 5509
'sovereign', 3782
'sovereign power', 964
'sovereignty', 3782
sovet, 9309
SOVIET, 9307
sow, 9388
'space, empty', 10463
'space, open', 7269
'Spanish gold coin', 1119
spar, 8019
SPAR, 8013

'standing in the way',
10611
'stand up', 8045
'stanza, concluding', 10650
'star', 7330
starboard, 8262
'starlike', 11226
Star-Spangled Banner, 4841
'starve', 6014
'state', 4524, 5780, 6175
STATE, 4597
'statehouse', 2152
'stateliness of bearing',
8294
'statement', 4550, 4874
'statement requiring
interpretation', 687
'statement worded in a
puzzling manner', 688
'state of being free', 4524
*State of Russia under the
Present Czar*, 6460
'state paper', 1297
'statistician', 112
'statue', 10105
status, 4595
'status, equal', 7966
'statute', 4526
'statute, body of a', 11353
staup-, 10319
staupilaz, 10321
staut-, 10262
'stay', 7113, 10997
'stay alive', 7113
'stay with as a guest',
11303
'steadfast', 7243
STEAK, 9900
'steal', 3146, 6636
'stealing', 6632, 7823
'steal into', 5300
stēap, 10318
'steel for striking fire',
5428
'steep', 2167, 4294
STEEP, 10050, 10317
STEEPLE, 10319
STEEPLECHASE, 10322
'steer', 1731
'steer-board', 8262
steg-, 9578, 9648, 9923,
10035
stegh-, 10037

steig, 10033
steig-, 9595, 9890, 9925,
9954, 9993, 10292
steik, 9907
steikja, 9907
steken, 9931
'stem', 10253
stengh-, 10038
stengjan-, 10039
STENOGRAPHY, 2830
stenos, 2831
stēop-, 10310
'step', 3382, 3444
'step-', 3715
STEP-, 10310
STEPBAIRN, 10312
STEPCHILD, 10051, 10312
STEPDAUGHTER, 10311
stēpel, 10321
STEPFATHER, 10311
'step heavily', 3431
'step lightly', 10597
STEPMOTHER, 10314
'step on repeatedly', 3434
STEPSON, 10311
steu, 10088
steu-, 9596, 10056, 10102,
10176, 10206, 10246,
10290, 10337
steup-, 10107
stewə-, 10339
sti-, 9889
stiborne, 10256
sticca, 9893
stice, 9897
-stice, 529
sticel, 9949
stician, 9893
stick, 9593, 9993, 10286
'stick', 2981, 9578, 9648,
9890, 9923, 9954, 9999,
10036, 10284
STICK, 9889, 9921
'sticker', 9935
'stick, heavy', 2586
STICKING, 9853
STICKLEBACK, 9947
stickler, 9950
stick or snee, 9944
'stick, pointed', 9966
'stick, short', 9714
'sticks, pointed', 9918
'sticky', 7086, 7113

-stīgāre, 9955
stigma, 10000
STIGMA, 10004
STIGMATA, 9853, 10006
STIGMATISM, 10012
stik-, 9894
stikiz, 9898
stikkōn, 9894
stile, 9874, 9952
STILETTO, 9875
stilo, 9874
'stilted', 4212
'stilts', 3439
stilus, 9858, 9886
STIMULANT, 9884
stimulus, 9879
STIMULUS, 9882
'sting', 9880, 9949
STING, 10039
stingan, 10039
stinguere, 9985
-stinguere, 9977
stingy, 10042
STINGY, 10041
STINT, 10238
'stipend, clergyman's', 5890
stipula, 10253
'stipulation', 6175, 11331
'stipulation, conditional',
11344
'stir', 798, 10211
'stir about', 10211
'stirred up', 789
stirrup, 9951
'stir up', 9957
'stir up fire', 10296
'stir up one's mind', 183
'stir up public interest',
177
STITCH, 9894
STITCHES, IN, 9898
stiti, 530
-stitium, 529
stiup-, 10308
stizein, 10001
stoborne, 10256
stoc(c), 10273
stock, 9593, 10284
STOCK, 10268
STOCKADE, 9576
'stockade for livestock',
2096

'strip of leaves', 5243
strippe, 9849
'strive', 5917
'strive after', 4268
'strived for', 5058
'strive together', 5064
'stroke', 1348, 9659, 9722, 9837, 10104
STROKE, 9660
'strong', 748, 912, 940, 968, 11742
STRONG, 9823
'strongest', 933
struck, 9691
'struck', 7504
STRUCK, 9657, 9685
-STRUCK, 9698
'structure', 4054, 9352
'structure, hollow', 8941
'structures, engineering', 11522
'structure, supporting', 10268
'struggle', 66, 10214
'struggle, one engaged in a', 94
'struggle, violent', 88
STRUNG, 9822
STUB, 10246
stub(b), 10248
*stubbaz, 10248
stubble, 10252
'stubble', 10253
'stubborn', 606
STUBBORN, 10255
stucchi, 10301
stucco, 10300
STUCCO, 10289
Stück, 10305
STUCK, 9905
STUDDINGSAIL, 10264
studēns, 10061
STUDENT, 10049, 10101
'student in a military or naval school', 2117
studēre, 10058, 10204
studie, 10069
STUDIO, 10076
STUDIOUS, 10087
studium, 10063, 10308
'study', 6597, 10060
STUDY, 10068
'studying', 10061

'study, place of', 10075
'stuff', 4103
*stug-, 10338
stugein, 10332
stugnos, 10333
stugos, 10333
*stukkaz, 10273, 10299
stukki, 10302
stulos, 9871
'stumble', 3421
'stumble, cause to', 9651
stump, 10245
'stump', 10247
'stun', 10096
'stunned', 10090
STUNSAIL, 10265
stunt, 10235
STUNT, 10234
*stuntaz, 10235
*stuntjan, 10241
stup-, 10103
*stūp-, 10325
stupefacere, 10096
stupefier, 10096
STUPEFY, 10095
STUPEFYING, 10087
STUPENDOUS, 10097
stupendus, 10098
stupēre, 10089
stūpian, 10325
'stupid', 10235
STUPID, 10051, 10093
'stupid person', 3951
stupidus, 10094
stupor, 10093
STUPOR, 10092
stutten, 10262
STUTTER, 10260
stuttr, 10238
Stux, 10328
'sty', 10785
styb(b), 10248
*stybbaz, 10248
STYGIAN, 10334
Stygius, 10334
styklbak, 9948
style, 9869
'style', 4190, 9874, 11450
STYLE, 9852
STYLET, 9877
stylos, 9871
'stylus', 2693, 9874
styntan, 10240

stȳpel, 10321
Styx, 10328
STYX, 10224, 10329
su, 9310
su-, 8675, 8748
*su-, 8754, 8912
sub, 8371
sub-, 639, 2054, 11903
subapostolic, 11920
subdere, 3526
'subdivision', 8220
subdūcere, 3523
'subdue', 11851
SUBDUE, 3522
'subheading of a book', 2188
subiugāre, 11852
subiugātus, 11852
subiungere, 11917
'subject in art', 4533
'subject to authority', 611
subjoin, 11944
SUBJOIN, 11916
SUBJOINDER, 11943
SUBJUGATE, 11850
SUBJUGATED, 11787
SUBJUGATION, 11835
SUBJUNCTIVE, 11881
SUBLUNAR, 7353
SUBLUNARY, 7353
'submissive', 3194
SUBORDINATE, 611
'suborn', 639
SUBORN, 637
subōrnāre, 639
'substance', 8514, 8645
'substance, lacking', 10463
'substance, of the same', 827
'substitute', 4310
subter, 5644
SUBTERFUGE, 5642
subterfugere, 5643
subterfugium, 5643
'subtract', 3474
'suburb', 4919, 5578
'suburbs', 5594
suc-, 2054
'succession, systematic', 1995
SUCCOR, 2052
succurrere, 2053

testudo, 9060
tetched, 6326
TETCHED, 6323
TETCHY, 6321
tête, 2340
tête-bêche, 2342
TÊTE-BÊCHE, 2336
tetora, 6840
tetra-, 6840
tetragrammaton, 2801
TETRAGRAMMATON, 2802
tetralogia, 6840
TETRALOGY, 6839
*teup-, 10108
'text, adorn a', 7332
th-, 4529
*th-, 11058
thanatos, 8747
'that', 533, 11094
'that is', 11267
'that is to say', 11389
thauma, 11570
thaumatos, 11570
THAUMATURGE, 11576
THAUMATURGY, 11570
the, 408
'theater, workings of', 11566
thēca, 4606
THECA, 4607
-theca-, 4613
The House That Jack Built, 3029
their, 9343, 11071
thēkē, 4605
them, 11073
thema, 4531
THEME, 4533
the nonce, 10727
then ones, 10727
theos, 9400
Æther, 4094
-ther, 11084
therapeia, 1639
there, 9343
'there', 910, 11149
thermal convection, 10706
THERMOGRAM, 2799
THERMOPHYTE, 1678
thēsauros, 4634
thēsaurus, 4638
THESAURUS, 4635
thesis, 4548, 4590, 4627
THESIS, 4551

'they are', 8709
'thicket', 7270
'thin', 9066
'thing', 11159
'thing done', 103
'things gathered up', 6718
'things, material', 1635
'things, natural', 1630
'things to be done', 4327
'think', 184, 645, 3221, 11193
'think logically, ability to', 649
'third party', 7906
thither, 11085
'thong', 9849
'thongs of oxhide', 1870
'thorn', 5475
'thoroughfare', 8442
THOROUGHFARE, 8420
'thoroughfare, broad', 2031
'thoroughly', 5089
'thought', 4522, 11184
'thought, creative', 6702
'thoughtless', 811
'thought, take careful', 185
'thousand', 1282
'thousand-leaf', 5242
'thousand thousand', 1286
thrē, 11055
'thread', 1039, 1344, 11235
'threadlike', 11234
THREE, 11055
'three men', 11763
'three, series of', 6837
'three-threaded', 1040
'thresh', 10179
thrice, 1053
thrie, 11055
'thrift and prudence, manage with', 1504
thrija, 11055
thrir, 11055
'thrive', 5171, 5218, 5259, 5286
'throat', 11839
'throat, base of the', 11839
'throat, inflammation of', 375
'throttle', 9833
'through', 2714, 4827, 5947, 6385, 6807, 7303, 7994, 8415, 9240, 10639

'throughout', 5089, 7303
'through the use of', 1465
'throw', 6342
'throw about jerkily', 5157
'throw head first', 2167
'throwing', 6344
'thrust', 9894, 9942
'thrust at', 10298
'thrust through', 10199
thunder, 704, 10180
thunor, 705
thura, 5603
thureoeidēs, 5602
thureos, 5602
thuroidēs, 5601
'thwart', 4250
THYROID, 5599
-ti, 8676
TICK, 4611
TICKET, 9927
TICKING, 4612
'tide', 4125
'tie', 1519, 6450
TIE, 3591
'tied together', 7201
'tie in a knot', 6453
Tierra del Fuego, 5451
*-tig, 1061
*tig-, 10034
tīgan, 3592
'tiger', 10027
TIGER, 10025
tighra-, 10028
tighri-, 10029
tight, 3593
'tight', 317, 347, 9737, 9813
'tighten', 9767
'tightening', 9733, 9767, 9827
'tight-fisted', 10041
tigra, 10027
tigras, 10026
tigre, 10026
tigrem, 10027
tigris, 10027
TIGRIS, 10031
tīke, 4610
tikke, 4611
tilde, 8669
'till', 1450

'tilled', 10981
'tilled (land)', 10980
'tiller of the soil', 1469
'tilling', 9119, 10973
'till the soil', 7774
tilsām, 11044
'tilting match', 11962
timbal, 10168
timbale, 10169
timbano, 10144
timbanon, 10143
timbene, 10145
'timber for roof of mine',
    10140
'timber, squared', 1568
**timbne*, 10145
timbre, 10145
TIMBRE, 10150
TIMBREL, 10148
'timeless', 11797
'time of day', 6923
'time-piece', 6921
'times, at all', 10565
TIMPANI, 10128
TIMPANIST, 10130
timpano, 10128
tinguere, 9991
'tiny', 10555
'tired', 11529
Tisch, 6360
'tissue, examination of',
    8861
'tissue, woody', 6534
tithenai, 4541, 4575
tittle, 8667
**tiuhan*, 3571
'to', 533, 663, 2316, 4263,
    4696, 8245, 9795, 10906
'to annoy', 8410
'to arms', 530
'tobacco', 2362
'tobacco, corporal's', 2363
'to cut again', 9532
TO-DO, 4489
'toe', 6273, 11998
TOE, 6317
'toe nail, sharp', 2584
togen, 3599, 10494
'together', 1442, 2422,
    6563, 6903, 7596, 9219,
    9310, 9355, 9405, 11561,
    11774, 12005
'togetherness', 9422

'together with', 183, 1288,
    3256, 7687, 7960, 9364,
    10654, 11870
toggen, 3571
togian, 3578
TOIL, 10054, 10215
toile, 10218
toilen, 10214
toiler, 10213
'toilet water', 10963
TOILING, 10049
toil(s), 10217
TOKEN, 6315
'tolerate', 8370
'toll a bell', 6490
tome, 1348
'tongue', 1205
'tongue (of a balance)', 127
tooillier, 10211
'tool', 7456, 8094, 11648
'tool, curved', 2895
'tool, cutting part of a',
    5283
'tool, digging', 1064
'tools', 476, 521
'tool, small pincerlike',
    1076
TOOTH, 2501
TOOTHSOME, 9296
'top against bottom', 2337
'topmost', 5680
'top of a buggy', 2229
'top of a wall', 2231
TOPOGRAPHY, 2831
Tor, 5517
'torch', 4401
'torment', 3583, 10735
'torment, mental', 355
torquēre, 10910
TORTICOLLIS, 10909
'torture', 9781, 10742
'tortured', 9788
tortus, 10910
'tossed', 789
'toss up and down', 175
'totter', 10517
'touchable', 5839
'touch, caressing', 9668
touched, 6327
'touch lightly', 9727
'touch playfully', 3872
'touch the emotions of',
    4265

touchy, 6325
tought, 3580
TOW, 3577
'toward', 2051, 2630, 3873,
    4263, 5309, 7995, 8095,
    8396, 9175, 9796, 10906,
    11085, 11975
towen, 3578, 10493
'town', 5581
'town, false', 5583
'tow rope', 6078
TOXICOPHOBIA, 5715
toxikon, 5716
toxon, 5717
'toy', 3865
trā-, 3462
'trace', 8361
'track', 3395, 10560
trade, 3395
'trade', 4341
TRADE, 3392
TRADED, 3400
'trademark', 6794
'trader', 8443
'trading place', 8444
'trading station', 4154
'tradition', 5931
TRADUCE, 3460
trādūcere, 3461
traduire, 3461
traeppe, 3414
'train (a horse)', 7515
'train, railway', 3574
TRAMP, 3431
**tramp-*, 3443
TRAMPLE, 3433
trampoli, 3439
trampolin, 3438
TRAMPOLINE, 3435
trampolino, 3438
trāns, 3462
'transact', 211
TRANSACT, 115
trānsāctum, 210
'transcendental, study of
    the', 1657
'transcript', 7692
TRANSECT, 9530
'transfixed', 9699
'transgress', 5569
'transgression', 8698
trānsigere, 210

'transitory', 10451
'translate', 3460
'translation, word-for-word', 3147
TRANSLUCENT, 7296
TRANSLUNAR, 7356
TRANSLUNARY, 7356
'transmigration of souls', 11019
'transmit', 3486
'transmitting', 10702
'transparent', 7004
'transport', 1900, 8258, 8437, 10658, 10690, 10747
TRANSPORT, 8353
trānsportāre, 8355
'transportation charge', 1908
'transported', 10702
'transport in a vehicle', 10525
'transpose letters', 2798
'transposition', 4582
TRANSVECTION, 10731
TRAP, 3413
trapp, 3419
trappa, 3419
TRAPPED, 3425
TRAPROCK, 3416
'travail', 10743
travailler, 10742
travel, 10743
'travel', 8420
'traveler', 8443, 10569
'traversed, capable of being', 8838
'tray', 775
trayas, 11056
'tread', 3405
TREAD, 3384
TREADLE, 3386
TREADMILL, 3387
TREASURE, 4640
'treasure room', 4634
'treasury of knowledge', 4636
'treatise', 2818, 6259
Treatise and discourse of the lawes of the forrest, 5552
'treatment, medical', 11592
tredan, 3403

'tree', 1567, 1625, 1667, 6532, 9367
'tree marten', 1584
'tree, olive', 3908
'trees, knower of', 11467
'tree trunk', 9593, 10268
TREFOIL, 5234
trei, 11056
treis, 11056
tremis, 11697
*trep-, 3414
trēs, 11056
*tresaurus, 4639
tresor, 4639
tresour, 4640
trēs virī, 11763
tretan, 3404
tria, 11056
'tribe', 1625, 1682
'tribe, subdivision of a', 11770
'tribunal', 5529, 6138
tribus, 1687
TRICEPS, 2177
'trick', 4209, 6466
'trickery', 451, 4209
tricot, 9714
TRICOT, 9716
tricoter, 9716
TRICYCLE, 10839
TRIFARIOUS, 4434
'trifles', 10618
'trifoliate leaf', 5236
trifolium, 5236
trilix, 1041
trillion, 1278
trilogia, 6844
TRILOGY, 6837
'trim', 3766, 8005
'trinket', 3736
trip, 10597
TRIP, 3421
tripāliāre, 10742
'triple-threaded', 1041
trippen, 3422
TRIPPING, 3424
'trip, short', 2033
trique, 9717
triquet, 9717
'trite', 4908
TRIUMVIRATE, 11761
triumvirātus, 11762
triumvir(i), 11762

triumvirōrum, 11762
trivia, 10619
TRIVIA, 10618
TRIVIAL, 10616
triviālis, 10613
'trivial objections, raise', 11130
trivium, 10612
TRIVIUM, 10624
trois, 11056
-tron, 10821
'troop', 9085, 9360
'troops', 9057
'troops, assembling of', 8050
'trophy, battle', 8971
TROT, 3406
troter, 3410
*trottare, 3410
trotten, 3411
trotter, 3411
TROTTER, 3407
trottōn, 3405
'trouble', 340, 1831, 10793
'trouble, causing', 9283
'troubled', 352, 790
'troublesome', 8408
TROUBLESOME, 9283
'trough', 3144
trousers, 9008
'true', 3244, 4381, 6134, 6404, 8710, 8736, 11469
'true, declare to be', 8716
'true, prove to be', 8716
'true-saying', 6116
'true, take for', 300
'true, that which is taken for', 301
'trunk, elephant's', 1864
'trunk of a tree', 11522
'trust, mutual', 8364
'trustworthy', 5831
'truth', 8711
'truth and wisdom, speaker of', 8713
'truth, self-evident', 305
'try', 138
'try out', 137
trys, 11056
'try to obtain', 5056
'try to seize', 5057
tt, 5880

-t(t), 2192
tū, 1013, 1051
TUB, 1082
tubbe, 1083
'tubular passage', 3546
tūcian, 3583
TUCK, 3581
tu(c)ken, 3582
TUCKER, 3585
TUCKERED, 3587
tud-, 10205
*tud-, 10205
tudes, 10207
tudicula, 10208
tudiculāre, 10210
*tud-ti-, 10219
TUG, 3567
'tug at', 3582
tuggen, 3571
tugon, 3572
*tugon, 3579
tumbanon, 10143, 10175
'tumor', 7126
tumpanizein, 10123
tumpanon, 10124
TUND, 10181
tundere, 10178, 10204
'tunic of chain mail',
   10937
*tupo-, 10110
tupos, 6794, 10104, 10175
tuptein, 10122, 10175
Tür, 5517
'turn', 1007, 1035, 1777,
   7387, 10773, 10872
'turn aside', 10600
'turned toward', 3304
'turn to profit', 8631
turos, 1783
tussis, 10220
TUSSIS, 10221
TUSSIVE, 10221
tvaer, 1018
tvau, 1018
tveir, 1018
tw-, 1009
twa, 1019
twā, 1012, 1017, 1051
twai, 1019
TWAIN, 1022
*twa-lif-, 1056, 7072
TWANG, 1075
'tweak', 1071

TWEAK, 1069
twee, 1016
TWEED, 1042
tweedle, 1002
TWEEDLEDEE, 995
TWEEDLEDUM, 994
TWEEL, 1042
TWEELED, 1044
TWEEZERS, 1076, 10084
twēgen, 1012, 1051
*twēgentig, 1061
twelf(e), 1055
'twelve', 1105, 1152
TWELVE, 1054, 7061
'twelve each', 1110
'twelve equals', 7921
'twelve fingers' breadths',
   1111
'twelve, of', 1106
'twelve peers', 7922
'twelve, pertaining to the
   number', 1104
'twelve, set of', 1151
twēne, 1017
TWENTY, 1060
twi-, 1253
TWI-, 1062
TWIBILL, 1064
'twice', 1191, 1233, 2330
TWICE, 1052
'twice a month', 1270
'twice as much', 1116
'twice a week, happening',
   1269
'twice a year', 1271
'twice-baked', 1250
'twice-cooked', 1234
'twice each year,
   happening', 1273
'twice folded', 1296, 1333
twiddle, 1004
TWIG, 1046
*twigga, 1048
*twik-, 1073
twili(c), 1038
TWILIGHT, 1063
'twill', 8453
TWILL, 1037
TWILLED, 1044
TWIN, 994
TWINE, 1029
TWINIGHT, 1067
twirl, 1005

'twist', 10910
TWIST, 1006
'twisted', 9830, 10910
'twist sharply', 1069
'twist to cut off blood',
   9835
TWIT, 11451
TWITCH, 1073
two, 1077, 1306
'two', 1062, 1089, 1138,
   1181, 1233, 1291, 1339,
   6814
TWO, 996, 1051, 1082
'two alternatives, hesitating
   between', 1159
'two, be (at)', 1159
'two, being', 1592
'two branches, divide into',
   1258
'two by two', 1214, 1287
'two by two, join', 1288
'two, consisting of', 1114
'two, each of', 11089
'two equals', 7936
'two, ever each of', 11091
'two eyes, using', 1199
'two feet, animal with',
   1197
'two-floor apartment', 1137
'twofold', 1137, 1297, 4434
'two-handled tub', 1086
'two-headed', 1206, 2174
'two hinged tablets', 1341
'two leave', 7063
'two left', 1054
'two left over', 7063
'two legs (and feet), stand
   having', 1198
'two materials, stuff made
   of', 1116
'two minds, of', 1161, 1593
'two months, every', 1270
TWONESS, 1011
'two objects, connecting',
   1050
'two objects, space
   separating', 1050
'two, of', 11086
'two of a kind', 7936
'two, of a number system
   based on', 1213
'two, one of', 11089

'two parties, supported by',
1211
'two parts,', 1027
'two parts, composed of',
1113, 1213
'two parts, cut into', 1209
'two parts, having', 1210
'two performers', 1099
'two performers, musical
composition for', 1100
'two persons, prearranged
combat between', 1177
'two plates, having', 1263
'two-pronged', 1259
'two remaining (over ten)',
1054
'two, roll of dice totaling',
1144
twos, 1019
TWOSOME, 994
'two sounds', 1344
'two-spot at dice or playing
cards', 1144
'two tens', 1060
'two terms, consisting of',
1215
'two-threaded', 1038
'two times', 1052
'two ways, in', 2330
'two weeks, happening
every', 1268
'two-wheeled velocipede',
1196
'two, which of', 11086
'two years, every', 1271
'two years, lasting', 1272
'two years, space of', 1272
tymber, 10156
TYMP, 10139
TYMPAN, 10137
TYMPANITES, 10131
tympanum, 10124, 10158
TYMPANUM, 10133
'type', 10113
TYPE, 10106
'typeface', 6793
TYPEWRITER, 10116
TYPICAL, 10118
TYPIFY, 10055, 10118
TYPIFYING, 10050
TYPIST, 10118
TYPOGRAPHY, 10118
typus, 10112

U

ubī, 11145
ubique, 11144
ubīquitās, 11144
UBIQUITY, 11143
-*ue*-, 3663
*uerg-, 11642
uevre, 7755
UGLIFY, 4369
'ugly', 3603
'ugly, make', 4369
-*üh*-, 2494
uisce, 8927
uisce beathadh, 8924
uisge beatha, 8924
-*ul*-, 5957
ulfr, 694
'ultimate reality, nature of',
1651
-*ulum*, 253
-*um*, 3616
'umbrella', 8026
UMPIRE, 7900
UMPIRES, 7897
'unaccompanied', 9227
'unadorned', 9234
'unadulterated', 9252
'unambiguous, render',
7013
'unbiased', 8572
'unbroken', 751
'uncertain', 1155
'uncertainty', 1169
'unchaste', 3598, 10493
'unclose', 2645
'uncomplicated', 9233
'unconcerned', 8570
'uncover', 2616
'uncover the neck', 10897
'uncreated', 11797
'uncultivated', 10396
'undecided', 1155
'under', 639, 2054, 4570,
8372, 11918
'underhand', 5645
'underhanded', 10605
'undershirt', 9230
'understand', 6517, 6591
'understandable', 7332
'understanding', 6600,
11393

'understanding, secret',
3879
'understand something
written', 678
'understood, easily', 7301
'undisciplined', 3597
'undivided', 889, 9227
'undo', 4249
UNDO, 4492
'undo a union', 11912
'undoing', 4426
'undone', 4248
'undress', 5794
'undressed', 9349
UNDUE, 5925
'undulate', 5328
'unearthly', 3937
'uneasiness', 795
'uneasy', 353
'uneasy, make', 4285
une paire, 7942
'unequal', 7902
'unexpected', 3248
'unfasten', 9623
'unfavorable', 8407
'unforseen', 11348
'unfulfilled', 7565
'unhappy', 4803
'unhappy fate', 10486
'unharmed', 784
'unhurt', 752
UNICYCLE, 10839
UNIFY, 4380
'uninhabited', 10342, 10399
'uninjured', 873
uninterested, 8575
UNINTERESTED, 8570
UNINTERESTING, 8557
'uninterrupted', 5091
'union', 550, 6006, 11792
'union, join in physical',
1290
'unique', 9157
'uniqueness', 9166
'unite', 6004, 11848, 11897,
11950
'united', 11868
'United Estates', 4594
'unit, particular and
discrete', 8555
'universal', 864
'universally', 866

'values, study of the nature of', 306
vāna glōria, 10434
vānēscere, 10445
vāni-loquentia, 10435
vāni-loquus, 10436
VANISH, 10455
vanissen, 10455
vanisshen, 10455
vānitantes, 10438
vānitāre, 10438
vanitās, 10429
'vanity', 10460
VANITY, 10427
'vanquish', 4250
vanta, 10497
vanter, 10439
vānus, 10424
'variegated', 8248
'varieties, of all', 4435
varit, 9307
vart, 8458
'vary irregularly', 5329
'vassal', 224
'vassals, assemblage of', 4901
VAST, 10422
vāstāre, 10416
vāstus, 10395
VASTY, 10421
Vater, 11051
'vaulted', 10709
VAUNT, 10441
VAUNTED, 10442
vē-, 10698
veage, 10589
vector, 10719
VECTOR, 10716
vectūra, 10671
vectus, 10658, 10702, 10736
vēda, 11465
VEDA, 11464
vedere, 11284
veduto, 11285
vega, 10788
'vegetable', 1669, 6529
'vegetables', 6528
veha, 10577
vehe-, 10697
vehemence, 10694
VEHEMENCE, 10686
vehemēns, 10687

vehement, 10686
'vehement, impulsively', 5074
vehere, 10658, 10689, 10736
VEHICLE, 10660
'vehicle (for moving things)', 10546
'vehicle, four-wheeled', 10528
'vehicle, four-wheeled passenger', 1909
'vehicle, wheeled', 3159
véhicule, 10661
vehiculum, 10661
veiage, 10589
'vein', 11841
veirdit, 6133
velo-, 3366
velocipede, 3366
VELODROME, 3365
vēmēns, 10688
vendetta, 6244
VENDETTA, 6245
VENGE, 6240
'vengeance', 6243
VENGEANCE, 6241
venger, 6239
vengier, 6239
venia dare, 5948
veoir, 11291
'veranda', 8278
'verbose', 7024
VERDICT, 6116
verdit, 6133
VERIFY, 4381
'verity', 8711
vermout, 11732
VERMOUTH, 11732
'verse, little', 10664
versicle, 10664
versus, 3304,
vērum, 6134
verus, 4381
'verve', 4964
ves heill, 881
'vessel', 2410
'vessel abandoned', 6990
'vessel, flat-bottomed', 1082
'vessel, hollow', 7395
'vest, embroidered', 512
vestisalba, 3963
'vestments', 5803

'vestments, Eucharistic', 7459
vetch, 10772
vĕtŭ, 9310
veue, 11290
'vex', 1836, 11526
VEX, 10744
vexāre, 10735
VEXATION, 10745
VEXATIOUS, 10745
-vey, 11358
vī-, 8822
via, 3551, 8838, 10574, 10608, 10642
via-, 8837
viable, 8838
VIABLE, 8833
via carrāria, 1915
VIADUCT, 3549, 10581
viage, 10590
viande, 8809
VIANDS, 8806
viāticum, 10587
VIATICUM, 10585
viāticus, 10588
vibrate, 8133
'victory', 5480
VICTUAL, 8819
victūālia, 8817
victūālis, 8817
victus, 8814
vide, 10386
VIDE, 11266
'videlicet', 11389
VIDELICET, 11267
vidēns, 11365
videō, 11264
VIDEO, 11265
vidēre, 11264, 11363
vie, 8832
'vie', 5064
Vieh, 7835
'view', 10838, 11288, 11315, 11371
VIEW, 11292
'view, at first', 4406
'view, beautiful', 3735, 11316
'viewer', 11296
'viewing', 8862
'view, mental', 11289
'vigor', 11646

'vigorous', 3775, 8787
'village', 1455
'village law', 1459
'village of South African
   natives', 2095
'villeinage', 1469
vim, 6237, 10579, 11780
VIM, 11775
vin-, 6235
vindex, 6234
vindicāre, 6234
VINDICATION, 6233
vindicta, 6242
VINDICTIVE, 6246
vinne, 5025
violāre, 11784
VIOLATE, 11783
VIOLATING, 11776
violātus, 11784
'violence', 6237
'violent', 10688
VIOLENT, 11776
violentus, 11782
'viper', 8133
VIPER, 8127, 8810
vīpera, 8128, 8812
vipere, 8812
vir, 11739
virāgō, 11743
'virago', 3603
VIRAGO, 11742
VIRILE, 11740, 11775
virīlis, 11741
VIRTUAL, 11757
virtuālis, 11760
VIRTUE, 11750
VIRTUOSO, 11754
virtuōsus, 11757
'virtuous', 8612, 11343,
   11443
'virtuous, indignantly',
   11443
virtūs, 11751
vis, 6237, 10579, 11276,
   11780
vis-, 11273
-VIS, 2872
VISA, 11274
visage, 11276
'visage', 4410
VISAGE, 11275
vīsāre, 11300
VIS-À-VIS, 11279

viser, 11283
vīsere, 11300
'visible', 11475
VISIBLE, 11274
Visigoth, 3824
vision, 11826
'vision', 11205
VISION, 11274
VISIONARY, 11274
'vision, faulty', 10015
'visit', 11306
VISIT, 11302
vīsitāre, 11301
VISITATION, 11303
VISOR, 11281
vista, 11286
'vista', 11292
VISTA, 11288
visto, 11285
VISUAL, 11274
vīsus, 11264, 11300
vīta, 8823
vitaile, 8818
vitaille, 8817
VITAL, 8824
'vitality', 11780
VITALITY, 8825
VITAMIN, 8825
vitamine, 8829
VITTLE, 8818
'vituperative', 10682
VIVA, 8795, 8842
vivace, 8788
VIVACIOUS, 8786
*vi(v)anda, 8808
vivant, 3649, 8759
vīvare, 8791
VIVARIUM, 8789
vivat, 8796
vīvāx, 8787
VIVE, 8796, 8843
vīvenda, 8807
VIVENDI, 8841
vīvere, 8772, 8814, 8840
VIVID, 8773
*vivipara, 8129
VIVIPAROUS, 8124, 8791
*vivipera, 8812
VIVISECTION, 8794
vivre, 8762
vīvus, 8771, 8852
viz, 11269
VIZOR, 11281

'vocabulary', 6728
vocāre, 10380
*vocitus, 10381
vocīvus, 10380
vodka, 8929
vogar, 10763
vogare, 10763
vogue, 10758
VOGUE, 10758
voguer, 10759
voiage, 10590
'voice', 1346, 2775, 4790,
   4828, 4859
'voice, far-off', 4814
'voice, female', 6050
'voice, good', 4846
'voice, male', 6049
'voice, with the living',
   8843
void, 10384
'void', 10380, 10424, 10463
VOID, 10340, 10385
voide, 10384
voie, 10643
voir, 11294
voit, 10384
VOITURE, 10670
voiture omnibus, 7732
volatile, 5840
VOLKSWAGEN, 10530
*vos, 1725
'votive offering', 4540
*vovis, 1726
voy-, 10642
VOYAGE, 10592, 10641
voyageurs, 260, 8306
VOYEUR, 11296
'V-shaped cut', 9560
vue, 11315
vuide, 10383
vuit, 10383
'vulgar', 9319

W

*wā-, 10345, 10424, 10480
wāch, 10544
Wacke, 10778
wacko, 10779
wāēge, 10550
wǣn, 10534
waes, 881

'whitehead', 11474
'whiten', 4018
'whiteness', 3957, 7391
'white of an egg', 3983
'white tablet', 3976
'whitewash', 4017
WHITHER, 11083
who, 11072
'who', 11102
WHO, 11060
'whole', 750, 787, 817, 851, 886
WHOLE, 868
'whole be thou', 904
'whole, concerning the', 864
'whole is greater than sum of parts', 863
'wholeness', 897
'whole, of the', 867
'wholesome effect, producing a', 762
'who-like', 11077
(w)holle, 890
'whom', 11131
WHOM, 11071
'whom, belonging to', 11069
'whom, by', 11131
'whom, of', 11069, 11111
WHOSE, 11069
WHY, 11074
wīago, 11410
wicga, 10770
'wicked, impiously', 4733
'wickedness', 10485
'wicket', 2983
wid-, 11469
widare, 11448
*(*w)idein*, 11244
widein, 11171
'wider, make', 4370
'widow', 6986
widtōr, 11172, 11245
WIELD, 964
wieldan, 966
'wife, faithful', 8787
-*wig*, 10772
-WIG, 10770
WIGGLE, 10571, 10771
wijssegger, 11408
'wild', 10402
'will', 923

'Will of God', 11336
win, 9295
'win at play', 3874
wi-n-d-no-, 11476
'wind, north', 3828
'window', 7319
'wind, south', 3806
'wind storm', 10818
'wine cellar', 4623
'wine, flavored', 11732
'wing', 4970, 5009, 5106, 8476
'winged', 5004
'wing-feather', 5002
'wing finger', 5112
'winglike', 5118
'wing, primitive', 5110
'wing, small', 4969
'winning', 9294
WINSOME, 9293
'wipe out by killing', 7015
wiro, 11774
wiros, 11738, 11778
wīs, 11173, 11404
wisa, 11450
wisdōm, 11406
WISDOM, 11167, 11405
'wise', 8690, 11173, 11340, 11420
WISE, 11403, 11433
-WISE, 11434
WISEACRE, 11383
WISECRACKS, 11418
wise(e)ard, 11420
'wise man', 11419
WISENHEIMER, 11417
wisent, 1757
'wish', 923
'wish for', 10497
'wishing of good fortune', 6160
wīssago, 11409
wīssaz, 11405
wis(s)on, 11451
WIT, 11388
witan, 11387, 11428, 11454
witan, 11448
witch, 11426
wītega, 11411
'with', 1652, 2423, 3334, 3878, 4440, 4566, 6563, 6903, 7596, 8868
'withdraw', 3524

'withdraw from', 10377
'wither', 6009
'within', 5501, 8896
'without', 399, 3599, 6756, 9423, 11619
'without equal', 7930
'without, from', 5511
'withstand', 8369
witnes, 11392
WITNESS, 11384
WITS, 11393
WITTINGLY, 11384
'witty', 3845, 4416
WITTY, 11403
'witty saying', 4417
WIVERN, 8135
wivre, 8134
wīzago, 11410
WIZARD, 11384, 11419
wleik-, 6994
wo, 11063
wogen, 10765
wogh-lo-, 10792
'wolf', 694, 11714
'wolf-man-wolf', 11714
'woman, domineering', 11743
'woman, good', 3639, 8787
'woman, heroic', 11742
'woman, loathsome', 3603
'woman, modest', 8610
'woman, old', 3709
'woman, strong', 8610
'woman, warlike', 11743
'womb', 9416
'wonder', 11571
'wondered at', 10099
'wonderful', 10098
Wonder of Words, 4798
wood, 11721
'wood', 6532
'wood, artificer in', 1986
'wooden objects, one who builds and repairs', 1987
'wood nymph', 9365
'wood sharpened at one end', 9919
'woods, outside', 5539
'wood, split piece of', 9047
'wood, turn into', 6534
worc, 11503
'word', 3648, 6146, 6694, 6724, 6753, 6792